Talking International Law

Talking International Law

Legal Argumentation Outside the Courtroom

Edited by
IAN JOHNSTONE AND STEVEN RATNER

OXFORD
UNIVERSITY PRESS

OXFORD
UNIVERSITY PRESS

Oxford University Press is a department of the University of Oxford. It furthers the University's objective of excellence in research, scholarship, and education by publishing worldwide. Oxford is a registered trade mark of Oxford University Press in the UK and certain other countries.

Published in the United States of America by Oxford University Press
198 Madison Avenue, New York, NY 10016, United States of America.

Library of Congress Cataloging-in-Publication Data
Names: Johnstone, Ian, 1960– editor. | Ratner, Steven, editor.
Title: Talking international law : legal argumentation outside the courtroom /
edited by Ian Johnstone and Steven Ratner.
Description: New York : Oxford University Press, 2021. | Includes index.
Identifiers: LCCN 2021027426 (print) | LCCN 2021027427 (ebook) |
ISBN 9780197588437 (hardback) | ISBN 9780197588451 (epub) |
ISBN 9780197588468 (digital-online) | ISBN 9780197588444 (updf)
Subjects: LCSH: International law. | International law—Political aspects. | United Nations.
Classification: LCC KZ3410 .T35 2021 (print) | LCC KZ3410 (ebook) | DDC 341—dc23
LC record available at https://lccn.loc.gov/2021027426
LC ebook record available at https://lccn.loc.gov/2021027427

DOI: 10.1093/oso/9780197588437.001.0001

1 3 5 7 9 8 6 4 2

Printed by Integrated Books International, United States of America

Note to Readers

This publication is designed to provide accurate and authoritative information in regard to the subject matter covered. It is based upon sources believed to be accurate and reliable and is intended to be current as of the time it was written. It is sold with the understanding that the publisher is not engaged in rendering legal, accounting, or other professional services. If legal advice or other expert assistance is required, the services of a competent professional person should be sought. Also, to confirm that the information has not been affected or changed by recent developments, traditional legal research techniques should be used, including checking primary sources where appropriate.

(Based on the Declaration of Principles jointly adopted by a Committee of the American Bar Association and a Committee of Publishers and Associations.)

To
Gabriela
and
Nancy, Ben, and Isabel

Contents

Acknowledgments

This genesis of this book probably began several decades ago as each of us made the trek from practicing international lawyer (for the UN and US government) to academic international lawyer. We had each participated in, witnessed, and been fascinated by the practice of international legal argumentation in political and other non-judicial settings and written separately about it. In 2018, we started talking about a new book on this topic, and we were fortunate to find both practitioners and scholars from around the world who shared our goal to provide greater understanding of this phenomenon across a range of issues. We thank all of them for taking the plunge with us.

We gathered with our contributors over two days in Ann Arbor, Michigan, in November 2019 to share insights and personal experiences across disciplines, subject areas, and institutions. We greatly appreciate generous support for that transformative workshop from the University of Michigan Law School, as well as superlative administrative assistance from Marielle Toonen-van Rooij. The editors also appreciate the excellent work of Irina Langenegger of the Fletcher School of Law and Diplomacy at Tufts University and Emma MacFarlane of the University of Michigan Law School in assisting us with the preparation of the index to this book.

In addition, our authors wish to thank the following individuals for research and other assistance with their chapters: Mackenzie Garrity, Philip Stekol, and Isabelle Janssen (Kathleen Claussen); Pegah Eftekhari and Anna Ver Beek (Monica Hakimi); Tsion Demissie Bergano (Namira Negm); Ellen Aldin (Steven Ratner); and Tabea Zimmermann and Franziska Scheppach (Lisbeth Zimmermann).

Finally, we greatly appreciate the support of our editors at Oxford University Press: Merel Alstein, Charlotte Holloway, and Emma Collison.

List of Contributors

Jutta Brunnée is the Dean & James M. Tory Professor of Law and University Professor at the Faculty of Law, University of Toronto. She was elected Fellow of the Royal Society of Canada in 2013, and Associate of the Institut de Droit International in 2017. In 2019, she taught at the Hague Academy of International Law.

Kathleen Claussen is Associate Professor at the University of Miami School of Law. Her research focuses on trade, investment, foreign relations and national security, and international dispute settlement, among other topics. She is a graduate of the Yale Law School, Queen's University Belfast, and Indiana University.

Monica Hakimi is the James V. Campbell Professor of Law at the University of Michigan Law School. Her work ties together the theory and practice of international law, particularly on issues relating to human and national security. She is a member of the Board of Editors of the *American Journal of International Law*.

Gina Heathcote is Professor of Gender Studies and International Law, School of Law, SOAS, University of London. She is the author of *Feminist Dialogues on International Law: Successes, Tensions, Futures* (2019) and *The International Law on the Use of Force: A Feminist Analysis* (2013). She co-authored *The Law of War and Peace: A Gender Analysis (Vol. 1)* (2021).

Hyeran Jo is Associate Professor of Political Science at Texas A&M University. She is the author of *Compliant Rebels: Rebel Groups and International Law* (2015). Her research has been supported by the US National Science Foundation, the Alexander von Humboldt Foundation, and the Howard G. Buffett Foundation.

Ian Johnstone is Professor of International Law at The Fletcher School of Law and Diplomacy, Tufts University. From 2018 to 2019, he served as Dean *ad interim*. Prior to joining Fletcher, Johnstone worked in the United Nations' Executive Office of the Secretary-General. His books include *The Oxford Handbook of International Organizations* (2016).

Edward Kwakwa is Assistant Director General, World Intellectual Property Organization (WIPO), Geneva. Before joining WIPO, he worked as Associate at the law firm O'Melveny and Myers. He has also held senior legal positions with the Commission on Global Governance, the Office of the United Nations High Commissioner for Refugees, and the World Trade Organization.

Stephen Mathias is the Assistant Secretary-General for Legal Affairs of the United Nations. Prior to taking up that position, he worked in various roles for the Office of the Legal Adviser at the US State Department.

Namira Negm is the African Union Legal Counsel. She was Ambassador of Egypt to Rwanda and Legal Adviser in New York and The Hague. She earned a PhD in International Law from the University of London and an LLM from King's College London.

Nicolas Perez is a Legal Officer in the Office of Legal Affairs of the United Nations. He also held similar positions for the United Nations in Kosovo and Afghanistan and, prior to joining the United Nations, was a legal adviser in the French Ministry of Defense.

Steven Ratner is the Bruno Simma Collegiate Professor of Law at the University of Michigan Law School. His recent wok addresses international law's linkages with political and moral philosophy, as well as business and human rights. He served on expert panels of the UN Secretary-General on accountability for human rights violations in Cambodia and Sri Lanka.

Scott P. Sheeran has worked in government, diplomacy, the military, and academia. He was a Senior Legal Counsel in the UN Security Council for 2015–2016, and previously a Vice Chair of the Sixth (Legal) Committee of the UN General Assembly. He has published primarily on the United Nations, international human rights and humanitarian law, and peacekeeping.

Bruno Stagno-Ugarte is Chief Advocacy Officer at Human Rights Watch and Affiliate Professor at Sciences Po. He was formerly Foreign Minister of Costa Rica, Ambassador to the United Nations, and President of the Assembly of States Parties of the International Criminal Court. He is a graduate of Georgetown University, the Sorbonne, and Princeton University.

Ingo Venzke is Professor for International Law and Social Justice at the University of Amsterdam and Director of the Amsterdam Center for International Law. His monographs include *How Interpretation Makes International Law* (2012), which won the book award of the European Society of International Law.

Wouter G. Werner is Professor of International Law at the Vrije Universiteit, Amsterdam, and Extraordinary Professor of International Law at the University of Curacao. His main research interests are in the field of international law and film, and the sources of international law. He is author of *Repetition and International Law* (2021).

Lisbeth Zimmermann holds the Chair of International Relations at Zeppelin University, Friedrichshafen. Her main research interests are norms and contestation in international relations, international organizations, dynamics of expertise, as well as peacebuilding. Her book *Global Norms with a Local Face: Rule of Law Promotion and Norm Translation* was published by Cambridge University Press in 2017.

PART I

1

International Legal Argumentation

Practice in Need of a Theory

Ian Johnstone and Steven Ratner

I. Introduction

In a decentralized global system that lacks the formal trappings of domestic governance systems, most disputes between and among states and non-state actors never reach either a domestic or an international courtroom for authoritative resolution. This state of affairs continues, even with the creation of new international tribunals in recent decades. Despite, indeed because of, the relative scarcity of judicial settlement of disputes, international legal argumentation remains pervasive, but notably in a range of *nonjudicial* settings. States, corporations, nongovernmental organizations (NGOs), and even guerrilla groups make claims in international legal terms in political bodies like the United Nations' organs or domestic parliaments, private diplomatic discussions, and public statements in formal and informal settings.

What purpose does such argumentation serve? What are its effects, intended and unintended? Who is engaging in the argumentation? Who is the audience? What, for that matter, counts as a legal argument and how is it different from other kinds of argument? These questions are not all new, but they have never been addressed systematically in one volume. Answering them is critical to a central goal for scholars and practitioners of international law and relations—to understand how international law actually operates in international affairs.

This book probes these and other questions related to the place of international legal arguments from a multi-perspectival lens. It brings together a group of scholars and practitioners from around the world who have either written about or engaged in international legal argumentation outside of courtrooms. We draw on various theoretical traditions that address the phenomenon of argumentation in international affairs, either as an element of legal theory or of international relations theory. Yet our approach is largely inductive, looking at the actual practice of legal argumentation in a variety of settings and issue areas. From the cases, we seek to identify patterns and common themes in why, where, how, and to what effect the language of law is used outside of courts. This fills a significant gap in scholarship on international law and international relations by exploring the microprocess of communication using international law.

Ian Johnstone and Steven Ratner, *International Legal Argumentation* In: *Talking International Law.* Edited by: Ian Johnstone and Steven Ratner, Oxford University Press. © Ian Johnstone and Steven Ratner 2021.
DOI: 10.1093/oso/9780197588437.003.0001

In this introduction, we will first describe existing theories that address argumentation in international affairs. These are not theories of argumentation per se, but rather areas of legal and international relations theory in which the phenomena of communications and argumentation are central. We then set out the questions our contributors were asked to consider in their essays. The introduction concludes with an overview of each chapter.

II. Argumentation: Theoretical Orientations and Gaps

Law is the language of international society. This proposition, though perhaps an overstatement (states communicate in ways other than through legal argumentation), captures an important feature of how states interact with each other, and increasingly with non-state actors. At least six bodies of scholarly literature address, directly or indirectly, argumentation in international affairs. Three are rooted in international law: compliance theory, interpretation theory, and critical legal theory. Three have found their way into international relations theory, although the first two have roots in other disciplines: communicative action, practice theory, and norm contestation. As the academic fields of international law and international relations have become intertwined, these schools have begun to borrow from each other. Yet they do not add up to a coherent theory. What is missing is a systematic focus on the invocation of *legal* norms during the conversation about compliance and other matters. This volume is designed to bring us a step closer to a full-blown theory of international legal argumentation.

A. Theories from International Law

1. Compliance Theory

Much of international legal theory focuses on compliance, precisely because coercive enforcement is rare in a decentralized international system. If not out of fear of sanctions, why do states comply with international law? Ever since H.L.A. Hart posited his internal acceptance theory of law, argumentation has been a prominent feature in theories of compliance. For a legal system to exist, sanctions are not necessary; the principal explanation for compliance is an internalized sense of obligation. Several prominent schools of legal thought have built on that insight. The New Haven School or policy-oriented approach associated with Myres McDougal and Harold Lasswell defines law as a "process of authoritative decision-making" characterized by communication between states,[1] often in response to international

[1] The methodology employed by McDougal and Lasswell is well captured in the following passage: "[t]he communications which constitute an international agreement, like all other communications, are functions of a larger context, and the realistic identification of the content of these communications must require a systematic, comprehensive examination of all the relevant features of that context, with conscious and deliberate appraisal of their significance." Myres McDougal, Harold Lasswell, and James Miller, *The Interpretation of Agreements and World Public Order: Principles of Content and Procedure* (New Haven and London: Yale University Press, 1967), 11.

incidents.[2] Incidents in particular provoke reactions of decision makers and legal authorities in the form of statements as well as deeds, resulting in back-and-forth argumentation about the legality of actions taken. Transnational Legal Process posits that international law acquires a certain "stickiness" through a process of interaction, interpretation, and internalization.[3] Legal argumentation permeates all three elements as governments engage with each other and with domestic actors in articulating what the law means and what compliance requires. And the management model of compliance sees international law as operating through a process of justificatory discourse: "the interpretation, elaboration, application and ultimately enforcement of international rules is accomplished through a process of (mostly verbal) interchange among interested parties."[4] States feel compelled to give reasons and justifications for their conduct; these justifications are reviewed and critiqued in various settings, particularly international institutions. The felt need to have those justifications accepted pushes states in the direction of compliance because, being bound up in an interdependent international system, they want to remain members in good standing in that system.

All three of these schools (New Haven, Transnational Legal Process, and the management model) have elements of both instrumentalism and constructivism in their theories of compliance. The instrumental account is that states obtain tangible benefits from participating in the system. Rules exert an impact on state behavior because states have an interest in reciprocal compliance by other states and in preserving a reputation for playing by the rules so other states will cooperate with them in the future or on other issues. The constructivist account is that membership in the international legal system generates a sense of obligation to comply with its rules and the felt need to be seen as complying. Engaging in legal argumentation to justify one's actions is a way of remaining a member in good standing.

None of these theories, it should be noted, depends on the interlocutors being truly persuaded of the merits of a rule. As Ryan Goodman and Derek Jinks have argued, state behavior can change through acculturation, the pressure to conform to the beliefs and norms of the surrounding culture.[5] The audience need not agree with or even assess the merits of the norm; what matters is the degree of identification it feels (or wants to feel) with some reference group.[6] In the geopolitical sphere, the referent group could be other great powers, regional neighbors, democratic countries, or the Global South.[7] Acculturation of this sort may lead to internal acceptance of the norm, but the behavior can change before or without that ever happening.

[2] W. Michael Reisman and Andrew R. Willard, eds., *International Incidents: The Law that Counts in World Politics* (Princeton: Princeton University Press, 1988).

[3] Harold Hongju Koh, "Why Do Nations Obey International Law?," *Yale Law Journal* 106 (1997): 2599 (book review).

[4] Abram Chayes and Antonia Chayes, *The New Sovereignty: Compliance with International Regulatory Agreements* (Cambridge: Harvard University Press, 1995), 118.

[5] Ryan Goodman and Derek Jinks, "How to Influence States: Socialization and International Human Rights Law," *Duke Law Journal* 54 (2004): 621, 638–645.

[6] Alastair Iain Johnston, "Treating International Institutions as Social Environments," *International Studies Quarterly* 45 (2001): 487.

[7] Courtney Fung, *China and Intervention in the UN Security Council* (Oxford: Oxford University Press, 2019).

For other legal scholars, true persuasion is central. Tom Franck's "fairness discourse" involves reasoning and communication on the basis of principles that combine procedural legitimacy and distributive justice.[8] Through this discourse, a sense of obligation is fully internalized by the targets of the communication: not only behavior but minds are actually changed. Steven Ratner goes furthest in developing a theory of persuasion by identifying four dimensions of a communications strategy: publicity (how public to be in the argumentation); density (how much law to invoke); directness (whether to appeal for compliance simply because it is the law, or because the law serves some higher purpose); and tone (how confrontational and accusatory to be).[9] Ratner does not claim that all persuasion aims to get a target to internalize a norm, but his model suggests what factors will make that more likely.[10]

2. Interpretation Theory

A growing body of literature considers argumentation through the lens of legal interpretation. All law, according to Ronald Dworkin, is fundamentally an exercise in interpretation.[11] In a domestic legal system, judges are the primary (though not sole) interpreters of the law. In the decentralized international legal order, interpretation occurs in a more diffuse process that includes adjudication, but also through the argumentation that occurs in quasi-judicial settings, the political organs of intergovernmental organizations, diplomatic conversation between states, government policy documents and statements, and the writings of practitioners, scholars, and engaged citizens in academic journals, blogs, and media outlets.

Many of those who proffer interpretations of the law in these settings are self-interested actors, such as the legal advisers to governments. This presents a conundrum. If "auto-interpretation" by self-interested actors is the norm, who decides what is the best interpretation of the law? Iain Scobbie draws on rhetorical theory to postulate that a set of ground rules for persuasive argumentation exists in the process of interpreting international law.[12] But he does not explain how those ground rules are administered in a horizontal legal system where there is no court to render authoritative decisions. Ian Johnstone does seek to explain that through the concept of an "interpretive community," an idea borrowed from literary theory that he applies to the

[8] Thomas M. Franck, *Fairness in International Law and Institutions* (Oxford: Clarendon Press, 1998), at 7, 14.

[9] Steven R. Ratner, "Persuading to Comply: On the Deployment and Avoidance of Legal Argumentation," in *Interdisciplinary Perspectives on International Law and International Relations: the State of the Art*, edited by Jeffrey L. Dunoff and Mark A. Pollack (New York: Cambridge University Press, 2013), 577. See also Steven Ratner, chapter 6, in this volume.

[10] For an earlier analysis of what makes arguments persuasive, see Stephen Toulmin, *The Uses of Argument* (Cambridge: Cambridge University Press, 1958).

[11] Ronald Dworkin, "Law as Interpretation," *Texas Law Review* 60 (1982): 27; Owen Fiss, "Objectivity and Interpretation," *Stanford Law Review* 34 (1984): 1325; Cass Sunstein, *Legal Reasoning and Political Conflict* (1996), 167; Richard H. Fallon, Jr., "The Meaning of Legal 'Meaning' and Its Implications for Theories of Legal Interpretation," *University of Chicago Law Review* 82 (2015): 1235, 1238–1239.

[12] Iain Scobbie, "Rhetoric, Persuasion and Interpretation in International Law," in *Interpretation in International Law*, edited by Andrea Bianchi, Daniel Peat, and Matthew Windsor (Oxford: Oxford University Press, 2015), 61. His summary of the ground rules is "start from a topic which is an object of agreement, pay attention to the audience's pre-conceptions, including its understanding of legitimate or proper argumentative methods, adapt the argument to the audience," at 62.

practice of international law.[13] The interpretive community is an amorphous constellation of actors that provides the assumptions, categories of understanding, and conventions of argumentation that make reasoned exchange about the meaning of a text possible. There are widely shared understandings and expectations about the relevant sources, processes, and argumentative techniques that characterize the international legal enterprise. One may question whether Article 38(1) of the International Court of Justice (ICJ) Statute fully exhausts all the so-called sources of international law, or whether Articles 31 and 32 of the Vienna Convention on the Law of Treaties (VCLT) provide adequate guidance on how to interpret treaties. But it is hard to claim that they are not central components of international legal practice. A competent lawyer would ignore these instruments at his or her peril.

Yet the interpretive community does more than simply set the parameters of discourse. It passes judgment on what constitutes the correct (or at least) best interpretation of the law. "Correctness" is not based on objective criteria, but rather is the outcome of an intersubjective, discursive process driven by the assumptions and categories of understanding that are embedded in the international legal discipline. What is a right or wrong interpretation can only be answered by other participants in the interpretive community.[14] More concretely, the impact of international law is felt through the weight of international legal opinion; that opinion is both shaped and measured through argumentation.

The participants in the legal discourse include officials and judges who are directly involved in the making, interpretation, and implementation of a particular legal norm. But it extends beyond them to all officials, legislators, judges, lawyers, scholars, and other nongovernmental actors who participate in some way in the field of international law or practice in which the interpretive dispute arises; as well as an amorphous constellation of stakeholders—what can be called transnational civil society—who listen to and critique the discourse that goes on within the inner circles.[15] As René Provost points out, non-state actors of various stripes—starting with the most "highly qualified publicists" (enshrined in Article 38(1)(d) of the ICJ Statute) and including NGOs such as the International Committee of the Red Cross (ICRC), and even non-state armed groups—engage in the process of interpretation.[16]

[13] Ian Johnstone, "Treaty Interpretation: The Authority of Interpretive Communities," *Michigan Journal of International Law* 12 (1991): 371. The term "interpretive community" was coined by literary theorist Stanley Fish. See Stanley Fish, *Is There a Text in This Class? The Authority of Interpretive Communities* (Cambridge: Harvard University Press, 1980). For a review of literature on legal interpretive communities, see Ian Johnstone, *The Power of Deliberation: International Law, Political and Organizations* (New York: Oxford University Press, 2011), 33–41. For later writing on the concept, see various chapters in *Interpretation in International Law, supra* note 12.

[14] Ingo Venzke, *How Interpretation Makes International Law* (Oxford: Oxford University Press, 2012), 366; Jean d'Aspremont, "The Multidimensional Process of Interpretation: Content-Determination and Law-Ascertainment Distinguished," in *Interpretation in International Law, supra* note 12, at 111, 114.

[15] Johnstone, *The Power of Deliberation, supra* note 13. See also Andraz Zidar, "Interpretation and the Legal Profession: Between Duty and Aspiration," in *Interpretation in International Law, supra* note 12, at 135; Jean d'Aspremont, "Wording in International Law," *Leiden Journal of International Law* 25 (2012): 575. See contra Gleider Hernandez, "Interpretative Authority and the International Judiciary," in *Interpretation in International Law, supra* note 12, at 166.

[16] René Provost, "Interpretation in International Law as a Transcultural Project," in *Interpretation in International Law, supra* note 12, at 300.

Much of the argumentation about interpretation is aimed at compliance, but the line between compliance with existing law and creating new law is blurry. Interpretation often involves refining, elaborating, or stretching the meaning of a legal term. At a minimum, it gives content to and thereby "hardens" inchoate norms. At a maximum, it is "constitutive of international law."[17] Moreover, even when the argumentation fails to produce clarity on the weight of international legal opinion, interpretative debates can provide structure and a modicum of stability to the international system. Legal argumentation is inherently confrontational, but not necessarily coercive. From one perspective, legal discourse is a battleground; from another, it is a bridge.[18] From the first, disputes over interpretation are an "argumentative battle for semantic authority."[19] The battle cannot be mitigated let alone resolved through legal language, because it is about whose language is the true language of international law.[20] From the second perspective, argumentation about interpretation is a vehicle for managing the conflicts that are inherent in any pluralistic society. Because it requires the offering up of arguments that fit within a wider context of intersubjective understandings about the rules of international life, it is a bridge if not to consensus and cooperation at least to peaceful coexistence.

3. Critical Legal Theory

Yet, as critical legal theorists remind us, not all participants in legal argumentation are equal: powerful actors dominate. Antonio Gramsci defined hegemony as domination not through brute force but through ideas—by developing an ideology that serves the interests of the powerful at the expense of the less powerful, but which the less powerful come to accept. Dominant actors do not impose order; they construct an order founded on values and ideas that work to their advantage, and then seek to legitimize that order through legal discourse that purports to be apolitical and universal.[21] Critical theorists stress that the structure of the international system is not fixed or immutable; it is a product of historical circumstances. It may be so enduring that it comes to be seen as natural, but it is not.

From this perspective, the distribution of power in the international system has a determining impact on the formulation, interpretation, and application of international law. The more powerful actors are better able to dictate the terms of legal debates, to win those debates, and to bear the reputational and other costs if they lose. More insidiously, legal argumentation does not constrain self-serving interpretations

[17] d'Aspremont, *supra* note 14, at 113. Duncan Hollis makes a related point when he speaks of "existential interpretation," which validates the existence of a rule by deciding whether it even counts as law. Duncan Hollis, "The Existential Function of Interpretation in International Law," in *Interpretation in International Law*, *supra* note 12, at 79.

[18] Venzke, *supra* note 14, at 356–360.

[19] d'Aspremont, *supra* note 14, at 113.

[20] Venzke, relying on Davidson, *supra* note 14, at 369.

[21] As Robert Cox put it, "Hegemony derives from the ways of doing and thinking of the dominant social strata of the dominant state or states insofar as these ways of doing and thinking have inspired emulation or acquired the acquiescence of the dominant social strata of other states. These social practices and the ideologies that explain and legitimize them constitute the foundation of the hegemonic order." Robert W. Cox with Timothy J. Sinclair, *Approaches to World Order* (Cambridge: Cambridge University Press, 1996), 517.

of the law by powerful actors, but rather legitimizes those interpretations by making them seem like a reflection of universally applicable community standards. Invoking the language of the law hides from view the fact that contestable political choices are being made.[22] To give an example, the UN Charter and many General Assembly resolutions enshrine two fundamental principles—"self-determination" and "territorial integrity"—which are often in conflict. Yet international law says little about how to resolve the conflict—about which people are entitled to assert the right to self-determination against states that claim territorial integrity. The principles are in fundamental contradiction, and there is nothing *within the law* to resolve the contradiction. International law is an elaborate argumentative structure that pretends to resolve these sorts of conflicts, but in the end it comes down to a matter of political choice. Moreover, critical legal theorists claim the argumentative structure is fundamentally incoherent as it vacillates perpetually between asserting that the law operates separate from the realities of power politics and asserting that it functions precisely because it is rooted in the political realities of state practice.[23] The project of critical legal studies in a nutshell is to examine the structure of legal argument to reveal that pattern, to reveal the inherent contradictions and hidden ideologies that run through all international law.[24]

A related critique concerns the power of experts. The critical literature spans both subject matter experts and legal experts. So, for example, economists in the World Bank and International Monetary Fund (IMF) are criticized for constructing structural adjustment policies that adhere to conventional economic wisdom with little regard for the distributional impacts. "Liberal peacebuilders" are accused of crafting programs and institutions that reflect Western conceptions of good governance and the rule of law without considering local perceptions of political legitimacy. In the field of international law, the claim is that legal discourse occurs among a closed circle of lawyers—the "self-appointed visionaries and arbiters of humanity's needs"[25]—who shut out perspectives that are beyond the mainstream through technical, formalistic, and ultimately obfuscating legal language. The invocation of legal expertise gets in the way of inclusive decision-making even when important value and political choices are being made.

4. The Missing Elements

Although all three of these theoretical orientations inform our understanding of why states make legal arguments and the effects thereof, none of them zeroes in on the actual microprocess of communication. The choices that international actors make between legal and nonlegal arguments (and the diversity of views about where to draw the line between them); the variety of motivations for and consequences of those

[22] Martti Koskenniemi, "The Politics of International Law," *European Journal of International Law* 1 (2000): 1.

[23] Martti Koskenniemi, *From Apology to Utopia: The Structure of International Legal Argument* (Cambridge: Cambridge University Press, 2009).

[24] David Kennedy, *International Legal Structures* (Baden Baden: Nomos Verlagsgesellschaft, 1987).

[25] Paul B. Stephan, "Comparative International Law, Foreign Relations Law and Fragmentation: Can the Center Hold?," in *Comparative International Law*, edited by Anthea Roberts, Paul B. Stephan, Pierre-Hugues Verdier, and Mila Versteeg (New York: Oxford University Press, 2018), 66.

choices; the relevance of the particular speaker, audience, and venue; the role of the thinness or thickness of the existing legal landscape in argumentation; and the implications for the direct targets of an argument as well as others who might hear it are among the critical issues that these theories leave out. Nor, generally, do they consider how and why non-state actors make legal arguments. To address these issues requires unpacking particular argumentative strategies in discrete settings, a task we set out to do in this book through our case studies offered from both scholarly and firsthand perspectives.

B. Theories from International Relations

1. Communicative Action

In indirect response to the critical theorists, Jürgen Habermas posits an ideal of legal argumentation that is not insular: "Legal discourse cannot operate self-sufficiently inside a hermetically sealed universe of existing norms but must rather remain open to arguments from other sources."[26] Though a philosopher and not an international relations theorist, Habermas has applied his theory of communicative action to the European Union.[27] His theory holds that there are at least three kinds of communicative behavior: bargaining based on fixed preferences; strategic argumentation, in which arguments are used to justify positions and induce others to change their minds; and "true reasoning," in which actors seek a reasoned consensus on the basis of shared understandings, where each actor not only tries to persuade but is also open to persuasion.[28] The last is Habermas's ideal of communicative action. It is not meant to describe an actual state of affairs, but its basic principles are presupposed in any linguistic communication.[29] It may be impossible to distinguish "true reasoning" from strategic argumentation, but even the latter can have beneficial effects. Jon Elster posits the "civilizing force of hypocrisy": even hypocritical arguments (seemingly impartial arguments that are really designed to hide one's self-serving motivations) often lead to principled and more equitable outcomes.[30] If the rhetoric changes with every shift in short-term interests, then it will be dismissed as "cheap talk," and the

[26] Jürgen Habermas, *Between Facts and Norms* (Cambridge: Polity Press, 1996), 230.

[27] Jürgen Habermas, *The Crisis of the European Union: A Response* (Cambridge: Polity Press, 2013).

[28] Thomas Risse, "'Let's Argue': Communicative Action in World Politics," *International Organization* 54 (2000): 1, 7–9. This is Risse's summary of Jürgen Habermas's *Theory of Communicative Action, Vol. 2* (New York: Beacon Publishing Group, 1985).

[29] Habermas argues that the ideal speech situation is embedded in the very nature of the discourse. "Insofar as participants understand themselves to be engaged in a cooperative search for common ground solely on the basis of good reasons, then they must—as a condition of the intelligibility of their activity—assume that the conditions of the ideal speech situation are satisfied." See Lars Lose, "Communicative Action and the World of Diplomacy," in *Constructing International Relations: The Next Generation*, edited by Karen Fierke and Knud Erik Jorgensen (London: Routledge, 2001), 179. See also Frank Cunningham, *Theories of Democracy: A Critical Introduction* (London: Routledge, 2002), 176.

[30] Jon Elster, "The Strategic Uses of Argument," in *Barriers to Conflict Resolution*, edited by Kenneth Arrow, Robert Mnookin, Lee Ross, Amos Tversky, and Robert Wilson (New York: Norton and Norton, 1995), 249. See also Diego Gambetta, "Claro!: An Essay on Discursive Machismo," in *Deliberative Democracy*, edited by Jon Elster (Cambridge: Cambridge University Press, 1998), 19, 23.

entire purpose of making impartial arguments is lost.[31] Presumably those who engage in the argumentation believe it serves a purpose (or else why bother) and therefore will feel some pressure to match deeds with words in order not to appear blatantly hypocritical.[32]

In a similar vein, deliberative democrats hold that in a well-functioning democracy, public policy should be decided not only through voting but also through the exchange of reasons that all those who are subject to them can accept.[33] This exchange of reasons will not always lead to agreement (that is why legislatures vote) but makes it easier to live with disagreement. If the matter is put to a vote, those who lose can at least feel all the relevant issues were aired and the interests of all stakeholders were considered.[34] Friederich Kratochwil, Thomas Risse, Michael Zurn, and others have sought to extend this line of thinking to international affairs.[35] They posit a logic of arguing, separate from but related to the logics of consequences and appropriateness.[36] According to the third logic, which is tied to the second, arguing helps to construct norms that reflect "appropriate" behavior and to determine whether the norms apply in a particular situation. Some deliberative democrats speak of multiple public spheres in which a range of opinions is developed and exchanged on matters of common concern: "a highly complex network that branches out into a multitude of overlapping international, national, regional, local and sub-cultural arenas."[37] International organizations are settings where a good deal of transnational deliberation occurs. Because international law is a concrete manifestation of shared (intersubjective) understandings about what constitutes acceptable behavior among states, the reasoned exchange that occurs there often has a legal character, although deliberative democrats tend not to acknowledge that point.

2. Practice Theory

Stretching from Ludwig Wittgenstein's philosophy of language, to Pierre Bourdieu's sociology, to Étienne Wenger's organization theory, to Emanuel Adler's communitarian

[31] Cf. Jack Goldsmith and Eric Posner, "Moral and Legal Rhetoric in International Relations: A Rational Choice Perspective," *Journal of Legal Studies* 31 (2002): 115; Jack L. Goldsmith and Eric A. Posner, *The Limits of International Law* (New York: Oxford University Press, 2005), 167.

[32] Thomas Risse's notion of argumentative self-entrapment makes the same point. Risse, *supra* note 28. See also Frank Schimmelfennig, *The EU, NATO, and the Integration of Europe: Rules and Rhetoric* (Cambridge: Cambridge University Press, 2003).

[33] Amy Gutmann and Dennis Thompson, *Democracy and Disagreement* (Cambridge, MA: Belknap Press, 1996).

[34] *Id.*

[35] Risse, *supra* note 28; Michael Zürn, "Democratic Governance Beyond the Nation-State: The EU and Other International Institutions," *European Journal of International Relations* 6 (2000): 183; Friedrich Kratochwil, *Rules, Norms and Decisions* (Cambridge: Cambridge University Press, 1989).

[36] On the logics of consequences and appropriateness, see James March and Johan Olsen, *Rediscovering Institutions* (New York: Free Press, 1989).

[37] Habermas quoted in Philip Schlesinger and Deirdre Kevin, "Can the European Union become a Sphere of Publics?," in *Democracy in the European Union: Integration through Deliberation?*, edited by Erik Oddvar Eriksen and Erik Fossum (London: Routledge, 2000), 211. See also Seyla Benhabib, ed., "Towards a Deliberative Model of Democratic Legitimacy," in *Democracy and Difference: Contesting the Boundaries of the Political* (Princeton: Princeton University Press, 1996), 74; John Dryzek, *Deliberative Global Politics* (Cambridge: Polity Press, 2006); James Bohman, "International Regimes and Democratic Governance: Political Equality and Influence in Global Institutions," *International Affairs* 73 (1999): 499, 506.

international relations, the concept of a community of practice has deep roots. It has found its way into the international law literature via Yves Dezalay and Bryant Garth, Jutta Brunnée and Stephen Toope, Jens Meierhenrich, and Anthea Roberts.[38]

To understand the relationship between legal argumentation and communities of practice, four elements of the concept are especially important. The first is "background knowledge," a term originally coined by John Searle.[39] This is similar to Wittgenstein's idea of "tacit knowledge" and to Habermas's notion of a "common lifeworld"—the background of shared assumptions, understandings, and practices that make meaningful communication possible. Searle put this in terms of interpretation. No rule is self-interpreting: a person must have contextual understanding to arrive at the correct meaning, and that contextual understanding draws on a cultural awareness, habits of mind, and presuppositions that those engaged in communication must share.

The second is the meaning of "practices." Adler and Pouliot define them as "socially meaningful patterns of action, which, in being performed more or less competently, simultaneously embody, act out, and possibly reify background knowledge and discourse in and on the material world."[40] A practice is not the same as either action or behavior:

> The concept of behavior evokes the material dimension of doing, as a deed performed in or on the world; then the notion of action adds an ideational layer, emphasizing the meaningfulness of the deed at both the subjective and intersubjective levels; and, finally, the term "practice" tacks another layer on the edifice or, better put, makes it hang together as one coherent structure, by pointing out the patterned nature of deeds in socially organized contexts.[41]

In the international law realm, Meierhenrich explains that practices are habitual, routinized behavior that facilitates a particular understanding of the world: "work activities . . . that are performed in a regularized fashion and which have bearing, whether large or small, on a social phenomenon, in our case, on the operation of international law."[42]

The third is the notion of shared discourse. Those who engage in a social practice share a common discourse, a way of speaking about the activities in which they are engaged that reflects a certain perspective on the world.[43] Law is a disciplined and specialized form of discourse. There are widely shared understandings and expectations

[38] For an excellent review of the philosophical and sociological roots of practice theory, see Jens Meierhenrich, "The Practice of International Law: A Theoretical Analysis," *Law and Contemporary Problems* 76 (2013): 1.

[39] John Searle, *Expression and Meaning: Studies in the Theory of Speech Acts* (Cambridge: Cambridge University Press, 1979).

[40] Emanuel Adler and Vincent Pouliot, eds., *International Practices* (New York: Cambridge University Press, 2011), 1, 4.

[41] *Id.* 5.

[42] Meierhenrich, *supra* note 38, at 19.

[43] Étienne Wenger, *Communities of Practice: Learning Meaning and Identity* (Cambridge: Cambridge University Press, 1998), 125–126.

about the relevant sources, processes, and argumentative techniques that characterize the international legal enterprise.

Fourth, being competent in the field is to possess "know-how"—a kind of knowledge that can only be acquired through practice.[44] Drawing on Wittgenstein's language theory and pragmatist philosophy, the idea is that knowledge and competence come from usage. We know the meaning of a word from how it is used. We understand the functioning of a professional discipline from how it is practiced.

Combining these four ideas and applying them to law, international law is an argumentative practice, competence in which depends on possessing a reservoir of background knowledge. One learns the law in part by studying it, but also by engaging in the practice. In so doing, one does not simply (or even primarily) learn black letter rules, but rather acquires tacit legal knowledge—the techniques of argumentation and interpretation that are embedded in the discipline. One internalizes a "certain perspective on the world," as well as a certain set of methods for reading texts and making claims based on those texts and the contexts in which they are encountered.

3. Norm Contestation

Finally, argument is a central feature of the burgeoning literature on "norm contestation." This literature stems from the work on norm diffusion pioneered by Martha Finnemore, Katherine Sikkink, and other constructivist international relations scholars.[45] While that work addresses how norms spread and become internalized, it does not focus on argumentation per se. Later research on norm contestation does. Antje Wiener defines contestation as "the range of social practices [that] discursively expresses disapproval of norms."[46] She starts from the assumption that, in democratic societies, the norms, rules, and principles of governance ought to be contestable at any given time by those governed by them (drawing on Habermas, among others). Contestation, while inherently confrontational, can generate legitimacy if it is regular and inclusive of all stakeholders.[47] Others take a similarly positive view of norm contestation as a way of generating shared understandings, echoing the deliberative democrats.[48] Even when the norms originate from a particular culture, such as liberal democracies, contestation can result in the extension of those norms

[44] Vincent Pouliot, "The Logic of Practicality: A Theory of Practice of Security Communities," *International Organization* 62 (2008): 255, 269.

[45] Martha Finnemore and Kathryn Sikkink, "International Norm Dynamics and Political Change," *International Organization* 52 (1998): 887; Thomas Risse and Kathryn Sikkink, "The Socialization of International Human Rights Norms into Domestic Practices: An Introduction," in *The Power of Human Rights: International Norms and Domestic Change*, edited by Thomas Risse, Stephen C. Ropp, and Kathryn Sikkink (Cambridge: Cambridge University Press, 1999), 1; Margaret Keck and Kathryn Sikkink, *Activists Beyond Borders: Advocacy Networks in International Politics* (Ithaca, NY: Cornell University Press, 1999).

[46] Antje Wiener, *Theory of Contestation* (New York: Springer, 2014), 1.

[47] *Id.* 10. See also Antje Wiener, "Contested Compliance: Interventions on the Normative Structure of World Politics," *European Journal of International Relations* 10 (2004): 189.

[48] Wayne Sandholtz, "Dynamics of International Norm Change: Rules Against Wartime Plunder," *European Journal of International Relations* 14 (2008): 101. Adam Bower, "Arguing with Law: Strategic Legal Argumentation, US Diplomacy, and Debates over the International Criminal Court," *Review of International Studies* 41 (2015): 337.

to other societies.[49] Although she does not use the term norm contestation, Monica Hakimi claims that communities are constructed as much by conflict as they are by agreement.[50]

Charlotte Epstein takes a less optimistic view of contestation. Echoing critical legal studies, she claims debates over norms are "generative structures that are always charged with relations of domination" and hence not a check on power but a reflection and perpetuation of it.[51] Another critical line of thinking sees norm contestation as a never-ending exercise—meaning is contested "all the way down." Holger Niemann and Henrik Schilinger question the very foundations of research on norms defined as shared understandings of appropriate behavior:

> [T]he almost mundane insight that norms have different meanings according to time, space, or social context leads to a fundamental conceptual problem in norm research. A contested norm, from this perspective, represents almost a contradiction in terms, as it is difficult to imagine that norms can be both contested and shared at the same time.[52]

They seek to turn norm research on its head by starting not with the established view of norms as "shared understandings" and norm contestation as the anomaly, but rather with contestation as the normal state of affairs and settling on an understanding is the anomaly.

Recent work on norm contestation focuses on outcomes. Nicole Deitelhoff and Lisbeth Zimmermann claim that contestation can either strengthen or weaken a norm, depending on the form of the contestation and context.[53] If the argumentation is about the application rather than the meaning of norm, then the consequences may not be severe, even if it does not produce agreement. If the contestation is about basic meaning, it will lead to decay. In a similar vein, Anette Stimmer questions the tendency to treat norm contestation and norm acceptance as binary categories. By distinguishing norm frames (justifications) from norm claims (to action), she identifies four possible outcomes from norm contestation: clarification of the norm, when there is agreement on the frame and claim; recognition of the norm, when there is agreement on the frame but not the claim; neglect, when there is agreement on the claim but not the frame; and impasse, when there is disagreement on both.[54]

[49] Amitav Acharya, "How Ideas Spread: Whose Norms Matter? Norm Localization and Institutional Change in Asian Regionalism," *International Organization* 58 (2004): 239; Lisbeth Zimmermann, "More for Less: The Interactive Translation of Global Norms in Post-Conflict Guatemala," *International Studies Quarterly* 61 (2017): 774.

[50] Monica Hakimi, "Constructing an International Community," *American Journal of International Law* 111 (2017): 317, 325. She quotes Bernard Yack for the proposition that if a practice of justice "structures nothing more than the way we engage in conflict with each other, it still reinforces the sense that we participate with others in a community."

[51] Charlotte Epstein, *The Power of Words in International Relations: Birth of an Anti-Whaling Discourse* (Cambridge, MA: MIT Press, 2008).

[52] Holger Niemann and Henrik Schilinger, "Contestation 'All the Way Down': The Grammar of Contestation in Norm Research," *Review of International Studies* 43 (2017): 29, 30.

[53] Nicole Deitelhoff and Lisbeth Zimmermann, "Things We Lost in the Fire: How Different Types of Contestation Affect the Robustness of International Norms," *International Studies Review* 22 (2020): 51.

[54] Anette Stimmer, "Beyond Internalization: Alternative Endings of the Norm Life Cycle," *International Studies Quarterly* 63 (2019): 270, 270–271.

4. The Missing Elements

International relations theories have offered important and influential insights on argumentation in international affairs. They complement the legal theories by addressing the microprocess of communication more directly. But despite decades of work on the issue, they have not tended to focus on the central concern of this book: the salience of *legality* to an argument. Norms are defined as standards of appropriate behavior for actors with a given identity. With some exceptions, whether the norms take a legal form is not of particular concern to most international relations (IR) theorists.[55] Moreover, they tend to elide the distinction between "soft" norms and "hard" norms. For legal theory, the distinction between soft law and hard law is important, in part because there is a debate over whether the first even exists and in part because there is a debate over whether the distinction has any bearing on compliance. For our purposes, the distinction is important because the type of norm may have an impact on the purpose, nature, and effects of the argumentation. It is our view, one that later chapters develop further, that international legal argumentation is different from other forms of normative argumentation, whether in its motivations or its effects. So we hope to fill in this important gap with this volume.

C. Theoretical Silences

Finally, we note that some theories or methods of international law and relations remain mostly silent about argumentation, legal or otherwise. Among the former, strict positivism stresses law's origin in and validity through certain discrete and formal "sources." The task of the lawyer is to identify the legal rules and then interpret them according to accepted modes of interpretation provided by the law (notably the VCLT). Argumentation, discourse, and persuasion are simply not seen as relevant to the inquiry—even though, of course, as a practical matter, the lawyer will be making her views about to the law to someone through an argument. Among the latter, realism and certain iterations of institutionalism both neglect the role of argumentation, and especially legal argumentation, in international affairs. For realists, structural forces about state power determine the outcomes of disputes between states, with international law playing a negligible role. Arguments about international law are just cheap talk. Even among institutionalists, those steeped in a rational choice model will accept the advantages of legalization as a way to reduce the costs of cooperation and increase the credibility of commitments, but the actual process by which those actors dispute what the norms mean is not particularly important.

These theories all share what might best be termed a *static* approach to international law. Law is something out there, to be found and applied by the positivists, and that may affect the behavior of global actors (or may not, according to the realists). While they accept that law changes over time, these approaches are static in that what

[55] A notable exception is Deitelhoff and Zimmermann's recent work that begins to explore how the legal character of norms affects the discourse about them. Nicole Deitelhoff and Lisbeth Zimmermann, "Norms Under Challenge: Unpacking the Dynamics of Norm Robustness," *Journal of Global Security Studies* 41 (2019): 2.

matters is the snapshot—not the underlying process that led to it, or the process that will follow from the law's invocation. It is our view, and indeed, that of the other theories we have discussed, that these static views are profoundly impoverished. They both oversell international law's relevance (by making its identification and application the only task for the lawyer) and undersell it (by seeing it strictly in terms of cost avoidance).

III. What This Book Adds

To fill in some of these gaps in the theoretical literature, we identify the central question as follows: How and why does international legal argumentation operate outside of courts? To answer that question we ask a number of subsidiary questions: What is a legal argument? Who engages in the legal argumentation? Why do they engage in it? Who is the audience? Where does it occur? And what is the effect? The existing literature, both theoretical and empirical, suggests some tentative answers.

What is a legal argument? This question is surprisingly difficult to answer. A minimal definition is an argument that explicitly invokes traditional sources of law and employs the standard techniques of interpretation. A maximalist definition would define it as an argument that in any way bears on law. The authors of this volume were not asked to adopt any particular definition, but to be explicit about the definition they use. We also asked the authors to compare legal to other forms of argumentation when helpful to illuminate what is distinctive about the former. These include policy-oriented, scientific, moral, religious, emotional, economic, and expedient arguments. Some found it useful to focus on the style of argument, for example, drawing on precedent or making analogies. Others considered explicit versus implicit argumentation. The latter can occur when a particular policy, decision, or act assumes a legal position, even if the legal claim is not articulated as such.

Who engages in legal argumentation? The principal "arguers" are representatives of states. Theory suggests we might observe a difference between powerful and weak states. The latter may be more inclined to make specific claims, insisting that the law is clear in order to tie down the powerful; the former may prefer vagueness, leaving them with the discretion to interpret and reinterpret the law in a manner that serves their preferences. Other important protagonists in legal argumentation include domestic actors: legislators, advocacy groups, civil society, academics, lawyers in private practice, and journalists. Prominent non-state actors at the international level are officials of intergovernmental organizations, representatives of international NGOs, multinational corporations, and armed groups.

Why do actors engage in legal argumentation? What motivates them, what purpose is the argumentation intended to serve? Here extant theory offers a range of possible answers. For some, it may be a genuine effort to persuade the interlocutor or other audiences of the merits of a legal claim. For others, the goal may be more strategic—to change behavior without caring whether the audience has been persuaded on the merits of the claim. For others still, it may be to build or preserve a reputation for law-abidingness, even if they do not expect to change anyone's mind or behavior. Legal argumentation can also legitimate (or delegitimate) action. It can lay the foundation for future changes in the law—either making new law or undermining the law that exists. It is also interesting to consider why actors avoid legal argumentation when legal issues are at stake. What is lost by engaging in legal argumentation?

Who is the audience? This question is closely tied to speaker and purpose. In most of the case studies, the audience is representatives of other states, whether they be allies, adversaries, or neutral. Indeed, it may well be that persuasion is not necessary for allies and not likely to succeed for adversaries, leaving the "undecided" as the real target. On occasion, officials of intergovernmental organizations may be the target, especially those who are in a position to provide diplomatic support or extract a diplomatic price. It may also be transnational NGOs, for example, human rights or humanitarian organizations, that participate in international legal discourse. Domestic actors are often the audience as well. These could be opposition groups (armed or otherwise), political parties, bureaucrats, leaders of civil society, religious leaders, or the general public.

Where, outside of courts, does legal argumentation occur? One common venue is the political organs of intergovernmental organizations, whether global, regional, or subregional. The UN Security Council figures prominently in this volume. A great deal of legal argumentation occurs in the European Union. The legal systems of other regional organizations are less fully developed, but the African Union, the Organization for Security and Cooperation in Europe, and the Association of Southeast Asian Nations are all sites for argumentation. It also occurs in quasi-judicial bodies, such as human rights treaty committees and alternative dispute resolution mechanisms. Other international venues include informal institutions such as the G7 and G20, conferences of states parties to treaties, and gatherings where new norms are developed, such as UN open-ended working groups and high-level panels. Bilateral diplomatic exchanges often include legal argumentation. At the domestic level, it can be heard in parliaments and executive agencies, as well as in public debates through the media, academic journals, blogs, and other organs of expert and public opinion. Where the argumentation occurs also impacts the form it takes: agreed written documents, unilateral public statements, private exchanges, or social media. An important question is who has access to the venues where argumentation occurs. Non-state actors, for example, have some access to intergovernmental organizations, but not as much as states. They may prefer more informal channels.

Finally, what are the effects of legal argumentation, intended and unintended? This is the hardest question to answer because clear causation is difficult to prove. Possible effects range from constraining behavior (compliance theory), enabling it (by signaling authority), or framing an issue (by casting it in legal terms).[56] Another effect could be to change the normative climate and thereby shape the future direction of a particular area of law. Legal argumentation may also promote the rule of law generally, cultivating a habit of seeking to resolve disputes and manage relations through the language of law rather than brute force. From the perspective

[56] Ian Hurd, *How to Do Things with International Law* (Princeton: Princeton University Press, 2017).

of critical theory, legal discourse can suppress or silence voices, obfuscate what is really at stake, and mask value choices behind the cloak of seemingly neutral legal language. Sometimes a good legal argument can have a bad moral effect and a bad legal argument a good one.

IV. Overview of the Volume

This book is overtly interdisciplinary, with perspectives from both international law and international relations. Its contributors include leading academics and seasoned practitioners, who collectively draw on theory and conceptual work, as well as real-world accounts of the way that international legal argumentation actually functions in practice. Each chapter focuses on a particular issue area, ranging from the *jus ad bellum* to trade to international whaling. Our hope and expectation is that a comparative analysis of the legal argumentation in each area, framed by the above questions, will illuminate this ubiquitous but not-well-understood feature of contemporary international affairs. The topics were deliberately chosen to provide a broad cross-section, but inevitably some important issue areas were left out. We describe three of those at the end of this chapter.

The second chapter in Part I of the book, by Ingo Venzke, combines theoretical accounts of the language of law in global politics with a review of the empirical work testing those accounts. He explains legal argumentation from the perspective of three logics of action and ties all three logics to the concept of legitimacy. He explores whether the language of law changes individual or collective attitudes toward certain actions or situations. Does a persuasive case for the legality of an action increase the level of approval for it? Venzke reviews several experimental studies that have inquired into the impact of invoking the law on public opinion, and finds the results to be mixed and ultimately unsatisfying. He identifies three areas for further empirical research: international law's distinctive claim to authority; the legitimacy effect of legal argumentation on non-US audiences; and law's function in enabling rather than constraining behavior. He concludes by highlighting the deep divides between the experimental work that has been done and legal scholarship of a more critical bent.

Part II comprises five chapters on legal argumentation about international peace and security. Monica Hakimi builds on her earlier work that suggests contestation over the *jus ad bellum* can actually help to build community. Her central claim in this chapter is that legal argumentation, even when the argument is not settled authoritatively (as is often the case), promotes three rule-of-law values: accountability for decisions about the use of force; respect for those affected by the decisions; and the fostering of relatively healthy transnational politics. In developing this claim, she challenges two extant theories of international legal argumentation: one that highlights the role of legal argumentation in lawmaking; the other, its function as an enforcement device. Neither theory, in Hakimi's view, adequately explains much of the argumentative practice about the *jus ad bellum* that does not—nor is it expected or intended to—result in authoritative resolution. If the benefits of legal argumentation were contingent on the matter being settled, then presumably little would be lost by disengaging from it when such resolution is out of reach. Her claim, to the contrary, is that much would be lost in terms of the three rule-of-law values described above.

Scott P. Sheeran draws on his experience as the Legal Adviser to the Permanent Mission of New Zealand to the United Nations in an analysis of legal discourse in the Security Council. He starts from the premise that, in this highly political and unequal body where diplomacy and the search for consensus are paramount, the role of international legal argumentation may seem modest. He highlights the disconnect between the positivist, disciplined methodology of most international lawyers and the institutional powers, practice, and processes of the Council. He claims that to understand the impact (or not) of international legal argumentation in the Council, one must pay close attention to the dominant (political) paradigm of argumentation that exists there, as well as the complex social interactions among its members. To promote international norms, and indeed the rule of law itself, an international lawyer operating in and around the Council must adopt a more contextual and flexible mode of argumentation founded on policy considerations and values as opposed to black letter rules.

In chapter 5, Gina Heathcote takes a critical look at the preambles to UN Security Council resolutions on women, peace, and security, starting with Resolution 1325 (2000). She argues that the preambles shape legal arguments on the issue by filtering out wider transnational feminist demands, and by filtering in the dominant normative commitments of the Security Council. The net result is that they articulate feminist approaches that emphasize women as victims of conflict-related sexual violence and as participants within decision-making structures, while downplaying the broader structural demands, such as anti-militarism and disarmament, of transnational feminist actors. She treats feminist protest and organizing itself as a form of legal argumentation, and calls this protest the "forgotten preamble" to the resolutions. More concretely, she considers the impact of the actual preambles (both in thematic and situation-specific resolutions) on the development of international law. She is critical of some contemporary feminist writing that, by attaching substantial legal weight to the preambles, contributes to the silencing of dissident feminist approaches that do not find their way into the texts.

Steven Ratner's chapter, unlike most others in the book, focuses on an issue area in which there is relatively little international law: cybersecurity. International legal argumentation in this field reflects at best a thin consensus, if not outright dissensus, at four levels: the existence of rules; the content of those rules; the desirability of new rules; and the content of any desired rules (as well as norms). This legal landscape results in a unique pattern of argumentation and persuasion by states and non-state actors both *ex ante*—in advocating for a regulatory scheme for cyber activity—and *ex post*, in reacting to and perhaps responding to a malicious act by another state or non-state actor. By taking out one of the key assumptions of existing studies on legal and normative argumentation, namely, an agreed set of rules, Ratner's chapter offers a distinctive perspective on the motivations and effects of legal argumentation in shaping debates and behavior outside of courts. States argue not only about the content of rules but also whether they even exist and, if not, whether new law or norms are needed. Ratner also considers the contributions of non-state actors (corporations, academics, and think tanks) to the construction of cyber norms. While Ratner's focus is on the use of legal argumentation to persuade, he discusses other purposes and effects as well.

The field of nuclear nonproliferation, by way of contrast, is characterized by a substantial amount of international law. Ian Johnstone focuses on the Nuclear Non-Proliferation Treaty (NPT) and presents a theory of legal argumentation as an intersubjective activity, underpinned by the principle of consent. Most arguments are about compliance, but often spill over into other kinds of legal arguments: What is the nature of the obligation, in what venue is the matter properly discussed, does existing law cover the situation, is new law needed? Through case studies of Article IV of the NPT on the "inalienable right" to peaceful nuclear energy, and Article VI on the obligation of the nuclear weapon states "to pursue negotiations in good faith" on disarmament, Johnstone finds evidence for several reasons why states engage in legal argumentation: to persuade another actor of the validity of a legal claim; to gain strategic benefits, such as the support of allies; and to stake out the moral high ground by affirming one's identity as "law-abiding." Regardless of motive, a noteworthy effect of legal argumentation is to change the normative climate surrounding a regime, possibly for the worse, but usually for the better because the argumentation is an implicit acknowledgment that the rules matter and they apply to all who engage in it.

Part III covers argumentation in areas of law that relate to human dignity. Bruno Stagno-Ugarte, who has served as Foreign Minister and as Permanent Representative of Costa Rica to the United Nations, writes about debates on mass atrocities in the UN Security Council. He focuses on two sets of actors: the members of the Security Council (both permanent and non-permanent) and the Secretary-General and Secretariat officials. He does not seek to demonstrate that legal argumentation is the best way to advance and achieve compliance with human rights (as nonlegal arguments may be more effective), but claims that legal arguments can have independent—if not sufficient—influence even in a political setting, due in part to the extraordinary powers of the Council to act on violations of international criminal, humanitarian, and human rights law, particularly under Chapter VII. Through case studies of Myanmar, Syria, and Yemen, he highlights the use, or avoidance, of legal language by actors within the Council to either capture, or—too often—dissimulate, the gravity of the crimes being perpetrated. He regrets that, by avoiding direct and specific language about the crimes being committed, actors minimize the effect of the legal argumentation, making it easier to avoid action.

Hyeran Jo's chapter focuses on the use of legal argumentation by non-state actors. Her issue area is the invocation of international humanitarian law (IHL) by non-state armed actors (NSAAs)—individuals or groups that fight for their political, economic, or social goals. She draws on a global sample of 364 NSAAs who operated from 1974 to 2010, at least 20 percent of whom engaged in some form of legal argumentation related to IHL. She asks: Why and when do they have an incentive to engage in international legal argumentation? What is the content of the legal argumentation and associated processes? What effects does it produce? Among the patterns she sees is the tendency of NSAAs to invoke legal arguments to claim the moral high ground vis-à-vis their government adversaries in order to gain support for their cause among international actors. She also observes the disparity among NSAAs in their access to interlocutors and venues where legal argumentation is common. Jo concludes with a set of observations about four possible effects of NSAAs' legal argumentation: persuasion, reciprocity, compliance, and peace.

Wouter Werner's chapter examines legal argumentation in and by the African Union (AU) in its long-standing dispute with the International Criminal Court (ICC) about whether the latter is biased against African countries. Building an analytical framework that draws on the institutional theory of law, legal expressivism, and the role of criminal law in the formation of communities, Werner focuses not on legal-technical questions such as head of state immunity, but rather on deeper political questions about recognition, respect, and equality. The AU has addressed these questions in a series of formal Decisions, adopted by its highest organ, the Assembly of Heads of State and Government. Werner treats the emotions expressed in these decisions as a type of legal argumentation, which have particular power because they articulate the collective stance of the AU and bestow it with the authority of law. Political struggles are thus articulated in the form of "argumentation through law" that attaches formal validity to claims about membership, recognition, and equality.

In her capacity as Legal Counsel of the African Union, Ambassador Namira Negm has been at the center of a wide range of political disputes with legal dimension. None have been more important to the AU than how it reacts to unconstitutional changes of government (UCGs). The Constitutive Act of the AU condemns UCGs and calls for the suspension of governments that come to power through unconstitutional means. In her analysis of the practice of the AU in implementing these provisions, Negm finds that legal argumentation has helped to facilitate the process of a return to constitutionality by suspended governments, enabling them to resume participation in the AU. The legal argumentation has revolved not only around the provisions in the Constitutive Act on UCGs but also those on democracy, later elaborated in the African Charter on Democracy, Elections and Good Governance. Reliance on AU legal texts helped to achieve AU consensus on how to respond and to marshal diplomatic efforts to persuade (or compel) those who come to power through unconstitutional means to step down. Negm concludes that the AU's consistent practice on this politically charged issue demonstrates the value of legal argumentation in promoting the rule of law, without resorting to adjudication.

Part IV is a cluster of chapters on cooperation in the global commons. Jutta Brunnée observes that argumentation regarding climate change is heavily concentrated in nonjudicial settings. Contemporary international environmental problems, because they are complex, multifaceted, long-term, and implicate multiple states and non-state actors, do not lend themselves to adjudication. Brunnée explores three interrelated shifts in the climate change regime, reflected in the differences between the 1997 Kyoto Protocol and the 2015 Paris Agreement: the move to a more decentralized "orchestration" model; the shift to more reliance on non-binding substantive terms supported by binding procedural terms; and the shift away from legal accountability practices toward nonlegal performance assessment. Informed by the interactional understanding of law she developed with Stephen Toope, Brunnée argues that the first two shifts, perhaps surprisingly, did not reduce the scope for legal argumentation in the regime, but the third did. While she considers the who, where, and why of legal argumentation, the main thrust of her chapter is to explore what constitutes a legal argument in the first place. A key point she makes is that interpretive reasoning characteristic of treaty law is not contingent on the formal nature of the norms; it applies to binding as well as non-binding terms of the climate treaties.

Lisbeth Zimmermann, a political scientist, uses a case study of the International Whaling Commission (IWC)'s whaling moratorium to contribute to the debates in international law and international relations theory about the distinctive qualities of legal argumentation and its distinctive effects on the conduct of global politics. She observes that in the field of environmental governance and environmental law, a similar debate exists about the quality and effects of scientific argumentation. Like international law, scholars have pointed out how "science" is used as a resource of authority and legitimacy in this field—and how scientific argumentation centrally shapes debates. Zimmermann studies the contestation of the commercial whaling moratorium as a way of exploring the different types of argumentation used in the IWC: legal, scientific, and other types of normative argument, including moral. She finds that legal and scientific argumentation (which are intertwined) dominate but that normative argumentation is surprisingly widespread. She compares the strategies of three opponents to the ban on commercial whaling (Japan, Norway, and Iceland) and concludes that different types of arguments are used by challengers for different ends and are influenced by the institutional settings in which they are deployed.

From his perch as the former Legal Counsel of the World Intellectual Property Organization (WIPO), Edward Kwakwa writes about international legal argumentation in the field of intellectual property. He looks at two processes in WIPO: the Uniform Domain Name Dispute Resolution Policy (UDRP), an alternative form of dispute settlement; and the Intergovernmental Committee on Intellectual Property and Genetic Resources, Traditional Knowledge and Folklore (IGC), an intergovernmental committee that has an explicit treaty-making or other norm-setting mandate. In the first, the legal argumentation by individuals and companies relies on strict administrative/quasi-judicial criteria in order to enhance their chance of winning cases. As a result, a body of jurisprudence has been established that facilitates greater certainty and predictability of decisions under the UDRP. In the IGC, a wider range of arguments is used, including moral, philosophical, economic, and even emotional, as well as legal. While legal argumentation is yet to result in a treaty or soft law instrument, it has shaped national and regional legislation on the protection of traditional knowledge.

International trade law benefits from a set of long-standing widely agreed rules that are subject to binding dispute settlement and enforcement in the World Trade Organization (WTO). Yet the reach of trade law has expanded to new areas of public policy and, as a result, argumentation about its content and contours occurs in multiple fora. This is the focus of Kathleen Claussen's chapter. She draws on two novel data sets of arguments growing out of recent events: first, state reactions to the Trump administration's imposition of special tariffs on steel and aluminum and on products from China; second, comments by US legislators in congressional debates during the Trump and Obama administrations. She calls the former "external trade law argumentation" and the latter "internal trade law argumentation." Both reveal that trade law argumentation appears across many settings and among diverse actors, directed at diverse audiences. However, a key difference between the two cases is the level of generality of the argumentation. States seeking to persuade other states to change their trade measures use rather low-intensity legal arguments, wrapping legal principles in broader political rhetoric. By contrast, the deployment of trade law argumentation in domestic settings by legislators is more nuanced, typically invoking specific aspects of international trade law in service of individual policy modifications.

The final chapter in Part IV, on privileges and immunities of international organizations, is written by UN Deputy Legal Counsel Stephen Mathias and Nicolas Perez, Legal Officer in the UN Office of Legal Affairs. They make the important observation that the Office of Legal Affairs (OLA) normally seeks to present, outside the courtroom, the exact same legal argumentation that lawyers and counsel would use in a courtroom even though it generally deals only with political entities, such as Permanent Missions, Foreign Ministries, and Ministries of Justice. The recognition of privileges and immunities can be sensitive for both member states and international organizations since it sometimes gives rise, within the general population and the media, to a feeling that the normal course of justice has not been followed in a given situation. They argue that a persuasive legal argument is one that is grounded in the clear obligations of UN member states under the Charter and the 1946 Convention on the Privileges and Immunities of the United Nations. But those arguments must be presented to the right national authorities, a task central to OLA. And the United Nations' power to persuade is linked to demonstrating to those audiences that all member states need to respect its privileges and immunities in order for the United Nations to carry out its vast array of tasks.

Legal argumentation beyond courts occurs in every area of law, and we were not able to cover all of them in this book. Other topics that strike us as especially worthy of further study include investment law, the law of the sea, and the law that bears on peace processes. A study of argumentation in investment law would be illuminating for several reasons: the parties to an investment dispute are a state and non-state actor; the disputes are often resolved through arbitration, where decisions are binding only on the parties yet a substantial body of jurisprudence is building up—influencing argumentation outside of the proceedings; and the legitimacy of the entire investment law system is being questioned, prompting legal argumentation that goes beyond interpretation and application of treaty terms. The law of the sea is also ripe for this sort of analysis, in part because it is based mainly on hard treaty law (the Law of the Sea Convention and Tribunal) but also customary law, which is especially important given that the United States is not a party. Moreover, even among parties, we are witnessing intensive argumentation outside the Tribunal and arbitral proceedings, especially as regards the South China Sea. The law that bears on peace processes holds special interest because the parties typically include at least one non-state actor, and it is not clear what, if any, international law applies. Moreover, some scholars have posited the emergence of an entirely new area of law—*jus post bellum*—while others have criticized the whole ideology behind "liberal peacebuilding" as a neocolonial enterprise. Thus argumentation over what international law principles apply (or should apply) to peace processes is intertwined with fundamental questions about whether international law is hegemonic.

The concluding chapter, in Part V, identifies a number of themes that run throughout the book. Rather than review each chapter in detail, we pull the threads together in an attempt to point toward a fully developed theory of legal argumentation. In so doing, we hope to lay the foundation for a rich agenda of further research on both the practice and theory of argumentation using international law.

2

Why Use the Language of the Law in Global Politics? On the Legitimacy Effects of Claiming to Act Legally

Ingo Venzke

I. Introduction

The language of international law has shaped many debates in global politics.[1] The legality of the 2003 US-led invasion of Iraq is a prominent example. Whether it was legal was a central question at the UN Security Council; it structured the speeches of many politicians when they addressed the public, and it was key to the claims that the public made in many market squares.[2] Why? What are the reasons for invoking the law? What are the underlying assumptions about its power? Do they hold?

Some public leaders—especially but not only of a populist bent—have shown little patience for international law, voicing outright disdain for international commitments instead.[3] For example, when President Donald Trump went on record after the United States, together with France and the United Kingdom, had struck against President Bashar al-Assad of Syria, arguably in retaliation of his use of chemical weapons, legal language was rarely heard. Here and elsewhere, a moral vocabulary prevailed: "The evil and the despicable attack left mothers and fathers, infants and children, thrashing in pain and gasping for air," Trump claimed. "These are not the actions of a man," he continued, "they are crimes of a monster instead."[4] But Trump intervened in a discursive field—debates about warfare—that often serves as an example for the prevalence

[1] As Steven Ratner points out in chapter 6 in this volume, the law has even done so when it has been rather thin, as is arguably the case in issues of cybersecurity. See more generally Friedrich Kratochwil, *The Status of Law in World Society: Meditations on the Role and Rule of Law* (Cambridge: Cambridge University Press, 2014); Nikolas M. Rajkovic, Tanja E. Aalberts, and Thomas Gammeltoft-Hansen, "Introduction: Legality, Interdisciplinarity and the Study of Practices," in *The Power of Legality: Practices of International Law and their Politics* edited by Nikolas M. Rajkovic, Tanja E. Aalberts, and Thomas Gammeltoft Hansen (Cambridge: Cambridge University Press, 2016); David Kennedy, *A World of Struggle: How Power, Law and Expertise Shape Global Political Economy* (Princeton: Princeton University Press, 2016) (showing the prevalence of legal discourse in the context of economic politics).

[2] See Ian Johnstone, "US-UN Relations after Iraq: The End of the World (Order) as We Know It?," *European Journal of International Law* 15 (2004): 813; Gerry Simpson, "The War in Iraq and International Law," *Melbourne Journal of International Law* 6 (2005): 167.

[3] Cf. James Crawford, "The Current Political Discourse Concerning International Law," *Modern Law Review* 81 (2018): 1.

[4] Donald J. Trump, "Statement by President Trump on Syria" (The White House, 2018).

Ingo Venzke, *Why Use the Language of the Law in Global Politics? On the Legitimacy Effects of Claiming to Act Legally*
In: *Talking International Law*. Edited by: Ian Johnstone and Steven Ratner, Oxford University Press.
DOI: 10.1093/oso/9780197588437.003.0002

of law in global politics. Struggles over legality—what is considered (il)legal—are recognized as a crucial site of warfare where gains and losses are experienced.[5]

One may also consider how Brexit has made many people conversant in both international and European law. Who, except for the experts, had ever heard of Article XXIV of the General Agreement on Tariffs and Trade (GATT) or of Article 50 of the Treaty of the European Union (TEU)? Boris Johnson quoted Article XXIV, paragraph 5(b) on BBC in one of his first appearances after he was elected prime minister, only to duck the interviewer's follow-up comment that paragraph 5(c) actually contradicts his plans.[6] Why this reliance (*vel non*) on the law?

In the present chapter, I focus on an assumption that underlies different approaches to answering that question, namely, that claims to legality have the capacity of changing individual or collective attitudes toward certain actions or situations.[7] I am interested, in other words, in international law's *legitimacy effects*—its impact on evaluative judgments about what is right and wrong. To be clear, my interest in this effect does not presuppose that those who invoke the law are themselves convinced by the law and deem it legitimate. Such a conviction may be one reason for invoking the law, but there are others.

Pioneering work has started to test the effect of invoking international law on public opinion, especially though experimental studies. That body of work answers one of this volume's structuring questions in the affirmative: the effect of legal versus non-legal argumentation on decision makers *can* be determined in an empirically convincing way.

I discuss this pioneering research against the background of different reasons for invoking the law that are embedded in different logics of action, and I enrich that discussion with insights from legal theory. This background adds important nuances to what has already been done, exposes gaps,[8] and instructs us on next steps. Three points will emerge in particular: First, more attention needs to be paid to distinctive

[5] See Monica Hakimi, chapter 3, in this volume. Research on this issue is often grouped under the notion of "lawfare." While propaganda is a timeworn dimension of warfare, lawfare is qualitatively different due to its reliance on *legal* language. Such a shift toward the law has gone hand in hand with an increasing role of lawyers. Consider the statement by General Jones, former NATO Supreme Allied Commander, Europe:

> It used to be a simple thing to fight a battle.... In a perfect world, a general would get up and say, "Follow me, men," and everybody would say, "Aye, sir" and run off. But that's not the world anymore, ... [now] you have to have a lawyer or a dozen. It's become very legalistic and very complex.

Quoted in Lyric Wallwork Winik, "A Marine's Toughest Mission," *Parade*, Jan. 19, 2003. Cf. Charles J. Dunlap, "Lawfare Today: A Perspective," *Yale Journal of International Affairs* 3 (2008): 146. It is fairly obvious that the notion of "lawfare" is itself employed strategically to discredit some uses of the law; see W.G. Werner, "The Curious Career of Lawfare," *Case Western Reserve Journal of International Law* 43 (2011): 61.

[6] The interview was with Andrew Neil on July 12, 2019, https://twitter.com/BBCPolitics/status/1149734201991806977.

[7] On attitudes as an evaluative response, see Gregory R. Maio, Geoffrey Haddock, and Bas Verplanken, *The Psychology of Attitudes and Attitude Change* (Thousand Oaks: Sage, 2018), 4 (summarizing different leading definitions of attitudes and identifying evaluation as the dominant aspect); cf. Alice H. Eagly and Shelly Chaiken, *The Psychology of Attitudes* (San Diego: Harcourt Brace Jovanovich College Publishers, 1993), 1 (defining attitudes as "a psychological tendency that is expressed by evaluating a particular entity with some degree of favor or disfavor.").

[8] On the existing theoretical literature on argumentation, as well as the gaps, see Ian Johnstone and Steven Ratner, chapter 1, in this volume.

features of legal claims, in particular law's claim to authority. Second, research has so far overwhelmingly focused on US public opinion and should expand to test effects among other audiences that probably hold different views about the role of law and public institutions. Third, existing research has probed international law's relevance by focusing on the constraints that it imposes and on hard cases as a litmus test. The law may be at least as important, however, in enabling action that would otherwise not be similarly available.

I will develop my argument about the prevalence of legal discourse and the underlying assumptions about its legitimacy effects in two main steps. I will first expand on the main reasons why actors invoke the law in public discourse, placing those reasons within three logics of action—consequentialism, appropriateness, and deference. Drawing on insights from legal theory, I will highlight the instrumental and formalist understandings of the law that are embedded in these explanations. Each of the three logics has a different take on the law's legitimacy effect, an effect that they, however, all share as an underlying assumption (Section II). This leads me, second, to an inquiry into the strength of that assumption and to a discussion of related experimental research. I thereby draw attention to the three main points for further inquiry—a better recognition of the law's distinctive claim to authority, of audiences' varying predispositions about the rule of law, and the law's enabling rather than constraining function in global politics (Section III). In conclusion, I will point to the deep divides that separate experimental methods from the critical legal research that has been most vocal in emphasizing law's legitimacy effects (Section IV).

II. Reasons for Invoking the Law

A. In the Aftermath of Legalization

Even if debates about the so-called legalization of world politics may now feel dated,[9] they still testify to a significant growth of international authority and increase in international legal commitments over the past decades.[10] Changes in the structure and scope of international law have been truly remarkable and are a crucial part of the condition for many legal arguments at present. Particularly noteworthy is the quantitative increase in international adjudication, which has gone hand in hand with a qualitative change toward greater judicial authority in international lawmaking, current backlashes notwithstanding.[11] Those developments made it possible for Friedrich

[9] Judith Goldstein et al., "Introduction: Legalization and World Politics," *International Organization* 54 (2000): 385.

[10] Armin von Bogdandy et al., eds., *The Exercise of Public Authority by International Institutions. Advancing International Institutional Law* (Heidelberg: Springer, 2010); Michael Zürn, *A Theory of Global Governance: Authority, Legitimacy, and Contestation* (Oxford: Oxford University Press, 2018); Armin von Bogdandy, Matthias Goldmann, and Ingo Venzke, "From Public International to International Public Law: Translating World Public Opinion into International Public Authority," *European Journal of International Law* 28 (2017): 115.

[11] Armin von Bogdandy and Ingo Venzke, *In Whose Name? A Public Law Theory of International Adjudication* (Oxford: Oxford University Press, 2014); Karen J. Alter, *The New Terrain of International Law: Courts, Politics, Rights* (Princeton: Princeton University Press, 2013).

Kratochwil to write in 2014 that "law now provides in large part the vocabulary for contemporary politics."[12] That continues to be the case even if the high times of codification and multilateral treaty-making were already over when Kratochwil penned those words.[13]

Law, however, has never been the only language of international politics, nor is its presence in public discourse a given over time, space, or issue area.[14] Legal language was rare, for example, in official discourses about Turkey's 2019 intervention into Northern Syria. One should in any case not mistake the prevalence of legal language as a victory for the rule of law and therefore be nostalgic in view of increasing disdain for international law among some world leaders. Nor is international law's discursive presence in global politics per se evidence of its power to convince actors or constrain action.[15]

Why legal discourses pervade many questions of global politics and *whether* the law constrains or convinces are related but separate questions. It may even be the case that international law has enjoyed popularity precisely because so many different things can be made of it—because it is arguably entirely malleable.[16] Whatever its overall strength, the argument that the law is so malleable cannot be brushed aside with the counterargument that it only makes sense to argue about something which is meaningful. There are many ways in which people might be led astray. It is for good reason that false consciousness is one of the main targets of critical work.[17] Put differently, it is simply not possible to gain much insight into why many actors argue about the law in global politics from the fact that they do.[18] The fact prompts the question: Why do they?

B. The Logic of Consequences

A first cut at the question of why actors invoke the law in global politics emphasizes the law's distribution of payoffs. The law matters for the way in which it allocates costs

[12] Kratochwil, *supra* note 1, at 1.

[13] Nico Krisch, "The Decay of Consent: International Law in an Age of Global Public Goods," *American Journal of International Law* 108 (2014): 1; Joost Pauwelyn, Ramses A. Wessel, and Jan Wouters, "When Structures Become Shackles: Stagnation and Dynamics in International Lawmaking," *European Journal of International Law* 25 (2014): 733.

[14] Lisbeth Zimmermann, chapter 13, in this volume, for instance, compares the relative salience of legal and scientific arguments in the International Whaling Commission, and Bruno Stagno-Ugarte, chapter 8, in this volume, notes that "non-legal arguments may be more effective" when it comes to the promotion of human rights.

[15] But see Ian Johnstone, *The Power of Deliberation: International Law, Politics and Organizations* (Oxford: Oxford University Press, 2011), 7 (suggesting that invocations of the law tesify to the fact that it matters).

[16] David Kennedy, *Of War and Law* (Princeton: Princeton University Press, 2006).

[17] On the role of ideology generally, Terry Eagleton, *Ideology: An Introduction* (New York: Verso, 2007); and in legal discourse specifically, see Duncan Kennedy, "The Hermeneutic of Suspicion in Contemporary American Legal Thought," *Law and Critique* 25 (2014): 91.

[18] I thus take a different view from Monica Hakimi, chapter 3, in this volume, who sees the prevalence of legal arguments as supporting the rule of law even when arguments cannot be authoritatively resolved. In short, I do not share her assumptions about the process of arguing. See in detail Ingo Venzke, *How Interpretation Makes International Law: On Semantic Change and Normative Twists* (Oxford: Oxford University Press, 2012), 214–222.

and benefits of different sorts. Actors invoke it because they want to enjoy the benefits that they receive through the law, or because they want to hold others to existing commitments. The use of legal arguments here is an extension of a process of continuous bargaining.[19] When it comes to maritime delimitation, for instance, legal claims determine the possibility to exploit natural resources and to exclude others from economic activity. When it comes to war and peace, assessments of legality may decide who lives and who dies during war, and who walks free or goes to prison if they take lives. In the field of investment law, the legality of host states' conduct determines their financial liability. The prevailing reason for invoking the law, these examples suggest, follows the logic of consequences—actors want to benefit from law's distribution of payoffs.[20]

This is not the place to digress into long-standing arguments about whether international law matters in consequentialist logic. That has been settled: it does.[21] It does not matter all the time, or for everyone in the same way. As a bottom line, however, a considerable part of international legal discourse cannot simply be cast aside as inconsequential rhetoric.[22] Moreover, while the prevalence of law in discourses of global politics does not *eo ipso* prove that the law matters, treating it as inconsequential rhetoric begs the question *why* law talk is so present all the same.[23] Why bother?

Two points require clarification. First, speaking the language of the law always has two dimensions: While actors seek to tap into the distribution of payoffs connected with determining the legality of certain action (e.g., what follows from an illegal use of force), making legal arguments also constantly contributes to shaping the law (what is, for instance, considered to be an illegal use of force?).[24] Particular legal arguments are a simultaneous expression of, on the one hand, the power that resides with specific actors to shape the law through their use of the law and, on the other hand, the power that resides within the structure of the law—the institution that shapes the chances that some legal arguments succeed and others fail.[25] Sticking to the metaphor of the language of international law, one can think of those two dimensions of speaking

[19] Cf. Harald Müller, "Arguing, Bargaining and All That: Communicative Action, Rationalist Theory and the Logic of Appropriateness in International Relations," *European Journal of International Relations* 10 (2004): 395; Jon Elster, "The Strategic Use of Arguments," in *Barriers to Conflict Resolution*, edited by K. Arrow et al. (New York: W. W. Norton, 1995), 236; Johnstone, *supra* note 15, at 17.

[20] James G. March and Johan P. Olsen, "Elaborating the 'New Institutionalism,'" in *The Oxford Handbook of Political Institutions*, edited by Sarah A. Binder and R.A.W. Rhodes (Oxford: Oxford University Press, 2008), 3.

[21] Friedrich V. Kratochwil, "How Do Norms Matter?," in *The Role of Law in International Politics: Essays in International Relations and International Law*, edited by Michael Byers (Oxford: Oxford University Press, 2000); Robert D. Keohane and Lisa L. Martin, "The Promise of Institutionalist Theory," *International Security* 20 (1995): 39.

[22] Jack L. Goldsmith and Eric A. Posner, *The Limits of International Law* (New York: Oxford University Press, 2005); Hans-Joachim Cremer, "Völkerrecht—Alles Nur Rhetorik?," *Zeitschrift für ausländisches öffentliches Recht und Völkerrecht* 67 (2007): 267.

[23] In agreement, Johnstone, *supra* note 15. Also see Steven R. Ratner, "Law Promotion beyond Law Talk: The Red Cross, Persuasion, and the Laws of War," *European Journal of International Law* 22 (2011): 459.

[24] Also see Steven Ratner, chapter 6, in this volume, highlighting the lawmaking dimension of legal arguments.

[25] See, in further detail, Venzke, *supra* note 18 (developing an understanding of legal argumentation as semantic struggle).

along the lines of the classic distinction between *langue*—structuring language—and *parole*—the act of speaking.[26]

Second, international law's institutional power not only constrains but also enables certain action—something that tends to be glossed over in much of the international relations literature and its emphasis on compliance.[27] One may consider the example of a bilateral investment treaty (BIT) between states "A" and "B" to illustrate both points. While the BIT imposes costs for breaches of certain standards of protection, it enables foreign investors to resort to international arbitration and opens up avenues for enforcement. When arguing about certain standards of protection—for example, whether A's environmental law reform amounts to an indirect expropriation—actors are subject to the institutional power of the underlying treaty and a mode of discourse which, once more, impacts the prospects of specific arguments succeeding or failing. At the same time, actors exercise power to the extent that they are able to shift those prospects with respect to the decision in the concrete case and for future arguments down the road.

Further examples stem from the frequent frame of reference for arguments about law talk, the laws of war. While those laws prohibit certain conduct, such as the direct targeting of civilians, they allow other actions, such as targeting civilians who take a direct part in hostilities, thus turning an act of killing into a legally sanctioned feat.[28] By referring to the law, actors tap into the way in which the law distributes gains and losses. They simultaneously try to pull the law onto their side and contribute to shaping and making the law within their practice.[29]

"Law's empire has less need for troops," Katharina Pistor writes in her analysis of private law and the making of capital. The law, she continues, "relies instead on the normative authority of the law, and its most powerful battle cry is 'but it is legal.'"[30] The way in which the law creates wealth and inequality by coding capital, Pistor argues, provides a powerful defense against those who want to challenge that distribution. Granting an appearance of legitimacy is one of law's key functions in Pistor's analysis, as in others.

The belief in the legitimacy of the law—of legal titles, wealth, and inequality that it creates—appears to be at the core of Pistor's arguments. Moreover, she places emphasis not on what is prohibited but on what is allowed and thereby legitimized.[31] Jean-Jacques Rousseau knew that as far back as 1775 when he wrote his *Discourse Upon the Origin and the Foundation of the Inequality among Mankind* of "[t]he first

[26] While recognizing that the former also shapes the latter and is not only structured by, see Ferdinand de Saussure, *Course in General Linguistics*, edited by Roy Harris (Chicago: Open Court, 1965); cf. Ingo Venzke, "Is Interpretation in International Law a Game?," in *Interpretation in International Law*, edited by Andrea Bianchi, Daniel Peat, and Matthew Windsor (Oxford: Oxford University Press, 2015), 352.

[27] But see Ian Johnstone, "The Security Council and International Law," in *The UN Security Council in the 21st Century*, edited by Sebastian von Einsiedel, David M. Malone, and Bruno Stagno Ugarte (Boulder: Lynne Rienne Publishers, 2015), 771; Ian Hurd, *How to Do Things with International Law* (Princeton: Princeton University Press, 2017).

[28] Nathaniel Berman, "Privileging Combat? Contemporary Conflict and the Legal Construction of War," *Columbia Journal of Transnational Law* 43 (2004): 1.

[29] Venzke, *supra* note 18; Kennedy, *supra* note 1.

[30] Katharina Pistor, *The Code of Capital: How the Law Creates Wealth and Inequality* (Princeton: Princeton University Press, 2019), 8, 161.

[31] Ingo Venzke, *International Law and the Spectre of Inequality* (Amsterdam: Amsterdam University Press, 2019).

man, who, after enclosing a piece of ground, took it into his head to say, 'This is mine,' and found people simple enough to *believe* him."[32] Since then, the sociological fact that legality begets legitimacy—that whatever is legal is legitimate, or at least okay—has only grown stronger.

The legitimacy effects of the law are important in the consequentialist logic. Legitimacy is the consequence that actors may be striving for in engaging in legal argumentation. As Nikolas Rajkovic suggests, debates about legality in war have brought to the fore that "the chief goal [of invoking the law] is to build social resonance, recognition and, ultimately, validation from a global audience of legal experts, public opinion, and sovereign decision-makers."[33] When Major-General Charles Dunlap fleshed out what he meant by the term "lawfare" in the early 2000s, he argued that parties to a conflict resort to the law in an attempt "to destroy the will to fight by undermining public support that is indispensable when democracies like the US conduct military interventions."[34] The reasons for invoking the law continue to be consequentialist, and the use of law, instrumentalist. At the same time, these accounts presume that what is considered right and wrong matters and that the law has something to do with that. The example of lawfare thus points beyond consequentialism toward a logic of appropriateness or deference.

C. The Logic of Appropriateness

A second cut at the question of why actors choose to talk international law emphasizes the logic of appropriateness and sees the use of international legal language not as an extension of processes of bargaining but of arguing.[35] The aim is not to materially induce but to persuade others to act, or at least to evaluate action, in a certain way.[36] This practice is supported by processes of socialization and a certain (legal) culture.[37] In using law in attempts to persuade, the reason for invoking the law continues to be consequentialist. But the presumption is that persuasion (through law) can impact beliefs and behavior.

The pervasiveness and appreciation of the rule of law plays an important role in those processes in domestic, supranational as well as international settings. *Ubi societas, ibi ius*, the old maxim goes—where there is society, there is law. As a

[32] Jean-Jacques Rousseau, "A Discourse upon the Origin and the Foundation of the Inequality Among Mankind," [1755], 18, https://www.gutenberg.org/cache/epub/11136/pg11136.html (italics added).

[33] Nikolas M. Rajkovic, "Performing 'Legality' in the Theatre of Hostilities: Asymmetric Conflict, Lawfare and the Rise of Vicarious Litigation" (unpublished manuscript), 7.

[34] Charles J. Dunlap Jr., "Law and Military Interventions: Preserving Humanitarian Values in 21st Century Conflicts," paper presented to the Humanitarian Challenges in Military Intervention Conference, Carr Center for Human Rights Policy, Washington, DC (November 29, 2001), 4, quoted in Rajkovic, *supra* note 33, at 18.

[35] Müller, *supra* note 19. In further detail, Venzke, *supra* note 18, at 214–222; Johnstone, *supra* note 15, at 17–21.

[36] See Hyeran Jo, chapter 9, in this volume, placing her analysis of the effect of legal argumentation within the logic of argumentation. Cf. Ryan Goodman and Derek Jinks, *Socializing States: Promoting Human Rights Through International Law* (Oxford: Oxford University Press, 2013), 21–31, on material inducement and persuasion as the related modes of influence.

[37] On appropriateness as a specific culture, see March and Olsen, *supra* note 20.

sociological fact, the rule of law reflects a normative program of living together through law. The underlying idea is that, in complex societies, discourses of legality often take the place of discourses of morality.[38] Two steps of the argument should be disentangled to understand invocations of international law from a logic of appropriateness: that legality begets legitimacy; and that legitimacy matters.

1. Legality Begets Legitimacy

"The most common form of legitimacy," Max Weber noted in the 1920s, "is the belief in legality."[39] When Niklas Luhmann picked up this claim, he criticized Weber, saying he had not actually shown how such legitimacy based on legality was sociologically possible.[40] Setting that task for himself, Luhmann emphasized the proceduralization that comes with resorting to legal language. Treating societal issues within the legal process chops them into pieces in a way that suspends tensions and abridges broader underlying questions, thus evoking that sense of rational-legal legitimacy that Weber was talking about.[41] It is precisely the possibility of legitimizing a decision in situations in which we cannot reason our way out, so to speak, that may well be the proper domain of law.[42] More recent scholarship, especially in social psychology, lends further support to the argument that legality does indeed induce legitimacy. It also emphasizes characteristics of the legal process.[43]

That legality does beget legitimacy—that something is considered right because it is legal and wrong when it is not—reflects a belief that is deeply rooted in many societies. The normative program that it reflects is most closely connected with (neo-)Kantian political philosophy and legal theory.[44] It holds high the idea of law as a means for ensuring legitimate rule, for ensuring individual as well as collective self-determination.[45] The law is used to constrain and enable action in vertical (private) and horizontal (public) relationships. Hans Kelsen developed his conception of law and defense of formal legal reasoning in this vein, as part of a democratic disposition—the legislator decides what is the norm.[46]

[38] On the ambition of facilitating legal discourses at the international level, Armin von Bogdandy, Matthias Goldmann, and Ingo Venzke, "From Public International to International Public Law: Translating World Public Opinion into International Public Authority," *European Journal of International Law* 28 (2017): 115.

[39] Max Weber, *Economy and Society* (Berkeley: University of California Press, 1978), 37.

[40] Niklas Luhmann, *Legitimation Durch Verfahren* (Berlin: Suhrkamp, 1983), 28.

[41] *Id.*

[42] See further text at *infra* note 82; Bas Schotel, "Multiple Legalities and International Criminal Tribunals: Juridical versus Political Legality," in *The Power of Legality: Practices of International Law and Their Politics*, *supra* note 1, at 210, 214 (arguing that "since all of what we do has politics in it in the sense that our decisions and actions are not fully guided by norms, we cannot 'reason our way out'. It means that there is a risk of coercion that cannot be fully understood, justified and curtailed by practical reasoning"). Cf. Johnstone, *supra* note 15.

[43] Avital Mentovich and Maor Zeev-Wolf, "Law and Moral Order: The Influence of Legal Outcomes on Moral Judgment," *Psychology, Public Policy, and Law* 24 (2018): 489. See also Monica Hakimi, chapter 3, in this volume, noting the importance of procedural legitimacy.

[44] Jürgen Habermas, *Between Facts and Norms: Contributions to a Discourse Theory of Law and Democracy* (Cambridge, MA: MIT Press, 1996).

[45] See Arthur Ripstein, *Force and Freedom: Kant's Legal and Political Philosophy* (Cambridge, MA: Harvard University Press, 2009).

[46] Hans Kelsen, *General Theory of Law and State* (Cambridge, MA: Harvard University Press, 1945).

Others, like Kelsen's national-socialist nemesis, Carl Schmitt, critiqued what Schmitt saw as empty formalism, decrying the degree to which legitimacy has effectively come to be used interchangeably with legality. But Schmitt, too, saw the degree to which legality in fact begets legitimacy.[47] Judith Shklar later coined the term "legalism" to refer precisely to "the belief that law is not only separate from political life but that it is a mode of social action superior to mere politics."[48] Other critical scholars have likewise drawn attention to the downside of law's legitimacy effects. The effect contributes to an appearance of a state of affairs as natural, necessary, and even just, they have argued—an appearance that they consider to be undeserved and to stand in the way of progressive change.[49]

2. Legitimacy Matters

The specific objectives of actors who invoke the law in the logic of appropriateness may again vary; arguments could be concerned with those actors' own action or with that of others, or with certain factual situations. The preceding examples of "lawfare" illustrate that. A great deal of research has highlighted the importance of legitimacy in understanding compliance in particular. While the emphasis on compliance across disciplines has perhaps been excessive, downplaying other important legal functions, compliance is certainly one concern that may underlie invocations of the law.[50] The point then is that actors should follow the law because it is the right thing to do.

Tom Tyler's work has supported the link between legitimacy and compliance, showing that legitimacy tends to be a better predictor for compliance than interest-based calculations.[51] In international legal scholarship, such a line of argument emerges in the works of Thomas Franck as well as Jutta Brunnée and Stephen Toope. Franck's seminal *The Power of Legitimacy Among Nations* once more testifies to the spirit of the 1990s, when it proclaims on its dust jacket that "[a]s frozen power blocs dissolve and the ideological steppes erode, a conflict-weary international community can expect to evolve more like other societies in which participants generally learn to

[47] Schmitt at the same time denounced that there are apparently no limits as to what can be (il)legal, arguing for a material conception of the constitution instead, one which was imbued with his nationalist belief in the "substantial content and force of the German nation": Carl Schmitt, *Legalität und Legitimität* (Berlin: Duncker & Humblot, 2012), 90 (my translation). Schmitt published his attack on legal legitimacy in the year before Hitler took power, then advancing to become, as is well known, the crown jurist of the Nazi regime.

[48] Judith N. Shklar, *Legalism* (Cambridge, MA: Harvard University Press, 1964), 8. Cf. Ingo Venzke, "Judicial Authority and Styles of Reasoning: Self-Presentation Between Legalism and Deliberation," in *Establishing Judicial Authority in International Economic Law*, edited by Joanna Jemielniak, Laura Nielsen, and Henrik Palmer Olsen (Cambridge: Cambridge University Press, 2016).

[49] Duncan Kennedy, *A Critique of Adjudication (Fin de Siècle)* (Cambridge, MA: Harvard University Press, 1997), 236; Roberto Mangabeira Unger, *What Should Legal Analysis Become?* (London: Verso, 1996); Roberto Mangabeira Unger, *False Necessity: Anti-Necessitarian Social Theory in the Service of Radical Democracy* (London: Verso, 2001). Cf. Ingo Venzke, "Cracking the Frame? On the Prospects of Change in a World of Struggle," *European Journal of International Law* 27 (2016): 831, http://ejil.oxfordjournals.org/lookup/doi/10.1093/ejil/chw036.

[50] Also see Steven Ratner, chapter 6, as well as Hyeran Jo, chapter 9, both in this volume. Cf. Robert Howse and Ruti G. Teitel, "Beyond Compliance: Rethinking Why International Law Really Matters," *Global Policy* 2 (2011): 127.

[51] Tom R. Tyler, "Procedural Justice, Legitimacy, and the Effective Rule of Law," *Crime and Justice* 30 (2016): 283. See also Weber, *supra* note 39, at 37 (linking legal legitimacy to compliance with those laws, "which are *formally* correct and which have been made in the accustomed manner").

obey the rules for the common good."[52] Its argument is straightforward enough: compliance with international law will increasingly depend on its legitimacy. That legitimacy, in turn, depends mostly on the belief that it "has come into being and operates in accordance with generally accepted principles of right process."[53] Those beliefs bestow the law with a legitimacy that contributes to explaining compliance with the law and that can account for the fact that claiming to act legally can impact individual and collective evaluative judgments.[54]

For their part, Brunnée and Toope start from the observation that the compliance pull of law is undervalued.[55] They focus on the sense of legal obligation that the law is supposed to generate, rely on the natural law theory of Lon Fuller, and subject the law to Fuller's eight criteria for legality.[56] For them, reasons for invoking the law in global politics connect to the logic of appropriateness. Invoking the law ought to remind others of their obligations and motivate corresponding behavior. Brunnée and Toope notably focus on the addressees of the law—those whose actions may actually be at issue—and not on larger audiences. Many invocations of international law are, however, not addressed to those who are supposed to comply but rather aim at (de)mobilizing allies and at shifting power and possibilities in a wider field of action.

Other work has taken law's legitimacy effects into account in such wider fields. Research on the International Criminal Court (ICC) has, for instance, placed emphasis on how legal arguments around it are aimed at mobilizing allies while demobilizing support opponents—also in the absence of any expectation that the ICC, or other actors like it, would actually get involved.[57] When courts or tribunals do get involved, consequences are not everything. Trade litigation shows that an expected authorization to suspend concessions does not fully explain that practice. Litigation is also pursued for the purpose of seeking recognition of what litigants believe to be right—a recognition that is provided through law.[58]

Especially when processes of persuasion are focused on the addressee of a norm, questions remain about the impact of invoking the law. The addressee may be an interested actor with fairly robust views of what is right and wrong, unlikely to be

[52] Thomas M. Franck, *The Power of Legitimacy Among Nations* (New York: Oxford University Press, 1990), 24.

[53] *Id.* 24, also at 19. As Ian Johnstone reminded me, Franck added a substantive dimension to his theory in his later *Fairness in International Law and Institutions* (Oxford: Oxford University Press, 1995).

[54] It is thus, of course, the case that the legitimacy effect of claiming to act legally depends on beliefs in the law's legitimacy. At the same time, that effect cannot simply be reduced to those background beliefs on which the law's legitimacy depends. That difference, or gap, that offers the law a genuine, irreducible effect is perhaps the main characteristic of a legal culture that marks many societies.

[55] Jutta Brunnée and Stephen Toope, *Legitimacy and Legality in International Law: An Interactional Account* (Cambridge: Cambridge University Press, 2010), 88. Also see Jutta Brunnée, chapter 12, in this volume.

[56] Brunnée and Toope, *supra* note 55, at 95–97.

[57] Wouter Werner, chapter 10, in this volume. Cf. Schotel, *supra* note 42, at 210: "[T]he legal statements are not so much directed at an opponent or counterparty. Rather, a proponent makes legal statements in order to mobilize his allies to enforce his claim against the opponent, and to de-mobilize the allies of the opponent who might otherwise assist him in fending off the enforcement by the proponent and his helpers." See also Cosette D. Creamer and Beth Simmons, "The Proof Is in the Process: Self-Reporting under International Human Rights Treaties," *American Journal of International Law* 114 (2019): 1, 37–39, on how committee reports mobilize civil society.

[58] Joseph A. Conti, "The Good Case: Decisions to Litigate at the World Trade Organization," *Law and Society Review* 42 (2008): 145 (distinguishing economic, political, and, notably, symbolic motivations for litigation).

persuaded by another actor's claims of legality.[59] Speaking about what is actually right and effective may actually be more promising language than invoking the law.[60] To get a fuller picture on the prevalence of law talk, the logic of deference should be considered.

D. Deference

While the logic of appropriateness places emphasis on persuasion and the connection between legality and legitimacy, the practice of invoking the law once more points beyond that emphasis. First, as much as persuasion—inducing agreement in substance—may be the aim, invoking the law may actually be understood as a demand to suspend individual substantive assessments and to defer to the law instead. The classic example is the aged road sign: "Buckle up—It's the law!" Do it, because the law says so (deference), not because it is necessarily the safe (consequentialism) or right (appropriateness) thing to do. Law makes a distinctive claim to authority. It offers content-independent reasons for action.[61] Its reasons for action collapse into neither institutional power and different enforcement mechanisms (physical coercion, at the extreme) nor into agreement in substance. Most conceptions of law certainly tie the law to minimal enforcement, and many require a minimal degree of moral justification.[62] Law's claim to authority, however, cannot be reduced to either of them. That concept of authority is at the heart of the logic of deference.

Second, there is often a curious gap, especially in research focused on legitimacy as a reason for compliance, with regard to how the law is put to use in the practice of arguing with it, about it. The law can, of course, not itself claim authority, but some actor must do so, supposedly on the law's behalf. More often than not, questions of what counts as law and what *is* the law are part of the argument.[63] Moreover, that argumentative space tends to be structured, to varying degrees, by international institutions that have the capacity to establish reference points that anyone wanting to make a legal argument cannot easily escape.[64] For example, it is difficult to argue about the legality of subsidies of Boeing or Airbus without referring to the (at least for now) defunct Appellate Body of the World Trade Organization, especially when its rulings on those matters make front-page news.[65]

59 Compare Ian Johnstone, chapter 7, in this volume, noting that those who are rather neutral are most likely to be persuaded.

60 See Ratner, *supra* note 23.

61 Stefan Sciaraffa, "On Content-Independent Reasons: It's Not in the Name," *Law and Philosophy* 28 (2009): 233.

62 Classically, Jeremy Bentham, *Of Laws in General* (London: Athlone, 1970).

63 See Steven Ratner, chapter 6, and Monica Hakimi, chapter 3, both in this volume.

64 On that distinctive feature of legal arguments, see Ian Johnstone, chapter 7, in this volume. Cf. Ingo Venzke, "Between Power and Persuasion: On International Institutions' Authority in Making Law," *Transnational Legal Theory* 4 (2013): 354.

65 E.g., "EU verleende illegale subsidies aan Airbus," *NRC*, May 15th, 2018, https://www.nrc.nl/nieuws/2018/05/15/eu-verleende-illegale-subsidies-aan-airbus-a1603014. Also see Kathleen Claussen, chapter 15, in this volume, on how international trade law has entered public discourse in the United States.

Granted, it would be rather far-fetched to think that public actors defer and suspend their own judgment when they invoke international law—and particular interpretations of it—in global politics. That is, however, not a prerequisite for the logic of deference to make sense in this context. Work on authority has traditionally focused too much on a dyadic relationship between the law or a particular actor claiming authority, on the one hand, and a specific addressee, on the other, with little acknowledgment of the crucial social context in which those claims are situated.

Public authority emerges when a broader social belief holds that an actor should do something because the law, and a particular actor interpreting the law, says so. Many societies have a legal culture that sustains such a belief, which also extends to global politics. It is decisive for the law's claim to authority that there is a social expectation that it be followed. What sustains its claim to authority is not its individual recognition in the specific case of its exercise, but its social recognition, which, as Luhmann noted, "does precisely not rest . . . on convictions for which one is personally responsible, but to the contrary on social climate."[66] At least parts of international law and its institutions enjoy the capacity to claim such authority.[67]

Consider the introductory example of debates about the legality of the 2003 invasion of Iraq, which turned on quite meticulous readings of Security Council resolutions. Neither George W. Bush nor Tony Blair, nor their respective legal advisers or other members of government, were convinced that those resolutions gave them what they wanted, namely, an unambiguous authorization to use force. Nor was their decision to go to war altered by the consequences they anticipated from being seen by many as lawbreakers. They referred to the law because it was socially expected of them, from their peers as well as the general public—paradoxically, yes, in this instance of its breach—to find support for their action through the law.

The mechanism through which that should work is similar to but not the same as persuasion and the logic of appropriateness. The expected effect here is not one of persuasion about what is appropriate but of changing registers from rightness to legality—that evaluative attitudes toward certain behavior or factual situations are shaped by what is legal, to the gradual exclusion of other considerations.

III. Testing the Legitimacy Effects of International Law

The three logics of action highlight different reasons for invoking the law in global politics. Actors seek to influence behavior and beliefs through material inducement, persuasion, and deference. In their distinct readings, each of the logics pointed to the law's legitimacy effects as an important part of their explanations. In this section, I turn to research that has set out to test these effects, especially through experimental studies (Subsection A). Against the background of the logics of action discussed in Section II, it appears that more attention needs to be paid to the distinctive claims

[66] Luhmann, *supra* note 40, at 34.

[67] See Kathleen Claussen, chapter 15, in this volume, on how international trade law is in this sense embedded domestically in the United States, including among members of Congress.

to authority, to audiences beyond the United States, and to the law's role in enabling rather than constraining action (Subsection B).

A. The State of Research

If an important reason for invoking the law is to sway larger audiences in their attitude toward certain actions or situations, what role do legal arguments actually play in that regard? Some research on the intersections among international law, international relations, and psychology has specifically turned to testing the effects of invoking international law, specifically on the general public's attitudes.[68] I structure the following discussion by focusing on the three main variables at issue—*what* has been claimed (contents), *who* has claimed it (source), and *toward whom* (audience).[69]

One of the leading questions has precisely been whether *legal* arguments, when compared with arguments of morality or expedience, have a differential impact on the public's beliefs. What would then explain such a differential impact—would it be the close connection between, if not conflation of, morality and legality, as embedded in the logic of appropriateness; or would claims to legality (partially) replace other considerations, as the logic of deference would suggest? The results on the law's legitimacy effect have so far been mixed, even partially contradictory, and questions remain as to what exactly explains the effects.

Geoffrey Wallace found that invoking international law does make a difference on the public's attitude. Building his study around the hard case of attitudes toward torture—a topic on which people hold relatively robust moral convictions—he found that referring to the fact that "[t]he United States has signed international treaties that do not allow the use of these methods under any circumstances" decreased agreement with the statement that "[t]he United States should use interrogation methods involving torture." Thirty-eight percent of those exposed to the international legal argument agreed with the proposition that the United States should use torture, while 44 percent agreed with it if they were not exposed to that claim—a decrease of 6 percent.[70] Wallace also found that the effect depended significantly on participants'

[68] Joshua D. Kertzer and Dustin Tingley, "Political Psychology in International Relations: Beyond the Paradigms," *Annual Review of Political Science* 21 (2018): 319 (offering an overview of political psychology in international relations; see esp. 325). See also Adam Chilton and Dustin Tingley, "Why the Study of International Law Needs Experiments," *Columbia Journal of Transnational Law* 52 (2013): 173. On the confluence of law and psychology, see Krin Irvine, David A. Hoffman, and Tess Wilkinson-Ryan, "Law and Psychology Grows Up, Goes Online, and Replicates," *Journal of Empirical Legal Studies* 15 (2018): 320.

[69] Compare the Laswell and Yale models of communication: Irving Lester Janis and Carl Iver Hovland, *Personality and Persuasibility* (3rd reprint, New Haven: Yale University Press, 1966); Joop van der Pligt and Michael Vliek, *Influence: Theory, Research and Practice* (Oxfordshire: Routledge, 2017), 6.

[70] Geoffrey P.R. Wallace, "International Law and Public Attitudes toward Torture: An Experimental Study," *International Organization* 67 (2013): 105, 119–120. A later study by Adam S. Chilton and Mila Versteeg used a different vignette and did not find a statistically significant effect from informing participants that the acts at issue would violate either international law or US Constitutional Law. Moreover, their results indicated an unexplained negative impact when participants were told that the acts violated both international and constitutional law, that is, levels of agreement in fact increased for that treatment group. Adam S. Chilton and Mila Versteeg, "International Law, Constitutional Law, and Public Support for Torture," *Research and Politics* 3 (2016): 1.

political orientation. While the percentage of agreement dropped by 11 percent among liberals, it only dropped by 1 percent among conservatives.[71]

In a similar study, Adam Chilton tested the impact of invoking the laws of war on levels of approval with the hypothetical decision of the US president "to continue the bombing campaign against the rebel forces because failing to do so would result in the loss of a strategic ally."[72] Further exposing participants to the claim that "continuing the bombing campaign of civilians would violate international law" led to a 9 percent decrease of approval. Chilton further found, however, that the effect was nearly the same if participants were exposed to the moral claim that "continuing the bombing of civilians would be immoral," which led to a 7 percent decrease of approval.[73] Moreover, the effect for combined exposure—that the bombing is both illegal and immoral—was almost the same as the international law effect. These results suggest, according to Chilton, "that information on the laws of war is a substitute for being told that the behavior in question would be immoral."[74] On the one hand, this suggestion may be understood to question the relevance and distinctive quality of international law—one might as well have referred to morality. On the other hand, however, it supports the law's legitimacy effect—it *can* serve as a substitute.

Sarah Kreps and Geoffrey Wallace compared legal claims about drone strikes with claims about their effectiveness and, at the same time, varied the source of the claims between the government (arguing in favor) as well as the United Nations and Human Rights Watch (HRW) (both arguing against).[75] They found a significant decrease of approval with drone strikes when participants were exposed to legal arguments against them by the United Nations (8%) or HRW (6%), and only a modest (1%) increase when the government argued in favor. Conversely, the impact of effectiveness-based claims was lower for the United Nations and HRW (decrease by 4%) and higher for the government (increase by 4%). Differences in beliefs about the source's credibility, the authors found, do not explain this variation. Rather, the authors speculate that the limited impact of claims made by the government, and effectiveness-based claims, are due to participants' prior exposure.[76]

Finally, several other studies have emphasized that any impact is mediated by preexisting preferences.[77] Stephen Chaudoin found that exposing participants to the claim that implementing protectionist trade barriers breached prior commitments

[71] Wallace, *supra* note 70, at 121–122.

[72] Adam S. Chilton, "The Laws of War and Public Opinion: An Experimental Study," *Journal of Institutional and Theoretical Economics* 171 (2015): 181. See also Adam S. Chilton, "The Influence of International Human Rights Agreements on Public Opinion: An Experimental Study," *Chicago Journal of International Law* 15 (2014): 110 (finding an effect of referring to prior treaty commitments in the field of human rights on public opinion).

[73] The difference between the legal and moral claim was statistically insignificant ($p = 0{,}74$).

[74] Chilton, "The Laws of War and Public Opinion: An Experimental Study," *supra* note 72, at 14.

[75] Sarah E. Kreps and Geoffrey P.R. Wallace, "International Law, Military Effectiveness, and Public Support for Drone Strikes," *Journal of Peace Research* 53 (2016): 830. Also see Naoko Matsumura, "A WTO Ruling Matters: Citizens' Support for the Government's Compliance with Trade Agreements," *Peace Economics, Peace Science and Public Policy* 25 (2019) (showing the difference of impact on attitudes between claims by a foreign government and an international quasi-judicial body).

[76] Kreps and Wallace, *supra* note 75, at 838 in further detail.

[77] Something that Wallace approaches by testing the moderating influence of political orientation on law's legitimacy effect.

only influenced the attitude of those who had no opinion on such a policy beforehand.[78] In a study among German parliamentarians, Burcu Bayram focused on participants' cosmopolitan social identity and their sense of obligation toward international law.[79] When participants were informed about benefits of breaching international legal commitments, the impact of that information was strongly mediated by their sense of obligation. Or, in her words: "cosmopolitan politicians' preferences for compliance are robust to information about compliance costs."[80] That is in line with what one would expect in a logic of deference—an at least partial suspension of individual assessments that is replaced by considerations of what is legal.

B. Next Steps

1. Law's Distinctive Claim to Authority

The discussion of research to date points to the following areas for further inquiry. First, questions remain with regard to the use of law when compared to other registers—in particular morality and efficiency. Existing studies are contradictory in some ways and wanting in others. Chilton's nonfinding of any significant differential impact of legal when compared to moral claims may well have been due to the fact that both claims were phrased in an almost identical way: "It is immoral [or: It is a violation of international law and the treaties that the United States has signed] to continue a bombing campaign when the expected loss of civilian life is excessive relative to the military advantage gained."[81] This almost identical wording had the advantage of isolating the argument's characterization as legal or moral. It is also true that the introductory vignette for all treatment groups already contained the information that "[a]ny continued bombing would result in excessive civilian casualties." Still, for the control group, excessive civilian casualties were one reason among others, whereas this reason was repeated, singled out, and thereby emphasized for both treatment groups. It is likely that the interventions among the treatment groups showed an impact when compared to the control group due to this repeated reason of excessive civilian casualties, rather than the claim's qualification as either legal or moral, and that this repetition, at the same time, overshadowed the difference between the legal and moral claims.

Insufficient attention has been paid to law's distinctive claim to authority, which, in contrast to other registers, stands in lieu of further justification—"buckle up," not because it's safe or right, but because it is the law. This is the idea at the heart of the logic of deference. This distinctive claim is all the more important when legal arguments *are not* readily evaluated by lay audiences and, even by expert audiences, *cannot be* easily translated into other registers of what is right or expedient. Consider, for instance, claims about Article XXIV, paragraph 5(b) of the GATT allowing for a free

[78] Stephen Chaudoin, "Promises or Policies? An Experimental Analysis of International Agreements and Audience Reactions," *International Organization* 68 (2014): 235.

[79] A. Burcu Bayram, "'Due Deference': Cosmopolitan Social Identity and the Psychology of Legal Obligation in International Politics," *International Organization* 71 (2017): S137.

[80] *Id.* S139.

[81] Chilton, "The Laws of War and Public Opinion: An Experimental Study," *supra* note 72.

trade agreement between the European Union and the United Kingdom post-Brexit and the conditions under which trade law would in fact stand in the way of such an agreement. Here the appeal is to the authority of the law and its quality as law. It does not stand in for another reason (like excessive killing in the previous example) that can easily replace it. This is what I meant when I talked about law's proper domain in legitimizing decisions when it is not possible to reason one's way out.[82] The claims in Chilton's as well as Wallace's study and the way in which those claims are paraphrased are, however, easily translatable into other registers of what is right or expedient.

Next steps for research should thus test the effect of more technical legal claims while continuing to be realistic about the actual usage of the law in public discourse—for example, of invoking Article XXIV 5(b) of the GATT or the trade legality of subsidies. One might expect that the effect of invoking the law on levels of perceived legitimacy would be higher when participants cannot easily substitute the claim of legality with their own judgment about what is right or expedient. The setup could in principle follow the design of past studies and likewise use experimental surveys, then expose the treatment group to the claim, for example, that imposing higher tariffs on steel would violate Articles I:1, II:1, and II:1(a) of the GATT and would be unjustifiable under Article XXI. What effect would that have on attitudes toward such action?

2. Predispositions of the Audience

Existing studies have paid attention to the role of respondents' political ideology in mediating the effects of using the language of international law. It would be useful to know whether those effects persist across different issue areas and among non-US audiences. In her study among German parliamentarians, Bayram notably did not find any significant effect of party-political ideology.[83]

Drawing on insights from the logics of appropriateness and deference, it may be expected that the effect of invoking international law is quite naturally mediated by more general beliefs about the legitimacy of the law to begin with, and of *international* law in particular. In his research on the legitimacy of international courts, Erik Voeten notably found that those courts' authority is, expectedly, strongly related to more general legal values and support for international institutions.[84] Given that these values and support levels vary within and across national and regional audiences, one may thus expect varying legitimacy effects of invoking international law.

Moreover, structurally similar studies on the legitimacy effect of domestic high court judgments have drawn attention to other moderating variables. Next to factors such as respondents' interest in politics, for example, they have consistently highlighted the influence of trust in public institutions.[85] These studies once more point to the importance of law's claim to authority and the sources of legitimacy that sustain it.[86]

[82] See *supra* note 42.

[83] Bayram, *supra* note 79, at S152.

[84] Erik Voeten, "Public Opinion and the Legitimacy of International Courts," *Theoretical Inquiries in Law* 14 (2013): 411.

[85] Rosalee A. Clawson, Elisabeth R. Kegler, and Eric N. Waltenburg, "The Legitimacy-Conferring Authority of the U.S. Supreme Court," *American Politics Research* 29 (2007): 566.

[86] Tom R. Tyler, "Psychological Perspectives on Legitimacy and Legitimation," *Annual Review of Psychology* 57 (2006): 375.

3. Law's Enabling Function

Existing research has almost exclusively focused on prohibitions of international law, on constraints on government actions. It may be that scholarship has been too absorbed by debates between realists and institutionalists, where the litmus test for international law's relevance has been to show that it constrains the powerful. Like some institutionalist literature on international relations, legal scholarship has, however, stressed that the law not only constrains but also enables action. One of law's main functions is to authorize action that would otherwise be illegal and thereby bestow it with an aura of legitimacy.[87]

Even though this enabling function is of primary interest in many explanations for the use of legal language, it has not yet been of similar concern in experimental research. It might be suggested that asking about the effect that something is allowed rather than prohibited is just the flipside of an identical question about its legality. However, in some contexts legal permissions may have a stronger effect than a prohibition. One might consider once more Wallace's study of the effects of branding certain practices as illegal torture on public attitudes (he found an overall drop in approval of 6%). What if the treatment group had been exposed to the claim that those practices were legal? It may well be that for some respondents the claim to legality would have undone an intuitive moral restraint (much more so than a claim to illegality would have changed a morally permissive attitude toward torture).

IV. Conclusions and Outlook

This book asks a straightforward question: Why is the language of international law so prevalent in global politics? My chapter seeks to answer that question by exploring how different logics of action emphasize different reasons for invoking the law and showing different understandings of what the law does. Those logics correspond to practices of bargaining, persuasion, and deference. In particular, the logic of deference that centers on claims to authority has not been fully explored in the academic literature, but in fact it is crucial to making sense of why law is used rather than other languages. I have argued that these logics of action share assumptions about the law's legitimacy effect, though read in distinct ways. I then discussed and critiqued research that probes this effect through experimental studies. My analysis demonstrates that further inquiries should pay closer attention to law's distinct claim to authority, to audiences' predispositions, and to law's enabling rather than constraining function.

Those inquiries would further probe the assumptions of critical scholarship, which has been most vocal in exposing the law's legitimacy effect while also being most skeptical about empirical methods to test this effect.[88] This would be fertile ground for further study, bridging two strands of thinking—behavioral and critical legal studies—that have developed in deliberate distance from one another.

[87] See *supra*, Section II.B.

[88] Kennedy, *supra* note 49.

PART II

3

Arguing about the *Jus ad Bellum*

Monica Hakimi

In January 2020, the United States conducted a targeted airstrike against Iranian General Qasem Soleimani, who at the time was on official business in Iraq. Soleimani had commanded an Iranian military unit that supported armed groups throughout the region, including in Iraq. He likely was involved, directly or indirectly, in countless incidents of low-level violence against the United States and its allies.[1] Nevertheless, the US attack on him was especially brazen and seemed to up the ante. It raised the possibility, or at least created some chatter, that the two countries were heading toward all-out war.

Most analysts who assessed the US action under the *jus ad bellum*—the body of international law that governs when states may use force across national borders—said that it was probably unlawful.[2] Although the *jus ad bellum* permits states to use force unilaterally in self-defense, it imposes certain conditions on the exercise of this right. And, most said, the United States did not appear to meet those conditions in this case. The United States did not try particularly hard to show that it did. In the days following the strike, President Donald Trump and other administration officials vacillated incoherently about their justification for using military force. They variously suggested that the action was justifiable to deter imminent attacks that Soleimani was plotting, that it was retribution for earlier attacks, and that it was just part of a broader geopolitical contest with Iran.[3] US officials did not provide the details to substantiate

[1] See, e.g., Alex Horton, "Soleimani's Legacy: The Gruesome, Advanced IEDs that Haunted U.S. Troops in Iraq," *Washington Post*, Jan. 3, 2020.

[2] E.g., Human Rights Council, Report of the Special Rapporteur on Extrajudicial, Summary, or Arbitrary Executions, UN Doc. A/HRC/44/38, para. 82 (June 29, 2020); Adil Ahmad Haque, "U.S. Legal Defense of the Soleimani Strike at the United Nations: A Critical Assessment," *Just Security*, Jan. 10, 2020, https://www.justsecurity.org/68008/u-s-legal-defense-of-the-soleimani-strike-at-the-united-nations-a-critical-assessment/; Marko Milanovic, "The Soleimani Strike and Self-Defence Against an Imminent Armed Attack," *EJIL:Talk!*, Jan. 7, 2020, https://www.ejiltalk.org/the-soleimani-strike-and-self-defence-against-an-imminent-armed-attack/; but cf. Stefan A.G. Talmon and Miriam Heipertz, "The U.S. Killing of Iranian General Qasem Soleimani: Of Wrong Trees and Red Herrings, and Why the Killing May Be Lawful after All," Feb. 2, 2020 (unpublished manuscript), https://papers.ssrn.com/sol3/papers.cfm?abstract_id=3530273 (arguing that the lawfulness of the operation depends on unknown facts); Geoffrey S. Corn and Rachel VanLandingham, "Lawful Self-Defense vs. Revenge Strikes: Scrutinizing Iran and U.S. Uses of Force Under International Law," *Just Security*, Jan. 8, 2020, https://www.justsecurity.org/67970/lawful-self-defense-vs-revenge-strikes-scrutinizing-iran-and-u-s-uses-of-force-under-international-law/ (same).

[3] See Mehrnusch Anssari and Benjamin Nussberger, "Compilation of States' Reactions to U.S. and Iranian Uses of Force in Iraq in January 2020," *Just Security*, Jan. 22, 2020, https://www.justsecurity.org/68173/compilation-of-states-reactions-to-u-s-and-iranian-uses-of-force-in-iraq-in-january-2020/ (collecting various US statements on the strike).

Monica Hakimi, *Arguing about the* Jus ad Bellum In: *Talking International Law.* Edited by: Ian Johnstone and Steven Ratner, Oxford University Press. © Monica Hakimi 2021. DOI: 10.1093/oso/9780197588437.003.0003

any of these justifications. At times, they even trafficked in conspiracy theories and lies.[4]

But if the United States acted in blatant disregard of the *jus ad bellum*, most other states declined to say so.[5] To be clear, states did not remain silent about the incident. Several indicated that they sympathized with one side or the other, and many encouraged the parties to de-escalate their tensions. However, the vast majority of states avoided taking a legal position on the US action or otherwise assessing it in law.

The question that I address in this chapter is: So what? What do we stand to lose when states fail to invoke and argue about the *jus ad bellum* in such cases? Two theories about the value of international legal argumentation are readily on offer in the scholarly literature. Although each approaches the issue from a slightly different perspective, they both suggest that legal argumentation is worthwhile insofar as the issue in dispute is authoritatively resolved.

The first theory highlights the role of legal argumentation in lawmaking.[6] A legal argument pushes the participants to focus on an issue, to crystallize their views, and eventually to settle the law's normative content. For example, the Soleimani strike was conducted against the backdrop of an ongoing debate about whether and, if so, when states may use defensive force anticipatorily—that is, before being victimized by an attack. Had states argued about the scope of the right of anticipatory self-defense in the context of the Soleimani incident, they might have made progress in defining it. By not having the argument, they lost a prescriptive opportunity.

[4] See Aaron Blake, "Pence's Dubious Tweet Tying Qasem Soleimani to 9/11," *Washington Post*, Jan. 3, 2020; Joseph Marks, Juliet Ellperin, and Drew Harwell, "Defense Secretary Esper Said He 'Didn't See' Evidence of an Iranian Plot to Attack Four Embassies," *Washington Post*, Jan. 12, 2020. On January 8, the United States finally submitted a report to the UN Security Council, asserting that it acted in self-defense, "in response to an escalating series of armed attacks in recent months" by Iran and Iranian-backed militia in the region, "in order to deter . . . further attacks," and "to degrade [Iran's] . . . ability to conduct attacks." Permanent Rep. of the U.S. to the U.N., Letter dated 8 January 2020 from the Permanent Representative of the United States of America to the United Nations addressed to the President of the Security Council, UN Doc. S/2020/20 (Jan. 9, 2020). This report was also half-baked and inconsistent with some of the things that the administration had said publicly. In particular, it did not claim that any Iranian attack was imminent. In March 2020, Paul Ney, the General Counsel at the US Department of Defense, elaborated on the US legal position in public remarks at Brigham Young University. Ney asserted that the question of whether an Iranian attack was imminent was a "red herring." See Paul C. Ney, "Legal Considerations Related to the U.S. Air Strike Against Qassem Soleimani," Address at Brigham Young University, Mar. 4, 2020 (transcript available at https://assets.documentcloud.org/documents/6808252/DOD-GC-Speech-BYU-QS.pdf). But in the days following the US action, administration officials themselves tried to justify the action by asserting that an Iranian attack was imminent. I do not address in this chapter whether the legal position that the United States eventually advanced satisfies the criteria for self-defense and renders the operation lawful. My goal instead is to appraise the shifting, incoherent, and at times fabricated justifications that the United States proffered in the immediate aftermath of the incident—when the world was actually paying attention.

[5] Anssari and Nussberger, *supra* note 3 (collecting state reactions).

[6] See, e.g., Ian Johnstone, *The Power of Deliberation: International Law, Politics, and Organization* (New York: Oxford University Press, 2011), 32. The idea that normative contests are part of the process for settling legal norms animates many theories of customary international law. It also has new energy in recent research on normative contestation in international relations. For an excellent overview of this research, see Nicole Deitelhoff and Lisbeth Zimmermann, "Norms under Challenge: Unpacking the Dynamics of Norm Robustness," *Journal of Global Security Studies* 4 (2019): 2.

The second theory posits that legal argumentation can be a useful enforcement device.[7] Invoking the law against a scofflaw is a way of condemning its violative conduct. Here, the legal argument is thought to have normative bite because the law's content is sufficiently settled for external actors to declare that the scofflaw violated it. The argument against the scofflaw articulates not just one possible view of the law but the correct view. So, if the United States acted unlawfully in targeting Soleimani, states could have invoked the *jus ad bellum* to condemn it. By not pushing a legal argument against the United States, they failed to enforce the law. They let the violation go without imposing normative or material repercussions on the United States.

Although these two theories each have some merit, they fail to account for much of the argumentative practice in the *jus ad bellum*. The *jus ad bellum* is known to be an extraordinarily open-textured body of law. Its content is in the ordinary course unclear, contested, and not authoritatively resolved. If the benefits of legal argumentation are contingent on its authoritative resolution, and if such resolution is regularly out of reach, then we would not lose much when states disengage from the *jus ad bellum*, as they mostly did in the Soleimani case.

But, I will argue, we actually lose quite a bit. My central claim is that arguments about the *jus ad bellum* are worthwhile, even when they do not lead to authoritative settlement and the law's content on the issue in dispute remains unresolved. They are worthwhile because they promote certain values that are associated with the rule of law. Legal arguments highlight that raw power is not a sufficient basis for making governance decisions. They serve to hold those who use force accountable for the decisions. They show respect to people who care about the decisions by providing reasoned accounts of what is happening and why. And they help to foster a relatively healthy politics about some of the most contentious things that states do in the world. All things being equal, we should value and try to stimulate this argumentative practice.

I. The *Jus ad Bellum*'s Constitutive Structure

States and other global actors routinely argue about the *jus ad bellum*'s content. They argue about how to interpret particular UN Security Council resolutions; about whether and, if so, when defensive force may be used anticipatorily or against non-state actors; about how to apply the requirements of proportionality and necessity that condition the right of self-defense; about whether unilateral humanitarian interventions can ever be lawful; and much more. Arguments about the *jus ad bellum* play out through its own constitutive structure—the processes and institutions for making and assessing use-of-force decisions. But the *jus ad bellum*'s constitutive structure is itself unstable. As a result, arguments about the *jus ad bellum* routinely put at issue not only what the law prescribes but also who may decide what the law prescribes and in what forum they may make that decision. This dynamic makes the *jus ad bellum* a

[7] E.g., Karen J. Alter, *The New Terrain of International Law* (Princeton: Princeton University Press, 2014), 19-23; Beth A. Simmons, *Mobilizing for Human Rights* (New York: Cambridge University Press, 2009), 14-17.

particularly open-textured and contentious body of law. It explains why arguments about the *jus ad bellum* are often not authoritatively resolved.

A. Unstable Foundations

The modern *jus ad bellum* derives from the UN Charter. Article 2(4) of the Charter prohibits states from threatening or using force "against the territorial integrity or political independence of any state, or in any other manner inconsistent with the Purposes of the United Nations."[8] This provision has long been understood to prohibit any use of force by one state in another without that latter state's consent. The Charter establishes only two exceptions. First, the UN Security Council has broad authority to "take such action by air, sea, or land forces as may be necessary to maintain or restore international peace and security."[9] The Council is a collective institution, so it has the potential to curb nationalistic impulses and advance policies that on the whole enhance human security. Second, Article 51 recognizes that states may use force unilaterally—that is, without going through the Council—in "individual or collective self-defense if an armed attack occurs."[10]

Although the Charter continues to establish the basic framework for the *jus ad bellum*, its original design never came to fruition. States did not satisfy their commitment, in Article 43, to place a standing set of armed forces under Council command. Without such forces, the Council cannot implement its own use-of-force decisions. It must rely on individual states to do that work—by authorizing them to use force when it decides that such force would advance international peace and security. The practical effect is that, even when the Council inserts itself into a situation, important decisions relating to the use of force are made by individual states. States that act pursuant to a Council authorization have some discretion to decide, at least in the first instance, how to conduct the operation.

Many analysts claim that the Council still must participate as much as possible in use-of-force decisions.[11] However, states have not consistently taken that view. They routinely battle over when and how the Council must participate in particular decisions. For example, the Council's failure to address certain security threats periodically creates pressure to act outside of it.[12] In the post–Cold War period, this dynamic has been most evident during humanitarian crises. States as a group have repeatedly indicated that they prefer such crises to be dealt with through the Council, but they have not always insisted on using the Council where it has stalled out. Many have instead tolerated or supported unilateral humanitarian interventions that have been

[8] UN Charter, art. 2, para. 4.

[9] *Id.* art. 42.

[10] *Id.* art. 51.

[11] E.g., Jules Lobel and Michael Ratner, "Bypassing the Security Council: Ambiguous Authorizations to Use Force, Cease-Fires and the Iraqi Inspection Regime," *American Journal of International Law* 93 (1999): 124, 125; Nico Krisch, "Article 42," in *The Charter of the United Nations: A Commentary*, edited by Bruno Simma, Daniel-Erasmus Khan, Georg Nolte, and Andreas Paulus, 3d ed. (Oxford: Oxford University Press 2012), 1330, 1342.

[12] E.g., GA Res. 377A (V), Uniting for Peace Resolution (Nov. 3, 1950); Int'l Comm'n on Intervention & State Sovereignty, *The Responsibility to Protect* (2001): 53–55.

conducted in the face of the Council's inaction. This ambivalence about the Council's role in humanitarian interventions has spawned a long-standing debate about the lawfulness of such actions.[13] Whatever position one takes in that debate, it itself—and the wishy-washy behavior that has generated it—reveal that the *jus ad bellum*'s constitutive structure is not as well-settled and centralized in the hands of the Council as many suggest. It is unstable and contestable in specific cases.

The instability in the *jus ad bellum*'s constitutive structure is also evident in the current debate about the use of defensive force against non-state actors. The debate is on its surface about the *jus ad bellum*'s content—the scope of the right to act in self-defense. However, the debate is also, and perhaps more fundamentally, about the *jus ad bellum*'s constitutive structure. It concerns the locus and allocation of decision-making authority in the *jus ad bellum*. The more expansively one defines the right of self-defense, the more authority shifts from the Council to individual states acting outside the Council. Again, the persistence and intensity of the debate reveal that the *jus ad bellum*'s constitutive structure is not settled in favor of the Council. Its terms are contested.

B. Loci of Authority

Although the *jus ad bellum* is not as centralized in the hands of the Council as many suppose, the Council remains the principal decision-making organ on the use of force. Three reasons help explain its prominence in the *jus ad bellum*. First, the Charter itself charges the Council with making peace-and-security decisions on behalf of all UN member states. It delegates decision-making authority to the Council.

Second, states and other global actors routinely affirm this authority. They regularly say and do things that establish the Council's primacy in the *jus ad bellum*, even though they often disagree about whether and how the Council ought to address particular situations. For example, after the Soleimani strike in January 2020, the Council hosted a ministerial-level "open debate" about how to maintain the *jus ad bellum*'s collective security system.[14] One dignitary after another spoke to uphold the Council's pride of place in the *jus ad bellum*. These participants expressed different views on precisely what the Council ought to do. They did not resolve the tension between the Council's primacy on the use of force and the carveout for self-defense. And they did not leave the meeting with any plan of action or authoritative text on the Council's proper role in the *jus ad bellum*. Still, the overall message was clear. It was for the Council to "reaffirm[] its primary responsibility for the maintenance of international peace and security under the Charter of the United Nations."[15]

The third reason for the Council's prominence is not particular to it. As Jacob Katz Cogan and I have explained in other work, international institutions have authority

[13] For recent evidence of the debate, see Christine Gray, "The Use of Force for Humanitarian Purposes," in *Research Handbook on International Conflict & Security Law*, edited by Nigel D. White and Christian Henderson (Cheltenham: Edward Elgar Publishing Ltd., 2013), 229, 253; Harold Hongju Koh, Address, "The War Powers and Humanitarian Intervention," *Houston Law Review* 53 (2016): 971, 1008–1010.

[14] UN Doc. S/PV.8699 (Jan. 9, 2020).

[15] UN Doc. S/PRST/2020/1 (Jan. 9, 2020).

in the *jus ad bellum* by virtue of their collective, deliberative, and structured processes for making decisions.[16] This authority is not entirely a function of the formal sources of law and is evident in the weight that international lawyers routinely ascribe to institutional pronouncements. Because the Council is the most active and prominent institution in the *jus ad bellum*, its pronouncements are regularly treated as authoritative. They are cited as evidence of positive law, even when they are not by their own terms binding.[17]

Other international institutions also have considerable authority in the *jus ad bellum*. For example, the positions that the International Court of Justice (ICJ) has taken on the *jus ad bellum* have been extremely influential. Although ICJ judgments are formally binding only in the cases presented, their authority radiates far beyond those cases. The ICJ's pronouncements are routinely taken to be positive law. The same goes for certain pronouncements of the UN General Assembly—most notably, the General Assembly's Declaration on Friendly Relations[18] and its definition of aggression.[19] These pronouncements have authority, even though they are not by their terms binding.

Because the Security Council and other international institutions have authority in the *jus ad bellum*, they play a critical role in establishing its content. Their normative positions on the *jus ad bellum* are widely, though not uniformly, accepted as positive law. However, there are limits to what these institutions can do to settle the *jus ad bellum*'s content. International institutions do not address every issue that arises in the *jus ad bellum*. Their normative positions are often ambiguous or open to multiple, conflicting interpretations. Even when the positions seem clear, states as a group might condone operations that deviate from them, raising questions about whether they (still) reflect positive law. And where an institution's authority is not formally established, it ultimately is contestable. For example, the United States has long rejected the ICJ position that some, low-level uses of force contravene Article 2(4) but do not trigger the Article 51 right to respond in self-defense. The US claim is that that position is not binding on or authoritative for it.

Decisions relating to the *jus ad bellum* are also made and appraised outside institutional settings, through a decentralized process that is commonly associated with customary international law but is also relevant to the interpretation and application of treaties. This process is messy and disjointed, and authority within it is not centered in any one place. Authority is instead shared among the many, uncoordinated participants. As such, the process does not easily lend itself to authoritative resolution. This does not mean that "anything goes" or that states may use the decentralized process to

[16] See Monica Hakimi and Jacob Katz Cogan, "The Two Codes on the Use of Force," *European Journal of International Law* 27 (2016): 257.

[17] For excellent overviews of the Council's authority, see José Alvarez, *The Impact of International Organizations on International Law* (Leiden: Martinus Nijhoff Publishers, 2017), 53, 366–369; Ian Johnstone, "The Security Council and International Law," in *The UN Security Council in the Twenty-First Century*, edited by Sebastian von Einsiedel, David M. Malone, and Bruno Stagno-Ugarte (Boulder: Lynne Rienner Publishers, 2016), 771. For an argument that the Council affects the lawfulness of particular operations, even when it does not formally authorize them, see Monica Hakimi, "The *Jus ad Bellum*'s Regulatory Form," *American Journal of International Law* 112 (2018): 151.

[18] GA Res. 2625 (XXV), Declaration on Friendly Relations (Oct. 24, 1970).

[19] GA Res. 3314 (XXIX) (Dec. 14, 1974).

establish authority for whatever they want to do. Rather, because authority rests with the collectivity, states that want it on their side must earn it from other participants in the process.[20] They must establish that their conduct is lawful.

Showing that is hard to do when a state contravenes settled law. For example, the prohibition of forcible annexations of foreign territory is deeply entrenched in the *jus ad bellum* (at least for now). A state that violates this prohibition is extremely unlikely to establish authority for its conduct through the decentralized decision-making process. The state might claim that the conduct is lawful, but the claim is unlikely to resonate with other actors. Most will appreciate that the acting state just violated the law.

The dynamic is different where there is a real contest about the authority to conduct a given operation. During a normative contest, states acting through the decentralized process routinely make ambiguous or contradictory legal arguments. Many stay silent on the law, use language that is opaque or noncommittal on the law, or support operations that are inconsistent with the positions that they themselves have taken in other contexts.[21] These discrepancies and ambiguities complicate efforts to resolve the legal issue in dispute. They suggest either that states have not collectively settled the law's content or that any settlement remains highly contingent. No one position has enough authority to stamp out the competing positions and establish the law's content. Thus, disagreements that play out mostly through the *jus ad bellum*'s decentralized process—without institutional support for one position or another—often lack authoritative resolution.

II. Arguing without Resolution

And yet, states and other global actors still have these disagreements. They argue about what the *jus ad bellum* prescribes, even when their arguments do not (and could not reasonably be expected to) lead to authoritative resolution. The legal arguments are had at different levels of generality. Sometimes, states focus on how to formulate the *jus ad bellum*'s general standards for entire categories of cases. Other times, they argue about how to apply an accepted standard to concrete facts. In either event, arguments about the *jus ad bellum* are in the ordinary course had but not resolved.

A. Arguments about the General Standards

As discussed, international institutions have considerable authority in the *jus ad bellum*. On some issues, they have articulated general standards that are widely accepted as law. But on other issues, their pronouncements are sparse and circumspect, and the governing standards remain contested.

[20] See W. Michael Reisman, Address, "International Lawmaking: A Process of Communication," *American Society of International Law Proceedings* 75 (1981): 101, 110 ("It is the audience, whether or not its members realize it, that endows the prescriber with the authority that renders his communications prescription.").

[21] For one account of why, see Namira Negm's contribution to this volume in chapter 11.

A well-known example concerns the use of defensive force against non-state actors.[22] Although key institutions have occasionally weighed in on this contest, their pronouncements have been cryptic or context-specific. For example, the Security Council has adopted two important resolutions on the issue—one immediately following the September 11, 2001, terrorist attacks,[23] and a second in the midst of an extensive military campaign against the so-called Islamic State in Iraq and Syria (ISIS).[24] Each resolution is ambiguous on the general question of when, if ever, states may act in self-defense against non-state actors. Likewise, the relevant ICJ judgments "reflect a considerable degree of uncertainty about the proper understanding of self-defence."[25] The institutional pronouncements thus do not establish a discernible, generally applicable standard for this context.[26]

The contest about the governing legal standard has instead played out through the decentralized decision-making process. In this process, states have advanced different, often ambiguous or incompatible positions on the use of defensive force against non-state actors. Several states have proclaimed that such force is lawful when the attack emanates from a state that is unable or unwilling to contain the threat. When states invoke this position in the context of discrete incidents, they usually are met with the silence or ambivalence of other states.[27] Yet the vast majority of states still have not endorsed the unable-or-unwilling position. They have signaled that, although they might at times support or tolerate discrete operations that can be justified under that position, they are on the whole unprepared to adopt it as the general standard of law.[28] Brazil and France each recently went out of its way to assert a strong contrary position—that defensive force against non-state actors is never or almost never permissible.[29]

Those who push for a particular position in this debate presumably do so because they want to earn authority for it or to deny authority to its competition. They might even succeed on the margins. For example, the number of states that accept the unable-or-unwilling position has increased over time, though it remains relatively small. However, despite the prominence of this contest over the past two decades, states have not settled the standard that governs the use of defensive force against

[22] I have discussed this contest in more detail elsewhere and draw on those works here. Hakimi, *supra* note 17, at 180–190; Hakimi and Cogan, *supra* note 16, at 278–283; Monica Hakimi, "Defensive Force against Non-state Actors: The State of Play," *International Law Studies* 91 (2015): 1.

[23] SC Res. 1368 (Sept. 12, 2001).

[24] SC Res. 2249 (Nov. 20, 2015).

[25] See Christian J. Tams, "Self-Defence against Non-State Actors: Making Sense of the 'Armed Attack' Requirement," in *Self-Defence against Non-State Actors*, edited by Christian Marxsen and Anne Peters (Cambridge: Cambridge University Press, 2019), 90, 158.

[26] See Hakimi and Cogan, *supra* note 16, at 279–283 (discussing other institutional pronouncements).

[27] See *id.* at 280–281.

[28] See, e.g., Jutta Brunnée and Stephen J. Toope, "Self-Defence Against Non-state Actors: Are Powerful States Willing but Unable to Change International Law?," *International and Comparative Law Quarterly* 67 (2018): 1.

[29] Mission of Brazil to the UN, Statement by H.E. Ambassador Mauro Vieira, Permanent Representative, to UN Security Council, Upholding International Law Within the Context of the Maintenance of International Peace and Security (May 17, 2018), https://drive.google.com/file/d/15CWYwX_G9K610xBWb7JmKelCOYHZDKSX/view; République Française, Droit International Appliqué Aux Opérations Dans le Cyberspace, at 10–11 (Sept. 9, 2019), https://www.justsecurity.org/wp-content/uploads/2019/09/droit-internat-appliqu%C3%A9-aux-op%C3%A9rations-cyberespace-france.pdf.

non-state actors.[30] They still act like having the contest matters. They fight about the *jus ad bellum*'s content or studiously avoid taking a clear position on it, with no authoritative resolution in sight.

B. Arguments about Discrete Cases

In other contexts, states argue not about how to formulate a general standard of behavior but about how to apply a given standard to concrete facts. Again, such arguments can be resolved in institutional settings. Take Russia's forcible annexation of Crimea. Although Russia argued that it was acting with the consent of the Crimean people and in support of their right to self-determination, that argument was overwhelmingly rejected in the UN Security Council.[31] A draft Council resolution called on "States to desist and refrain from actions aimed at the partial or total disruption of the national unity and territorial integrity of Ukraine, including any attempts to modify Ukraine's borders through the threat or use of force."[32] That draft resolution did not pass only because of Russia's veto. The UN General Assembly then adopted a very similar resolution.[33] In this case, international institutions helped resolve the law's content, as applied to the facts.

But here again, authoritative resolution is hard to come by outside of institutional channels. An illustrative example is the contest about the 2011 operation that instituted a regime change in Libya. The Security Council had adopted Resolution 1973 on the understanding that Libya's longtime leader, Muammar Gaddafi, was about to commit atrocities. Resolution 1973 authorized states "to take all necessary measures ... to protect civilians and civilian populated areas [in Libya] under threat of attack."[34] The United States, the United Kingdom, and France then led a coalition of NATO and other states to implement that resolution. Soon afterward, these states acknowledged that they sought to depose Gaddafi.[35] The legal question was whether a regime change fell within the scope of Resolution 1973—more precisely, whether removing Gaddafi was necessary to protect civilians from harm.

Security Council resolutions are usually interpreted by reference to the Council's contemporaneous intentions.[36] But when the Council adopted Resolution 1973, it did not offer a coherent position on the scope of its own authorization. At the time, France argued that the resolution was broad and permitted states to take "all measures

[30] Some analysts have suggested otherwise. They have tried to distill from the mix of claims and counterclaims the "correct" legal standard. E.g., Nico Schrijver and Larissa Van Den Herik, "Leiden Policy Recommendations on Counter-Terrorism and International Law," paras. 29, 32 (Apr. 1, 2010); "The Chatham House Principles of International Law on the Use of Force in Self-Defense," *International & Comparative Law Quarterly* 55 (2006): 963, 963–964, 970. But the evident disharmony on this issue reveals that states have not coalesced around a single standard.

[31] UN Doc. S/PV.7138 (Mar. 15, 2014).

[32] SC Draft Res., UN Doc. S/2014/89 (Mar. 15, 2014).

[33] GA Res. 68/262, paras. 5–6 (Mar. 27, 2014).

[34] SC Res. 1973, para. 4 (Mar. 17, 2011).

[35] See Steven Lee Myers, "Allies Renew Demands for Qaddafi to Give Up Power," *New York Times*, Mar. 29, 2011.

[36] See Michael C. Wood, "The Interpretation of Security Council Resolutions," *Max Planck Yearbook of United Nations Law* 2 (1998): 73, 92.

necessary, over and above the no-fly zone, to protect civilians and territories."[37] Other states contended that Gaddafi had "lost all legitimacy" and had to go.[38] However, China and Russia underscored "that many questions had not been answered in regard to provisions of the resolution, including ... what the limits of the engagement would be."[39]

Once the operation was underway, states variously invoked Resolution 1973 to argue that a regime change was or was not lawful. The three states that led the operation insisted that they were acting consistently with the resolution. US President Barack Obama, UK Prime Minister David Cameron, and French President Nicolas Sarkozy co-authored an opinion piece, published in several major newspapers, that justified the regime change by reference to Resolution 1973. They explained that, although the resolution's mandate was "not to remove Qaddafi by force," "it [was] impossible to imagine a future for Libya with Qaddafi in power."[40] Cameron separately argued that the operation was "in line with UN resolution 1973 and [was] about preventing a loss of civilian life by targeting Gaddafi's war-making machine."[41] NATO Secretary General Anders Rasmussen likewise asserted that NATO was acting "in strict conformity with both the spirit and the letter of the UN security council motion."[42] UN Secretary-General Ban Ki-Moon said something similar—that the "military operation done by NATO forces was strictly within 1973."[43]

But Russia repeatedly claimed that a regime change fell outside the scope of Resolution 1973 and was unlawful.[44] Further, the African Union appeared before the Security Council to express its "deep concern about the dangerous precedent being set by one-sided interpretations of [the resolution] ... and about the consequences that may result for international legality."[45] And while the Arab League had been instrumental in pushing for the resolution's no-fly zone, its Secretary-General later indicated that the operation had gone too far.[46] In the end, global actors repeatedly invoked Resolution 1973 to argue for and against the lawfulness of the regime change,

[37] UN Doc. S/PV.6498, at 3 (Mar. 17, 2011).

[38] *Id.* at 4, 7, 8 (statements by Germany, Portugal, and Colombia).

[39] Press Release, Security Council, Security Council Approves "No-Fly Zone" over Libya, Authorizing "All Necessary Measures" to Protect Civilians by Vote of 10 in Favour with 5 Abstentions, UN Press Release UN Doc. SC/10200 (Mar. 17, 2011); see also UN Doc. S/PV.6498, at 6 (Mar. 17, 2011) (statement of India) (asserting that there was not "clarity about details of enforcement measures, including who will participate and with what assets, and how these measures will exactly be carried out").

[40] Opinion, Barack Obama, David Cameron, and Nicolas Sarkozy, "Libya's Pathway to Peace," *New York Times*, Apr. 14, 2011.

[41] David Hughes and Diana Pilkington, "Nato Action 'In Line' with Policy, Says Cameron," *Independent*, May 1, 2011.

[42] Helen Pidd, "Nato Rejects Russian Claims of Libya Mission Creep," *Guardian*, Apr. 15, 2011 (internal quotation marks omitted).

[43] UN Secretary-General, Press Conference by Secretary-General Ban Ki-Moon at United Nations Headquarters, UN Doc. SG/SM/14021 (Dec. 14, 2011).

[44] See, e.g., Pidd, *supra* note 42; Gleb Bryanski, "Putin: Libya Coalition Has No Right to Kill Gaddafi," *Reuters*, Apr. 26, 2011; Mary Dejevsky, "Putin Attacks Britain and US for 'Violating Libya Resolution,'" *Independent*, Nov. 12, 2011.

[45] UN Doc. S/PV.6555 at 4 (June 15, 2011).

[46] See Michael Slackman, "Dislike for Qaddafi Gives Arabs a Point of Unity," *New York Times*, Mar. 21, 2011; interview with Amr Moussa, "The Goal in Libya Is Not Regime Change," *New York Times*, Mar. 23, 2011.

without any prospect of authoritative resolution. They argued about but did not in any meaningful sense settle the *jus ad bellum*'s content in this case.

III. Rule of Law Values

We can now return to the question that I presented at the beginning of this chapter: Does the argumentative practice in the *jus ad bellum* have any value, if it proceeds without meaningful resolution?[47] As discussed, the two most prominent theories on international legal argumentation suggest that the answer is no—that a legal argument matters only insofar as it is authoritatively resolved. "If no one can say with authority what the law is," Ian Johnstone has asked rhetorically, "what would be the point of making legal arguments at all?"[48]

Yet a substantial body of legal and political philosophy suggests that legal argumentation is itself worthwhile. Jeremy Waldron's work is especially instructive. He explains that a lot of what we value in law is that it commits us "to a certain method of arguing about the exercise of public power."[49] Legal arguments have a particular structure and style. Most importantly, they center on questions of authority. They prioritize certain texts, norms, and methods of analysis. They offer reasons for positions that purport to reflect not just the speaker's own idiosyncratic preferences but the interests and values of a broader group. They tie the reasons to the facts. And so forth. Arguments can be more or less "legalized" depending on the extent to which they display these qualities.[50] But—and this point is worth underscoring—an argument need not use a derivation of the word "law" or invoke any particular text or norm to be legal in kind. What makes it a legal argument is its structure and style. The key philosophical insight is that legal argumentation is desirable, even when it does not settle an issue in dispute or perceptibly change behavior on the ground. It is desirable because it promotes certain values that are associated with the rule of law.

Some might resist this idea. They might contend that, in order for the *jus ad bellum* to advance the rule of law, it must above all else establish relatively precise conduct rules that are consistently applied to constrain governmental discretion. If the *jus ad bellum* does not establish such rules—if it just provides the material for states to argue about the rules, without resolving what the rules are—then, the reasoning would go, it must fall short of the rule of law ideal; it would not meaningfully constrain the people in power.

But as Waldron has shown, that conception of the rule of law is not the only available one. Other conceptions prioritize legal argumentation as a critical dimension of the rule of law. Waldron explains that law is worthwhile not only because it sometimes

[47] This part of the chapter draws heavily on Monica Hakimi, "Why Should We Care About International Law?," *Michigan Law Review* 118 (2020): 1.

[48] Johnstone, *supra* note 6, at 7.

[49] Jeremy Waldron, "The Rule of Law as a Theater of Debate," in *Dworkin and His Critics*, edited by Justine Burley (Malden: Blackwell Publishing, 2004), 319, 330.

[50] Lisbeth Zimmermann's contribution to this volume in chapter 13 also discusses the qualities of legal argumentation, focuses on the dimension of authority, and recognizes that the line between legal and nonlegal argumentation is not so stark.

establishes conduct rules that constrain official discretion or make life predictable but also, and "at least as important," because of "what we do in law with the norms that we identify."[51] "We do not just obey [legal norms] or apply the sanctions that they ordain."[52] "[W]e use our sense of what is at stake in their application to license a continual process of argument ... about what it means to apply [the law] faithfully."[53]

In an ideal world, we might want the *jus ad bellum* both to establish stable conduct rules that constrain state discretion and to foster a culture of legal argumentation and debate. But as a practical matter, these two dimensions of the rule of law routinely push in different directions. Prioritizing law's argumentative practice often means tolerating greater levels of discretion, unpredictability, and inconsistency in the law's application. Law best fosters justification and debate by staying pliable and contestable—such that people with competing perspectives can tap into and argue through it—not by establishing fixed conduct rules that are mechanically applied. So, there are trade-offs inherent in the rule of law. These trade-offs cannot meaningfully be assessed in the abstract because they depend on the interests and values at stake in a given area of legal regulation and on the political economy in which the law operates. In some contexts, establishing clear and settled conduct rules, with little room for debate, might seem essential. In others, it will be oppressive or impracticable. The critical point for now is that, even if we on balance prefer clarity and settlement, that option is not always available. As discussed, authoritative settlement in the *jus ad bellum* is often beyond reach. Still, the *jus ad bellum*'s argumentative dimension has real, if somewhat intangible, value.

To be clear, my claim here is about the social effects of legal argumentation. I am not saying that the actors who argue about the *jus ad bellum* do so in order to promote the rule of law. Although some of them might, I suspect that many of them do not. Global actors might argue about the *jus ad bellum* for any number of reasons, including reasons that are self-interested and cynical, and because they want their preferred positions to be law.[54] However, no matter their internal motivations, their arguments about the *jus ad bellum* contribute in meaningful ways to the rule of law. The more legalized the arguments are, and the more seriously others engage with them, the greater their contribution to the rule of law is likely to be.[55]

A. Authority

At the most basic level, legal arguments signal that material power is not a sufficient basis for governing. Those who have the power to make particular governance

[51] Jeremy Waldron, "The Concept and the Rule of Law," *Georgia Law Review* 43 (2008): 1, 56.

[52] *Id.*

[53] *Id.* Some readers might claim that, if international law only structures an argumentative practice, without resolving what ought to be done, it does not operate as law. I disagree; international law's role here might be more constitutive than it is regulative—it might mostly structure the argumentative practice—but it is still quintessentially legal in nature. See *id.*

[54] On the "self-interested and cynical" use of legal argumentation, see Ian Johnstone and Steven Ratner, chapter 1, in this volume.

[55] On some of the challenges to proving the effects of legal argumentation, see Ingo Venzke's contribution to this volume in chapter 2.

decisions must show not only that they *can* implement the decisions but that they *may*—that they have authority to do what they want to do. In the *jus ad bellum*, the relevant authority rests beyond the jurisdiction of any one state. Those who want it have to earn it from other global actors. When they argue about whether they have it, they indicate, even if only implicitly, that it exists and that it matters. It matters enough for them to fight over it. Arguments about the *jus ad bellum*'s content thus reinforce and preserve the expectation that use-of-force decisions must be rooted in some authority that resides at the international level.

This authority works differently depending on whether the arguments are resolved. In cases of settlement, the legal argument helps to confer authority on particular normative positions. For example, the widespread rejection of Russia's argument on Crimea helped establish that it acted unlawfully. Absent a meaningful settlement, the authority that is generated through the argumentative practice might not attach to any one position. It might instead be systemic. It might reinforce the general proposition that use-of-force issues are properly resolved not by any one state but by the collectivity of them.[56]

Consider a concrete example. In 2017, the United States attacked a Syrian airfield after evidence surfaced that the Syrian regime had used chemical weapons against its people. The United States did not try to justify the attack under the *jus ad bellum*'s general standards. It did not claim to be acting pursuant to the Security Council's authorization, in self-defense, or with the Syrian government's consent. Some analysts have taken this to mean that it simply did not present a legal argument for its conduct.[57] But it did; remember, as argued above, that what makes an argument legal in kind is its structure and style.

The United States tried to justify its exercise of military power against Syria by reference to Syria's "[w]idespread violations of international law."[58] It invoked several international legal texts to argue that it was upholding not just its own priorities but the interests and values of the group. It alluded to background norms of behavior when it asserted that it used force only as a last resort, only after the "exhaustion of all reasonably available peaceful remedies," and only as "necessary and proportionate to the aim of deterring and preventing the future use of chemical weapons by the Syrian government."[59] It also appeared before the Security Council—the international institution that has a legal mandate in this area—to explain its conduct and subject its reasoning to external scrutiny.[60] In short, the United States conceded that it was not entitled to

[56] I have explained in other work that, when states take their arguments to the Council and try to earn its support for their own positions, they also help affirm its authority in the *jus ad bellum*. They do so, no matter whether the Council ultimately takes a stand on the question presented. In any event, the effort to obtain its support signals that its support matters—that states continue to afford it a pride of place in the *jus ad bellum*, even if they do not give it as large a role in use-of-force decisions as they might. Here again, the authority that is constituted through the argumentative practice is not particular to any one normative position but systemic. It reinforces the Council's institutional standing in the *jus ad bellum*. *See* Hakimi *supra* note 17, at 184.

[57] Ingo Venzke's contribution to this volume in chapter 2 makes this claim about the US justification for the copycat action that it, the United Kingdom, and France conducted against Syria in 2018.

[58] See Kristina Daugirdas and Julian Davis Mortenson, "Contemporary Practice of the United States Relating to International Law," *American Journal of International Law* 111 (2017): 781, 783.

[59] *Id.* at 784.

[60] UN Doc. S/PV.7919 (Apr. 7, 2017).

attack Syria just because it could. It recognized that any authority for its operation would have to come from other states. And it made a pitch to them to earn this authority. These are the ingredients of a legal argument.

We might disagree about whether the US argument was sufficient to establish its authority—whether the operation was, in the end, lawful. Yet no matter how we answer that question, we should appreciate that the United States advanced a legal argument that, by its very nature, treated the authority that exists at the international level as relevant. In doing so, it helped to reinforce this authority.

B. Accountability

Because international legal authority rests with the collectivity, and states that want it on their side must earn it from other actors, arguing with them about whether they have it is a way of holding them accountable for their decisions. When a state seeks to establish its authority—when it makes a legal argument to support what it has done—it effectively empowers other actors either to confer authority on or to deny authority to it. The legal argument thus becomes a tool for legitimizing or delegitimizing its behavior in law.

Take the unresolved legal contest about the regime change in Libya. The states that argued that the operation went beyond the scope of Resolution 1973 helped to undercut its authority. By pressing this legal argument, they communicated that the NATO-led coalition had not fully established authority for the operation. The legal argument worked to delegitimize the regime change in the eyes of many audiences.[61]

In some circumstances, having a legal argument might constrain whether or how a state exercises its military power. A state that cannot reasonably justify a use-of-force decision might choose to do something else. But whether or not the legal argument affects a state's operational behavior, it is a way of holding the state's feet to the fire. The argument pushes the state to explain and try to justify the decision to the various external constituencies that are paying attention.

The Soleimani strike offers a useful contrast. Although Iran and Iraq each complained to the Security Council that the United States had acted unlawfully,[62] the United States communicated, through its evident lack of seriousness about the legal enterprise, that it was not particularly invested in justifying its conduct in law. Moreover, the vast majority of other states did not press it to do so. The result was that the *jus ad bellum* seemed not only materially but also normatively irrelevant. It did not constrain the decision to use force, but neither did it serve to legitimize or

[61] For evidence that this contest put in doubt the lawfulness of the regime change, see, for example, Yasmine Nahlawi, "The Legality of NATO's Pursuit of Regime Change in Libya," *Journal on the Use of Force and International Law* 5 (2018): 295; Patrick C.R. Terry, "The Libya Intervention (2011): Neither Lawful, Nor Successful," *Comparative and International Law Journal of Southern Africa* 48 (2015): 162.

[62] Letter dated 3 January 2020 from the Permanent Representative of the Islamic Republic of Iran to the United States addressed to the Secretary-General and the President of the Security Council, UN Doc. S/2020/13 (Jan. 3, 2020); Identical Letters dated 6 January 2020 from the Permanent Representative of Iraq to the United Nation addressed to the President of the Security Council, UN Doc. S/2020/15 (Jan. 6, 2020).

delegitimize the action in law. By not having the legal argument, states did not hold the United States accountable for its action.

C. Respect

Legal argumentation is also a way of showing respect to those who care about or are affected by particular decisions. The argument treats people like they are not just pawns in a geopolitical game of chess but individuals who deserve an account of what is happening and why, and who might themselves have views to share. "Even if compliance is not the issue," Frederick Schauer has explained, "giving reasons [for governance decisions] is still a way of showing respect for the subject, and a way of opening a conversation rather than forestalling one."[63] Mark Tushnet has made a similar point. Arguing in law "express[es] respect for people as reasoning (and reasonable) beings," which "does seem an unqualified human good."[64]

In trying to justify the Libya operation under international law, Obama, Cameron, and Sarkozy recognized that they owed various audiences an explanation for their conduct. They conceded that they were not entitled to depose Gaddafi just because they had the military power to do so. They explained that their action was based on general principles that, though contested, reflect a considered view of the public good, not, for example, their own personal vendettas. And they acknowledged and addressed competing normative positions. Of course, many would have preferred for them not to have ousted Gaddafi. But given that they did, their legal arguments at least informed others of what they were doing and why, and invited various actors around the globe to think about their logic, to voice objections, and to demand a reasoned response.

The Soleimani case is again different. The Trump administration's changing and untethered justifications expressed not respect but contempt for those who expected a reasoned account of what it did. Don't take my word for it; take US Republican Senator Mike Lee's. He claimed that the administration's closed-door briefing to Congress was "insulting and demeaning" for the way it tried to stifle, rather than engage seriously in, a reasoned discussion.[65] To be clear, Lee's complaint was not about the legal or policy merits of the Soleimani strike. He emphasized that he supported the Trump administration and admired what he saw as its overall restraint in dealing with Iran. His complaint was that the administration was not serious about publicly justifying its action in law. The administration's message, according to Lee, was that "we need to be good

[63] Frederick Schauer, "Giving Reasons," *Stanford Law Review* 47 (1995): 633, 658.

[64] Mark Tushnet, "Critical Legal Studies and the Rule of Law," Harvard Pub. Law, Working Paper No. 18-14 (2018): 12, https://papers.ssrn.com/sol3/papers.cfm?abstract_id=3135903; see also Waldron, *supra* note 51, at 23, 24 (explaining that law "is a mode of governing people that treats them with respect," which it does in large part through its argumentative practice).

[65] Catie Edmondson, "Mike Lee, a G.O.P. Senator, Calls Administration's Iran Briefing 'Insulting,'" *New York Times*, Jan. 8, 2020 (quoting Senator Lee). For a full recording of Lee's media appearance, see "Senator Mike Lee Calls Iran Briefing 'the Worst' in Nine Years in the Senate," *C-Span*, Jan. 8, 2020, https://www.c-span.org/video/?c4844034/senator-mike-lee-calls-iran-briefing-the-worst-years-senate.

little boys and girls and not debate this in public."[66] For Lee, that message was "absolutely insane," just plain "wrong," and again "insulting."[67]

D. Transnational Politics

Finally, the *jus ad bellum*'s argumentative practice can help constitute a decent politics beyond the borders of any one state.[68] It enables people in disparate parts of the world to engage together on the global governance issues that they all care about, while structuring in relatively positive ways how they engage. Again, legal arguments have a particular structure and style. The participants use the law's various resources—texts, norms, methods, and institutions—to explain how their positions are consonant with the interests or values of a group.[69] The argument thus pushes them to grapple with the politics of the group.

To be sure, the participants might disagree about which policies best promote the public good. Their disagreements might at times run so deep that they cannot definitively or authoritatively be resolved. And their legal positions will almost certainly be informed by their own interests or passions. Still, there is value to putting them in conversation with one another and pushing them to "see themselves as belonging to the same political association … [and] sharing a common symbolic space."[70] As others have explained, "debate over principle, over the common good and justice, is a distinctive and invaluable moment of political life."[71] It acquires a "depth and seriousness of purpose" not because it is detached from or just a cloak for the participants' preferences but because it involves the "dissonant intertwining of principle and interest."[72] In trying to define their own priorities in relation to the group's, the participants must in some way contend with the politics of the group. They must confront what is at stake in concrete decisions not just for themselves but for others who care about the decisions.

The claim that the unable-or-unwilling position is law has spawned nearly two decades of intense debate. This debate has played out in manifold arenas—some domestic, others international—and among a broad range of actors. Although the participants have plainly been motivated by their own interests and values, they have also argued about principle; they have pushed for their priorities to be reflected in the *jus ad bellum*'s shared "fund of public normative references."[73] And though the

[66] Edmondson, *id* at 64 (internal quotation marks omitted).

[67] *Id.* (internal quotation marks omitted).

[68] I have argued in other work that international law plays an important role in constituting political communities beyond the state. See Monica Hakimi, "Constructing an International Community," *American Journal of International Law* 111 (2017): 317.

[69] See, e.g., K.N. Llewellyn and E. Adamson Hoebel, *The Cheyenne Way: Conflict and Case Law in Primitive Jurisprudence* (Norman: University of Oklahoma Press, 1941), 277 (explaining that, in law, "claims get made and urged in terms of the Order" and "tend powerfully to be set up as serving the welfare of the relevant Entirety").

[70] Chantal Mouffe, *On the Political* (Abingdon: Routledge, 2005), 20.

[71] Don Herzog, *Poisoning the Minds of the Lower Orders* (Princeton: Princeton University Press, 1998), 152.

[72] *Id.*

[73] Frank Michelman, "Law's Republic," *Yale Law Journal* 97 (1988): 1493, 1513.

proponents of the unable-or-unwilling position have not much changed their position as a result of the debates, their critics evidently still want to argue with them about it and focus the world's attention on it, rather than passively accept it as inevitable. The critics want these states to contend with their opposing views.

IV. Conclusion

Arguments about the *jus ad bellum* are not only routine but worthwhile. They are worthwhile, even when, as is often the case, they are not authoritatively resolved. They still help to promote rule of law values. They foster the expectation that sheer power is not a sufficient basis for making use-of-force decisions. They help to hold the people in power accountable for such decisions. They show respect for those who care about the decisions by providing a reasoned account of what is happening and why. And they foster a relatively healthy politics about some of the most devastating things that states do in the world. We should push global actors to engage in this argumentative practice, even when authoritative resolution is beyond reach.

Some might object that, in the absence of authoritative resolution, legal argumentation is not a virtue but a vice. When a militarily powerful state makes a legal argument, the objection would go, it too easily cloaks its own policy preferences in the authority of law; it manipulates the law's normative valence to bolster its contentious, even lawless behavior. This objection misses the mark. In the circumstances that we are discussing, the *jus ad bellum*'s content is sufficiently unsettled that the authority to make particular decisions is, at least to some extent, up for grabs. Because this authority ultimately rests with the collectivity, states that want it on their side must earn and fight for it. They must establish to external audiences that their decisions are appropriate exercises of military power. There is little evidence that they can successfully do this simply by advancing a legal claim.

Of course, one might still worry that a militarily powerful state will too easily harness the law's authority for its own contentious policies. The answer is not to push the state to ignore the law or to concede that its conduct falls outside of the law, in the realm of ordinary politics. The answer is to encourage other actors to argue with it in law—to insist that it needs authority for the use of force, to demand that it provide good reasons for its decision, to hold it accountable when its reasons fall flat, and to press it to grapple with competing perspectives. By contrast, insisting that its decision falls outside the law would mean accepting that, once it uses force as it pleases, it need not explain or justify the decision to the people who are affected. It's not clear why that result would be a victory for the rule of law or would make the world a better place.

4

Argumentation in the UN Security Council

International Law as Process

Scott P. Sheeran

I. Introduction

The UN Security Council is the central global stage for mitigating international conflict and for managing cooperation on threats to international peace and security. The Council is a critical body in the decentralized international legal system. As the Council must exercise its powers in accordance with the UN Charter and is consistently responding to violations of international law, it is also a key forum for international legal argumentation. The Council is relatively unique in that it creates, interprets, and enforces international law.

Much of the legal literature concerning the Council is rooted in the traditional or orthodox positivist approach to international law. As a result, this focuses typically on the extent of the Council's legal powers by reference to the UN Charter's empowering provisions, and concludes that the Council is not "unbound by law."[1] When faced with a legal-related challenge in the Council, the lawyers participating in or observing its actions will often seek to find "the correct legal answer."

The Security Council, however, is essentially a political organ and operates in a political context. As this author can attest, the reality is that lawyers working on the Council spend their time engaging with and persuading those who are not committed to the legal discipline and those who are not part of their "interpretive community." Moreover, the nucleus of decision-making in the Council is the veto of the five permanent members. Diplomacy is paramount, as are negotiation and consensus. The role of international legal argumentation can feel modest.

The international legal argumentation in the Council is usually grounded in the disciplinary methodology of lawyers and their common paradigm. However, the institutional powers, practice, and processes of the Council cannot be comprehensively and convincingly explained in simple positivist terms. While legal reasoning in traditional adjudicative settings is analytically detailed and determined, reasoning in the Council's political settings is conceptually open and fluid, and naturally interdisciplinary given the audience. A theory of international legal argumentation concerning the Council, therefore, must pay attention to the Council's dominant paradigm of

[1] International Criminal Tribunal for the Former Yugoslavia, Appeals Chamber, Prosecutor v. Dusko Tadic (Appeal Judgement), IT-94-1-A (July 15, 1999), para. 29.

Scott P. Sheeran, *Argumentation in the UN Security Council* In: *Talking International Law*. Edited by: Ian Johnstone and Steven Ratner, Oxford University Press. © Scott P. Sheeran 2021. DOI: 10.1093/oso/9780197588437.003.0004

argumentation, its complexity of social interactions, and the principle of effectiveness in persuasion.

Legal argumentation in the Council can be made optimally effective only when the actual role of international law is better understood. This chapter seeks to highlight the assumptions and presuppositions of many international lawyers, which in the Council context are often regrettably antithetical to the influence of legal argumentation. To promote international norms, and indeed the rule of law itself, requires the international lawyer to adopt a more contextual and flexible mode of argumentation.

The chapter addresses the issue of legal argumentation in the Council in four main parts. Section II demonstrates the relationship of international law to international relations and diplomacy in the system of thought, argument, and decision-making predominant in the Council. Section III explores international law in the Council as a process, underpinned by diplomacy and consensus, rather than only a series of rules to interpret and apply. Section IV discusses the characteristics of the argumentation and decision-making in the Council, including key challenges and the areas of most legal relevance. Section V explains that policy considerations and values are an essential foundation of effective international legal argumentation. Finally, the chapter concludes with a few key observations and reflections.

II. The Relationship of International Law to International Relations in the Security Council

A starting point is to consider the characteristics and culture of the UN Security Council that shape its processes of argumentation. There is a relatively common set of patterns of analysis and decision-making used by governments, as informed by their various advisers, officials, and politicians, both in the national capitals and in New York. The impact of international legal argumentation cannot be determined without better appreciating the nature of the Council. For the author, a member of New Zealand's Council team in 2015–2016, the opportunity to engage in Council argumentation and negotiations, and to consider the Council's outcomes and decisions, left a lasting impression.

A. Legal Argumentation and the Assumptions of International Law

International law provides a remarkable degree of commonality of structure and method and is relatively well institutionalized. There is a large cadre of scholars and practitioners globally who share the identification of a set of treaties, customary rules, international judicial decisions, formal institutions, and practices of reasoning and argument. Legal argumentation can be especially powerful because its structure and method are widely understood and accepted *within* the discipline.

International lawyers adopt a learnt and unconscious approach to the complex process of legal argumentation. It is a specialized form of rhetoric concerned with the interpretation of facts, legal terms, and concepts and is underpinned by the aims of the law and the parties concerned. More importantly, as Iain Scobbie notes, legal argumentation "is essentially instrumental because it aims to have a practical effect" and "by its nature it aims at securing the assent or adhesion of those to whom the argument is addressed rather than demonstrating the truth of the proposition or interpretation advanced."[2]

International law is not the predominant methodology or discipline relevant for the Security Council and its participants, nor for their mode of argumentation. International relations and its broader home field of political science are essential. Yet there is a long tradition of viewing international law and relations as separate areas of social activity. The development of international law as well as its pedagogy have reinforced this division. International law is a system that fits within another system, namely, international relations. A key obvious difference is that international relations does not share the same commitment to the obligatory nature of international law.

B. Legitimacy through International Law

International law still plays an important role in international relations thinking for both theorists and practitioners through its *legitimating* effect. It is a widely held view that legitimation aids international governance by reducing opposition and encouraging compliance. In this regard, international relations theory often focuses upon the legitimacy of international institutions, rather than of international law.

Many scholars have suggested that the pervasive use of international legal argumentation demonstrates an efficacy and legitimacy of international law which cannot be explained in instrumentalist terms. This assessment is underpinned by a variety of different perspectives, many of which relate to compliance in a decentralized legal order. Abram and Antonia Chayes and Thomas Franck emphasize "justificatory discourse" and "fairness discourse," respectively, to explain compliance with international law.[3] Harold Koh says that international law becomes part of a state's "internal value set."[4]

The UN Security Council is constantly striving for legitimacy, including a number of the permanent members (P5) due to their privileged position. While the Council is an institution that has inherent legitimacy, primarily due to the UN Charter, it also obtains legitimacy by applying international law (e.g., responding to illegal use of force and human rights and humanitarian suffering). Accordingly, the Council and its members can enhance the legitimacy of their position by claiming that they are acting consistent with international law.

[2] Iain Scobbie, "Rhetoric, Persuasion, and Interpretation in International Law," in *Interpretation in International Law*, edited by Andrea Bianchi, Daniel Peat, and Matthew Windsor (Oxford: Oxford University Press, 2015), 64.

[3] See Abram Chayes and Antonia Chayes, *The New Sovereignty: Compliance with International Regulatory Agreements* (Cambridge, MA: Harvard University Press, 1996); and Thomas Franck, *Fairness in International Law and Institutions* (Oxford: Clarendon Press, 1995).

[4] Harold Hongju Koh, "Why Do Nations Obey International Law?," *Yale Law Journal* 106 (1997): 2599, 2603.

C. Realism vs. Normativity in the Security Council

The effectiveness of international legal argumentation must be informed by recognition that the Council is an institution with strong roots in the realist tradition of international relations. A scholarly consensus is that the United Nations' design reflected a world of great powers as the primary means to keep the peace and not to address justice. The most core principles of the UN Charter, including concerning the Council, are the sovereign equality of states, non-intervention in the affairs of other member states, the peaceful settlement of disputes, and the non-use of force. The United Nations' main role was to prevent future wars, and the Council was intended to be the most important organ, managed by the great powers, whose own interests would be protected by their so-called veto power.

The veto power is fundamental to the Council. It was based in the assumption, informed by realism, that the United Nations as an entity of sovereign states would work effectively only when its most powerful members conferred on it sufficient competence. To borrow Rosalyn Higgins' words, "power and authority coincide" in the Council, and the veto is central to that intersection of power and law.[5] However, this power can override authority and may be exercised contrary to normative values. As observed by Anjali Patil in her study *The UN Veto in World Affairs, 1946–1990*: "We have to acknowledge that nations big and small are going to consider it their 'duty' to advance their own interests even at the cost of suffering among other peoples."[6]

D. Diplomacy and International Legal Argumentation—Consensus vs. Adjudication

Diplomacy is central to the paradigm of the UN Security Council. It has significant consequences for the use of international legal argumentation. The diplomatic underpinnings of the United Nations' political processes have been mostly neglected in the literature on the United Nations. Diplomacy is the primary method of decision-making in Council. The veto looms large, and nothing operative or binding can be done without agreement of the five permanent members of the Council. Diplomacy as both a process and a tool of decision-making is fundamentally different to legal adjudication and engages the interaction of realism and normativity. This process is well described by Andrew Cooper, Jorge Heine, and Ramesh Thakur:

> Decision-makers therefore have to strike a balance among the different interests and actors, between domestic demands and international imperatives, between principle and pragmatism, between idealistic values and material interests, between what is

[5] Rosalyn Higgins, *Problems and Processes: International Law and How We Use It* (Oxford: Clarendon Press, 1994), 4, 15.

[6] Anjali Patil, *The UN Veto in World Affairs, 1946–1990: A Complete Record and Case Histories of the Security Council's Veto* (Sarasota: UNIFO Publishers, 1992), 694.

> the expedient and what the right thing to do, between the national constituency and the international community, and between the immediate, medium, and long terms.[7]

The institutional context of UN multilateral diplomacy is more favorable to the role of international law than traditional inter-state diplomacy. It is broadly guided by the UN Charter's principles, offsetting somewhat the unfavorable position of the weaker parties. However, what is decisive in Council discussions is not the merits of legal argument but diplomacy and obtaining the consensus of those with political power, primarily the P5. The multilateral process is consensus-driven and not adjudicatory of the law, and interpretation is implicit in the measures adopted.[8]

For example, New Zealand during its term led a successful initiative that the chairs of the Council's subsidiary bodies would be selected in a process including the elected members. This role had previously been the sole domain of the P5, which rotated the facilitation of these decisions and allocated the chairing roles to elected members. New Zealand, for example, despite having different national priorities and initial preferences for committee chairing, was appointed to chair the ISIL (Islamic State in Iraq and the Levant) (Da'esh)–Al-Qaeda and Afghanistan sanctions committees.

In the course of pursuing this initiative, New Zealand found that one P5 member in the Council was unwilling to relinquish the P5's privileged role, despite its lacking any normative basis in the UN Charter. In the end, an improvement could only be attained by thinking creatively, with the P5 member agreeing provided that the process be "facilitated jointly by two members of the Security Council working in full cooperation" (i.e., meaning one P5 member and one elected member). While New Zealand was comfortable using specific language concerning the division of responsibilities, the P5 member concerned was not.

The Council and its members also notably at times engage in "polylateral diplomacy." This is a term of growing recognition, which describes the diplomacy between state and non-state representatives.[9] The influential Council members have regular engagement with nongovernmental organizations (NGOs), for example, Security Council Report, Human Rights Watch, and International Crisis Group. These NGOs, and particularly human rights NGOs, are significant and robust users of legal argumentation to pursue their objectives, although not always with success.

New Zealand during its term initiated the negotiation of Council Resolution 2286 (2016) concerning the protection of medical facilities and personnel in conflict situations. This involved significant engagement and coordination with key NGOs that initially were quite concerned about the initiative. Their reservations were that a Council resolution would detract from rather than assist their important work. However, the heads of the International Committee for the Red Cross and Médecins Sans Frontières ultimately supported the resolution and were invited briefers at the

[7] Andrew Cooper, Jorge Heine, and Ramesh Thakur, "Introduction: The Challenges of 21st-Century Diplomacy," *The Oxford Handbook of Modern Diplomacy*, edited by Andrew Cooper, Jorge Heine, and Ramesh Thakur (Oxford: Oxford University Press, 2013), 21.

[8] Oscar Schachter, "The UN Legal Order: An Overview," in *The United Nations and International Law*, edited by Christopher Joyner (Cambridge: Cambridge University Press, 1997), 9.

[9] Geoffrey Wiseman and Soumita Basu, "The United Nations," in *Diplomacy in a Globalising World*, edited by Pauline Kerr and Geoffrey Wiseman (Oxford: Oxford University Press, 2013), 329.

Council's meeting for its adoption. While the resolution's main value was to raise the political profile of this important issue, the lawyers' role was essentially to ensure there were no "backwards steps" in the many restatements of the applicable law throughout the resolution.[10]

E. Individual Participants in Security Council Argumentation and Decision-Making

The UN Security Council is not an island, and each member takes into account a range of factors in reaching its national positions on the agenda issues. However, the processes of Council argumentation and decision-making are relatively exclusionary and primarily grounded in the members' interactions, especially in New York. The Council holds public debates, but the true negotiations happen behind closed doors in "informal consultations," and more often bilaterally. The culture of diplomacy ensures that much of the real argumentation is kept out of the public eye. As observed by the author, Council members are therefore not particularly accountable for the nature and quality of their arguments, including weak normative arguments.

The dominant influence of politics and realism has naturally shaped the Council's individual participants, and consequently, the role of international lawyers. Martti Koskenniemi noted during his involvement in Finland's term on the Council in 1989–1990 that the international lawyer was midlevel in ranking and importance in the Finnish team of diplomats. He indicated that this was similar to other Council members. By the time of New Zealand's term on the Council in 2015–2016, the diplomatic ranking of international lawyers was still largely the same, but the importance of the lawyer's role appeared to have declined, and particularly for the elected members (as both Finland and New Zealand were).

The "experts" who dominated the working-level discussions on situations before the Council, including on draft resolutions, were mid-to-junior-level diplomats with a political and policy background. During New Zealand's term, there was only one resolution discussion for which all Council members' legal advisers uniformly took responsibility. This resolution concerned the International Criminal Tribunals for Rwanda and the former Yugoslavia and the Mechanism for International Criminal Tribunals. As this author discovered, it was primarily a negotiation based on administrative issues, working methods, appointments, and budget.[11] The Council's "Informal Working Group on International Tribunals" in which the legal advisers participated was not permitted to discuss the International Criminal Court, as such discussion was discouraged by China, Russia, and other members. In addition, given that many of the

[10] SC Res. 2286 (May 3, 2016). For example, preambular para. 9 stated: "*Recalling also* the obligation under international humanitarian law to distinguish between civilian populations and combatants, and the prohibition against indiscriminate attacks, and the obligations to do everything feasible to verify that the objectives to be attacked are neither civilians nor civilian objects and are not subject to special protection, including medical personnel their means of transport and equipment, and hospitals and other medical facilities, and *recalling further* the obligation to take all feasible precautions with a view to avoiding and in any event minimizing harm to civilians and civilian objects."

[11] For example, see SC Res. 2256 (Dec. 22, 2015), and SC Res. 2329 (Dec. 19, 2016).

Council's procedural issues are not governed by formal rules but rather are decided by "practice" and consensus, the management of these issues tended to be led in each Council team by the "political coordinator" role.

From the UN Secretariat side, almost all issues on the Council's agenda were led and briefed by the Department of Political Affairs and the Department of Peacekeeping Operations (as they were called at the time). In New Zealand's two years on the Council, the UN Legal Counsel never once spoke to the Council, in either a formal or informal context. In this regard, the UN Secretariat also contributed to the modest profile of international law's contribution in the work and problem-solving of the Council. At a working lunch of Council legal advisers that New Zealand decided to host, a common theme for many was the challenge of relevance in their missions. This author took a leading role in the diplomacy for several of New Zealand's achievements on the Council—on working methods, sanctions, and early warning—and with regard to these initiatives had little direct involvement with other legal advisers, whether of Council members or the UN Secretariat.

F. Realism vs. Normativity in the Security Council—The Haitian Cholera Epidemic Example

A striking example in the UN Security Council of the dominance of realism over normativity concerns the peacekeeping operation the Council mandated that caused a cholera epidemic in Haiti. Members of the UN peacekeeping operation in Haiti introduced a virulent strain of cholera to Haiti as a consequence of the release of untreated sewage into a main river and water source. The resulting epidemic is estimated in three years to have killed 8,000 people and infected another 670,000 people.[12] Despite the development of clear evidence linking the cholera to UN peacekeepers, the Council and the UN Secretariat were unwilling to accept or address the legal claims and remedies.

This reflected realism over normativity, diplomacy over adjudication, and a general *lack of* national interest. The US government pays for 30 percent of the UN peacekeeping budget and would ultimately pay for 30 percent of any reparations (which were claimed as hundreds of millions of US dollars). Any acceptance of responsibility and liability would set a costly precedent. The United States is also the main host nation for the United Nations and has seen many legal claims against the Organization in its courts, including on the Haiti issue. France had a tangled history with Haiti, including on slave reparations. The United Kingdom had little interest in Haiti in terms of their bilateral relationship and was also concerned about the precedent of UN liability. Russia and China did not support a human rights focus on reparations; and China had limited sympathy for Haiti in light of its recognition of Taiwan.

The UN Legal Counsel reinforced the rejection of claims by providing a legal position that appeared to be contrary to any reasonable and objective interpretation of

[12] Rosa Freedman and Nicolas Lemay-Hébert, "The Security Council in Practice: Haiti, Cholera, and the Elected Members of the United Nations Security Council," *Leiden Journal of International Law* 32 (2019): 1.

the applicable law.[13] The legal advice ensured that the consequences of the release of raw sewage leading to the cholera outbreak fell under the United Nations' immunities. This appeared to contradict the 1946 Convention on the Privileges and Immunities of the United Nations. This Convention includes the undertaking that "[t]he Secretary-General shall have the right and the *duty* to waive the immunity of any official in any case where, in his opinion, *the immunity would impede the course of justice* and can be waived without prejudice to the interests of the United Nations."[14] The UN Secretariat invoked immunity as the "consideration of these claims would necessarily include a review of political and policy matters."[15] This meant that the victims could not lodge any claims against the United Nations. This provided significant assurance to many policymakers.

The elected members engaged, but mostly only cautiously and moderately, given the P5 position and the UN Secretariat position. The main actors pushing the issue were two NGOs—one Haiti-based, one US-based—and a few Western academics. While New Zealand was on the Council, the author was lobbied by the academics, without participation of any officials from the government of Haiti (which has a mission in New York) or anyone who was Haitian or connected to a Haitian NGO.

Without being simplistic, a shift occurred when the balance of interests changed. After many meetings and lobbying of the UN Secretariat leadership, the UN special rapporteur on extreme poverty and human rights, Philip Alston, unusually but very effectively published an unprecedented and damning report against the United Nations. Alston wrote that the United Nations' Haiti cholera policy "is morally unconscionable, legally indefensible and politically self-defeating" and the Organization's continued denial and refusal of reparations to the victims "upholds a double standard according to which the U.N. insists that member states respect human rights, while rejecting any such responsibility for itself."[16] The UN special rapporteur's arguments were heavily based on principles of international law.

At the time of the UN special rapporteur's report, Secretary-General Ban Ki-Moon was nearing the end of his ten-year term. The Haiti cholera incident was a difficult issue for Ban Ki-Moon's legacy. The Secretary-General very shortly after the Alston report announced a "significant set of new UN actions," and then in his final month of office apologized to the Haitian people and committed to contain cholera and provide remedies in some form, but without accepting any legal responsibility.[17]

Shortly thereafter, the Council renewed the UN peacekeeping mission's mandate in Haiti and did little more than "note" in the preamble of its resolution (i.e., language

[13] For an alternative view, see the discussion on Haiti and UN immunities in Stephen Mathias and Nicolas Perez, chapter 16, in this volume, particularly Section II.C, "Protecting the Immunity of the Organization Itself."

[14] Convention on the Privileges and Immunities of the United Nations, adopted by the General Assembly of the United Nations, Feb. 13, 1946, 1 UNTS 15, sec. 20 (emphasis added).

[15] Letter from Patricia O'Brien, UN Under Secretary-General for Legal Affairs, to Brian Concannon, Director of the Institute for Justice and Democracy in Haiti (Feb. 21, 2013), http://opiniojuris.org/wp-content/uploads/LettertoMr.BrianConcannon.pdf.

[16] UN Human Rights Council, Report of the Special Rapporteur on extreme poverty and human rights (Aug. 26, 2016), UN Doc. A/71/367, at 2, https://undocs.org/A/71/367.

[17] Jonathan Katz, "U.N Admits Role in Cholera Epidemic in Haiti," *New York Times*, Aug. 17, 2016, https://www.nytimes.com/2016/08/18/world/americas/united-nations-haiti-cholera.html.

often indicating a lack of positive endorsement, cf. "welcomes") "the intention of the Secretary-General to develop a package that would provide material assistance and support to those Haitians directly affected by cholera."[18] To date, there has been insufficient action on the proposed $2.2 billion plan. Six months after Ban Ki-Moon's announcement, the United Nations had received pledges of around only $9 million to address the problem.[19]

Rosa Freedman, one of the legal academics involved in the Haiti advocacy campaign, concluded of her experience that "[i]n vying for positions of influence inside the Security Council, diplomatic practices follow less logical reasonings and strategic calculus than being driven by general narratives diplomats perceive as legitimate."[20] In essence, diplomats and UN officials did not respond in a significant way to traditional international legal argumentation. This revised response of the United Nations may be seen critically as more focused on public relations to counter the legal argumentation than reflecting political will to actually address an injustice. As the foregoing regrettably indicates, international legal argumentation was not effective in persuading the Council to respond and take action.

III. Diplomacy and International Law as Process

The theories of international law based on the "law as process" idea, which incorporates elements of international relations thinking, are influential for legal argumentation in the Council.[21] The law as process approach is a reaction to legal formalism and the purported separation of legal reasoning (i.e., application of norms to facts) from other normative, policy, or political considerations. The "arguments," which characterize the law, rules, and adjudication, stand in juxtaposition to "process," which is more relevant to diplomacy, negotiation, and consensus.

International law is an instrument of diplomacy, and diplomacy is a means to advance international law; they are mutually reinforcing. Diplomacy provides its own distinct social process, which can be complicated and opaque. While legal argumentation is common in the Council context, achieving consensus (e.g., avoiding the veto) is driven primarily by political positions and national interests, rather than by normative positions. To be influential requires international lawyers to have a broader disciplinary and political understanding. The diplomatic process does not have the inherent structure of adjudication, as decision makers lack relevant information, act under severe time pressures, and are lobbied by a diversity of interest groups and other constituencies.

To provide an example, New Zealand played a significant role in supporting the adoption of Resolution 2272 (2016) on combating sexual exploitation and abuse (SEA) by UN peacekeepers. This resolution was an initiative of the United States, which led

[18] SC Res. 2313 (Oct. 13, 2016).

[19] Agence France-Presse, "UN Haiti Cholera Fund Fails to Draw Pledges," *Business Insider*, Feb. 25, 2017, https://www.businessinsider.com/afp-un-haiti-cholera-fund-fails-to-draw-pledges-2017-2.

[20] Freedman and Lemay-Hébert, *supra* note 12, at 4.

[21] In respect of international law as process, see Higgins, *supra* note 5, at 1–10.

the negotiations. The applicable UN standards for SEA were relatively clear, but there was an ongoing lack of implementation and accountability. The resolution was negotiated under urgency in the Council and was controversial, as some major troop contributing countries are generally resistant to UN involvement in accountability of their forces. The final resolution adopted included a Council request to the Secretary-General to replace member state peacekeeping forces responsible for a pattern of SEA for which there had been insufficient national follow-up and accountability.[22]

An important part of building support for the resolution was finding ways to neutralize objections by reference to the many UN instruments on this topic. This required a lawyer's familiarity and mastery of the regime of commitments and arrangements for SEA in UN peacekeeping (i.e., General Assembly resolutions, UN Model Status of Forces Agreement, UN Model Memorandum of Understanding between the UN troop contributors, Victims Assistance Strategy, and so on). Many experts in the negotiation (in which the author was again the only legal adviser) did not have a national position (or even a personal professional position) committed to human rights or justice. However, most broadly accepted the need to ensure consistency with the relevant UN instruments that had been agreed by UN member states, and particularly by the UN General Assembly. While the UN instruments were very helpful, they also codified the United Nations' lack of authority to immediately investigate serious allegations of SEA without the troop contributing countries' consent.[23]

A. The Primary Rule of Law (and Diplomacy)—The Veto

The most important law or rules to consider for the Council's argumentation are those which are constitutive. These define the actors and structure the processes by which those actors interact and make decisions. The most essential rule of law in the Council is naturally the veto, as reflected in Article 27(3) of the Charter. It can be objectively verified, as it is a matter of simple binary fact rather than a legal interpretation—that is, whether there is consensus among the P5 or not. The veto is a procedural rule that has transformed to effectively become a political principle of consensus, which is applied across a wide ambit of the Council's work.

In light of this institutionalized need for consensus, Council diplomats and lawyers need to master a multidimensional kind of chess game, with significant innovation and understanding of stakeholders' interests and positions. This was well illustrated in respect of Council Resolution 2231 and the Joint Comprehensive Plan of Action (the Iran nuclear deal), which the Council adopted under New Zealand's presidency in July 2015. The most critical element necessary to reach agreement on Iran's sanction relief was the so-called "snap back" provision.[24] It projected the veto forward to a

[22] SC Res. 2272 (Mar. 11, 2016), paras. 3 and 4.

[23] See UN General Assembly, Report of the Special Committee on Peacekeeping Operations and its Working Group (June 9, 2008), UN Doc. A/61/19/Rev.1, Annex II ("Revised Draft Model Memorandum of Understanding between the United Nations and [Participating State] Contributing Resources to [the United Nations Peacekeeping Operation]"), Articles 7 quarter, quinquiens, and sexiens, https://documents-dds-ny.un.org/doc/UNDOC/GEN/N08/372/78/pdf/N0837278.pdf?OpenElement.

[24] See the discussion on the JCPOA and also the "snap back" provision in Ian Johnstone, chapter 7, in this volume, particularly Section IV.B, "The Joint Comprehensive Program of Action (JCPOA)."

future moment in time and decision, by providing that sanctions would be reimposed on Iran following an allegation of significant nonperformance, unless the Council unanimously agreed otherwise.

Legal argumentation in the judicial and adjudicative setting is predicated on binding decision-making by the arbiter. In diplomacy, by contrast, it is necessary to construct argumentation in a manner that builds momentum toward an agreement of all the parties. International legal argumentation may be delivered in a principled or absolutist manner (e.g., legal accountability for international crimes), which can risk alienating "the other side" from the diplomatic process of negotiation, concession, and consensus. Yet there is a need to proactively build coalitions of interest and to uncover the motivations of other interlocutors. In respect of the worst conflict situations before the Council, it is usually the regional players that can apply the most influence. In New Zealand's term on the Council in relation to the South Sudan conflict, this was the African Union, the Intergovernmental Authority on Development, and Sudan's neighbor Uganda. To obtain the support of the African Union, for example, involved more listening than expounding, and flexibility rather than potentially rigid legal positions.

B. Social Processes and Culture over Rules

Furthermore, the Council's processes can actually create normative expectations that are independent of rules and positively impact on the culture of the Council's members. As Philip Allott suggests, the law is an ever-changing set of retained acts of social willing.[25] In the Council context, decisions are not self-executing or easily enforceable, and political will and personal commitment are required to move an issue forward. The lawyer's faith of the power of the text is easily misplaced if, for example, there is little political buy-in or support for the particular words in a resolution.

As New Zealand discovered, even the UN Secretariat could refuse to follow legal obligations prescribed in a binding Chapter VII resolution agreed by the Council. In the process of New Zealand's chairing of the ISIL–Al-Qaida sanctions regime, it became clear that the Ombudsperson's office had been set up improperly by the UN Secretariat. The Ombudsperson is an independent and impartial office that reviews requests from individuals and groups seeking to be removed from the UN terrorist designation list. The office did not have the required independence from the UN Department of Political Affairs (in budget, staffing, and so on). New Zealand was able to secure language in a Council resolution, requesting the Secretary-General to "make the necessary arrangements to ensure [the Ombudsperson's] continued ability to carry out its mandate in an independent, effective and timely manner, and to provide the Committee an update on actions taken in six months."[26] Unfortunately, that request did not resolve the problem, as while the UN Secretariat accepted there were independence problems, its general position was that any changes to arrangements

[25] See Philip Allott, "Reconstituting Humanity—New International Law," *European Journal of International Law* 3 (1992): 219, para. 12.1.

[26] See SC Res. 2253 (June 27, 2015), para. 59.

required a Council consensus (which made this destined to fail, given some Council members' hostility to the office).

If international lawyers understand that the Council's process and culture can be more normatively powerful than its rules, this reshapes the method and focus of the legal argumentation. As Friedrich Kratochwil states: "Actors are not only affected by rules, but they also change by their practice the normative structures within which they act."[27] For these reasons, efforts on legal argumentation must be accompanied by attention to building support, good will, and the culture in the Council and beyond. This might comprise regular consultation with the UN Secretariat department that will implement the proposed resolution, or the chair of the UN sanctions committee's regular briefings with interested and affected member states.

C. Case Study—Responsibility to Protect and Protection of Civilians

The concepts of Responsibility to Protect (R2P) and the "protection of civilians" mandate provide a good example of the need to understand the Council's social processes and culture over rules. R2P is a concept well known to most engaged in international law and international relations. It was most developed in the period leading up to the 2005 World Summit and was agreed in the Outcome Document.[28] R2P was intended to address the shortcomings associated with humanitarian intervention and the Council's failures to protect people from mass atrocities, such as occurred under the United Nations' watch in Rwanda and Srebrenica. R2P was supported by many international lawyers, including for the purpose of creating a greater expectation on the international community and the UN Security Council, given its central role, to intervene as a last resort in mass atrocity situations.

The supporters of R2P promoted it as an "emerging guiding principle" grounded in "sovereignty as responsibility," and with the threshold for international involvement being met if a state was "unwilling or unable to fulfil its responsibility" to act against mass atrocities on its territory.[29] Despite the best efforts of supporters—including the Group of Friends, the International Coalition, and the Global Centre for R2P—the concept was never embraced by the Non-Aligned Movement (an influential group of 120 mostly developing states) and was opposed by notable figures such as Noam Chomsky.[30] A key reason was that, in the absence of any veto reform, R2P would likely be selectively applied and inherently politically biased. The Council never directly cited the concept of R2P. The concept's support was eroded by the divisive Council vote in favor of authorizing intervention in Libya, which was followed by an overly

[27] Friedrich Kratochwil, *Rules, Norms, and Decisions on the Conditions of Practical and Legal Reasoning in International Relations and Domestic Affairs* (Cambridge: Cambridge University Press, 2013), 61.

[28] GA Res. 60/1, 2005 World Summit Outcome (Oct. 24, 2005), para. 138.

[29] International Commission on Intervention and State Sovereignty, *The Responsibility to Protect: Report of the International Commission on Intervention and State Sovereignty* (ICISS Report) (Ottawa: International Development Research Centre, 2001), paras. 2.24, 2.31.

[30] Noam Chomsky, *The New Military Humanism: Lessons from Kosovo* (London: Pluto Press, 1999), 10.

broad interpretation of the international coalition's mandate to use force, resulting in Muammar Gaddafi's removal from power.

The Council's "protection of civilians" mandate is by contrast a successful example of the social process of normative construction in the Council. This mandate concerns the authority and responsibility provided by the Council under Chapter VII to a UN peacekeeping operation to use "all necessary means" (i.e., force), within the limits of its capabilities and areas of deployment, to protect civilians under imminent threat of physical violence, without prejudice to the responsibility of the host government. The vast majority of UN peacekeepers in the field now routinely have this mandate. While not without its problems, principally the patchy implementation by under-resourced UN peacekeepers, the concept is a success story in the Council.

The "protection of civilians" mandate has become widely accepted. This has led to a fairly consistent pattern of the Council providing a clear mandate to protect people in instances of serious violations of human rights and humanitarian law.[31] The mandate has fitted well with the Council's politics and created few tensions with the veto or broader concerns of Council intervention and selectivity. This contrasts with the approach for R2P, which focused on arguing directly for a rules-based regime with an expectation of intervention when required. Protection of civilians appears to be simply a policy or mandate option for the Council. The concept has developed a normative character and automaticity in the Council's practice for UN peacekeeping operations. This has led to UN normative statements that it may be an inherent obligation on UN peacekeepers even in situations where it is not mandated.[32]

A key reason the protection of civilians concept was embraced, including by major troop contributing countries to UN peacekeeping, and therefore by the whole Council, was the concept's endorsement by the UN General Assembly.[33] This resulted from a sustained campaign of socialization, with inclusive workshops and discussions with UN members and experienced peacekeepers, including from the Global South, and many others, over the course of more than five years. The Special Committee on Peacekeeping Operations (the C34) initially rejected the concept, and only came to embrace it later, after further and continued dialogue.

Prior to this development in the Council, there was no rule of law on the "protection of civilians," and in reality, nor is there today. A traditional approach to international legal argumentation—that international human rights and humanitarian law require the Council to act—would not have been effective at bringing about such an important and valuable normative development. For example, there is little doubt the protection of civilians mandate was central in South Sudan to UN peacekeepers' actions, which likely prevented atrocities, including potentially even acts of genocide.

[31] Scott Sheeran and Catherine Kent, "Protection of Civilians, Responsibility to Protect, and Humanitarian Intervention: Conceptual and Normative Interactions," in *Protection of Civilians*, edited by Haidi Willmot, Ralph Mamiya, Scott Sheeran, and Marc Weller (Oxford: Oxford University Press, 2016), 42–46.

[32] High-Level Independent Panel on United Nations Peace Operations, Uniting Our Strengths for Peace: Politics, Partnerships and People, UN Doc. A/70/95 (June 16, 2015), para. 90.

[33] UN General Assembly, Report of the Special Committee on Peacekeeping Operations and its Working Group, UN Doc. A/63/19 (Mar. 24, 2009), paras. 125–128.

This provides pause for thought in focusing argumentation to the Council on its obligations to stop international crimes.[34]

IV. The Characteristics of Legal Argumentation in the Security Council

In light of establishing the dominant paradigm of the Council, and the overarching focus on diplomacy in the process, it is necessary next to consider the more detailed elements of the Council's argumentation and decision-making. The Council's political nature and diplomatic process provide the overarching context for the particular methods of legal argumentation. A starting point is a typology of the issues most subject to international legal argument, and the extent and manner to which they can be influenced by that legal argument.

A. Typology of Issues for International Legal Argument

Broadly speaking, there are four main aspects of the Council's work in which international law, and by extension legal argumentation, is particularly relevant. First is whether a situation before the Council engages violations of international law. The primary examples of such violations are the Charter's prohibition against the use of force, violations of international humanitarian and human rights law, and of peace agreements and mandates of international forces—for example, UN peacekeeping missions or UN-authorized forces.

Second is whether a situation constitutes a "threat to international peace and security," which is grounds for the Council's power to impose binding measures under Chapter VII of the Charter. In practice, this may be a question for the Council to debate, or it may simply be inferred and flow naturally from the Council agreeing on specific actions to take under Chapter VII.

Third is the scope of the Council's powers to impose binding measures for a situation and on member states. This includes measures for conflict resolution, peacekeeping, targeted sanctions, mediation and good offices, international criminal justice, boundary dispute resolution, reparations, and so on.

Fourth, and related but distinct, is the interpretation of the operative or legal effect of the Council's decision. This matters both *before* and *after* the Council adopts its decision. From this author's experience, this is where legal argumentation is most valuable. In situations in which the Council has a sufficiently common political or policy intent, this needs to be translated into a text. That text will need to appropriately use the prior precedent of the Council and must be interpreted by lawyers globally in a manner that the Council intended. A draft resolution may have unintended side effects, or may not do what its proponents like to say that it does. Naturally, given

[34] For a contrasting view, see Bruno Stagno-Ugarte, chapter 8, in this volume, for a discussion of Council members not speaking directly enough about obligations to stop international crimes.

the diplomatic process and its underlying politics, often a Chapter VII resolution text is "constructively ambiguous," permitting more than one plausible interpretation in order to achieve agreement.

While the legal argumentation is important in debating the Council's jurisdiction, powers, and decisions, in practice these are ultimately decided at a political level. The most difficult politically sensitive issues concern not the lawfulness of the Council's decisions but rather its capacity and the wisdom of its decisions. Legal argumentation may not therefore be paramount for the *constraining* role of law, but is more important for the *constructive* or *enabling* role. As almost all Chapter VII resolutions of any importance are under the penholdership of the P3 (i.e., the United States, the United Kingdom, and France), and negotiated first with Russia and China, it is the P5's legal advisers who play an important role here.

The *ex post facto* interpretation of Council resolutions is a challenging task. There are numerous occasions in which Council resolutions have become central to a judicial process, especially before of the International Court of Justice (ICJ).[35] In this formal adjudicative setting, the granularity of international legal argumentation becomes essential and much more relevant. As stated in the ICJ's *Namibia* advisory opinion: "The language of a resolution ... should be carefully analysed before a conclusion can be made as to its binding effect ... [and] having regard to the terms of the resolution to be interpreted, the discussions leading to it, the Charter provisions invoked and, in general, all circumstances that might assist in determining the legal consequences of the resolution of the Security Council."[36]

The vast majority of Security Council resolutions are not interpreted by international courts and tribunals. For governments, foreign ministries, and others, it can be difficult to determine the precise meaning and legal implications of a Council resolution. This relates especially to whether the resolution or parts thereof lead to specific binding obligations. The terms "decides," "requires," "demands," "requests," and "authorizes" are clearer in their binding effect and do not lead to many difficulties of interpretation. Other terms such as "calls upon" and "urges" are less clear.[37]

Furthermore, there are also systemic challenges for the influence of international legal argumentation in the Council. These are closely related to the Council's dominant paradigm of international relations and the diplomatic process. They are reflected in three main ways—the lack of adjudication, the Council's selectivity and inconsistency, and divergence in law and practice—as well as in other characteristics of the Council.

[35] For example, see Legal Consequences for States of the Continued Presence of South Africa in Namibia (South West Africa) notwithstanding Security Council Resolution 276 (1970), Advisory Opinion, 1971 ICJ Rep., at 16; Accordance with International Law of the Unilateral Declaration of Independence in Respect of Kosovo, Advisory Opinion, 2010 ICJ Rep., at 403; Application of the Convention on the Prevention and Punishment of the Crime of Genocide (Bosnia and Herzegovina v. Serbia and Montenegro), Judgment, 2007 ICJ Rep., at 43; Legal Consequences of the Construction of a Wall in the Occupied Palestinian Territory, Advisory Opinion, 2004 ICJ Rep., at 136.

[36] *South West Africa* (Advisory Opinion), *id.* p. 53, para. 114. The Court similarly addressed this issue in *Kosovo* (Advisory Opinion) *id.* p. 403, para. 94.

[37] Loraine Sievers and Sam Daws, *The Procedure of the UN Security Council* (Oxford: Oxford University Press, 2014), 382.

B. Lack of Adjudication and Determinacy of Legal Argumentation

There is a challenge that the Council is lacking as an authoritative arbiter of international law. Legal argumentation, therefore, does not have the same primary role as in a judicial process. Flawed legal interpretations are unlikely to be objectively adjudicated and rejected, but rather may blend into the political rhetoric and decision-making.

In 2015, UN Secretary-General Ban Ki-Moon visited the Western Sahara and referred to its "occupation" by Morocco. Morocco took swift and robust countermeasures, including withdrawal of its consent for the deployment of various UN peacekeepers to the mission in Western Sahara. The fact the ICJ and the UN Legal Counsel had previously indicated that Morocco did not have sovereignty over Western Sahara meant that Morocco's consent was not required for deployment of UN peacekeepers, as New Zealand pointed out to Council members.[38] Indeed, it was legally irrelevant. However, that was out of step with the politics and practical necessity of Moroccan cooperation for Western Sahara and on other bilateral issues for the P3, and was essentially ignored in the Council's attempts to resolve the problem.

The Council is required to act in accordance with the UN Charter's principles and purposes.[39] However, as Michael Wood, another former Council legal adviser suggests, these appear in practice as largely policy principles and are not judicialized (as suggested by the ICJ in the *Namibia* advisory opinion).[40] They are broad and general, and at times in tension with each other. Ian Johnstone notes about key Charter principles that "State sovereignty is an important principle, but so is the promotion of human rights. Territorial integrity is fundamental, but so is self-determination. An important question then is who decides how to balance these competing principles."[41]

At the San Francisco Conference of 1945, which founded the United Nations, it was decided that each UN organ interpret such parts of the Charter as are applicable to its functions. This led to Hans Kelsen observing that "the Council is not bound strictly to comply with existing law."[42] The combination of the unique interpretive tools for the UN Charter—that is, the implied powers doctrine and enhanced role of practice as reflective of law—means that it is difficult to imagine a Council decision that would be politically agreed but considered unlawful. There is no doubt that decisions of the Council have gone beyond the Charter's text and drafters' intent, for example, in areas such as general legislating of counterterrorism obligations in the absence of being able to agree to a multilateral treaty, and binding decisions on state borders and reparations.

38 Advisory Opinion on Western Sahara, 1975 ICJ Rep., 12; Letter dated Jan. 29, 2002 from the Under-Secretary-General for Legal Affairs, the Legal Counsel, addressed to the President of the Security Council, UN Doc. S/2002/161 (Feb. 12, 2002).

39 UN Charter, art. 25.

40 Sir Michael Wood, "The Security Council's Powers and Their Limits," Hersch Lauterpacht Memorial Lectures, Lecture 2 (Nov. 8, 2006), 7, https://www.lcil.cam.ac.uk/sites/www.law.cam.ac.uk/files/images/www.lcil.law.cam.ac.uk/Image/Publications/2006_hersch_lecture_2.pdf.

41 Ian Johnstone, "The Security Council and International Law," in *The UN Security Council in the 21st Century*, edited by Sebastian von Einsiedel, David Malone, and Bruno Stagno-Ugarte (Boulder: Lynne Rienner, 2015), 784.

42 Hans Kelsen, *The Law of the United Nations* (New York: Frederick Praeger, 1951), 275.

Political checks and balances are therefore more central to controlling the Council's exercise of powers. Notwithstanding the ICJ's decision in the *Lockerbie* and *Bosnian Genocide* cases, which some scholars have called the "expressive mode of review,"[43] the ICJ has never placed a formal limit on the jurisdiction and powers of the Council. This state of affairs has consequences for legal argumentation in the Council.

C. Selectivity and Inconsistency of Legal Argumentation

In the Council, the legitimating effect of legal argumentation is regrettably undermined by the inconsistent manner of its use. The selective use of argument and contradictory positions, both within and across agenda items, are a hallmark of Council practice. This selectivity, especially by the P5, is related to which situations to address, the framing of a Council issue, and determining the Council's options for action. As Johnstone notes:

> Consistency may seem a simplistic pursuit, but it is also a fundamental principle of justice ... The problem is that in the realm of international politics, perfect consistency is not possible: power matters and inequalities in power inevitably result in inconsistency.[44]

During the author's term on the Council, Russia often argued that the P3 were hypocritical in their positions, including on normative issues. It is ironic that China and Russia are actually more consistent, albeit not in a way favored by most international lawyers, in their use of legal argumentation (i.e., favoring sovereignty, non-intervention, non-use of force). All Council members use international legal rhetoric to mask or rationalize behavior driven by self-interest. For example, this includes Russia's construction of a largely implausible self-determination rationale for its annexation of Crimea. The veto guaranteed that the Council would never have an opportunity to decide on that legal argument (only the individual Council members could, without the Council's legitimacy).

For the P3, the problem is well described by Jack Goldsmith and Eric Posner's observation of states' arguments: "Their legal or moral justifications cleave to their interests, and so when interest change, so do the rationalizations."[45] In the case of the renewal of the Western Sahara peacekeeping mission mandate in 2016, the P3 voted in favor of Resolution 2285, which was in Morocco's rather than in Western Sahara's interests. The P3 also put pressure on other Council members, including New Zealand, to vote in favor. New Zealand and others' objections related to international law—that is, the human rights monitoring mandate, recognition that Morocco's consent to the UN peacekeeping operation was not required, and the need for a meaningful process for self-determination. The objections were overwhelmed by considerations of

[43] Jose Alvarez, "Judging the Security Council," *American Journal of International Law* 90 (1996): 28.
[44] Johnstone, *supra* note 41, at 787.
[45] Jack Goldsmith and Eric Posner, *The Limits of International Law* (Oxford: Oxford University Press, 2005), 169.

national interests, including bilateral cooperation with Morocco on counterterrorism and migration issues. Uruguay, Venezuela, Angola, the Russian Federation, and New Zealand did not vote in favor of the resolution. During the next Council discussion where the P3 sought to (genuinely) stand up for matters of human rights, their arguments were approached with more skepticism.

D. Divergence in Law vs. Practice

A particular challenge for legal argumentation concerns situations in which the Council's accepted practice has developed inconsistently with legal rules. This contradiction and its implications may not always be apparent to international lawyers unfamiliar with the Council. For example, Article 27(3) of the Charter provides that the P5 cannot veto a decision under Chapter VI on peaceful settlement of dispute, or Article 53 on regional arrangements, if they are "a party to the dispute." There are regrettably many examples of the P5 doing just that and the Council accepting this practice (e.g., Russia in respect of Georgia and Ukraine, the United States in respect of Libya). New Zealand considered using Article 27(3) in its argumentation after Russia successfully pushed an urgent draft resolution on the conflict in Ukraine through the Council for adoption.[46] However, in an instance immediately prior to New Zealand's term, Lithuania had considered this very same argument also, but was advised by a P3 member not to make this argument.

The P5 dominance in the Council also creates a *de facto* veto on procedural issues in many instances. This is despite the fact that Article 23 of the Charter makes clear there is no veto on procedural matters. A prime example is the Security Council President's program of work—that includes the issues that will be discussed by the Council that month—which is effectively subject to veto.

E. Non-Legal Elements that Impact Legal Argumentation

Equally, there is a range of non-legal elements with a significant impact on the reception of legal argumentation. These elements tend to reflect the dominant influence of international relations, diplomacy, and national interests, which in a simple sense reduces the effect of legal argumentation. For example, a compliance-based theory of international law suggests that, in light of the highly politically sensitive issues in the Council, member states will privilege the outcome that they seek over any reputational damage (e.g., as the preceding P3 and Morocco resolution example demonstrates). While the non-legal elements relevant to legal argumentation vary, four such elements are worth emphasis.

First is the degree of political sensitivity and national interest on the issues in question. In New Zealand's time on the Council, for example, the most politically charged issues were Palestine, Syria, Ukraine, North Korea, Iran, the downing of flight MH-17,

[46] SC Res. 2202 (Feb. 17, 2015).

and Srebrenica. In the Council's history, these issues have collectively attracted many vetoes, including two vetoes during New Zealand's presidency of the Council for July 2015.[47]

Second is the current climate in the Council among the P5, that is, whether it is one of cooperation or confrontation and "payback." During New Zealand's term, the two vetoes during its first presidency reflected a difficult environment of increased likelihood of political interests trumping normative values. It was in this context that Russia vetoed a commemorative resolution on the anniversary of Srebrenica because it included the word "genocide" (even though the International Criminal Tribunal for the former Yugoslavia and the Council had already recognized it was a genocide), and on the basis of lack of consultation by the United Kingdom (the penholder) on the draft resolution.

Third is the general resistance, including by China and Russia, to the Council being too quick to take up country situations and impose a Council view on human rights and domestic affairs. For this reason, it took six months of lobbying to get the Council to agree to merely visit Burundi in 2016 at a time when there was constant reporting on serious human rights violations and increasing security problems. In terms of the Council's conflict prevention role, this was too slow and missed an opportunity to shape the situation. The reticence appeared to have less to do with Burundi than with the general precedent of the Council's measures of conflict prevention. Legal argumentation in this context actually increased the resistance to Council agreement.

Finally, there is arguably also a general resistance to acceding to normative argumentation, to the extent that it may imply the Council accepts an *obligation* to act. As indicated previously, there are international lawyers, states, and NGOs which argue that R2P engages the necessity to act. In addition, arguments of norms *jus cogens* (i.e., peremptory) and positive obligations to prevent genocide can have the same effect, with the latter even a concern for countries such as the United States, which have domestic legal consequences arising from invoking the term "genocide."

This is an area, even more than others, subject to very fine judgments of strategy and diplomacy. There is no doubt that legal argumentation—in the media, by NGOs, in the UN membership, and in the Council—can help to create pressure for the Council to act. However, it is also fair to say that an argument based on a strong and public focus on human rights victims by a powerful Council member like the United States—that is, that the Council must intervene to protect the victims—may make it harder for countries like Russia and China to accede to an intervention.

This legal argumentation creates a precedent of which some Council members are wary and can be instrumentalized in future (an example would be France's argument that the Council should use the "responsibility to protect" as a basis for intervening in Myanmar after that government's inadequate response to Cyclone Nargis in 2008). In a general sense, "quiet diplomacy" may need to precede "naming and shaming," because the latter does not easily lead to the Council's consensus. This author has seen in the Council examples in which it appeared a Council member placed more emphasis

[47] See the UN Security Council draft resolution on the genocide in Srebrenica, UN Doc. S/2015/508 (July 8, 2015); UN Security Council draft resolution on the downing of MH-17, UN Doc. S/2015/562 (July 29, 2016).

on its own portrayal in the media than on constructively contributing to a negotiated solution.

For an outsider, it is easy to be ignorant of overarching dynamics of decision-making in the Council. As Colin Keating notes: "In many respects, on major issues the Council has become either a vehicle for political theatre, when the P5 cannot agree, or a tool for the ratification and formalisation of decisions already taken privately by the P5."[48] This unfortunate reality requires that international lawyers inside and outside the Council improve their situational awareness and lateral thinking in order for their legal argument to have instrumental impact.

V. The Policy Underpinnings of International Legal Argumentation

The preceding sections generally indicated the limits to legal argumentation in the Council and exposed assumptions of the traditional legal approach. This section discusses the most important lessons from practice for effective legal argumentation. Ironically, these may be simplistically misunderstood as "not to argue legally." However, as previously identified in Scobbie's description, legal argumentation is instrumentally designed for practical effect, and its success is measured by persuasion of the audience addressed. In the Council context, this means the ensuring legal argument's persuasion of nonlawyer diplomats and government officials, including by harnessing their paradigm and language, in order to influence the Council's decisions.

A. International Law's Concomitance with Underlying Policy and Values

It is necessary for international lawyers to consider the policy or values that underlie the law. The drafters of a legal rule normally have a two-layer intention: to address in specific dètail an issue of immediate concern, and also to advance a broader policy goal or value. As Higgins notes: "Policy considerations, although they differ from rules, are an integral part of that decision making process which we call international law; the assessment of so-called extralegal considerations is *part of the legal process*."[49] There is logic in the law to follow, rather than just a logic in following the law. In relation to the UN Charter, the underlying principles include sovereignty, peaceful resolution of conflicts, and human dignity.

The international lawyer may struggle to create a commitment among policymakers that Article 1(3) of the Charter, through Article 25, binds the Council to human rights obligations. However, it may be more productive to seek to create commitment to the values represented, for example, via the concept of "protection of civilians." This

[48] Colin Keating, "Power Dynamics: Between Permanent and Elected Members," in *The UN Security Council in the 21st Century*, *supra* note 41, at 145.
[49] Higgins, *supra* note 5, at 5.

allows the international lawyer to draw on a broader range of tools, including practice and precedent, normative behaviors from other fora and communities, as was the case for the development of the protection of civilians mandate.

The international lawyer's dilemma is reflected in Koskenniemi's well-known opposition—from apology to utopia. Arguably, in the Council this manifests in whether to be formalist and absolutist and have limited influence, or to be pragmatic and achieve imperfect but modestly better outcomes in line with normative values. It is a difficult line to walk. But it is incorrect to claim that a more flexible approach robs the lawyer's argument of its normative impact. The goal is to find the right balance of upholding values with pragmatic incrementalism that helps make lives better. It is certainly easier in the Council to take a legal position that is binary and purist, but also to be ineffective in influencing the Council's decisions and, therefore, normative values and peoples' lives.

B. Case Example—Situational Awareness Briefings to the Council

The establishment of situational awareness briefings in the Council provides an example of how understanding the policy behind the legal argumentation can assist its persuasiveness.

In the first five months of 2009, it is estimated that over forty thousand people were killed in northern Sri Lanka in the final stages of its civil war. The United Nations was deployed in Sri Lanka and had access to significant and concerning information leading up to the apex of the conflict. According to the United Nations' own review afterward, the conflict included serious violations of international human rights and humanitarian law. This conflict was never placed on the Council's agenda.

A *Report of the Secretary-General's Internal Review Panel on United Nations Action* (known as "the Petrie report") was commissioned as an independent assessment. This report was damning for the Organization. Despite the clear and well-founded concerns, the UN Secretariat and Secretary-General chose not to brief the Council, and accordingly, a key recommendation of the Petrie report was: "[T]he Secretary-General should make more regular and explicit use of his Security Council convening authority under Article 99 of the Charter."[50] Article 99 of the UN Charter provides: "The Secretary-General may bring to the attention of the Security Council any matter which in his opinion may threaten the maintenance of international peace and security." Based on the Petrie report, the Secretary-General approved a reform agenda that he called the "Human Rights Up Front" (HRUF) initiative. The Petrie report's key recommendation that was left largely untouched by the HRUF initiative was Article 99.

New Zealand, at the author's initiative, launched a campaign of diplomacy and lobbying with the UN Secretariat and Council members, which resulted in the

[50] United Nations, Report of the Secretary-General's Internal Review Panel on United Nations Action in Sri Lanka (Nov. 2012), at 34, https://digitallibrary.un.org/record/737299?ln=en.

establishment of a new "situational awareness" briefing.[51] This was to enhance the Council's conflict prevention and preventive diplomacy, using the information the UN Secretariat had through their field presences, but which most Council members did not. The intent was a regular briefing to Council members, focused on burgeoning situations and potential conflict, provided by the UN Secretariat outside of the Council's official program of work. A regular briefing for the Council would make it harder for a Sri Lanka–type failure to occur again. This initiative was sensitive and initially rejected by the UN Secretariat. It took almost a year of determined and delicate efforts to finally get the UN Secretariat to agree to offer the briefings.

While the situational awareness initiative had a normative basis in the Charter, the overwhelming focus of the argumentation deployed related to the underlying policy rationale of Article 99, rather than expressly to Article 99 itself. Furthermore, the argument (and even the briefing's title) was deliberately framed not to invoke human rights or R2P. A more traditional mode of international legal argument would likely have faced resistance, both to the specific initiative and to human rights, R2P, and obligations under Article 99. New Zealand ensured that other Council members would champion these briefings after it departed the Council, and the situational awareness briefings did continue. In 2018, the ten elected Council members and five incoming elected members conducted an ambassadorial-level démarche on the UN Secretary-General to request early situational awareness briefings, as the Secretariat had ceased providing them.

C. Case Example—Transitional Justice in the Central African Republic

In the Council, the accountability for violations of international law is one of the most difficult types of issues on which to attract support or consensus. This is underpinned by a long-standing debate of "peace versus justice." As practice demonstrates, the Council clearly privileges the former over the latter. The reasons are as Kenneth Weisbrode states: "The pursuit of justice first requires peace. Ignoring this particular natural law, realists say, results in the spread of neither peace nor justice."[52]

In the case of the Central African Republic (CAR), a situation before the Council, New Zealand tried to introduce a different approach to pursuing the goals of accountability and human rights. The CAR had emerged from civil war with weak systems of governance and a legacy of significant violence between the Séléka and Anti-Balaka aligned groups, which reflected a Muslim and Christian divide. The New Zealand approach was based on engaging the Council members with arguments in favor of the benefits of bottom-up political solutions, intercommunity dialogue, and community-based dispute resolution and reconciliation. The stated goal was the ending of the

[51] UN Deputy Secretary-General Jan Eliasson's remarks at the Annual Gareth Evans Lecture on the Responsibility to Protect and Mass Atrocity Prevention (Dec. 8, 2016), https://www.un.org/press/en/2016/dsgsm1031.doc.htm; Security Council Report, October 2019 Monthly Forecast (Sept. 30, 2019), https://www.securitycouncilreport.org/monthly-forecast/2019-10/conflict-prevention.php.

[52] Kenneth Weisbrode, "Diplomacy and Politics," in *Global Diplomacy: Theories, Types, and Models*, edited by Alison Holmes and Simon Rofe (Abingdon: Routledge, 2015), 131.

conflict and maintaining peace. By contrast, the common arguments of "criminal accountability" tended to attract the support of less than half of the Council's members.

The New Zealand effort was intended to rebalance the almost exclusive push for a narrow top-down centralized criminal court (which continued unsuccessfully at time of writing) over a broader-based process of transitional justice.[53] Second, it sought greater political support and resources from the Council for community-based transitional justice than would be possible for a special criminal court in the CAR that was barely supported by the government. The practical effect on the ground for the two courses of action was not really comparable.

While the UN special rapporteur on the promotion of truth, justice, reparation, and guarantees of non-recurrence at the time, and UN political officials, were supportive of the New Zealand objective, the UN human rights officers and NGOs largely were not. Some of the UN human rights officers who were consulted and included in the initiative ended up actively and clandestinely resisting the initiative. These human rights officers were not malicious. They too were committed to improved normative outcomes, but had a different paradigm, priorities, and understanding of what would attract political backing from the Council and CAR government (i.e., rather than just from fellow human rights advocates).

D. Case Example—Draft Resolution on an Israel-Palestine Peace Process

During its term, New Zealand prepared and proposed a draft resolution for progressing a peace process for Israel and Palestine. The resolution was designed around clear parameters for setting up a diplomatic process designed to build political momentum, rather than addressing specifically what either side laid down as its "red lines" in public statements (which doomed any negotiation to fail). Accordingly, neither side was happy with the New Zealand draft resolution. However, it was necessary to be realistic in order to lead to any diplomatic progress. The primary intent was to attract the political support (and avoid the veto) of the US administration.

A key element of the balance and effectiveness of the draft resolution was inclusion of an operative paragraph that temporarily suspended the ability of the Palestinians to request International Criminal Court (ICC) investigations. This reflected a concept set out in Article 16 of the Rome Statute. The Council could hold out this possibility (Palestine eventually self-referred to the ICC in May 2018) in exchange for Israel genuinely participating in the peace process. It appeared to be precisely the kind of tradeoff, for conflict resolution purposes, that Article 16 in the Rome Statute was intended to address.

It was the civil society community that reacted strongly and lobbied against the draft resolution on the basis of the ICC reference. This led to a meeting between New Zealand and civil society representatives which was tense and searching, both at the practical level and the conceptual and normative levels. The primary objection from

[53] For an alternative view, see Bruno Stagno-Ugarte, chapter 8, in this volume, and his discussion of the ICC.

civil society was that this would damage the ICC and the precedent would be used by African states for President al-Bashir of Sudan. In this case, the NGOs were using essentially extralegal considerations arguably not aligned with the policy intent of Article 16 in their legal argumentation.

VI. Conclusion

International legal argumentation as traditionally understood is not highly relevant in the UN Security Council. Diplomacy, negotiation, and consensus drive the outcomes. This chapter's aim was not to criticize, but rather to empower, the role of international legal argumentation. This is particularly in light of the principle of effectiveness. It requires a serious acceptance of the contextual limits of international law in the Council in order to better comprehend what can be achieved normatively.

To have influence in the Council, international lawyers must think and argue laterally and embrace law as a social process. The leveraging of extralegal factors—arising from international relations, diplomacy, policy considerations, and international values—ultimately shapes the output of the legal process itself. There is still an important role for those who can maintain pressure and describe what the Council ought to do legally, shining a light on the significant normative dissonance between the Charter and practice. However, within the Council and especially on the real-life situations before it, this does not promote the aims of international law, nor does it reduce human suffering and save lives. International lawyers must to learn to instrumentalize international relations and politics, rather than be the unwitting victims of the reverse.

5
Protesting the Preamble

Normative Pronouncements and Feminist Jurisprudence in the Security Council

Gina Heathcote

I. Introduction

When Alaa Saleh took to the streets of Dafur, to sing as part of the street protests that began after the arrest of Sudanese President Omar Al-Bashir in 2019,[1] the image of her, dressed in white and leading the chants, traveled the world. Saleh's demands were simple: freedom, peace, and justice. Subsequently, Saleh was one of three Sudanese women who addressed the UN Security Council at the annual meeting in October 2019 on women, peace, and security (WPS). Saleh spoke on behalf of Sudanese youth and spoke of Sudanese women's participation in the protests for peace alongside cofounder of the Women for Peace Initiative, Samah Jamous, and member of the women's rights coalition MANSAM, Huda Ali.[2]

I am interested in the flow of knowledge from transnational feminist praxis on the ground to the transformation of that knowledge through international institutions. Within those knowledge flows lie spaces of legal argumentation from voices raised in protest to the legal text. Of specific interest is the function of the preambles within international legal texts and their capacity to filter out some knowledge and to transform the perspectives of one community to align with dominant forms. I examine two aspects of the preambles to Security Council resolutions in this chapter. First, the filtering out of wider transnational feminist demands that continue to reside in the space of protest. Second, the filtering in of the dominant normative commitments of international institutions and, in both instances, the role of the preamble in shaping the normative frame for legal argument. I examine how Security Council preambles become an articulation of feminist approaches that emphasize women as victims (of conflict-related sexual violence) and as participants within decision-making structures while downplaying the structural changes, such as commitments to antimilitarism, peace, wider justice agendas, and disarmament, framed by transnational feminist actors.

[1] For details, see Wouter Werner, chapter 10, in this volume.

[2] UN Women, "From Sudan to the Security Council: Sudanese Women Lead Drive for Change," Nov. 7, 2019, https://www.unwomen.org/en/news/stories/2019/11/feature-sudanese-women-lead-drive-for-change.

Gina Heathcote, *Protesting the Preamble* In: *Talking International Law*. Edited by: Ian Johnstone and Steven Ratner, Oxford University Press. © Gina Heathcote 2021. DOI: 10.1093/oso/9780197588437.003.0005

Through the examination of Security Council preambles, I argue for feminist protest as a form of legal argumentation. I explore how feminist protest might be understood as the overlooked preamble to WPS that makes impenitent demands on international legal responses to militarism and insecurity. My approach is drawn from an understanding of the legal and the normative as iterative of each other, given meaning through legal interpretation.[3] As such, the legal effect of WPS resolutions is not only understood through the text of operative paragraphs but also through the normative universe they stem from. That normative universe, I argue, includes the content within the preamble as well as the histories of feminist organizing that come to be only partially included in the resolutions. In order to analyze the forms of legal argumentation deployed in the Security Council, in feminist legal spaces, and in the resolutions, I center the preamble to evidence the silencing of dissident feminist approaches and the elision between normative and legal arguments within international law. It is easy to dismiss the preamble as just that, preambular, non-legal, and thus insignificant to the development of law.[4] However, the changing practice of the Council not only in terms of the length of preambles but, perhaps more importantly, the content of the preamble from strictly legal to a combination of legal and normative justifications benefits from closer scrutiny.

This chapter provides an entry point for asking what sort of work the preambles of Security Council resolutions do. Michael Wood argues that "given the way that SC resolutions are drafted, less reliance can be placed upon the preambular language of resolutions as a tool for the interpretation of the operative part."[5] However, the changing nature of contemporary preambles—and thus the efforts and input invested into the preamble—suggests interactions between the normative and legal in Security Council resolutions, including what preambles add and, perhaps, what they distract from. If the normative encompasses the larger patterns of beliefs and assumptions that circulate across a community, the legal is a specific expression of the normative. At the same time, the legal remains distinct from the normative due to its prescriptive content. Many lawyers understand law and the legal, as the precise rules within a system, and yet, as this book attests, lawyers also understand the legal as produced within a specific normative universe.[6] In this chapter I examine the different normative universes that combine to shape Security Council resolutions on WPS and the role of the preamble in refining the wider normative agenda of transnational feminisms into a shape amenable to the Security Council. Thematic resolutions, including on WPS, from the Security Council are understood as normative, in the sense of holding something other than binding legal obligations through the incorporation of beliefs and

[3] Robert Cover, "Nomos and Narrative," *Harvard Law Review* 97 (1983): 4.

[4] Also see Scott P. Sheeran, chapter 4, in this volume, on the complex social interactions and political dimensions of Security Council practice.

[5] Michael Wood, "The Interpretation of Security Council Resolutions: Revisited," *Max Planck Yearbook of United Nations Online* 20 (2017): 1, 34.

[6] See further, in particular, Kathleen Claussen, chapter 15, Monica Hakimi, chapter 3, and Ian Johnstone, chapter 7, all in this volume.

assumptions. Yet this does not preclude elements of a thematic resolution acquiring specific legal force.

I use the ten WPS resolutions as an example of the changing normative content, the traveling of content between thematic and situation-specific resolutions, and the potential legal consequences of often repeated preamble framings and phrasings. I consider how the resolutions on WPS are an important illustration of the risks of the continued development of normative agendas via the Security Council and its ever-growing preambular material. I examine these risks in terms of the spaces of forgetting, that is, where preambular material may be discarded for its (assumed) lack of legal meaning, and as spaces of legal argumentation with the potential to crystallize into future customary international law, while also developing interpretations of existing treaty law. Contemporary feminist writing has begun to make claim to this crystallization of legal content in the preambles of WPS resolutions,[7] which has implications for international lawyers as a form of legal argument in and of itself. At the same time, the risks of feminist engagement with the Security Council are identified, where a partial, potentially damaging, form of gender law reform emerges as a consequence.

The chapter proceeds in the following manner. Section II provides a short introduction to the expanding preambles of Security Council resolutions. I track the content and expansion of resolutions to examine the normative work performed by preambles and the development of the WPS resolutions. In Section III, I look at contemporary feminist accounts of the Security Council's WPS framework, where arguments with regard to the legal, as opposed to normative, value of the ten resolutions as a co-joined body of law have begun to appear. This is distinct from analysis of the legal impact of operative paragraphs.[8] In Section IV, I draw in the substantial feminist critiques of the WPS resolutions to understand the risks for feminist projects of pursuing either a normative or legal agenda within the Security Council. These are legal developments that, I argue, often ignore and actively "forget" feminist histories and feminist knowledge production—both past and present—that is deeply rooted in antimilitarist struggles and, through feminist protest, challenges the Security Council and its five permanent members' propensity to rely on the use of force and the circulation of arms as a means to peace.[9] To conclude the chapter, I argue for feminist protest—historical and contemporary—as the forgotten preamble to WPS that makes unrepentant demands on a global system that uses law to underscore war and which has consistently misused feminist messages as a normative weapon.

[7] Christine Chinkin and Madeleine Rees, "Commentary on Security Council Resolution 2467: Continued State Obligation and Civil Society Obligation on Sexual Violence in Conflict," LSE WPS Working Paper Series (July 2019), http://www.lse.ac.uk/women-peace-security/assets/documents/2019/reports/WPS-Commentary-Report-online.pdf.

[8] Gina Heathcote, "Feminist Politics and the Use of Force: Theorising Feminist Action and SC Resolution 1325," *Socio-Legal Review* 7 (2011): 23.

[9] See further Anna Stavrianakis, "Towards a Postcolonial, Anti-Racist, Anti-Militarist Feminist Mode of Weapons Control," in *New Directions in Women Peace and Security*, edited by Soumita Basu, Paul Kirby, and Laura Shepherd (Bristol: Polity Press, 2020).

II. On Expanding Preambles of the UN Security Council

Security Council resolutions are structured through a preamble and a series of operative paragraphs. The preamble of resolutions situates them in relation to prior resolutions and relevant treaty material and, when the resolution is issued under Chapter VII of the UN Charter, offers evidence of the binding quality of the operative paragraphs. Although not often regarded as creating legal obligations for states, the preamble is not only an important part of the resolution, it is also a form of legal argumentation. That is, the preamble gives evidence of, and articulates, the legal and factual situation, from which the operative paragraphs emerge. Following the *Namibia* case, it is clear the Council's decisions must be "adopted in conformity with the purposes and principles of the Charter and in accordance with its Articles 24 and 25."[10] That is, Articles 24 and 25 of the UN Charter give legal meaning to decisions within any given resolution, which might also contain recommendations. The ten resolutions on WPS are generally regarded as thematic, recommendatory, and non-binding. However, Christine Chinkin and Madeleine Rees argue that the continued production of WPS resolutions indicates a crystallization of some provisions into customary international law, while noting the use of references to additional, existing laws in the preambles of these resolutions.[11] Here I examine, first, the changing nature of Security Council resolutions over the life of the institution and, second, the placement of the WPS resolutions within that history.

A. Security Council Preambles over Time

A simple quantitative check gives a sense of how the use of preambles has evolved. In 2000, in the first WPS resolution, Resolution 1325, the preamble consists of eleven paragraphs that take up just over one page of the resolution. In contrast, the preamble of the ninth resolution on WPS, 2467 of April 23, 2019, consists of twenty-five paragraphs, just over three pages in length. Before 1990 (and prior to the development of thematic resolutions) the preambles to resolutions were around one or two paragraphs in length and sometimes nonexistent. For example, Resolution 678 from November 30, 1990, authorizing military force in the event of Iraq's noncompliance with the Council's demand to withdraw its troops from Kuwait, has a preamble of three short paragraphs (in fact, one sentence each in length). In contrast, Resolution 2490, September 20, 2019, renewing the mandate of UNITAD in Iraq, consists of a preamble just over a page in length—including six long paragraphs—and a mere four operative paragraphs. It is now not unusual for a resolution preamble to far exceed the length of the operative paragraphs—a reverse of pre-1990 practice.

At the commencement of the Security Council's work, in Resolution 1, January 25, 1946, the preamble begins with a reference to the UN Charter's authorization of the Council to establish a military staff committee under Article 47. This is the substance

[10] Legal Consequences for States of the Continued Presence of South Africa in Namibia (South West Africa) notwithstanding Security Council Resolution 276 (1970) 1971 ICJ Rep., at 16, para. 115.
[11] Chinkin and Rees, *supra* note 7, at 7–9.

of the preamble of the first Council resolution: an underpinning of the legal authority given to the institution to act under Chapter VII. In the subsequent half century, the role of any Security Council commentary prior to the operative elements of resolutions (i.e., the preamble) remains largely explanatory—explaining the situation before the Security Council or establishing the legal authority with which the Security Council acts. For example, Resolution 83, June 27, 1950, authorizing the use of force (or assistance "as may be necessary") against North Korea, contains a five-sentence preamble that identifies an Article 39 breach of the peace, the prior call by the Council for North Korea to cease hostilities and withdraw their forces, and the statements from the UN Commission on Korea, before asserting the request from the Republic of Korea for assistance. That is, the preamble in Resolution 83 establishes the legal grounds on which the Council has chosen to act. Compared to contemporary preambular material, not only is this a relatively brief text but it is also qualitatively different. Resolution 678, November 30, 1990, authorizing the use of force to protect Kuwait in the event of Iraqi noncompliance with the resolution, provides similar preambular content—affirming the capacity of the Council to act through the referencing of former resolutions on the situation before it, noting, in particular, Iraq's noncompliance with Resolution 660 and invoking its own authority under the Charter—essentially recording the legal authority to act.

By the mid-1990s, preambular length had changed significantly, as had the content of preambles to increasingly invoke the wider situation and normative force behind the resolution. For example, Resolution 866, September 22, 1993, establishing the creation of UNOMIL in Liberia, includes a preamble of over a page in length, consisting of thirteen paragraphs. At this point, the content of the preamble roughly aligns with earlier resolutions: establishing the antecedents to the resolution, including previous relevant resolutions, Secretary-General reports, the actions and recommendations of relevant regional bodies (ECOWAS, African Union), and legal documents, such as the peace agreements. However, by the end of the 1990s, the shift from direct legal references in the preamble toward the inclusion of broader normative claims had commenced, reflecting the changing political dimensions that saw the Security Council actively and deeply engaged with an increased number of situations after the end of the Cold War. In Resolution 1214, December 8, 1998, on the situation in Afghanistan,[12] the preamble continues well into the second page of the resolution and includes general statements on human suffering, the ethnic and religious nature of the conflict, and, for the first time in a resolution, "its deep concern at the continuing discrimination against girls and women."[13] The latter is explicitly linked to both international human rights and humanitarian law. What is new is the shift from a legal assertion to an expression of "concern."[14] Resolution 1214 thus marks the commencement of the transition from the use of the preamble to underpin the legal authority for the Security Council's actions toward a combination of legal and normative claims.

[12] SC Res. 1214 (Dec. 8, 1998).
[13] *Id.*, preamble.
[14] See further Wouter Werner, chapter 10, in this volume.

B. Thematic Resolutions

The development of thematic rather than situation-specific resolutions also begins to appear during the final decade of the twentieth century. In Resolution 868, September 29, 1993, on peacekeeping, the Council endorses the Secretary-General's *An Agenda for Peace*. It is a relatively short resolution acknowledging the report and endorsing the protections for peacekeepers and peacekeeping operations recommended in the report.[15] The second thematic resolution from the Council is Resolution 984 (April 1, 1995) on the non-proliferation of nuclear weapons.[16] With the exception of Resolution 1121, July 22, 1997 (on the creation of the Dag Hammarskjöld Medal), the next thematic resolutions were not adopted until 1999—Resolution 1261 (August 25, 1999), on the protection of children in armed conflict, and Resolution 1265 (September 17, 1999), on the protection of civilians in armed conflict.[17] Various resolutions—on refugees and on illicit arms flow in Africa, on international terrorism and international peace and security—while focused on a region do address wider concerns of the Security Council over the same period.[18] In the year 2000, the Council issued five thematic resolutions, including Resolution 1325, on WPS. By 2019, the Council issued seven thematic resolutions in a single calendar year, although the annual average between 2010 and 2019 has been five.

This emergence of thematic resolutions has in turn resulted in a shift toward a form of normative pronouncement within the preamble of situation-specific resolutions, even when they are relatively short. For example, Resolutions 2516 and 2517 of March 30, 2020, in which the Council renews the existing mandate for missions in Somalia (2516) and Sudan (2517), both include references to "sovereignty, territorial integrity, political independence and unity."[19] This language is neither uniform nor consistent in all mandate renewals but mimics the language of Article 2 of the UN Charter, giving it a distinctly legal resonance. This older, consistent legal framing thus remains, but as the thematic resolutions multiply, so does the normative framing within some situation-specific resolutions. In the preamble of Resolution 2489, the Council refers to the need for a "comprehensive and inclusive Afghan-led" peace process, while Resolution 2488 refers to "peace, security, justice, reconciliation, inclusivity and development" in the preamble.[20] If the established approach of the Security Council has always centered the signaling of legal authority in the preamble, the emergence of additional language that is not legal, evidencing wider normative considerations and a subtle expansion of the content of preambles, is of interest. Given the rise of thematic resolutions over the same period, the normative assertions of these general resolutions flow into situation-specific resolutions via the preamble.

15 SC Res. 868 (Sept. 29, 1993); An Agenda for Peace.

16 Treaty on the Non-Proliferation of Nuclear Weapons, 1968, 729 UNTS 161.

17 SC Res. 1121 (July 22, 1997); SC Res. 1261 (Aug. 25, 1999); SC Res. 1265 (Sept. 17, 1999).

18 SC Res. 1172 (June 6, 1998); SC Res. 1189 (Aug. 13, 1998); SC Res. 1208 (Nov. 19, 1998); SC Res. 1209 (Nov. 19, 1998).

19 SC Res. 2516 (Mar. 30, 2020); SC Res. 2517 (Mar. 30, 2020).

20 SC Res. 2488 (Sept. 12, 2019).

C. Women, Peace, and Security

Within this shift from legal statements to normative claims in the preambles, the ten WPS resolutions have seen the Security Council deploy feminist-derived messages as a normative weapon. That is, the Council has used the WPS resolutions to underscore its own legitimacy after a period, at the beginning of the millennium, when questions were raised as to the Security Council's continued effectiveness.[21] In addition, the WPS agenda has been refined by the Council to slowly become a process of forgetting the transnational feminist origins behind the law. While the first WPS resolution, 1325, was informed by the work of civil society actors, subsequent resolutions have developed their own repertoire of language and terminologies. Consequently, the WPS resolutions demonstrate the changing ways in which the Security Council perceives and performs its role, as well as the interplay between legal and normative forms. When considered in terms of legal argumentation, developments *within* the resolutions—the expansion of normative statements—and developments *around* the resolutions—understandings of their legal meaning and effect—both help track how the WPS framework has been used by feminist actors to assert a feminist agenda and by the Council's members to assert a separate Security Council agenda, sometimes aligned with the former and yet always partial.

The first WPS resolution had a preamble aligned with Security Council practice at the time—about a page in length and largely (although not only) making links between the work of the Council and adjunct legal structures and obligations.[22] By 2019, in Resolution 2467, the preamble extends over the first three pages of the resolution and links to other legal documents, recalls and repeats earlier resolutions, and makes normative statements about gendered violence within armed conflict and post-conflict. The legal significance of these developments has received some attention in feminist writing on WPS. Attempts to assert the legal value, and thus potential, of the various resolutions on WPS, including through the language of the preambles, emerges as a form of legal argumentation.[23]

III. Normative Content and Legal Argumentation

Dianne Otto notes the enthusiasm of some feminist actors to hold the WPS resolutions as having binding legal force.[24] That is, early in the development of the WPS agenda, a misunderstanding as to the legal quality of Council resolutions decided under Chapter VI was apparent within wider feminist networks. This misperception within feminist spaces had advantages, in that feminist actors lobbied states (and

[21] Dianne Otto, "The Security Council's Alliance of Gender Legitimacy: The Symbolic Capital of Resolution 1325," in *Fault Lines of International Legitimacy*, edited by Hilary Charlesworth and Jean-Marc Coicaud (Cambridge: Cambridge University Press, 2010).

[22] SC Res. 1325 (Oct. 30, 2000).

[23] Chinkin and Rees, *supra* note 7, at 12–14.

[24] Dianne Otto, "Exile of Inclusion: Reflections on Gender Issues in International Law over the Last Decade of the Twentieth Century," *Melbourne Journal of International Law* 10 (2009): 11.

continue to do so) via the language of the WPS agenda with conviction that the origins of the resolutions in the Security Council gave them binding legal force. In 2020, this continued to a degree, with an influential scholarly text announcing "1325 bound the international community . . . [a]s such, it was a ground-breaking commitment by the SC."[25] The language of being bound and a commitment from the Council gives the impression of a binding legal obligation, despite the soft law nature of 1325 as a thematic resolution. Otto notes that her anxiety about the failure of feminist actors to appreciate the distinction between Chapter VI and Chapter VII resolutions might be "unduly legalistic" given the work of feminist actors, in civil society and in nongovernmental organizations, to use the resolutions in transformative and innovative ways to build legal change.[26] This transnational feminist "misreading" of the WPS resolutions is reminiscent of other sites of feminist praxis that use the ambiguous space of legal language and soft law to inform practice and legal change.[27]

Catherine O'Rourke argues that feminist engagements with international law need to be understood as driven by normative and political motivations beyond the "pursuit of legal obligations and state compliance."[28] O'Rourke questions the motivations for academic critique of the UN system that ignores "what these international law norms for gender equality mean to the feminist activists who engage them," advocating for increased attention to the "insights from local feminist advocacy, transnational feminist organizations and feminists within the institutions of international law."[29] While the overlap between feminist activist, academic, and international lawyer is a difficult one to untangle, the continued choice to engage with international law and to pursue the development of normative agendas, such as is seen in the production of preambles, has potentially far-reaching consequences for all feminist actors. In addition, understandings from feminist scholars and actors that the legal quality of the resolutions is less important than the change undertaken in their name suggests a two-tier life for the resolutions: their work in legitimating the Security Council's activities and their function within transnational feminist spaces. These distinct interpretative communities "meet" in the world of WPS.[30]

A. Finding Legal Meaning in Security Council Preambles

The agitation (protest) from civil society that pursued legal change, although outside of the legal institutional structures, constructs a form of legal argument that helps explain the limitations of gender law reforms through the WPS framework. Drawing again on Robert Cover, feminist praxis—from academic to activist spaces—constructs

[25] Soumita Basu, Paul Kirby, and Laura Shepherd, "WPS: a Critical Cartography," in *New Directions in Women, Peace and Security*, edited by Soumita Basu, Paul Kirby, and Laura Shepherd (Bristol: Polity Press, 2020), 1.

[26] Otto, *supra* note 24, at 12.

[27] Gina Heathcote, *Feminist Dialogues on International Law: Successes, Tensions, Futures* (Oxford: Oxford University Press, 2019), 156–157.

[28] Catherine O'Rourke, "Feminist Strategy in International Law: Understanding Its Legal, Normative and Political Dimensions," *European Journal of International Law* 28 (2018): 1019, 1021.

[29] *Id.* 1021.

[30] On interpretive communities, see Ian Johnstone and Steven Ratner, chapter 1, in this volume.

a normative universe. The preamble to Security Council resolutions then draws in some elements of that universe to the exclusion of other elements. In particular, the embedding of women's rights within larger social justice/peace projects, feminist antimilitarism, and commitments to disarmament—while prominent in transnational feminist work—are absent in the normative universe framed through the preamble. Following Cover, the dissent and the difference in these normative worlds, or differing narratives on gendered insecurity, remain an important space of legal meaning and interpretation.[31]

In quite a different vein, Chinkin and Rees argue in their commentary on Resolution 2467 that the consolidation of legal language across multiple WPS resolutions, as well as local level or domestic legal implementation, ultimately creates new international law, as custom.[32] Chinkin and Rees describe the preamble of Security Council resolutions in the following way: "it essentially states its purpose, aims, and justification and locates it within existing legal and political structures."[33] Chinkin and Rees note that the preamble of Resolution 2467 "opens the door for interpretation of the Operative Paragraphs in ways that civil society can make good use of them to further State and institutional implementation."[34] Chinkin and Rees further argue that the reference to existing (treaty-based) legal obligations within the text of resolutions helps embed the legal effect of Council outputs.[35] With regard to specific legal obligations that Chinkin and Rees draw out of Resolution 2467—CEDAW (including the Optional Protocol) and the Geneva Conventions—these references are found in the preamble.

Although writing is sparse on the legal status of the preambles to Security Council resolutions, Chinkin and Rees's approach considers the potential legal force of preambles. Perhaps the iteration of ten resolutions on WPS gives them a greater propensity to signal binding legal commitments. Wood's account of Security Council practice, in contrast, argues that the political reality of the Council's membership leads "to the ambiguities inherent in political compromise and consensus, not to clarity."[36] A history of unanimous endorsement from states on WPS texts seems to negate this argument, at least in relation to the perceptions of states as to which issues ought to be addressed via the WPS resolutions. The consensus on WPS ended, however, during the drafting of Resolution 2467, when objections from China, Russia, and the United States led to an adapted draft being concluded and, ultimately, abstentions from China and Russia in the final vote. US objections rested on the broad approach to the provision of reproductive and sexual health services that potentially included abortion services, while China and Russia expressed concern at the increasing expansion of the WPS agenda, including the creation of the Informal Expert Group on Women, Peace and Security (IEG) related to sexual violence in conflict.[37] These different normative

[31] Robert Cover, "Violence and the Word," *Yale Law Journal* 95 (1986): 1601, 1616–1618.
[32] Chinkin and Rees, *supra* note 7, at 7.
[33] *Id.* 12.
[34] *Id.* 14.
[35] *Id.* 7.
[36] Wood, *supra* note 5, at 12.
[37] See further: "In Hindsight: Negotiations on Resolution 2467 on Sexual Violence in Conflict," *What's in Blue*, May 2, 2019, https://www.whatsinblue.org/2019/05/in-hindsight-negotiations-on-resolution-2467-on-sexual-violence-in-conflict.php.

communities, obviously, also have their own internal tensions and disagreements. Likewise, transnational feminist spaces are not uniform in their approaches to what constitutes gender law reform. Accounts of the meaning and effect of the preamble and of WPS thus emerge as varied and present an additional range of legal argument with no settled or agreed positions.

B. Situation-Specific Resolutions, WPS, and the Preamble

The ambiguity surrounding the legal status and function of Security Council preambular paragraphs is further complicated by analysis of situation-specific resolutions where the normative framings found in thematic resolutions are adapted and refined. For example, the Security Council resolutions on the situation in Libya attracted analysis of the text of the preamble as having an impact on the potential crystallization of the Responsibility to Protect doctrine into customary international law.[38] Importantly, although often characterized as an instance of the Council "authorising" military force via the responsibility to protect doctrine, scholars are quick to highlight that the phrase "responsibility to protect" is not used in the operative paragraphs of Resolution 1973 authorizing military force but rather in the preamble.[39] In fact, legal arguments about the existence of the responsibility to protect under international law are more likely to refer to the General Assembly's Summit Outcome Document, in which states make clear that the powers of the Security Council to authorize military force include the capacity to respond to a range of security threats such as occurred in Libya in 2011.[40] Similarly, Resolution 1368, adopted after the terrorist attacks in the United States in 2001, flags Article 51 of the UN Charter in the preamble but is generally not regarded as offering more than recognition of the existing right of states to act in self-defense, as opposed to legal authority on this point.[41]

Legal argumentation, as traditionally understood, is the process of establishing that a law or legal obligation exists, the way that obligation should be interpreted, and the legal authority the obligation stems from. In the condemnation of terrorist attacks (1368) and the authorization of military force against Libya (1973), the changing security environment is reflected in the invocation, through the preamble, of new legal developments rather than consolidation of new legal obligations via preambular material. In 2001, this happens in a short, legally focused preamble that parallels the post-9/11 use of force against terrorist actors. In 2011, the responsibility to protect is invoked in a lengthy preamble that signals a larger agenda around responding to the ongoing violence in Libya. Both preambles constitute a legal argument for what comes next—the operative paragraphs—placing the resolution in a normative universe that propels toward a specific interpretation and the construction of *nomos*. I am interested in both the traditional legal approach to Security Council resolutions, which

[38] SC Res. 1970 (Feb. 26, 2011); SC Res. 1973 (Mar. 17, 2011).

[39] Marie-Eve Loiselle, "The Normative Status of the Responsibility to Protect after Libya," *Global Responsibility to Protect* 5 (2013): 317.

[40] 2005 World Summit Outcome Document, GA. Res. 60/1 (Sept. 16, 2005).

[41] SC Res. 1368 (Sept. 12, 2001).

does not ascribe significant legal value to the preamble, and the expansion of the content of preambles suggesting a wider purpose for the preamble than was previously understood.

Resolutions 1368 and 1970 do not invoke the WPS framework, although in both cases gendered experiences of violence are significant in the conflicts, highlighting, then, a further aspect of the preamble as a space of forgetting, or overlooking, as much as it is a space invoking a normative universe. While the resolutions on WPS might be replete with commitments to their application in situation-specific resolutions, these are filtered out of preambles of many such resolutions, including the two mentioned above on Afghanistan and Libya. In sum, the arguments for the WPS as embedding legal obligations, crystallizing as customary international law via the preamble, demonstrates the collision of different normative agendas rather than a satisfying legal argument for the transformation of peace and security laws through WPS frames.

IV. The Security Council as Site of Gender Law Reform

Otto analyzes the "footholds for feminist change" that emerge from engagement within international institutions, in particular, the Security Council, to conclude that "un-crisis," or feminist, thinking

> requires supporting the activism of women outside the mainstream institutions of law and politics as well as carving out spaces on the inside. The institutionalisation of feminist ideas will always extract a price of compromise and dilution, even more so in a crisis; but the damage to long term feminist goals can be mitigated by outside movements of women, in coalition with others, demanding that emergencies be re-mapped through a feminist lens.[42]

The emergence of feminist gains inside institutional spaces has attracted feminist questions about the legitimacy and value of the Security Council as a place for gender law reform.[43] Chinkin and Rees's argument that the preamble to Security Council resolutions might also signal potential law, *lex ferenda*, through the capacity to crystallize into custom must be understood then as having implications for Security Council resolutions generally, which in turn may have the effect of narrowing the scope of gender law reform. Both international lawyers and feminist actors might consider the structural constraints of any institutional practice before any ad hoc agenda for consolidated legal obligations is pursued.

Beyond the question of whether a preamble could provide evidence of a crystallizing norm, there is need for feminist interrogation of what it means to pursue and

[42] Dianne Otto, "Remapping Crisis through a Feminist Lens," *University of Melbourne Law School Research Series* (2011): 5.

[43] Also see: Dianne Otto, "Power and Danger: Feminist Engagement with International Law through the UN SC," *Australian Feminist Law Journal* 32 (2010): 97; Dianne Otto, "Beyond Stories of Victory and Danger: Resisting Feminism's Amenability to Serving Security Council Politics," in *Rethinking Peacekeeping, Gender Equality and Collective Security*, edited by Gina Heathcote and Dianne Otto (London: Palgrave MacMillan, 2012).

assert the legal potential of Security Council preambles. That is, if the preamble of WPS resolutions can, over time, acquire legal significance, then feminist international lawyers need to reflect on how this form of legal argument lends itself to application to other areas of the Security Council's work. For example, the resolutions on countering terrorism and violent extremism also deploy preambles of increasing length, with reference to an array of established legal obligations *and* normative assertions. While WPS resolutions are thematic, most resolutions on the threat of terrorism are situation-specific. Since 2015, the WPS resolutions have cross-referenced the counterterrorism resolutions, drawing aspects of the two agendas into alignment.[44] Both the WPS and the counterterrorism work in the Security Council draw from particular worldviews, or normative visions, of international peace and security and raise questions about what gets left out and which states influence the text. The crossing over between the two agendas through the cross-referencing of resolutions in the preambles demonstrates how the non-legally binding preamble does more legal "work" than an assertion of a wider normative framework. The coordinated approach to WPS and counterterrorism also constructs the legal frame that future arguments might be articulated through, where future WPS resolutions move further from their origins within transnational feminist praxis and closer to counterterrorism approach and/or the agendas of specific global powers.

Ultimately, the development of extensive preambles to Security Council resolutions remains a curious thing, as it is not clear what legal consequences flow. In some ways, contemporary preambles are an attempt to draw attention to Council action as a force for "good," justifiable and based on larger principles and legal obligations within international law: a form of legal argumentation. Not only is this not required, the shifting between the legal and the normative within preambles is unsettling, precisely because of the potential of the preamble to become evidence of *opinio juris* or state practice through repetition. In thematic, Chapter VI resolutions, such as WPS where the open debate formula collates the views of many states, this adds transnational feminist tensions to existing political tensions within the Security Council. The preamble becomes an iteration of a very specific feminist politics that traces women as victims (of conflict-related sexual violence) and as potential participants (of decision-making structures) while ignoring the widescale structural changes needed to mobilize solutions, including a commitment to antimilitarism and disarmament. At one level, this is no different from the pursuit of consensus in international law generally and in the Security Council specifically; however, the diversity of feminist positions outside of the Council becomes co-opted as the reasons behind the WPS agenda, as well as the actual demands of those actors, are left outside of the institution.

Furthermore, for feminist or any other civil society actors to assume that the turning of the Security Council toward their interests is guaranteed to continue is belied by the drafting of Resolution 2467. Unlike earlier resolutions on WPS, Germany was the penholder.[45] As noted above, the United States expressed objections to the draft and

[44] Gina Heathcote, "SC Resolution 2242 on WPS: Progressive Gains or Dangerous Development?," Special Issue on Gender and Security *Global Society* 34 (2018): 374.

[45] "The Penholder," *Security Council Report*: Research Report #3, Dec. 21, 2018, https://www.securitycouncilreport.org/atf/cf/%7B65BFCF9B-6D27-4E9C-8CD3-CF6E4FF96FF9%7D/Penholders.pdf.

threatened to veto it if it was put to a vote. Previously both the United Kingdom and the United States had taken the lead on resolutions and debates on conflict-related sexual violence (the focus of Resolution 2467), and resolutions consistently received the full support of Council members. Resolution 2467 marked the end of unanimous support from member states for WPS resolutions. The position taken by the United States is an important reminder of the political restraints on the legal outputs of the Council. A feminist agenda that seeks to affirm the legal potential of a non-binding text must tread carefully in a global environment of increasingly repressive and nationalist states with very narrow perceptions of women's rights and of gender.

There is a need to hold the "outside" and "inside" of institutional spaces as interconnected rather than distinct. A failure to do so limits the capacity to voice a challenge to contemporary legal and political institutions as always outside of those structures and the incremental "footholds" for change as within institutions. In addition, any critique of the Security Council must address at least two different levels of its work. First, the persistent structural bias within the institutions of international law and, second, the larger outputs the institution produces. The study of Security Council preambles illustrates not only the dangers of unqualified acceptance of the structures and methods of international institutions but also the potential flow of feminist arguments into other areas of the Council's work that might be actively anti-feminist, such as the counterterrorism resolutions. Structural bias feminisms require an "excavation" to look under the surface of laws and legal structures to expose the deep-set gender norms that inform and construct the work of international institutions and international law. Thinking about the legal value of Security Council preambles requires a composite analysis of the structural restraints on any legal outputs from the Council—not only interrogation of what work its outputs on WPS "do" in terms of producing gender law reform but also how this work underpins the larger work and methods of the Council. The pursuit, then, of enhanced legal value for WPS resolutions, including the preambles to these resolutions, requires attention to the unlikelihood of the Council articulating gender beyond narrow versions of feminism *and* the potential impact such developments hold for the Security Council itself.

At the same time, feminist analysis of Security Council outputs over twenty years has focused on resolutions concerning women, peace, and security, to the exclusion of resolutions on specific situations. Analysis of situation-specific resolutions suggests WPS resolutions do more "work" than simply produce a set of normative statements on women and gender. The 2018 and 2019 resolutions on Sudan and South Sudan present a good example. Here I add to the discussion of the Libyan and Afghanistan resolutions, mentioned above, through a focus on the preambles of recent situation-specific resolutions.

Resolution 2445, November 15, 2018, on Sudan and South Sudan has a preamble that extends over two pages with dense background information on the conflict and includes mentions of Resolutions 1325 and 2242:

> *Further recalling* resolutions 1325 (2000) and subsequent resolutions on women, peace, and security and emphasizing that persistent barriers to full implementation of these resolutions will only be dismantled through dedicated commitment to women's empowerment, participation, and human rights, and through concerted

> leadership, consistent information and action, and support, to build women's engagement in all levels of decision-making, also recalling resolution 2242 and its aspiration to increase the number of women in military and police contingents of United Nations peacekeeping operations.[46]

This paragraph is fascinating for the normative content it picks up and develops beyond the direct reference to Resolution 1325 and the subsequent WPS resolutions. For example, terms such as "persistent barriers," "dedicated commitment," and "consistent information and action," as well as the language of "aspiration," are a form of argument that is normative, in the sense of not relying on direct legal content for their articulation, and, instead, drawing in perceptions and values. As such, it can be seen how the normative content of the thematic resolutions is carried, and adapted, in situation-specific resolutions via the preamble. At the same time, the eight additional WPS resolutions, also with nuances of language and changing content, are not mentioned. Consequently, the study of preambles and WPS must include the preambles of situation-specific resolutions to understand which aspects "travel," and are expanded, from the thematic resolutions. The preamble of Resolution 2445 shows an emphasis on women's participation in decision-making and peacekeeping operations, an agenda reiterated in operative paragraph 18 of the resolution.[47] Other situation-specific resolutions draw attention, via the preamble, to the provisions for responding to conflict-related sexual violence. Given that the various WPS resolutions address both conflict-related sexual violence and women's participation, it is curious that some resolutions draw attention to one but not the other. In Resolution 2445, the focus is narrowed to an agenda on women's participation, although reports of sexual violence from the region have been documented.[48] A study of gender law reform and the development of legal content in preambles thus requires analysis of when and where the Council further expands WPS content across its large oeuvre of work and what selectivity occurs in these expansions. This research might also parallel understandings of colonial histories of engagement in colonial territories under the guise of civilizing through gender law reform, as women's bodies have a long history of providing the justification for foreign interventions whether military or otherwise.[49]

The study of additional institutional outputs for feminist actors, however, cannot be as selective as only drawing attention to the placement of WPS text in situation-specific resolutions. The absence of this content also matters. Resolution 2479, June 27, 2019, on Sudan and South Sudan, has an extremely brief preamble and no reference to the WPS framework.[50] Resolution 2479 identifies the situation in Sudan and South Sudan as a threat to international peace and security and establishes the resolution as a Chapter VII resolution. The operative

[46] SC Res. 2445 (Nov. 15, 2018).

[47] *Id.*

[48] Report from Nobel Women's Initiative, "Survivor's Speak Out: Sexual Violence in Sudan," Nobel Women's Initiative (2013), https://nobelwomensinitiative.org/wp-content/uploads/2013/12/Survivors-Speak-Out-Sudan-web.pdf?ref=218.

[49] Anne McClintock, *Imperial Leather: Race, Gender and Sexuality in the Colonial Context* (London: Routledge, 1995).

[50] SC Res. 2479 (June 27, 2019).

paragraphs, also brief, contain the decision to extend the mandate of the international force in Sudan and South Sudan. In contrast, Resolution 2445 references Chapter VII within operative paragraph one only, extending the mandate for the force; the remainder of the resolution is therefore clearly under Chapter VI. As I have discussed elsewhere, it is standard practice of the Security Council to leave off any incorporation of the WPS framework when authorizing military force.[51] The distinction between the authorization of military force and the construction of post-conflict peace is gendered, where work on WPS is expected to wait until the crisis moment has passed. Ultimately, an account of the legal and normative content of WPS resolutions cannot progress without an analysis of both where WPS content travels into other resolutions and where it does not. The continued distinction between the preambular content of Chapter VI and Chapter VII resolutions might, in particular, mark a significant emerging practice of separating the normative (i.e., Chapter VI) from the legally binding (i.e., Chapter VII) content of resolutions.

Feminist "footholds" within the Security Council do not happen in isolation from the larger work of the Council. Resolutions on Sudan and South Sudan present women's participation as an external value "brought" to the region by the international community in utter ignorance of the persistence and forms of regional structures and organizations that are inclusive of spaces for gender-balanced women's leadership. The preamble of Resolution 2445 does work in reinforcing gender and women's rights as part of the civilizing force of international law rather than as transnational, varied, and active in challenging multiple spaces of oppression and power, actively forgetting Alaa Saleh's presence at the Council only a few weeks prior. Cover's understanding of the relationship between normative and legal orders assists here, as the space of legal interpretation and what Cover describes as the "problem of meaning in law" functions such that, "legal hermeneutics or interpretation . . . is commonly associated with one rather narrow kind of problem that confronts officials and those who seek to predict, control, or profit from official behavior."[52] The WPS resolutions, in their operative paragraphs and in the preamble, as well as the feminist agendas that are never included in the legal text, form a *nomos* that questions the possibility of feminist law reform while also signaling important features of the relationship between the normative and the legal and, therefore, how legal argumentation is framed. In particular, feminist protests reflect a commitment to a quite different *nomos*, one that centers disarmament, one that attends to antimilitarism, and one that configures feminist change through appeals to peace and justice that do not collapse back into a preoccupation with women's lives in isolation from the communities in which gendered harms materialize.

[51] Gina Heathcote, "Humanitarian Intervention and Gender Dynamics," in *Oxford Handbook on Gender and Conflict*, edited by Naomi Cahn, Dina Haynes, Fionnuala Ni Aolain, and Naha Valji (Oxford: Oxford University Press, 2018).

[52] Cover, *supra* note 3, at 6.

V. Protest as Legal Argumentation

The traveling of feminist knowledge from protest to the Security Council to resolutions on WPS provides an opportunity to understand what knowledge (narrative) travels from transnational feminist spaces to international law and what gets filtered out. The language of Resolution 2467 on WPS, adopted after Alaa Saleh addressed the Council, repackages the voices of those who addressed the Council and offers no prescriptions for actual change. This understanding is further filtered when the Council returned its focus to Sudan, two weeks later, addressing the situation in Abyei in Resolution 2497. This resolution was debated and drafted without the Sudan representatives who had previously been invited into the WPS debate and with only the standard reference to 1325 in the preamble and the inclusion of gender and sexual violence in the list of human rights abuses.

Transnational feminist approaches to peace and security are filtered via WPS resolution preambles, narrowed into the format of the main text of the resolutions, and then diluted further in situation-specific resolutions. This practice demonstrates how the legal text dictates the future narratives of the *nomos*, leaving some framings as outside of the normative universe of the Council even at the moment where there is a performance of bringing diverse voices into law, such as the invitation to Sudanese activists to speak to the Council. The study of legal argumentation, thus, must look outside of the prescriptions held within the legal text to understand the plural normative worlds that emerge at the institution voicing strategies for inclusion. Saleh's voice, her protest, her song, were invited in and yet the words that the Security Council issued on WPS ignored the structural change Sudanese protests demanded and, in resolutions on Sudan, ignored the intertwined relationship between women, peace, and security.

This study of preambles leads me to an account of feminist protest, such as Saleh's image in 2018, as an alternative preamble to WPS resolutions, that hold legal arguments derived from the history of feminist transnational organizing and that speak to power from outside of traditional legal forms. This study challenges the understanding that legal interpretation derives from a very specific, shared normative space, as it becomes clear that the political frames that inform Security Council resolutions are not the same as the origins of the texts within feminist histories of engaging through protest. While the Security Council calls for the increased participation of women in negotiations, peace agreements, and post-conflict processes, what is silenced is the voices of women who act and speak throughout peacetimes and conflict to challenge the insecurity they experience in the everyday. Chinkin writes:

> Again we are asking the wrong question. We should not ask how the participation of more women in peace-making processes and peacekeeping missions can be achieved but rather participation in what? In the structures of patriarchy? And how can those structures be transformed to deliver a sustainable, feminist peace?[53]

[53] Christine Chinkin, "Are We Asking the Right Questions? Reframing Peace and Security," *LSE WPS Blog*, Mar. 4, 2019, https://blogs.lse.ac.uk/wps/2019/03/04/1805/.

I have argued that the preamble functions as a filtering out of the diversity of feminist organizing (protest) and the unrepentant demands for different approaches to international peace and security.

The WPS resolutions are simultaneously evidence of Cover's claim that "law and narrative are inseparably related. Every prescription is insistent in its demand to be located in discourse—to be supplied with history and destiny, beginning and end, explanation and purpose,"[54] and evidence of the failures of international lawyers, feminist and otherwise, to understand the political domain as more than the dynamics of the Council itself. While Wood deems the preamble to be less reliable as a tool of interpretation, I have shown the interplay between the legal and the normative and the work that preamble does in shaping the normative, including in terms of what is excluded.[55] In particular, the forms of feminist agitation—protest—that portend the creation of gender law reform remain poorly understood and significantly undermined when viewed from the text of the resolutions themselves. The Council's shift toward the framing of a normative agenda via the expansive use of preambles is significant in this filtering.

Feminist protest is a space of engagement with law that often speaks and enacts the unspeakable. Sylvia Tamale writes in her analysis of (naked) protest, "[t]he law is an important instrument in shaping and scripting our gendered bodies. Society 'reads' women's bodies along the landmarks forged by the law."[56] While Tamale's argument specifically engages the embodied meanings of naked protest in Uganda, her argument about the meaning and force of women's bodies as a challenge to the oppressive laws of the state have resonance across contexts (and protests). The striking image of Saleh, in Khartoum in 2018, returns: preceded by feminist protest that centered on female clothing choices, the centering of women's bodies and self-representation were part of the resistance and response to the repressive state. Similarly, the protests of Indian women in Manipur, naked in public to protest the killing and rape of a young woman while holding the banner "Indian Army Rape Us," shows an engagement between state, law, and women as a means of speaking that which law continues to fail to speak.[57] In fact, the spectrum of issues contained in the Security Council resolutions on WPS have histories in transnational feminist and women's protests, from the Campaign against Nuclear Disarmament to Greenham Common to Liberian feminist demands for inclusion in peace processes through the sitting-in spaces otherwise occupied by those formally gathered at the peace talks. Women's participation, the prevention of gender-based violence, protection from gender-based violence, and the shaping of post-conflict recovery processes, the four pillars of WPS, all start in the mobilization of women's and feminist networks, local, regional, transnational, that voice dissent with the status quo.[58]

[54] Cover, *supra* note 3, at 5.

[55] Wood, *supra* note 5, at 34.

[56] Sylvia Tamale, "Nudity, Protest and the Law in Uganda," *Feminist Africa* 22 (2017): 52, 79.

[57] Sumi Madhok, "Coloniality, Political Subjectivation and Gendered Politics of Protest in a 'State of Exception,'" *Feminist Review* 119 (2018): 56.

[58] Felicity Ruby, "SC Resolution 1325: A Tool for Conflict Prevention?," in *Rethinking Peacekeeping, Gender Equality and Collective Security*, *supra* note 44, at 173.

Articulating feminist protest as preamble creates an opportunity for transnational feminist approaches to law to develop two important methods. The first is a reimagining of the persistence of calls for both inside and outside strategies within feminist legal writing, to see that which happens "outside" of institutions, whether scholarly critique or protest, as inflecting and influencing the insider, institutional spaces of gender law reform—and vice versa. Second, in response to the larger impact of the changing practice of the Council and the nonfeminist developments that might emerge from the expansion of normative content in the Council's output, the protest as preamble is a reminder that the normative and ethical commitments that inform WPS are on the streets, in bodies and the everyday. They are legal arguments that challenge the status quo. Feminist protest continues to articulate a challenge to the global system, which has been unable to look beyond military intervention as a solution and, in the example of the Security Council, misusing feminist messages as a normative weapon.

6

Persuasion About/Without International Law

The Case of Cybersecurity Norms

Steven Ratner

Few global cooperation problems seem to match cybersecurity when it comes to the need for some kind of multilateral regulation. The combination of highly effective viruses and malware; sophisticated state and non-state perpetrators of malicious acts; the actual and potential harm to individuals, companies, and state infrastructure; the difficulties of identifying the source of those acts; and the limitations of uncoordinated regulation by individual states put cybersecurity, along with climate change, at the top of any list of global cooperation problems. Yet compared to the other subjects in this volume—whether the use of force, human rights, or even international environmental law—cyber-international law, and thus argumentation based on it, is characterized by at best a thin consensus, if not outright dissensus. Disagreements operate at four levels—the existence of rules; the content of those rules; the desirability of new rules (in particular as opposed to non-binding norms); and the content of any desired rules (as well as norms). This legal landscape results in a unique pattern of argumentation and persuasion by states and non-state actors both *ex ante*—in advocating for a regulatory scheme for cyber-activity—and *ex post*, in reacting to and perhaps responding to a malicious act by another state or non-state actor.

My goal in this chapter is to conceptualize the process of legal argumentation in this unusual setting—to understand how and why states and non-state actors, in a thin normative environment, deploy international law, or its absence, to persuade other states and accomplish other goals. It thus seeks to focus on the purpose and the modalities of such a use of legal rules. At the same time, it also hopes to uncover some possible effects of these choices on the regulation of cybersecurity. By taking out one of the key assumptions of existing studies on legal and normative argumentation, namely, an agreed set of rules, this theoretical move can reveal more of the motivations and effects of international legal argumentation in shaping debates and behavior outside of the judicial setting.

My argument will proceed in three parts. Section I describes the extant legal landscape on cybersecurity. It shows where states seem to have achieved some consensus on rules or norms as well as where they differ. It also points out the regulation of these issues by non-state actors. Section II offers an analysis of the process of argumentation used by states. It adopts a view of multilevel persuasion, as states argue about the existence of rules, their meaning, the need for new law or norms, and the content of desired rules or norms. It offers an explanation for states' choice to invoke law, how they do so,

Steven Ratner, *Persuasion About/Without International Law* In: *Talking International Law*. Edited by: Ian Johnstone and Steven Ratner, Oxford University Press. © Steven Ratner 2021. DOI: 10.1093/oso/9780197588437.003.0006

and the results thereof in the normative universe of cybersecurity. Section III applies this framework to non-state actors making claims about current or future international law. In the case of cybersecurity, these key actors are corporations, academics, and think tanks (some with close relationships with states or international organizations). Section IV draws out some of the larger implications of the cybersecurity example for understanding the role of legal rules in international discourse.

For purposes of this chapter, I will adopt the definition of cybersecurity offered by Martha Finnemore and Duncan Hollis, namely, "the protection of information and communication technologies from unauthorized access or attempted access."[1] Thus cybersecurity is not limited to so-called cyberwarfare, but encompasses a range of threats by, and responses to, malicious software. Second, I will not consider the broader issue of cyber-governance, that is, which body should regulate the internet. Third, I will use the term "legal argumentation" to refer to any claim that concerns or references international law, that is, toward the broad end of the spectrum of conceptions of legal argumentation identified in chapter 1. I will also distinguish between rules, by which I mean legally binding duties (or rights or entitlements); principles, namely, legal concepts that typically entail a number of legal rules (e.g., sovereign equality or a state's jurisdiction over its territory); and norms, formally non-binding guides to conduct. Lastly, most of my analysis focuses on the use of legal argumentation to persuade, but I acknowledge and discuss other purposes and effects.

I. Surveying the Legal Landscape

A. Key Landmarks

I would identify four key markers regarding international law's treatment of cybersecurity.

1. A Handful of Treaties

First, states have prepared a small number *of treaties that directly address cybersecurity issues*. The most significant is the 2001 Budapest Convention on Cybercrime, prepared by the Council of Europe but with membership extending beyond it.[2] The convention obligates states to criminalize certain cybercrimes and provides for law enforcement cooperation; it is supported by several monitoring and technical support committees under Council auspices. The Shanghai Cooperation Organization and the African Union have adopted their own conventions—though the former is limited to defining certain threats and

[1] Martha Finnemore and Duncan Hollis, "Constructing Norms for Global Cybersecurity," *American Journal of International* Law 110 (2016): 425, 431.

[2] Details of Treaty No. 185, Council of Europe, Nov. 23, 2001, https://www.coe.int/en/web/conventions/full-list/-/conventions/treaty/185. The treaty has forty-one COE parties and eighteen non-COE parties (including the United States, Australia, and Japan). See generally Jonathan Clough, "A World of Difference: The Budapest Convention on Cybercrime and the Challenges of Harmonization," *Monash University Law Review* 40 (2014): 698.

calling for cooperation and covers only its six member states, and the latter covers only e-commerce and privacy protection and has only five parties (and is not in force).[3] The only global treaties even indirectly referring to cybersecurity are the Constitution of the International Telecommunication Union and the associated Radio Regulations, which prohibit "harmful interference" by radio stations (although both were drafted long before the era of the internet).[4]

2. Existing Legal Rules Apply, Up to a Point

Second, the deliberations of states to date point to a consensus by states that *(some) existing rules of international law apply to cyber-activity*, or, more precisely, that the use of the internet by state or non-state actors does not per se insulate those actors from extant rules and the consequences for their violation. The best evidence of this consensus are the two final reports of the Group of Governmental Experts on Developments in the Field of Information and Telecommunications in the Context of International Security (GGE), convened pursuant to General Assembly Resolution 68/243. The GGE, with governmental experts from fifteen (later twenty) states—including most key players in the cybersecurity debates—agreed on this premise early in its work, with its 2013 report stating, "International law, and in particular the Charter of the United Nations, is applicable and is essential to maintaining peace and stability and promoting an open, secure, peaceful and accessible ICT [information and communications technology] environment."[5]

In 2015, the GGE managed to elaborate on this starting point a bit, mentioning certain rules or principles of customary international law (without using that term to describe them): for example, states have jurisdiction over infrastructure on their territory; sovereignty, sovereign equality, non-intervention, as well as human rights obligations, apply; states "must not use proxies" to violate international law; and states "must meet their international obligations" regarding acts attributable to them." At the same time, the consensus was weaker on some aspects. Rather than mentioning the Charter's right of self-defense, the GGE simply stated that the Charter applies "in its entirety," and noted "the inherent right of states to take measures consistent with international law"; and rather than reiterating a state's duties under international humanitarian law (IHL) treaties and custom, the GGE simply "noted … the principles of humanity, necessity, proportionality, and distinction."[6] Rather than endorsing a duty on states to engage in due diligence to prevent harmful acts by non-state actors,

[3] Agreement between the Governments of Member States of the Shanghai Cooperation Organization on Cooperation in the Field of International Information Security, June 16, 2009, https://ccdcoe-admin.aku.co/wp-content/uploads/2018/11/SCO-090616-IISAgreement.pdf; African Union Convention on Cyber Security and Personal Data Protection, June 27, 2014, https://au.int/sites/default/files/treaties/29560-treaty-0048_-_african_union_convention_on_cyber_security_and_personal_data_protection_e.pdf (not yet in force).

[4] Constitution of the International Telecommunication Union, 2019, art. 45(1).

[5] Report of the Group of Governmental Experts on Developments in the Field of Information and Telecommunications in the Context of International Security, June 24, 2013, para. 19, UN Doc. A/68/98; see also Report of the Group of Governmental Experts on Developments in the Field of Information and Telecommunications in the Context of International Security, July 22, 2015, para. 24, UN Doc. A/70/174 [hereinafter 2015 GGE Report].

[6] 2015 GGE Report, *supra* note 5, at para. 28.

sometimes claimed to be a norm of customary international law,[7] the document says that states "should seek to ensure that their territory is not used by non-State actors to commit such acts."

Beyond the GGE, UN political organs have by consensus reaffirmed the importance of respect for human rights in cyberspace, including a resolution of the Human Rights Council and a privacy-specific resolution of the General Assembly.[8] In the fall of 2018, France, backed by a group of corporations and institutions, issued the "Paris Call for Trust and Security in Cyberspace." One key provision goes beyond the GGE by stating: "international law, including the United Nations Charter in its entirety, *international humanitarian law and customary international law* is applicable to the use of information and communication technologies."[9] Although non-binding, the Paris Call has been endorsed by sixty-seven states, though not the United States, Russia, or China.[10]

Implicit in the GGE's mention of some rules or principles of customary international law—sovereign equality, non-intervention, territorial-based jurisdiction, nonuse of proxies, and due diligence—is its silence on whether other rules of customary law also apply to cybersecurity policy or whether new rules of custom have emerged. For instance, the United States, the United Kingdom, and France have claimed in official statements that international law rules on countermeasures allow a state to breach international law in response to an illegal act committed through cyber-means.[11] They have also asserted that rules on attribution of conduct apply in the cyber context.[12] However, states are not usually so forthright with their views on specific applications of international law to cybersecurity. States may be deploying illegal (or legal) measures in response to prior illegal (or legal) acts, but they have generally (including those three states mentioned above) refrained from offering a legal rationale for their reaction or nonreaction, making *opinio juris* difficult to discern, a

[7] See Tina Stephens and Duncan French, ILA Study Group on Due Diligence in International Law, Second Report, International Law Association, July 2016, at 5, https://www.ila-hq.org/index.php/study-groups?study-groupsID=63; Robin Geiss and Henning Lahmann, "Freedom and Security in Cyberspace: Shifting the Focus away from Military Responses towards Non-Forcible Countermeasures and Collective Threat-Prevention," in *Peacetime Regime for State Activities in Cyberspace: International Law, International Relations, and Diplomacy*, edited by Katharina Ziolkowski (Tallinn: NATO CCDCOE, 2013), 621, 635–636.

[8] See, e.g., HRC Res. 38/7 (July 5, 2018); GA Res. 73/179 (Jan. 21, 2019).

[9] "Paris Call for Trust and Security in Cyberspace," Nov. 12, 2018, https://pariscall.international/en/call (text in italics is not found in the GGE reports).

[10] https://pariscall.international/en/supporters.

[11] See, e.g., Jeremy Wright, "Cyber and International Law in the 21st Century," Government of the United Kingdom, May 23, 2019, https://www.gov.uk/government/speeches/cyber-and-international-law-in-the-21st-century; Revue stratégique de cyberdéfense, Secrétariat Général de la Défense et de la Sécurité Nationale, Feb. 12, 2018, at 82–83, http://www.sgdsn.gouv.fr/uploads/2018/02/20180206-np-revue-cyber-public-v3.3-publication.pdf; see generally Brian Egan, "International Law and Stability in Cyberspace," *Berkeley Journal of International Law* 35 (2017): 169, 177–178; Ann Väljataga, *Tracing opinio juris in National Cyber Security Strategy Documents* (Tallinn: NATO CCDCOE, 2018).

[12] See, e.g., Egan, *id.*, at 176–177; Wright, *id.* Attribution rules are so-called secondary rules in that they do not involve duties per se, but rather identify the bases and consequences of violations.

point to which I will return later. That silence is also a challenge to the identification of subsequent practice under the UN Charter or the Geneva Conventions.[13]

The failure of states to agree on a detailed elaboration of the rules of international law in the cybersecurity context became painfully obvious at the GGE's 2017 meeting. Western states pushed for a more specific list than that offered up in 2015, but faced resistance from China, Russia, Cuba, and other states. Among the areas of disagreement were whether to include in the final report the applicability in the cyber context of the right of self-defense and specific rules of IHL.[14] The GGE issued no report that year, and the process fractured in 2018 and 2019 when the General Assembly passed two resolutions—one (proposed by Russia), endorsing thirteen "international rules, norms and principles of responsible behavior of States" and creating a large "open-ended working group" (OEWG) to further study the question (with the authority to "introduce changes" to the rules, norms, and principles);[15] and another (proposed by the United States) omitting any list of agreed rules or norms and creating a new GGE to continue to study these issues.[16]

3. Norms Beyond Rules

Third, states also seem to agree that any rules of international law need to be *supplemented by (non-binding) norms*, with some convergence on desirable norms. Thus, the 2015 GGE Report lists eleven important "recommendations for consideration by States for voluntary, non-binding norms, rules or principles [note their usage of "rules" and "principles"] of responsible behavior of states," including the need for cooperation among states, the need to consider all information in determining attribution, a prohibition on knowing use of a state's territory for unlawful acts, and a ban on illegal activity that intentionally damages critical infrastructure or computer emergency response teams of other states.[17]

Yet whether any of these proposed norms have gained actual acceptance, even in a non-binding way, remains an open question. As Toni Erskine and Madeline Carr

[13] See Dan Efrony and Yuval Shany, "A Rule Book on the Shelf? Tallinn Manual 2.0 on Cyberoperations and Subsequent State Practice," *American Journal of International Law* 112 (2018): 583, 649; Barrie Sander, "The Sound of Silence: International Law and the Governance of Peacetime Cyber Operations," in *11th International Conference on Cyber Conflict: Silent Battle*, edited by T. Minarik et al. (Tallinn: NATO CCDCOE, 2019), 361.

[14] Cf. Michele Markoff, Explanation of Position at the Conclusion of the 2016–2017 UN Group of Governmental Experts (GGE) on Developments in the Field of Information and Telecommunications in the Context of International Security, United States Mission to the United Nations, June 23, 2017, https://usun.usmission.gov/explanation-of-position-at-the-conclusion-of-the-2016-2017-un-group-of-governmental-experts-gge-on-developments-in-the-field-of-information-and-tele/; Declaration by Miguel Rodriguez, Representative of Cuba, at the Final Session of the Group of Governmental Experts on Developments in the Field of Information and Telecommunications in the Context of International Security, *Just Security*, June 23, 2017, https://www.justsecurity.org/wp-content/uploads/2017/06/Cuban-Expert-Declaration.pdf ("dangerous reinterpretation of the norms of international law and the Charter") [hereinafter Cuba Statement].

[15] GA Res. 73/27 (Dec. 5, 2018).

[16] See GA Res. 73/266 (Dec. 22, 2019). See generally Anders Henriksen, "The End of the Road for the UN GGE Process: The Future Regulation of Cyberspace," *Journal of Cybersecurity* 5 (2019): 1; Alex Grigsby, "The United Nations Doubles Its Workload on Cyber Norms, and Not Everyone Is Pleased," *Council on Foreign Relations Blog*, Nov. 15, 2018, https://www.cfr.org/blog/united-nations-doubles-its-workload-cyber-norms-and-not-everyone-pleased.

[17] 2015 GGE Report, *supra* note 5, at para. 13.

(citing Mervyn Frost) have pointed out, a norm exists only when an actor sees a need to "justify, excuse, rationalize, hide, or deny any deviation from it."[18] While certainly some states have denied engaging in cyberattacks, neither their actions—their actual compliance with these proposed norms—nor their words constitute any general acceptance of these norms.[19]

4. Participation by Non-State Actors

Lastly, the legal landscape is characterized by significant regulation and calls for it by *non-state actors*. At a basic level, all communications work through a privately developed technical protocol; domain names are established by ICAAN, a private multistakeholder organization.[20] Expert groups like the Global Commission on the Stability of Cyberspace (GCSC) (funded by governments) have proposed norms too. The GCSC has proposed nine norms of cybersecurity, including a duty to prevent vulnerabilities, a ban on "offensive cyber-operations," and a ban on operations meant to disrupt elections.[21] Some corporations seek a greater role in cybersecurity regulation, notably Microsoft's call for a "digital Geneva Convention."[22] And the ICRC has called for a norm protecting medical facilities from cyberattacks.[23] Finally, academics have offered their views on the state of international law and urged adoption of norms or rules. The most ambitious was the so-called Tallinn Manual process, where a group of predominantly Western experts produced a two-volume set of international law views.[24]

B. Conditioning Factors

The thin, uneven fiber of international law regarding cybersecurity can be traced to at least four structural features of malicious cyber activity. First is the relatively new use and mutating forms of malicious activity over the internet. States are

[18] Toni Erskine and Madeline Carr, "Beyond 'Quasi-Norms': The Challenges and Potential of Engaging with Norms in Cyberspace," in *International Cyber Norms: Legal, Policy & Industry Perspectives*, edited by Anna-Maria Osula and Henry Roigas (Tallinn: NATO CCDCOE, 2016), 87, 93.

[19] See Melissa Hathaway, "When Violating the Agreement Becomes the Customary Practice," in *Getting Beyond Norms: New Approaches to International Cyber Security Challenges*, edited by Fen Osler Hampson and Michael Sulmeyer (Waterloo: Centre for International Governance Innovation, 2017), 5.

[20] See, e.g., Finnemore and Hollis, *supra* note 1, at 460–461.

[21] See Global Commission on the Stability of Cyberspace, "Norms Through Singapore," The Hague Center for Strategic Studies & The East West Institute, Nov. 2018, https://cyberstability.org/wp-content/uploads/2019/04/singaporenew-digital.pdf.

[22] See Brad Smith, "The Need for a Digital Geneva Convention," Microsoft, Feb. 14, 2017, https://blogs.microsoft.com/on-the-issues/2017/02/14/need-digital-geneva-convention/.

[23] ICRC, "Norms for responsible State behavior should build on international law," Feb. 11, 2020 (statement to UN Open-Ended Working Group).

[24] See, e.g., Efrony and Shany, *supra* note 13; Jean d'Aspremont, "Cyber Operations and International Law: An Interventionist Legal Thought," *Journal of Conflict and Security Law* 21 (2016): 575; Oliver Kessler and Wouter Werner, "Expertise, Uncertainty, and International Law: A Study of the Tallinn Manual and Cyberwarfare," *Leiden Journal of International Law* 26 (2013): 793. For another academia-driven process, see the three statements on cyber operations against the health care sector and foreign elections issued through the Oxford Process on International Law Protections in Cyberspace, https://elac.web.ox.ac.uk/the-oxford-process-on-international-law-protections-in-cyberspace.

still seeking to understand both what they want to prevent and what they want to conduct or allow. States with greater vulnerability to malicious acts (including through less ability to attribute them successfully), or less interest in carrying them out—the cyber "have-nots"—may seek heavier regulation, such as a binding treaty or control by an intergovernmental organization like the International Telecommunication Union. States with stronger capacities—the cyber "haves"—may prefer no new rules, as well as prove reticent to issue formal legal opinions, *ex ante* or *ex post*.[25]

Second are political and ideological cleavages across states. To simplify a bit, Western states have seen the internet as a vehicle for their values of freedom of expression and free flow of commerce. To them, cybersecurity is about responding to threats to these values (such as stealing company data) or responding to other threats (such as attacks on a state's critical infrastructure) in a way that preserves these values. Their starting point is limited governmental involvement in cyberspace. Authoritarian states—Russia, China, the Gulf States, and others—see the internet as an instrument of their key values, namely, security and order.[26] For them, cybersecurity—or "information security" as they call it—means protecting the state and its monopoly of power; it demands a heavy governmental hand to prevent private actors from eroding state authority. Threats include the sorts of expression that Western states wish to preserve, notably political speech. Thus, agreeing on new norms or rules—or even on the applicability of existing rules—requires overcoming different starting points. Some of this inter-state fissure may be more a manifestation of great-power rivalries, for example, between the United States and the European Union on the one hand, and China (or Russia, or both) on the other.[27] These ideological battles may also discourage participation by, or have the effect of discounting the views of, developing states—a phenomenon that, as pointed out by scholars identified with Third World Approaches to International Law, permeates other subject areas.[28] As will be seen below, nearly all the governmental positions on international law concerning cybersecurity have emanated from Northern states.[29]

Third is the difficulty of identifying the source of malicious activity in a timely manner, or at all. For rules or norms to affect behavior, their addressees must either

[25] See generally Henriksen, *supra* note 16; Sander, *supra* note 13, at 369–370.

[26] See, e.g., Doctrine of Information Security of the Russian Federation, Ministry of Foreign Affairs of the Russian Federation, Dec. 5, 2016, para. 2(c), https://www.mid.ru/en/foreign_policy/official_documents/-/asset_publisher/CptICkB6BZ29/content/id/2563163 ("the information security of the Russian Federation . . . is the state of protection of the individual, society and the State against internal and external threats, allowing to ensure [*sic*] the constitutional human and civil rights and freedoms, the decent quality and standard of living for citizens, the sovereignty, the territorial integrity and . . . development of the Russian Federation, as well as defence and security of the State").

[27] For further evidence, see GA Res. 74/247 (Jan. 20, 2020) (adopting by vote of 79–60–33 a Russia-proposed resolution to begin drafting a new cybercrime convention).

[28] See, e.g., Ntina Tzouvala, "TWAIL and the 'Unwilling or Unable' Doctrine: Continuities and Ruptures," *AJIL Unbound* 109 (2016): 266.

[29] For an attempt to survey Latin American views, including explanations for lack of transparency, see Organization of American States Inter-American Juridical Committee, Improving Transparency: International Law and State Cyber Operations—Fifth Report, Aug. 7, 2020, OAS Doc. CJI/doc. 615/20.rev.1.

comply voluntarily, as a result of various dynamics described in the introduction to this volume, or face consequences for noncompliance. Assuming malicious actors will not do the former, the latter becomes difficult if targets of attacks or independent observers cannot identify them or, for non-state actors, their ties with states. The obstacles to attribution are not unique to cybersecurity—they are a staple of *jus in bello* and *jus ad bellum*—but they present a greater technological challenge. This attribution problem casts a pall over lawmaking if states believe the rules they are developing cannot be meaningfully invoked or enforced due to technological limitations.[30]

Last is the desire by states for secrecy on at least three fronts: (a) States will not want to discuss their *capabilities* for conducting disruptive cyber activity (even if they believe them to be legal). This confidentiality can lead to vague, unproductive, or dishonest discussions of permitted or prohibited conduct. (b) States may not want to reveal their *intelligence methods* for identifying sources of malicious activity, resulting in a lack of public identification even when they know them. Indeed, they may not even acknowledge that they have been the target of a malicious activity so as to convince the originator that it achieved its goal without detection; or they may prefer nonacknowledgment to avoid escalating tensions. (c) States may not want to reveal whether they have *responded* to a malicious activity, whether because they may not wish the target of a response to know its source or because such acknowledgment might escalate tensions.

This penchant for secrecy is central to this chapter's focus on legal argumentation. It will particularly affect whether states choose to invoke international law to defend their own programs, to protest a malicious cyber operation, or to defend a counteroperation.[31] In a word, when states are reluctant to publicly state the facts about a capability or operation—Can they or do they plan to deploy X malware? Did they fall victim to Y malware? Have they deployed Z malware in response?—they will a fortiori see little point in making legal arguments, whether to declare the originator's activities unlawful or their own responses lawful.

* * *

Cybersecurity thus represents a unique challenge to any appraisal of purpose (and also the effect) of legal argumentation outside the courtroom. It requires dispensing with three assumptions in most analyses of legal argumentation: (a) an agreed legal framework, even if states differ on their interpretations of the law; (b) institutions with broad acceptance to serve as fora for contestation about existing law and new law; and (c) a starting point of willingness to deploy legal argumentation to advance particular policy goals. Without these elements, how does international law affect the motives, modalities, and effects of argumentation at the international level?

[30] For an excellent case study, see Tomohiro Mikanagi and Kubo Macák, "Attribution of Cyber Operations: An International Law Perspective on the *Park Jin Hyok* Case," *Cambridge International Law Journal* 9 (2020): 51.

[31] See Sander, *supra* note 13.

II. Multilevel Persuasion and Legal Argumentation

In prior work on persuasion and international law, I examined two nonjudicial institutions that deployed legal argumentation for the purposes of persuading states and non-state actors to alter their policies to conform with legal rules—the Organization for Security and Cooperation in Europe's (OSCE's) High Commissioner on National Minorities (HCNM) and the International Committee of the Red Cross (ICRC). Their strategy was not simply one of invoking the rules—law talk—to persuade them to comply, but was far more nuanced. Scrutiny of their work gave rise to a broader theory, namely, that the argumentative strategies of any international actor seeking to persuade another to act in accordance with international law were determined by four factors: the nature of the compliance dispute (including the severity of violations), the nature of the parties (including their amenability to legal argumentation and internal coherence), the traits of the persuading entity (if different from one of the parties), and the setting of the persuasive process (e.g., bilateral vs. multilateral, public vs. private).[32]

Based on these inputs, an argumentative strategy aimed at compliance with international law varies along four dimensions: (a) confidentiality versus publicity of communications; (b) the density of legal rules, that is, the amount and specifity of law to invoke; (c) directness of a claim, that is, demanding compliance because of a legal duty as compared to invoking advantages to the legally required behavior; and (d) the tone of argumentation, that is, a persuader's confrontational versus conciliatory stance. Thus, the ICRC urges compliance with IHL through a strategy that often relies on (a) secrecy, (b) ambiguity about the law's requirements, (c) avoidance of law talk, and (d) a nonconfrontational tone.[33] The effects and effectiveness of these strategies is another question, though the ICRC claims many successes.

A. Beyond the Compliance-based Model

This model to assess the deployment of legal argumentation to advance compliance with the law assumed the existence of some agreed body of rules—human rights law (and in particular the law concerning minority rights) for the OSCE HCNM, and IHL for the ICRC. But as noted earlier, the case of cybersecurity dispenses with that assumption. If we think that the model is still useful in this setting, it suggests that a new input must be added—namely, the *density of the legal landscape*. Argumentation through law aimed at compliance with law will depend a great deal on how much law is out there.[34]

[32] See generally Steven R. Ratner, "Law Promotion Beyond Law Talk: The Red Cross, Persuasion, and the Laws of War," *European Journal of International Law* 22 (2011): 459. See Hyeran Jo, chapter 9, in this volume, for development of some of these ideas regarding non-state actors.

[33] *Id.* 492–493.

[34] Thus, as Jutta Brunnée points out in chapter 12, in this volume, the shift in argumentation around climate change to soft law and procedural norms stems from the paucity of strong, substantive duties to reduce greenhouse gases.

But a thin legal landscape affects the entire process of persuasion more profoundly. I would argue that the absence of a detailed legal framework for cybersecurity has meant that instead of states identifying law violations and then using persuasive strategies *to foster compliance*, they are spending most of their efforts trying to persuade other parties *to adopt a particular position on what the law is or should be.*[35] The absence of a consensus on most of the law shifts the legal argumentation away from a focus on compliance—for what is compliance if we fail to agree much on the law?—and toward the content of the law.

How does this type of legal persuasion work? Essentially, states invoke the law in a process of *multilevel persuasion*: (1) to persuade others about whether international law *currently has rules* governing a particular cyber activity; (2) to persuade others about the *meaning or interpretation* of those rules; (3) to persuade others about the *need for new law versus non-binding norms*; and (4) to persuade others about the *desired content* of new law. In a legal landscape with a thicker set of rules, the first of these is simply not necessary; and, as for the third and fourth, states will likely argue less about the need for and content of new law if the law already has numerous rules.

The argumentative practice with respect to cybersecurity shows actors engage in the first two levels of persuasion—about the existence and meaning of current law—in two separate phases—*ex ante* as states and non-state actors discuss legal rules or norms prospectively and abstractly, that is, not in response to a specific malicious activity; and *ex post* as they communicate in response to a malicious act. Each phase can take place in different venues, from bilateral communications to international organizations or even business conferences. The third and fourth levels of persuasion—about the need for and content of new rules—has typically transpired only in the *ex ante* context, which is not surprising since in the *ex post* context states are more concerned with responding to an attack and deterring future attacks than with describing the best new normative landscape.

In order to map this schema onto the practice, I will organize the discussion that follows into these two phases. I will attempt to describe what states are doing, why they are doing it, and the effects of each form of legal argumentation.

B. Legal Persuasion *Ex Ante* (before a Malicious Activity)

1. Persuasion about the Existence and Meaning of International Law (Levels 1 and 2)

Many debates among states at the *ex ante* phase are characterized by a disagreements about whether international law has rules governing cybersecurity, including permissible measures that a state can take on its own as well as in response to the actions of other states. States invoke international law at Level 1 to (a) claim that the law *already regulates* a particular cyber activity, or (b) to *deny* that it does. For example, the United States, the United Kingdom, and France have offered statements that international law

[35] States pursue this goal even when the law is clear, as seen, for instance, in Ian Johnstone's account of efforts toward a treaty banning nuclear weapons, chapter 7, in this volume. But where the law is not clear or thick, this goal assumes particular salience.

already has many rules in place, whether treaty law like the UN Charter or the Geneva Conventions, or customary international law, such as the rules on state responsibility. Some of these claims have been accepted—witness the consensus in the GGE over the list of rules in its 2015 report. But when the claims about the state of the law get more specific, for example, about self-defense, countermeasures, or the need to protect human rights—they face resistance, as seen in the 2017 debacle. Non-state actors have made expansive claims about its coverage and meaning, most ambitiously in the Tallinn Manuals.[36]

A state's Level 1 argument to demonstrate that the law *applies* may include interpretations of the law—Level 2 persuasion. For example, Australia, France, and the Netherlands have each put forth impressive papers with detailed interpretations of international law rules (including, in Australia's case, hypothetical scenarios in which it applies those interpretations).[37] In other situations, leading officials have given speeches. One move during Level 2 persuasion is to emphasize what the law *does not prohibit*. Thus, for example, the United Kingdom claims that the principle of sovereignty does not contain prohibitions beyond those in the duty of non-intervention; and that countermeasures need not be symmetrical.[38] And the United States, France, and other states have emphasized the norms of attribution do not require a state to reveal its sources of information.[39] In these contexts, law is invoked and interpreted to stress its absence of prohibitions.

The rhetorical methods of states and non-state actors claiming that the law already exists entails an unstated default move, namely, the use of analogies: cyber activity X is already regulated by legal regime L1 because X resembles in some important way other activity (A1) regulated by regime L1; and X is regulated by regime L2 because of similarities between X and other activity (A2) regulated by L2. Actors will argue, if only implicitly, about whether cybersecurity is more like A1 (e.g., armed conflict) or A2 (e.g., excessive enforcement jurisdiction)—a classic common law discourse. And they will interpret each rule in L1 and L2 with reference to its meaning in regulating activities A1 and A2, respectively. By the same reasoning, those denying the existence of law will reject those analogies.

[36] See *Tallinn Manual 2.0 on the International Law Applicable to Cyber Operations*, edited by Michael N. Schmitt (Cambridge: Cambridge University Press, Feb. 2017), 2 (manual as expression of the experts "as to the state of the law"), 4 ("rules . . . reflect customary international law (unless they expressly reference a treaty)").

[37] Australia Non-Paper: Case Studies on the Application of International Law in Cyberspace, Australia Ministry of Foreign Affairs and Trade, 2020, https://unoda-web.s3.amazonaws.com/wp-content/uploads/2020/02/australian-international-law-case-studies-final-5-february-2020.pdf; Droit International Appliqué aux Opérations dans le Cyberpace, Ministère des Armées, Sept. 9, 2019, https://www.defense.gouv.fr/content/download/565895/9750877/file/Droit+internat+appliqu%C3%A9+aux+op%C3%A9rations+Cyberespace.pdf [hereinafter French Statement]; Appendix: International Law in Cyberspace, Government of the Kingdom of the Netherlands, July 5, 2019, https://unoda-web.s3.amazonaws.com/wp-content/uploads/2020/02/appendix-Internaional-law-in-cyberspace-kingdom-of-the-netherlands.pdf [hereinafter Netherlands Statement].

[38] Wright, *supra* note 11. See also Government of Estonia, President of the Republic at the Opening of Cycon 2019, May 29, 2019, https://www.president.ee/en/official-duties/speeches/15241-president-of-the-republic-at-the-opening-of-cycon-2019/index.html (endorsing collective countermeasures).

[39] See Egan, *supra* note 11; French Statement, *supra* note 37, at 11.

However reflexive the practice may be for lawyer, the use of analogies and the particular analogy chosen reflect choices to link certain features or concepts of cyberattacks and responses to existing categories of law.[40] Hollis has pointed out that among the shortcomings of analogical reasoning in the cyber context is its failure to recognize that certain facets of cyber operations are so different from analogs regulated by an existing body of law that reliance on that law will yield ineffective legal rules.[41] Yet analogical claims remain common, as seen in the UK and US statements.

States' motivations in claiming or denying the existence of extant law and in offering their interpretation of it are not difficult to surmise. For example, regarding an affirmative claim, the US claim that self-defense already regulates some malicious cyber activity is meant to preserve its options and signal its willingness to deploy both counteroperations and the use of military force (although the United States, unlike France, has not elaborated its interpretation of self-defense in much detail). With respect to a claim of denial, the Cuban rejection of the applicability of *jus in bello* is meant to delegitimize military responses as well as lay the groundwork for their own view that cybersecurity needs new rules.

2. Persuasion about the Need for New Law vs. Norms (Level 3)

State claims about the coverage or meaning of existing law can serve as a predicate to claims about the need for new law or norms.

a. The Link to Persuasion about the State of Existing Law

We can somewhat simplistically map claims about existing law and claims about the need for new law into four permutations, with corresponding examples from state practice.[42]

- Existing bodies of law do not apply, so new *legal rules are* needed: At the 2017 GGE meeting, the claims by Cuba that some of the *jus ad bellum* and *jus in bello* did not apply to cyber activity and responses grounded its call for an "internationally legally binding instrument to respond ... to the significant existing legal gaps in the context of cybersecurity."[43] China has rejected the applicability of rules of state responsibility and called for "new international legal instruments commensurate with the characteristics of cyberspace, with a view to maintaining peace in cyberspace, instead of using legal instruments as a tool to pursue accountability and punishment unilaterally new law."[44]

[40] Barry Sander, "Cyber Insecurity and the Politics of International Law," *ESIL Reflections* 6 (2017): 1, 4. As Monica Hakimi discusses in chapter 3, in this volume, US attempts to analogize various perceived threats to armed attacks under Article 51 have met with mixed results.

[41] Duncan Hollis, "Re-Thinking the Boundaries of Law in Cyberspace," in *Cyber War: Law and Ethics for Virtual Conflicts*, edited by Jens David Ohlin et al. (Oxford: Oxford University Press, 2015), 29, 146–155.

[42] This schema is somewhat stylized insofar as, based on the GGE's consensus, no state rejects the applicability of all international law, and all states agree on the need for both some new law (or interpretations) and new norms.

[43] Cuba Statement, *supra* note 14.

[44] China's Contribution to the Initial Pre-Draft of OEWG Report, 5–6, https://front.un-arm.org/wp-content/uploads/2020/04/china-contribution-to-oewg-pre-draft-report-final.pdf.

- Existing bodies of law do not apply, so new *non-binding norms* are needed: Iran's submission to the Open-Ended Working Group in 2020 questioned whether existing international law applied to cyber-security and that extant law "has not been able to preserve the ICTs peaceful nature." It called for states to develop new "norms, rules, and principles."[45]
- Existing bodies of law *apply*, but new *non-binding norms* are needed: The GGE's position in 2015 seems to endorse this view by advocating early in its report the importance of new non-binding norms.[46] The report nowhere calls on states to develop new legal rules, but rather includes a section at the end with a nonexhaustive list of "how international law applies" to cybersecurity and notes that "common understandings on how international law applies to State use of ICTs are important for promoting" an open and secure internet.[47]
- Existing bodies of law apply, but new *legal rules* (or interpretations thereof) are needed. The 2018 speech by the UK Attorney-General included both a detailed interpretation of existing law as applied to the cyber context and a call for "defining the appropriate principles of international law to apply to cyberspace," calling for a "rules-based international order."[48] This position puts an emphasis on legally binding rules. But it is also a bit vague. It could simply call for more detailed elaboration of what existing rules (e.g., on self-defense or state responsibility) mean. The quote above suggests that the GGE has endorsed this position, which is consistent with the elaboration of non-binding norms. (The line between new interpretations and new law is thin indeed.) But it could mean more than that—the derivation of completely new rules unique to the cyber context (e.g., rules of attribution different from those in the Articles on State Responsibility). After the breakdown of the 2017 GGE, the United States was critical of states that opposed "clear and direct statements on how certain international law applies to states use of ICTs," including *jus ad bellum*, *jus in bello*, and countermeasures.[49] Although the United States seems more interested in interpreting existing law and not creating new law, China both accepts the applicability of some (but not all) existing international law, and also seems keen for new rules, for example, a convention on cyberspace.[50]

So states seem to be trying to persuade one another to go down different routes and grounding those arguments in both the applicability or absence of law currently. And this mode of argumentation also reflects calculated thinking by states. In the case of the United States, for instance, interpretation of existing rules (that the United States helped develop, of course) gives the United States a strong hand as an important state

[45] Preliminary reflection by the Islamic Republic of Iran, Apr. 2020, paras. 10–11, https://front.un-arm.org/wp-content/uploads/2020/04/iran-preliminary-on-oewg-pre-draft-15-april-2020-1.pdf.
[46] 2015 GGE Report, *supra* note 5, at para. 10.
[47] *Id.* paras. 28–29.
[48] Wright, *supra* note 11.
[49] Markoff, Explanation of Position, *supra* note 14, at para. 2.
[50] Zhixiong Huang and Kubo Macák, "Towards the International Rule of Law in Cyberspace: Contrasting Chinese and Western Approaches," *Chinese Journal of International Law* 16 (2017): 1, 9; Ma Xinmin, "What Kind of Internet Order Do We Need?," *Chinese Journal of International Law* 14 (2014): 399, 401–403.

to justify its own policies. Its voice would be less during the prescription of wholly new rules, which might end up inconsistent with its interests.[51] So it invokes the law to persuade other actors *not* to make new law.

b. The Balance of Law and Norms

Whatever their views about the applicability of existing law, states may be quite imprecise about the balance of law and norms they prefer for the future. France's 2018 cyber defense policy calls for "des options de régulation ou de norms internationales informelles," and its policy freely speaks about "les règles et norms."[52] Both the Russia-sponsored and US-sponsored 2018 General Assembly resolutions call for the new workings groups to "develop" (the Russian draft) or "study" (the US draft) "norms, rules and principles of responsible behavior of States ... as well as how international law applies to the use of information and communications technologies."[53] The Shanghai Cooperation Organization's 2015 call for a "international code of conduct for information security," which has gotten very little traction, is unclear about its legal status.[54]

States' views of the relationship of norms to existing law can prove puzzling. The GGE claims that "norms do not seek to limit or prohibit action that is otherwise consistent with international law,"[55] which suggests that new norms are meant to regulate only conduct *not* governed by international law. Yet one of the key functions of norms is indeed to limit, in a non-binding way, states' freedom of action otherwise enjoyed under international law.

With regard to state *motivations*, prior theoretical work on soft law argues that states will seek formally non-binding norms (or vague but legally binding rules, another form of softness) in areas characterized by uncertainty about the issue or states' views on the best mode of regulation.[56] States will push norms over a treaty or identification of custom where they wish a new regulatory architecture to preserve flexibility for themselves—where they cannot achieve agreement on detailed rules or implementation procedures.

But the *effects* of these preferences extend beyond the norms or rules ultimately adopted, and thus beyond the immediate goal of the argument. When states argue to other states to adopt law or norms, that advocacy itself can prove transformative in ways not intended by—or at least not reflecting the primary motivation of—the speakers. First, persuading that new *law* (or at least new interpretations thereof) is needed (as, for instance, in the British Attorney General's speech) frames the issue as

[51] Cf. Henriksen, *supra* note 16, at 5 (on why states might not favor detailed regulations).

[52] Revue stratégique de cyberdéfense, *supra* note 11, at 84–85.

[53] GA Res. 73/27, para. 5; GA Res. 73/266, para. 3.

[54] Letter dated 9 January 2015 from the Permanent Representatives of China, Kazakhstan, Kyrgyzstan, the Russian Federation, Tajikistan and Uzbekistan to the United Nations addressed to the Secretary-General, UN Doc. A/69/723 (Jan. 13, 2015).

[55] 2015 GGE Report, *supra* note 5, at para. 10.

[56] Gregory Shaffer and Mark A. Pollack, "Hard and Soft Law," in *Interdisciplinary Perspectives on International Law and International Relations: The State of the Art*, edited by Jeffrey L. Dunoff and Mark A. Pollack (Cambridge: Cambridge University Press, 2013): 197, 213–214. As Jutta Brunnée points out in chapter 12, in this volume, debates over this balance are central to the trajectory of international law on climate change.

requiring *predictability* regarding permissible conduct and *identification* of law followers and breakers. Predictability and identification of compliers/violators are two sides of the same coin. States favoring law see it as generating strong expectations on states, promoting predictability; with that predictability comes the stigma on those violating those expectations. With norms, these features are attenuated.[57]

Second, law talk at the prescription stage frames the issue in an *epistemological* sense. By calling for new law or more detailed elaboration of existing law, states signal their preference for a certain type of expertise for future cyber-regulation, one requiring facility with existing rules and the ability to craft future rules. Lawyers are central to this process. Norms, on the other hand, can be developed and drafted by policy experts (though lawyers in foreign ministries will typically take a crack at them).[58] When states advocate for norms, they convey, "We can work this issue out without the lawyers" (though lawyers will probably end up being involved as a practical matter). This epistemological framing can affect the atmosphere of a prescriptive process, even promoting a collegial effort by an epistemic community of experts.[59] The choice to involve lawyers may lead to a new dialogue—or argumentation—between them and technical experts.

C. Legal Persuasion *Ex Post* (after a Malicious Act)

States also make choices about whether to invoke international law on cyber activity not just *ex ante*, *in abstracto*, but in the aftermath of particular incidents.[60]

1. Patterns and Motivations of Law vs. Norm Invocation

Consider the following four incidents, where states admitted that they had been the victim of an attack and indeed identified its source, thus overcoming the incentives to secrecy:

(1) In the 2014 attack against Sony, the United States publicly attributed the act to North Korea and characterized it act as a violation of "international norms" but not international law.[61]

(2) After the 2016 Russian hacks in connection with the US election, President Obama identified the source of the attacks and spoke of the need to "oppose Russia's efforts to undermine established international norms of behavior."[62]

[57] Cf. Kubo Macák, "From Cyber Norms to Cyber Rules: Re-engaging States as Law-makers," *Leiden Journal of International Law* 30 (2017): 877, 896 (calling on states to be more explicit in interpretations of the law in order to promote *opinio juris*).

[58] The same dynamic can be seen in Lisbeth Zimmermann's account of the choices to engage in legal versus scientific argumentation in the context of the ban on whaling, chapter 13, in this volume.

[59] See generally Peter Haas, "Do Regimes Matter? Epistemic Communities and Mediterranean Pollution Control," *International Organization* 43 (1989): 377.

[60] See generally W. Michael Reisman and Andrew R. Willard, *International Incidents: The Law that Counts in World Politics* (Princeton: Princeton University Press, 1988).

[61] U.S. Department of State, "Condemning Cyber-Attack by North Korea: Press Statement," Dec. 19, 2014, https://2009-2017.state.gov/secretary/remarks/2014/12/235444.htm.

[62] White House, Statement by the President on Actions in Response to Russian Malicious Cyber Activity and Harassment, Dec. 29, 2016, https://obamawhitehouse.archives.gov/the-press-office/2016/12/29/statement-president-actions-response-russian-malicious-cyber-activity.

(3) In the 2017 WannaCry global attack, the United States and the United Kingdom attributed the attack to North Korea, and while neither state accused North Korea of violating international law, the UK Foreign Office stated that "international law applies online as it does offline. The United Kingdom is determined to identify, pursue and respond to malicious cyber activity . . . imposing costs on those who wish to attack us in cyberspace."[63]

(4) In October 2018, the United Kingdom attributed cyberattacks directed at the Organization for the Prohibition of Chemical Weapons and other targets to Russia and called it a "flagrant violation of international law."[64]

In the first two cases, international law was not invoked; in the third case, it was invoked without a claim that it was violated; and in the final case, a reacting state claimed a legal violation. This diversity of argumentation is not new—it is precisely the dimension of directness discussed in the compliance-based model, whereby a persuading entity may or may not mention the law or identify an act as a violation. Under that paradigm, the victim state's purpose is to persuade the other state to change its conduct. It may argue in terms of law or norms, but nonrecurrence is the goal. But the state has a second goal—to persuade others of its views *about the state of the law*, in particular, what it views as illegal versus merely a violation of norms. This goal is not inconsistent with the compliance-based model, but it is far less often the goal of the persuading entity in that context.

Yet because the law is so undeveloped, the motivations for these choices are difficult to discern. With respect to the first two statements, the US avoidance of law talk in 2014 and 2016 could be based on a view that (1) international law does not regulate the conduct; (2) international law regulates the subject, but that the attacker did not violate the law (only non-binding norms); (3) international law regulates the subject, the attacker violated the law, but, for diplomatic reasons, it is preferable to invoke merely a violation of international norms; or (4) it is not in the US interest to take a position on whether the law regulates the conduct.[65] (These hypotheses can also help explain why a state may choose not to react at all or fail to attribute responsibility.[66])

[63] UK Foreign Commonwealth Office, "Foreign Office Minister Condemns North Korean Actor for WannaCry Attacks," Dec. 19, 2017, https://www.gov.uk/government/news/foreign-office-minister-condemns-north-korean-actor-for-wannacry-attacks. For a later episode, see U.S. Department of the Treasury, "Treasury Targets North Korea for Multiple Cyber Attacks," Sept. 6, 2018, https://home.treasury.gov/news/press-releases/sm473 ("disruptive and harmful cyber activity that is inconsistent with the growing consensus on what constitutes responsible state behavior in cyberspace").

[64] UK Government, "U.K. Exposes Russian Cyber Attacks," Oct. 4, 2018, https://www.gov.uk/government/news/uk-exposes-russian-cyber-attacks. See also Netherlands Ministry of Defence, "Netherlands Defence Intelligence and Security Service disrupts Russian cyber operation targeting OPCW," Oct. 4, 2018 (Russian operations "undermine the international rule of law"). The United States publicly attributed cyberattacks in 2020 to Russia and in 2021 accused (albeit somewhat obliquely) Russia of "violat[ing] well-established principles of international law, including respect for the territorial integrity of states." White House Fact Sheet: Imposing Costs for Harmful Foreign Activities by the Russian Government, Apr. 15, 2021, https://www.whitehouse.gov/briefing-room/statements-releases/2021/04/15/fact-sheet-imposing-costs-for-harmful-foreign-activities-by-the-russian-government/.

[65] These hypothesis assume that the state thought about the question of law versus norms.

[66] See Sander, *supra* note 13, at 369–370, 372–373 (US failure to protest espionage against Office of Personnel Management as implicit acceptance of cyber-espionage).

In addition, the United States not only spoke in terms of norms and not law; it did not even identify the norms—even those in the 2015 GGE report that it had accepted.[67]

With respect to the third statement, the United Kingdom's invocation without blame, the United Kingdom would seem to want to signal that international law applies in cyberspace, but the avoidance of blame could be accounted for by any of the four explanations just mentioned. As for the final statement, where the United Kingdom blamed Russia for a law violation (the only episode to date involving such a direct claim), the United Kingdom was nonetheless unwilling to identify the specific rules violated. One interpretation is that the United Kingdom believed that the law had been violated, but was unsure about which rule was violated—a somewhat remarkable posture to take, but perhaps a testing of the waters to see how others might react. Another is that it was sure which rule had been violated but did not want to identify the Russian hack as a violation of that rule to preserve its own freedom of action for the future.[68]

While the data set is small, the rarity with which we witness invocation of law—compared to the alternatives of silence, condemnation without mention of norms, and condemnation with mention of norms but not law—suggests that, in situations where the law is contested in basic respects, states will exercise caution in making claims about violations of international law.[69] Those same states seem willing to make claims *ex ante* about the meaning of existing law, but in responding to an attack they express a reluctance to link their view of the law to a specific factual situation. We thus witness a *duality* of law invocation—assertive in one phase and cautious in another. This duality might be based on internal bureaucratic politics within states, where states have enough time to develop a position for a forum like the GGE, but *ex post* lack the time for careful consideration of whether the law has been violated.

2. Effects of Law vs. Norm Invocation

The effects of invoking law versus norms *ex post* have several dimensions, some intended and some not. As for deterring malicious conduct, the perpetrators of such attacks may care equally little for a claim of violation of norms as a claim of violation of international law. Or they may care just as much.[70] As for the other audiences, states generally understand that the law is in its early phases in terms of fleshing out the meaning of existing law and prescribing new law. Yet even in that environment—perhaps especially there—when a state argues in terms of international law after a violation (even if that state is not clear about which law has been violated), it sends a signal of seriousness about the violation.

[67] See Martha Finnemore and Duncan Hollis, "Beyond Naming and Shaming: Accusations and International Law in Cybersecurity," *European Journal of International Law* 31 (2020): 969.

[68] In addition, a victim state would not go out of its way *ex post* to say that the attack was legal even if it believed it was. The US invocation of international law, and the specific rule of territorial integrity, in the 2021 White House Fact Sheet, *supra* note 64, may portend a greater willingness to accuse a state of violating a specific rule *ex post*.

[69] States may exercise caution for political reasons even when the law is clear, as seen in Namira Negm, chapter 11, and Bruno Stagno-Ugarte, chapter 8, both in this volume.

[70] Cf. Ratner, *supra* note 32, at 496–498 (hard/soft law distinction often irrelevant to persuasion strategies).

More important for our purposes, law invocation sends a signal not only about the particular act, or the need to comply with the law. Rather, it indicates that the state making that claim has *made up its mind about something that the law prohibits*. From a doctrinal viewpoint, we simply call this *opinio juris*. But from the perspective of the persuasive process, it can be a pivotal moment for creating shared expectations in an environment where states disagree so much on the law governing cybersecurity. As might be heard in a foreign ministry legal office, "So France thinks that behavior is illegal? That's important. Let's see what others say." Where states are just exploring what existing law prohibits, a decision to invoke the law, even if the state has not fully figured out its meaning, signals both an interest in participation in the lawmaking process and a readiness to identify law violations. The state also shows some willingness to tie its hands in responding to future episodes by treating like cases alike (with a caveat for self-interested interpretations).

Of course, judging by the record to date, most states *ex post* are *not* invoking law and thus not sending that signal. Instead, when they claim, as does the United States, that the conduct is merely inconsistent with norms, they offer a weaker condemnation about the conduct (although one that could be counteracted if the states retaliates). But invocation of *norms* also sends a signal about that state's view of the contours of the *law*. What signal? I would hazard to guess that the most likely signal is that the victim state simply does not believe that the activity is clearly illegal insofar as the law does not regulate the conduct (explanation 1 in Section II.C.1 above). Careful observers reading the state's reaction might consider the other explanations behind a state's claim that an act violated only international norms. But it would seem that invoking merely norms sends a signal of caution, and even a reluctance to treating like cases alike.

Yet a state's decision to invoke norms does not signal full nonparticipation in the prescriptive process and can still have effects. Finnemore and Hollis describe a condemnation without invocation of, or an attempt to enforce, international law as an "accusation." They regard accusations as "an opening bid, aimed at a particular community, indicating not just the accuser's disapproval of the cited operation, but often, too, its proposal (perhaps implicit) that all such conduct should be barred"[71]—and thus that like cases should be treated alike in the future. States can make accusations when there are no extant norms.[72] Both invocation of law and of norms serve what they call a constitutive functions, even if the former is a more vocal and law-generating "opening bid."

The same state might even invoke law in some situations and norms in others, a phenomenon Dan Efrony and Yuval Shany refer to as "optionality."[73] While politically motivated decisions to invoke law or not are "part and parcel of international law's structural DNA,"[74] optionality is more likely in the cybersecurity context because

[71] Finnemore and Hollis, *supra* note 67, at 14.

[72] *Id.* 28.

[73] Efrony and Shany, *supra* note 13, at 648–649. For other examples of actors switching back and forth between legal and other arguments, see Lisbeth Zimmermann, chapter 13, and Hyeran Jo, chapter 9, both in this volume.

[74] Nicholas Tsagourias, "The Slow Process of Normativizing Cyberspace," *AJIL Unbound* 113 (2019): 71, 74.

states have an additional incentive to opt out of invoking the law. They do not want to contribute to *opinio juris* (or subsequent practice under a treaty) if they want to keep their options open about future policy. Where the law is less settled, this opt-out keeps the law in flux and slows down the prescriptive process.

III. Non-State Actors and Legal Argumentation

Non-state actors already play a role in regulating cyberspace, through dynamics quite distinct from the argumentative strategies of armed groups discussed in Hyeran Jo's chapter in this volume. Some have gone further than states in persuading at all three levels about the applicability and content of international law and the need for new norms or rules. In addition, some of these actors have begun to persuade at a fourth level, about the detailed *content of new norms or rules*.

A. Persuasion at the First and Second Levels: The Tallinn Manual

The most publicized non-state effort regarding the application and interpretation of existing law is the Tallinn Manual process. Whereas states could only agree at the GGE in 2015 on a short list of international law rules that apply in cyberspace, with ambiguous formulations at times, the experts preparing the Tallinn Manuals identified 154 rules. The document relies centrally on the analogical approach to make both uncontroversial conclusions (a diplomatic mission's inviolable archives include electronic data)[75] and those pushing contemporary understandings (an absolute requirement of due diligence on states to prevent malicious cyber activity).[76] The overwhelming message sent by the process, and Tallinn 2.0 in particular, is one of certainty about a vast range of rules as already governing cyber operations.

Tallinn's reliance on the first two levels of persuasion is not surprising given its non-state origins. Indeed, the credibility of the process hinges on its assertion that it is the product of experts drawing out logical implications, typically based on analogies, of existing rules.[77] Jean d'Aspremont has criticized the Tallinn process for its lack of candor in serving as an active intervention by lawyers in the prescriptive process.[78] Under the guise of administering existing rules, he claims the authors stretched them to advance their own purposes. Whether the interpretations are safe or stretches, the Tallinn experts certainly sought to persuade others to adopt their understanding of the law.[79]

Tallinn's strategy of purporting to identify and interpret existing law is coupled with a complete absence of persuasion at the third level—whether international law needs

[75] *Tallinn Manual 2.0*, *supra* note 36, at 219.
[76] *Id.* 30.
[77] For a criticism of the makeup of those experts, see Kessler and Werner, *supra* note 24, at 802–807.
[78] d'Aspremont, *supra* note 24.
[79] Kessler and Werner, *supra* note 24 (criticizing alignment with US interests).

new rules. In a sense, this is an odd omission, for international lawyers ought to be the first to spot the need for new rules. Tallinn's authors might have regarded such a step as a policy, not legal, move. But the message Tallinn's drafters leave by producing such a large volume is that international law is *already adequate* to address the challenges of cybersecurity. Tallinn's authors might claim that the volume shows only that the law is already there, not that its rules are substantively right for cyberspace, but the effect of such a volume is to suggest that law reform is not needed.

States, for their part (at least those that have spoken on the issue), do not seem to be swallowing that message. Efrony and Shany show no invocation of the rules in Tallinn and few claims by states that would suggest that they have internalized the rules.[80] One particular disagreement concerns the Manual's claim that cyber operations can be illegal for violating the sovereignty of other states independent of any other violation, a claim already rejected by the United Kingdom and United States (but accepted by the Netherlands and France).[81] An unofficial Chinese response criticized the particular rules based on *jus ad bellum* and *jus in bello*.[82] And the gap between the GGE report's list of rules and Tallinn's suggests that states are not as confident as Tallinn's drafters about the content of existing law.

B. Persuasion at the Third and Fourth Levels: Microsoft and the Global Commission

Other non-state players have gone well beyond the Tallinn drafters regarding future rules and norms. Both Microsoft and the GCSC have argued that international law needs to be supplemented and have offered suggestions in that regard. In the case of Microsoft, Brad Smith's 2017 call for a Digital Geneva Convention (Smith is an international lawyer too) implies that existing law regarding state-sponsored cyberattacks is inadequate and that new law (and not merely norms) is needed.[83] Microsoft has also called for norms in the form of pledges by industry to prevent and respond to cyberattacks, working through a private organization, akin to the ICRC.[84]

The Global Commission has characterized the current international regulation of cybersecurity as inadequate,[85] and called for new norms. The Commission set a goal using a "bottom up" methodology to: (1) identify what it calls "operational norms," based upon which it will (2) develop a set of principles for cyberstability, then (3) propose some "clearer understanding of what the international peace and security

[80] Efrony and Shany, *supra* note 13.

[81] See Wright, *supra* note 11; Paul C. Ney, Jr., "DOD General Counsel Remarks at U.S. Cyber Command Legal Conference," U.S. Department of Defense, Mar. 2, 2020, https://www.defense.gov/Newsroom/Speeches/Speech/Article/2099378/dod-general-counsel-remarks-at-us-cyber-command-legal-conference/; Netherlands Statement, *supra* note 37, at 2; French Statement, *supra* note 37, at 6–7.

[82] Huang and Macák, *supra* note 50, at 32.

[83] See Smith, *supra* note 22 ("a convention that will call on the world's governments to pledge that they will not engaged in cyberattacks on the private sectors, that they will not target civilian infrastructure").

[84] *Id.* Microsoft and others eventually created the CyberPeace Institute, https://cyberpeaceinstitute.org.

[85] Global Commission on the Stability of Cyberspace, "Norm Package Singapore," Nov. 2018, at 6, https://cyberstability.org/wp-content/uploads/2018/11/GCSC-Singapore-Norm-Package-3MB.pdf ("many nations still see [cyberspace] as an unconstrained arena for conflict").

architecture needs to do to meet that definition" of cyberstability, followed by (4) a set of proposals on implementing this goal.[86] Instead, it completed its work with stage 1, with its package of eight norms "to accompany and reinforce" those in the UN GGE reports.[87]

Yet one of its norms relies extensively on legal argumentation to support it: "Non-state actors should not engage in offensive cyber operations and state actors should prevent and respond to activities if they occur."[88] In a commentary to this proposed norm, the Commission cites and explains several international law rules as supporting it—including rules of state responsibility, "the principle of due diligence under international law," and the law of countermeasures and measures of retorsion "to incentivize the state to comply with its obligation of due diligence."[89]

Thus, the non-state actor relies on existing legal *rules* (or purported rules in the case of due diligence), to support the development of a non-binding *norm*. This move suggests that the Commission believed that a proposal for a new norm would be aided by some legal support for it in extant notions of state responsibility and due diligence. This choice can be contrasted with the GGE, whose proposed norms are offered *before* the discussion of extant international law and do not rely on law at all in proposing norms. It is also at odds with the trajectory we normally ascribe to norms and rules, that is, that norms come first and ground rules.

The corporate and think-tank mixing proposals for rules and norms—and norms based on rules (rather than the reverse)—is, in the end, not surprising given their own place in the cybersecurity prescriptive process. Unlike the Tallinn drafters, they do not see their role as limited to, or limited by, existing law. Both Microsoft's Cyber Geneva Convention and cyber-ICRC are out-of-the-box thinking to create entirely new rules and institutions, and the Global Commission's norms package seeks to build up norms in a process parallel to the GGE—and one that may become increasingly important if the GGE itself remains paralyzed.

Finally, the involvement of non-state actors at the fourth level of persuasion (identifying new norms and rules) should not obscure the professed commitment by states to take the lead on this task. Both the GGE and OEWG processes set such prescriptive activity as their goal, even as states differ on the balance of norms and law (or legal interpretations). States certainly show no interest in delegating argumentation about future law or norms to academics, companies, or multistakeholder groups. At the same time, one can see only very slow progress at the United Nations—with no formal endorsement by the United Nations as a whole of any of the norms suggested by the GGE. Indeed the GGE, OEWG, and, eventually the General Assembly itself are likely

[86] *Id.*

[87] Global Commission on the Stability of Cyberspace, *Advancing Cyberstability: Final Report* (Nov. 2019), Appendix B.

[88] *Id.* 45.

[89] Global Commission on the Stability of Cyberspace, "Additional Note to the Norm Against Offensive Cyber Operations by Non-State Actors," Nov. 2018, https://cyberstability.org/wp-content/ uploads/2018/11/Additional-Note-to-the-Norm-Against-Offensive-Cyber-Operations-by-Non-state-Actors-Norm-Package-Singapore.pdf.

to become fora where non-state actors try to persuade states of the merits of their proposals (with the OEWG already welcoming NGO input into its work).[90]

IV. Implications for Theories of Argumentation and Compliance

The process of invoking or not invoking international law in conversations about the regulation of cybersecurity isolates a generally hidden variable in discussions about legal argumentation—the thickness of the legal landscape. The above analysis has worked along two axes— (1) the distinction between argumentation about cybersecurity law and norms *ex ante* versus *ex post*; and (2) the distinctions among argumentation about the applicability of existing law, its interpretation, the need for new law versus norms, and the content of new norms or law. A diverse set of patterns has been revealed with respect to the phases and levels of persuasion.

Most intriguingly, the cybersecurity case study demonstrates the possibilities for states and non-state actors to invoke the law even when there is not very much law upon which states have agreed. Yet the disincentives to invoking law are also strong, suggesting that states are more likely to engage in the optionality identified by Efrony and Shany when the legal landscape is thin and the norms are contested at the most basic level. States' motivations for invoking or not invoking the law will depend on the phase and level of argumentation, but also on their own cyber-capabilities and vulnerabilities, ideologies, and broader strategic interests. These factors can interact in strange ways, as one cyber-power (the United States) sees existing law as adequate and prefers only new norms, while another cyber-power (China) wants a new legal framework, at least in part. As for the effects of these choices on other parties involved in cybersecurity, these choices send signals distinct from getting them to comply with the rules.

Although the regulation of cybersecurity is sui generis in some respects, the theoretical insights in this chapter can be generalized to cover other areas of law with significant disagreement about the existence and content of rules. I would offer several tentative implications of the cybersecurity practice for theories of argumentation and compliance:

1. Where the law is fundamentally contested in terms of the application or meaning of rules, compliance becomes less important to states, and thus less a goal of the persuasive process. State persuasion is oriented toward convincing other actors of what the underlying rules are or should be. Other subjects with thin landscapes include artificial intelligence and even such traditional subjects as conflicts of jurisdiction. Theories of compliance that focus on why states follow *accepted rules* need to be rethought to understand the motivations and effects of legal argumentation oriented to the *future of rules*.[91]

[90] For the various NGO reports, see "Open-ended Working Group," United Nations, https://www.un.org/disarmament/open-ended-working-group/.

[91] See chapter 3, in this volume, by Monica Hakimi, making a similar point about the *jus ad bellum*.

2. Realism and institutionalism rely on fixed features of the persuader and persuadee to explain the motivation for and effects of persuasion.[92] The former would see states as offering self-serving claims about whether the law applies and where it should go, without any serious commitment to existing or future rules. The arguments over law and norms at the United Nations and elsewhere are simply cheap talk to mask a desire for maximum flexibility and projection of power. Indeed, realism might explain the position of the cyber-haves, or even a have-not like Cuba.

3. Institutionalism's focus on reducing transactions costs through rules and institutions would see states as attempting to find some common ground to regulate cybersecurity and would view the UN process more seriously. Institutionalist scholarship on hard versus soft law or norms also helps us better see why states prefer one versus the other. All other things being equal, states will more likely want a clear elaboration of existing international law, invoke hard law in response to a violation, and prefer hard law over norms as a future governance strategy if they seek a more predictable, verifiable, sticky, and enforceable regulatory framework to advance their interests in cybersecurity. If they want to keep their options open, they will be less likely to do all of those, and prefer norms over law. But the hard law/soft law literature does not explain why a state would choose to be expansive in characterizing the law *ex ante* and yet cautious in identifying legal violations *ex post*.

4. Constructivism would see the choices states make as both (a) grounded in their norm-generated identity (motivations); and (b) contributing to a norm cascade with respect to new norms (effects). Thus, the views of the Western states regarding cybersecurity, *ex ante* and *ex post*, originate in their identity-based commitments to the free flow of ideas; and those of China, Russia, and others in their attachment to the norm of state control over information. Constructivism would also see the ongoing claims as potentially leading to the creation of new norms. For instance, certain norms proposed in the GGE 2015 report, the Paris Call, and the GCSC Singapore package, for example, due diligence regarding private actors or nonuse of cyberattacks against critical infrastructure, may be on the cusp of a cascade (although constructivism tends to be backward-looking rather than predictive). Constructivism does not, however, offer much explanatory punch on the motivations for or effects of invoking law versus norms (*ex ante* or *ex post*) because it generally downplays the distinctions between them.

5. Thus, the phased nature of legal argumentation over cyberspace is an aspect of argumentation that requires more theoretical consideration. Even where norms are not so contested, we may see two phases of argumentation, such as in human rights law or IHL. One input into the compliance-based model seems particularly important for understanding how law invocation works in the different phases, namely, the *venue* for argumentation. The *ex ante* phase often involves claims to a centralized body like the GGE, where states try to shape the law through a process leading to a consensus-based document. Diplomats are face to face in trying to craft a common position about the application and meaning of existing law and the need for new norms or rules.

[92] Steven R. Ratner, "Persuading to Comply: On the Deployment and Avoidance of Legal Argumentation," in *Interdisciplinary Perspectives on International Law and International Relations*, *supra* note 56, at 568, 571–572.

Politically sophisticated actors will shape their message with that audience in mind.[93] And the result (effect) will be a compromise document, one that glosses over many interpretive differences (like the GGE reports). (Some *ex ante* claims are not part of a centralized process, for example, individual cybersecurity strategies issued by states, or speeches by senior officials. When they are not working toward a common goal, they can afford to be more detailed in their claims, but also less compromising.)

On the other hand, a statement in response to a violation, at the *ex post* phase, is not part of a face-to-face, consensus-driven process.[94] Like most protests, the *ex post* response is both directed at one state and directed at all states, as well as domestic audiences. The claiming state might be sure that the immediate target gets the message—by, for example, delivering it directly to its ambassador or foreign ministry, or if it really wants to be clear, by accompanying the message with an actual cyber-response. But it cannot gauge the effects on the broader community of states or domestic constituencies. (If states wish to coordinate a collective *ex post* response, an additional layer of persuasion takes place among the responding states.)

6. Theories of compliance or argumentation should also take more account of the levels of persuasion. In particular, at each level of persuasion, we see an outcome whereby states are conveying (whether intended or not) something important and distinct about *international law itself*. A statement at the first and second levels that international law's rules prohibit, permit, or require a certain kind of conduct—including identifying a violation *ex post*—reaffirms the *relevance* of international law as a regulatory framework. States are saying that the system has rules, and that they need to be followed. A claim that a body of international law does not apply, or that only non-binding norms apply, is a statement that the law is somehow inadequate. Legal or non-legal argumentation at the first and second levels thus has a sort of constitutive or existential effect—international law governs because states think it governs. This effect is not surprising as a doctrinal matter, for international law is mostly based on consent, but signaling to other actors of its adequacy or inadequacy matters for how we think about international law's relevance.[95]

As for the third level, a state's assertion of a need for law versus norms is not only, as hard/soft law theory points out, a reflection of state's preferences to lock in certain rules, but a statement about international law's *potential* to govern an issue. When the United Kingdom, or even Microsoft, calls for more legal rules, it is a statement of faith in international law. When the GGE or the GCSC emphasizes the need for new norms, they offer a message in favor of some constraints on future conduct, but they ultimately see law as the wrong route to follow. To get a sense of the consequences for international law, one might imagine if, at the time of the drafting of the UN Charter, states left out Article 2(4) and instead included a political declaration, or a preambular paragraph, about the undesirability of the use of force in international relations. That

93 See generally Ian Johnstone, *The Power of Deliberation: International Law, Politics, and International Organizations* (Oxford: Oxford University Press, 2011) (concerning the Security Council).

94 At the same time, some venues are designed for *ex post* responses, notably the UN Security Council, as discussed by Bruno Stagno-Ugarte, chapter 8, and Scott P. Sheeran, chapter 4, both in this volume.

95 A point also made by Monica Hakimi, chapter 3, in this volume.

message would reflect their own interests, but it would also be a setback for law as a firm constraint on state behavior.

7. Lastly, as for the argumentation strategies of non-state actors, constructivism helps isolate their role in the creation of norms and norm cascades; some of the key non-state actors, like Microsoft or the GCSC, qualify as norm entrepreneurs. But in the case of cybersecurity, the Tallinn experts, who do not quite fit the label of norm entrepreneur, have also proved relevant insofar as some governments have felt obliged to disagree with them in public statements. While the composition or candor of the Tallinn experts has elicited criticism, many other experts and expert bodies, such as UN special rapporteurs or treaty bodies, seem accepted without criticism. All experts invoke law as part of a process of persuasion, often making expansive claims that international law already offers rules governing particular conduct. In that context, scholars of international law and international relations scholars can do more to develop tools for evaluating the legitimate roles of experts and other non-state actors in persuading states about current and future law.

7

Nuclear Non-Proliferation Law

Why Argue and to What Effect?

Ian Johnstone

I. Introduction

Legal argumentation outside of courts occurs among a multitude of actors in a multiplicity of settings. Legal advisers to foreign ministries are key players, but politicians, diplomats, bureaucrats, academics, businesses, and organs of civil society are also involved. It occurs at the inter-state level, either in intergovernmental organizations or directly through bilateral exchanges and unilateral statements. It is also prevalent at the domestic level, in political debates, through the workings of interagency processes, and in the broader public discourse. The legal claims and counterclaims may be either explicit, through the interpretation of legal texts, or implicit through policy proposals and actions.

As I aim to demonstrate in this chapter, the management of nuclear non-proliferation is affected by a diffuse discursive process, centered on the Treaty on the Non-Proliferation of Nuclear Weapons (NPT). At the international level, the discourse takes place partly in formal institutions (like the UN Security Council, the International Atomic Energy Agency, and the NPT five-yearly review conferences), partly in informal institutions (like the Nuclear Suppliers Group and the Nuclear Security Summits), and partly in diplomatic conversation where actions are justified, explained, critiqued, and condemned in legal terms. It also occurs at the domestic level and in formal institutions (such as legislatures and executive branch decision-making fora) but also through think-tank analyses, in academic conferences, and in opinion pieces of major media outlets.

This chapter focuses on treaty law and views legal argumentation as an intersubjective activity, underpinned by the principle of consent. Parties to a treaty have committed, at least rhetorically, to treat the legal instrument as a shared frame of reference. Those engaged in interpretation feel compelled to proffer arguments that resonate with the other parties to the legal instrument, based on a broadly shared understanding of the enterprise in which the instrument is encountered. This is what enables them to speak to rather than past each other.

An advantage of focusing on treaty law as opposed to custom or general principles of law is that, when arguments about the meaning of a treaty term arise, there is

Ian Johnstone, *Nuclear Non-Proliferation Law* In: *Talking International Law*. Edited by: Ian Johnstone and Steven Ratner, Oxford University Press. © Ian Johnstone 2021. DOI: 10.1093/oso/9780197588437.003.0007

little doubt that the arguments are about "law."[1] Moreover, they are usually tied to a relatively straightforward question of compliance, the sort of question that—at the domestic level—would normally be resolved in a court. Yet, as we shall see, arguments about compliance often spill over into other kinds of legal arguments: What is the nature of the obligation, in what venue is the matter properly discussed, does existing law cover the situation, is new law needed?

From that theoretical starting point, I turn to an analysis of two NPT articles. The first is Article IV, which stipulates an "inalienable right" to peaceful nuclear energy. This was at issue when proposals for international control of the nuclear fuel were being debated. It has also been a critical source of contention in the Iran case. The second is the obligation in Article VI for all parties "to pursue negotiations in good faith" on disarmament. Whether nuclear state parties to the NPT have fulfilled that obligation has been a long-standing source of debate. It also been a focal point in argumentation about the merits of the Treaty on the Prohibition of Nuclear Weapons. I consider several possible reasons why states have engaged in extensive legal argumentation about those provisions in nonjudicial settings. These include: persuasion, to convince another actor of the validity of a legal claim; for strategic reasons, to gain the support of allies and neutralize adversaries; or to stake out the moral high ground and affirm one's identity as "law-abiding." I also consider the effects of legal argumentation. I find evidence that argumentation about compliance can lead to new law or, at a minimum, impacts the normative climate in which future argumentation occurs.

II. A Theoretical Perspective

This chapter, unlike some of the other chapters in this volume, employs a narrow conception of legal argumentation—namely, an argument that explicitly invokes traditional sources of law, employs the standard techniques of interpretation, and seeks to determine whether behavior is consistent with the law. Thus my starting point is that legal argumentation is mainly about compliance, and it occurs because law requires interpretation, a core feature—perhaps *the* core feature—of all law.[2] Many legal disputes are decided in tribunals, and recent years have seen the "judicialization" of international law.[3] Yet most international legal disputes never get to court. Rather they play out in a discursive process that occurs in formal and informal settings. The principal participants in this legal discourse are the representatives of governments, but officials of international organizations and nongovernmental actors also play a role. Some members of the legal "interpretive community"[4] are lawyers; many are not.

[1] The nuclear non-proliferation field is in some ways the polar opposite of the cybersecurity field addressed by Steven Ratner, chapter 6 in this volume, in the sense that there is a fairly dense body of law.

[2] Ronald Dworkin, "Law as Interpretation," *Texas Law Review* 2 (1982): 527. See also Cass Sunstein, *Legal Reasoning and Political Conflict* (New York: Oxford University Press, 1996), 167.

[3] Karen Alter, *The New Terrain of International Law: Courts, Politics and Rights* (Princeton: Princeton University Press, 2014); Cesare Romano, Karen Alter, and Yuval Shany, eds., *The Oxford Handbook on International Adjudication* (New York: Oxford University Press, 2014).

[4] See Johnstone and Ratner, chapter 1 of this volume. See also Ian Johnstone, *The Power of Deliberation: International Law, Politics and Organizations* (New York: Oxford University Press, 2011), ch. 3.

While legal argumentation tends to be mainly about compliance, there are other reasons for it.[5] In this chapter, I am especially interested in how argumentation about compliance can lead to the creation of new law. The line between interpreting existing law and making new law is blurry. Many treaties are open-textured, the "ordinary meaning" of which is not self-evident and whose application to new fact situations is not a technical exercise. Interpretation of disputed terms can give content to inchoate norms.[6] It may even be "constitutive of international law."[7]

As the cases I explore demonstrate, argumentation about compliance can lead to the creation of new law in another way. The complicated terms of the Joint Comprehensive Program of Action (JCPOA) regarding Iran's nuclear program are partly the result of argumentation about the Article IV right to peaceful nuclear energy. Similarly, the Treaty on the Prohibition of Nuclear Weapons (TPNW) emerged from sharp differences of opinion about the requirements of Article VI of the NPT: those who support the TPNW see it as a step toward fulfilling the disarmament requirements of Article VI; those who oppose it see it as contrary to the article. Moreover, both the TPNW and the JCPOA can be seen as extensions of legal argumentation about the NPT. In that sense, they are legal arguments in themselves.

A. Motives and Effects

As noted above, a number of motives for legal argumentation can be posited. The first is to actually *persuade* others of the correctness of one's argument.[8] In terms of Jürgen Habermas's theory of communicative action, this is sincere argumentation, in which the speaker seeks to persuade and is open to persuasion. The second is *strategic*.[9] Legal arguments are deployed for instrumental reasons, for example, to gain the support of allies or neutralize adversaries. Whether the listener is actually persuaded of the merits of the argument is secondary; it is enough that a strong legal case will make it easier for the ally to support the course of action than if the action were widely perceived to be in violation of the law.[10] A third possible purpose of legal argumentation

[5] It is worth noting that none of the chapters in this volume view legal argumentation as mere "cheap talk," with no real impact on the conduct of international affairs. See Jack L. Goldsmith and Eric A. Posner, *The Limits of International Law* (New York: Oxford University Press, 2005), ch. 6.

[6] Duncan Hollis makes a related point when he speaks of "existential interpretation," which validates the existence of a rule by deciding whether it even counts as law. Duncan Hollis, "The Existential Function of Interpretation in International Law," in *Interpretation in International Law*, edited by Andrea Bianchi, Daniel Peat, and Matthew Windsor (Oxford: Oxford University Press, 2015), 79.

[7] Jean d'Aspremont, "The Multidimensional Process of Interpretation: Content-determination and Law-Ascertainment Distinguished," in *Interpretation in International Law*, *supra* note 6, at 113; Jean d'Aspremont, *Epistemic Forces in International Law: Foundational Doctrines and Techniques of International Legal Argumentation* (Cheltenham, UK: Elgar International Law, 2015). See also Ingo Venzke, *How Interpretation Makes International Law* (Oxford: Oxford University Press, 2012).

[8] Steven R. Ratner, "Persuading to Comply: On the Deployment and Avoidance of Legal Argumentation," in *Interdisciplinary Perspectives on International Law and International Relations: The State of the Art*, edited by Jeffrey L. Dunoff and Mark A. Pollack (New York: Cambridge University Press, 2013), 577–578.

[9] Jon Elster, "The Strategic Uses of Argument," in *Barriers to Conflict Resolution*, edited by Kenneth Arrow et al. (New York: W.W. Norton, 1995), 249; Adam Bower, "Arguing with Law: Strategic Legal Argumentation, US Diplomacy and Debates over the ICC," *Review of International Studies* 41 (2015): 337.

[10] As Monica Hakimi argues in chapter 3, in this volume, a good deal of legal argumentation occurs without any real prospect of persuading one's adversaries.

is to affirm one's *identity* as a law-abiding global citizen, behaving in a manner that is expected by one's domestic constituency or global referent group.[11] Unlike strategic argumentation, which is explained by rational choice theory and the logic of consequences, identity-driven argumentation is associated with social constructivism and the logic of appropriateness. A more critical perspective sees legal argumentation as a way of *masking* the political choices being made by powerful actors. To argue that the law requires (or prevents) a course of action is a way for hegemons to advance their goals in a seemingly neutral way, maintaining the fiction that the law applies to all equally and that all are equal under the law.

For all of those purposes, the principal audience for the legal argumentation is other governments—allies, adversaries, or those in between (neutrals). If the purpose is persuasion, neutrals are the most likely target, because allies probably do not need to be persuaded and adversaries are not likely to be won over by a good argument. If the purpose is strategic, all three could be the target: allies and neutrals who need a good excuse to join the cause; adversaries, whose support among other countries needs to be undercut. The need to win or undercut support shows that, in addition to government officials, public opinion may be a target. If, for example, Japan is pressured by the United States to *not* join the TPNW, the Japanese public may need to be persuaded that staying out of the nuclear ban treaty is consistent with the NPT. Domestic public opinion is also an audience for identity-based arguments. Japan's position on nuclear weapons is wrapped up in its identity as a pacifist country that suffered through Hiroshima and Nagasaki. Legal arguments about the NPT or TPNW may be designed to reinforce, or transform, that identity.

What motivates a state to deploy a legal argument in a particular situation is hard to discern, though not necessarily impossible. Easier to discern—though still at times elusive—is the effect. Regardless of motives, legal argumentation has the potential to change the normative climate and therefore the politics that surround a regime. It may happen suddenly, if, for example, a tipping point is reached; or it may occur over time as the terms of debate change and behavior shifts incrementally. A changed normative climate is one in which the boundaries of what is considered proper behavior for actors with a given identity has moved.[12] Sometimes the argumentation can cause hard norms to soften. More often, the movement is in the opposite direction: the argumentation causes soft law to harden. The flow tends to be from soft to hard because the argumentation itself is tacit acknowledgment that there are rules and that they apply to all parties engaged in the argumentation.[13] This is true regardless of whether

[11] On the notion of status and referent groups, see Alistair Iain Johnston, "Treating Institutions as Social Environments," *International Studies Quarterly* 45 (2001): 487; Courtney Fung, *China and Intervention in the UN Security Council* (Oxford: Oxford University Press, 2019). Fung draws on the work of Paul Larson and William Wohlforth, *Status and World Order* (Cambridge: Cambridge University Press, 2014).

[12] Peter Katzenstein, "Introduction: Alternative Perspectives on National Security," in *The Culture of National Security*, edited by Peter Katzenstein (New York: Columbia University Press, 1996), 5; Martha Finnemore and Kathryn Sikkink, "International Norm Dynamics and Political Change," *International Organization* 52 (1998): 887.

[13] Kate Shaw made a similar point in explaining the value of the Trump impeachment proceedings being fought using the language of law: "The Trump administration has shown little interest in adhering to settled norms and practices of governance; indeed, it has frequently evinced contempt for institutions that might serve as rivals or act as genuine checks on the president. But to the extent that the president's lawyers choose to make their arguments for the rest of the trial in mostly legal terms, they will be acceding to the

the arguments are genuine, strategic or hypocritical. As François de La Rochefoucauld famously said, "hypocrisy is the homage vice pays to virtue." There is an important difference between saying "the rules don't matter" and saying "the rules matter and, as I interpret them, I am complying—you are not."

B. Legal Argumentation as an Intersubjective Activity

Legal argumentation is distinct from other forms of argumentation (such as moral discourse, political discourse, or appeals to emotion) because international law, in principle, is the product of agreement among those bound by it. It is not necessarily more powerful, but it has an intersubjective quality that does not exist in those other forms. To call legal argumentation an intersubjective activity means that those engaged in it are committed, at least implicitly, to making arguments that resonate with other parties to the legal instrument—even if they disagree with the substance of the arguments. Arguments are understood as relevant (or resonate) when they are founded in a broadly shared view of the nature of the enterprise in which the instrument is encountered. The enterprise may be as broad as "the maintenance of international peace and security" (if the text is a UN Security Council resolution) or "protecting the inherent dignity of the human person" (if the text is a human rights treaty) or "limiting the spread of nuclear weapons" (if the text is the NPT). It is that shared understanding that renders reasoned discourse—argumentation—possible. Otherwise the whole idea of arguing would be nonsensical. Why argue about how to interpret the law if the assumption is that interpretation is entirely subjective, the law means whatever the interpreter says it means? Conversely, if the law has some inherent, "objective" meaning, why would legal argumentation occur at all? Could the meaning not simply be extracted from the text?[14]

This understanding of legal discourse, when applied to treaty law, is saying nothing more (or less) than that in signing and ratifying a treaty, states have consented to treating it as a shared frame of reference.[15] It is not saying that the arguers share common values, let alone that they have equal power, capabilities, or expertise. Nor is it saying they agree on what each treaty term means at the time of adoption.[16] Rather, the legal argumentation is a signal to one's interlocutor: "I accept that we are bound by this set of rules and, while we may disagree about what the rules require, I am willing to live by them and expect you to do the same. So, bearing in mind why we agreed to those rules in the first place, let's talk about what they mean." In an intersubjective approach to interpretation, the search for meaning is neither purely subjective, nor

requirements of the institutional setting in which they are operating. And in doing so they will be implicitly acknowledging that the rules do apply to the president and his surrogates, and that law continues to matter." Kate Shaw, "Will Trump's Defenders Pass the Test of Legitimacy?," *New York Times*, Jan. 28, 2020.

[14] Stanley Fish makes this point about literary interpretation. Stanley Fish, *Is There a Text in this Class? The Authority of Interpretive Communities* (Cambridge: Harvard University Press, 1980).

[15] I am grateful to Ingo Venzke for this point.

[16] Many treaties, especially multilateral treaties, are "disagreements reduced to writing." Philip Allot, "The Concept of International Law," *European Journal of International Law* 10 (1999): 31.

purely objective, but a collectively meaningful activity.[17] That being said, the notion of equal, freely given consent is problematic. Often states are under great pressure to adopt a treaty (for example, a peace agreement) and have little choice but to consent. Moreover, materially powerful states can make the choice to join a treaty more freely than weaker states—they have options. Nevertheless, as a matter of international legal theory, consent matters.[18]

C. Legal Argumentation as a Structured Activity

Legal interpretation is not only intersubjective, it is highly structured, much more so than literary interpretation,[19] the practice of diplomacy,[20] or security relations.[21] There are widely shared understandings and expectations about the relevant sources, processes, and argumentative techniques that characterize the international legal enterprise. As noted in the introduction to this volume, engaging in legal argumentation is inherently confrontational, but there are two ways of looking at the confrontation—as a battleground or as a bridge. Either way, the discursive process is dynamic and iterative. Those who engage in it may have different motives for doing so, and they may or may not achieve what they hoped. The legal argumentation may be triggered by an incident, such as the US withdrawal from the Iran nuclear deal. Or the discourse could be built into a structural feature of the regime, such as the five-yearly review conferences of the NPT. In all cases, it is not a semantic free-for-all: those who are most effective display competence or "know-how" in the "practice" of legal argument.[22]

III. The Nuclear Non-Proliferation Regime

A. The NPT

The nuclear non-proliferation regime is composed of a dense web of multilateral treaties and institutional arrangements designed to prevent the spread of nuclear weapons, as well as their delivery systems. The NPT is the centerpiece of the regime.

[17] See Johnstone and Ratner, chapter 1 in this volume. Gerald Postema draws an analogy to friendship: "The history of a friendship is a common history and the complex meaning of the relationship is collectively constructed [by the friends] over the course of the history.... To regard the meaning of that relationship as the private interpretive construct of one or the other, or some ideal of such constructs, fails to recognize the common perspective and discourse which structure the relationship." Gerald Postema, "'Protestant' Interpretation and Social Practices,'" *Law and Philosophy* 6 (1987): 283, 309–310.

[18] Samantha Besson, "State Consent and Disagreement in International Law-Making: Dissolving the Paradox," *Leiden Journal of International Law* 29 (2016): 289; Duncan Hollis, "Why Consent Still Matters—Non-State Actors, Treaties and Changing Sources of International Law," *Berkeley Journal of International Law* 23 (2005): 137.

[19] Fish, *supra* note 14.

[20] Ivor Neumann, "Returning Practice to the Linguistic Turn," *Millennium* 31 (2002): 627.

[21] Emanual Adler, "The Spread of Security Communities: Communities of Practice, Self-Restraint and NATO's Post-Cold War Transformation," *European Journal of International Relations* 15 (2008): 195.

[22] On "practice theory," see Johnstone and Ratner, chapter 1 in this volume.

It has been supplemented by an array of other legal instruments and institutional arrangements. Some of these instruments are the product of legal argumentation about NPT norms and themselves have become the subject of legal argumentation.

Adopted in 1968 and in force since 1970, the NPT currently has 189 adherents, including all five declared nuclear weapon states: China, France, Russia, the United Kingdom, and the United States. The only countries that are not parties are India, Israel, and Pakistan. North Korea announced its withdrawal in 2003, but that has never been formally accepted by the depositories (the United States, the United Kingdom, and Russia) or the International Atomic Energy Agency (IAEA). The NPT has two types of parties: nuclear weapons states (NWS) and non-nuclear weapon states (NNWS). The main obligation on the non-nuclear powers is to not acquire, manufacture, or possess such weapons and to accept a system of IAEA safeguards on all peaceful nuclear activities. The nuclear powers in turn commit not to transfer nuclear weapons or devices to any recipient, while agreeing to assist in the peaceful development of nuclear energy by sharing nuclear equipment, materials, and technology. To further balance the equation between nuclear haves and have-nots, the former undertake to pursue negotiations in good faith toward nuclear disarmament. Thus there are three pillars of the NPT: non-proliferation (embodied in Articles I–III), peaceful nuclear energy (embodied in Articles IV and V), and disarmament (Article VI). Virtually every one of these articles has been the subject of interpretive disagreements and thus legal argumentation.[23]

B. Venues for Legal Argumentation about Non-Proliferation

These debates occur in a variety of settings. One is the IAEA, whose twin aims are to promote the safe use of nuclear power and ensure that any nuclear assistance is not used to further a military purpose. The second goal is realized through a system of safeguards, spelled out in an agreement the IAEA reaches with each NPT party. The system is designed to deter the diversion or theft of "significant quantity" of nuclear materials (defined as enough to make one crude bomb) through the threat of early detection and public exposure. Because the IAEA failed to detect Iraq's clandestine nuclear program before 1991, its board of governors endorsed more vigorous safeguards, now embodied in an Additional Protocol, giving the IAEA authority to inspect countries for undeclared nuclear facilities.

Enforcement of the NPT, like the treaties on the proliferation of chemical and biological weapons, occurs through the UN Security Council. The basic authority of the Council stems from its general powers conferred in the UN Charter, especially those under Chapter VII. Most but not all proliferation matters get to the Security Council through the IAEA, whose board of governors *must* report violations of safeguards agreements to the Council. The Security Council has used its enforcement powers to condemn nuclear tests by India and Pakistan, to impose a comprehensive disarmament regime on Iraq in the aftermath of its invasion of Kuwait, to impose

[23] For a summary of some of the debates, see Johnstone, *supra* note 4, at 116–122. For a fuller analysis, see Daniel Joyner, *Interpreting the Nuclear Non-Proliferation Treaty* (New York: Oxford University Press, 2011).

sanctions on North Korea and Iran, and to adopt Resolution 1540 in 2004, designed to stop weapons of mass destruction from falling in the hands of terrorists. The Council has also adopted a number of thematic resolutions on non-proliferation and disarmament.[24]

Another key institution in the regime is the NPT conferences that occur every five years to "review the operation of this Treaty with a view to assuring that [its] purposes are being realized" (Article VIII). These review conferences have become a critical venue for argumentation about the treaty. They often conclude with consensus statements. At the 2000 review conference, thirteen "practical steps" toward implementation of Article VI of the NPT were agreed to—including "urgent" ratification of the Comprehensive Test Ban Treaty and an "unequivocal undertaking" to accomplish the total elimination of nuclear weapons. The political atmosphere had soured by 2005, and no substantial declaration came out of that review conference. The atmosphere improved with US President Barack Obama's election in 2008, setting the stage for a relatively successful 2010 review conference. The final document that year included specific action plans on non-proliferation, disarmament, and peaceful uses of nuclear energy. It also proposed steps for implementing a 1995 resolution calling for a weapons of mass destruction free zone (WMDFZ) in the Middle East. Between 2010 and 2015, the atmosphere turned sour again, and the 2015 review conference failed to produce a consensus outcome document with any substance.

The nuclear non-proliferation regime includes a number of other elements: five regional nuclear weapons free zones; test ban treaties; an International Court of Justice (ICJ) Advisory Opinion on the Legality of the Threat or Use of Nuclear Weapons;[25] the Nuclear Suppliers Group, a cartel of suppliers of nuclear material, reactors, equipment, and technology; the Proliferation Security Initiative; and a variety of initiatives to address the threat of nuclear terrorism.[26]

To summarize, nuclear non-proliferation is a complex regime with elements that range from hard to soft law and from formal institutions to informal arrangements. At the time of writing, it was not in good shape. Divisions over how to manage North Korea's and Iran's nuclear programs remained high, and the risk of further proliferation was palpable. When Iran hinted that it could withdraw from the NPT,[27] Crown Prince Mohamed Bin Salman said Saudi Arabia would follow suit.[28] US-Russia arms control agreements were on shaky ground. The 2020 NPT review conference (postponed until 2021 due to COVID-19) was headed for failure. These and other developments were symptomatic of a polarized geopolitical atmosphere that generated legal fireworks in all the formal and informal institutions associated with the NPT, to which I now turn.

[24] SC Res. 984 (Apr. 11, 1995); SC Res. 1887 (Sept. 24, 2009); SC Res. 2310 (Sept. 23, 2016).

[25] The ICJ has also been involved in a number of contentious proceedings, but none got to the merits.

[26] Four nuclear security summits from 2010 to 2016; the Cooperative Threat Reduction (the Nunn-Lugar) program, which expanded into the Global Partnership against the Spread of Weapons and Material of Mass Destruction; and the Global Initiative to Combat Nuclear Terrorism.

[27] Iran first hinted at that in April 2018 and repeated the threat in May 2019, https://www.reuters.com/article/us-iran-nuclear-rouhani/iran-warns-trump-it-might-withdraw-from-non-proliferation-treaty-idUSKBN1HV0MY.

[28] https://www.aljazeera.com/programmes/insidestory/2019/04/saudi-arabia-nuclear-190404212819023.html.

IV. Article IV of the NPT: The Nuclear Fuel Cycle and Iran

Article IV of the NPT reads as follows:

1. Nothing in this Treaty shall be interpreted as affecting the inalienable right of all the Parties to the Treaty to develop research, production and use of nuclear energy for peaceful purposes without discrimination and in conformity with Articles I and II of this Treaty.
2. All the Parties to the Treaty undertake to facilitate, and have the right to participate in, the fullest possible exchange of equipment, materials and scientific and technological information for the peaceful uses of nuclear energy . . .

The article falls on the "hard" end of the spectrum of soft to hard law.[29] It is relatively precise, its obligatory nature is clear, and it engages third-party oversight by the IAEA. Yet there has been no shortage of debate over interpretation of Article IV. For our purposes, the practical issue at stake can be stated succinctly: Does "the inalienable right" to peaceful nuclear energy include the right to enrich uranium or to reprocess spent fuel to obtain plutonium? The facilities that are used to produce low enriched uranium for nuclear power plants can also be used to produce highly enriched uranium for bombs. Similarly, plutonium can be used for both power plants and bombs. The policy dilemma is clear. A permissive reading of Article IV would enable NPT parties to get close to the threshold of being able to build a bomb and then withdraw from the treaty. A restrictive reading would deny NNWS the indigenous capacity to build peaceful nuclear programs, gutting one limb of the "grand bargain."

For suppliers, the question is whether Article IV represents a commitment to facilitate and guarantee the right of NNWS to participate in *all* types of nuclear cooperation, or whether the suppliers have discretion to deny access to sensitive technology to countries of proliferation concern. If the "inalienable right" is interpreted *not* to include the right to enrich uranium or reprocess plutonium but simply access to peaceful nuclear energy, then Article IV can be satisfied by providing external sources of nuclear fuel. Alternatively, if the right to enrich or reprocess is interpreted to be conditional on Articles I, II, and III, then the Article IV issue comes down to whether an NPT party has violated one of those other obligations. If, alternatively again, the "inalienable right" is truly unconditional, then the legal issue comes down to *intention*: Is the state seeking to enrich uranium or reprocess fuel for peaceful purposes or to build a bomb?

The ambiguities in Article IV were apparent even to its drafters. The *travaux préparatoires* reveal that attempts to clarify the language were deliberately rebuffed by the United States and the Soviet Union.[30] This does not render Article IV

[29] Kenneth Abbott et al. "The Concept of Legalization," *International Organization* 54 (2000): 401. For an earlier iteration of "legalization" criteria, see W. Michael Reisman, "The Concept and Functions of Soft Law in International Politics," in *Essays in Honour of Judge Taslim Olawale Elias*, edited by Emanuel Bello and B.A. Ajibola (New York: Springer, 1992), 135.

[30] Zhang Xinjun, "The Riddle of the Inalienable Right," *Chinese Journal of International Law* 5 (2006): 647, 647.

uninterpretable, as Zhang Xinjun claims, but it does mean the ambiguity cannot be resolved by reference to the intent of the drafters because their intentions diverged.

A. International Control of the Nuclear Fuel Cycle

This debate played out in a generic way in 2004, when US President George W. Bush decried the "loophole" in the NPT that enabled states like North Korea and Iran to produce nuclear weapons material under cover of civilian nuclear programs.[31] He proposed that Nuclear Suppliers Group members refuse to sell enrichment and reprocessing equipment to any state that did not already have full-scale functioning enrichment and reprocessing plants, while promising that the world's leading nuclear exporters would ensure that states have "reliable access at reasonable costs to fuel for civilian reactors." The US representative to the 2004 PrepCom followed up by stating: "Under President Bush's proposals ... nations could use peaceful nuclear power as anticipated by the Treaty, but not to produce fissile material for nuclear weapons. *The Treaty provides no right to such sensitive fuel cycle technologies* [emphasis added]."[32] These statements represent an implicit interpretation that the "inalienable right" to peaceful nuclear energy in Article IV could be limited, in effect prioritizing non-proliferation over the other two pillars when it comes to interpreting ambiguous language.[33]

This implicit interpretation was followed by explicit interpretations by the United States and other NWS representatives at the 2005 NPT review conference. US delegate Stephen Rademaker said, "[T]he language of Article IV is explicit and unambiguous: states asserting their rights to receive the benefits of peaceful nuclear benefits must be in compliance with their obligations under Articles I and II of the NPT."[34] The French representative brought Article III into the equation by stating, "I wish to recall ... the conditions required to have the right to nuclear power within the meaning of Article IV of the Treaty, namely: compliance with the obligations to ensure non-proliferation and implement IAEA safeguards on the one hand; and the pursuit of 'peaceful purposes' on the other."[35] At the 2008 PrepCom for the 2010 review conference, the five NWS issued this joint statement:

[31] Remarks by President George W. Bush on Weapons of Mass Destruction Proliferation delivered at Fort Lesley J. McNair, Feb. 11, 2004.

[32] Statement by US Under Secretary of State for Arms Control and International Security John Bolton to the Third Session of the Preparatory Committee for the 2005 Review Conference of the NPT. "The NPT: A Crisis of Non-Compliance," New York, Apr. 27, 2004.

[33] Joyner, *supra* note 23, at 43.

[34] Statement by Stephen Rademaker, US Assistant Secretary of State for Arms Control to the 2005 Review Conference of the NPT, New York, May 2, 2005.

[35] Statement by François Rivasseau to the 2005 Review Conference of the NPT, May 5, 2005. See also statement of US Representative to the 2004 PrepCom for the 2005 NPT Review Conference, Andrew Semmel: "the inalienable right to develop nuclear energy is not an entitlement but rather flows from demonstrable and verifiable compliance with Articles I, II and III of the Treaty." Geneva, Switzerland, May 7, 2003.

> We welcome the work of the International Atomic Energy Agency on multilateral approaches to the nuclear fuel cycle and encourage efforts towards a multilateral mechanism to assure access for all countries to nuclear fuel services *as a viable alternative* to indigenous development of enrichment and processing [emphasis added].

Describing multilateral approaches to the fuel cycle as an "alternative" to indigenous capabilities is in effect a denial that the NNWS have the right to enrich and reprocess.

The idea for a multinational fuel bank came from IAEA Director-General Mohamed ElBaradei, who in 2005 called for a five-year moratorium on the creation of facilities for uranium enrichment and plutonium separation, pending creation of a mechanism whereby all sensitive fuel cycle facilities would be placed under international control. After several years of sharp debate on the issue, the IAEA board of governors finally approved the idea in November 2009, though not unanimously: eight countries were opposed, and three abstained. The debate was partially conducted on policy grounds (i.e., whether it was wise to allow all countries to develop this indigenous capacity), but the legal issue was prominent. Those in favor of ElBaradei's proposal claimed it was consistent with the NPT; those opposed argued that the arrangement could erode Article IV by inhibiting their right to develop their own nuclear fuel cycle.

The opposition of developing NNWS was expressed in other settings as well.[36] At the 2008 PrepCom, the Non-Aligned Movement (NAM) stated collectively: "Concerns related to nuclear non-proliferation should not in any way restrict the inalienable right of all states to develop all aspects of nuclear science and technology for peaceful purposes."[37] The representative of Egypt objected to attempts to "reinterpret Article IV in a manner that restricts the ability of NNWS to benefit from their rights by creating artificial categories of 'sensitive' and 'non-sensitive' nuclear technologies or 'responsible' and 'irresponsible' states."[38]

At the 2010 RevCon, the final document came down on the side of a permissive reading of Article IV. It stated that "nothing in the treaty shall be interpreted as affecting the inalienable right" to develop peaceful nuclear energy, and that "each country's choices and decisions should be respected, without jeopardizing its policies or international cooperation agreements" (para. 31). That was the end of debate about a multinational nuclear fuel cycle arrangement, but argumentation over Article IV continued in the particular context of Iran's nuclear program.

[36] At the 2010 NPT review conference, NAM states would not support any specific multinational fuel cycle proposal because they perceived the initiatives as challenging their "inalienable rights." See also Joyner, *supra* note 23, at 55–60, for an analysis the debates in NPT PrepComs and RevCon.

[37] Statement by the Delegation of the Republic of Indonesia on behalf of the Non-Aligned Group to the NPT at the Second Session of the Preparatory Committee for the 2010 NPT Review Conference on Cluster 3 issues, Apr. 28–May 9, 2008. See also Working Papers the NAM submitted to the 2019 PrepCom, NPT/CONF.2020/PC.III/WP.11, Mar. 21, 2019, and NPT/CONF.2020/PC.III/WP.18.

[38] *Id.*

B. The Joint Comprehensive Program of Action (JCPOA)

Iran never supported the idea of a multinational fuel bank, because that would be tantamount to conceding that it did not have the right to enrich uranium itself. Ever since the IAEA confirmed the existence of clandestine nuclear facilities in Natanz in February 2003, Iran has insisted on that right.[39] It did not waver on that in the twelve years of diplomacy and pressure (including Security Council sanctions) that led to the JCPOA, and it was a key point of contention in the negotiations. The JCPOA, finalized in July 2015, is a political commitment between Iran and the P5+1 (Germany).[40] It requires Iran to reduce its holdings of lightly enriched uranium by 98 percent for fifteen years (selling the excess to Russia). It is entitled to keep 2 percent but is prohibited from enriching that beyond 3.67 percent—nowhere near high enough to produce a bomb.[41] It must put two-thirds of its centrifuges in storage for ten years. And it must convert its plant in Arak to render it incapable of producing plutonium. Iran also agrees to abide by the IAEA Additional Protocol. In exchange, the P5+1 agree to lift multilateral and unilateral sanctions.

The JCPOA was endorsed by the Security Council in Resolution 2231 of 2015, which "calls upon" all states to take action commensurate with implementation of the plan. The resolution terminated the sanctions on Iran but includes a provision that if a participating state notifies the Security Council of nonperformance by another participant, the Security Council must vote on a draft resolution to *continue termination* of the sanctions. If the resolution does not pass, the old sanctions "snapback." The effect is that one of the P5 alone can use its veto power to trigger reimposition of the sanctions by blocking a resolution to keep the termination of the sanctions in place.

The positions of the key players in the negotiations can be summarized as follows: Iran insisted on the right to enrich; the United States insisted there was no such right; and the Europeans were somewhere in the middle.[42] In the moments of more constructive negotiations with the E3 (Germany, France, and the United Kingdom), Iran was amenable to making concessions on safeguards and other matters, but always in exchange for the European recognition of its Article IV rights. Thus in 2003, when the E3 visited Iran, Chief Negotiator Hassan Rouhani said he was willing to consider implementation of the Additional Protocol and to cooperate with the IAEA *if* the E3 accepted Iran's right to peaceful nuclear technology. Conversely, when in 2005 the European Union proposed that Iran commit not to pursue fuel cycle technologies for at least ten years and the E3 would provide access to fuel through third parties, newly elected President Mahmoud Ahmadinejad rejected it as a denial of Iran's right to enrich.[43]

[39] See generally Tarja Cronberg, *Nuclear Multilateralism and Iran: Inside EU Negotiations* (Abingdon on Thames: Routledge, 2017).

[40] It was not put in the form of a legally binding agreement because neither the United States nor Iran would have been able to get legislative support for ratification of a treaty.

[41] Before the 2015 deal was reached, Iran produced uranium enriched to 20 percent, a fraction of the 90 percent needed for nuclear weapons.

[42] Cronberg herself participated in the negotiations. Cronberg, *supra* note 39, at 1 and 53.

[43] *Id.* 27.

For the United States, on the other hand, uranium enrichment by Iran was a red line. While there was no proof that Iran had produced fissile material or diverted fuel to military purposes, the George W. Bush administration saw enrichment as evidence of Iran's military intentions.[44] The Obama administration loosened the rigid "zero enrichment" policy but never explicitly accepted that Iran had a right to enrich. The E3 took a more nuanced position, arguing that Iran had forfeited its right to enrich by failing to fully report its nuclear activities to the IAEA, implying it could reclaim the right if it came back into compliance with its safeguards obligations.[45] Together, they persuaded the Security Council to impose sanctions and demand that Iran suspend its enrichment activities.

In the end, the JCPOA itself fudged the issue, allowing both sides to maintain their positions of principle. The agreement does not include a specific reference to the "right to enrich." Instead, it speaks of "the right to peaceful use of nuclear technology," enabling the United States to avoid conceding that right. But because it allows some enrichment, Iran could claim the JCPOA validated its position that Iran has the right to enrich under the NPT.[46]

The story did not end there. US President Trump renounced the JCPOA in May 2018. He claimed Iran was not in compliance "with the spirit of the deal," though he never charged Iran with violating its letter.[47] He added other complaints, unrelated to the deal, calling Iran a "fanatical," "radical" regime, that supports terrorism, foments instability in the Middle East, and "spreads death, destruction and chaos."[48] He branded the nuclear deal "one of the worst and most one-sided in US history," which would allow Iran to "sprint to nuclear weapons" when the restrictions end in ten or fifteen years. The new deal the Trump administration called for in 2019 would have covered Iran's ballistic missile program, alleged support for terrorism, regional behavior, and foreign hostages, as well as the nuclear program, suggesting Trump was more concerned with Iran's overall behavior than its nuclear program per se.[49] NPT Article IV did not factor heavily into the renunciation because Trump was more intent on condemning the deal as an Obama travesty than delving into legal niceties.

Iran's first reaction to the US renunciation was to insist on full compliance by all. A year later it announced that it would enrich uranium to 5 percent, higher than the 3.67 percent agreed to in the JCPOA. It said it would continue to reduce its commitments to the deal every sixty days unless Britain, France, Germany, China, and Russia provide sanctions relief.[50] This culminated in a decision by Iran in January 2021 to

[44] *Id.* 53. The US position was articulated in various settings, including the 2008 NPT PrepCom and the 2010 RevCon.

[45] *Id.* 54.

[46] Statement by General Hassan Firouzabadi, Aug. 9, 2015, quoted in *id.* 55.

[47] Others, including Secretary of State Rex Tillerson and Secretary of Defence James Mattis, said Iran had not violated the terms of the deal. See, e.g., "Mattis Says Iran 'Fundamentally' in Compliance with Nuclear Deal," *Reuters*, Oct. 3, 2017, https://www.reuters.com/article/us-usa-iran-nuclear/mattis-says-iran-fundamentally-in-compliance-with-nuclear-deal-idUSKCN1C82GK.

[48] White House, "Remarks by President Trump on Iran Strategy," Oct. 13, 2017, https://trumpwhitehouse.archives.gov/articles/president-trump-announces-iran-strategy/.

[49] US Working Paper, "The US Approach to the 2019 Preparatory committee Meeting," NPT/CONF.2020/PC.III/WP41, Apr. 26, 2019.

[50] "Iran Nuclear Deal: Government Announces Enrichment Breach," *BBC*, July 7, 2019, https://www.bbc.com/news/world-middle-east-48899243. In May, President Hassan Rouhani had delivered a televised speech announcing Iran would no longer abide by limits on its stockpiles of low enriched uranium and of

enrich uranium to 20 percent, well above the agreed limit but well short of the 90 percent required to build a bomb. It also made the JCPOA a topic of conversation at the 2018 and 2019 PrepComs, claiming the United States was in breach of its NPT Article IV obligations by reimposing sanctions.[51] And it lobbied hard to delete language in the consensus recommendations that were meant to come out of the 2019 PrepCom on the importance of Iran's compliance with the JCPOA, after several countries objected to calling only on Iran to implement the deal and not the United States. Instead, the draft noted the strong support for the continued implementation of the deal and added a reference to Security Council Resolution 2231.[52]

The denouement was the failed effort of the Trump administration to invoke the sanctions "snapback" provision in Resolution 2231. Paragraph 11 allows a single "JCPOA participant" to trigger reimposition of the sanctions. Despite having withdrawn from the JCPOA, the United States claimed it was still a "participant" in the deal and therefore could invoke the snapback. Virtually every other member of the Council disagreed. Nevertheless, when no new resolution was adopted to continue termination of the sanctions, the United States claimed they were back on and warned other nations to comply.[53] That was greeted with a collective shrug not only by the Council but by the UN membership as a whole.[54] This is a good example of bad legal argumentation whose only effect was to put President Trump's clumsy unilateralism on display and to complicate the ability of President Joe Biden to negotiate with Iran on returning to the original terms of the deal.[55]

C. Arguing about Article IV: Purposes and Effects

It is hard to state with certainty what motivated any of the protagonists to engage in legal argumentation about either the nuclear fuel cycle or the JCPOA. But inferences can be drawn from the circumstances. In the generic debates on the nuclear fuel cycle,

heavy water; could resume construction on the unfinished Arak nuclear reactor; and could resume uranium enrichment to levels above the 3.67 level allowed by the JCPOA. Alicia Sanders-Zakre, "NPT Looks Ahead to 2020 Review Conference Without Consensus Recommendations," Arms Control Association, May 10, 2019.

[51] James Martin Center for Nonproliferation Studies, "Daily Summaries of NPT PrepCom 2019," Day 6–7 and right of reply, https://nonproliferation.org/npt-prepcom-2019-live-cns-updates/#summaries. At both PrepComs Iran submitted lengthy working papers that implicitly criticized the US sanctions as a violation of Article IV. See NPT/CONF.2020/PCII./WP/25, Apr. 9, 2018; and NPT/CONF.2020/PC.III/WP.3, Mar. 14, 2019.

[52] Sanders-Zakre, *supra* note 50.

[53] For statements made by President Donald Trump, Secretary Mike Pompeo, and the Treasury Department, see United States Institute for Peace, "The Iran Primer: US Snapback Sanctions Go into Force," Sept. 21, 2020. https://iranprimer.usip.org/blog/2020/sep/21/us-snapback-sanctions-go-force-0.

[54] Lara Jakes and David Sanger, "Instead of Isolating Iran, US Finds Itself on the Outside over Nuclear Deal," *New York Times*, Sept. 2, 2020. An earlier draft resolution by the United States to extend the arms embargo against Iran lost in the Security Council by a vote of 2 in favor (the United States and the Dominican Republic), 2 against (China and Russia), and 11 abstentions (including France, Germany, and the United Kingdom).

[55] Thomas Pickering, "The US 'Snapback' Against Iran—Bad Politics and Flawed Law," *Just Security*, Sept. 28, 2020, https://www.justsecurity.org/72591/the-us-snapback-against-iran-bad-politics-and-flawed-law/.

the United States, Russia, and the IAEA Director-General were all on the same side. It is conceivable that they were hoping to *persuade* others to accept their interpretation of Article IV—not Iran, perhaps, but other members of the IAEA Board of Governors and participants in the NPT review conference. It was an issue on which reasonable arguments could be made on all sides, and many states had a stake in the outcome. This tells us something about the distinctive power of legal argumentation over pure policy arguments. The geopolitical stakes were high, and the world's two most militarily powerful states were in agreement. And yet simply asserting their policy preferences, even if cast as serving the greater good of non-proliferation, was not likely to persuade the IAEA Director-General to join the cause nor states that may someday want to develop a nuclear energy program, let alone Iran. By addressing the legal issue head on—and proposing a mechanism that could plausibly satisfy the requirements of Article IV—the states advocating for a multinational fuel bank were more likely to persuade others to support the arrangement. That the effort to establish the fuel bank was unsuccessful does not mean it was not a motive for the legal argumentation.

There were also *strategic* reasons for using legal arguments in the fuel cycle debate. Russia, for example, had much to gain from insisting that Article IV could be satisfied as long as all states had access to low-enriched uranium because it sought to position itself as host of the low-enriched uranium reserve.[56] Conversely, members of the NAM had good strategic reasons for not adding to their "second-class citizen" status as nuclear have-nots by creating a further division between those allowed to develop sensitive technologies and those not.

Connecting the nuclear fuel cycle debate with its own program, Iran used generic legal arguments on "the right to enrich" in the NPT review conferences to win support for its position in the negotiations that led to the JCPOA. With respect to the JCPOA, the United States used legal arguments (rather than purely security arguments) to ratchet up pressure on Iran in the Security Council and IAEA. The E3 were in the interesting position of trying to split the difference—in the P5+1 talks and in the Security Council. Splitting the difference, among other things, meant trying to reconcile the diametrically opposed legal positions on the right to enrich.

Finally, we see evidence of *identity* playing a role in the argumentation. Tarja Cronberg claims Iran's rejection of the demand to suspend enrichment (by the United States, the E3, and ultimately the Security Council) was "an act of resistance."[57] Homeira Moshirzadeh, an Iranian scholar, argues that Iran's nuclear policy was driven not by security nor by economics, but as a matter of identity, shaped by "discourses of independence, justice and resistance."[58] By insisting on its legal rights in the face of intense pressure, Iran was upholding its image as a fierce opponent of Western double standards. Its ability to project that image depended on standards all have supposedly agreed to. If the law were different—if Article IV did not exist—it would have

[56] When and IAEA Expert Group presented options for international control of the nuclear fuel cycle in 2005, Russia picked up on the idea and in 2007 established a center where a reserve of low-enriched uranium fuel was to be stored and made available, under IAEA control, to IAEA member states. IAEA Expert Group report on "Multilateral Approaches to the Nuclear Fuel Cycle," Feb. 22, 2005.

[57] Cronberg, *supra* note 39, at 67.

[58] Homeira Moshirzadeh, "Discursive Foundations of Iran's Nuclear Policy," *Security Dialogue* 38 (2007): 521.

been harder for Iran to make a principled case. Conversely, because Article IV exists, it would have been awkward for Iran to knuckle under. Upholding what it sees as an "inalienable right" endorsed by positive international law is a powerful political tool at home and abroad—not simply because of the instrumental benefits from being able to enrich, but because it is a symbol of status. Indeed, by that logic, Iran would have no interest in a multinational fuel cycle arrangement *even if* it believed that would guarantee it of an adequate supply of low enriched uranium.

It is never easy to separate the various motives, and conceivably all were at play. In Iran's case, identity-based motives seem to interact with strategic motives and persuasion. That could explain why, despite appeals in Iran's parliament in 2005 and again in 2012 to withdraw from the NPT, Iran did not do so.[59] Doing so would have reinforced its status as a great regional power, putting it on the same footing as Israel, India, and Pakistan. But it would undermine its ability to insist on its legal rights while accusing the United States of hypocrisy. If it were to withdraw from the NPT, it would lose the legal and moral high ground.

What was the effect of the legal argumentation? It seems that interpretation of Article IV was consequential in debates about both the multinational fuel bank and the JCPOA. It essentially derailed the former, despite being pushed by some powerful actors. And the right to enrich permeated the negotiating process on the JCPOA, with impact both on the ability to reach an agreement and on the final shape of the deal. Specifically, fudging the "right to enrich" issue in the text of the JCPOA made it possible to agree on that deal without resolving the generic disagreement about Article IV of the NPT. The hope and expectation was that over the subsequent ten to fifteen years Iran would once again become a member in good standing of the nuclear nonproliferation regime with the same rights as all other parties.

Stepping back from the concrete impact, the legal argumentation altered the normative climate. The consensus at the end of the 2010 NPT review conference was that multilateral nuclear fuel cycle mechanisms should be pursued but in a way that did not undermine Article IV rights. This consensus followed six years of legal argumentation about what Article IV meant, pitting the NWS against the NNWS. If material power and policy preferences were all that mattered to nuclear politics, then the NWS would have won the argument. Having lost it, it will be that much harder to revive in the future because the normative context has been altered.

Similarly, the compromise over the right to enrich embodied in the JCPOA—which was the product of legal argumentation—had the effect of putting in abeyance arguments about Article IV.[60] That made it easier to preserve the momentum on nonproliferation the Obama administration had generated. The US renunciation of the JCPOA was a setback, although it is interesting that the Trump administration did not use legal arguments to justify doing so (a backhanded compliment to the law, given how weak the legal arguments were). If anything, the "right to enrich" is stronger than ever given that the United States is relatively exposed on the issue following the snapback debacle.

[59] Cronberg, *supra* note 39, at 68.
[60] I am grateful to Steve Mathias for this observation.

Stepping even further back, all the argumentation may, paradoxically, have strengthened the non-proliferation regime. Monica Hakimi makes the interesting point that communities are constructed as much by conflict as they are by agreement.[61] She quotes Bernard Yack for the proposition that if a practice "structures nothing more than the way we engage in conflict with each other, it still reinforces the sense that we participate with others in a community."[62] Arguing is different from other modes of confrontation such as coercion or even hard bargaining in that it implicitly acknowledges the protagonists are in some sort of relationship. They argue to define—and perhaps change—the terms of that relationship, not to end it.

V. Article VI and the Treaty on the Prohibition of Nuclear Weapons

Article VI is even more imprecise than Article IV:

> Each of the Parties to the Treaty undertakes to pursue negotiations in good faith on effective measures relating to cessation of the nuclear arms race at an early date and to nuclear disarmament, and on a treaty on general and complete disarmament under strict and effective international control.

Does it impose a legal obligation at all, or is it a political goal? If an obligation, is it to pursue negotiations in good faith or "to pursue in good faith *and bring to a conclusion*" such negotiations, as the ICJ opined.[63] What—if anything—does the term "good faith" add? How does one interpret "effective measures" and "at an early date"?

A. Disarmament

In the negotiations that produced the NPT, many NNWS wanted the treaty to include concrete measures on nuclear disarmament.[64] The NWS resisted, and in the US and Soviet drafts the only references to disarmament were in preambular paragraphs. Mexico produced the first draft of what became Article VI, supported by

[61] Monica Hakimi, "Constructing an International Community," *American Journal of International Law* 111 (2017): 317, 325.

[62] Bernard Yack, *The Problem of a Political Animal* (Los Angeles: University of California Press, 1993), 43.

[63] The ICJ in its Advisory Opinion on The Threat and Use of Nuclear Weapons, 1996 ICJ Rep., at 26, said the latter, but this appears in cursory form at the end of the opinion, and it is not directly connected to the question it was asked by the General Assembly. Christopher Ford, a US official, questions the validity of the conclusion. Christopher Ford, "Debating Disarmament: Interpreting Article VI of the Treaty on the Non-Proliferation of Nuclear Weapons," *Non-Proliferation Review* 14 (2007): 401. The refusal of the ICJ to clarify the question in the later case brought by the Marshall Islands case demonstrates that it is not realistic to rely on courts to settle the matter.

[64] Gro Nystuen and Torjborn Graff Hugo, "The Nuclear Non-Proliferation Treaty," in *Nuclear Weapons Under International Law*, edited by Gro Nystuen, Stuart Casey-Maslen, and Annie Golden Bersagel (Cambridge: Cambridge University Press, 2014), 374, 383.

Egypt, Canada, and Sweden. It was eventually watered down, so much that some countries—including Brazil—abstained on the vote to adopt the NPT in the General Assembly.[65]

Despite a clear divergence among the NWS and the NNWS (and within the NNWS) on what Article VI means, their styles of argumentation are similar. The NWS tend to avoid substantive debate and simply claim that all arms control agreements are evidence that the obligation has been met. Occasionally US officials will make explicit interpretive statements, such as Christopher Ford, US representative at the 2007 and 2008 PrepComs, who wrote at the time the only legal *obligation* contained in Article VI is to "pursue" negotiations in good faith, leaving open the possibility that "such negotiations might not take place, let alone succeed."[66] More often, the United States and the other NWS obfuscate.[67]

While most of the NNWS are adamant that the NWS are not meeting their Article VI obligations, they tend not to engage in pointed legal argumentation either. Thus at the 2008 PrepCom, the Indonesian representative speaking for the Non-Aligned Group lamented the modernization programs of the nuclear states, "illustrating a *trend* of vertical proliferation and non-compliance by NWS towards their commitments under Article VI of the NPT" (emphasis added).[68] New Zealand, speaking on behalf of the New Agenda Coalition (Brazil, Egypt, Ireland, Mexico, New Zealand, South Africa, and Sweden), stated that the modernization programs "contradict the spirit of the disarmament and non-proliferation obligations."[69]

Efforts have been made to give Article VI content at the NPT review conferences. At the 2000 review conference, the parties agreed on thirteen "practical steps for the systematic and progressive efforts to implement Article VI." At the 2010 RevCon, they agreed on a sixty-four-point action plan that includes twenty-two items on disarmament. As guidance on implementation of the NPT,[70] consensus documents that come out of these review conferences constitute subsequent practice within the meaning of Article 31 of the Vienna Convention on the Law of Treaties (VCLT) and therefore are to be considered in interpreting its provisions. Whether those interpretations of Article VI stand the test of time depends on subsequent behavior of the parties. As it turns out, both the thirteen steps and the twenty-two actions are in limbo given the failure of the 2015 RevCon to reach agreement on disarmament measures (or anything else).

[65] *Id.* at 386.
[66] Ford, *supra* note 63, at 72.
[67] Joyner, *supra* note 23, at 69 and 95.
[68] Statement of the Ambassador of Republic of Indonesia on behalf of the Group of Non-Aligned States at the 2008 PrepCom to the 2010 NPT RevCon, Apr. 28, 2008.
[69] Statement of the Permanent Representative of New Zealand on behalf of the NAC to the 2008 PrepCom of the 2010 NPT RevCon, Apr. 28, 2008.
[70] Wilfrid Wan, "Why the 2015 NPT RevCon Fell Apart," United Nations University, May 28, 2015.

B. Treaty on the Prohibition of Nuclear Weapons

The TPNW presents a good case study because its supporters see it as a step toward fulfillment of Article VI obligations. Its detractors say the opposite: it undermines good faith efforts to work on disarmament and therefore is incompatible with Article VI.

The push for the TPNW corresponded to deepening disappointment with the NWS on arms control and disarmament. Failure to ratify the Comprehensive Test Ban Treaty (CTBT) by the United States and China has long been a source of consternation, and there have been hints that the United States will "unsign" it.[71] US withdrawal from the Intermediate Nuclear Forces Treaty in August 2019, ostensibly in response to Russian violations, has added to the tensions. Signs that the Trump administration would not extend the 2010 New START made matters even worse in 2020, but the Biden administration quickly did so in 2021.

The failure of the 2015 review conference was in part because the United States, the United Kingdom, and Canada opposed a March 2016 deadline for convening a conference on the establishment of a WMD-free zone in the Middle East, with Canada insisting that any such meeting include Israel, a non-NPT party. While the disagreement on the WMDFZ was the coup de grâce, there were other fissures between the NWS and the NNWS—mainly about the lack of progress on nuclear disarmament.[72] There was wide support for the humanitarian impact movement, which had gained momentum in three conferences in Oslo (March 2013), Nayarit (February 2014), and Vienna (December 2014). At the third of these, Austria introduced the so-called "humanitarian pledge," which makes an explicit connection between the humanitarian consequences of the use of nuclear weapons and Article VI of the NPT:

> We call on all states parties to the NPT to renew their commitment to the urgent and full implementation of existing obligations under Article VI, and to this end, to identify and pursue effective measures *to fill the legal gap* for the prohibition and elimination of nuclear weapons and we pledge to cooperate with all stakeholders to achieve this goal [emphasis added].

The assertion that there is a "legal gap" in Article VI itself is a legal argument, with which not every state (especially the United States) agrees. At the 2015 review conference a total of 185 states joined statements on the humanitarian consequences of nuclear weapons use, and 70 states had endorsed the humanitarian pledge.[73] By October

[71] The US Director of the Defense Intelligence Agency raised the possibility, after accusing Russia of "probably not adhering to its nuclear testing moratorium in a manner consistent with the 'zero yield' standard." Daryl Kimball, "Nuclear Testing and Comprehensive Test Ban Treaty Timeline," Arms Control Association, June 2019. Countries that have signed but not ratified the treaty, which includes the United States and China, are obliged by international law (specifically, the VCLT) not to take actions that would defeat its object and purpose. "Unsigning" CTBT, as the United States did the Rome Statute of the ICC, would liberate the United States from that obligation. Ted Bromund, "Alleged Russian Violations of the CTBT Make New Case for US Withdrawal," Heritage Foundation, June 1, 2019.

[72] Tariq Rauf, "The 2015 NPT Review Conference: Setting the Record Straight," SIPRI, June 5, 2015. William Potter, "The Unfulfilled Promise of the 2015 NPT Review Conference," *Survival* 58 (2016): 151.

[73] William Potter, "Disarmament Diplomacy and the Nuclear Ban Treaty," *Survival* 59 (2017): 75, 84.

2019, 127 states had endorsed the pledge, and another 23 voted for a UN General Assembly resolution in favor of it.[74]

The failure of 2015 NPT review conference represented a turning point for the advocates of the treaty. Seeking a venue where decisions are taken by majority vote, not consensus, they turned to the General Assembly. In 2016, the First Committee charged an Open-Ended Working Group "to substantively address concrete effective legal measures, legal provisions and norms that will need to be concluded to attain and maintain a world without nuclear weapons."[75] Negotiations on the text began in March 2017 with 130 states participating. On July 27 of that year, it was adopted in the General Assembly by 122 states. In October 2020, the fiftieth country ratified the TPNW, paving the way for it to come into force on January 22, 2021.

The process leading to the treaty is noteworthy for the extent of legal argumentation and the rather nuanced positions taken. To begin with, the International Committee of the Red Cross (ICRC) was instrumental in the success of the humanitarian initiative.[76] A speech made by its delegate at the 2010 NPT review conference highlighted not only the humanitarian consequences of nuclear weapons use but also its incompatibility with humanitarian law. This and later interventions by the ICRC—a highly credible nongovernmental organization (NGO)—became central to the message of the International Campaign to Abolish Nuclear Weapons (ICAN) and an important refrain in many of the speeches made by government representatives.

Second, the 150 countries that have in one way or another endorsed the humanitarian pledge accept the idea there is a "legal gap" in Article VI. Not every NNWS agrees that the TPNW is the way to fill that gap: most from the Global South support it; most of the United States' military allies do not.[77] Nevertheless, it is highly plausible that the long-standing discourse around Article VI gave impetus to the push for the ban treaty.

Third, just as with the NNWS, there are some differences of opinion among the NWS. In the General Assembly debates, only the US ambassador challenged the assumption that there was a "legal gap" in the disarmament provisions of the NPT.[78] The United States sought to persuade NATO allies to vote against the General Assembly resolution by sending a memo that presented a line-by-line analysis of how the proposed text of the ban would conflict with NATO doctrine and planning.[79] The United Kingdom and France were less adamant than the United States, but the P3 were unified in opposing the ban. They made a rather restrained joint statement, emphasizing the ongoing relevance of all 2010 NPT Rev Con action items.

Russia, on the other hand, was less restrained:

[74] https://www.bmeia.gv.at/en/european-foreign-policy/disarmament/weapons-of-mass-destruction/nuclear-weapons/vienna-conference-on-the-humanitarian-impact-of-nuclear-weapons/.

[75] Potter, *supra* note 73, at 88.

[76] Rebecca Davis Gibbons, "The Humanitarian Turn in Nuclear Disarmament and the Treaty on the Prohibition of Nuclear Weapons," *Non-Proliferation Review*, July 5, 2018, at 33–34.

[77] The only European countries that have expressed support are Austria, Ireland, and Lichtenstein. New Zealand signed and ratified it.

[78] Potter, *supra* note 73, at 93.

[79] United States Non-Paper: "Defense Impacts of Potential United Nations General Assembly Nuclear Weapons Ban Treaty," Annex 2, NATO Committee on Proliferation, Oct. 17, 2016.

> The Russian spokesperson ... characterised [the treaty-ban resolution] as a "destructive" and "hasty" initiative that would undermine the NPT.... Moreover, he argued that the possession of nuclear weapons by the five NPT NWS was "absolutely legitimate" and that efforts to delegitimise their possession would be "illegal under a new mythical agreement". Adoption of L.41, he asserted, would create "two parallel regimes with opposed goals" that would endanger the NPT and run the risk of "plunging the world into chaos".[80]

Russia's view that the TPNW would undermine the NPT permeated the debates leading to the adoption of treaty and continues to this day. All five NWS collectively refused to participate in the first humanitarian conference in Oslo and made a joint statement that it would divert attention from more practical steps. The Norwegian government's intention in hosting that conference was to promote the humanitarian initiative, not the ban treaty. It was only after Oslo that a group of states and NGOs began to meet to discuss the TPNW. Tension on that issue emerged at the second conference in Nariyata, the tone of which is nicely summarized by Rebecca Gibbons. The Mexican chair

> called for "a diplomatic process" toward "a legally binding instrument" outlawing nuclear weapons, asserting that "Nayarit is a point of no return." The chair's statement brought the tension over the goal of the humanitarian conferences to the fore. Some participants ... wanted to begin discussing what they saw as the next logical step in the movement: a nuclear-weapon-ban treaty. Other officials at Nayarit advocated pursuing disarmament through the NPT, not a ban treaty, a process that the German envoy noted required ... and "maintaining a dialogue with the Nuclear Weapon States."[81]

At the 2018 PrepCom, France and Russia made strong statements denouncing the TPNW, arguing in effect that it is contrary to Article VI because it will undermine more realistic efforts to achieve the goal of disarmament. France said: "The TPNW could undermine the NPT ... by creating an alternative and contrary standard. As it dissociates itself from the goal of complete and general disarmament, which is central to Article VI of the NPT, the Treaty could lead to a race to develop conventional capabilities and consequentially military escalation."[82] The Russian representative said the treaty "will undermine long-term efforts aimed at real nuclear disarmament."[83] The United States went a step further by distributing a working paper called "Creating the Conditions for Nuclear Disarmament," which listed resolution of the North Korea and Iran crises, a declaration of Israel's right to exist, adherence to the IAEA Additional Protocol, and compliance by Russia with its arms control obligations as measures that "would create the trust that is a pre-requisite for Article VI."[84] In a nod to the power

[80] Potter, *supra* note 73, at 93–94.
[81] Gibbons, *supra* note 76, at 21–22.
[82] Statement of the Ambassador of France at the 2008 PrepCom to the 2010 NPT RevCon, Apr. 28, 2008.
[83] Statement of the Ambassador of Russia at the 2008 PrepCom to the 2010 NPT RevCon, Apr. 28, 2008.
[84] Arms Control Association, "Reporting on the 2018 NPT Prep Com," May 7, 2018.

of words, at the 2019 PrepCom the United States changed the name of its initiative to "Create an Environment for Nuclear Disarmament" as an effective measure within the meaning of Article VI, in order to signal that it was not imposing conditions on its disarmament obligations.[85] France, the United Kingdom, China, and many NATO states said they would not support the TPNW because "it undermines the good faith efforts to work on disarmament in the NPT context, and attempts to be a 'shortcut' to disarmament."[86]

On the other side of the debate, at the 2018 PrepCom, the New Agenda Coalition (led by New Zealand) presented its own working paper stating forcefully that the TPNW is consistent with—even an extension of—Article VI, while referring to all the commitments made on disarmament at earlier RevCons, including the thirteen steps (2000) and twenty-two actions (2010).[87] At the 2019 PrepCom, two dozen states welcomed the TPNW, emphasizing that it complemented Article VI of the NPT. The NAM said the TPNW "closes a legal loophole" and is a legal measure to advance disarmament.[88] And in their national statements, many NNWS said it "is a legally binding mechanism that supports Article VI."[89] A similar exchange occurred at the April 2, 2019, High Level UN Security Council meeting, when France, the United Kingdom, and the United States criticized the TPNW, while six others welcomed its adoption and emphasized its compatibility with the NPT.

Shortly before the fiftieth ratification of the treaty was received (the number required for it to come into force), the United States sent a non-paper to a large number of countries urging them to withdraw.[90] The letter states:

> Although we recognize your sovereign right to ratify or accede to the Treaty on the Prohibition of Nuclear Weapons (TPNW), we believe that you have made a strategic error and should withdraw your instrument of ratification or accession.

The US non-paper claimed that the TPNW was "dangerously counterproductive" to the NPT. This is an interesting formulation. It does not specifically state that the parties to the TPNW are violating their NPT obligations, but by calling it "counterproductive," the United States implied that it would be counter to the "good faith" requirement in Article VI. Beatrice Fihn, Executive Director of ICAN, dismissed the nuclear powers' claim that the treaty interferes with the NPT, stating as follows:

> The Nonproliferation Treaty is about preventing the spread of nuclear weapons and eliminating nuclear weapons, and this treaty implements that. There's no way you

[85] James Martin Center for Nonproliferation Studies, "Daily Summaries of NPT PrepCom 2019," *supra* note 51, Days 4–5.

[86] *Id.* 6.

[87] "Article VI of the NPT: Working Paper Submitted by New Zealand on behalf of the New Agenda Coalition (Brazil, Egypt, Ireland, New Zealand and South Africa)," NPT/CONF.2020/PC.II/WP13, Mar. 15, 2018.

[88] *Id.* 4.

[89] *Id.* 6.

[90] Daryl Kimball, "The Nuclear Ban Treaty: A Much Needed Wake-up Call," *Arms Control Today*, Nov. 2020.

> can undermine the Nonproliferation Treaty by banning nuclear weapons. It's the end goal of the Nonproliferation Treaty.[91]

Meanwhile fifty-six former leaders, foreign ministers, and defense ministers from twenty-two NATO countries plus Japan and South Korea wrote an open letter to their own governments urging them to join the TPNW. The letter included the following language:

> As states parties, we could remain in alliances with nuclear-armed states, as nothing in the treaty itself nor in our respective defence pacts precludes that. But we would be legally bound never under any circumstances to assist or encourage our allies to use, threaten to use or possess nuclear weapons.... The prohibition treaty is an important reinforcement to the half-century-old Non-Proliferation Treaty.[92]

Again, without opining directly on the implications for Article VI of the NPT, the letter contains notable legal argumentation.

C. Arguing about Article VI: Purposes and Effects

Until the TPNW, the debates about Article VI were rather wide open. Given that the language is imprecise and its object and purpose in relation to other parts of the treaty is contested, there is less scope for strong claims about compliance. In that context, engaging in careful legal reasoning (outside of courts) was not likely to be persuasive. The adequacy of steps taken to meet the commitment tend to be the subject of more overtly political than legal argumentation. Yet debates about Article VI did factor into the decision to pursue a ban treaty. The TPNW did not come out of the blue; it was born of dissatisfaction with the progress on disarmament and the tendency of the NWS to downplay the legal character of their obligation under Article VI. Conceivably, some fence-sitter states were persuaded to sign and ratify the TPNW because of that. It is less likely that persuasion worked in the opposite direction: namely, that the nuclear umbrella states (US allies in NATO and the Pacific) chose not to join *because* they were persuaded by the argument that Article VI was nothing more than a political aspiration.

The evidence on the strategic or instrumental purpose of legal argumentation about Article VI is mixed. On the part of some engaged in the debate, the purpose was to fend off demands to engage in deeper disarmament (mainly the NWS); on the part of others, it was to resist pressure on non-proliferation by pointing to lack of progress on disarmament. Prior to the TPNW, the battle lines were clear and not many states were likely to bend for reputational or other reasons. The push for a TPNW was meant to

[91] Edith Lederer, "US Urges Countries to Withdraw from the UN Nuclear Ban," *Washington Post*, Oct. 21, 2020, https://www.washingtonpost.com/world/the_americas/us-urges-countries-to-withdraw-from-un-nuke-ban-treaty/2020/10/21/21918918-13ce-11eb-a258-614acf2b906d_story.html.

[92] ICAN, "56 Former Leaders and Ministers of US Allies Urge States to Join the Nuclear Weapon Ban Treaty," Sept. 21, 2020, https://www.icanw.org/56_former_leaders.

change that. The strongest advocates did not expect any of the NWS to join, but they hoped to put the nuclear umbrella states in a quandary, making it harder to dodge questions about what was required to advance the disarmament agenda. Conversely, many of those umbrella states were driven by a desire to maintain a dialogue with nuclear weapon states rather than a deep-seated belief in the correctness of their legal position. Adoption of the TPNW may change that: it may alter the cost and benefit calculations of some states. Some umbrella states—Norway, for example—may wish to resume leadership of the humanitarian initiative by throwing their weight behind the treaty as a step toward Article VI disarmament.[93] Conversely, some of the supporters of the treaty may discover they have an interest in closer ties with one or more NWS and will seize on the argument that it undermines Article VI (and the NPT as a whole) to switch sides.

Identity factors also impacted the legal argumentation of some states. New Zealand, one of the few states not from the Global South to have signed and ratified the treaty, has long been a leader on non-proliferation and disarmament in the Pacific region and globally.[94] It was one of the first states to sign the NPT and has been very active in pushing for a comprehensive nuclear test ban. Leading the efforts on the TPNW burnished its image as a small state that can punch above its weight in international affairs. Switzerland, home of the ICRC, pushed the humanitarian initiative in the 2010 and 2015 NPT review conferences. It voted for the TPNW in the General Assembly but in 2018 decided not to sign or ratify it, opting to participate as an observer and then reconsider at the end of 2020. It is plausible that Switzerland's identity as a neutral state and leader on humanitarian law affected its positioning. Japan has neither signed nor ratified the TPNW, but one can imagine it some day throwing its weight behind the treaty given the country's history and self-image as a leader on nuclear disarmament.

At the same time, the TPNW will not change much from a practical point of view in the near term. When the treaty came into force in January 2021, the only states that had ratified it were not close to acquiring nuclear weapons. Its proponents well understood that would be the case. But one way or another it will have an impact on the broader normative climate. Ramesh Thakur believes the ban treaty will have a powerful impact "by reshaping . . . the cluster of laws, norms, rules, practices and discourse that shape how we think about and act in relation to nuclear weapons."[95] There are multiple reasons why states choose to go nuclear or to abstain from doing so. Security is part of the equation, but "the nuclear taboo," domestic politics, bureaucratic bargaining, great power prestige, history, technological know-how, and other factors come into the equation as well.[96] If the possession of nuclear weapons is delegitimized

[93] This is even more true of Sweden, which is not a member of NATO and so not formally under the "umbrella" of the United States.

[94] See speech by former Prime Minister Helen Clark, "New Zealand as a Disarmament Leader," Oct. 1, 2007, https://www.wagingpeace.org/new-zealand-as-a-disarmament-leader/.

[95] Ramesh Thakur, "The Nuclear Ban Treaty: Recasting a Normative Framework for Disarmament," *The Washington Quarterly* 40 (2017): 71, 82. See also Merav Datan and Jurgën Scheffran, "The Treaty Is Out of the Bottle: The Power and Logic of Nuclear Disarmament," *Journal of Peace and Disarmament* 2 (2019): 114.

[96] Scott D. Sagan, "Why Do States Build Nuclear Weapons: Three Models in Search of a Bomb," *International Security* 21 (Winter 1996/1997): 54.

incrementally through increasing accessions to the TPNW, that will add one more to the constellation of factors that could tip the scales in favor of a more robust NPT. Even if the accessions do not increase, some of the nuclear umbrella states could be prompted to launch new disarmament initiatives, such as Sweden's "stepping-stone" approach.[97]

Or it could have the opposite effect. It is possible the TPNW will make the climate for non-proliferation and disarmament worse, by driving a wedge between the nuclear umbrella states and the rest of the NNWS. The effect of the legal argumentation that led to the TPNW may in the end make it harder to reach common understanding on what Article VI requires.

VI. Conclusion

It is risky to generalize about the purposes and effects of legal argumentation from one case, especially nuclear non-proliferation, but the following observations can be made.

First, there are multiple reasons why states engage in legal argumentation outside of courts. As the case studies show, it could be to persuade, to affect instrumental calculations of interest, or to assert one's identity. The purposes are not mutually exclusive, and more than one may be at play at any given time.

Second, a not-always intended effect of legal argumentation about compliance is to produce new law. The terms of the JCPOA are the result—at least in part—of debates about the interpretation of Article IV of the NPT on the right to enrich. The TPNW is the result—at least in part—of debates about interpretation of Article VI of the NPT, and whether the step-by-step approach of the NWS meets their obligation to "pursue negotiations in good faith" on disarmament. Moreover both these legal instruments are themselves a form—not merely an outcome—of legal argumentation about the treaty that spawned them: the JCPOA embodies a claim (albeit ambiguous) about the right to enrich uranium pursuant to Article IV of the NPT; the TPNW embodies a claim about the meaning of Article VI of the NPT. Neither ends the argument; they continue it.

Third, the quality of legal argumentation matters. A "good" legal argument—in our case, one that fits with intersubjective understandings of what legal interpretation entails—can have a significant impact on political dynamics; a "bad" legal argument, less so. The United States' clumsy attempt to invoke the Iran sanctions snapback provision is a case in point.

Fourth, legal argumentation, regardless of the purpose, can affect the broader normative climate in which future argumentation occurs—for better or worse. The deteriorating international security environment in 2020 did not bode well for the future of the NPT and nuclear non-proliferation generally. But the intensive ongoing

[97] Ann Linde, "Swedish Initiative Aims to Strengthen the NPT," *Arms Control Today*, Mar. 2020, https://www.armscontrol.org/act/2020-03/features/swedish-initiative-aims-strengthen-npt.

debates about what the NPT means suggest the parties have not given up on it as a frame of reference for engaging with each other on non-proliferation issues. More worrying will be when those legal debates end, marking the demise of an intersubjective approach to interpretation and the consensual relationship among the parties that approach signifies.

PART III

8

Mass Atrocity Crimes and Human Rights Discourse at the UN Security Council

Three Case Studies

Bruno Stagno-Ugarte

Words matter. As thousands of people were killed or maimed in Rwanda in 1994, the international community debated whether the crimes being committed amounted to the crime of genocide. Egregious crimes had been amply documented, yet it was important for many in the international community to agree on a common characterization of the crimes as more than "ethnic killings," "carnage and slaughter,"[1] a "killing field," "hacking, spearing and shooting,"[2] or "torrent of widespread killings" and "massacres of civilians."[3] The UN Security Council, for example, agreed to a consensus formulation twenty-two days into the killings, stating that "the killing of members of an ethnic group with the intention of destroying such a group in whole or in part constitutes a crime punishable under international law."[4] While the word "genocide" was not used, key elements of its definition were explicitly employed to characterize the situation in Rwanda.

This chapter concentrates on the most egregious and heinous human rights violations, specifically those crimes that are listed and defined in the Rome Statute of the International Criminal Court (ICC) and their intersection with the UN Security Council as the body mandated with the primary responsibility for the maintenance of international peace and security. It will look at how various actors use legal discourse in the Council to argue whether such crimes are happening in situations on its agenda, and whether such discourse successfully advances, or not, action by the Council to address these crimes.[5] The role of legal or paralegal discourse within this fifteen-member body is of interest due to its expansive and intrusive powers of implementation and adjudication of international humanitarian and human rights law. The Council has referenced or determined facts, named parties, highlighted or characterized violations, targeted perpetrators, and/or established situation-specific

[1] UN Doc. S/PV.3368 (Apr. 21, 1994). Terms used by Nigeria.
[2] *Id.* Terms used by Djibouti.
[3] UN Doc. S/1994/470 (Apr. 20, 1994). Terms used by the Secretary-General.
[4] UN Doc. S/PRST/1994/21 (Apr. 30, 1994).
[5] This chapter employs a narrow conception of legal argumentation: "an argument that explicitly invokes traditional sources of law, employs the standard techniques of interpretation, and seeks to determine whether behavior is consistent with the law." See Ian Johnstone, chapter 7, in this volume.

Bruno Stagno-Ugarte, *Mass Atrocity Crimes and Human Rights Discourse at the UN Security Council* In: *Talking International Law*. Edited by: Ian Johnstone and Steven Ratner, Oxford University Press. © Bruno Stagno-Ugarte 2021.
DOI: 10.1093/oso/9780197588437.003.0008

international criminal or special tribunals or referred situations to the ICC.[6] The interplay of norms and politics in the deliberative processes of the Council is important as it largely determines whether or not the Council acts in meaningfully addressing and ideally deterring mass atrocity crimes. This interplay, especially as it relates to ICC-listed crimes, is not a rarity within the Council due to the "tragic irony of this age of human rights"[7]—the Council is at present seized of several situations where such crimes have likely been perpetrated—and the higher stakes that come with an exponential resort to Chapter VII (enforcement) powers.[8]

Despite its uneven composition, with five veto-wielding permanent members and ten non-permanent members elected for nonrenewable two-year terms, the Security Council is a space for both public and nonpublic negotiation and communication, and thus argumentation, between states and other actors with formal standing before the Council. Unfortunately, it is also an opaque body where most of the argumentation happens out of view, in closed-door informal meetings or consultations, or within similarly opaque subsidiary bodies, with only a fraction occurring in public Council meetings.[9] Council members, however, are unequally dependent on argumentation and persuasion, as permanent members ultimately have the option of using the veto, or threat thereof, to forestall a decision or action they deem contrary to their interests. As the threat of use or use of the veto furthermore does not require justification, permanent members can opt to withdraw from argumentation while preempting an adverse outcome.

In addition to Council members, this chapter will focus on one other set of key actors, the Secretary-General and wider UN Secretariat, as together they play an important role in framing the debates in the Council, through reports, briefings, and recommendations. Although infrequently invoked, the Secretary-General has the power to bring a situation to the attention of the Council under Article 99 of the UN Charter and has been expressly invited by the Council to do so in "cases of serious violations of international law."[10] Although Article 97 describes the Secretary-General as the "chief administrative officer" of the United Nations, Article 99 provides the Secretariat with a strategic opening to initiate or engage in Council deliberations on situations of concern. Cumulative practice since Secretary-General Trygve Lie (1946–1952) first successfully tested the confines of Article 99 has allowed the office to grow into more than "a glorified clerk," to quote U Thant (1961–1971), and to leverage the "unwritten moral responsibility which every Secretary-General bears not to turn a

[6] Bruno Stagno-Ugarte and Jared Genser, "Evolution of the Security Council's Engagement on Human Rights," in *The United Nations Security Council in the Age of Human Rights*, edited by Jared Genser and Bruno Stagno-Ugarte (New York: Cambridge University Press, 2014), 3.

[7] "The tragic irony of this age of human rights—where greater numbers are enjoying human rights than perhaps ever in history—is that it has been repeatedly darkened by outbursts of indiscriminate violence and organized mass killings." Kofi Annan, "No Government Has the Right to Hide Behind National Sovereignty to Violate Human Rights," *The Guardian*, Apr. 7, 1999.

[8] Peter Wallensteen and Patrik Johansson, "The UN Security Council: Decisions and Actions," in *The Security Council in the 21st Century*, edited by Sebastian von Einsiedel et al. (New York: International Peace Institute, 2016), 28.

[9] Since 2010, the highest percentage of public meetings was recorded in 2018 (67.4%), the lowest in 2013 (48.3%).

[10] SC Res. 1366 (Aug. 30, 2001).

blind eye when innocent civilian lives are placed in jeopardy on a large scale," to quote Kurt Waldheim (1972–1981).[11] Despite no formal authority,[12] the UN Secretariat, and the Secretary-General more specifically, is "an influential participant in the legal discourse that infuses much of global politics."[13] In the public meetings of the Council, the Secretary-General, or designated representatives, can set the stage by laying out the facts, invoking the norms, and calling the alleged crimes by the legal terms that characterize them. The Secretary-General can be a prominent legal actor, as best demonstrated by the "use of smaller rifles," as Lie called the many legal opinions he issued to insert himself in Council proceedings.[14] The UN Secretariat is supposed to be an impartial player, a provider of facts, informed analysis, and recommendations rooted in UN Charter values,[15] yet Council members may assign unequal weight to the "objective" situation as presented by the Secretariat and instead narrate—or argue—it differently, including by disputing the facts and/or opposing the recommendations presented by the Secretariat.

This chapter does not seek to demonstrate that legal argumentation is the best way to advance and achieve compliance with human rights, as non-legal arguments may be more effective, especially within an eminently political body as the Security Council, where national interests are frequently at play. Yet legal arguments can have independent—if not sufficient—influence even in a political setting, due in part to the extraordinary powers of implementation and adjudication of international humanitarian and human rights law the Council possesses, particularly under Chapter VII. In addressing ICC-listed crimes, this chapter specifically focuses on the use, or avoidance thereof, of legal language by actors within the Council to either capture, or—too often—dissimulate, the gravity of the crimes being perpetrated. Particular attention will be paid to actual references to ICC-listed crimes, as these terms, when specifically applied to situations that shock the conscience of humanity, prefigure accountability and the withdrawal of impunity from perpetrators. Between these two extremes, there are a number of shades of gray, as actors may only reference elements or incidents of a specific crime without uttering the crime itself, thus minimizing its effect. In addition, they may use the passive voice in referencing elements or incidents, or even one or more of the crimes, thus avoiding attribution. As actors may also make unprincipled use of the crimes and invoke them for political purposes in cases that may not meet the necessary thresholds or elements, the chapter limits its examination to three contemporary cases where there is substantial evidence and opinion that one or more ICC-listed crimes have been committed.

[11] *Id.* 121, 122.

[12] Secretary-General Kofi Annan put it succinctly: "In the end, the only means I have is reason and persuasion." William Shawcross, *Deliver Us from Evil: Peacekeepers, Warlords and a World of Endless Conflict* (New York: Simon and Schuster, 2000), 278.

[13] Ian Johnstone, "The Role of the UN Secretary-General: The Power of Persuasion Based on Law," *Global Governance* 9 (2003): 442.

[14] Thomas M. Franck, *Nation Against Nation: What Happened to the U.N. Dream and What the U.S. Can Do About It* (Oxford: Oxford University Press, 1985), 126-127.

[15] Dag Hammarskjöld put it most eloquently: "I am not neutral as regards the Charter; I am not neutral as regards facts [. . .] In relation to interests, there I do claim that there is no insurmountable difficulty for anybody with the proper kind of guiding principles in carrying through such neutrality one hundred percent." Dag Hammarskjöld, *To Speak for the World* (Stockholm: Atlantis, 2005), 101.

The chapter is guided by evidence limited to a few case studies and specific time frames within each. It covers three country-specific situations (Myanmar, Syria, Yemen), selected using two criteria: first, the UN Secretariat, through individual offices or special procedures or mandates, determined at some point that the abuses perpetrated in each situation amounted to one or more ICC-listed crimes, and, second, each specifically brings into play one or more of the permanent members. The first condition ensures that the argumentative interplay of norms and politics relates to an agenda item where ICC crimes have been determined to have occurred at some stage of the deliberative process within the Council. The second condition ensures that the interplay of norms and politics is geopolitically balanced by examining situations where different permanent members are politically—and at times also militarily—tied. It thus provides a lens for analyzing their adherence to the universality of human rights norms in showing how they characterized violations perpetrated by their allies: China as the main ally within the Council of the Tatmadaw–Aung San Suu Kyi regime (Myanmar); Russia as principal arms provider to the Bashar Al-Assad regime and as a military ally in the conflict since April 2015 (Syria); and France, the United Kingdom, and the United States as principal arms providers to the Saudi Arabia–led military coalition and main providers of intelligence and guidance for its strikes (Yemen).

The chapter treats the Security Council as a relatively closed "interpretive community" where "legal argument is part of a broader discursive process."[16] The use, and abuse, of norms and terms within the Council serves varying purposes: explanation or justification, persuasion or promotion, or dissimulation of crude national interest.[17] The approach here is fundamentally inductive, based on situations that have recently tested the resolve of the Council to maintain international peace and security while ensuring or enforcing compliance with international human rights law. The cases studies are structured chronologically to identify any significant changes in legal discourse and, more specifically, invocation of norms or terms over time. Methodologically, the chapter is therefore not tied to a general theory of international relations on state compliance with international law or commitment to accountability for mass atrocity crimes. Neither is it based on a theory of communicative action but guided simply by the evidence that emerges from the case studies.

I. Syria: The Price of Inconsistency in Crimes against Humanity Discourse

The Security Council first considered the situation in Syria—in a public meeting—on April 27, 2011, when the Under-Secretary-General for Political Affairs reported on 350 to 400 civilians killed by "security forces and their supporters" and called for an "independent, transparent and effective investigation into the killings."[18] He spoke of

[16] Ian Johnstone, "Security Council Deliberations: The Power of the Better Argument," *European Journal of International Law* 14 (2003): 437.

[17] Abram Chayes and Antonia Handler Chayes, *The New Sovereignty: Compliance with International Regulatory Agreements* (Cambridge: Harvard University Press, 1995), 119.

[18] UN Doc. S/PV.6524 (Apr. 27, 2011), at 2–4.

"siege-like conditions" and the "use of artillery fire against unarmed civilians, door-to-door arrest campaigns, the shooting of medical personnel who attempt to aid the wounded, raids against hospitals, clinics and mosques and the purposeful destruction of medical supplies and arrests of medical personnel." While some Council members gave credence to the gravity of the abuses committed by the government employing a wide array of terms—"disproportionate force" (Colombia), "unacceptable brutality" (France), "ongoing repression" (Gabon), "systematic use of force" (Germany), "abhorrent violence" (United States)—others highlighted the primacy of national sovereignty and downplayed the situation. Some opted for passive terms such as "incidents" and "events" (China), "suffering" (Russia), or "loss of life" (South Africa), used non-situation-specific language such as "we condemn the use of force against unarmed demonstrators wherever it occurs" (Brazil), or kept silent (India, Lebanon). Yet by August 3, as the toll on civilians continued to mount, the Council consensually[19] characterized the abuses as "widespread violations of human rights and use of force against civilians" and called for compliance with "obligations under applicable international law."[20]

Efforts to consider options under Article 41 of the UN Charter (sanctions) doomed the first draft resolution (S/2011/612) tabled on the situation in Syria, as China and Russia vetoed the text on October 4, 2011.[21] Because the draft condemned the "continued grave and systematic human rights violations and the use of force against civilians" by the Al-Assad regime, Russia took issue with the "unilateral, accusatory bent against Damascus" and what it deemed to be a regime change agenda akin to the one pursued by the North Atlantic Treaty Organization (NATO) against the Muammar Gaddafi regime in Libya under the guise of the emerging norm of the responsibility to protect.[22] South Africa echoed this sentiment in speaking of "a hidden agenda aimed at once again instituting regime change" and stating that "resolutions have been abused, and their implementation has gone far beyond the mandate of what was intended." On the other hand, the United Kingdom and the United States were the first Council members to employ the term "crimes against humanity," echoing the language used by the Human Rights Council,[23] with Bosnia and Herzegovina using the less precise "crimes."

Yet on January 31, 2012, when the Security Council met at ministerial-level, US Secretary of State Hillary Clinton chose the legally vague "campaign of violence" and "brutality,"[24] while UK Foreign Secretary William Hague used the superlative "gravest of crimes." Both failed, however, to join France and Germany, which now opted for "crimes against humanity." Four days later, despite support by all other Council members, China and Russia vetoed a draft resolution (S/2012/77) that referenced "continued

19 In a novel procedural move, Lebanon "disassociated" from the presidential statement.

20 UN Doc. PRST/2011/16 (Aug. 3, 2011).

21 UN Doc. S/2011/612 (Oct. 4, 2011). Brazil, India, Lebanon, and South Africa abstained.

22 UN Doc. S/PV.6627 (Oct. 4, 2011). "The situation in Syria cannot be considered in the Council separately from the Libyan experience. The international community is alarmed by statements that compliance with Council resolutions on Libya in the NATO interpretation is a model for the future actions of NATO in implementing the responsibility to protect."

23 HRC Res. S-17/1 (Aug. 23, 2011).

24 UN Doc. S/PV.6710 (Jan. 31, 2012), at 13.

widespread and gross violations of human rights."[25] Only France and the United States employed the term "crimes against humanity" in statements following the failed vote.

A. Inconsistency: Take Two

The UN Secretariat first referenced ICC-listed crimes in a Security Council public meeting on February 28, 2012, when the Under-Secretary-General for Political Affairs cited the findings of the Human Rights Council–mandated Commission of Inquiry on Syria[26] regarding "widespread, systematic and gross human rights violations amounting to crimes against humanity."[27] The Secretary-General repeated the reference at the March 12 ministerial meeting, yet only Colombia and France employed the language. Despite the UN Secretariat seemingly coalescing around an explicit invocation of crimes against humanity, both the United Kingdom and the United States now failed to do so: Hague repeated a vague reference to "crimes" and Clinton opted for "horrific campaign of violence that has shocked the conscience of the world."[28] Other Council members selected diverse language: "rampant violence and human rights abuses" (Azerbaijan), "overwhelming repression and violence" (Germany), "ruthless campaign of repression" (Portugal), and "human rights are violated on a massive scale" (Togo). Others made no reference to the level of violence and used the opportunity to cast doubt on "such concepts as regime change" (Pakistan) or "hasty demands for regime change" (Russia). Some states explicitly or implicitly criticized NATO instead for its no-fly zone operations in Libya: "no party is to interpret [resolutions] in anyway it wants, let alone take action that exceeds Council mandates" (China), "selective or partial interpretation of a mandate" (India), "massive bombings" and "civilian casualties" (Russia), and "pursue self-interest and execute regime change" (South Africa).

As such, it is not surprising that, albeit calling on the Al-Assad regime to "end the use of heavy weapons in population centers," the presidential statements adopted on March 21 and April 5 contained vague references to "a serious human rights crisis"[29] and "violence and human rights violations,"[30] respectively, compared to the stronger language agreed to on August 3, 2011. These statements were casualties of the conflation some Council members made between regime change and the responsibility to protect, suspecting that any invocation of atrocity crimes would open the door to a Libya-like "interpretation" of the Council mandate.

The first two Syria-related resolutions adopted by the Security Council on April 14 and 21, 2012, condemned the "widespread violations of human rights" perpetrated by Syria as well as "any human rights abuses by armed groups" and recalled that those responsible shall be held accountable.[31] No Council members employed

[25] UN Doc. S/2012/77 (Feb. 4, 2012). Unlike UN Doc. S/2011/612, this draft resolution was supported by Brazil, India and South Africa. Lebanon was no longer a non-permanent member.

[26] UN Doc. A/HRC/19/69 (Feb. 22, 2012).

[27] UN Doc. S/PV.6725 (Feb. 28, 2012), at 2.

[28] UN Doc. S/PV.6734 (Mar. 12, 2012), at 5, 9.

[29] UN Doc. S/PRST/2012/6 (Mar. 21, 2012).

[30] UN Doc. S/PRST/2012/12 (Apr. 5, 2012).

[31] SC Res. 2042 (Apr. 14, 2012) and SC Res. 2043 (Apr. 21, 2012).

the term "crimes against humanity," opting instead for a wide array of characterizations: "human rights violations" (Azerbaijan, Portugal) and "atrocities" and "crimes" (Colombia, Germany), with the P3 employing colorful but legally vague language to depict the atrocities committed by the Bashar Al-Assad regime only. France, for example, used "barbaric repression," "heinous deeds," and "lethal behavior," identifying specific abuses, such as arbitrary arrests, forced disappearances, sexual violence, and torture, "all of which [...] have been committed systematically and on a large scale." The United Kingdom employed "unimaginable brutality" and referenced how the regime had "murdered, arbitrarily detained, tortured, abused and terrorized innocent civilians," while the United States opted for "barbaric campaign of violence" and "murderous rampage." Other Council members selected more indeterminate terms such as "acts of violence" (China), "bloodshed" (Morocco), "too many casualties" (Russia), or just plain "violence" (India, South Africa).[32]

At the August 30, 2012, Security Council meeting, the Deputy Secretary-General cited "recent accounts of possible war crimes" and called for those responsible to be held "accountable for gross human rights violations, war crimes and crimes against humanity."[33] Only Guatemala referenced one of the ICC crimes, albeit in conditional terms—"actions that could be later classified as war crimes"—while France, Germany, and the United Kingdom explicitly referenced the ICC, albeit using the generic "crimes." Yet by the April 18, 2013 briefing, the UN Secretariat was using a varying array of terms, instead of rallying behind a common message. Only the Special Representative for Sexual Violence employed "crimes against humanity and war crimes," while the Office for the Coordination of Humanitarian Affairs (OCHA) and the Special Representative for Children and Armed Conflict opted for weaker formulations: "obligations to protect civilians and to abide by international humanitarian law" and "disproportionate use of force [...] without any precautionary measures and with the use of indiscriminate weapons."[34] The same would be the case with the July 16 briefing, with OCHA using "open and blatant violations of the rules of war," while the UN Refugee Agency (UNHCR) made no reference whatsoever to abuses or crimes.[35] The Office of the High Commissioner for Human Rights echoed the terms used earlier by the Deputy Secretary-General in stating that "in Syria today, serious human rights violations, war crimes and crimes against humanity are the rule," adding an appeal for the Council to refer the situation to the ICC. The Under-Secretary-General for Political Affairs opted for "international crimes" at the August 20 briefing.[36]

The alleged use of chemical weapons in Syria did not bring an end to the varying terminology employed by the UN Secretariat. At the September 27, 2013, Council meeting, the first at which Council members considered the Ghouta chemical weapons attack (August 21, 2013), the Secretary-General spoke generically of "that crime" and "a catalogue of horrors in Syria,"[37] while OCHA employed "violations of international humanitarian law and violations and abuses of human rights" at the October

[32] UN Doc. S/PV.6751 and UN Doc. S/PV.6756 (Apr. 14 and 21, 2012).
[33] UN Doc. S/PV.6826 (Aug. 30, 2012).
[34] UN Doc. S/PV.6949 (Apr. 18, 2013), at 3, 7–8.
[35] UN Doc. S/PV.7000 (July 16, 2013), at 3.
[36] UN Doc. S/PV.7020 (Aug. 20, 2013), at 4.
[37] UN Doc. S/PV.7038 (Sept. 27, 2013), at 3.

25 briefing.[38] On February 22, 2014, the Secretary-General now reported "brutal violence and indiscriminate attacks, including the use of heavy weapons, aerial bombings, mortars and car bombs in populated areas," as well as "massacres and atrocities" and "countless killings, disappearances, the horrendous use of barrel bombs and torture on a massive scale,"[39] yet did not reference any of the ICC-listed crimes previously cited by the Deputy Secretary-General, the Under-Secretary-General for Political Affairs, the High Commissioner for Human Rights, or the Special Representative for Sexual Violence. His silence was particularly inexplicable—and inexcusable—as the Council meeting began with the adoption, by consensus, of Resolution 2139, which stressed that some of violations committed in Syria "may amount to war crimes and crimes against humanity."[40] While the Secretary-General used only the generic "obligations under international humanitarian law," Argentina and Jordan used "crimes against humanity," while Chile, Lithuania, and Nigeria employed "war crimes and crimes against humanity." The United States shied away from enunciating any ICC crimes, albeit speaking of "crimes that are so horrific, so systematic and so recurrent that they have lost some of their power to shock the conscience." None of the remaining Council members echoed the terms used in Resolution 2139, including two of the main drafters (Australia and Luxembourg).

B. Inconsistency: Take Three

At the May 22, 2014, meeting, the Deputy Secretary-General, speaking for the Secretary-General, changed tune and explicitly used "gross human rights violations, crimes against humanity and war crimes," recalling that the High Commissioner for Human Rights had "repeatedly called" for a referral of the situation in Syria to the ICC, "the appropriate venue for the fight against impunity in Syria," according to the Commission of Inquiry on Syria.[41] The mention of ICC-listed crimes was welcomed by several Council members—and probably helped by the Council's consideration at the same time of a draft resolution to refer the situation to the ICC. Some states also referenced one or more crimes, including Argentina, Lithuania, the United Kingdom, and the United States ("war crimes and crimes against humanity"); Chile, Jordan, and Luxembourg ("genocide, war crimes and crimes against humanity"); and Rwanda ("genocide, war crimes, ethnic cleansing, and crimes against humanity").

Unfortunately, OCHA failed to seize on this forward movement toward a shared characterization of the crimes at the June 26, 2014, briefing, speaking of "targeted or indiscriminate attacks on civilians, in densely populated areas, in violation of the most fundamental principles of international humanitarian law," yet generically recalling that "targeting or indiscriminately attacking vulnerable civilians constitutes a war crime."[42] At the next Council meeting, on July 14, the Council adopted Resolution

[38] UN Doc. S/PV.7049 (Oct. 25, 2013), at 2.

[39] UN Doc. S/PV.7116 (Feb. 22, 2014), at 2.

[40] SC Res. 2139 (Feb. 22, 2014). The resolution contains the most robust human rights language to date of any Council statement or product on Syria.

[41] UN Doc. S/PV.7180 (May 22, 2014), at 2.

[42] UN Doc. S/PV.7212 (June 26, 2014), at 2–3.

2165, which established a new precedent in authorizing cross-border aid delivery into Syria without the consent of the government. Yet only Lithuania used "war crimes and crimes against humanity," with Luxembourg employing "crimes" and "starvation as a weapon of war," while other members at best employed legally vague characterizations: "cynical manipulation of humanitarian aid" (Australia), "siege and starvation tactics" (United Kingdom), and "denial of aid and starvation, sickness and misery [...] as yet another weapon" (United States).[43] OCHA publicly briefed the Council five additional times in what remained of 2014, yet not once did it reference one or more of the ICC-listed crimes—save to make reference to abuses committed by Daesh.[44]

Notwithstanding the non-invocation of the Rome Statute crimes by OCHA, Resolution 2191, adopted on December 17, 2014, recalled that "some of the violations and abuses committed in Syria may amount to war crimes and crimes against humanity."[45] The three drafters (Australia, Jordan, Luxembourg) carefully steered the renewal of cross-border humanitarian delivery, thus ensuring that Resolution 2191 adhered to the terms referenced in Resolution 2139. Since Resolutions 2139 and 2191, however, the only other Syria-related resolutions that have referenced ICC-listed crimes are subsequent periodic renewals to Resolution 2139. Those addressing the use of chemical weapons, such as Resolutions 2209, 2235, 2314, or 2319, used only "serious violation of international law."[46]

One of the apparent lessons of the tragedy in Syria is that Security Council members and the UN Secretariat were inconsistent in employing the term "crimes against humanity," opting at times for language that while colorful is legally less powerful. They also seemed to operate at cross-purposes at times, for when the UN Secretariat seized on the term, Council members tended to use other characterizations, and vice versa. With such inconsistent application and argumentation for the use of the term, it is not surprising that the UN Secretariat was largely unsuccessful in convincing Council members—including those members most politically inclined to do so, namely, the P3—to adhere to a specific crime to legally characterize the violations perpetrated in Syria, and more specifically, by the Al-Assad regime.

The continued failure of the Security Council to address ICC crimes in Syria led the General Assembly, acting at the initiative of Liechtenstein, to creatively stretch the meaning of Article 11 of the UN Charter and start filling the void in adopting Resolution 71/248 on December 21, 2016. The resolution not only stressed that crimes

[43] UN Doc. S/PV.7216 (July 14, 2014), at 2, 4, 7, 10.

[44] UN Doc. S/PV.7342 (Dec. 15, 2014), at 4.

[45] SC Res. 2191 (Dec. 17, 2014). It also recalled "legal obligations under international humanitarian law and international human rights law, as well as all the relevant decisions of the Security Council, including by ceasing all attacks against civilians and civilian objects, including those involving attacks on schools, medical facilities and the deliberate interruptions of water supply, the indiscriminate use of weapons, including artillery, barrel bombs and air strikes, indiscriminate shelling by mortars, car bombs, suicide attacks and tunnel bombs, as well as the use of starvation of civilians as a method of combat, including by the besiegement of populated areas, and the widespread use of torture, ill-treatment, arbitrary executions, extrajudicial killings, enforced disappearances, sexual and gender-based violence as well as all grave violations and abuses committed against children."

[46] SC Res. 2209 (Mar. 6, 2015); SC Res. 2235 (Aug. 7, 2015); SC Res. 2314 (Oct. 31, 2016); SC Res. 2319 (Nov. 17, 2016).

perpetrated in Syria "may constitute war crimes and crimes against humanity" but it more importantly opened different routes for accountability through the establishment of the International, Impartial and Independent Mechanism for Syria (IIIM) with an unprecedented mandate—for a General Assembly subsidiary body—to

> collect, consolidate, preserve and analyse evidence of violations of international humanitarian law and human rights violations and abuses and to prepare files in order to facilitate and expedite fair and independent criminal proceedings, in accordance with international law standards, in national, regional or international courts or tribunals that have or may in the future have jurisdiction over these crimes, in accordance with international law.[47]

II. Yemen: One-Sided Discourse and Alleged War Crimes

The armed conflict in Yemen is a telltale example of one-sided discourse in action, in which political interests color references to legal norms regulating the conduct of war. On April 14, 2015, almost three weeks into the Saudi Arabia and the United Arab Emirates co-led military intervention against the Houthis and their allies in Yemen, the Security Council adopted Resolution 2216, a text initiated by Jordan, then a non-permanent member but also a member of the military coalition. It was therefore not entirely surprising that the text—notwithstanding a call on "all parties to comply with their obligations under international law, including applicable international humanitarian law and human rights law"[48]—only singled out the Houthis, a total of eleven times, including by unilaterally imposing or reinforcing measures under Chapter VII. Jordan presented the resolution as sending a "strong and firm message to the Houthis"[49] and was joined in its one-sided discourse by the United Kingdom expressing "support for the Saudi-led military intervention" and condemnation of the Houthis. Russia, on the other hand, highlighted the imbalance of the text by abstaining on the resolution and castigating its sponsors for failing to impose measures, most notably an arms embargo, on all parties. Other Council members (Bolivia, Chad, France, Lithuania, Malaysia, New Zealand, United States) voting for the resolution underscored that "all parties" needed to abide by their international humanitarian law and human rights law obligations. Adding context to these obligations, only Bolivia expressed specific condemnation for attacks on schools and hospitals, while Chad additionally referenced attacks on civilian infrastructure and camps for refugees and displaced persons.

At the next briefing on Yemen, on July 28, 2015, OCHA characterized the impact of the conflict on civilians as "catastrophic" and spoke of "parties"—not "all parties"—continuing to "fail to meet their responsibilities under international humanitarian law and international human rights law."[50] It was therefore not clear whether the plural

[47] GA Res. 71/248 (Dec. 21, 2016). Adopted by 105 votes, with 15 against and 52 abstentions.
[48] SC Res. 2216 (Apr. 14, 2015).
[49] UN Doc. S/PV.7426 (Apr. 14, 2015), at 8.
[50] UN Doc. S/PV.7494 (July 28, 2015), at 1.

form was indirectly meant to refer to both sides of the conflict or just the Houthis and their allies. The Special Envoy of the Secretary-General for Yemen made no significant mention in regard to obligations arising from the conduct of the war at the next briefing, on November 11, although he did refer to "grave breaches of international humanitarian law" and "horrific violence" at the December 22 briefing, albeit in the passive voice, without referencing parties.[51] At the same briefing, the Assistant Secretary-General for Humanitarian Affairs continued to employ the plural indefinite form of parties used by OCHA earlier, maintaining the ambiguity as to what parties were concerned. Also participating in the briefing on December 22, but unlike all other UN Secretariat briefers, the High Commissioner for Human Rights brought clarity to the scope of the parties and to the type of crimes committed. He challenged ongoing attempts by some Council members to cast the Houthis and their allies as the main perpetrators of crimes in Yemen, denouncing a

> continuation of heavy shelling from the ground and the air in areas with high concentration of civilians, as well as continued destruction of civilian infrastructure—in particular hospitals and schools—by all parties to the conflict, although a disproportionate share appeared to be the result of civilian strikes carried out by coalition forces.

He also called for "an international investigation into credible allegations of violations of international humanitarian law and human rights law, as well as a call for accountability for the perpetrators of such crimes." He moreover "strongly encouraged" Yemen to ratify the Rome Statute or to at least "urgently accept its jurisdiction," thus signaling that the abuses amounted to the crimes covered by the Rome Statute.

The differences in language by three different UN officers at the December 22, 2015, briefing undermined the unity of the message on accountability. The continued ambiguity by the Special Envoy or OCHA in identifying the parties ran contrary to the clarity and specificity offered by the High Commissioner. Although such differences could have been part of a carefully scripted and agreed upon division of labor, the statements were not coordinated,[52] and they aligned with the mandates of each office more than they advanced a common communication strategy against impunity for egregious crimes. Neither the Special Envoy or OCHA could have been surprised by the elements highlighted by the High Commissioner, as he had already used similar language and called for the same recommendations at the September 2015 Human Rights Council session.

Despite these briefings, and the clarity brought to the fore by the High Commissioner in particular, Jordan continued to cast the Houthis and their allies as the sole concern, while France made no reference to any party whatsoever. The United Kingdom shifted somewhat from its earlier one-sidedness, repeating the wording of Resolution 2216, calling on "all parties ... to fulfill their obligations under international humanitarian law." Other Council members, however, referencing specific weapons or targets,

[51] UN Doc. S/PV.7596 (Dec. 22, 2015), at 3.

[52] Personal interviews with UN officials involved in preparing and/or delivering the statements, Mar. 11, 2020.

hinted at alleged crimes committed by the coalition (Chile, Lithuania, Malaysia, New Zealand, Spain), with Chile and Malaysia also echoing some of the stronger calls made by the High Commissioner in support of an independent investigation. Lithuania was the only Council member to use the term "war crimes," while the United States "urge[d] the Saudi-led coalition to ensure lawful and discriminate targeting and to thoroughly investigate all credible allegations of civilian casualties."

It was only at the February 16, 2016, briefing that OCHA finally referenced, in passing and without any information on casualties, a "Saudi-led coalition airstrike," otherwise referring to "indiscriminate bombing and shelling by the parties" and emphasizing the "duty of care in the conduct of military operations to protect all civilian persons and objects."[53] On April 20, the Secretary-General released the annual Children and Armed Conflict report, lamenting a sixfold increase in the number of children killed and maimed due to the conflict in Yemen in 2015 relative to 2014. It attributed 60 percent of the casualties to the Saudi Arabia–led coalition versus 20 percent to the Houthis.[54] It moreover temporarily listed the Saudi Arabia–led coalition as a party to Annex I of its report, colloquially known as the "list of shame," before the Secretary-General caved in to political pressure and removed the coalition "pending review."[55]

A. The October 8, 2016, Double Airstrike

It took the October 8, 2016, Saudi-led coalition double airstrike on a funeral in Sana'a, leading to more than one hundred forty people killed and five hundred fifty injured, for the one-sided discourse to change temporarily. The Special Envoy finally named the "Arab coalition" for "a tragic and painful attack."[56] Yet, as the Special Envoy himself acknowledged at the October 31 briefing to the Council, in an apparent attempt to soften the statement, the coalition had already taken responsibility for the attack, conducted a preliminary investigation, and recommended action against those involved and a revision of its rules of engagement. Moreover, the Special Envoy did not call for an independent investigation but only the need for the coalition joint incident assessment team "to complete the investigations," thus toeing a line that was markedly different from the October 9 call by the Secretary-General, in a press statement, for a "prompt and impartial investigation."[57]

OCHA, which similarly briefed the Council and referenced the October 8 strikes, hinted at the disproportionate share of civilian deaths due to coalition attacks, stating that "there is no equivalence between those killing with air power, available only to one side of the fight, and those on the other side killing with land-based weaponry." In addition to stating that "perpetrators on all sides must be held responsible for the legions of violations of international humanitarian law," OCHA stressed the need for

53 UN Doc. S/PV.7622 (Feb. 16, 2016), at 2.
54 UN Doc. A/170/836–S/2016/360 (Apr. 20, 2016), at 27–28.
55 UN Doc. A170/836/Add.1–S/2016/360/Add.1 (June 24, 2016).
56 UN Doc. S/PV.7797 (Oct. 31, 2016), at 2.
57 Statement by the Secretary-General, Oct. 8, 2016.

"effective, independent investigations into allegations of war crimes,"[58] the first such reference to war crimes made by OCHA in the context of Yemen in its briefings to the Council. As on previous occasions, the UN Secretariat sent mixed signals: the Special Envoy merely called for the coalition to "complete" its own preliminary investigations, whereas OCHA—in close alignment with the High Commissioner for Human Rights and the Secretary-General—called for an independent investigation.

The October 8 double airstrike by the Saudi-led coalition was a short-lived watershed moment for some Council members. Uruguay was explicit in characterizing the strikes as a "terrorist attack" more than a war crime, with the intent of casting more opprobrium on the attack.[59] Uruguay also openly spoke to the one-sidedness of the Council, lamenting that it "has not been able to issue even a statement condemning the horrendous attack." Uruguay drew a contrast with the war in Syria, stating that "we cannot condemn aerial attacks that kill civilians in Syria but remain mute in the face of similar attacks in Yemen. There is no place for double standards." This was echoed by Venezuela and Russia, with the latter speaking of "cynical double standards" and castigating the United Kingdom, "a country with a clear material interest in extending the military conflict," as the lead drafter (penholder) of Council products on Yemen. More specifically, Russia criticized the penholder for drafting a "toothless" draft press statement for the Council in response to the October 8 attack, calling it "not simply broadly general, but openly weak [...] it was not stated who made the strike, even though the coalition had already accepted responsibility."[60]

On the opposite end, omitting any reference to the October 8 attack, were China, Egypt, Japan, Malaysia, Spain, and Ukraine, although the latter three generically condemned attacks against civilians. France and Senegal referred to the attack in passing while failing to name a perpetrator. Both the United Kingdom and the United States condemned the attack and named the coalition, yet couched their condemnation in positive terms. The United Kingdom was "shocked and appalled" by the attack and stressed that "there must be accountability for that attack," yet remained silent on an independent investigation, supporting instead the self-investigation conducted by the coalition as "a positive step." It also expressed "disappointment and regret" that the Council had failed to adopt its draft press statement, "which would have strongly condemned the attack"—a euphemism, as the text did not name the perpetrator.[61] The United States, for its part, similarly refrained from calling for an independent investigation, stating that it looked "forward to further reporting" from the coalition. It also underscored—avoiding any mention of legal norms or terms—that the coalition needed to "take all feasible measures to reduce civilian casualties and target precisely, including verifying targets against a no-strike list."[62]

[58] UN Doc. S/PV.7797 (Oct. 31, 2016), at 2.

[59] Uruguay was scathing in its criticism of the Saudi-led coalition: "Allow me to make special reference to the terrorist attack—I repeat, the terrorist attack—carried out on 8 October in Sana'a ... I refer to it as a terrorist attack because [...] if it walks like a duck and talks like a duck, with its distinctive quack, then we must acknowledge that it is, in fact, a duck." *Id.* at 10.

[60] *Id.* at 22.

[61] *Id.* at 11.

[62] *Id.* at 17.

B. The Deafening Silence

Tellingly, at the next Council meeting, on January 26, 2017, accountability language had all but disappeared. This was surprising as Council members were by then apprised of the final report of the Panel of Experts to the 2140 Yemen Sanctions Committee. The report covered abuses committed by all parties, but dealt at length with ten coalition attacks it investigated:

> In 8 of the 10 investigations, the Panel found no evidence that the air strikes had targeted legitimate military objects. For all 10 investigations, the Panel considers it almost certain that the coalition did not meet international humanitarian law requirements of proportionality and precaution in attack. The Panel considers that some of the attacks may amount to war crimes.[63]

With the exception of OCHA, which would at subsequent briefings dramatically ramp up its calls for accountability, and Uruguay, a consistent voice for avoiding "double standards on this matter,"[64] all other Secretariat briefers or Council members went silent on accountability. By August 18, 2017, Under-Secretary-General Stephen O'Brien would stress "that even wars have rules, and even wars have their limits, or at least they should have." He moreover stressed that "we must not get hung up on the semantics of who is a party, who is a proxy and who denies being involved. All the perpetrators and their facilitators of this hideous Yemen war know who they are." Having by then given up on the Council regarding the accountability angle, O'Brien called on the Human Rights Council "to act." The Special Envoy of the Secretary-General, on the other hand, made no calls for accountability, save relating to the May 22, 2017, attack on his own convoy.[65]

Uruguay, a lonely voice for accountability for all parties, repeatedly stressed that the Council "has all the competencies required to establish impartial and transparent mechanisms for investigating the violations of international humanitarian law [. . .] committed by both parties to the conflict."[66] Despite its unsuccessful appeals for Council action, Uruguay ultimately was pleased to see the Human Rights Council—not the Security Council—establishing a Group of Eminent Experts (see below) to monitor the human rights situation in Yemen, including "violations and abuses committed by all the parties to the conflict since September 2014."[67]

As this summary examination of Security Council meetings on Yemen shows, despite Resolution 2216's call on "all parties" to abide by their international humanitarian law obligations, there was a determined effort by some Council members to cast the Houthis as the main—or sole—perpetrators of egregious crimes, notwithstanding mounting evidence that the Saudi-led coalition was primarily responsible for the killing and maiming of civilians and for striking schools, hospitals, and other

[63] UN Doc. S/2017/81, at 51–52. The letter was publicly released on January 27, 2017, but it had been privately shared with Council members on January 11 through the 2140 Yemen Sanctions Committee.
[64] UN Doc. S/PV.7871 (Jan. 26, 2017), at 7.
[65] UN Doc. S/PV.7954 (May 30, 2017), at 4.
[66] UN Doc. S/PV.7999 (July 12, 2017), at 7–8.
[67] UN Doc. S/PV.8066 (Oct. 10, 2017), at 6.

civilian sites. They were largely successful in avoiding any uncomfortable references to the coalition, using their prerogatives as penholders (Jordan, United Kingdom) to ensure that any such references were drowned in ambiguous mentions of "parties." Except for the High Commissioner for Human Rights, the UN Secretariat largely played along, either keeping silent (Special Envoy) or similarly employing ambiguous language at first (OCHA). The Secretary-General, under pressure by Saudi Arabia, undermined the technical integrity of the monitoring and reporting mechanism that underpins the Children and Armed Conflict agenda due to political considerations. Despite reporting that "six times as many children were killed and maimed in 2015 [. . .] and five times as many were recruited into fighting" in Yemen compared to 2014, and that children "must always come first," the Secretary-General acknowledged that "objections to the annual report forced me to make a difficult decision": removing the Saudi Arabia–led coalition from the annexes.[68] This political intervention of what had been a robust technical monitoring and reporting mechanism undermined the universal applicability of the norms and the legitimacy and objectivity of the mechanism.

The remarkable paucity in references to alleged war crimes in Yemen to characterize the violations committed by the coalition continued apace. With the notable exception of an isolated reference by the Under-Secretary-General for Humanitarian Affairs (October 31, 2016), the UN Secretariat shied away from the term "war crimes." It did not even embrace the term following the release of the January 27, 2017, report by the Panel of Experts servicing the 2140 Yemen Sanctions Committee. Within the Council, only Lithuania used the term (December 22, 2015), with Uruguay opting for the added opprobrium of "terrorist attack" (October 31, 2016). Most other members either used generic references to "violations to international humanitarian and human rights law," or, worse, remained silent on coalition violations (China, Egypt, Japan, Jordan, Malaysia, Spain, Ukraine) or urged improvement in conduct by the parties in an apparent attempt to preempt independent investigations (United Kingdom, United States).

C. Vindication of the Few

Those making use of the term "war crimes" were not only vindicated by the January 27, 2017, report issued by the Panel of Experts but also, belatedly, by the August 28, 2018, report released by the Group of Eminent Experts on Yemen.[69] In its report, the Panel concluded that the government of Yemen and the coalition, including Saudi Arabia and the United Arab Emirates,

> may have conducted attacks in violation of the principles of distinction, proportionality and precaution that may amount to war crimes [and] have committed acts that

[68] UN Doc. S/PV.7753 (Aug. 2, 2016), at 3. Pursuant to Resolutions 1379 (2001), 1882 (2009), 1998 (2011), and 2225 (2015), parties that commit grave violations affecting children in situations of armed conflict on the agenda of the Council are liable to be listed in the annexes to the annual report of the Secretary-General on Children and Armed Conflict.

[69] Group of Eminent International and Regional Experts on Yemen established by Human Rights Council Res. 36/31 (Sept. 29, 2017).

> may amount to war crimes, including cruel treatment and torture, outrages upon personal dignity, rape and conscripting or enlisting children under the age of 15 or using them to participate actively in hostilities.[70]

The Panel was categorical in its conclusion that these incidents

> raise serious concerns about the targeting process applied by the coalition. If there are errors in the targeting process that effectively remove the protections provided by international humanitarian law, these would amount to violations. These may, depending on the circumstances, amount to war crimes by individuals at all levels in the member states of the coalition and the Government, including civilian officials.

At the time of writing, the Security Council continues to unilaterally identify the Houthis for certain violations of international humanitarian and human rights law while keeping silent on coalition-led abuses, notwithstanding a growing body of evidence.[71] In sum, despite strongly worded calls by the High Commissioner, Lithuania, and Uruguay invoking Rome Statute crimes, and credible reporting by its own Panel of Experts, the Council failed to take any meaningful action in addressing the alleged war crimes and related abuses perpetrated by the Saudi-led coalition in Yemen. Ultimately it was the Human Rights Council, at the initiative of the Netherlands, that answered those calls in mandating the establishment of the Group of Eminent Experts. The Secretary-General, on the other hand, again delisted the Saudi-led coalition on June 9, 2020, despite the evidence presented in the latest annual report on Children and Armed Conflict,[72] and the non-cessation of all violations for a period of at least one reporting cycle, as mandated by Resolution 1882.

III. Myanmar: Ethnic Cleansing, Crimes against Humanity, Genocide, or None of the Above

The Security Council deliberations on the situation in Myanmar, following the August 25, 2017, attacks by the Arakan Rohingya Salvation Army against military outposts and the subsequent campaign unleashed by the army (Tatmadaw) against the Rohingya minority, provide a revealing example of how legal terms and norms are brought to the fore in what are essentially political deliberations. On September 11, addressing the Human Rights Council, the High Commissioner for Human Rights declared that "the situation cannot yet be fully assessed but the situation remains or seems a textbook example of ethnic cleansing." The choice of the term was interesting in that ethnic cleansing has not been recognized as an independent crime under

[70] UN Doc. A/HRC/39/43 (Aug. 28, 2018), at 15–16.
[71] SC Res. 2511 (Feb. 25, 2020); SC Res. 2564 (Feb. 25, 2021).
[72] Children and Armed Conflict: Report of the Secretary-General, UN Doc. A/74/845-S/2020/525 (June 9, 2020).

international law, although it can constitute a crime against humanity, can be assimilated to war crimes, and can fall within the meaning of genocide.[73]

Speaking at the first meeting of the Security Council on Myanmar on September 28, 2017, the Secretary-General refrained from using the term "ethnic cleansing," opting for more understated formulations, mostly in the passive voice, such as "indiscriminate firing," "use of force . . . must respect human rights obligations under international law," or "lethal force, even in situations of emergency, must be commensurate with the threat to the public order."[74] The closest he came to referencing ethnic cleansing was a passive voice reference to "there seems to be a deeply disturbing pattern to the violence and the ensuing large movements of an ethnic group from their homes." On the other hand, the United States and France, as well as Bangladesh, sought to give credence to the claims that ethnic cleansing was happening, albeit using different formulations. Whereas the United States characterized the situation as "a brutal sustained campaign to cleanse the country of an ethnic minority," France was more assertive in stating that "ethnic cleansing is happening today in western Burma" and referencing alleged "massive violations of human rights that may constitute crimes against humanity." Bangladesh was even more categorical in stating that the atrocities committed "amount to crimes against humanity" and reminding the Council that the High Commissioner for Human Rights considered the situation to be "a textbook example of ethnic cleansing."

On the other end of the spectrum, Russia and Myanmar sought to draw a dividing line between politically and emotionally charged terms and legal definitions. Russia asked for "restraint and objectivity in the assessment of ongoing events" and cautioned that "we need to be very precise in using terms like 'genocide' and 'ethnic cleansing.' " Myanmar dismissed the use of these terms as the product of "subjective and emotionally charged accounts," highlighting that "ethnic cleansing and genocide are serious charges that should not be made lightly." Driving the point home, it also stressed that no such assertions should be made "without first undertaking a legal review and making a judicial determination."

Following consultations and negotiations, Security Council members agreed to a presidential statement, co-drafted by France and the United Kingdom, that sought to balance these two conflicting accounts by providing a road map for evaluating progress, while expressing "grave concern over reports of human rights violations and abuses in Rakhine state, including by the Myanmar security forces, in particular against persons belonging to the Rohingya community."[75] In typifying the abuses, the statement blended non-legal terminology such as "killing of men, women and children" and "sexual violence and abuse and violence against children" with calls to ensure there was no more "excessive use of military force" and broad appeals for respect of "obligations and commitments to respect human rights."

[73] See Letter from the Secretary-General to the President of the Security Council, UN Doc. S/1994/674 (Feb. 10, 1993); and Letter from the Secretary-General to the President of the Security Council, UN Doc. S/1994/674 (May 27, 1994); and SC Res. 780 (Oct. 6, 1992).

[74] UN Doc. S/PV.8060 (Sept. 28, 2017), at 2.

[75] UN Doc. S/PV.8085 (Nov. 6, 2017).

On December 12, 2017, the Security Council met again, with the Under-Secretary-General for Political Affairs continuing to sing the tune of the Secretary-General with non-legal references to a "vicious cycle of discrimination, violence and displacement." The Special Representative of the Secretary-General on Sexual Violence, however, spoke of terror "seemingly aimed at the extermination and removal of the Rohingya as a group" and added later, in the passive voice, that "ethnic cleansing must never be allowed to achieve its goal." Neither referenced the finding made by the High Commissioner for Human Rights that the crimes against the Rohingya were "characteristic of genocide," thus potentially undermining the authority or credibility of the claim. Only Uruguay openly endorsed this finding, with France and the United States preferring to use "ethnic cleansing," and in the case of the former, references to acts that "could amount to crimes against humanity." Sweden was somewhat more categorical in stating that the "acts of violence strongly indicate that crimes against humanity have been committed," adding that it was "important that the facts and circumstances on the ground be fully established," a task that it said fell on the Human Rights Council–mandated Fact-Finding Mission.[76]

At the next debate on Myanmar, on February 18, 2018, neither the Assistant Secretary-General for Political Affairs nor the High Commissioner for Refugees briefing the Council used the term "ethnic cleansing," opting, respectively, for vague references to "large scale acts of violence" and "violence and destruction, following decades of repression and exclusion."[77] While briefing the Council on August 28, a year into the mass killings, the Secretary-General could still not utter ICC-listed crimes, notwithstanding the release of the report by the Fact-Finding Mission for Myanmar and its legal findings:

> [T]here is sufficient information to warrant the investigation and prosecution of senior officials in the Tatmadaw chain of command, so that a competent court can determine their liability for genocide in relation to the situation in Rakhine State [and] crimes against humanity [. . .] committed in Kachin, Rakhine and Shan States, principally by the Tatmadaw.[78]

Instead, the Secretary-General quoted a generic reference to "gross human rights violations and abuses . . . [which] undoubtedly amount to the gravest crimes under international law."[79] While keeping a safe distance from the term "genocide," some Council members adhered to the term "ethnic cleansing" (Equatorial Guinea, France, Kuwait, the United Kingdom, the United States), with France even claiming precedence in using the term "almost a year ago."[80]

On October 24, 2018, the Security Council was briefed by the chairman of the Fact-Finding Mission. The United Kingdom, speaking for the nine states that supported

[76] Independent International Fact-Finding Mission for Myanmar established by Human Rights Council Res. 34/22 (Mar. 24, 2017).

[77] UN Doc. S/PV.8179 (Feb. 13, 2018).

[78] Report of the Independent International Fact-Finding Mission for Myanmar, UN Doc. A/HRC/39/64 (Sept. 12, 2018), paras. 87, 88.

[79] UN Doc. S/PV.8333 (Aug. 28, 2018), at 3.

[80] UN Doc. A/72/PV.4 (Sept. 19, 2017).

the invitation to the Mission to brief the Council, highlighted that its report recommended that the Council "ensure accountability for crimes under international law committed in Myanmar," while reminding Council members that "ensuring the prevention of such crimes—genocide, war crimes and crimes against humanity—is one of the reasons why the United Nations and the Security Council were established in the first place."[81] Speaking about genocidal intent, France highlighted that the report concludes "that on the basis of 'reasonable inference', there are factors 'that have allowed genocidal intent to be established,'" whereas the Netherlands stated that the Mission "concludes that, on reasonable grounds, the factors allowing the inference of genocidal intent are present."

Although Secretary-General António Guterres is to be commended for bringing the situation in Myanmar to the attention of the Security Council,[82] in avoiding the term "ethnic cleansing" he had already invoked in an opinion piece,[83] he missed the opportunity to give it further credence. Moreover, he refrained from invoking the term within the Council, while deeming it appropriate for the court of public opinion. Such avoidance to refer to specific crimes contrasts, for example, with the celerity and clarity with which Kofi Annan alerted the Security Council to "various categories of international crime [*sic*]" being perpetrated by Indonesia in East Timor following the August 30, 1999, consultation on independence.[84] It also contrasts with the overtly legal framing provided by Dag Hammarskjöld in 1960, who—informed of the killing of several hundred Balubas in the Kasai region (present-day Democratic Republic of the Congo)—alerted the Council to "a most flagrant violation of elementary human rights [that] have the characteristics of the crime of genocide since they appear to be directed towards the extermination of a specific ethnic group."[85] Unlike Guterres, both Annan and Hammarskjöld promptly and explicitly pointed to atrocity crimes albeit addressing situations with lower thresholds of violence and doing so in an era that predated the Rome Statute, the "emerging norm" of the Responsibility to Protect, and the commitment to the Human Rights Up Front initiative. Moreover, despite the evidence brought forth by the monitoring and reporting mechanism and the non-cessation of all violations for a period of at least one reporting cycle, as mandated by Resolution 1882, Guterres unilaterally decided to delist the Tatmadaw from the latest annual report on Children and Armed Conflict,[86] the very same party that is mainly responsible for the ethnic killing of the Rohingya.

At the time of writing, the Security Council continues to fail to meaningfully address the ongoing crimes against the Rohingya. Instead, the Human Rights Council has taken the lead, first through the establishment of a Fact-Finding Mission (March 24, 2017), and then through the establishment of an International Impartial Mechanism for Myanmar (IIMM) (October 3, 2018), with an unprecedented quasi-prosecutorial

[81] UN Doc. S/PV.8381 (Oct. 24 2018). Statement on behalf of Côte d'Ivoire, France, Kuwait, the Netherlands, Peru, Poland, Sweden, the United Kingdom, and the United States.

[82] Letter from the Secretary-General to the President of the Security Council, UN Doc. S/2017/753 (Sept. 2, 2017).

[83] António Guterres, "The Rohingya are Victims of Ethnic Cleansing," *Washington Post*, July 10, 2018.

[84] UN Doc. S/PV.4043 (Sept. 11, 1999), at 2.

[85] UN Doc. S/PV.896 (Sept. 9, 1960), para. 101.

[86] Children and Armed Conflict: Report of the Secretary-General, *supra* note 72.

mandate for a Human Rights Council subsidiary body.[87] In addition, the Prosecutor of the ICC has initiated an investigation into crimes against the Rohingya within the jurisdiction of the Court in which at least one element occurred on the territory of neighboring Bangladesh, a state party to the Rome Statute (November 14, 2019).[88] And following an application by The Gambia to the International Court of Justice alleging that the crimes against the Rohingya violate the Convention of the Prevention and Punishment of the Crime of Genocide, the Court issued provisional measures ordering Myanmar to prevent all acts under Article 2 of the Convention (January 23, 2020).

IV. Conclusion

The Security Council has played an important role in the implementation of international humanitarian and human rights law in situations on its agenda, at times also in effect adjudicating or predetermining judicial assessment by denoting specific facts, naming specific parties, highlighting specific violations, or targeting specific perpetrators.[89] It has also established ad hoc international criminal tribunals (Yugoslavia, Rwanda)[90] or special tribunals (Sierra Leone, Lebanon)[91] and referred, to date, two situations to the ICC (Sudan, Libya).[92] It has also imposed arms embargoes, mandated the use of force—including to apprehend alleged criminals[93]—imposed war reparations,[94] and demanded the extradition of alleged criminals and terrorists.[95] It is therefore not surprising that the eminently political negotiations within the Council may include legal arguments. The case studies indicate that Council members regularly invoke minimal—generic and at times anemic—references to traditional sources of international humanitarian and human rights law. At times, a few members are inclined to add more meaningful case-specific and actionable demands, including accountability, to address serious human rights violations. Very few members are inclined to denounce alleged ICC crimes, to characterize them as such in unequivocal legal terms, and do so consistently across time and space.

[87] HRC Res. 39/2 (Oct. 3, 2018). The IIMM has a mandate to "collect, consolidate, preserve and analyze evidence of the most serious international crimes and violations of international law committed in Myanmar since 2011, and to prepare files in order to facilitate and expedite fair and independent criminal proceedings, in accordance with international law standards, in national, regional or international courts or tribunals that have or may in the future have jurisdiction over these crimes, in accordance with international law." At 2.

[88] On November 14, 2019, Pre-Trial Chamber III authorized the Prosecutor to proceed with the investigation, positively responding to the request dated July 4, 2019, by the Prosecutor to open an investigation into alleged crimes falling within ICC jurisdiction.

[89] Georg Nolte, "The Different Functions of the Security Council with Respect to Humanitarian Law," in *The United Nations Security Council and War*, edited by Vaughan Lowe et al. (Oxford: Oxford University Press, 2008), 519.

[90] SC Res. 808 (Feb. 22, 1993); SC Res. 827 (May 25, 1993); SC Res. 955 (Nov. 8, 1994).

[91] SC Res. 1315 (Aug. 14, 2000); SC Res. 1664 (Mar. 29, 2006); SC Res. 1757 (May 30, 2007).

[92] SC Res. 1593 (Mar. 31, 2005); SC Res. 1970 (Feb. 26, 2011).

[93] SC Res. 837 (June 6, 1993).

[94] SC Res. 674 (Oct. 29, 1990); SC Res. 687 (Apr. 3, 1991); SC Res. 692 (May 20, 1991).

[95] SC Res. 748 (Mar. 31, 1992); SC Res. 1054 (Apr. 26, 1996).

Unlike moral grandstanding, to which most Security Council members have become inured, legal argument can have independent, if insufficient, impact. However, its impact is limited by the eminently political nature of the interpretive community—the fifteen-member Council—where legal arguments must at best coexist, and at worst collide, with political interests generally. More specifically, legal arguments are also often heavily, if not entirely, compromised by double standards that lead to uneven invocation or application of applicable law across situations, and thus raise questions of impartiality, accuracy, and legitimacy. The cases described in this chapter illustrate the selective hypocrisy of the P3 in relation to the crimes of the Saudi-led coalition in Yemen and that of Russia in relation to the crimes of the Al-Assad regime in Syria. Since the Council has only adopted one presidential statement to address the plight of the Rohingya—no draft resolutions have been tabled to date—any double standards by China have been less in the open in relation to Myanmar. In all three cases, the Council has failed to mandate investigations of atrocity crimes, impose targeted sanctions against perpetrators—with the exception of the Houthis and their allies—and, save for Syria, create meaningful pressure on the parties most responsible for the crimes committed, namely, the Saudi-led coalition and the Tatmadaw.

Permanent members, however, do not have a monopoly on hypocrisy. The case studies show that, notwithstanding increasing evidence of alleged ICC-listed crimes, or determinations by UN-mandated bodies that such crimes were likely or actually committed, Security Council members and the UN Secretariat continued to engage in rhetorical exercises that devalue and obfuscate the facts of the crimes perpetrated. While expecting perfect consistency for any norm may be unrealistic, the case studies show anything but consistency, with expediency being the norm, not the exception. By substituting legally imprecise or politically passive language for crimes with international definitions and thresholds,[96] such language of substitution not only detracts and distracts. More generally, it devalues the currency of applicable international law and the overall coherence of and adherence to the normative systems in place.

While some Council members may indeed want to devalue international human rights and criminal law, they remain a minority. More problematic are those Council members, and the UN Secretariat, that despite claiming to be strongly committed to international human rights norms and accountability, fail to rise to the occasion and prefer abstraction and substitution instead of precision and affirmation. It also is inimical to the promotion of accountability, as it casts a legal or political penumbra on the scale and scope of the crimes (threshold substantiality) and the issue of appropriate venues to ensure that those responsible are brought to justice. The international legal frameworks listing and defining such crimes or the jurisdiction of relevant accountability mechanisms are reduced to one policy option among others at best, or as prescriptions that are subject to the discretion of the Council at worst. This is all the more concerning as, unlike other areas that have a "thin normative environment,"

[96] Unlike other bodies of law, the applicable international law is not an extraordinarily "open-textured body of law" whose "content is […] unclear, contested, and not authoritatively resolved," see Monica Hakimi, chapter 3, in this volume. The substitutions are therefore not likely the product of Security Council actors "think[ing] and argu[ing] laterally and embrac[ing] law as a social process," see Scott P. Sheeran, chapter 4, in this volume.

there is both density and specificity in the law to invoke and the demands for compliance by the alleged perpetrators because of legal duty.[97]

As demonstrated by the case studies, non-permanent members are more inclined to insert criminal law discourse into Security Council debates, and more importantly for the purposes of this chapter, references to crimes or elements thereof, than permanent members. This aligns with their prominent role in creating the "Arria-Formula meetings" (Venezuela), an informal mechanism for Council members to interact with outsiders with no formal standing before the Council, or add thematic issues with human rights dimensions to the Council agenda: children and armed conflict (Portugal),[98] protection of civilians (Canada),[99] and women, peace, and security (Bangladesh).[100] It also aligns with a longer history of non-permanent members seeking meaningful engagement by the Council on ongoing atrocity crimes: Croatia, New Zealand, Nigeria, Spain (Rwanda, 1994); Austria, Costa Rica, Mexico (Sri Lanka, 2009). However, as they are limited by the UN Charter to a two-year nonrenewable term, their efforts have limited continuity at best, as was the case with Lithuania and Uruguay, to cite the most prolific in invoking ICC-listed crimes in the case studies covered in this chapter. Most of these states either opt for abstraction or substitution in terms, or the invocation of the primacy of national sovereignty as a sacrosanct principle that overrides any liability for the commission of atrocity crimes.

Indeed, the question of regime change, seen as the ultimate challenge to national sovereignty, unfortunately crept into Security Council deliberations following the NATO operation against the Gaddafi regime in Libya, clearly affecting deliberations regarding Syria. The emerging norm of the responsibility to protect has been construed by some Council members to be a bellwether of regime change, and the invocation of ICC crimes to be a means to that end: an important part of the justificatory discourse behind regime change. Russia, albeit not alone, has been the most explicit in making the argument that attempts to invoke the responsibility to protect "lay the ultimate groundwork for eventual outside military intervention."[101]

The chapter has also sought to bring to the fore the role of the Secretary-General, and wider UN Secretariat, as an important set of players in Security Council discussions by virtue of being the "intendant of the Charter."[102] Yet, as seen with the case studies, the Secretary-General has largely failed to invoke the full legal power of international humanitarian and human rights norms and terms within the Council, keeping a safe distance from denouncing ICC crimes that carry criminal liability and instead employing less legally robust language. At times, the UN Secretariat seems to have preferred, wittingly or unwittingly, a division of labor—with the Secretary-General or other high-level Secretariat briefer shunning legal characterization, while other Secretariat briefers clearly denounce specific crimes. While such a division of labor may be grounded in a tactical decision to either balance or preserve political

97 See Steven Ratner, chapter 6, in this volume, for a more detailed development of thin normative consensus or dissensus.

98 SC Res. 1261 (Aug. 25, 1999).

99 UN Doc. S/PRST/1999/6 (Feb. 12, 1999), and SC Res. 1265 (Sept. 17, 1999).

100 SC Res. 1325 (Oct. 31, 2000).

101 UN Doc. S/PV.7180 (May 22, 2014).

102 Franck, *supra* note 14, at 119.

space for the Secretary-General, it inevitably sends mixed signals, as any substitution in terms undermines or collides with legal clarity, substantiality, and specificity. As Uruguay stated in one of the meetings on Yemen, "if it walks like a duck and talks like a duck, with its distinctive quack, then we must acknowledge that it is, in fact, a duck."[103] Yet the Secretariat at times employs diverse and diffuse terms to avoid calling it a duck within and across briefings on the same situation.

As the case studies also show, especially the case of Syria, the UN Secretariat can also be remarkably inconsistent in adhering to a specific legal term, walking back rhetorically from previously enunciated ICC crimes, despite an ever-increasing civilian toll. It can also be of different minds in identifying parties responsible for the commission of specific crimes, at times using abstract and passive references to "parties" or to "crimes" for safe distance. This preference for abstraction and substitution probably arises from an aversion to identify perpetrators, a politically sensitive issue, and more so when Council members, and especially permanent members, have different allegiances to the parties on the ground. As for the argument that not naming perpetrators, or crimes for that matter, helps the Secretariat build political rapport with the parties responsible, the proof of the alleged benefits of such silence should at the very least outweigh the costs in terms of accountability and nonselectivity. Yet the Secretariat has never made that case, just as it has not explained the benefits accrued from delisting the Saudi-led coalition and the Tatmadaw from the annexes of the recent Children and Armed Conflict report.

Ultimately, when the Security Council fails to meaningfully address atrocity crimes, other UN organs can substitute themselves, within their respective mandates, for the Council. For Syria, the Human Rights Council mandated the Commission of Inquiry on Syria and the General Assembly established the IIIM for Syria; for Yemen, the Human Rights Council mandated the Group of Eminent Experts; and for Myanmar, the Human Rights Council established the IIMM and The Gambia seized the International Court of Justice. These repeat substitutions are an alarming signal that the Security Council, due to internal divisions primarily among the permanent members, has lost its ability to be adaptable in addressing mass atrocities, both procedurally and substantively. While in the past the Council dramatically expanded its authority, redefining sovereignty and creating a panoply of tools unimaginable at the adoption of the UN Charter, at present other organs are adapting for the perceived loss of Council authority and translating principle into practice. These substitutions cannot rely on the Chapter VII powers of the Council and are therefore weaker than a like response mandated by the Council, though they are significant in terms of their capacity to attribute crimes to specific perpetrators and announce the withdrawal of impunity, thus potentially deterring other actual or potential perpetrators.

Without Security Council members feeling comfortable denouncing, as appropriate, ICC crimes in the first place as part of their argumentative and deliberative process, there seems to be little prospect of them considering larger "legislative" decisions to either advance compliance with international human rights law or deterrence of crimes that shock the conscience of humanity. The Council could clearly

[103] UN Doc. S/PV.7797 (Oct. 31, 2016).

play a much larger role in advancing and protecting human rights, including through quasi-legislative acts, even though the General Assembly is the organ mandated to encourage "the progressive development of international law and its codification."[104] The Council has at times substituted itself for the General Assembly in establishing new obligations through resolutions that are "legislative" in nature and that apply to all states, not just the specific situation the Council is seized of. Yet the Council, to date at least, has confined its "legislative" overreach to two domains: counterterrorism (Resolutions 1257, 1373, 2178) and non-proliferation (Resolution 1540).[105] As much as Council members have argued or accepted that Council-established or reinforced norms are essential to bolster wider counterterrorism and non-proliferation efforts, they have shied away from extending that same argument to bolster deterrence of and accountability for ICC-listed crimes.

George Kennan, one of the fathers of political realism, wished that "there be a bit more of morality in our concepts of what is legal, and more attention to legality in our concepts of what is moral," avoiding the "tendency to fall back on both of these extremes when it suits our purpose to do so."[106] Unfortunately, we are still left wishing, as too often Security Council members and the UN Secretariat defer to politically passive language in lieu of harnessing the full legal and moral force of legal discourse. This may be self-serving but ultimately also self-defeating, as tools and norms that could assist the Council address serious and heinous crimes are—confirming what devil Screwtape teaches nephew Wormwood—kept out.

[104] UN Charter, art. 13(a).
[105] Bruno Stagno-Ugarte, "Security Council Diplomacy on the Protection of Civilians," in *Protection of Civilians*, edited by Haidi Willmot et al. (Oxford: Oxford University Press, 2016), 305.
[106] George F. Kennan, *American Diplomacy* (Chicago: Chicago University Press, 1984), vii.

9

Non-State Armed Actors and International Legal Argumentation

Patterns, Processes, and Putative Effects

Hyeran Jo

Non-state armed actors (NSAAs) are groups or individuals who militarily fight with state actors to achieve their economic, political, or social goals. Their armed struggle or military methods often brand them as outlaws, which could be said to locate them in a sense outside the realm of international law.[1] Rather surprisingly to some people, though, some NSAAs *have* engaged in international legal argumentation. In their bid for a new nation without apartheid, the African National Congress (ANC) declared in 1980 that it would adhere to the Geneva Conventions,[2] and subsequently deposited its declaration with the International Committee of the Red Cross (ICRC).[3] The Polisario Front, the liberation movement in Western Sahara, filed a case in 2012 at the European Court of Justice concerning the 2000 EU-Morocco Association Agreement.[4] More recently, in 2019, the delegation from the Islamic Emirate of Afghanistan (IEA), also known as the Taliban, spoke about their views and positions on international law in a regional conference at Moscow.[5] Many other armed groups, more than one hundred

[1] An important historical exception is the national liberation movements' participation in the negotiation of the Additional Protocols in 1977. See Giovanni Mantilla, "The Political Origins of the Geneva Conventions of 1949 and the Additional Protocols of 1977," in *Do the Geneva Conventions Matter?*, edited by Matthew Evangelista and Nina Tannenwald (New York: Oxford University Press, 2017), 35 . See also Emma Stone Mackinnon, "Contingencies of Context: Legacies of the Algerian Revolution in the 1977 Additional Protocols to the Geneva Conventions," in *Contingency in International Law: On the Possibility of Different Legal Histories*, edited by Ingo Venzke and Kevin Jon Heller (Oxford: Oxford University Press, forthcoming 2021).

[2] Oliver Tambo, "Statement on Signing Declaration, on behalf of the ANC and Umkohonto we Sizwe, adhering to the Geneva Convention of 1949 and Protocol 1 of 1977, at the Headquarters of International Committee of the Red Cross, Geneva, November 28, 1980," http://theirwords.org/media/transfer/doc/za_anc_mk_1980_02-fdcf14f6a39d5c73ebee6318a8568ad5.pdf.

[3] See Churchill Ewumbue-Monono, "Respect for International Humanitarian Law by Armed Non-state Actors in Africa," *International Review of the Red Cross* 88 (2006): 864, 905. The formal depositary for ratifications of the Geneva Conventions is the Swiss government, but many national liberation movements ended up depositing their declarations with the ICRC. On this point about depositary, see Noelle Higgins, *Regulating the Use of Force in Wars of National Liberation* (Leiden: Brill, 2009), 119–120.

[4] T-512/12 *Front Polisario v. Council* (2015) Judgment of the General Court (Eighth Chamber) of Dec. 10, 2015; Front populaire pour la libération de la saguia-el-hamra et du rio de oro (Front Polisario) v. Council of the European Union (see para. 25 in "Procedure and forms of order sought").

[5] Islamic Emirates in Afghanistan, "Complete Transcript of Speech Delivered by Delegation of Islamic Emirate in Moscow Conference," *Voice of Jihad*, Feb. 5, 2019, http://alemarahenglish.com/?p=41268. The original version on the Taliban website was taken down as of March 2020. The full screenshot of the

Hyeran Jo, *Non-State Armed Actors and International Legal Argumentation* In: *Talking International Law*. Edited by: Ian Johnstone and Steven Ratner, Oxford University Press. © Hyeran Jo 2021. DOI: 10.1093/oso/9780197588437.003.0009

fifty of them, have expressed their commitments to international humanitarian law (IHL), according to the Their Words database that curates the IHL commitments by NSAAs.[6] These examples amply demonstrate that NSAAs *are* indeed part of international legal argumentation processes. More general questions then arise. Why and how do some NSAAs explicitly and purposefully choose to engage in international legal argumentation?

In this chapter, I present the patterns and processes of NSAA legal argumentation mainly from my ongoing research on the documents related to humanitarian commitments expressed by the global sample of NSAAs from 1974 to 2010.[7] Approximately 20 percent of groups, 64 out of 364, in that period have expressed something related to IHL. The sample includes only NSAAs that generated at least twenty-five battle deaths annually in fighting against national governments, leaving out other classes of militants, such as some terrorists who are not insurgents, purely criminal gangs, or paramilitary groups. It is therefore possible that more than 20 percent of armed groups expressed some form of arguments related to IHL that the database does not capture. Also, the documents are usually published by the leadership of those armed organizations, so the sample leaves out some legal arguments potentially made by individuals in the rank and file.[8]

Using the analysis of the assembled global sample, I add a deeper textual analysis with research on the contextual factors of the NSAA legal argumentation. I also add updates from recent years with regard to some selected groups (e.g., Taliban in Afghanistan, National Transitional Council in Libya) that are relevant to recent developments in international legal argumentation. The latter part of this chapter is devoted to a discussion of the putative effects of legal argumentation. The effects are presented as plausible hypotheses drawing on various literatures on legal argumentation, communicative action, and compliance[9]—hence the subtitle "putative effects."

complete web page available on file with the author. The transcript was also archived by the Long War Journal at https://www.longwarjournal.org/archives/2018/11/at-moscow-conference-taliban-refers-to-itself-as-the-islamic-emirate-61-times.php.

[6] The Their Words database was collected by the Geneva Call, a Geneva-based humanitarian organization, publicly available at http://theirwords.org/. The database was assembled using primary and secondary documents related to IHL and NSAAs. Primary sources include ICRC archive, Geneva Call's own archive, as well as soft law documents. The secondary sources include cover scholarly articles or other published works. For full disclosure, the author is currently serving on an advisory board related to the Geneva Call's research project, but there should be no conflict of interests. This author's duty involves only advising on research projects, with no financial compensation.

[7] The time frame was restricted by the availability of other related quantitive data in this particular analysis. The sampling procedure and associated data set are described in Hyeran Jo et al., "Signaling Restraint: International Engagement and Rebel Groups' Commitment to International Law," *International Interactions*, Jan. 18, 2021, https://www.tandfonline.com/doi/abs/10.1080/03050629.2020.1814761.

[8] This inclusion criteria of any statements related to international law produced by relevant organizations (in my case, non-state armed groups) is aligned with the inquiry method by Edward Kwakwa, chapter 14, in this volume (for the study of the World Intellectual Property Organization), Stephen Mattias and Nicolas Perez, chapter 16, in this volume (for the study of the United Nations Office of Legal Affairs), and Namira Negm, chapter 11, in this volume (for the study of the African Union). The key difference however will be the core fact that NSAAs are squarely non-state organizations, which might condition them to invoke legal rules less than associated moral and political dimensions.

[9] For a review of these bodies of literature, see Ian Johnstone and Steven Ratner, chapter 1, in this volume.

Understanding legal argumentation by NSAAs is important because of the human security implications. From the policy perspective, NSAAs that engage in international legal argumentation have the potential to change behavior consistent with international legal principles,[10] presumably for better humanitarian outcomes of restrained violence, saving lives, and producing peace. Studying the patterns, processes, and effects of the legal argumentation by NSAAs will also contribute to our understanding of the "work" of international law,[11] of which debates and conflicts are an essential part.

I. A Maximalist Definition of Legal Argumentation

According to the introductory chapter of this volume by Steven Ratner and Ian Johnstone, the minimal definition of legal argumentation is "an argument that explicitly invokes traditional sources of law and employs the standard techniques of interpretation." The maximum definition is "an argument that in any way bears on international law." On the spectrum between the minimum and maximum definition of legal argumentation, this author adopts the maximum definition in studying the legal argumentation by NSAAs. This means that the subsequent discussion will involve not only the NSAAs' direct invocation of treaty law (e.g., mention of the Geneva Conventions or specific articles) but also legal instruments that NSAAs have created (e.g., humanitarian commitments to eschew the use of anti-personnel mines),[12] as well as NSAAs' references to local norms or principles closely related to IHL (e.g., the civilian immunity principle in internal codes of conduct).[13]

In the subsequent discussion, NSAAs' legal argumentation will include statements that do not explicitly invoke a legal source. While many of the NSAAs' arguments map onto legal rules, these utterances may not invoke the law directly and explicitly. For example, an NSAA's arguments related to civilian immunity and the duty to avoid civilian death is discussed even if an NSAA does not directly invoke the Fourth Geneva Convention. The boundaries of argumentation are equally broad in a sense that the discussion includes any statement or contention about IHL principles and norms made by NSAAs. Expressions on the acceptance of law are treated as part of NSAA legal argumentation if they convey the implicit information that NSAAs intend to abide by IHL—in expressions of support for the law—potentially to convince the audience that might think otherwise. Disputes, debates, and objections related to IHL and made by NSAAs are also considered to be legal arguments as they convey rebuttals or reveal discrepancies and lay bare differences in precepts and premises—in expressions of disapproval of the law.

[10] Kristian Gleditsch et al., "International Conventions and Nonstate Actors: Selection, Signaling, and Reputation Effects," *Journal of Conflict Resolution* 62 (2016): 346.

[11] Monica Hakimi, "The Work of International Law," *Harvard International Law Journal* 58 (2017): 1.

[12] Anthea Roberts and Sandesh Sivakumaran, "Lawmaking by Non-State Actors: Engaging Armed Groups in the Creation of IHL," *Yale Journal of International Law* 37 (2012): 107.

[13] Note that Kathleen Claussen, chapter 15, in this volume also explicitly considers underlying principles in her study of trade law.

The key advantage of the maximalist definition of legal argumentation is its coverage and breadth in discussing the context and process of NSAAs' legal argumentation. Per Monica Hakimi's observation in chapter 3 of this volume, power, interests, and values are inherent features of international legal argumentation. In the fight against the national government authority, NSAAs will be invariably attuned to these political settings of their armed struggles. The maximalist definition allows me to examine the full breadth of NSAAs' legal argumentation with respect to their contents. Also, in terms of who is making the international legal arguments, when we restrict the discussion to the minimum definition of explicit references to law in a narrow sense, we would miss a big chunk of the NSAA population because they simply do not swim in the world of international law in a strict legal sense. In humanitarian commitments of NSAAs featured in the Their Words database, approximately 20 percent of insurgents have produced soft law documents related to IHLs and norms.[14] Even within that committer set, traditional argumentation techniques such as invoking treaties or presenting precedents are rare. The empirical practice of NSAAs warrants adoption of the maximal definition of legal argumentation because the contents of NSAA legal argumentation are often very thin in terms of explicit legal references, but thick in terms of implicit references to legal norms and principles.[15] Studying NSAAs' legal argumentation using the maximalist definition will give a fuller picture not only of NSAA practice but also of the phenomenon of legal argumentation generally—how it is used, by whom, for what purposes, and to what effects.

The maximalist definition of legal argumentation carries a disadvantage, too, as it risks expanding and stretching the boundaries of "legal" too much. If we adopt the minimal definition and confine our discussion to cases where explicit invocation of law is made, the empirical boundary would be clearly marked. The adoption of the maximalist definition of legal argumentation means sometimes crossing unclear boundaries to include norms and principles related to law. To minimize the risk of expanding the boundaries of "legal" too much, I make an effort to distinguish between specific references to law itself (which is less common in the context of NSAA legal argumentation) and the invocation of principles that are clearly reflected in the law but also reflected in other normative sources (e.g., warrior codes, ethical codes).

II. The Context of NSAA Legal Argumentation

NSAAs have been traditionally excluded from formal international lawmaking; they have voices but no votes.[16] The structure of international relations sometimes inhibits them from partaking in legal argumentation in formal venues. The very nature of the international lawmaking process has opened up the space for some NSAAs to voice

[14] Jo et al., *supra* note 7, at 6.

[15] This view of legal argumentation is consistent with the "purposive interpretation of law," which emphasizes social and political contexts of where legal interpretation is made. Aharon Barak, *Purposive Interpretation of Law* (Princeton: Princeton University Press, 2015).

[16] René Provost, "Asymmetrical Reciprocity and Compliance with the Laws of War," in *Modern Warfare: Armed Groups, Private Militaries, Humanitarian Organizations, and the Law*, edited by Benjamin Perrin (Vancouver, BC: UBC Press, 2012), 17.

their arguments *outside* the courtroom.[17] NSAAs are expected to be active in legal argumentation not only because of the structural factors of international politics but also because of the legal uncertainty.[18] Legal uncertainties are replete in the practice of IHL where the fog of war is thick[19] and when NSAAs often lack the awareness and legal apparatus to judge IHL principles and practices.[20] The uncertainty gives NSAAs an opportunity to take part in the international legal argumentation process by generating their own interpretations of law and sometimes by challenging its normative framework.

In rare cases, NSAAs have presented their legal argumentation inside the courtroom. At the International Criminal Court (ICC), Jean-Pierre Bemba, the former commander in chief of the Mouvement de Libération du Congo, defended his case in terms of the Rome Statute,[21] arguing no involvement and thus no command responsibility.[22] Lawyers representing the Polisario, the liberation movement in Western Sahara, invoked self-determination in presenting their case at the European Court of Justice. The case concerned the EU-Morocco Fisheries agreement that affected the Polisario's political and economic interests in the disputed territory. Accordingly, the Polisario's argument was framed in terms of EU law and international law.[23] As the long-time insurgent group in Sri Lanka, the LTTE challenged its designation in the United States as a foreign terrorist organization at a US court, which also illustrates that some NSAAs do take their cases to court.[24] Yet, other than in a handful of cases, the majority of legal argumentation by NSAAs takes place outside of the courtroom.

The majority of NSAAs will choose to stay outside of the international legal argumentation zone. They might stay silent because they lack capacity. For example, some might not have a legal affairs department or political divisions that could carry

[17] On the notion of "interpretative space," see Eveline Feteris, *Fundamentals of Legal Argumentation: A Survey of Theories on the Justification of Judicial Decisions* (Dortrecht: Springer, 2017).

[18] Risse observes that "arguing processes are more likely . . . when rule of the game is not clear"; Thomas Risse, "Let's Argue! Communicative Action in World Politics," *International Organization* 54 (2000): 1, 33. For the social dimension as part of legal argumentation, see also Richard Nobles and David Schiff, "Legal Argumentation: A Sociological Account," *Jurisprudence* 8 (2016): 52.

[19] Uncertainty is highlighted for example in the definition of civilians. See, e.g., Emily Crawford, *Identifying the Enemy: Civilian Participation in Armed Conflict* (Oxford: Oxford University Press, 2015).

[20] If a humanitarian's knowledge and understanding is not perfect, we cannot expect NSAAs to be aware and argue effectively about IHL. On this point, see the recent survey of humanitarians in Rob Grace, "Humanitarian Negotiation with Parties to Armed Conflict: The Role of Laws and Principles in the Discourse," *Journal of International Humanitarian Legal Studies* 11 (2020): 68.

[21] Here, the legal argumentation of Bemba's defense inside the courtroom resembles standard legal argumentation, entailing active interpretation about legal provisions, the meaning of words, purposes of a rule. See Diane Marie Amann, "In Bemba and Beyond, Crimes Adjudged to Commit Themselves," *EJIL Talk!*, June 13, 2018.

[22] Judgment on the Appeal of Mr. Jean-Pierre Bemba Gombo against Trial Chamber III's Judgment Pursuant to Article 74 of the Statute, ICC-01/05-01/08-3636, June 8, 2018.

[23] The Polisario's representative, Mohamed Sidati, commented during the interview with EURACTIV, "The ruling makes clear, as with the case of December 2016 that the fisheries agreement between the EU and Morocco cannot be applied to Western Sahara or its adjacent waters; doing so would be a violation of international law and the right to self-determination of the people of Western Sahara." https://www.euractiv.com/section/economy-jobs/news/morocco-fisheries-pact-must-not-include-western-sahara-eu-court-confirms/.

[24] People's Mojahedin Org. of Iran v. United States Department of State, 182 F. 3d 17 (D.C. Cir. 1999). The LTTE had filed suits in the District of Columbia arguing that the group is a legitimate political organization in Sri Lanka and that they had been denied due process.

out international legal argumentation. They might avoid legal arguments because of their religious ideology. Given this heterogeneity, ranging from the vocal to the silent, this chapter pays attention to the differences within the categories of NSAAs, as they are relevant to the topic of international legal argumentation. As Gina Heathcote observes in chapter 5 of this volume, silence, voice, and filtering out can be an all-important part of understanding various aspects of legal argumentation. In understanding NSAAs' legal argumentation, in particular, the heterogeneity within the data set is important, as NSAAs come in various stripes. Defined as militants who take up arms to achieve their political or social objectives outside of the state apparatus, NSAAs include secessionist groups (or national liberation movements), rebel groups (or insurgents), terrorists, or criminal gangs.[25] Some are more likely to invoke international law than others within and across these categories. Despite overlaps among the categories or nomenclatures,[26] some patterns emerge, as discussed in what follows.

III. Word Patterns

One way to uncover the structure of legal argumentation is to start with its basic building blocks, namely, words. The choice or "bag of words"[27] reveals the patterns of words that undergird the arguments. It is also a good way to identify broad themes embedded in the arguments. Although the words do not reveal the connections between or across words and ignore nuanced use in sentences, it is a useful way to cut cross the structures at the basic level.

Using the tools of text analysis,[28] my research team[29] looked at approximately six hundred documents in the humanitarian commitment database in order to uncover the basic patterns in word choices among the NSAAs[30] in the Their Words database.[31] Figure 9.1 plots two categories of NSAAs' words: (1) words related to international humanitarian norms, and (2) words related to "political demands." In terms of the probability of a particular topic appearing in a document, we see humanitarian norm-related words (e.g., "right," "children," "people," or "human") increasing over time, while rebels' political demands related words (e.g., "nation" or "govern") are decreasing. The graph shows some recognitions among NSAAs about norms related

[25] The nomenclature is not strictly legal and sometimes involves political labeling, but nonetheless, the differences are useful to note here.

[26] Secessionists are often part of insurgent groups. See David Cunningham, Kristian Skrede Gleditsch, and Idean Salehyan, "Non-State Actors in Civil Wars: A New Dataset," *Conflict Management and Peace Science* 30 (2013): 516. On the overlap between rebel groups and terrorist groups, see, e.g., Hyeran Jo, *Compliant Rebels: Rebel Groups and International Law in World Politics* (Cambridge: Cambridge University Press, 2015); Sara Polo and Kristian Gleditsch, "Twisting Arms and Sending Messages: Terrorist Tactics in Civil War," *Journal of Peace Research* 53 (2016): 815. On terrorist groups as criminal gangs, see James Piazza and Scott Piazza, "Crime Pays: Terrorist Group Engagement in Crime and Survival," *Terrorism and Political Violence* 1-23 (Nov. 2017).

[27] In standard jargon in text analysis literature.

[28] David Blei, "Probabilistic Topic Models," *Communications of the ACM* 55 (2012): 77.

[29] I specifically thank Soren Jordan for his research assistance on text analysis.

[30] The detailed procedures and methodological details can be found in Jo et al., *supra* note 7, at 6.

[31] *Id.*

to IHL. At the very least, these instances serve the purpose of signifying that some NSAAs do engage in international legal argumentation.

Figure 9.2 presents two word clouds, one from 1981 and the other from 2014, again based on the documents in Their Words database.[32]

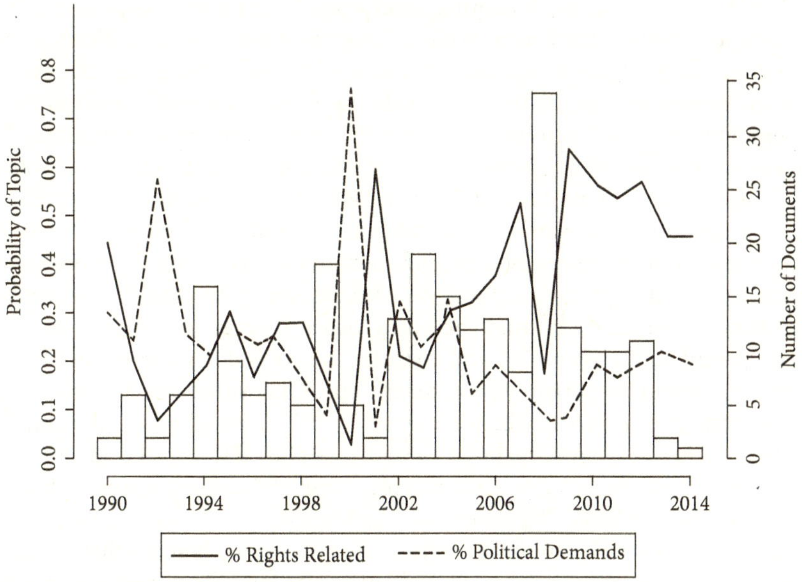

Figure 9.1 "Bag of NSAAs' Words"
Political Demands and Humanitarian References

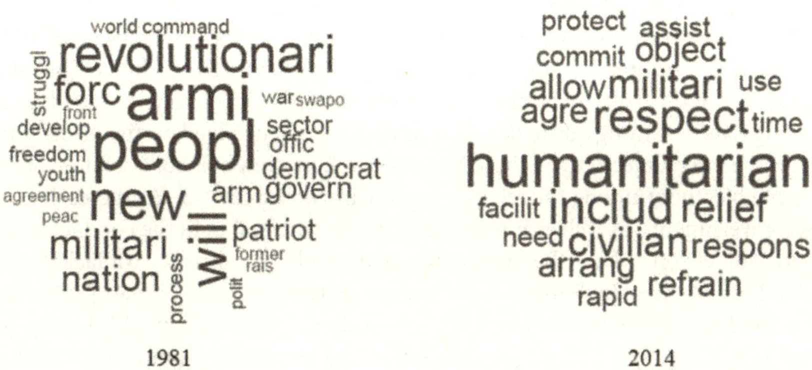

Figure 9.2 Then and Now
Word-Snapshots in NSAA Documents, 1981 and 2014

32 Figure 9.2 is reproduced from Hyeran Jo, "International Humanitarian Law on the Periphery: Case of Non-state Armed Actors," *Journal of International Humanitarian Legal Studies* 11 (2020): 97.

The two word clouds give us some snapshots of IHL-related documents in 1981 and 2014 issued by NSAAs. The word cloud of 1981 is based on two documents. The first is the "SWAPO Declaration to the International Committee of the Red Cross" from the South West Africa People's Organization (SWAPO), a national liberation movement in Namibia. The year 1981 was an important one for the SWAPO. At that time, the SWAPO had been actively fighting against South Africa for independence since the 1960s, and in 1978, the United Nations recognized the SWAPO as Namibia's representative. The 1981 document came in this context where the group expressed its intent to "respect and be guided by the rules of the four Geneva Conventions." As a group fighting for self-determination, the SWAPO did not miss mentioning "nation" as one of the key words in the document. The second document is the "Political Agreement between the FMLN and Youth for Military Army of New Constitution,"[33] by the Farabundo Martí National Liberation Front (FMLN) in El Salvador. In this document, the FMLN expresses its commitment to the Geneva Conventions and the humane treatment of prisoners of war. As a Marxist group, the FMLN frequently reminds us of its Marxist roots, using the words such as "people" or "revolutionary."

Fast forward to the year 2014 and consider the collection of words used by the National Coalition of Syrian Revolutionary and Opposition Forces, often called the Free Syrian Army (FSA). The word cloud of 2014 is based on the document titled "Declaration of Commitment on Compliance with IHL and the Facilitation of Humanitarian Assistance." The cloud is replete with IHL-related words such as "respect," "protect," "civilians," "humanitarian," and "relief." The words evoke the norm of civilian immunity in IHL. In the document, the FSA explicitly states that "we affirm our responsibility to respect International Humanitarian Law at all times" and lists its responsibilities within the ambit of IHL. It is also instructive to note that in the same year, the FSA released the document titled "Communiqué to Eliminate Sexual Violence," where the FSA leadership, both the political arm of the Syrian Opposition Coalition, as well as the military wing, Supreme Military Council, made a pledge, "in accordance with the UN Security Council Resolution 2106."[34]

The ultimate meaning of these documents might lie in the intersubjective understanding and interpretation of the texts and words, as emphasized by Ian Johnstone in chapter 7 of this volume. In the treaty context, Johnstone observed, shared understanding is rather strong due to the prior consent among involved parties, usually state actors. The intersubjectivity in these NSAA documents might involve a different kind of intersubjectivity among the relevant parties, including the NSAAs themselves, national governments, as well as international actors with stakes in the conduct of warfare in conflict zones. How that intersubjectivity would be construed (or lack thereof) is what I turn to next. In doing so, I discuss the contexts in which NSAAs proffer their subjective legal argumentation, and how international actors are involved in the process of producing NSAAs legal argumentation and ultimately producing intersubjective meaning of those documents.

[33] The original title is "Acuerdo Político entre el FMLN y la Juventud Militar para la Constitución del Nuevo Ejército."

[34] See Point 6. The document is available at https://www.un.org/sexualviolenceinconflict/wp-content/uploads/2020/02/Communique_to_end_Sexual_Violence-Syria.pdf.

IV. Invoking the Roots and Claiming the Moral High Ground

At their foundation, NSAAs' international legal argumentation cannot be divorced from the question of why they initiated armed conflicts in the first place. The insurgents among NSAAs often make the connection between government repression and rebellion. NSAAs, whenever they invoke some IHL-related arguments, are quick to imply that their actions are justified because they have just cause. Consider the example of the Taliban delegation's remark during the regional conference in Moscow in 2019,[35] where the group mentions its "legitimate right of defense":

> Our beloved country, Muslim and Mujahid nation have been burning in the flames of fire for the past four decades. Their spiritual and material assets have been robbed and looted; they have been prevented from progress and hundreds of thousands of people have been displaced. Poverty and destitution are another main misfortune that the Afghan people are faced with due to war. The fundamental cause of all these disasters is interferences and invasions of foreigners. It is worth mentioning that throughout the history Afghan Mujahid Nation has resorted to its *legitimate right of defense* against each invasion, which is still going on under the leadership of the Islamic Emirate of Afghanistan against the current invasion for the last 17 years.

Another fairly common feature of international legal argumentation by NSAAs is what I call the "J'accuse" principle. NSAAs "accuse" national governments or opposing parties as violators of international law, partly in order to assert their status as a relative complier to international law. Claiming the moral high ground, some NSAAs often justify their actions by comparing their behaviors to those of the government that they are fighting. In this setting and framing, moral *is* legal, within the bounds of what is legitimate by social moral standards. NSAAs' argumentation per se may not explicitly include moral arguments, but they bring a moral dimension to the debate over IHL issues. In these cases, NSAAs exploit the uncertainty of law and sometimes act as an arbiter of truth.

The argument made by the National Transitional Council (NTC) in Libya serves as an example. At the height of the Libyan civil war that started in February 2011, the NTC media (@NTC_of_Libya) released a tweet on June 2011: "In defiance of international law, Colonel Gaddafi's authorities committed the most serious crimes possible against the Libyan people.#Libya" (1:46 p.m., June 7, 2011).[36] This delegitimization of the opposing side blurs the boundaries of legal, moral, and political in the context of international legal argumentation.

An additional example comes from the Fuerzas Armadas Revolucionarias de Colombia—Ejército del Pueblo (FARC-EP). In June 2008, FARC had the following

[35] Emphasis added by the author. The excerpt is from Islamic Emirates in Afghanistan, "Complete Transcript."

[36] The original tweet can be found at https://twitter.com/NTC_of_Libya/status/78171104727941120?s=20, requoted at Eleonora Mattiacci, "How Twitter and Other Social Media Can Draw the US into Foreign Interventions," *The Conversation*, Apr. 3, 2019, https://www.pri.org/stories/2019-04-03/how-twitter-and-other-social-media-can-draw-us-foreign-interventions.

"appeal to soldiers, police, officers and non-commissioned patriots" in a press release.[37]

> 5- . . . the ***State forces*** to kill his own brothers: popular leaders, trade unions, peasants and the left, for which they organize groups of hitmen and paramilitaries.
>
> 6- In ***our Internal Statutes*** and Regulations, full respect for the physical and moral integrity of every military who falls prisoner in combat.[38]

In this statement, touching upon the topic of the wartime behavior related to combat and taking prisoners, the FARC is comparing the government's behavior (in point 5) to its own behavior (in point 6). The contrast provided by FARC is stark: the government with "corrupt generals" is employing "hitmen and paramilitaries," while the FARC, with "internal statutes and regulations" treats enemy government soldiers with "respect." The friends and foe division[39] is apparent in this document, as well as many other documents of the FARC.

In terms of content, the above quote does not directly mention international law, although the treatment of prisoners and civilians is part of IHL. The points laid out in the document are not straight from relevant treaties or the jurisprudence of related cases. Rather, the document *indirectly* invokes norms consistent with IHL—of treating enemy soldiers humanely. Similarly, in its disciplinary code, "estatutos," in 1978 (modified in 1982, 1993, and 2007),[40] FARC released the list of crimes under the movement (Article 3) related to civilian protection, such as murder, rape, and stealing from the civilian population. The document also laid out the penalties and the detailed procedures to determine penalties (Article 5). These instances collectively demonstrate that FARC, as an NSAA, participates in international legal argumentation, albeit in an indirect manner.

V. Local Interpretations

NSAA legal argumentation often reveals a struggle over discrepancies between local norms and global norms. The Moro Islamic Liberation Front (MILF), which primarily fought for the political autonomy and possible secession in the Mindanao region of the southern Philippines, provides one example of local interpretation of global norms. In an interview with the United Nations, the MILF spokesman Eid Kabalu pointed out a difference between international law's prescription of fifteen as the minimum age for combatants[41] and the MILF's own local standard of thirteen as the age

[37] For the collection and translations of original FARC documents, I thank Maria Paula Abadia.

[38] FARC, "Llamamiento a Soldados, Oficiales y Suboficiales Patriotas" (2008), available at the CeDeMa (Centro de Documentación de los Movimientos Armados: Center for the Documentation of Armed Movements), http://www.cedema.org/ver.php?id=2685 (emphasis added by this author).

[39] As noted in Sarah Nouwen and Wouter Werner, "Doing Justice to the Political: The International Criminal Court in Uganda and Sudan," *European Journal of International Law* 21 (2011): 941.

[40] FARC, "Estatutos," http://www.farc-ep.co/pdf/Estatutos.pdf.

[41] The ICC Statute considers fifteen as the cutoff age, and many international standards use eighteen as a cutoff.

of adulthood, following the norm in the Islamic community.[42] Kabalu further justified the MILF's actions in the same interview. His argument conveys the group's willingness to engage and argue with international law, augmented with justifications of the group's own societal values and standards.

> We adhere to the standards set by the UN . . . while there is no forced conscription among our ranks, there are certain definitions that are different from [the Western norms]. These children identified so far by UNICEF are not really fighting on the frontlines, but are helping in MILF communities. It is an obligation for anyone born into the struggle to help achieve our goal of a Muslim homeland.

The Taliban in Afghanistan provides another example of local interpretation of IHL, as seen in various versions of its internal code of conduct, *Layeha*.[43] Take one passage from the 2009 version of *Layeha*, discussing the principle of distinction between combatants and civilians.

> [A]ll mujahideen must do their best to avoid civilian deaths and injuries and damage to civilian property.[44]

Although the passage includes religious elements (e.g., mujahideen), the reference to civilian immunity is linked to IHL. The expression of IHL in local settings carries important implications for the legal argumentation on the humanitarian actor's side: instead of emphasizing differences between Islamic law and non-Islamic law, IHL legal argumentation can make good use of commonalities written in NSAAs' internal codes of conduct, as long as they are consistent with core IHL principles.

In the same version of *Layeha*, "Section 4. Concerning those who provide logistical support or [carry out] construction for the enemy" entails a discussion about a driver working for a government (or "infidels"). The provincial official has the authority to judge the driver's fate.

> 20. If a driver is arrested while he is transporting supplies to the infidels, the provincial official shall decide whether to punish, exchange or release him.

In the 2010 version of *Layeha*, however, the same issue is dealt with differently. A driver who provides logistical support to the enemy is to be executed summarily, instead of being judged by the "provincial official."

[42] In an interview with IRIN, "Philippines: Moves to End Use of Child Soldiers, But Problem Persists," Apr. 8, 2011, https://www.refworld.org/docid/4da3f6542.html.

[43] For the analysis of *Layeha* and political context, see Yoshinobu Nagamine, *The Legitimization Strategy of the Taliban's Code of Conduct* (New York: Palgrave Macmillan, 2015); Hyeran Jo and John Niehaus, "Through Rebel Eyes: Rebel Groups, Human Rights, and Humanitarian Law," *Law and Contemporary Problems* 81 (2018): 101.

[44] The cited texts are from Kate Clark, "The Layha. Calling the Taleban to Account," *Afghanistan Analysts Network* (2011), https://www.afghanistan-analysts.org/publication/aan-papers/the-layha-calling-the-taleban-to-account/, in particular Appendix 1. The Taleban Codes of Conduct in English.

> 24. Drivers who transport supplies for the infidels—during that transportation and if the mujahedin are well-informed that they are transporting [supplies] for the infidels or their enslaved administration—shall be killed and their vehicles burned.

The shift appeared to have come when, in 2009, the Taliban was in desperate need of internal discipline after it experienced many organizational upheavals. The changed IHL discussion highlights how local interpretations of IHL are subject to changing situations in warfare.

Fast-forward ten years and consider the Taliban in the midst of talks on potential negotiations with President Donald Trump. A Taliban delegation at an international conference in Moscow spoke of its views on IHL in a section of the speech entitled "protection of civilian casualties."[45]

> Often, the Islamic Emirate of Afghanistan has postponed its military operations due to the risk of civilian causalities, but the Americans and their friends carry out night raids on civilian houses, make blind bombardments and use heavy weapons in civilian places, even they arrest people from cities on the basis of suspicion and then kill them under punishment and torture. Now, with the new American policy, bombardment and night raids have further increased which in turn has increased the graph of civilian casualties as well; albeit most of the media do not publish these reports and these incidents remain nonregistered. Some media outlets and some directions attempt to hide the original perpetrators of civilian casualties which further embolden the perpetrators to continue their crimes.
>
> Islamic Emirate of Afghanistan has taken the following practical measures for the prevention of civilian casualties:
>
> 1. In order to prevent civilian casualties, Mujahidin are provided with guidelines by scholars on regular basis and independent seminars are held in this regard.
> 2. Delegations pay visit to Mujahidin circles from time to time in order to investigate incidents of civilian casualties and prosecute the perpetrators.

The timing is noteworthy. The announcement came with the political demands to "finish the sanctions or rewards," rebuking America and its allies as having "no excuse avoiding the talks for peace." Like the FARC example, the friend-foe analogy is engrained in the discussion, painting the image of "occupiers" and "liberators." The rhetorical technique exhibited here is in connection to the broad international legal argumentation made in the document. In conjunction with the above-mentioned policy, on its official group website, both in Pashtun and English, the Taliban includes the IEA commissions such as "Commission for Prevention of Civilian Casualties and Complaints" and "Commission for Agriculture, Livestock, Ushr and Zakat."[46] Political

[45] This excerpt is from Islamic Emirates in Afghanistan, "Complete Transcript."

[46] Voice of Jihad (official IEA website), http://alemarahenglish.com/?p=41268. The screenshot is on file with the author.

motives aside,[47] the organizational structure also attests that the IEA is an example that could potentially show how international law is interpreted locally on the ground.

The IEA delegation speech is also addressed to the humanitarian community, adding "we guarantee your security" and deliver assistance to the "needy people living in areas under the control of the Islamic Emirate." This signifies that the IHL principle of protecting humanitarian personnel appears to be known to the group. That such argumentation was made during an international conference also shows that the IEA delegation publicly engages in IHL-related debates. The Taliban's speech highlights that even some Islamic armed groups engage in international legal argumentation in some fashion.

VI. Process

The process of NSAA legal argumentation usually entails a series of events, sometimes together, other times separately. NSAAs acquire knowledge of international law; interact with participants in the international law community (such as international humanitarian actors); and participate in international legal argumentation by drafting documents with explicit or implicit references to law, making legal commitments, or, on rare occasions, appearing in judicial venues such as international courts.

Not all NSAAs enter the communicative process of international legal argumentation. Who participates and who does not? *Capacity* looms large as a participation condition for NSAA legal argumentation. Sufficiently resourceful NSAAs have political machines to gain awareness of international law and to get the message out to the public. Some NSAA organizations feature spokespersons within relevant divisions of the movement, such as public relations, media, or legal affairs units.[48] These NSAAs acquire knowledge about international law through interaction with nongovernmental organizations (NGOs), or because their leaders include former members of a state's military apparatus.[49] Such NSAAs are able to produce documents with packages of "international law language" that are delivered to the international arena. In contrast, resource-poor NSAAs like the Rohingya lack the capacity to participate in legal argumentation with ease. The Arakan Rohingya Salvation Army (ARSA) marches in the rainy jungle with flip-flops and wooden machetes.[50] In these poor conditions, we cannot expect much on the legal front.

[47] Rebel governance literature in political science deals with this question of why non-state armed groups would build institutions for civilian population. See, for instance, Megan Stewart, "Civil War as State-Making: Strategic Governance in Civil War," *International Organization* 72 (2018): 205.

[48] For diplomatic activities of insurgent groups, see Reyko Huang, "Rebel Diplomacy in Civil War," *International Security* 40 (2016): 89.

[49] Tanisha Fazal, *Wars of Law: Unintended Consequences in the Regulation of Armed Conflict* (Ithaca: Cornell University Press, 2018).

[50] In the video entitled "Inside the Rohingya Resistance" supplemental to the article by Jamie Tarabay, "Who Are Myanmar's Militants? Five Questions about ARSA," *CNN*, Dec. 6, 2017, https://www.cnn.com/2017/09/12/asia/arsa-rohingya-militants-who-are-they/index.html.

Ideology imposes another important participation condition for NSAA legal argumentation. Argumentation is essentially a system of premises leading to claims, and an underlying belief system can affect the core premises. The premises presented by non-state actors are often based on religious or ideological beliefs, which are reflected in the legal argumentation patterns. Marxist rebels often present arguments that describe international law as a set of hegemonic rules. Some consider the production of international law to be dominated by powerful states,[51] implying that they are not obliged to follow international law *in toto*. Jihadists or extremist Islamic groups often reject international law on religious grounds, as they consider international law to be a body of rules made by "takfir"—non-believers of Islam.[52] By contrast, moderate Islamists seem to accept an overlap between Islamic principles and IHL. These religious and ideological groundings are important elements of non-state actors' legal argumentation processes. To some NSAAs, ideology dictates the outright rejection of international legal argumentation, leading to the situation where some refuse to take part in it.

How NSAAs formulate legal arguments may also depend on their experience outside the movement. NSAAs whose members come from state military backgrounds may take what they learned in their prior positions[53] and engage in legal argumentation.[54] Interaction with outside actors is also important. The interactional approach to understanding international law emphasized by Jutta Brunnée in chapter 12 of this volume is very much in evidence here. International actors, such as international humanitarians, disseminate knowledge about IHL to NSAAs. The process of participation in a legal arena by NSAAs is often facilitated by international actors, such as mediators, who actively engage NSAAs in terms of humanitarian commitments in peace agreements[55] and bring them into the realm of international law. One example of NSAA legal argumentation as a dialogue takes place during the ICRC's detention visits. Another is the negotiation of action plans[56] between NSAAs and the Office of the Special Representative of the Secretary-General for Children and Armed Conflict (SRSG/CAAC) at the United Nations, with the aim of reducing the number of child soldiers. A third example is the Deed of Commitment[57] between NSAAs and the Geneva Call to increase the humanitarian commitments by NSAAs.[58] In

[51] For the citation of FARC statement defining IHL as "the dominating class of the dominating states in the world," see Jo, *supra* note 32, at 10.

[52] See the discussion in John Kelsay, *Arguing the Just War in Islam* (Cambridge: Harvard University Press, 2007).

[53] Tanisha Fazal, "Rebellion, War Aims, and the Laws of War," *Daedalus* 146 (2017): 71.

[54] Here, the assumption is that the invocation of legal argumentation necessitates gaining some knowledge about international law, especially laws of war in this case of non-state armed groups.

[55] On international engagement in peace processes, see Desirée Nilsson, "Anchoring the Peace: Civil Society Actors in Peace Accords and Durable Peace," *International Interactions* 38 (2012): 243. See also Christine Bell, *Peace Agreements and Human Rights* (Oxford: Oxford University Press, 2003).

[56] As of 2020, about fifteen groups have signed the action plans to ban the use of child soldiers.

[57] The Deed of Commitment is a formal humanitarian commitment, often in document form, made by NSAAs. The Deeds started with anti-personnel mines issue and expanded to the issues related to child protection and sexual violence. So far, about sixty groups have signed the Deeds to ban the anti-personnel mines.

[58] At the same time, these sets of discussions potentially involving legal argumentation among involved parties are difficult to study in-depth as most the documents and persuasion processes are often confidential and off limits to outside researchers. Interview with anonymous official at the ICRC; interview with anonymous official at the UN special office on children and armed conflicts.

these situations, NSAAs have pursued strategies of drafting legal instruments such as unilateral statements or bilateral agreements with governments and international organizations.

Different NSAAs choose a variety of *venues* in which to make legal arguments. Some choose the formal institutional route. NSAAs could deposit their intention to abide by the Geneva Conventions with the ICRC, as the African National Congress did.[59] They can bring their claims to an international court, as the Polisario did.[60] Other groups submit their arguments via unilateral declarations or bilateral agreements with intergovernmental organizations or NGOs.[61] The choice of venues can be partly explained by the capacity and willingness of NSAAs. When NSAAs have the capacity to unleash legal resources[62] and if they believe they would benefit from legal argumentation either politically or socially, they might have more incentives to choose formal institutions rather than informal venues. NSAAs engaging in international legal argumentation may believe they have something to gain in terms of legitimacy and thus might choose more formal venues. Acting like a state can be a strong incentive when their legal space is substantially restricted in comparison to states. States have common fora, such as the UN Security Council, to argue their legal positions,[63] or express legal arguments in fora negotiating international treaties. Recent research on rebel diplomacy[64] backs up the observation that secessionist groups often engage in high-level legal argumentation and even go to courts.

VII. Effects of Legal Argumentation

Compared to the patterns and processes described above that can be studied with concrete examples, the precise effects of NSAA legal argumentation are harder to specify due to the difficulty of establishing the causality. In what follows, I synthesize the existing literature and propose some plausible pathways by which NSAA legal argumentation can have an impact. Specifically, I propose four potential effects generated by NSAA legal argumentation: a persuasion effect, a reciprocity effect, a compliance effect, and a peace-inducing effect.

[59] Tambo, *supra* note 2.

[60] Front Polisario v. Council of the European Union (European Court of Justice, Cases T/512/12 (2015) and C-104/16 P (2016)).

[61] For the examples and details of these potential lawmaking activities by NSAAs, see Roberts and Sivakumaran, *supra* note 12.

[62] The Polisario case shows that when there is jurisdictional opportunity, non-state armed actors use judicial strategies.

[63] Ian Johnstone, "Security Council Deliberations: The Power of the Better Argument," *European Journal of International Law* 14 (2003): 437. See also Scott Sheeran, Gina Heathcote, and Bruno Stagno-Ugarte's contributions to this volume in chapters 4, 5, and 8, respectively.

[64] The following two works show the diplomacy conducted by insurgents globally, including some legal actions: Huang, *supra* note 48; Fazal, *supra* note 53.

A. Persuasion Effect

In assessing the persuasion effect, the key dimensions of persuasion are important. Relevant aspects include the nature of the dispute, the characteristics of the persuading entity, the characteristics of the entity being persuaded, and the persuasion process.[65] Following the theoretical framework set out by Steven Ratner in chapter 6 of this volume, I analyze NSAAs' potential persuasion effects in four dimensions: (1) the nature of the parties (i.e., NSAAs' audiences), (2) the nature of the compliance (i.e., what NSAAs attempt to persuade), (3) the traits of the persuading entity (i.e., diversity in NSAAs' capacity and willingness), and (4) the setting of the persuasive process (i.e., medium by which the persuasion is conveyed).

The first dimension of persuasion strategies involves the nature of the parties. The persuasion effect will be generated when the NSAAs' legal argumentation influences the action or belief of the key audience who receive legal arguments, be it international actors, the domestic populace, or within-group soldiers. In this context, NSAAs are persuaders and audiences are persuadees.

The second dimension—the nature of the compliance dispute—concerns what NSAAs try to persuade the aforementioned audiences to do. The goal of persuasion on the part of NSAAs is to convince the other party that the NSAA is international-law-regarding and part of the international community. At a minimum, NSAA legal argumentation should convey the message that "we speak your language," or signal some conformity to existing international law. Among the three logics of legal argumentation suggested by Ingo Venzke in chapter 2 of this volume, namely, consequentialism, appropriateness, and deference, the logic of appropriateness would be strongly at play. In a similar vein, Wouter Werner in chapter 10 of this volume observes that recognition, respect, and equality are important elements of interpretive practice of international law. When NSAAs express conformity to international law, it can be read as a sign of "recognition" of and willingness to fit into the existing order. At a maximum, some NSAAs might invoke and thereby endorse the law in order to sway the action of international actors to support them.[66]

The third dimension that can determine the persuasion strategy is related to the traits of the persuading entity. The engagement of NSAA legal argumentation might demonstrate that they are viable actors, potentially law-abiding and potentially following the principles embodied in humanitarian law or human rights. Legal argumentation then might generate effects consistent with NSAAs' strategic purpose to demonstrate their relative strength and political viability in the midst of fighting against oft-corrupt and oft-law-disregarding governments.

The fourth dimension is the setting in which the persuasive process occurs. It can also affect the degree of persuasiveness of NSAAs' legal argumentation. Some might

[65] The subsequent discussion is heavily influenced by the signaling models in game theory within political science and economics discipline. Also, the structure follows the theory of persuasion in legal argumentation laid out in Steven R. Ratner, "Law Promotion beyond Law Talk: The Red Cross, Persuasion, and the Laws of War," *European Journal of International Law* 22 (2011): 459.

[66] Research has demonstrated the connections between the NTC's tweets and the US support in Libya. Benjamin Jones and Eleonora Mattiacci, "A Manifesto, in 140 Characters or Fewer: Social Media as a Tool of Rebel Diplomacy," *British Journal of Political Science* 49 (2017): 739.

argue that NSAAs' unilateral declarations or bilateral agreements with international organizations or NGOs are not persuasive on the grounds that none of those are formally binding in the same sense as treaties. There may be, however, certain settings where the NSAAs' legal argumentation could be persuasive—for example, if the argumentation involves direct engagement with international actors, such as UN sub-organs (e.g., SRSG/CAAC) or NGOs (e.g., Geneva Call). Suppose an NSAA commits to a bilateral agreement with an international humanitarian organization. In this case, we could expect the NSAA legal argumentation to be persuasive in influencing some international actors that participated in the process of arguing with the NSAA. When the MILF engaged in legal argumentation in formulating their internal code of conduct called "General Order,"[67] the insurgent group showed its commitment to IHL by laying out concrete step-by-step plans, often with timelines, to implement within the rank and file of the MILF command. With these specific commitments, MILF's legal argumentation would carry some persuasive power in the eyes of international actors with respect to the obligation to reduce the number of child soldiers. The argumentation was embedded in negotiations, interactions, and deliberations between the international organization community and NSAAs, and therefore would be more credible and persuasive to the international community. So, in this case, the members of the international community might be expected to update their beliefs about the group and further engage NSAAs for a better humanitarian outcome.

An NSAA's legal argumentation could also be persuasive in advance of peace negotiations. The very fact that NSAAs are making arguments related to IHL or human rights law before peace negotiations would indicate that the armed actors, or at least a faction of them, are going through a moderation period. Often coupled with ceasefire agreements and peace agreement commitments, these kinds of peace-negotiation NSAA legal arguments send a strong signal that an NSAA might be moving away from exercising violence as the only option. The documents produced near peace talks therefore will carry some persuasive weight, compared to the legal argumentation made outside of peace negotiations, which might not be taken seriously by international actors.

According to the calculation on the part of an NSAA invoking law, this signaling via legal argumentation during the peace process might distinguish it from other NSAAs. The act of international legal argumentation will separate out the participating NSAA from the pack as a moderator of peace and a law-abiding interlocutor that could be trusted. The Mouvement National pour la Libération de l'Azawad (MNLA) in Mali is one such example. The group had an active record of interaction with humanitarian actors in terms of devising soft law (e.g., deeds of commitment). It is instructive that the group, with two other armed groups in northern Mali, signed the Algiers Peace Accord in June 2015.[68]

[67] "Supplemental General Order in support of the Action Plan between the MILF and the United Nations in the Philippines regarding the Issue of Recruitment and Use of Child Soldiers in the Armed Conflict in Mindanao," http://theirwords.org/media/transfer/doc/1_ph_milf_biaf_2009_13-d74703efad5c37df5ab9842bc87e67a2.pdf.

[68] For the trajectory of the Malian conflict involving MNLA, see Arthur Boutellis and Marie-Joelle Zahar, "A Process in Search of Peace: Lessons from the Inter-Malian Agreement," International Peace Institute (June 2017), https://www.ipinst.org/wp-content/uploads/2017/06/IPI-Rpt-Inter-Malian-Agreement.pdf.

Other kinds of NSAA legal argumentation will not be persuasive. NSAAs often accuse the government of violations of IHL and human rights law. These kinds of arguments are too abundant and cheap to make, imposing little cost on NSAAs. This low cost creates a situation where invoking the law is not enough to persuade international actors. Many NSAAs would issue such statements or remarks to the extent that they can. Since the legal argumentation could as easily come from law-disregarding as law-abiding NSAAs, international actors would not change their beliefs based on them. In addition, accusations in these documents are often buttressed by factual claims that are not verified, and the weight of the evidence is difficult to validate. Therefore, NSAAs' accusations about the opponent's IHL violations have no particular persuasive value.

It is also possible that NSAAs' claims outside of a courtroom can be persuasive because evidentiary standards are low, and even bad legal arguments can carry weight. In the rivalry context among the multiple NSAAs in particular, the signaling to the potential intervener might be persuasive to some extent. Benjamin Jones and Eleonora Mattiacci, for example, show how the NTC's law references with their messages (sometimes false) of their victories conditioned intervention decisions of the United States. In these situations, a bad legal argument can be persuasive from the perspective of outside actors under certain circumstances.

B. Reciprocity Effect

Suppose NSAAs are engaged in international legal argumentation with international humanitarian actors. The governments might reason that "the rebels are engaging in legal argumentation; I might want to do that too." The NSAAs' legal argumentation that disparages state practice might prompt some autocratic states to react, effectively generating tit for tat in a positive cycle of legal argumentation. That is what the Sudanese government did in response to the Darfuri groups signing onto the deeds of commitment to ban the use of anti-personnel mines.[69] In a similar vein, Idriss Abu Garda, the former commander of the Justice and Equality Movement, voluntarily appeared at the ICC in 2009,[70] while Omar al-Bashir staged cat-and-mouse games and stirred controversies in South Africa. In this case, the NSAAs' engagement in legal argumentation and surrounding events brought the spotlight on the al-Bashir regime, which was isolated by the international community. This reciprocal effect might not have been intended by NSAAs, but nonetheless a positive cycle of reciprocity is a potential effect of an NSAA's international legal argumentation.

[69] Gleditsch et al., *supra* note 10.

[70] For the surrounding circumstances and related statements, see Nouwen and Werner, *supra* note 39, at 958.

C. Compliance Effect

A body of literature, much of it in the realm of state politics, shows how legal argumentation can impact compliance through reputation and/or socialization, where those who engage in legal argumentation come under pressure to match deeds with words.[71] When Bruno Stagno-Ugarte, in chapter 8 of this volume, discusses the UN Security Council's avoidance of explicit international criminal law language and preference for passive political pledges, his discussion implies that state actors are concerned about the power of explicit legal language to generate the need for action. In much the same way, NSAAs' international legal argumentation has a potential to generate pressure for compliance with international law. Words are not deeds, so legal argumentation alone may not directly lead to compliance. However, some exchange of legal argumentation between NSAAs and international actors has the potential to produce compliance.

One example of this dynamic can be illustrated with the work by the SRSG/CAAC at the United Nations. The Office has been engaging NSAAs for two decades to stop child soldiering. NSAAs' legal argumentation with the Office, by way of negotiating action plans and concrete steps and timelines, becomes the steppingstone for further engagement, mainly through the demobilization, disarmament, and reintegration (DDR) of child soldiers. The MILF had to go through an internal deliberation and argumentation process before signing onto the 2009 UN Action plan. The deliberation of local religious leadership facilitated the argumentative process, as a UNICEF report explicates in the following paragraph:[72]

> However, the process leading to the adoption of the Action Plan was more challenging than expected. The MILF's concern lay with the difference between the age of maturity in the perspective of Islam and the definition of a child under international law. To ensure the Action Plan received full acceptance by its forces from a religious point of view, the MILF first consulted its Darul Ifta (Religious Council), which deliberated and confirmed that the Action Plan did not contravene Islamic teachings and principles, and endorsed the agreement for signing by the MILF leadership. This mitigating step by the MILF leadership minimised possible resistance to the legitimacy of the Action Plan among the commanders and elements, greatly facilitating its implementation in later years.

[71] Ian Johnstone, *The Power of Deliberation: International Law, Politics and Organizations* (New York: Oxford University Press, 2011), esp. 47–48. The idea of "argumentative entrapment" is from Thomas Risse, "International Norms and Domestic Change: Arguing and Communicative Behavior in the Human Rights Area," *Politics & Society* 27 (1999): 526. On the idea of acculturation and pressure to conform, see Ryan Goodman and Derek Jinks, *Socializing States: Promoting Human Rights through International Law* (New York: Oxford University Press, 2013).

[72] UNICEF, "Children in Armed Conflict: Philippines. Processes and Lessons Learned 2009–2017, Action Plan on the Recruitment and Use of Children in Armed Conflict, United Nations and the Moro Islamic Liberation Front" (2017), at 20, https://www.unicef.org/philippines/media/881/file/Children%20in%20Armed%20Conflict:%20Philippines.pdf.

D. Peace-Inducing Effect

NSAAs' legal argumentation can engender meaningful changes in global security in terms of reduced and restrained violence in non-international armed conflicts, as well as ending those conflicts. The incentives for international legal argumentation can be stronger near peace talks when NSAAs adopt a stance of moderation and want to appeal to international audiences for international support. Ultimately, the NSAAs' participation in international legal argumentation has the potential to be the harbinger for peace agreements.

At a minimum, international legal argumentation by NSAAs can be a signal of restraint in wartime behavior. It is often a meaningful signal that NSAAs are willing to be engaged, although not necessarily a sign that they will exercise restraint. The form and result of humanitarian engagement depends on what happens in between. The prospects for wartime restraint will depend on whether the intention to follow international rules or conform to international norms is genuine and whether those arguments have teeth in the actual practice of armed groups through either socialization among ranks or enforcement across ranks. The willingness in the NSAAs' leadership, socialization patterns among individual armed actors,[73] and the mode of international engagement to assist the process are key to realizing the gains of legal argumentation for the purpose of achieving peace.

Whether legal argumentation can lead to peace in the form of absence of violence will depend on a variety of factors. For example, the presence of NSAA commitments in peace agreements will be important, as the literature on treaty designs show.[74] The participation of NSAAs in peace processes, with the add-on of international legal argumentation featured during negotiations, will be important. The follow-up by the international community will be helpful if it comes with assistance in DDR processes or peacekeeping mechanisms, so that the conflict environment would be favorable to a durable peace with civilian protection.[75]

The MILF in the Philippines provides an example of how legal argumentation can connect with the path to peace. In 2014, the MILF concluded a peace agreement with the Philippines government, the Comprehensive Agreement on Bangsamoro. In the agreement, the MILF achieved some political autonomy in exchange for decommissioning its armed wing, the Bangsamoro Islamic Armed Forces. The MILF case illustrates that NSAAs' international legal argumentation can be read as a prelude to those subsequent changes from armed movement to political settlement.

[73] Dara Cohen, "Explaining Rape During Civil War: Cross-National Evidence (1980–2009)," *American Political Science Review* 107 (2013): 461.

[74] Michaela Mattes and Burcu Savun, "Fostering Peace After Civil War: Commitment Problems and Agreement Design," *International Studies Quarterly* 53 (2009): 737.

[75] On a related result on the effect of peacekeeping on conflict outcomes and civilian protection, see Lisa Hultman, Jacob Kathman, and Megan Shannon, "United Nations Peacekeeping and Civilian Protection in Civil War," *American Journal of Political Science* 57 (2013): 875.

VIII. Conclusion

The examples and analyses presented in this chapter demonstrate that NSAAs are indeed part of international law encompassing "a constant process of communication over conduct and consequences."[76] Just as with states, NSAAs appear to engage in international law for the purpose of advancing their political and military interests.[77] Just as with states, there appear to be imbalances as to who gets to advertise their position through the international legal argumentation processes.

Since making legal arguments publicly requires knowledge and bureaucratic capacity, some NSAAs are able to pursue those legal argumentation strategies, while others are not. The inequality in opportunity structure suggests international legal argumentation may be a privileged exercise. Intentional engagement by humanitarian actors ameliorates this situation by contacting weak and marginalized groups. Silent groups also include those that refuse to participate in international legal argumentation on the ground that the law is based on Western norms and ignores their own religious principles or societal structures. Extremists seem to exaggerate the differences, but legal argumentation made by moderate Islamic groups suggests that debates are possible. These engagements are more likely to occur during the period of moderation near peace negotiations when NSAAs pursue the double-pronged strategy of talking while fighting.

The analysis also points to the importance of legal argumentation strategies by humanitarian actors. In encountering the spectrum of NSAAs, humanitarians can reach out first to those who are engage-able, with clear interlocutors who have a willingness to engage. With this first set, humanitarians might succeed by actively engaging them with soft law strategies or monitoring. With those groups that reject the very foundations of international law, differentiated argumentation strategies might be necessary. It might be better not to talk law but to emphasize their underlying belief systems and start with the similarities and commonalities between those belief systems and international law. Much like what Scott Sheeran (in chapter 4 of this volume) observed, straightforward legal argumentation, at times, might backfire. In politically laden settings, diplomatic language might carry more persuasive weight than direct legal arguments. Humanitarians have learned over time the practical value of adopting non-legal language that reflects the values embedded in legal rules.[78] Persuasion or dissuasion strategies involving non-legal language should be considered when NSAAs differ in their origins and goals. Recognizing the heterogeneity among the set of NSAAs is the first step to enable "the work of international law,"[79] that is, to create and moderate conflicts in order to narrow the differences and to recognize the value of engaging NSAAs in international legal conversations.

[76] Steven R. Ratner, "Persuading to Comply: On the Deployment and Avoidance of Legal Argumentation," in *Interdisciplinary Perspectives on International Law and International Relations: The State of the Art*, edited by Jeffrey L. Dunoff and Mark A. Pollack (New York: Cambridge University Press, 2012), 568.

[77] Lisa Wedeen, *Ambiguities of Domination: Politics, Rhetoric, and Symbols in Contemporary Syria* (Chicago: Chicago University Press, 2015).

[78] As theorized in Ratner, *supra* note 76, and observed in ICRC, *The Roots of Restraints in War* (Geneva: International Committee of the Red Cross, 2018).

[79] Hakimi, *supra* note 11.

The patterns and processes of NSAAs' legal argumentation hint at future directions for international engagement. Suppose some armed groups invoke the Geneva Conventions and signal their intention to be part of the discourse used by the international community. This participation in international legal argumentation could potentially pave the way for future interactions by other international actors via mediation or humanitarian engagement. The content NSAAs convey will be important also for devising a global security policy; understanding what kind and content of legal justification is employed by NSAAs will help us to better understand NSAAs. The content will also shed light on the extent to which international law is relevant and in what ways beyond the realm of states.

10
Argumentation through Law
An Analysis of Decisions of the African Union

Wouter Werner

I. Introduction

"It never gets boring," Teresa Reinold wrote some two years ago, referring to the (then) latest decision of the African Union (AU) on the International Criminal Court (ICC).[1] For over a decade, relations between the two organizations have been tense. The ICC has issued a series of judgments, mostly against African states that refused to arrest and hand over the then incumbent president of Sudan, Omar al-Bashir.[2] The AU, for its part, repeatedly accused the ICC of having an "African bias," of lack of respect for sovereign immunity, and for its detrimental influence on peace processes in countries such as Sudan or Kenya. Underlying these concerns is frustration that the ICC shows a lack of respect and willingness to seriously engage with the AU's critiques. On several occasions, these complaints were voiced through the adoption of formal legal documents. In a series of "Decisions," the AU has set out why it feels let down by the ICC (and the UN Security Council) and has expressed the need to respect the unity and dignity of the African continent.

Decisions by the AU are part of a larger practice of legal argumentation. In and outside the courtroom, African and other states, ICC officials, academics, and non-governmental organizations (NGOs) have exchanged legal arguments about topics such as the Court's jurisdiction, the immunities of heads of state, the formation of customary law, and the scope and impact of Security Council resolutions. There is no question that these are important legal issues, for the ICC, the AU, and international law generally. However, underlying these more technical questions of law lie highly

[1] Teresa Reinold, "African Union v International Criminal Court: Episode MLXIII (?)," *EJILTalk!*, Mar. 23, 2018, https://www.ejiltalk.org/african-union-v-international-criminal-court-episode-mlxiii/.

[2] Corrigendum to the Decision Pursuant to Article 87(7) of the Rome Statute on The Failure by the Republic of Malawi to Comply with the Cooperation Requests Issued by the Court with Respect to the Arrests and Surrender of Omar Hassan Ahmad Al Bashir, ICC-02/05-01/09-139-Corr, Dec.13, 2011; Decision on the Failure by the Republic of Malawi to Comply with the Cooperation Requests; Decision pursuant to Article 87(7) of the Rome Statute on the refusal of the Republic of Chad to comply with the cooperation requests issued by the Court with respect to the arrest and surrender of Omar Hassan Ahmad Al Bashir, ICC-02/05-01/09-140-ENG, Dec. 13, 2011; Decision on the Cooperation of the Democratic Republic of the Congo Regarding Omar Al Bashir's Arrest and Surrender to the Court, ICC-02/05-01/09-195, Apr. 9, 2014; Decision under Article 87(7) of the Rome Statute on the noncompliance by South Africa with the request by the Court for the arrest and *surrender of Omar Al-Bashir*, ICC-02/05-01/09-302, July 6, 2017; Judgment in the Jordan Referral re Al-Bashir Appeal, ICC-02/05-01/09-397-Corr, May 6, 2019.

Wouter Werner, *Argumentation through Law* In: *Talking International Law.* Edited by: Ian Johnstone and Steven Ratner, Oxford University Press. © Wouter Werner 2021. DOI: 10.1093/oso/9780197588437.003.0010

political questions regarding recognition, equality, and respect. The AU does not just disagree with the ICC on the interpretation of law. As it has stated repeatedly, it feels it is not being taken seriously, not being heard, and not being recognized as an equal partner in the fight against impunity.[3]

What interests me is that these "feelings" are not only expressed in informal ways, for example, through press statements, but are also expressed in legal form, in formal Decisions taken by the supreme organ of the AU, the Assembly of Heads of State and Government. The Decisions do not contain elaborate arguments about the proper interpretation or application of law. In that sense, they are different from legal argumentation as understood traditionally. However, as I will argue in more detail, it does make sense to include them in a study on legal argumentation. First, they express what underlies the more doctrinal debates on the application of the ICC Statute, rules of customary law, or the powers of the Security Council. By choosing to use a formal legal instrument to communicate about issues, the AU gives the more technical debates their political bite. Second, the fact that the AU opted for "Decisions" has implications for the commitment of member states. AU Decisions, after all, constitute one of the sources of AU law, which member states are bound to respect. In that sense, it makes a big difference whether the Union expresses its concerns via formal Decisions or through informal statements. In this context, it is important to note that one of the recurring elements in AU Decisions has been the need to stick to a common position in relation to the ICC. This makes it possible to endow the concerns with the authority that comes with a common position expressed in legal form. There are good reasons for the AU to use legal decisions to appeal to emotions outside the courtroom. Through such appeals, the Union seeks to (re)claim membership, respect, and dignity while also fostering unity among African states.

Before I analyze the decisions of the AU in more detail, I will set out my theoretical framework, based on the institutional theory of law, legal expressivism, and Emile Durkheim's reflections on the role of criminal law in the formation of communities. I use this framework because it helps to illuminate one of the characteristic features of the Decisions of the AU: the expression of feelings of frustration, concern, and disappointment, together with a commitment to fight impunity. Taken together, these theoretical lenses support the claim that, although emotions play a role in various legal fields, they are of particular importance in the field of international criminal law. The first section lays the basis for the second, where I will focus in more detail on the content of the Decisions by the AU. I will conclude the chapter by returning to some of the questions posed by the editors of this volume.

[3] For some it may seem odd to ascribe feelings to an international organization, as if I am anthropomorphizing it. Of course, I am aware of the difference between humans and abstract entities such as organizations. Still, I think it makes sense to speak of "feelings" when it comes to international organizations such as the African Union. In the first place, the "feelings" that are central to this chapter are the formally expressed feelings, as set out in Decisions adopted by the African Union. Just like an organization "takes decisions" or "recommends," it is capable of formally expressing feelings and emotions. The question is not whether the organization "really" has these feelings, just like the question is not whether the organization "really" has taken a decision. Within the system of law, the feelings exist as institutional fact if they are created in accordance with the relevant power conferring rules. I will return to this point in Section II, where I discuss the institutional theory of law.

II. Beyond Norms: Emotions and Communities in International Criminal Law

A. Institutional Theory

My analysis of AU Decisions is inspired by three streams of literature. The first is the institutional theory of law, as developed from the late 1980s onward. The theory was introduced by Neil MacCormick and Ota Weinberger, who joined forces when they discovered they had been working on similar topics, although coming from two rather different intellectual traditions.[4] Both authors emphasized the need to analyze law in terms of "institutions" instead of rules of conduct and competence only. An institution, as MacCormick set out, combines three types of rules: (1) institutive rules, spelling out under what conditions a new institutional legal fact is created (e.g., the conditions that create the institutions of marriage, ownership, or an armed conflict under humanitarian law); (2) consequential rules, spelling out which other rules become applicable when a new institutional fact is created; and (3) terminative rules, spelling out under which conditions an institutional fact ceases to exist.[5] The idea that law consists of institutions and institutional facts was further developed by Dick Ruiter, who used it to distinguish two concepts: validity and binding force.[6] Often, the question whether something is "valid law" is confused with the narrower question whether there is a legally binding norm, rule, or principle. Of course, law does consist of norms, rules, and principles. However, there is no reason to assume a priori that law is *only* about that. As Ingo Venzke has argued in chapter 2 of this volume, one of the core functions of law is to enable certain forms of conduct. Rules of law make it possible to behave in ways "that would otherwise not be similarly available." I would add to this that power-conferring rules in law make it possible to express oneself in ways that would not be otherwise available. Just a cursory look at treaties, judgments, or resolutions illustrates this point.

Take, for example, the Security Council resolution on Yemen that was adopted on February 25, 2020 (SC Res. 2511). The resolution is created in accordance with the rules of competence set out in the UN Charter, a valid treaty under international law. However, only a small portion of the resolution consists of "binding decisions" or binding norms. Most of the text communicates the stance of the Security Council toward the situation in Yemen: the Council "reaffirms its commitment," expresses "alarm" about the presence of Al-Qaeda and Daesh, "emphasizes" the importance of humanitarian assistance, "affirms" that sexual violence can be an international crime—and so forth. This is done not only in the preamble to the resolution, as may be expected, but also in the operative part, following the explicit mention that it is "acting under Chapter VII of the Charter of the United Nations." Following the institutional theory developed by Ruiter, all these expressions possess validity under international law, even though they do not create binding obligations. Their validity is

[4] See especially Neil MacCormick and Ota Weinberger, *An Institutional Theory of Law: New Approaches to Legal Positivism* (Dordrecht: Reidel Publishing, 1986).

[5] *Id.*

[6] Dick Ruiter, *Institutional Legal Fact: Legal Powers and Their Effects* (Dordrecht: Springer, 1993).

derived, in a classical Kelsenian or Hartian way, from the power-conferring rules of the legal system. They are, in other words, legally valid expressions of concern, legally valid confirmations of existing obligations, legally valid hortatory acts pressuring or nudging states, and so forth. They exist as institutional legal facts, endowed with the authority of the legal system.

B. Expressivism in International Criminal Law

The separation of bindingness and validity dovetails with a second theoretical strand I rely on, namely, theories of expressivism developed in the field of international criminal law. These theories focus on the different messages that are communicated through the language and procedures of international criminal law. These messages are connected to a wide variety of functions assumed by international courts and tribunals. A cursory look at some of the websites reveals an image that international courts and tribunals present to the world: they do not just issue arrest warrants and try individuals; they also engage in peace-building, recording history, changing the course of international law, truth-telling, and conciliation.[7] Although such lofty ambitions have been criticized,[8] they do appear time and again, especially in high-profile cases involving international criminal law.[9]

The expressive potential of international criminal law has not gone unnoticed by practitioners. An example inside the courtroom can be found in David Crane's opening statement in the case against Samuel Hinga Norman Moinina Fofana Allieu Kondewa, leader of the Kamajors militia that supported the Sierre Leone government in its fight against the Revolutionary United Front in the late 1990s. Crane begins by claiming to speak on behalf of "mankind," which has to reconstitute itself in the face of the atrocities committed in Sierra Leone: "On this solemn occasion, mankind is once again assembled before an international tribunal to begin the sober and steady climb upwards toward the towering summit of justice." This can only be done if humanity can overcome impunity and strike back passionately against the transgressors. In Crane's words, mankind needs to put an "end to the life of that beast of impunity, which howls in frustration and shrinks from the bright and shining spectre of the law." In this way, humanity rediscovers itself through the boundaries set by the law. Deviance is translated into "crimes, the most grievous of acts that a person can be

[7] I checked the websites of the ICC, the International Criminal Tribunal for the Former Yugoslavia, and the Special Court for Sierra Leone: https://www.icc-cpi.int/about; https://www.icty.org/en/about; https://www.icc-cpi.int/about.

[8] See, e.g., Arendt's insistence that trials should only be about the guilt of the defendant: Hannah Arendt, *Eichmann in Jerusalem: A Report on the Banality of Evil* (London: Penguin Classics, 2006).

[9] See, e.g., the discussion on the use of film and images in the Nuremberg trials in relation to the portrayal of the defendants in the press. For this argument, see Ulricke Weckel, "Watching the Accused Watch the Nazi Crimes: Observers' Reports on the Atrocity Film Screenings in the Belsen, Nuremberg and Eichmann Trials," *London Review of International Law* 6 (Mar. 2018): 45. For a more general analysis of the screening of "Nazi concentration camps," see Lawrence Douglas, "Film as Witness: Screening Nazi Concentration Camps Before the Nuremberg Tribunal," *Yale Law Journal* 105 (1995): 449; for a more general analysis of the "show part" of international criminal trials, see Martti Koskenniemi, "Between Impunity and Show Trials" *Max Planck Yearbook of United Nations Law* 6 (2002): 1.

charged with by mankind."[10] The example shows the close link between the (felt) need to express the basic values of international criminal law and the appeal to emotions. When it comes to questions how "we," humanity, or mankind, should respond to "them," transgressors of the basic values that hold the world together, it is practically impossible not to invoke emotions, not to include pathos. This brings me to the third theoretical influence on my analysis, the work of Durkheim.

C. International Criminal Law and the Constitution of Communities

Crane's opening statement may be exceptional in its style and tone, but it does reflect a more general aspect of international criminal law. The statement repeatedly refers to concepts such as "mankind" or "humanity." In other words: it is the global community in whose name crimes are prosecuted and whose interests are at stake in fighting impunity. The invocation of a global community also appears regularly outside the courtroom. Take, for example, the 2018 speech delivered by the president of the ICC, Judge Chile Eboe-Osuji, to the General Assembly of the United Nations. The president recites the preamble of the Rome Statute, which speaks of "common bonds that unite all peoples," as well as the never-ending threat of "unimaginable atrocities that deeply shock the conscience of humanity." In order to fight these atrocities, the president states, it is necessary to promote a "rules-based order," where international crimes are "prosecuted and punished—'properly.' "[11]

The reference to the "crimes that shock the conscience of humanity" echoes Durkheim's emphasis on the "collective conscience" in domestic criminal law.[12] According to Durkheim, criminal law and punishment fulfill essential functions in the (re)constitution of a collectivity. Criminal law responses carve out the moral boundaries of a community, while enhancing social cohesion within the group through regulated yet "passionate" reactions to deviant behavior. Through its responses to criminal behavior, a collectivity (re)discovers its outer limits and identity; the moral boundaries that cannot be transgressed. Those who challenge these boundaries must be marked as transgressors in order to preserve the bonds that keep a group together. The identity of a group is secured through an emotional and forceful reaction against beliefs and acts "we do not, and cannot, permit to raise (their) head with impunity."[13] What is at stake in criminal law are not just the injuries suffered by the direct victim but also the integrity of the "collective conscience" that needs to be defended against its enemies.

[10] The Opening Statement of David M. Crane, The Prosecutor Special Court for Sierra Leone, June 3, 2004, In the International Criminal Trial for Crimes against Humanity, War Crimes and Other Serious Violations of International Humanitarian Law Against Samuel Hinga Norman Moinina Fofana Allieu Kondewa (Case No. SCSL-03-14-I), http://www.rscsl.org/Documents/Press/OTP/prosecutor-openingstatement060304.pdf.

[11] Speech of the ICC President to United Nations General Assembly, Oct. 29, 2018, https://www.icc-cpi.int/Pages/item.aspx?name=181029-pres-stat-un.

[12] Emile Durkheim, *The Division of Labor in Society* (New York: The Free Press, 1960, fourth print, translation by George Simpson). Originally published in 1893 as "La Division du Travail Social."

[13] *Id.* 97–98.

Durkheim's take on criminal law explains the often-repeated vocation of international criminal law to "end impunity" for crimes that shock the conscience of humanity.[14] This is not just a matter of redress for those who directly suffer from atrocities; it is also a matter of (re)constituting and (re)storing the common bonds that hold the global community of peoples together.[15] Those who transgress the boundaries of the global community commit crimes "against humanity" and deserve to be stigmatized and punished as such.[16] Because it fulfills a core function in the attempt to constitute a global community, international criminal law is a field where law and emotion often work in tandem.

The expressive power of international criminal law also means that a great deal is at stake for those who *contest* the way in which the boundaries of the common conscience are drawn. One may challenge, for example, the crimes that are used to delineate the contours of the moral core of humanity. As Kamari Clarke has shown, it was by no means obvious that only the three (now four) crimes covered by the Rome Statute would be those that shock the conscience of humanity. If other crimes were included, other acts would (also) have been singled out as requiring a passionate legal response.[17] The current debate on the "African bias" of the ICC, she contends, should be viewed through this lens: "It has to do with which crimes can be pursued, which agents can be held responsible, whether Africa's violence can be managed by African countries, and whether the crimes of the Rome Statute are sufficient to address the root causes of violence in Africa's political landscape."[18]

Much is also at stake for those against whom the ICC has issued arrest warrants. Contesting an arrest warrant by the ICC is often more than just trying to escape prosecution. It is also an attempt to fight the stigma of having acted beyond the scope of humanity, of transgressing the moral bonds that, to paraphrase the ICC Statute, hold a delicate international society together. Those fighting the stigma almost unavoidably seek to turn the tables. For those challenging the arrest warrants, it is the Court that endangers the delicate balance that holds societies together peacefully. The imposing of legal stigmata itself is presented as the core of the problem.

In the next section, I will analyze a set of responses to some of the ICC's most controversial arrest warrants, those against the then-incumbent president of Sudan as

[14] For an application of Durkheim's sociology to international criminal law, see Mark Osiel, *Mass Atrocity, Collective Memory and the Law* (London: Routledge, 2017); Frédéric Mégret, "Practices of Stigmatization," *Law and Contemporary* Problems 3/4 (2003): 287; Immi Tallgren, "The Durkheimian Spell of International Criminal Law?," *Revue interdisciplinaire d'études juridiques* 71 (2013): 137.

[15] This is also visible in, for example, Hannah Arendt's epilogue to *Eichmann in Jerusalem*, where she sets out why Eichmann deserves to be put to death. Arendt's justification goes beyond the fate of his direct victims, referring in addition to the very idea of a global community of people as well as every "member of the human race": "Just as you supported and carried out a policy of not wanting to share the earth with the Jewish people and the people of a number of other nations—as though you and your superiors had any right to determine who should and who should not inhabit the world—we find that no one, that is, no member of the human race, can be expected to share the world with you. This is the reason, and the only reason, you must hang." Arendt, *supra* note 8, at 279.

[16] In this context, it is interesting to recall the jurisprudence of the European Court of Human Rights, where torture is set apart from other forms of "degrading or inhumane treatment" because of the specific stigma attached to torture.

[17] Kamari Maxine Clarke, *Fictions of Justice: The International Criminal Court and the Challenge of Legal Pluralism in Sub-Saharan Africa* (Cambridge: Cambridge University Press, 2009).

[18] ICC Forum, Invited Experts on Africa Question, https://iccforum.com/africa.

well as those against the persons believed to be responsible for the post-election violence in Kenya in 2007–2008. These arrest warrants exacerbated a lingering frustration about the way in which the ICC targeted African states, how they interfered with peace processes, and pressured states to act in contravention of rules on state immunity. One of the ways in which the AU responded to the ICC was through the adoption of formal legal instruments, Decisions. In this way, the AU used the power-conferring rules of its Constitutive Act to express a position that is valid for all its members. Speaking with a single pan-African voice, the Decisions allowed the Union to forcefully express its stance toward the ICC (and the UN Security Council) and to present it in a formal legal act. Like many other instruments in international law (think of the example of the Security Council discussed above), the Decisions of the AU include emotive appeals regarding basic values, identity, and respect.

III. AU Decisions and Legal Expressivism

A. Preliminary Remarks

To illustrate how emotions are communicated through law, but outside the courtroom, I have selected a series of Decisions by the AU on the ICC. I realize that the AU is not the only voice coming from Africa. States have disagreed on the desirability of withdrawing from the ICC,[19] different branches of government in African states may hold different opinions, and several African human rights NGOs have indicated their continued support for the Court. As I will set out in more detail below, the existence of various voices has been precisely one of the reasons for the AU to emphasize the need to "speak with one voice" and to guard the unity of the continent. And indeed, Decisions by the AU represent the formal voice of the Assembly, comprised of all member states of the Union, and thus come with legal authority.

My starting point is 2009, the year of the arrest warrant against al-Bashir. The arrest warrant grew out of Security Council Resolution 1593 (2005), which referred the situation of Sudan to the ICC. The Security Council, acting under Chapter VII of the UN Charter, had determined that the situation in Darfur constituted a threat to international peace and security and referred it to the ICC for investigation. The ICC investigation eventually led to several cases against Sudanese government officials, Janjaweed leaders, and leaders of the Resistance Front. By far the most controversial case concerned the then-incumbent president of Sudan, Omar al-Bashir.[20] He was the first sitting president indicted by the ICC and the first person charged by the ICC with the crime of genocide.

Legally speaking, the arrest warrant was controversial. Although Sudan was not a party to the ICC Statute, the statute allows for the referral of non-parties to the Court by the Security Council. Nevertheless, as head of state, al-Bashir would

[19] Assembly of the African Union, Decision on the International Criminal Court, 28th Ordinary Session, Doc.EX.CL/1006 (XXX) (Jan. 30–31, 2017). Elise Keppler, "AU's 'ICC Withdrawal Strategy' Less than Meets the Eye, Opposition to Withdrawal by States," *Human Rights Watch*, Feb. 1, 2017, https://www.hrw.org/news/2017/02/01/aus-icc-withdrawal-strategy-less-meets-eye.

[20] Warrant of Arrest for Omar Hassan Ahmad Al Bashir, ICC-02/05-01/09, Mar. 4, 2009.

normally be entitled to immunity from arrest should he travel to other states. The question was (and remains) whether this immunity was set aside by the combined effect of the Security Council referral and the arrest warrant of the ICC.[21] Politically, the arrest warrant spurred debates on the effects of ICC interventions on peace processes, the African bias of the ICC, and the reluctance of the Security Council to seriously engage with arguments brought up by African states.[22]

Like all beginnings, my starting point is somewhat arbitrary. The current dispute between the AU and the ICC has multiple roots, including the negotiations in Rome, colonialism, decolonization, lobbying by targeted heads of state, the Sudan referral by the Security Council, and the refusal by that same Council to take the concerns expressed by the AU seriously. Depending on where one starts, the story looks and evolves differently. At the same time, the choice for 2009 is not random. The arrest warrant against al-Bashir was a turning point in the relationship between the ICC and the AU and has given rise to a series of cases before the ICC.[23]

AU Decisions, by their very nature, are a form of legal communication. They are adopted by the Assembly, the "supreme organ of the Union" (Article 6), in accordance with the formal decision-making procedures set out in the Constitutive Act of the Union ("by consensus or, failing which, by a two-third majority of the Member States"; Article 7). However, that does not necessarily mean that all sections of AU Decisions contain legally binding elements. Just like Security Council resolutions, Decisions of the AU are filled with other elements, including the expression of emotions and claims about identity and membership. Such elements can only be taken seriously in legal analysis if the question of legal validity is separated from the question of binding force. The elements in the Decisions are legally valid, as they have been issued in accordance with the proper power-conferring rules under a valid treaty in international law. Yet their content is quite diverse and goes beyond normative prescriptions.

Especially in resolutions pertaining to the ICC, AU Decisions have been utilized to express the stance of the Union and to condemn the behavior of other institutions and states. They do revolve around what happens in the courtroom, including arrest warrants that are issued and states that are reprimanded for not arresting al-Bashir. Yet they do not contain in-depth doctrinal analyses, as the AU did, for example, in its submission in the case against Jordan.[24] Instead, they present a formally validated and consistent narrative that seeks to challenge the attempts by the ICC to impose stigmata in the name of the shocked conscience of humanity.

[21] See, *inter alia*, the case law mentioned *supra* note 2.

[22] See, *inter alia*, Sarah M.H. Nouwen and Wouter G. Werner, "Doing Justice to the Political: The International Criminal Court in Uganda and Sudan," *European Journal of International Law* 21 (2011): 941.

[23] *Supra* note 2.

[24] The African Union's Submission in the Hashemite Kingdom of Jordan's Appeal Against the Decision under Article 87(7) of the Rome Statute on the NonCompliance by Jordan with the Request by the Court for the Arrest and Surrender [of] Omar Al-Bashir, ICC-02/05-01/09-370.

B. Decisions by the AU

I have analyzed eighteen Decisions adopted by the AU on the ICC between 2009 and 2020. The list of Decisions can be found in the annex to this chapter. In the following, I will set out how these Decisions express the anxieties of the AU on issues of membership, recognition, and dignity.

1. Joining the Fight against Impunity

My starting point is an element in all Decisions of the AU: the reiteration of the AU of its commitment to fight impunity. The reiteration appears in seventeen out of the eighteen Decisions, the only exception being Decision 586 (XXV) of June 14–15, 2015. This Decision, however, starts out by "taking note" of previous Decisions on the ICC and by "recalling" Decision 547, which does contain a reiteration of the commitment to the fight against impunity. In this context, the term "re-iteration" is interesting. The term indicates that, apparently, the commitment was already "iterated" (repeated) before and is now repeated again. Going back, however, there is no first "repetition" of the commitment, only "re-iterations." This gives the commitment the aura of being eternal, or at least it presents the AU's dedication to fight impunity as something that was always already there.

Given the expressive power of international criminal law, it is not surprising to find in all Decisions reiterations of the commitment to fight impunity. After all, when the ICC goes after individuals, it unavoidably sends out a message about larger communities as well. International crimes are almost invariably policy crimes, involving groups of people and often rooted in political programs.[25] Prosecuting individuals then involves delegitimizing broader political programs and structures as well. When the ICC determines that states have failed to arrest someone against whom it has issued an arrest warrant, it does more than identify the violation of a technical legal rule. It signals that a state is unable or unwilling to cooperate to fight impunity for the greater good of humanity as a whole. As the Appeals Chamber in a recent judgment regarding the Jordan referral decided, a failure to cooperate with the Court implies that a state refuses to live up to its obligations to the international community. After all, the Appeals Chamber argued, the duty to cooperate "reinforces the obligation *erga omnes* to prevent, investigate and punish crimes that shock the conscience of humanity (. . .) and it is this *erga omnes* character that makes the obligation of State Parties to cooperate with the Court so fundamental."[26]

This puts the constant reiterations of the commitment to fight impunity in the context of a struggle over recognition and membership. The reiteration signals that the AU is as dedicated as the Court to restore the shocked conscience of humanity. At the same time, the Union signals that the ICC does not hold a monopoly on the protection

[25] For an analysis of the tension between the collective nature of international crimes and the attempt to single out individuals under international criminal law, see, *inter alia*, Mark Drumbl, "Collective Violence and Individual Punishment: The Criminality of Mass Atrocity," Washington & Lee University School of Law Scholarly Commons, https://scholarlycommons.law.wlu.edu/cgi/viewcontent.cgi?article=1035&context=wlufac.

[26] Appeals Chamber, Situation in Darfur, Sudan, in the Case of The Prosecutor v. Omar Hassan Ahmad Al-Bashir, Judgment in the Jordan Referral re Al-Bashir Appeal, ICC-02/05-01/09OA2, May 6, 2019.

of humanity's conscience. The reiteration of the commitment to fight impunity is invariably accompanied by a reference to the Constitutive Act of the AU, and often more specifically to Article 4(h), which asserts a right to intervene in a member state in case of war crimes, genocide, and crimes against humanity. The duty to the conscience of humanity is thus related to the specific position of the AU and its commitment as set out in the Constitutive Act.

2. Reinforcing African Unity

The reference to the position and commitment of the AU adds two additional layers to the struggle between the AU and the ICC. In the first place, the Decisions present an altogether different image of the international community that is fighting crimes. The ICC invokes a global community transcending sovereign states and the rules that regulate their interactions—it is "humanity" or "mankind" whose interests are at stake, and it is up to the Court to draw the boundaries of that community. The AU, for its part, sees a world of sovereign states dedicated to fight impunity while respecting traditional rules of international law. In this world of sovereign states, there is room for regional approaches, such as that of the AU. This points to the second layer: the community of African states. By constantly referring to the Constitutive Act of the AU, the Decisions also seek to reinforce the unity of the member states of the AU. This point is reinforced by frequent references to the need to "speak with one voice"[27] or to comply with "the position" or the "Decisions" of the Assembly.[28]

The reference to African unity gets more bite when it is related to the issues of respect and dignity, as mentioned above. The actions of the Court, the Security Council, and the Prosecutor are related, not only to issues such as immunity or balancing prosecution and peace but also to the dignity and integrity of the continent that would be at stake. Thus, some Decisions "[u]nderscore that the AU and its Member States reserve the right to take any further decisions or measures that may be deemed necessary in order to preserve and safeguard the dignity, sovereignty and integrity of the continent."[29] In this way, the AU links the struggle over the nature of the international community as a whole to the need to cling to the Union as a community of African states. Its Decisions, in other words, are Janus-faced. One part is looking outward, informing the world at large that the AU is as committed to fighting crimes as the ICC, albeit on different terms. The other part is looking inward, calling upon states to speak with one voice in order to prevent the ICC's image of "humanity" from undermining the dignity and unity of the continent.

3. Recognition

The idea of a community of African states that deserves to be taken seriously on the international plane recurs in several other ways across the Decisions. In eight Decisions,

[27] See, e.g., Doc.Assembly/AU/Dec.270 (XIV); Doc.Assembly/AU/Dec.269 (XV); Doc.Assembly/AU/Dec.334 (XVI).

[28] See, e.g., Doc.Assembly/AU/Dec.547 (XXIV); Doc.Assembly/AU/Dec.590 (XXVI); Doc.Assembly/AU/Dec.616 (XXVII).

[29] Doc.Assembly/AU/13 (XIII), July 1–3, 2009, para. 12; see also para. 9 of Doc.Assembly/AU/13 (XXI), May 26–27, 2013.

for example, the Assembly expresses dissatisfaction with the refusal of the Security Council to defer proceedings against al-Bashir or Kenyan officials, as provided in Article 16 of the ICC Statute. The reason for the AU's request for a deferral is spelled out in several Decisions: prosecution would hamper the peace process in Sudan and the political processes in Kenya, and may conflict with customary rules on head of state immunities. The language chosen to formulate the AU's position is telling. The Union "cautions," "notes with grave concern," "expresses concern," and "reiterates its requests to the Security Council." The AU here uses its formal decision-making powers to communicate to the Security Council what it seeks and why it does so.

However, there is more at stake than warning the Council about possible consequences of indictments. In a number of Decisions, the AU expresses its frustration, because it does not feel it is taken seriously or heard by the Security Council. The frustrations are rooted in the experiences of leaders and representatives of African states. Yet they also exist in legally valid form, as the officially sanctioned frustration of the AU. In this way, the frustrations are presented as the common experience of the member states, legally sanctioned and communicated to the outside world. In its Decision of January 30–31, 2017, for example, the AU "decides that the Open Ended Ministerial Committee discontinue any further engagement with the United Nations Security Council as no tangible result will come out of the exercise due to the *recalcitrant position* of some members of the UNSC" (emphasis added).[30] This helps explain the strong emotional language found across several Decisions when they talk about the Security Council. The AU is not just "disappointed" or "dissatisfied"; it is "deeply disappointed," it "deeply regrets" (four times), and even expresses "deep grief." The image that emerges is that of a Union whose members feel stigmatized by the ICC, insufficiently protected by rules on immunity, and not being taken seriously in the AU's attempts to address these issues at the United Nations.

4. The Prosecution

A last example concerns the position of the Prosecution within some of the AU Decisions. In five Decisions, the Assembly expresses unease and disagreement with arrest warrants, as they are believed to undermine peace, stability, and the rule of law. Thus in its Decision of January 30–31, 2015, the Assembly challenges "the wisdom of the continued prosecution against African Leaders."[31] These challenges spring from the Union's concern about the effects of prosecution on peace and political processes, as mentioned above. They also arise from concerns about international immunity law, as reconfirmed in several Decisions. The Decision of July 1–3, 2009, even stated that African state parties to the Rome Statute should prepare guidelines and a code of conduct for the exercise of the Prosecutor's discretionary powers.[32]

However, just as with decisions of the Security Council, the underlying issue is one of respect and recognition. The text of a few Decisions goes beyond expressing concerns by singling out specific persons and agents, in what I can only understand as handing out "counter-stigmata." Consider the language in the Decision of July

[30] Doc.EX.CL1006 (XXX), para. 3.
[31] Doc.Assembly/AU/18 (XXIV), para. 4.
[32] Doc.Assembly/AU/13 (XII), para. 11.

25–27, 2010: "Mr. Moreno Ocampo who has been making egregiously unacceptable, rude and condescending statements. . . ."[33] . . . Six years later, the AU "takes note with concern of the obstinacy of the ICC by the so-called 'Principals of the Court' comprising the Prosecutor, the Registrar and the President of the ICC, which continues to privilege the views of civil society over clearly held positions of African Member States . . . the disturbing dismissive disregard of the decisions of the 14th ASP by the Prosecution. . . ."[34] Where the ICC singles out specific individuals, and thereby the political structures they represent, the AU singles out the prosecutor in particular, and thereby the office and structures that she or he represents.

The reiteration of the AU's commitment to fight impunity in accordance with its Constitutive Act is thus more than a perfunctory signal. In a nutshell, it sets out how the Union sees itself as belonging to the moral community that is dedicated to fighting international crimes. In line with the arguments presented by Venzke and Hakimi in this volume, the authority of the law is used to present the African Union as a responsible member of the global community. All the while, the Decisions highlight the different approaches adopted by the African Union. The ICC does not hold a monopoly on how the international community is to be understood nor how the fight against impunity should be conducted. At the same time, the reiteration contains a call upon African states to speak with one voice (that is: the voice of the Assembly) in order to defend what the AU has called the "dignity . . . of the continent." In that sense, it is also the prelude to the more emotive aspects, such as its "concern" or "deep disappointment."

5. The ICC Responding

The calls for respect by the AU did not go unnoticed at the ICC. The Court held several meetings and retreats with representatives of the AU. It also dedicated a special issue of its online forum to the question "Is the International Criminal Court targeting Africa inappropriately?," where it invited experts to reflect on this question. The experts held different opinions, with some of them criticizing the setup or the functioning of the Court.[35] The ICC also responded more directly by means of its Presidency. On May 29, 2013, the Presidency published a press statement, which directly engages with the question of dignity and respect. The statement opens with a diplomatic gesture, "The International Criminal Court acknowledges and respects the AU's important role as the continent's main regional organization," while ending on a cooperative note: "[The ICC] remains fully committed to a constructive and cooperative relationship with the African Union."[36] The middle part of the press statement, however, does little to ease the concerns and anxieties of the AU. It mainly sets out that the ICC works independently within its mandate, is unable "to take political factors into account," and takes decisions "not based on regional or ethnic considerations." The AU is reassured that the ICC complements national jurisdictions and that it does so on the basis of fair,

33 Doc.Assembly/AU/10 (XV), para. 9.

34 Doc.EX.CL/952 (XXVIII), Jan. 30–31, 2016.

35 See ICC Forum, Mar. 2013–Jan. 2014, https://iccforum.com/africa.

36 Press Release: ICC underlines impartiality, reiterates commitment to cooperation with the African Union, May 29, 2013, ICC-CPI-20130529-PR908. For a similar message, see Press Statement: Oct. 2, 2013, ICC-CPI-20130529-PR908.

legal proceedings. The Presidency, moreover, explains that the ICC "is autonomous from the United Nations and does not participate in the Security Council's decision-making," while allowing states to challenge all Decisions in accordance with the rules set for the Court. While the Presidency thus starts by confirming respect for the AU, the rest of the statement reads more as an attempt to refute criticisms.

As may be gathered from the examples given above, the ICC has not responded to the Decisions by the AU by adopting decisions of its own. This reflects an institutional asymmetry between the AU and the ICC. In theory, the ICC Assembly of State Parties could also adopt a formal "Decision" contesting the critiques voiced by the AU. However, given the prominence of African states in the Assembly of State Parties, this is not a viable course of action. Where AU Decisions are taken by intergovernmental bodies composed of member states, the ICC organs that are engaged in the debate are individual Court officials, or groups of Court officials. It is not surprising, therefore, that ICC responses took quite a different form, such as press statements and blog posts. Of course, inside the courtroom the situation was different: in a series of judgments, the ICC expressed its views on what it means to be a member of an international community that seeks to fight impunity. It is exactly this imagery that the AU sought to question through a different legal form, the Decision.

IV. Concluding Reflections

By way of conclusion, let me return to some of the questions posed by the editors of this volume. I will start with perhaps the most important question: What do we hope to learn? As it would be pretentious to claim that I know what the reader has learned or should learn from this chapter, let me rephrase this question: What did I learn from writing this piece? Most important, it took me to places that are often overlooked in the analysis of the relation between the ICC and the AU. Instead of focusing on the umpteenth round of debates on the obligation of states to arrest and hand over suspects to the ICC, I turned to a series of Decisions adopted by the Assembly of the AU. Formally speaking, these Decisions constitute valid law, being one of the sources of the legal order of the AU. They express the position of the Union, and thus are more than the sum of the views of fifty-five individual member states.

However, the Decisions hardly contain legal arguments in the traditional sense. Instead, they express the stance of the AU toward the ICC and the Security Council, including an expression of the state of mind of the Union on several issues (e.g., the Union is "concerned," "deeply disappointed," etc.). This does not mean they are less important. Nor does it mean they have no relevance for the more doctrinal debates on matters related to arrest warrants issued by the ICC. On the contrary, the Decisions I analyzed address questions that go to the heart of international criminal law, as they concern the constitution of the international society as well as the recognition and dignity of its members. The AU's choice to use the formal category of "Decisions" has much to do with the need to speak with one voice in the struggles with the ICC. Decisions address at least two audiences: internally, they point at the common position that states have formally agreed upon; externally, they function as signals that they formally (re)present how the AU feels about matters of international criminal law. Again, these characteristics do not make them less legal—they just point to what gives the more technical aspects of international criminal law their political bite.

My chapter was based on a textual analysis, which makes it difficult to answer another question posed by the editors: Why does legal argumentation outside the courtroom occur? Still, I think it is safe to say that the use of legally valid Decisions reflects an intention on the part of the AU to strengthen unity among its members. The Decisions were not only addressed to outsiders such as the ICC or the Security Council. They also constituted attempts to rally AU members together against what the AU perceived as a lack of respect on the part of the ICC and the Security Council. Again, what was at stake were issues of membership and dignity; this time, however, the relevant community was the community of African states. The use of the legal form to express the position of the AU was thus far from arbitrary.

Last but not least is the question: Why is this an important issue? At the level of the AU-ICC disputes, attention to the emotions that are involved is crucial. If lawyers talk only of legal formalities such as the mandate of the ICC, its formal independence, and the like, they will do little to bring the two institutions together. In fact, they may very well intensify the problem, because the issues that the AU feels most strongly about are not addressed. At a more general level, it is important to make lawyers and researchers aware of the importance of emotions in legal argumentation. Decisions of the AU are by no means unique when it comes to expressing emotions: across the board, states and international organizations communicate how they feel about political issues in resolutions, decisions, or agreements. Ignoring these aspects would be practically unwise and academically untenable.

Annex

Analyzed Decisions and Declarations of the Assembly of the African Union Concerning the ICC

Twelfth Ordinary Session 1–3 February 2009, AU—Decision on the Application by the International Criminal Court (ICC) Prosecutor for the Indictment of the President of the Republic of The Sudan ICC

Thirteenth Ordinary Session 1–3 July 2009, AU—Doc. Assembly, AU13 (XIII)—Decision on the Meeting of African States Parties to the Rome Statute of the ICC

Fourteenth Ordinary Session 31 January–2 February 2010, AU—Doc. Assembly, AU8 (XIV)—Decision on the Report of the Second Meeting of States Parties to the Rome Statute on the ICC

Fifteenth Ordinary Session 25–27 July 2010, AU—Doc. Assembly, AU10 (XV)—Decision on the Progress Report of the Commission on the Implementation of Decision Assembly /AU/Dec.270 (XIV)

Sixteenth Ordinary Session 30–31 January 2011, AU—Doc. EX.CL639 (XVIII)—Decision on the Implementation of the Decisions on the International Criminal Court (ICC)

Seventeenth Ordinary Session 30 June–1 July 2011, AU—Doc. EX.CL670 (XIX)—Decision on the Implementation of the Assembly Decisions on the International Criminal Court

Eighteenth Ordinary Session 29–30 January 2012, AU—Doc. EX.CL710 (XX)—Decision on the Progress Report of the Commission on the Implementation of the Assembly Decisions on the ICC

Nineteenth Ordinary Session 15–16 July 2012, AU—Doc. EX.CL731 (XXI)—Decision on the Implementation of the Decisions on the International Criminal Court (ICC)

Twenty-First Ordinary Session 26–27 May 2013, AU—Doc. Assembly, AU13 (XXI)—Decision on International Jurisdiction, Justice and The International Criminal Court (ICC)

Extraordinary Session of the Assembly of the African Union 12 October 2013—Decision on Africa's Relationship With the International Criminal Court (ICC)

Twenty-Second Ordinary Session 30–31 January 2014 AU—Doc. Assembly, AU13 (XXII)—Decision on the Progress Report of the Commission on the Implementation of the Decisions on the ICC

Twenty-Fourth Ordinary Session 30–31 January 2015, AU—Doc. Assembly, AU18 (XXIV)—Decision on the Progress Report of the Commission on the Implementation of Previous Decisions on The ICC

Twenty-Fifth Ordinary Session 14–15 June 2015, AU—Decision on the Update of the Commission on the Implementation of Previous Decisions on the International Criminal Court

Twenty-Sixth Ordinary Session 30–31 January 2016, AU—Doc. EX.CL952 (XXVIII)—Decision on the International Criminal Court

Twenty-Seventh Ordinary Session 17–18 July 2016, AU—Doc. EX.CL987 (XXIX)—Decision on the International Criminal Court

28th Ordinary Session of the Assembly of the Union, 30–31 January 2017, AU—Doc. EX.CL1006 (XXX)—Decision on the International Criminal Court

30th Ordinary Session of the Assembly, 28–29 January 2018, AU—Doc. EX.CL1068 (XXXII)—Decision on the International Criminal Court

32nd Ordinary Session of the Assembly, 10–11 February 2019, AU—Doc. EX.CL1138 (XXXIV)—Decision on the International Criminal Court

11

The Sanctions Regime of the African Union in Response to Unconstitutional Changes of Government

Namira Negm

I. Introduction

The term "coup d'état" comes from French and found its way into the English dictionary in the seventeenth century. The term means "stroke of state" or "sudden change at the summit of the state." It is defined by Pat McGowan and Thomas Johnson as "events in which existing regimes are suddenly and illegally displaced by the action of relatively small groups, in which members of the military, police, or security forces of the state play a key role, either on their own or in conjunction with a number of civil servants or politicians."[1]

Although "coup d'état" is widely used, the African Union (AU) in its Constitutive Act avoids using it and instead uses the term "unconstitutional change of government" (UCG). The intent of the drafters might have been to avoid getting into legal and political quandaries while identifying, on a case-by-case basis, whether the acts committed constituted a coup or not. It is easier to prove the occurrence of a UCG than a coup.

At the United Nations, it is possible to adopt resolutions requesting states to restore constitutional government in cases of a UCG. But the UN Charter does not explicitly provide for sanctions in the event of a UCG. Chapter VII of the UN Charter is entitled "Action with Respect to Threats to the Peace, Breaches of the Peace, and Acts of Aggression," under which sanctions are referenced in Articles 41 and 42.[2] These sanctions are to be imposed by the United Nations in cases that endanger international peace and security. Yet if the UCG is not perceived by the members of the UN Security Council to constitute such a threat, the Council will not impose sanctions.

In contrast, Article 4(p) of the AU Constitutive Act[3] condemns and rejects UCGs, while Article 30 stipulates that "Governments which shall come to power through unconstitutional means shall not be allowed to participate in the activities of the Union."[4] By virtue of these articles, the AU has the capacity to impose sanctions on

[1] Isaaka K. Souare, "The AU and the Challenge of Unconstitutional Changes of Government in Africa," *Institute for Security Studies Papers* 197 (2009): 16.

[2] UN Charter, art. 42.

[3] African Union Constitutive Act, Lomé, Togo, July 11, 2000, art. 4(p).

[4] *Id.* art. 30.

Namira Negm, *The Sanctions Regime of the African Union in Response to Unconstitutional Changes of Government*
In: *Talking International Law.* Edited by: Ian Johnstone and Steven Ratner, Oxford University Press.
DOI: 10.1093/oso/9780197588437.003.0011

governments that assume power through unconstitutional means regardless of the implications for peace and security. Moreover, the Peace and Security Council Protocol has also tackled UCGs as inherited from the predecessor of the AU, the Organization of African Unity (OAU), which adopted a resolution on the matter. The OAU, realizing the weakness of the UCG, adopted and implemented decisions to condemn and sanction a UCG to pressure unconstitutional governments to change their course of action without recourse to courtrooms.

This chapter explores the AU's perspective toward UCGs occurring on the continent and how legal argumentation is invoked in discussions about the imposition of sanctions should a member state be found in breach of the relevant rules. It highlights the innovative ways in which legal argumentation is used in a highly political and volatile environment. It demonstrates a practical and progressive approach that takes into consideration not only peace and security but also the quest of African peoples for democracy and good governance.

II. Legal Basis for the OAU/AU Sanctions Regime for UCGs

A. Background

In the decades following independence, Africa suffered a rising number of coups d'état, which were an obstacle to stability, development, and democracy. For more than thirty years, between the 1960s and 1990s, governments changed in Africa mainly through coups d'état. During this period, Africa witnessed more than two hundred successful and failed coups.[5] Even though the OAU followed the principle of "[n]on-interference in the internal affairs of States,"[6] the widespread practice of launching coups as a means to change governments on the continent prompted African leaders to come together and take a stand against UCGs.

In 1997, the OAU adopted Assembly Declaration No. AHG/Decl. 5 (XXXVI), entitled "Decision on Unconstitutional Changes of Government in Africa," in which the African heads of state and government condemned the coup d'état in Sierra Leone and rejected the unconstitutional change of a democratically elected government.[7] This Declaration was the first document that articulated the OAU's stance on UCGs. It marked a significant move from mere condemnation of violent coups and the assassination of political leaders, laying the foundation for a proper policy framework on UCGs.[8] The Declaration set out an official position of the OAU on UCGs in its member states.

[5] Ionel Zamfir, "Actions of the African Union against Coup D'état, at a Glance," *European Parliamentary Research Service*, Apr. 2016, at 1, https://www.europarl.europa.eu/thinktank/en/document.html?reference=EPRS_ATA(2016)580878.

[6] Organization of African Unity Charter, Addis Ababa, Ethiopia, May 1963, art. III (2).

[7] Organization of African Unity Assembly, Declaration on the Framework for an OAU Response to Unconstitutional Changes of Government, 36th Session, Doc.AHG/Decl.5 (XXXVI) (July 10–12, 2000) [hereinafter Lomé Declaration].

[8] See Lomé Declaration, *id.* preamble para. 6, where it notes that the Assembly has agreed to put forward elements such as (a) a set of common values and principles for democratic governance; (b) a definition of what constitutes an unconstitutional change; (c) measures and actions that the OAU would progressively

In 1999, the OAU Assembly issued a Decision on UCGs that further paved the way for a general policy framework on responding to UCGs. It called on leaders of member states that came to power through UCGs after the Harare Summit of 1997 to constitutionalize and legalize their position by going through the proper channels, and it provided them with a deadline, which was the following summit in the year 2000.[9]

In July 2000 the Assembly of Heads of State and Government of the OAU at their 36th Ordinary Session came up with a more concrete and elaborate stance on UCGs through the Lomé Declaration on the Framework for an OAU Response to Unconstitutional Changes of Government (Lomé Declaration).[10] The Declaration identified what constitutes and qualifies as a UCG. It established a sanctions regime that could be triggered in response to unconstitutional changes. The implementation of the Lomé Declaration was the responsibility of the Central Organ of the OAU Mechanism of Conflict Prevention, Management and Resolution.[11]

The Lomé Declaration became the basis for the illegality of UCGs, which was subsequently enshrined in the Constitutive Act of the AU.[12] Article 4 of the Constitutive Act stipulates that "the Union shall function in accordance with the following principles ... (p) condemnation and rejection of unconstitutional changes of governments." Moreover, to act in a speedy manner in cases of a UCG, the Peace and Security Council of the African Union (PSC), established in 2004, was empowered to impose sanctions in cases of a UCG as per the criteria provided in the Lomé Declaration.[13] In the same vein, the African Charter on Democracy, Elections and Governance, adopted in January 2007,[14] provided for a broader framework for the definition of "UCG" as it added scenarios that would be considered UCGs. It also introduced additional types of sanctions to be imposed on governments and individuals involved in infringements of the principle of democratic changes of government.[15] The Charter builds on Articles 3(g) and 4(m) of the Constitutive Act, which call for the promotion of democratic principles and institutions as well as good governance.

A. Legal Instruments

In order to understand the role of legal argumentation in the AU's approaches to UCGs, it is important to set out in more detail the key documents addressing this issue.

take to respond to unconstitutional change of government; and (d) an implementation mechanism, as a policy framework to guide the Organization on matters concerning UCG.

[9] Organization of African Unity, Assembly Decision on Unconstitutional Changes of Government, 35th Session, Doc.AHG/Dec.142 (XXXV), Algiers, Algeria (July 12–14, 1999), 1, para 1 [hereinafter AHG Dec. 142].

[10] Lomé Declaration, *supra* note 7.

[11] *Id.* Preamble.

[12] Constitutive Act, art. 2.

[13] African Union Protocol Relating to the Establishment of the Peace and Security Council of the African Union, July 9, 2002, art. 2.

[14] African Charter on Democracy, Elections and Good Governance, Addis Ababa, Jan. 30, 2007, at 19 (the Charter had not entered into force at the time of writing this chapter).

[15] *Id.* ch. 8, arts. 23–26.

1. The Lomé Declaration

The Lomé Declaration identified certain situations as constituting a UCG:

1. a military coup d'état;
2. intervention by mercenaries to replace a democratically elected government;
3. replacement of a democratically elected government by armed dissident groups and rebel movements; and
4. the refusal by an incumbent government to relinquish power to the winning side after free, fair, and regular elections.[16]

In the event of a UCG, the Lomé Declaration provides for a number of sanctions to be imposed by the OAU against a government that unlawfully ascends to power, including:

1. condemnation of the UCG and denial of recognition of the unlawful government;
2. suspension from the OAU policy organs' activities;
3. a request to the government to restore the constitutional order within a maximum of six months; and
4. after the lapse of a six-month period, the imposition of sanctions by the Central Organ of the OAU Mechanism for Conflict Prevention, Management and Resolution, including trade restrictions, visa denials, and restrictions on government-to-government contacts.[17]

2. The Constitutive Act of the AU

One of the objectives of the AU is to "promote democratic principles and institutions, popular participation and good governance."[18] To complement this objective, the Constitutive Act "condemns and rejects unconstitutional changes of government."[19] This is a significant departure from the OAU's policy of caution in dealing with UCGs, essentially a shift from the principle of non-interference to a robust approach for dealing with UCGs that are perceived to be a threat to peace and stability on the continent.

The Constitutive Act reflects the unwillingness of the Union to tolerate the continuation of regimes that come to power unlawfully in any of its member states. Hence under Article 30,[20] it is authorized to suspend such a government from participating in the activities of the Union. Article 30 uses the verb "shall" when it demands suspension of the unlawful government to stress the vigor of the intent of the negotiators—such a government "shall not be allowed" to participate in the activities of the Union.[21] Article 23 empowers the Assembly of Heads of State and Government to impose further sanctions, such as the denial of transport and communications links with other

[16] Lomé Declaration, *supra* note 7, at 3.

[17] *Id.* at 4–5.

[18] Constitutive Act, art. 3(g).

[19] *Id.* art. 4(p).

[20] Article 30 of the Constitutive Act states, "Governments which shall come to power through unconstitutional means shall not be allowed to participate in the activities of the Union."

[21] *Id.*

member states and other measures of a political and economic nature if the unlawful government remains in breach of the decisions of the Union.[22] These provisions are meant to impose political and developmental costs on the government in question. Politically, the suspended government loses the right to attend any AU meetings and to present candidates to AU elected positions. It also loses the support of the AU's member states for previously endorsed candidatures within the international system, such as the United Nations. Nor is it permitted to introduce new candidatures until the sanctions are lifted. On the development side, the unlawful government is not entitled to receiving any technical assistance from AU programs in trade, industry, environment, agriculture, and so forth.[23]

All these measures contemplated under the Constitutive Act are designed to compel the unlawful government to restore constitutional democracy and to take actions against the perpetrators who led the disturbance of peace. This is meant both as a deterrent to other states and as a preventive measure against escalation of such situations into armed conflicts that threaten neighboring countries that may be faced with an influx of refugees and might be dragged into the conflict.[24]

3. The Protocol Relating to the Establishment of the Peace and Security Council

The Peace and Security Council (PSC) is the AU organ responsible for the prevention, management, and resolution of conflicts. It is the successor of the Central Organ of the OAU and as such assumed its responsibilities under the Lomé Declaration.[25] Under Article 7(g) of the Protocol, the PSC has the power to impose sanctions in cases of a UCG. It affirms the responsibility of the PSC to uphold the principles of the Constitutive Act and implement the Lomé Declaration. Even states that are not parties to the PSC Protocol are subject to the rules on UCGs; because the prohibition is derived from the AU Constitutive Act, it is binding on all AU member states. Consequently, the PSC can impose sanctions on any member state, regardless of whether it had ratified the Protocol.[26]

The PSC Council has fifteen members elected by the Executive Council of the Union based on equitable regional representation and rotation.[27] Under Article 7(1) of the Protocol, the chair of the African Union Commission (AUC) is to work in conjunction with the PSC and undertake all the activities and decisions, including approving "modalities for intervention by the Union in a Member State, following a decision by the Assembly" and "institut[ing] sanctions whenever an unconstitutional change of

[22] *Id.* art. 23.

[23] Mikael Eriksson, "Supporting Democracy in Africa-African Union's Use of Targeted Sanctions to deal with Unconstitutional Changes of Government," Swedish Defence Research Agency Department of Defence Analysis, 2010, at 84. These sanctions are imposed on the basis of Article 23 of the Constitutive Act, which provides that the Assembly can impose any "other measures of a political and economic nature."

[24] Appiah F. Afriyie and Jisong Jian, "An Investigation of Economic Sanctions and Its Implications for Africa," *Journal of Politics and Law* 11 (2018): 74.

[25] PSC Protocol, arts. 2 and 7.

[26] See, e.g., PSC 151th meeting on the situation in the Islamic Republic of Mauritania, Doc.PSC/MIN/Comm.2 (CLI), New York (Sept. 2008), http://www.peaceau.org/uploads/mauritaniacommeng.pdf.

[27] According to Article 8 of the Protocol, each member has one vote; where the Council fails to reach consensus, a two-thirds majority is needed to decide on substantive matters. Decisions of the Council are binding on all AU member states as the former acts on behalf of the later.

government takes place in a Member State." Under Article 10, the AUC is mandated to "bring to the attention of the Peace and Security Council any matter, which, in his/her opinion, may threaten peace, security and stability in the Continent," and follow up on the implementation of PSC decisions.

4. The African Charter on Democracy, Elections, and Governance

Finally, and most recently, the adoption of the Charter on Democracy, Elections and Governance in 2007 demonstrates the AU's commitment to fight any form of UCG by providing an expanded legal framework to strengthen the legal regime imposed in these cases. Once operational, the Charter will in effect convert the Lomé Declaration into a treaty while also expanding it. The Charter identifies UCG as one of the main causes of insecurity, instability, and conflict; hence, it prohibits, condemns, and rejects it. It also expands the Lomé definition of UCG by adding "any amendment or revision of the constitution or legal instruments, which is an infringement on the Principles of democratic change of government."[28]

The Charter also introduces broader measures to be taken by the PSC, including the barring of perpetrators of the UCG from participating in the constitutional election held in the aftermath of the UGC "or hold any position of responsibility in political institutions of their State,"[29] as well as the possibility of prosecution before a competent court for their crimes.[30] It also leapt ahead by classifying the UCG as a "crime against democracy" and urging member states not to provide a safe haven for perpetrators of such a crime. Article 25(8) requests member states to bring the perpetrators to justice, or if it is impossible to do so, extradite them. Article 25(6) empowers the Assembly to take additional measures and impose sanctions on states in which a UCG took place. In addition, the imposition of sanctions may extend to member states that support and/or instigate a UCG in another member state.

Upon coming into force, the Charter will be a comprehensive legal document in dealing with UCGs in a broader context. It also provides the AU with more robust legal grounds to continue promoting democratization on the continent while maintaining peace, security, and stability. The Charter thus extends the move of the OAU from the principle of non-interference in the internal affairs of its member states to the measures adopted in the Lomé Declaration.[31]

Moreover, as part of the attempt to promote good governance on the continent, which usually requires a preventive measure against UCGs, the AU recently merged the African Peer Review Mechanism (APRM) into its system. The main objectives of this process are to ensure that the policies and practices of member states that accede to the instrument "conform to the agreed political, economic and corporate governance values, codes and standards contained in the African Union Declaration on Democracy, Political, Economic and Corporate Governance."[32] This demonstrates

[28] African Charter on Democracy, Elections and Good Governance, *supra* note 14, art. 23(1).

[29] *Id.* art. 25(4).

[30] *Id.* art. 25(5).

[31] Lomé Declaration, *supra* note 7, Preamble.

[32] The New Partnership for Africa's Development (NEPAD) The African Peer Review Mechanism (APRM), Key Document, 2003, para. 2, https://www.aprm-au.org/publications/partnership-for-africa-nepad-and-aprm/.

that the AU takes a comprehensive approach to the legal and political contexts as they complement each other. Governments that fail in good governance and democracy open the door to UCGs. So the AU within its reform process is trying to ensure that the mechanisms in place assist states in development, such as the African Union Development Agency,[33] and in promoting democracy and good governance through the APRM. Then, in the event that these mechanisms are not sufficient and a UCG takes place, the legal regime of sanctions applies.

C. Modalities of AU Responses to UCGs

1. Stages of Involvement

Over the years, the AU has developed a normative approach on how to deal with UCGs. In principle the AU condemns and rejects any UCGs taking place on the continent; however, the imposition of sanctions comes in stages.[34] The *first stage* is to classify the situation as a UCG. Once this fact is established, the PSC will issue an official statement condemning and rejecting the UCG.[35] While deciding on the legal classification, policy organs sometimes seek the opinion of the AU Legal Counsel[36] to provide a legal perspective based on the AU rules and other relevant international law, such as human rights when applicable, in order to assist them in making their decisions. Thereafter, the PSC calls for the speedy return of constitutional order and gives the concerned government a period of up to six months to restore it.[37] The PSC assesses the situation in the country to determine how much time should be given to restore constitutional order.

Normally, the communiqué is delivered after the AU decides that a UCG took place. In some circumstances, the AU chooses to take a step back in order to assess the situation and may refrain from adopting any measures for political reasons. However, when the PSC believes that the UCG would bring great suffering to the country, it adopts proactive measures. For instance, when a UCG took place in Mauritania on August 6, 2008, the PSC met the following day and issued a communiqué condemning the UCG and demanding that power be handed over to the constitutionally elected government.[38] In the same vein, when the president of Mauritania, who was ousted in 2008, had previously staged a coup and took over the government on August 3, 2005, the PSC met and issued a statement on August 4, 2005, condemning the UCG and calling on the military to hand over power to the civilian transitional

[33] Assembly Decision on the Transformation of the NEPAD Planning and Coordinating Agency (NPCA) into the African Union Development Agency (AUDA), 31st Ordinary Session, Doc.Assembly/AU/2 (XXXI), Nouakchott, Mauritania (2018).

[34] See, e.g., PSC Protocol art. 27, and the Charter art. 3(g).

[35] Constitutive Act, art. 4(P).

[36] Executive Council Decision, Third Ordinary Session July 4–8, 2003, Maputo, Mozambique, EX/CL/Dec.34 (III), Doc.Assembly/AU/Dec.22, referred to as Maputo Decision of (2003), that set the mandates of the African Union Commission and its offices.

[37] PSC Protocol, art. 7.

[38] African Union Peace and Security Council Communiqué of the 144th Meeting, Doc.PSC/PR/Comm.(CLIV) (Aug. 7, 2008), http://www.peaceau.org/uploads/2008-144-comm-c1e.pdf.

government.[39] The AU applied different approaches in dealing with UCGs that took place in the same country (Mauritania) at different times. This practice demonstrates that it analyzes the circumstances surrounding each UCG on a case-by-case basis, taking into account whether the ousted government was democratically elected. This factor largely influences the decisions of the AU to either condemn the coup and call for the restoration of the constitutionally elected government or condemn the coup and demand that democratic elections be held.

During the *second stage*, the interval to return to constitutional order, the AU intensifies diplomatic efforts in order to help the parties concerned reach an amicable solution. While political mediation is ongoing, and depending on the developments, the PSC through consecutive communiqués may maintain the threat to impose stricter measures based on Article 7(g) of the PSC Protocol. If the mediation does not bear fruit and the situation continues to deteriorate, the PSC may conclude that it is no longer in a position to compromise for fear of internal and regional escalation and will invoke Article 7(g) to suspend the concerned state from the Union.[40]

The debate surrounding the AU's inaction over the situation in Zimbabwe demonstrates that the AU's stance can be ambiguous at times. Some argue that the AU's silence concerning the "military takeover" that took place in Zimbabwe on November 14, 2017, shows that the AU operates on political rather than on legal grounds. They maintain that if the AU had adhered to its own principles and policies, it would have condemned what was clearly a violation of constitutional order by the military and imposed sanctions on the coup makers.[41] A counterargument is that the AU followed its principles by remaining silent on the situation in Zimbabwe. In fact, the military did not oust President Robert Mugabe; Mugabe was still formally in power. To make matters more complicated, he was seen exchanging pleasantries with army leaders and performing some activities as head of state.[42] Thus, for the AU, imposing sanctions at that time would have been unlawful. The events that followed demonstrated that there was no military takeover or unconstitutional action on the part of the military, as Mugabe was given an ultimatum by his own party either to resign or risk impeachment under Zimbabwe's constitution.[43] Following pressure by his party, Mugabe finally resigned on November 21, 2017. Vice President Phelekezela Mphoko became acting president until the ruling party, Zanu-PF, nominated Emmerson Mnangagwa as president, as provided in the constitution.[44]

Both of these arguments have merit from a legal standpoint; yet the AU is a political organization, and the decisions adopted by the policy organs, whether the Assembly

[39] PSC, Statement of the 36th meeting of the PSC on the situation in Mauritania, Doc.PSC/PR/Stat.(XXXVI)-(ii) (Aug. 4, 2005), http://www.peaceau.org/uploads/mauritaniaeng.pdf.

[40] See, e.g., PSC, Communique of 854th meeting on the situation in Sudan, Doc.PSC/PR/Comm.(DCCCXLIV) (June 6, 2019), http://www.peaceau.org/uploads/psc.854.comm.sudan.6.6.19.pdf.

[41] Philip Roessler, "How AU Got It Wrong on Zimbabwe," *News 24*, Nov. 8, 2017, https://www.news24.com/Africa/Zimbabwe/how-au-got-it-wrong-on-zimbabwe-20171208.

[42] "There Was No Coup in Zimbabwe; Mugabe 'Submitted His Resignation Willingly,' Says AU," *How Africa News*, Dec. 24 2017, https://howafrica.com/there-was-no-coup-in-zimbabwe-mugabe-submitted-his-resignation-willingly-says-au/.

[43] Nicole Beardsworth, Nic Cheeseman, and Simukai Tinhu, "Zimbabwe: The Coup That Never Was, and the Election That Could Have Been," *African Affairs* 118 (2019): 580.

[44] *Id.*

or the PSC, are adopted based on political considerations and require a minimum of a two-thirds majority of member states to support it. No one-size-fits-all rule can be applied to every situation.

The *last stage* in the AU sanctions regime is intervention. The AU draws a connection between the violation of constitutional order and the maintenance of peace and security on the continent, even though that connection is not explicit in the Constitutive Act. UCGs are perceived to be recipes for crisis, which warrant military intervention as a last resort if economic and diplomatic sanctions are not likely to succeed. In The Gambia, for example, when former President Yahya Jammeh refused to hand over power after losing the elections on December 1, 2016, the PSC called on Jammeh to step down. His refusal to do so, as well as the drastic measures he took in order to remain in office, put the country in crisis, at which point the PSC issued another communiqué on January 17, 2017, supporting the Economic Community of West African States (ECOWAS)'s threat to intervene militarily to return the country to constitutional order.[45]

2. Authority and Consistency in AU Action

There is a continued debate regarding the legality of the AU's authority to intervene militarily in a member state to restore constitutional order without prior authorization of the UN Security Council, as stipulated in Chapter VIII of the UN Charter. Some scholars argue that it is unlawful under Chapter VIII for a regional or subregional organization to intervene militarily in any state without prior authorization from the Security Council.[46] Others note that the Council does not perceive such interventions to be in contravention of the Charter, as seen in its support for the interventions after they occurred, or through its silence by not condemning them.

As mentioned, for the AU, taking action on UCGs is designed to maintain peace and security. Thus, the policy organs of the AU resort to both political and legal solutions in order to avoid a crisis, as opposed to the United Nations, which does not treat UCGs per se as a threat to peace and security and rarely authorizes military intervention in those circumstances.[47] Furthermore, in many cases, the Security Council may be reluctant to rapidly intervene in UCG situations until it perceives the coup as endangering international peace and security. As its practice indicates, the AU acts upon its own initiative to intervene or authorize Regional Economic Communities (RECs) to intervene when a crisis occurs in a member state. The Security Council has on occasion endorsed or commended AU interventions after they occur.

The normative and institutional fundamentals introduced (and to some extent applied) by the AU are comprehensive, unique, and ambitious in comparison to the OAU or non-African organizations. The AU has followed a relatively consistent practice

[45] PSC 647th meeting, on the post-election situation in The Islamic Republic of The Gambia, Doc. PSC/PR/Comm. (DCXLVII) (Jan. 13, 2017), http://www.peaceau.org/uploads/647.psc.comm.gambia.13.01.2017-1.pdf.

[46] *Id.*

[47] Catherine Maia and Anatole Ayissi, "Peace through Constitution: The Importance of Constitutional Order for International Peace and Security," *African Yearbook of International Law Online/Annuaire Africain de droit international Online* 19 (2011): 201, 202.

with regard to UCGs. As mentioned, one of the AU's core principles, stipulated in Articles 3(g) and 4(m) of the Constitutive Act, is the promotion of democratic principles and institutions as well as good governance[48]—neither of which can be achieved without free and fair elections. As a consequence, the AU has always attempted to give effect to both principles, namely, the rejection of UCGs and the promotion of democracy. So, for example, when there is an unconstitutional change of government in the name of democracy, or with democratizing effects, the AU takes a nuanced approach.

From the practice of the AU's intervention during UCGs, one can observe that this nuanced approach is often supported by legal argumentation. While the AU as an institution or actors within the AU might resort to political argument, they endeavor to sing the same tune using legal argumentation. They seek to link arguments for restoration of a constitutional system with the promotion of democracy, as well as peace, security, and stability. Typically, when the AU adopts a decision on a specific case, political argumentation is mixed with legal argumentation. For instance, identification of the exact chain of events that occur in a country in order to classify the situation as a UCG is not solely legal but also factual and political. Countries supporting the change of government in a specific case may argue that the change is supported by the people or by different members of the international community. In such cases, other states will argue on the basis of the law, that if the change did not follow the constitution in the said case, it constitutes a UCG and merits condemnation from the PSC, followed by sanctions to restore the constitutional regime and democracy. So although implementation of the rules occurs on a case-by-case basis where political arguments play a role, the outcomes are mostly harmonized because of legal argumentation. These legal arguments are grounded in Articles 3(g) and 4(p) of the AU Constitutive Act, which rejects and condemns UCGs irrespective of who carries them out.[49] The AU also applies a broad interpretation of what constitutes UCGs as part of the responsibility of the AU to promote democracy, good governance, and constitutionalism.

D. Cases Where Sanctions Were Imposed within the OAU/AU Context

The AU practice on coups d'état on the continent has been relatively consistent since the first imposition of sanctions on Sierra Leone by the OAU. Member states subjected to AU sanctions pursuant to AU legal instruments on UCGs are the Central African Republic, Guinea-Bissau, Mauritania, Togo, Madagascar, Guinea, Côte d'Ivoire, Mali, Egypt, Burkina Faso, and, the latest one, Sudan.[50] For the purpose of this chapter, three cases will be analyzed where sanctions were imposed by the AU and rendered effective in bringing the states on track to reinstitute good governance based on the rule of law and constitutional reforms.

[48] Constitutive Act, art. 3(g).
[49] *Id.* arts. 3(g), 4(p).
[50] Zamfir, *supra* note 5, at 2.

1. Sierra Leone

Sierra Leone suffered from a civil war that lasted for seven years. A peace accord was concluded between the Revolutionary United Front (RUF) and the then sitting government. In 1996, multiparty elections took place, where Ahmed Tejan Kabbah of the Sierra Leone People's Party (SLPP) won.[51] However, just a year later, the RUF, who were not satisfied with the outcome of the elections, staged a coup that forced the democratically elected government to seek refuge in neighboring Guinea.[52] Following that coup, at the 33rd OAU Summit, the African leaders jointly and unequivocally condemned and rejected coups or any UCG on the continent. They resolved to maintain a united official stance on this issue from that moment forward, "particularly, as regards to the measures applicable in similar situations occurring in Member States."[53]

The Sierra Leone case was the first to provoke a strong response from OAU member states, as they "saw the coup as a double setback: for both the peace process in the country and the democratic process there in particular, and on the continent as a whole."[54] Moreover, only President Kabbah was permitted to attend the meeting in Harare in May 1997.[55] In February 1998, ECOWAS intervened to reinstate President Kabbah. The OAU effort, alongside that of ECOWAS and the United Nations, to mediate between the RUF and SLPP finally bore fruit in 2002 when the civil war was declared over by President Kabbah.[56]

This progress led to a more concerted effort by the Union to institutionalize and legalize measures against UCGs on the continent. At the 1999 Algiers Summit, the OAU took a step forward by adopting two Decisions, AHG/Dec.141 (XXXV) and AHG/Dec.142 (XXXV).[57] These Decisions set the tone for the stance of the OAU and later the AU on UCGs with regard to democracy, respect for human rights, good governance, and establishing a stable government contributing to conflict prevention on the continent.[58] Decision 142 specifically called upon governments of member states that came to power through unconstitutional means to constitutionalize and legalize their power through democratic elections before the next ordinary session of the Assembly.[59] Thus, the UCG of Sierra Leone can be considered as a turning point for the African regional organization's legal framework on UCGs that came afterward.

2. Togo

In 1967, General Gnassingbé Eyadéma, the president of Togo, came to power through a coup and managed to stay in power until his sudden death in 2005.[60] In 1993, he

[51] Clotilde Asangna, "An Examination of the Sierra Leone War," *African Journal of Political Science and International Relations* 11 (2017): 103.

[52] Souare, *supra* note 1, at 4.

[53] *Id.*.

[54] *Id.*

[55] *Id.* at 5. See also OAU Assembly Decision on Unconstitutional Changes of Government, 35th Session, Doc.AHG/Dec. 141 (XXXV) (July 12–14, 1999), 1 [hereinafter AHG Dec. 141]; Lomé Declaration, *supra* note 7, Preamble.

[56] Ibrahim Abdullah, ed., *Between Democracy and Terror: The Sierra Leone Civil War* (Dakar: Council for the Development of Social Science Research in Africa, 2004).

[57] AHG Dec. 142, *supra* note 9, at para. 1.

[58] AHG Dec. 141, *supra* note 55; AHG Dec. 142, *supra* note 9.

[59] *Id.*

[60] Souare, *supra* note 1, at 12.

introduced a multiparty constitution and organized an election in which he appeared to be the winner, until he passed away after thirty-eight years in power.[61] According to the Togolese constitution, the president of the National Assembly, Fambaré Natchaba Ouattara, should have assumed power as an interim president for sixty days, during which an election was to be organized.[62] However, in violation of the constitution, Faure Gnassingbé, the son of the late President Eyadéma, was installed as president through a coup staged by the armed forces.[63] The armed forces justified their actions by claiming that Ouattara was out of Togo, while in fact he was blocked from entering the country.[64] In an attempt to legitimize the presidency, on February 6, 2005, the National Assembly, dominated by Gnassingbé's party, claimed to have removed Ouattara and appointed Gnassingbé as president. The Assembly further amended the constitution to allow Gnassingbé to continue ruling without holding elections until the end of the tenure of his father in 2008.[65]

In a communiqué of February 7, 2005, the PSC condemned the coup and "the constitutional modifications intended to legally window dress the *coup d'état*."[66] It further noted that the succession of office was done in breach of both the Togolese constitution and AU instruments such as the Lomé Declaration and the Protocol establishing the PSC. The PSC called for immediate action to restore the constitutional order or it would impose sanctions on the unlawful government based on Article 7(g) of the Protocol.[67] The National Assembly restored the constitutional provision to organize elections in sixty days, but kept Gnassingbé in power, which the AU considered to be unconstitutional.[68] As a result, on February 25, 2005, the AU suspended Togo from its activities until it restored constitutional order. It rejected any elections organized under conditions set by "de facto authorities in Togo."[69] It demanded that Gnassingbé resign to make way for a constitutionally elected government. Further, the AU endorsed ECOWAS's imposition of an arms embargo and travel ban on leaders of the coup. It also called upon ECOWAS to take the necessary measures to fully restore the constitutional order in Togo.[70] Under mounting pressure from the AU and ECOWAS, Gnassingbé resigned as president and handed over power to the new president of the National Assembly, Abass Bonfoh, as interim president of Togo, an action based on the Togolese constitution.[71] In April 2005, an election was held in which Gnassingbé appeared to be the winner.[72] Hence, the AU lifted its

[61] Adewale Banjo, "Constitutional and Succession Crisis in West Africa: The Case of Togo," *African Journal of Legal Studies* 2 (2008): 147.

[62] Togo's Constitution 1992 with Amendments 2007, art.65, https://www.constituteproject.org/constitution/Togo_2007.pdf.

[63] Banjo, *supra* note 61, at 151.

[64] PSC, Brief on the Evolving Situation in Togo (Feb. 21, 2005), 1.

[65] Banjo, *supra* note 61, at 151.

[66] PSC, Communiqué of the 25th Meeting, Doc.PSC/PR/Comm. (XXV) (Feb. 25, 2005), 1.

[67] *Id.*

[68] Banjo, *supra* note 61, at 151.

[69] PSC, Communiqué of the 25th Meeting, *supra* note 66, at 2.

[70] *Id.*

[71] *Id.*

[72] Eki Yemisi Omorogbe, "A Club of Incumbents? The African Union and Coups d'État," *Vanderbilt Journal of Transnational Law* 44 (2011): 123.

sanctions and Togo rejoined the Union's activities, having fulfilled the conditions set forth.[73]

This is another case where the mounting political pressure from the AU and subregional institutions like ECOWAS bore fruit in ensuring respect for the rule of law. Rejecting the unconstitutional government and denying assistance to the leaders that assumed power illegally led to the restoration of legality. Legal argumentation played an important role in fashioning the balanced measures the AU took to resolve the situation. While rejecting the UCG in Togo pursuant to Articles 4(p) and 30 of the Constitutive Act, the AU also sought to uphold democratic principles pursuant to Articles 3(g) and 4(m).

3. Sudan

The Sudan case is an even better example of the balanced approach the AU takes, seeking to reconcile constitutionality with democracy when the two conflict. On December 19, 2019, the people of Sudan took to the streets of Khartoum in major protests and civil disobedience that lasted for eight months. The persistent protests forced the then president of Sudan, Omar al-Bashir, out of office on April 11, 2019, after thirty years in power.[74] Upon ousting al-Bashir, the military took power and created a Transitional Military Council (TMC) to rule the country.[75] Protestors continued the uprising. They demanded that the TMC hand over power to a civilian transitional government.[76]

a. The PSC Response and Results

On April 15, 2019, the PSC issued a Communiqué on the Situation in Sudan. In the communiqué, the PSC expressed the "AU's conviction that the military take-over is not the appropriate response to the challenges facing Sudan and the aspirations of its people."[77] It characterized the arrest of al-Bashir, suspension of the constitution, dissolution of the National Assembly, and creation of the TMC—which imposed a three-month state of emergency and two-year transitional period—as a UCG.[78] It condemned and rejected the seizure of power by the military through unconstitutional means. It then called upon the military to step down and hand over power within fifteen days—not back to al-Bashir but to a civilian-led transitional government, according to "the will of the people and constitutional order."[79] Should the TMC fail to comply, the PSC threatened to suspend Sudan from participating in

[73] PSC, Communiqué of the 30th Meeting, Doc.PSC/PR/Comm. (XXX) (May 27, 2005), 1, http://www.peaceau.org/uploads/communiqueeng-30th.pdf.

[74] Kimiko de Freytas-Tamura, "Sudanese Protests, After Days of Violence, Turn Anger over Bread toward Bashir," *New York Times*, Dec. 24, 2018, https://www.nytimes.com/2018/12/24/world/africa/sudan-protests.html.

[75] *Id.*

[76] "Sudan: Huge Crowds Call for Civilian Rule in Biggest Protest Since Bashir Ousting," *The Guardian*, Apr. 19, 2019, https://www.theguardian.com/world/2019/apr/19/sudan-huge-crowds-call-for-civilian-rule-in-biggest-protest since-Bashir-ousting.

[77] PSC, Communiqué of the 840th meeting on the situation in Sudan, Doc.PSC/PR/Comm. (DCCCXL) (Apr. 14, 2019), http://www.peaceau.org/uploads/840-psc-communique-sudan.eng.pdf.

[78] *Id.*

[79] *Id.*

activities of the Union based on Article 7(g) of its Protocol, until full constitutional order was restored. Further, it called upon all stakeholders to engage in an inclusive consultative process to ensure a smooth transition to democracy through free and fair elections.[80] In these circumstances, the TMC was compelled to negotiate with the civilian opposition to form a joint transitional government during April and May 2019.[81]

In consultations with the PSC, the AUC chairperson, Moussa Faki Mahamat, appointed Professor Hassan Lebbat as his special envoy for Sudan to assist the parties in coming to an agreement on the formation of the transitional civilian government. This was accompanied by shuttle diplomacy carried out by Egypt as chair of the AU, Ethiopia as chair of the Intergovernmental Authority on Development (IGAD), and the AUC chairperson. Those efforts bore fruit, and an interim civilian arrangement was established to govern until elections. Following this development, the PSC issued another communiqué on April 30, 2019, extending the deadline for the resignation of the TMC.[82]

The PSC noted that "gradual progress has been made in the negotiations" and gave an additional sixty days for the TMC to transfer power to the civilian led transitional government, during which time the PSC urged all parties to quickly complete the negotiations and agree "on the composition of a civilian-led Transitional Authority." The communiqué further requested that the AU's relevant instruments and policies on UCGs be complied with while negotiating the terms of the transition. Should Sudan fail to do so, the PSC expressed its readiness to impose the full range of sanctions as empowered by Article 7(g) of the PSC Protocol.[83] This legal argumentation—that is, invoking the various legal instruments concerning UCGs—shaped the PSC's nuanced approach, demanding not a return to the constitutional order that existed before the seizure of power by the military but rather a new, more democratic order where rule of law would be respected. Here the process was as important as the substance of the transition. Principles of democracy and good governance as stipulated under the Constitutive Act and other relevant legal instruments were applied in the processes and plans, leading to the desired result.

In another communiqué adopted by the PSC on May 27, 2019, it emphasized once again "that the solution to the challenges facing the Sudan should be forged within an African-led process, based on decisions of the relevant AU policy organs, in collaboration with the region, through the IGAD." In this context, the Council reiterated its call on all partners to provide their support to Africa's approach on the situation prevailing in the Sudan.[84] The AUC chairperson was mandated to follow up on the ground and report on the progress to the Council every three weeks, based on which the Council

[80] *Id.*

[81] Samy Magdy "New Ruling Sudan Military Council Promises Civilian Cabinet," *AP News*, Apr. 14, 2019, https://apnews.com/b00ee252cf4c4d08b2d0a88380df2696.

[82] PSC, Communique of 846th meeting on the Situation in Sudan, Doc.PSC/PR/Comm. (DCCCXLVI), Tunis, Tunisia (Apr. 30, 2019), 1, http://www.peaceau.org/uploads/psc-com-sudan-30-april-2019-eng.pdf.

[83] *Id.* para. 6.

[84] PSC, Communique of 852nd meeting on the Situation in Sudan, Doc.PSC/PR/Comm. (DCCCXLII), Addis Ababa, Ethiopia (May 27, 2019), 1, http://www.peaceau.org/uploads/psc.852.comm.sudan.27.05.2019lll.pdf.

would issue a communiqué on the way forward. It also called upon "external actors" to refrain from interfering in Sudan so as to avoid further exacerbating the situation.[85]

The negotiations between the TMC and civilian opposition were halted when the Rapid Support forces (a Sudanese paramilitary force) killed protestors in Khartoum on June 3, 2019.[86] The AUC chairperson condemned the violence against the peaceful protesters and called "for an immediate and transparent investigation in order to hold those responsible accountable" and for the TMC to protect civilians. In addition, he reiterated the PSC's call for all stakeholders to return to the negotiations in order to move toward a "civilian-led Transitional Authority."[87] Based on these last actions, the PSC could not allow the violence to continue out of fear of escalation in the region. Consequently, on June 6, 2019, it suspended Sudan from AU activities until the "effective establishment of a civilian government."[88]

On July 5, 2019, a verbal agreement was reached between the parties, and on July 17, 2019, they committed to form an eleven-member Sovereign Council of five civilians and five military members chosen by the two parties, and one civilian chosen jointly. They also agreed on a transitional period of three years and three months during which the military and civilians would take turns holding the presidency, culminating in democratic elections.[89] Consequently, on August 20, 2019, the TMC was dissolved and the Sovereign Council was appointed. The following day, Dr. Abdullah Hamdok, the previous Executive Secretary of the UN Economic Commission for Africa, was appointed prime minister to serve for the first half of the transition period.[90] The PSC then lifted the sanctions and put an end to the suspension of the participation of Sudan in AU activities on September 6, 2019.[91]

b. Effects on Sudan's Participation in the Activities of Union

In analyzing this case, it is important to consider the effect of the suspension of Sudan on its participation in the AU's activities. Although it might seem a modest action, it significantly affected the interests of Sudan. For example, the PSC was holding meetings to consider the renewal of the AU Mission in Darfur, and Sudan was not allowed to participate in the meeting.[92] Sudan requested a legal opinion regarding the PSC's decision. A high-level delegation from Sudan visited the AU Legal Counsel to seek a

[85] *Id.* para. 8.

[86] Leah Asmelash and Faith Karimi, "What's Going on in Sudan and What the US Is Doing about It—Explained," *CNN*, June 13, 2019, https://www.cnn.com.

[87] AU Commission Chairperson Statement on the situation in Sudan (June 3, 2019), http://www.peaceau.org/uploads/auc-sudan-03-juin-2019-.pdf.

[88] PSC, Communique of 854th meeting on the situation in Sudan, *supra* note 40. The PSC noted that "should the Transition Military Council fail to hand-over power to a civilian-led Transitional Authority, the Council shall, without any further delay, automatically impose punitive measures on individuals and entities obstructing the establishment of the civilian-led Transitional Authority."

[89] "Our Revolution Won: Sudan's Opposition Lauds Deal with Military," *Aljazeera*, July 5, 2019, https://www.aljazeera.com/news/2019/07/sudan-military-council-opposition-reach-power-sharing-agreement-190705013332385.html.

[90] "Sudan Transition: Abdalla Hamdok Appointed New Prime Minister," *BBC News*, Aug. 21, 2019, https://www.bbc.com/news/world-africa-49425702.

[91] PSC, Communique of the 875th meeting on the situation in Sudan, Doc.PSC/PR/Comm.(DCCCLXXV) Addis Ababa, Ethiopia (Sept. 6, 2019), http://www.peaceau.org/uploads/eng.875.psc.communique.sudan.6.9.2019.pdf.

[92] SC Res. 2479 (June 27, 2019).

solution or a path to enable their representation in the PSC meetings. They argued that Sudan was the main stakeholder in the Darfur Mission and it would be affected directly by the PSC decision. The Legal Counsel advised them to direct their demands, interests, and concerns to the Director of the Peace and Security Department in order to bring them to the attention of the PSC. Hence, she confirmed that the PSC communiqué did not allow them to participate in the activities of the Union.

Another way in which Sudan was affected concerned its candidatures in international organizations. A question arose as to whether the African Civil Aviation Commission (AFCAC) should continue to provide support to Sudan for election to the International Civil Aviation Organization (ICAO) Council during the ICAO General Assembly. Another question was whether AU member states should continue to support the Sudanese candidate for the position of International Organization for Migration (IOM) Director. Recall that the June 6, 2019, PSC communiqué suspended Sudan from "*all AU activities*."[93] AFCAC requested clarification on whether that decision automatically affected Sudan's membership in all AU specialized agencies. In addition, AFCAC needed to know whether the decision of the AU policy organs that had endorsed Sudan's candidacy for the elections in ICAO could still be implemented. Based on the opinion, AFCAC would or would not urge its members and partners to support Sudan's candidature.

The AU Legal Counsel issued a legal opinion that clarified that the suspension decision was to be implemented by all AU organs and specialized agencies. Hence Sudan should not be allowed to participate in AFCAC activities. Regarding Sudan's candidature to the IOM Director-General position and the ICAO, the opinion balanced the obligation of the AU Commission to implement the policy organ's decision with the concern that taking the time to go through the process of picking another candidate might result in Africa losing the seats. The Legal Counsel concluded that elections held outside the AU are not to be considered AU activities; hence they do not fall under the sanctioned activities by virtue of Rule 37(4)(e) of the Rules of Procedure of the AU Assembly of the Union:

> Whenever an unconstitutional change of Government takes place, the Chairperson and the Chairperson of the Commission shall . . . immediately suspend the Member State from the Union and from participating in the organs of the Union, provided that exclusion from participating in the organs of the Union shall not affect that State's membership of the Union and its obligations towards the Union.[94]

The rule stipulates that the member in question is to be suspended "*from participating in the organs of the Union*." By implication, any activities that are not of the Union's organs are not covered by the suspension. The article also clarifies that the suspension shall not affect the membership status of the state, thereby providing an additional argument as to why the state can participate in activities that do not involve the organs of the Union.

[93] PSC, Communique of the 854th meeting, *supra* note 40.
[94] Rules of Procedure of the Assembly of the Union, 2002, Rule 37(4)(e).

In addition, the Legal Counsel relied on Rule 12(2) of the Rules of Procedure of the AU Ministerial Committee on Candidatures within the International System, which states "by virtue of Article 4(p) of the Constitutive Act, candidatures of States or nationals of States under suspension shall not be considered."[95] A state suspended from the AU's activities at the time of submission of candidates (or its own candidacy) for an international post shall not be eligible to submit a candidate. However, where a state had submitted its candidate for consideration by the Committee and endorsement by the Executive Council as the AU candidate prior to being subjected to sanctions, the AU's support for that candidate remains until the Executive Council adopts a new decision to change candidates. Legally, the body that issued the endorsement decision is alone competent to change its decision, and the PSC is not higher than the Executive Council. Moreover, both elections were imminent, and the AU and its member states had invested considerable effort campaigning for Sudan's candidatures as Africa's candidatures. Hence, the loss would not be a Sudanese loss but rather an African one.

Thus, while the suspension of Sudan prohibited the unconstitutional government from presenting candidates on behalf of Sudan for AU endorsement, it did not invalidate the AU's decisions to support candidatures previously presented by the former government. This position was maintained until the Executive Council in Niamey decided to withdraw AU support to the candidatures in the international system of suspended member states.[96]

The AU played a crucial role in delegitimizing the TMC through the invocation of the AU's own legal norms and stood firm with the people of Sudan in demanding a civilian transitional government to take over. Furthermore, it upheld the AU's commitment to bring African solutions to African problems based on the rule of law and principles of democracy and good governance.

III. Conclusion

The history of Africa that led to bloodshed and instability instigated a robust course of action by the AU in order to put an end to violence, bring peace to the continent, and focus on the development and prosperity of its peoples. This could not and would not have been possible without rules to be invoked when peace and security are threatened by UCGs. Since the Sierra Leone case in 1993 and the action taken by the then OAU, fighting against UCGs became one of the top priorities for the AU.

In the Lomé Declaration, the Constitutive Act, the PSC Protocol, and consecutive decisions by its policy organs, the AU built a sanctions system to ensure respect for the rule of law. Did Africa need a courtroom to remind the culprits in a coup d'état of the rule of law? The answer is a simple NO. The objectives that underpin the condemnation of UCGs are the AU's commitment to democratization and good governance. Hence it adopted a consistent practice of condemning the UCGs

[95] Rules of Procedure of the AU Ministerial Committee on Candidatures, 2006, Rule 12(2).

[96] Executive Council, Decision on the Report of the Ministerial Committee on African Candidatures in the International System, 36th Ordinary Session, Doc.EX.CL/Dec.1067 (XXXV), Niamey, Niger (2019).

regardless of the type of government that had been ousted. This firm legal position is important to prevent the use of political argumentation to justify breaches of the law. In simple terms, UCGs should not be used to bring about change *and* guidelines for democratization and good governance should be followed; otherwise bringing stability and building institutions on the continent will be deemed impossible. Africa experienced that road after independence, with almost all the coup leaders promising democracy and good governance, yet it did not work. Over the long term, it brought instability in Africa. This is why the AU sought and was able to find a path to support democracy and good governance through the rejection of UCGs, legally and politically.

In adopting a nuanced approach to implementing the rules relating to UCGs and the promotion of democracy and good governance, the AU followed a fairly consistent practice. As demonstrated through the case studies, it usually started with a condemnation and demands either for the reinstatement of a democratically elected government or, if the overthrown government had not been democratically elected, for a transitional civilian government to be established and a free and fair election to be held.

When AU demands are not met, sanctions and intervention follow. However, some of these measures are usually resisted by the targeted government, while local and regional civil society organizations welcome them. The sanctions regime of the AU is relatively successful, as it sides with the people in their call for democracy. Hence, the AU gains popular support for itself, with the diplomatic efforts it employs through its own envoys combined with the pressure of sanctions forcing coup plotters to succumb to following a path to democracy.

Thus, African states, through the AU, have managed to establish a sophisticated system of rules—some hard law and some soft—to use when necessary. This legal system complemented a realpolitik approach that made it effective and efficient in putting an end to cases of UCG. The reliance on AU legal texts has been valuable in gaining AU consensus on its responses and in marshaling diplomatic efforts to persuade (or compel) those who come to power through unconstitutional means to step down and hand power over to the people.

Despite criticism of the current sanctions system, it is still the most effective on the continent. The Constitutive Act in Article 4(h) went further than the UN Charter to protect the rule of law by all means, even by military intervention, when deemed necessary. While this provision is of fundamental normative importance, the combined effect of Articles 3(g), 4(m), 4(p), and 30 have been more consequential as a practical matter. Decisions of the AU policy organs are political decisions, but they are based on rules incorporated in the Constitutive Act and other AU instruments. The legal and political implications of the decisions adopted either by the Assembly or the PSC to impose sanctions are severe. The suspension of participation in the activities of the Union causes major disruption and sometimes affects the direct interests of states, which adds to the pressure on the unlawful governments to return to the rule of law in order to have the sanctions against them lifted. In brief, the African experience proves that promoting respect for the rule of law can be executed outside of the courtroom.

PART IV

12
Legal Argumentation in the Evolving Climate Regime

Jutta Brunnée

I. Introduction

Notwithstanding the relative rise of international courts and tribunals, it seems fair to say that the bulk of international legal argumentation unfolds in the course of interstate diplomacy, UN practice, treaty negotiations, and interactions under the auspices of treaties and codification projects and in a growing range of state and non-state arenas. In international environmental law, legal argumentation is even more heavily concentrated in such nonjudicial settings. A relatively small number of judicial decisions were influential in delineating the conceptual cornerstones of the field, supporting the development of customary law on transboundary impacts.[1] Despite some increase in international judicial activity over the last two decades, adjudication has played a very limited role in the field overall.[2]

The reason for this picture is simple: the vast majority of international environmental problems are not amenable to resolution on the basis of typically broad-stroked customary norms, such as the harm prevention rule, or through judicial settlement. That is because most contemporary international environmental problems are complex, multifaceted, long-term, and regional or global in nature, and implicate multiple states and innumerable non-state actors. Given the limits of adjudication in the context of such polycentric problems,[3] the most common arenas for legal argumentation are the institutions and compliance mechanisms of various kinds of international environmental regimes.[4] States remain central in shaping these discourses. But

[1] See Jutta Brunnée, "Procedure and Substance in International Environmental Law," *Collected Courses of the Hague Academy of International Law*, 405, ch. 3, http://dx.doi.org/10.1163/1875-8096_pplrdc_A9789004433007_02 (first published online: 2019).

[2] Daniel Bodansky, "The Role and Limits of the International Court of Justice in International Environmental Law," in *The Cambridge Companion to the International Court of Justice*, edited by Carlos Esposito and Kate Parlett (Cambridge: Cambridge University Press, first published online: June 15, 2020, last revised Aug. 12, 2020) (on file with author), 1.

[3] Lon L. Fuller, "The Forms and Limits of Adjudication," *Harvard Law Review* 92 (1978): 353.

[4] Jutta Brunnée, "The Rule of International (Environmental) Law and Complex Problems," in *The International Rule of Law: Rise or Decline?*, edited by Heike Krieger, Georg Nolte, and Andreas Zimmermann (Oxford: Oxford University Press, 2019), 211.

Jutta Brunnée, *Legal Argumentation in the Evolving Climate Regime* In: *Talking International Law*. Edited by: Ian Johnstone and Steven Ratner, Oxford University Press. © Jutta Brunnée 2021. DOI: 10.1093/oso/9780197588437.003.0012

non-state actors have established themselves as influential participants in environmental regimes and in a variety of other transnational or subnational arenas.[5]

No other issue illustrates the importance of nonjudicial arenas for legal argumentation around complex environmental challenges better than climate change. Although there has been an uptick in domestic and human rights–based climate litigation,[6] international judicial processes have played virtually no role to date.[7] The UN climate regime, anchored in the 1992 UN Framework Convention on Climate Change (UNFCCC),[8] remains the primary arena for international legal argumentation around climate change.

For that reason alone, it offers a productive setting in which to explore some of the questions around which this volume is built. Even more conducive to these purposes is the fact that the climate regime has undergone a significant evolution, encapsulated in a shift in approach from the 1997 Kyoto Protocol[9] to the 2015 Paris Agreement.[10] While the Paris Agreement, like the UNFCCC and the Kyoto Protocol, is a treaty under international law,[11] its provisions represent a significant softening of the climate regime's legal framework. This softening, however, is not simply a matter of shifting emphasis from legally binding to non-binding terms, although that is part of the mix. Rather, what I am referring to as "softening" involves three interrelated shifts.

First, the climate regime evidences a shift from a model in which the treaty serves as centralized forum for inter-state standard setting and accountability practices, epitomized by the Kyoto Protocol, to a more decentralized model in which the treaty helps "orchestrate" a range of state and non-state practices,[12] epitomized by the Paris Agreement. Second, the climate regime, like other multilateral environmental agreements, has always emphasized procedural requirements and relied upon non-binding standard setting, but the Paris Agreement marks a decisive turn toward non-binding substantive terms, supported by binding procedural terms.[13] Finally, the Paris

[5] See Sarah Mason-Case, "On Being Companions and Strangers: Lawyers and the Production of International Climate Law," *Leiden Journal of International Law* 32 (2019): 625.

[6] See, e.g., Joana Setzer and Rebecca Byrnes, *Global Trends in Climate Change Litigation: 2019 Snapshot* (London: Grantham Research Institute on Climate Change and the Environment and Centre for Climate Change Economics and Policy, London School of Economics and Political Science, 2019), http://www.lse.ac.uk/GranthamInstitute/publication/global-trends-in-climate-change-litigation-2019-snapshot/; Lennart Wegener, "Can the Paris Agreement Help Climate Litigation and Vice Versa?," *Transnational Environmental Law* 9 (2020): 17, 18.

[7] See Brunnée, *supra* note 1.

[8] United Nations Framework Convention on Climate Change, May 9, 1992, 1771 UNTS 107 (entered into force Mar. 21, 1994) [hereinafter UNFCCC].

[9] Kyoto Protocol to the United Nations Framework Convention on Climate Change, Dec. 10, 1997, 2303 UNTS 162 (entered into force Feb. 16, 2005).

[10] Paris Agreement to the United Nations Framework Convention on Climate Change, Dec. 12, 2015, (2016) 55 International Legal Materials 740 (entered into force Nov. 4, 2016).

[11] See, e.g., Daniel Bodansky, "The Legal Character of the Paris Agreement," *Review of European, Comparative & International Environmental Law* 25 (2016): 142.

[12] See Kenneth W. Abbott, "Strengthening the Transnational Regime Complex for Climate Change," *Transnational Environmental Law* 3 (2013): 57; Thomas Hale, "'All Hands on Deck': The Paris Agreement and Nonstate Climate Action," *Global Environmental Politics* 16 (2016): 12.

[13] See, e.g., Marion Lemoine-Schonne, "Substance et Procédure en Droit International du Climat," in *Substance et Procédure en Droit International Public: Dialectique et Influences Croisées*, edited by Ioannis Prezas (Paris: Éditions Pédone, 2016), 19, 34–45.

Agreement suggests a shift away from legal accountability practices toward non-legal performance assessment.[14]

Paying attention to these three strands of the climate regime's evolution allows for a more nuanced assessment of the extent to which the softening of its approach is likely to affect the patterns of legal argumentation. I argue that only the third shift—the move to performance assessment—stands to reduce the scope for legal argumentation in the regime. The Paris Agreement's decentralized approach and its increased reliance on non-binding or procedural terms are unlikely to diminish the salience of legal argumentation.

My argument is informed by the interactional understanding of law that I developed in my work with Stephen Toope.[15] This practice-focused account posits that law emerges from social interaction, when norms assume specific traits of legality and actors respect these criteria of legality in the application and interpretation of the relevant norms—that is, when they sustain a practice of legality. Legal argumentation is a key part of this practice of legality. The criteria both constrain what can be argued in legal terms and lend distinctive persuasiveness to legal argumentation, thereby helping to shape the practices of participants in a given legal regime as well as its evolution.

Of course, arguments about the science, economics, and politics of climate change are inevitably prominent as actors debate the need for more ambition under the climate regime. But legal argumentation is ubiquitous, by virtue of the treaty-based norms around which the regime revolves.[16] Specifically, I suggest that treaty-based argumentation is likely to involve procedural or interpretive reasoning. That reasoning, in turn, is shaped by the requirements of the law of treaties. The rules of treaty law, I argue, instantiate the criteria of legality that I posit, such that treaty-based procedural and interpretive reasoning can serve as proxies for legal argumentation. As I will show, this point holds in relation to binding as well as non-binding terms of the climate treaties. The argumentative patterns in the climate regime are in line with the assumption of the interactional account that the traits and practices of legality that generate law are not contingent on the formal legal nature of the relevant norms.[17]

In this chapter, I focus on the mitigation-related aspects of the climate regime, leaving aside issues related to climate adaptation, climate finance, and loss and damage due to climate change. I consider argumentation by both state and non-state

[14] See, e.g., Christopher Campbell-Duruflé, "Accountability or Accounting? Elaboration of the Paris Agreement's Implementation and Compliance Committee at COP 23," *Climate Law* 8 (2018): 1. See also William Nordhaus, "The Climate Club: How to Fix a Failing Global Effort," *Foreign Affairs*, May/June 2020, https://www.foreignaffairs.com/articles/united-states/2020-04-10/climate-club (arguing that the Paris Agreement's voluntary, penalty-free nature is one of its major structural defects).

[15] See, e.g., Jutta Brunnée and Stephen J. Toope, *Legitimacy and Legality in International Law: An Interactional Account* (Cambridge: Cambridge University Press, 2010); Jutta Brunnée and Stephen J. Toope, "Interactional Legal Theory, the International Rule of Law, and Global Constitutionalism," in *Handbook of Global Constitutionalism*, edited by Anthony Lang and Antje Wiener (Cheltenham: Edward Elgar, 2017), 170; "International Law and the Practice of Legality: Stability and Change," *Victoria University of Wellington Law Review* 49 (2010): 429.

[16] On the role of treaties in framing argumentation among parties, see also Ian Johnstone, chapter 7, in this volume (focusing on the Treaty on the Non-Proliferation of Nuclear Weapons).

[17] See also Wouter Werner, chapter 10, in this volume (illustrating that legal validity and binding force are not necessarily coextensive).

actors. However, my primary focus is on argumentative patterns among state parties to the climate treaties.

The chapter will proceed as follows. In Section II, I sketch the salient features of the interactional understanding of international law from which I derive the concept of legal argumentation used in the chapter. In Section III, I canvass the three shifts highlighted above. In Section IV, I explore the patterns of legal argumentation in the climate regime, and, in Section V, I assess what impact, if any, the three shifts have had, or are likely to have, on them. In Section VI, I pull together the key conclusions that my exploration of the climate regime suggests for this volume's inquiry into legal argumentation outside the courtroom. The chapter touches on many of the questions that animate this volume: Who engages in legal argumentation, why and with what effects; who is the audience for legal argumentation; what are the arenas in which it occurs? The main thrust of its conclusions, however, pertains to what constitutes a legal argument in the first place.

II. Interactional International Law and Legal Argumentation

Over the last twenty years, Stephen Toope and I have developed what we call an "interactional" understanding of international law, connecting insights from constructivism in international relations and practice theory to the legal theory of Lon Fuller. Fuller's account of domestic law struck us as productive for international law because it recognizes and explains the essential "horizontality" of law.[18] It is thus helpful in confronting head-on the persistent critique that international law lacks many of the hierarchical structures of authority that are commonly seen as characteristic of law. Fuller's work illustrates that what, in the context of domestic law, is often assumed to be a vertical relationship (of authority and subordination) is better understood as a reciprocal relationship between citizens and government.[19] For international law, where states are subjects, lawmakers, and administrative agencies, the notion of reciprocity highlights the fact that legality is a collective enterprise. Constructivism provides a useful complement to this interactional understanding of law because it offers insight into the emergence, maintenance, and operation of social norms.[20] Practice theory, in turn, illuminates the dynamic interplay between actors pursuing their ends and legal norms enabling, guiding, or constraining them in these pursuits.[21] It helps us

[18] Lon L. Fuller, *The Morality of Law*, rev. ed. (New Haven: Yale University Press, 1969).

[19] Lon L. Fuller, "Human Interaction and the Law," *American Journal of Jurisprudence* 14 (1969): 1; reprinted in Kenneth I. Winston, ed., *The Principles of Social Order: Selected Essays of Lon L. Fuller*, rev. ed. (Oxford: Hart Publishing, 2001), 211.

[20] See Jutta Brunnée and Stephen J. Toope, "Constructivism and International Law," in Interdisciplinary *Perspectives on International Law and International Relations: The State of the Art*, edited by Jeffrey L. Dunoff and Mark A. Pollack (New York: Cambridge University Press, 2013), 119.

[21] See, e.g., Christian Bueger and Frank Gadinger, *International Practice Theory: New Perspectives*, 2d ed. (Basingstoke: Palgrave Macmillan, 2018); Jeffrey L. Dunoff and Mark A. Pollack, "Practice Theory and International Law," in *Research Handbook on the Sociology of International Law*, edited by Moshe Hirsch and Andrew Lang (Cheltenham: Edward Elgar, 2018), 252.

understand international law as a distinctive practice, rooted in and sustained by distinctive modes of argumentation.

Drawing on these influences, the framework has three interrelated elements. First, it posits that legal norms arise in the context of social norms based on shared understandings. Second, what distinguishes law from other types of social ordering is not simply provenance from a formal source, but adherence to a series of criteria of legality most comprehensively described by Fuller: generality, promulgation, nonretroactivity, clarity, noncontradiction, not asking the impossible, constancy, and congruence between rules and official action.[22] When norm creation meets these criteria and when, third, there exists what we call a practice of legality (norm application that also satisfies the legality requirements), actors can pursue their purposes and organize their interactions through law. In other words, social interaction, whether channeled through formal sources or through informal norm-building practices, generates law when norms assume traits of legality. The criterion of "congruence," in this reading, is pivotal. It encapsulates more than conformity of conduct with existing norms and highlights that actors must also respect the requirements of legality in the application, interpretation, and justification of actions on the basis of the relevant norms. That is what we mean when we speak of a practice of legality. Legal argumentation is a key part of that practice.

In such a practice-based account, the boundaries between norm creation and norm application are fluid.[23] The criteria of legality highlight traits that distinguish legal norms, but they also discipline norm application. For example, while "congruence" and "constancy" may appear to be focused on norm application, they equally speak to norm creation. Norms that envisage ad hoc decisions or fluctuating standards, and thus fail to project "constancy," are unlikely to emerge as legal norms and attract practices of legality. At the same time, the criteria of legality matter in norm application. Since legal norms are practice-based, they ultimately emerge and persist through norm application that treats them as law. For example, at times it is through implementation and legal argumentation in the course of interpretative or justificatory processes that norms acquire the requisite clarity. Sometimes norm application may even constitute "promulgation," such as when parties further develop treaty terms through their practice,[24] or when customary law emerges through a consistent and widespread practice of legality.[25]

The criteria of legality thus play a central role in shaping the patterns of a practice of legality, providing the parameters for legal argumentation and enabling interpretation along similar standards. Because the interactional law framework illuminates the role of horizontal legal practices, it is especially useful in considering international

[22] See Fuller, *supra* note 18.

[23] See Jutta Brunnée, "The Sources of International Environmental Law: Interactional Law," in *The Oxford Handbook of the Sources of International Law*, edited by Samantha Besson and Jean d'Aspremont (Oxford University Press, 2017), 960, 962–963, 964.

[24] See, e.g., Anthony Aust, *Modern Treaty Law and Practice*, 3d ed. (Cambridge: Cambridge University Press, 2018), 215 (on the interpretation through subsequent practice of Article 27(3) of the UN Charter).

[25] See also Monica Hakimi, "Making Sense of Customary International Law," *Michigan Law Review* 118 (2020): 1487, 1491 (arguing that customary law does not flow in on/off fashion from formal secondary rules, but emerges organically from "what global actors use and receive as [custom] in the everyday practice of law," such that customary international law is best understood as "a real-world sociological phenomenon").

legal argumentation outside judicial settings. It serves both to widen and to sharpen the analytical focus in a few ways. First, it widens our optic since both "hard" and "soft" norms in the conventional sense can be appreciated as law in this account.[26] Accordingly, given its focus on criteria and practices of legality rather than purely source-based indicators, the framework speaks both to argumentation on the basis of formally binding norms, such as customary or treaty law, and to argumentation on the basis of non-binding norms. For the same reason, it can accommodate argumentative practices by state and non-state actors. Second, the interactional law framework sharpens our focus because its criteria of legality zero in on the features that distinguish legal argumentation from other modes of argumentation and that enhance the persuasiveness of legal argumentation.

III. The Evolution of the International Climate Change Regime

When the UN climate regime was launched with the adoption of the UNFCCC in 1992, it followed what had by then established itself as the conventional wisdom for environmental treaty design—the "framework-protocol" model. The model was a response to the previously mentioned complexity of many international environmental issues and the need to gradually build consensus among participants with often widely diverging priorities. To these ends, a framework treaty enshrines the regime's objective and its guiding principles and procedural obligations, and establishes treaty bodies and decision-making rules. Typically, concrete substantive obligations are inserted into the regime at a later stage, through supplementary treaties, usually referred to as protocols. While separate treaties, protocols are legally connected to the framework, sharing its objectives, principles, and decision-making rules.[27]

The UNFCCC and its Kyoto Protocol neatly map onto the framework-protocol approach. The Paris Agreement introduced the three shifts in approach that I highlighted in the introduction. Although these shifts are intertwined, I examine them in sequence, so as to lay the groundwork for Section IV of the chapter.

A. From Centralization to Orchestration

The Kyoto Protocol contained binding emission reduction targets, as well as procedural obligations to allow for compliance assessment and a compliance review mechanism. In keeping with the UNFCCC's core principles of common but differentiated responsibilities and respective capabilities (CBDRRC) and developed country leadership,[28] the protocol did not enshrine emission reduction commitments for

[26] See Brunnée, *supra* note 23, at 981–982.

[27] See Daniel Bodansky, Jutta Brunnée, and Lavanya Rajamani, *International Climate Change Law* (Oxford: Oxford University Press, 2017), 57, 85–94.

[28] See UNFCCC, *supra* note 8, preamble and art. 3.1.

developing countries, a feature that later became a major point of contention among parties.[29]

The Kyoto Protocol is emblematic of the "centralized" model of environmental regime building. Substantive commitments are negotiated among parties and enshrined in the treaty. Party performance is then assessed through a treaty-based compliance review process and by a designated compliance body. Because of these features, the approach has also been described as "top-down."[30] But such centralized standard-setting and accountability is difficult to achieve at a global scale. Hence, the quest for a commitment regime that would oblige both developed and developing countries resulted in the change in approach that is now embodied in the 2015 Paris Agreement.

The Paris Agreement resembles the Kyoto Protocol to the extent that it is a treaty in its own right but operates under the umbrella of the UNFCCC, pursues its objective, and relies upon its principles and decision-making procedures. In terms of substantive commitments, however, it represents a significant departure from the Kyoto Protocol's top-down approach. There are no legally binding and centrally reviewed emission reduction commitments in the Paris Agreement. Instead it relies on a "bottom-up" approach to emissions mitigation, with individual countries making "nationally determined contributions" (NDCs), aimed at achieving the agreement's goal of keeping temperature increases beyond pre-industrial levels at "well below 2° C" and, ideally, below 1.5°C.[31]

The Paris Agreement's emphasis on bottom-up action is reflected not only in the inter-state commitment regime. The agreement also focuses on orchestration of climate action, by engaging sub-state and non-state actors in a much more expansive fashion than did the Kyoto Protocol. To be sure, non-state actors were always highly visible in the climate regime. Experts networks and nongovernmental organizations (NGOs) have long provided input into and feedback on negotiations and states' emissions performance. The Paris Agreement, however, specifically acknowledges the role of a much wider range of "non-Party stakeholders" in the bottom-up action required to address climate change.[32] It taps into a series of existing initiatives under the banner of a Global Climate Action Agenda, encompassing voluntary initiatives by sub-state governmental actors like cities and regions and business actors and civil society actors.[33]

B. A Shifting Blend of Procedure and Substance, and Binding and Non-Binding Elements

The climate regime's shift from centralization to orchestration went hand in hand with a shift in the types and legal nature of state commitments. As noted, the Kyoto

[29] Bodansky et al., *supra* note 27, at 105–108.

[30] *Id.* at 23, 163.

[31] *Id.* at 23, 214–215.

[32] See UNFCCC, Adoption of the Paris Agreement, Decision 1/CP.21, FCCC/CP/2015/10/Add. 1, 2 (Jan. 29, 2016), at paras. 118–122, 133–136; and see generally Hale, *supra* note 12, at 14.

[33] See Harro van Asselt, "The Role of Non-State Actors in Reviewing Ambition, Implementation, and Compliance under the Paris Agreement," *Climate Law* 6 (2016): 91, 98–99.

Protocol built on the UNFCCC by enshrining binding emission reduction targets for individual parties, along with detailed procedural obligations intended to ensure transparency of performance. The protocol's binding terms were supplemented by detailed standards and guidelines adopted in nonlegally binding form through plenary body decisions.[34]

Blending procedure and substance and binding and non-binding terms, then, has always been a feature of the UN climate regime. In the Paris Agreement, however, the nature of the blend has changed. The only substantive obligation the agreement imposes on states is the broadly framed obligation of conduct to "pursue domestic mitigation measures, with the aim of achieving the objectives" of their NDCs.[35] Crucially, the NDCs themselves are not binding under international law. Parties merely commit themselves to preparing, communicating, and maintaining successive NDCs, guided by the nonlegally binding normative expectations that a party's NDC reflect its "highest possible ambition" and its CBDRRC, and that successive NDCs represent a "progression" over time.[36] In other words, the Paris Agreement requires parties to have an NDC, but does not render their content obligatory.

Aside from the obligation to pursue domestic mitigation measures, parties' obligations under the Paris Agreement are procedural in nature. Thus, in communicating their NDCs, parties are required to "provide the information necessary for clarity, transparency and understanding," in accordance with decisions adopted by the Conference of the Parties (COP).[37] Parties must also "account for" their NDCs and, in doing so, must "promote environmental integrity, transparency, accuracy, completeness, comparability, and consistency, and ensure the avoidance of double-counting," again in accordance with guidance adopted by the COP.[38]

C. From Legal Accountability to Performance Assessment

The declared goals of the Kyoto Protocol's noncompliance procedure (NCP) were to "facilitate, promote and enforce compliance" with the protocol.[39] In relation to noncompliance with the parties' binding emissions targets, the NCP set out fixed "consequences to non-compliance," to be applied by the enforcement branch upon a finding of noncompliance.[40] All told, the NCP was set up to ensure systematic and predictable

[34] See Jutta Brunnée, "COPing with Consent: Lawmaking under Multilateral Environmental Agreements," *Leiden Journal of International Law* 15 (2002): 1, 26–29.

[35] See Paris Agreement, *supra* note 10, art. 4.2.

[36] *Id.* arts. 3, 4.3.

[37] *Id.* art. 4.8. For simplicity's sake, I will refer to all plenary bodies as "COP," even though the plenary bodies of the Kyoto Protocol and Paris Agreement are referred to as "Conference of the Parties serving as the meeting of the Parties" to the Protocol/Agreement.

[38] *Id.* art. 4.13.

[39] See UNFCC, Procedures and Mechanisms Relating to Compliance under the Kyoto Protocol, Decision 27/CMP.1, FCCC/KP/CMP/2005/8/Add.3 (Mar. 30, 2006), 92 at 93, Sec. I (Kyoto Protocol NCP), https://unfccc.int/resource/docs/2005/cmp1/eng/08a03.pdf (emphasis added).

[40] See Kyoto Protocol NCP, *supra* note 39, 102, Sec. XV.5.

compliance assessment in relation to the agreement's core substantive obligations and related procedural obligations.

The changed structure of the Paris Agreement's commitment regime is reflected in its three-part approach to accountability.[41] First, the agreement provides for a relatively robust transparency mechanism. Pursuant to the procedural obligations canvassed in the previous subsection, each party must provide emission inventories and reports on progress toward and implementation of its NDC. All inventories and reports then undergo expert review.[42] Second, this transparency mechanism is complemented by a "global stocktake," focused on parties' collective performance toward the treaty objective and temperature goals.[43] The process is explicitly not focused on individual performance.[44] It is meant only to offer "non-policy prescriptive consideration of collective progress" that parties may consider in the "updating and enhancing, in a nationally determined manner, of their actions and support."[45]

The third component of the Paris Agreement's performance assessment approach is a "mechanism to facilitate implementation and promote compliance," with a compliance committee that is to be "expert-based and facilitative in nature and function in a manner that is transparent, non-adversarial and non-punitive."[46] Thus, whereas the Kyoto Protocol experimented with an enforcement-oriented approach, the Paris Agreement's compliance mechanism returns to a managerial approach.[47] The mechanism is focused almost exclusively on parties' compliance with their procedural obligations. It can be triggered by a party "with respect to its own implementation of and/or compliance with any provision of the Paris Agreement."[48] The compliance committee itself can initiate the process only to determine whether or not a party has communicated or submitted a required NDC, report, or information at all.[49] The committee may not assess whether parties are complying with the requirements concerning the content or form of submissions. Furthermore, the committee may not issue findings of noncompliance concerning individual parties, only "findings of fact."[50]

[41] For an overview, see Lavanya Rajamani and Daniel Bodansky, "The Paris Rulebook: Balancing International Prescriptiveness with National Discretion," *International & Comparative Law Quarterly* 68 (2019): 1023, 1025–1027.

[42] See Paris Agreement, *supra* note 10, arts. 4.8 and 4.13, 13.

[43] See *id.* art. 14. And see UNFCCC, Matters relating to Article 14 of the Paris Agreement and paragraphs 99–101 of Decision 1/CP.21, Draft Decision—/CMA.1, FCCC/CP/2018.L.16 (Dec. 14, 2018) [hereinafter Matters relating to Article 14].

[44] See Matters relating to Article 14, id. para. 14.

[45] *Id.*

[46] See Paris Agreement, *supra* note 10, arts. 15.1 and 15.2.

[47] Abram Chayes and Antonia Handler Chayes, *The New Sovereignty: Compliance with International Regulatory Agreements* (Cambridge, MA: Harvard University Press, 1996).

[48] See UNFCCC, Modalities and procedures for the effective operation of the committee to facilitate implementation and promote compliance referred to in Article 15, paragraph 2 of the Paris Agreement, Draft Decision—/CMA.1, FCCC/CP/2018/L.5 (Dec. 14, 2018), para. 5 [hereinafter Modalities and procedures for compliance], para. 20.

[49] *Id.* para. 22(a).

[50] *Id.* para. 30(e).

IV. International Legal Argumentation and the Climate Regime

A. Patterns of Legal Argumentation

Since the UN climate regime is treaty-based, the rules of treaty law frame interactions pertaining to the application, interpretation, and further development of the regime. As I have shown elsewhere, the bulk of the rules set out in the Vienna Convention on the Law of Treaties (VCLT) instantiate the criteria of legality and insist upon their application to inter-state agreements.[51] For example, procedural rules, such as those pertaining to consent, entry into force, and amendments, promote the requirements of clarity, nonretroactivity, reasonableness, and promulgation, among others.[52] The rules on treaty interpretation, in turn, promote all of the requirements of legality—generality, promulgation, clarity, noncontradiction, nonretroactivity, constancy over time, reasonableness, and congruence.[53] As a result, legal argumentation is coded into the argumentative patterns of the treaty-based climate regime.[54] My point here is not that only procedural or interpretive reasoning on the basis of the VCLT amounts to legal argumentation. Clearly, legal argumentation can also invoke customary law, general principles, or non-treaty-based soft law. Rather, my point is that because procedural and interpretative reasoning occurs against the backdrop of the VCLT, importing the criteria of legality, they provide good examples of legal argumentation.

Below, I explore three typical patterns of legal argumentation. First, in promoting or defending particular positions, parties deploy *interpretive reasoning* to argue for or against preferred understandings of existing treaty terms, or for or against new terms. To these ends, in line with the canons of the VCLT,[55] parties invoke other parts of the regime, such as principles in the UNFCCC, as interpretative context or to illuminate the object and purpose of the treaty at hand. By the same token, given the evolving nature of climate regime, argumentation in relation to one of the climate treaties is inextricably linked not only to prevailing interpretations of the others but also to the past practice of parties in the regime and to the negotiating history.[56] I will use the interpretive battles surrounding the CBDRRC principle to illustrate these dynamics.

Second, parties invoke both *binding and non-binding parts* of the regime in their legal argumentation, often blending the two. Interpretative recourse to non-binding treaty terms is not a particularity of the practice in the climate regime, of course. It is fully in line with the canons of the VCLT. A treaty's preamble, objective, guiding

[51] See Vienna Convention on the Law of Treaties, Jan. 27, 1980, 1155 UNTS 1155 (entered into force Jan. 27, 1980) [hereinafter VCLT]. And see Brunnée and Toope, *Legitimacy and Legality*, *supra* note 15, at 49–50. Examples include the rules on: written form (clarity); entry-into-force and registration (promulgation, clarity); reservations and amendments (generality, clarity); nonretroactivity; successive treaties and peremptory norms (noncontradiction); fundamental change in circumstance (reasonable demands); termination and suspension (constancy over time); *pacta sunt servanda* and peremptory norms (congruence).

[52] Brunnée and Toope, *id.*

[53] *Id.*

[54] See also Mason-Case, *supra* note 5, at 632–633 (speaking of a "culture of legality" that pervades diplomatic conferencing around climate change).

[55] VCLT, *supra* note 51, arts. 31, 32.

[56] See Bodansky et al., *supra* note 27, at 94.

principles or annexes, for example, are important parts of its interpretative context.[57] In turn, when parties adopt non-binding standards to flesh out or implement the terms of a treaty, it is unsurprising that the treaty interpretation methods apply to those standards as well. Such decisions may also constitute subsequent agreements regarding the interpretation of a treaty within the meaning of the VCLT.[58] To explore these patterns, I will consider the role of decisions by the climate agreements' COPs.

A third common argumentative approach in the climate regime, often deployed when parties seek to advance or stall regime progress, is to draw upon *procedural rules* concerning the development of new terms. The long-standing disagreements concerning the decision-making formula for the climate regime and its struggle with the resulting default to a consensus practice provide a good illustration.

1. Argumentation Invoking Treaty Principles

The UNFCCC stipulates that "[i]n their actions to achieve the objective of the Convention ... , the Parties shall be guided" by a set of principles, including the proposition that they "should protect the climate system ... in accordance with their common but differentiated responsibilities and respective capabilities."[59] Although the CBDRRC principle is not phrased in obligatory terms, it has played a key role in the parties' argumentative patterns over the years. For the first two decades of the regime's evolution, developing country parties successfully invoked the principle to resist taking on legally binding emission reduction commitments. The principle's impact is reflected most prominently in the Kyoto Protocol's exclusive focus on emissions targets for industrialized and transition countries.[60]

Early in the negotiation process for a post-Kyoto, long-term climate agreement, the parties to the convention adopted a decision, dubbed the "Bali Action Plan," that required their "shared vision" for global climate action to be "in accordance with the provisions and principles of the convention, in particular the principle of common but differentiated responsibilities and respective capabilities."[61] At the time, developing countries, especially those with rising emissions, tended to take the position that the Kyoto Protocol reflected the correct approach to differentiation, making a binary distinction between developed and developing countries. China, for example, argued that

> [t]he principle of "common but differentiated responsibilities" between developed and developing countries is the keystone of the Convention and the Bali Action Plan. Any further sub-categorization of developing countries runs against the Convention itself and is not in conformity with the consensus reached at Bali.[62]

[57] See VCLT, *supra* note 51, art. 31(2).

[58] See *id.* art. 31(2)(a). And see International Law Commission (ILC), Draft conclusions on subsequent agreements and subsequent practice in relation to the interpretation of treaties, with commentaries (A/73/10, para. 51), in *Yearbook of the International Law Commission, 2018*, vol. II, Part Two, at 82–93 (Part 4, Conclusion 11: Decisions adopted within the framework of a Conference of States Parties).

[59] See UNFCCC, *supra* note 8, preamble and art. 3.1.

[60] See Brunnée and Toope, *Legitimacy and Legality*, *supra* note 15, at 155.

[61] See UNFCCC, Bali Action Plan, Decision 1/CP.13, FCCC/CP/2007/6/Add. (Mar. 14, 2008), 1, 3.

[62] See UNFCCC, Ideas and proposals on the elements contained in paragraph 1 of the Bali Action Plan. Submissions from Parties, Paper No. 5: China, FCCC/AWGLCA/2008/MISC.5 (Oct. 27, 2008), at 34.

Industrialized countries, by contrast, tended to favor differentiation within groups and argued that it was not precluded by the UNFCCC. For example, Australia argued that

> [t]here is considerable variation in the circumstances of the 191 countries in the UNFCCC. Accordingly, there can be many different approaches to differentiating and grouping countries according to such circumstances.[63]

When China and India emerged as major greenhouse gas emitters, however, their preferred bright-line differentiation between developed and developing countries was increasingly at odds with the thrust of both the CBDRRC principle and the objective of the climate regime (to avert dangerous human-induced greenhouse gas concentrations in the atmosphere). The persuasive power of China and India's legal arguments against mitigation commitments based on CBDRRC diminished accordingly.[64] Indeed, then US Secretary of State Hillary Rodham Clinton noted at the time that she "completely" understood arguments about per capita emissions, but that the argument "loses force" as developing countries became major emitters.[65] Regardless, the United States and other industrialized countries redoubled their efforts to dilute the interpretative role of CBDRRC in the climate regime, maintaining that

> [n]ew sight on the differentiation among Parties is required . . . , based on . . . advances in scientific knowledge and changing social and economic situation in the world [*sic*].[66]

The debate continued over the course of several years.[67] China and India sought to maintain the interpretive relevance of CBDRRC by securing references to it in all decisions and instruments pertaining to the further development of the climate regime. Industrialized countries sought to avoid explicit references to the principle, so as to diminish its interpretive role. An uneasy compromise, indicative of the gradually shifting argumentative tide, is reflected in the negotiating mandate for what became the Paris Agreement. The mandate made no reference to CBDRRC, nor did it repeat the convention's language that developed countries should "take the lead" in combating climate change.[68] However, the convention principles were implicitly

[63] See UNFCCC, Views Regarding the Work Programme of the Ad Hoc Working Group on Long-term Cooperative Action under Convention. Submissions from Parties, Australia, FCCC/AWGLCA/2008/MISC.1/Add.2 (Mar. 20, 2008), at 7–8.

[64] Brunnée and Toope, *Legitimacy and Legality*, *supra* note 15, at 164–166.

[65] See also Glenn Kessler, "Clinton, Indian Minister Clash over Emissions Reduction Pact," *Washington Post*, July 20 2009 (citing the US Secretary of State).

[66] See UNFCCC, Ideas and Proposals on paragraph 1 of the Bali Action Plan, Revised Note by the Chair, FCCC/AWGLCA/2008/16/Rev.1 (Jan. 15, 2009), para. 22(h) (citing Australia, New Zealand, the Russian Federation, and the United States).

[67] For a compact overview, see Bodansky et al., *supra* note 27, at 26–30.

[68] *Id.* at 114.

incorporated by the stipulation that the agreed legal outcome of the negotiations would be "under the convention."[69]

The Paris Agreement reflects the eventual success of the efforts to defuse CBDRRC as an argumentative barrier to a genuinely global approach to climate change, with emissions commitments by all states. The principle does appear in the Paris Agreement.[70] But the addition of the clause "in the light of different national circumstances" imports the idea that differentiated responsibilities are not categorical but contextual, and not immutable but dynamic, evolving as national circumstances change.[71] In other words, the addition further softens the principle by undercutting the static, binary interpretation of CBDRRC previously advanced by developing countries. Furthermore, differentiation is not a one-size formula in the Paris Agreement, but tailored specifically to each issue (i.e., mitigation, adaptation, finance, transparency, and so forth). With respect to emissions mitigation, parties can self-differentiate through their NDCs, subject to the normative expectations of progression and highest possible ambition.[72]

Of course, political and economic factors played a significant role in the evolution of the climate regime. Without the participation of China as the single largest national emitter, the Obama administration could not have supported the Paris Agreement. Nonetheless, the CBDRRC example illustrates the influence that treaty norms have on argumentative patterns and treaty development. Promulgated terms, whether binding or non-binding, become points of reference, reinforcing argumentation that is consistent with those terms and undercutting argumentation that is not.[73] The efforts by the United States and other states to shift the normative understandings surrounding CBDRRC speak volumes to their awareness of the principle's significance in legal argumentation under the climate regime. The Paris Agreement's amendment of the CBDRRC principle and its self-differentiation approach to mitigation effectively defused the interpretive battles that long stalled the negotiation of a global emissions regime.

2. Argumentation Blending Binding and Non-Binding Rules

A second example may serve to highlight the pervasive interplay between binding and non-binding terms in the climate regime's argumentative patterns. Under the Kyoto Protocol, standards adopted by means of COP decisions complemented the inventory or reporting obligations in the treaty and provided specific parameters for compliance assessment.[74] COP decisions are non-binding, unless the relevant treaty authorizes binding decision-making.[75] In relation to the protocol's emissions trading mechanism, the protocol asked the plenary body to adopt "principles, modalities, rules and guidelines."[76] Relying on the reference to "rules," which did not appear in

[69] See UNFCCC, Establishment of an Ad Hoc Working Group on the Durban Platform for Enhanced Action, FCCC/CP/2011/9/Add. 1, 2 (Dec. 11, 2011), para. 2 (agreeing to develop "a protocol, another legal instrument or an agreed outcome with legal force under the convention applicable to all parties").

[70] See, e.g., Paris Agreement, *supra* note 10, preamble and art. 2.2.

[71] See Bodansky et al., *supra* note 27, at 220–221.

[72] *Id.* at 29–30.

[73] See also Wouter Werner, chapter 10, in this volume (discussing, in the context of the African Union, the practice of recalling or reiterating earlier decisions or documents).

[74] See Kyoto Protocol, *supra* note 9, arts. 5.1, 7.1, and 7.4.

[75] See Brunnée, *supra* note 34, at 21–31.

[76] See Kyoto Protocol, *supra* note 9, art. 17.

any of the protocol's other enabling clauses, and asserting the importance of binding standards for the integrity of emissions trading, some parties and academic observers argued that the protocol had provided authority for binding rule-making.[77] Indeed, the Kyoto Protocol delegated to COP decisions much of the detail needed to make key terms of the protocol, such as those pertaining to emissions trading, operational.[78] Still, some parties resisted the argument that the mere reference to "rules" enabled the adoption of a binding emissions trading regime,[79] fearing a precedent for binding decision-making by COPs without the explicit authority that is normally required.[80] Some parties were also concerned about the use of "shall" language in plenary body decisions, arguing that such language should be reserved for instruments capable of binding effect.[81] This back and forth about the legal valence of COP decisions itself provides examples of legal argumentation, as parties deploy interpretive reasoning (distinguishing the term "rules" from "principles, modalities and guidelines" and seeking to preserve the distinction between "shall" and "should") as well as procedurally oriented arguments (seeking to preserve the formal consent requirements for treaty-based lawmaking).[82]

Today, parties routinely adopt both "shall" and "should" terms by means of COP decisions. For example, under the Paris Agreement,[83] parties adopted a series of decisions with additional guidance on communicating and accounting for NDCs.[84] Among other things, the COP decided that "Parties shall account for their nationally determined contributions in accordance with the guidance contained in annex II."[85] In turn, Annex II to this decision lists the information parties are to provide and, in relation to methodological consistency, indicates in factual terms what parties are expected to do ("Parties . . . provide . . .") and "should" do, respectively.[86] In other words, the Paris Agreement weaves an intricate web of binding and non-binding standards. The agreement itself obligates the parties ("shall") to act in accordance with decisions adopted by the COP. The relevant COP decision, stipulates what parties "shall" do, in accordance with an Annex that, for its part, includes mandatory as well as "should" terms.[87]

Thus, although the baseline assumption remains that COP decisions are non-binding,[88] the Paris Agreement guidance illustrates that parties often settle on mixed

[77] See, e.g., Robin Churchill and Geir Ulfstein, "Autonomous Institutional Arrangements in Multilateral Environmental Agreements: A Little-Noticed Phenomenon in International Law," *American Journal of International Law* 94 (2000): 623, 639.

[78] See Kyoto Protocol, *supra* note 9, arts. 3.4, 5.1, 6.2, 7.4, 8.4, 12.7, 16–18.

[79] Personal observation.

[80] For examples, see Brunnée, *supra* note 34, at 21–23.

[81] Personal observation.

[82] On significance of the use, or nonuse, of established legal terms see also Bruno Stagno-Ugarte, chapter 8, in this volume (on states, in the context of UN Security Council sessions, using a variety of terms while avoiding reference to the concept of crimes against humanity).

[83] See *supra* notes 37–38 and accompanying text.

[84] See UNFCCC, Katowice Climate Package, https://unfccc.int/process-and-meetings/the-paris-agreement/paris-agreement-work-programme/katowice-climate-package.

[85] See UNFCCC, Decision 4/CMA.1: Further guidance in relation to the mitigation section of decision 1/CP.21, FCCC/PA/CMA/2018/3/Add.1 (Mar. 19, 2019), para. 13.

[86] *Id.* Annex II, paras. 1 and 2(b) and (d).

[87] For a detailed exploration, see Rajamani and Bodansky, *supra* note 41.

[88] See, e.g., ILC, *supra* note 58.

signals regarding legal valence, obscuring the disagreements regarding the status of the guidance adopted by the COP. In fact, the UN press release about the outcome referred to "the adopted guidelines package, called the 'rulebook' by some."[89] All parties accept the importance of standards adopted by COP decision for the functioning of the regime. They reason with the terms of such decisions in keeping with rules of treaty interpretation, and their practice suggests acceptance that some parts of decisions designate mandatory conduct, whereas others are recommendatory.[90] In other words, notwithstanding the uncertain formal status of standards adopted by COP decisions, parties frequently invoke them in their legal argumentation, and they shape state conduct in much the same way as do binding terms.[91] The interactional account, with its emphasis on criteria and practices of legality rather than formal status, illuminates how such a, at first glance, counterintuitive pattern can arise and endure.

3. Argumentation Invoking Rules of Procedure

A third common argumentative pattern in the climate regime can be found in practices around procedural rules. The rules of procedure governing climate regime's plenary bodies, governing matters such as participation, agenda setting, and voting, provide a good example.[92] When the rules of procedure were adopted, the parties were unable to agree on whether and under what conditions decision-making by majority vote should be possible. As a result, the COP defaulted to the UN practice of decision-making by consensus.[93] This consensus practice has hobbled the climate regime over the years, enabling individual parties to stall or derail the adoption of decisions supported by the majority of parties.

The 2009 Copenhagen meeting of the parties offers one of the starkest illustrations of this dynamic. The meetings were originally meant to result in the adoption of a formal agreement on post-Kyoto climate action, but the disagreements among parties were too deep to be bridged during the meeting.[94] Furthermore, parties favoring a long-term agreement covering both developed and developing countries were concerned that the consensus practice would make it impossible to adopt any text that charted a course in this direction. Hence, in the final hours of the meeting, the leaders of twenty-eight states, including all of the major economies and emitters, hammered out a blueprint for a global commitments regime, dubbed the Copenhagen Accord.[95] The group had hoped that a COP decision could then bring this blueprint under the umbrella of the UNFCCC. But a handful of developing countries, including Bolivia,

[89] "At COP24, Countries Agree Concrete Way Forward to Bring the Paris Climate Deal to Life," *UN News*, Dec 15, 2018, https://news.un.org/en/story/2018/12/1028681.

[90] See Brunnée, *supra* note 34, at 26, 32.

[91] The phenomenon of actors blurring the boundaries between binding and nonbinding terms is not unique to climate law, of course. See, e.g., Steven R. Ratner, "Persuading to Comply: On the Deployment and Avoidance of Legal Argumentation," in *Interdisciplinary Perspectives on International Law and International Relations*, *supra* note 20, at 568 (arguing that compliance with formal law may at times be best promoted by invoking soft law).

[92] See UNFCCC, Draft Rules of Procedure of the Conference of the Parties and its Subsidiary Bodies, FCCC/CP/1996/2 (May 22, 1996).

[93] See Bodansky et al., *supra* note 27, at 75.

[94] See Brunnée and Toope, *Legitimacy and Legality*, *supra* note 15, at 204.

[95] See Bodansky et al., *supra* note 27, at 76, 110.

Sudan, Tuvalu, and Venezuela, objected that the accord had been negotiated outside of the normal process of the climate regime.[96] Given the refusal of these states to support the adoption of the accord through a decision, the COP merely took note of it.[97]

The consensus practice is hard to dislodge from the climate regime, not least because adopting a different decision-making rule would require consensus. And so parties continue to work with the practice, as well as draft rules of procedure. Rules of procedure are crucial to providing predictability and legitimacy of decision-making. As a result, such rules engender robust, widely supported practices of legality. Indeed, after the Copenhagen meeting, notwithstanding the broad support for the Copenhagen Accord, the UNFCCC Secretariat felt compelled to clarify that, since the plenary body had "neither adopted nor endorsed" the accord, "its provisions do not have any legal standing within the UNFCCC process"; it was "a political agreement, rather than a treaty instrument subject to signature."[98]

The episode illustrates the salience of argumentation grounded in procedural rules on decision-making. Parties often wield procedural arguments to stall progress in a direction that does not accord with their preferred substantive positions. Some parties are keen to maintain the consensus rule because it grants them this very blockage power. At Copenhagen, those parties unhappy with the thrust of the Copenhagen Accord were well aware that once adopted, even if through a non-binding COP decision, the accord would become an interpretive reference point and pull argumentative patterns toward regime development. Indeed, it stands to reason that this is precisely why the states seeking to push the regime forward sought to bypass the normal process to put in place a textual steppingstone for future negotiations. It is worth adding that the key elements of the Copenhagen Accord were brought into the climate regime the following year, through a series of decisions adopted at the next meeting of the parties.[99] In fact, once embraced by the parties, procedurally and substantively speaking, these elements became the foundation for the Paris Agreement and its bottom-up approach.[100]

B. Participants in Legal Argumentation

While the primary focus of this chapter is on inter-state argumentative patterns, legal argumentation is employed not only by state parties to the climate treaties but also by a broad range of non-state actors engaged in the regime. The annual meetings of the parties to the climate treaties are flanked by a multitude of "side-events" organized by think tanks, NGOs, and academic experts, and attended by thousands of governmental and nongovernmental participants.[101] Some of these events are concerned

[96] See *id.* at 111–112.

[97] *Id.*

[98] See UNFCCC—Executive Secretary, "Clarification to the Notification of 18 January 2010," Jan. 25, 2010, https://unfccc.int/files/parties_and_observers/notifications/application/pdf/100125_noti_clarification.pdf.

[99] See Bodansky et al., *supra* note 27, at 112.

[100] *Id.* at 29, 214.

[101] See *id.* at 95–96.

with technical or policy issues, but many focus on legal matters, such as assessments of the binding effect of parts of the Paris Agreement or the legal interplay between the UNFCCC and other international agreements.[102] In addition, a diverse range of some two thousand civil society organizations and more than one hundred intergovernmental organizations are accredited with the climate regime as observers.[103] Legal academics are advisers to, or even members of, state delegations. Some NGOs also offer legal advice to state delegations, notably delegations from smaller, less well-resourced states.[104] Other organizations seek to put pressure on state parties, highlighting weak positions and procedural or substantive failures, and providing proposals for language to be included in instruments under negotiation.[105] For example, NGOs actively participated in the debates surrounding CBDRRC traced above.[106] To the extent that non-state argumentation in the international arena is aimed at state delegations, it tends to mirror the patterns of legal argumentation among states.

Within many states, domestic NGOs apply similar pressure to national or local governments. Sometimes, the goal is primarily to "shame" a government for dragging its heels on climate action. In that context, an international commitment may be invoked to enhance the pressure on the government. When the goal is to communicate the gravity of government inaction to a broader audience, a full legal argument will often not be needed. It will suffice to signal to that audience that the government's failures are not merely bad for the climate but are also in bad faith or even illegal. Sometimes, however, domestic actors will argue in some detail that domestic action falls short of the legal requirements of the climate regime. For example, Canadian NGOs highlighted the gap between domestic action and Canada's binding emissions target under the Kyoto Protocol.[107] When Canada declared to domestic and international audiences that it would not take the steps required to meet its Kyoto target,[108] academic experts pointed to Article 26 of the VCLT and called on Canada to withdraw from the treaty.[109]

[102] See, e.g., International Institute of Sustainable Development, "Coverage of Selected Side Events at the Marrakech Climate Change Conference—November 2016," https://enb.iisd.org/climate/cop22/enbots/17nov.html.

[103] On the prerequisites for observer status, see UNFCCC, *supra* note 8, art. 4.7; and UNFCCC, *Draft Rules of Procedure*, *supra* note 92, Rules 6–7.

[104] See, e.g., Lawyers Responding to Climate Change (LRI), https://legalresponse.org/about-us/. And see Mason-Case, *supra* note 5, at 630–631 (describing how NGOs get directly involved in negotiations by providing state delegations with legal advice).

[105] See van Asselt, *supra* note 33, at 96.

[106] See Brunnée and Toope, *Legitimacy and Legality*, *supra* note 15, at 158–159 (referring to submissions by the International Trade Union Confederation and various environmental groups, including Greenpeace and the World Wildlife Fund).

[107] See, e.g., Friends of the Earth Canada, "Canada Violating UN Climate Change Pacts," Oct. 31, 2006, https://foecanada.org/2006/10/canada-violating-un-climate-change-pacts-foe-international/.

[108] See Clare Demerse, Matthew Bramley, and Dale Marshall, "Canada in Bali: A Backgrounder on the 2007 UN Climate Negotiations," Nov. 22, 2007, https://climateactionnetwork.ca/wp-content/uploads/2011/06/pembina-bali-backgrounder-2007.pdf.

[109] See, e.g., Geneviève Dufour, "Le retrait du Canada du Protocole de Kyoto et le droit international public—Droit de dénonciation, abus de droit et responsabilité international," *Revue Québécoise de droit international* 25 (2012): 29. Canada did announce its withdrawal from the Protocol in 2011. See "Canada Pulls Out of Kyoto Protocol," *CBC News*, Dec. 12, 2011, https://www.cbc.ca/news/politics/canada-pulls-out-of-kyoto-protocol-1.999072.

V. The Shifts in the Climate Regime and Their Impact on Legal Argumentation

In Section III of this chapter, I highlighted the shifts that the Paris Agreement introduced into the climate regime, resulting in a softening of its legal framework. In Section IV, I explored three common patterns of inter-state legal argumentation in the climate regime: interpretive argumentation invoking treaty principles, argumentation blending binding and non-binding terms, and argumentation invoking rules of procedure. Further, I suggested that international legal argumentation is also deployed by non-state actors operating in the international arena, and sometimes even in a domestic context. I can now pull these different strands together and consider the implications of the climate regime's overall softening for legal argumentation concerning the regime. As suggested earlier, this softening of the regime is brought about by three shifts in its structure and approach. The following discussion will illustrate why two of these shifts seem unlikely to affect legal argumentation, while the third stands to reduce the space in which it can occur.

A. From Centralization to Orchestration

The shift from the Kyoto Protocol's centralized/top-down regulation to the Paris Agreement's decentralized/bottom-up approach as such does not appear to have had a discernible effect on legal argumentation, at least not as between treaty parties. Given the Paris Agreement's strong procedural obligations and its reliance on the climate regime's rules of procedure, it is safe to say that legal argumentation in relation to procedural issues will remain as salient as it has been under the UNFCCC and the Kyoto Protocol. As for substantive matters, it seems unlikely that either the bottom-up or the nonlegally binding nature of NDCs will bring about a significant shift away from legal argumentation. As we have seen, although the parties do distinguish between binding and non-binding elements of the climate regime, legal argumentation in the regime has drawn upon both. Two of my examples illustrate this point: the protracted argumentation around the (non-obligatory) CBDRRC principle, and the arguments concerning standards adopted by COP decision. All indications are that these argumentative patterns will extend to the bottom-up elements of the regime. At least insofar as parties' NDCs are subject to normative expectations enshrined in the Paris Agreement, such as the notions of ambition and progression, it does not appear that parties consider their NDCs to exist in a law-free zone.

However, whereas decentralization among state parties may not entail a retreat from legal argumentation, the attendant shift to orchestration of multilevel action may well have this effect as far as non-state actors are concerned. The various sub-state and non-state climate initiatives in existence today are less likely to give rise to international legal argumentation than has been the case when non-state actors participate in the regime itself.[110] While these initiatives may be loosely related to the Paris

[110] See *supra* notes 102–106 and accompanying text.

Agreement and even contribute to NDC implementation, the majority of them do not appear to be specifically focused on the terms of the agreement.[111] The mere mention of the 1.5°C or 2°C temperature target, or of the Paris Agreement as a whole—both ubiquitous in policy and public discourse and in press reports—does not by itself amount to international legal argumentation. It is conceivable, of course, that within a given sub- or non-state initiative legal reasoning develops over time, for example, by treating the temperature goal and the Paris Agreement's normative expectations of progression and ambition as reference points against which to interpret standards of conduct and assess positions and actions. But in the framework proposed here, a mere reference to law would not turn an argument into a legal argument, unless accompanied by the traits of legal reasoning that I have described.

B. Shifting Blend of Procedure and Substance, and Binding and Non-Binding Elements

The shift in inter-state commitments from a top-down to a bottom-up model has entailed not only that commitments are nationally determined rather than subject to negotiation but also that these commitments are nonlegally binding. The Paris Agreement's greater emphasis on non-binding commitments is unlikely to bring about a retreat from legal argumentation, for several reasons. First, the examples provided in Section III show that robust patterns of legal argumentation around non-binding terms are well entrenched in the practices of the climate regime. Second, under the Paris Agreement, substantive standards remain tied to procedural standards. What has changed is the mix of procedure and substance, and binding and non-binding standards. As also shown earlier, the climate regime has long been familiar with non-binding standards, adopted by COP decision, complementing binding procedural or substantive rules.[112] Under the Paris Agreement, such non-binding, complementary standards remain relevant. Their main purpose now is to flesh out and reinforce the agreement's procedural obligations, so as to ensure transparency with respect to the parties' non-binding substantive efforts—their NDCs.[113]

Two features of the Paris Agreements mitigation-related commitments are worth considering more closely. First, most of the agreement's substantive standards are not binding, but framed as non-binding normative expectations. Second, the agreement's single substantive obligation is an open-textured obligation of conduct.[114]

1. Non-Binding Substantive Standards

This aspect of the bottom-up approach seems unlikely to reduce recourse to legal argumentation. In the practice of the climate regime, non-binding standards commonly attract legal argumentation, as I have shown in relation to the principle of CBDRRC

[111] See Benoit Mayer, *The International Law on Climate Change* (Cambridge: Cambridge University Press, 2018), 255.

[112] See *supra* Section III.B.

[113] See *supra* notes 38 and 83–87 and accompanying text.

[114] See *supra* note 35 and accompanying text.

and the parties' routine reliance on terms adopted by plenary body decision.[115] The debate surrounding the "downgrading" of existing NDCs provides another excellent illustration, and speaks directly to the role of the Paris Agreement's normative expectations.

When the United States, upon the election of President Trump, considered options for retreat from the Paris Agreement, some former government lawyers, and some academics, argued that agreement permitted parties to dial back their existing NDCs.[116] The argument was that Article 4.11, which provides that a party "may at any time adjust its existing nationally determined contribution with a view to enhancing its level of ambition," did not explicitly prohibit downgrading, thereby allowing it.[117] Since the NDCs as such were nonlegally binding, the argument went, a party would not violate its obligations under the Paris Agreement by weakening its NDC.[118]

The argument regarding the NDCs themselves, and their content, is correct, of course. More interesting for our purposes is the proposition that the Paris Agreement actually permitted downgrading. A number of points are worth highlighting. To begin with, given the wording of Article 4.11, even if considered in isolation, the claim that downgrading is allowed because not explicitly prohibited is dubious. What is more, it runs counter to the rules of treaty interpretation and the requirement that an individual treaty provision be interpreted in the context of the treaty as a whole and in light of its object and purpose.[119] Through the rules of interpretation, the temperature goals of the treaty and its normative expectations (progression and highest possible ambition) become parameters for the interpretation of Article 4.11. Seen in this context, it is clear that Article 4.11 permits upward, but not downward, adjustment of an NDC.[120]

This interpretive reasoning informed what appears to be the majority view on the issue.[121] It had traction notwithstanding the non-binding nature of the normative expectations and, indeed, was animated by a desire to preserve these expectations as yardsticks for parties' substantive efforts.[122] Perhaps most interesting is that the proponents of downgrading were intent on claiming that it was *permitted* by the treaty. It appears that it was not enough to be able to say that no obligations would be violated.

[115] See *supra* Section IV.A.1 and 2.

[116] See John Schwartz, "Debate over Paris Climate Deal Could Turn on a Single Phrase," *New York Times*, May 2, 2017, https://www.nytimes.com/2017/05/02/climate/trump-paris-climate-accord.html (citing Todd Stern, former US Climate Envoy, for the view that negotiators had written the flexibility to downgrade into the Paris Agreement). And see Center for Climate and Energy Solutions (C2ES), "Legal Issues Related to the Paris Agreement," May 2017, https://www.c2es.org/site/assets/uploads/2017/05/legal-issues-related-paris-agreement.pdf.

[117] See C2ES, *id.*

[118] *Id.*

[119] See VCLT, *supra* note 51, art. 31. See also Lavanya Rajamani and Jutta Brunnée, "The Legality of Downgrading Nationally Determined Contributions under the Paris Agreement," *Journal of Environmental Law* 29 (2017): 537, 547 (on the negotiating history).

[120] Rajamani and Brunnée, *id.* at 59, 547–548.

[121] See, e.g., Mayer, *supra* note 111, at 119; LRI, *supra* note 104, https://legalresponse.org/legaladvice/interpretation-of-article-4-11-paris-agreement/; Robin Eckersley, "COP23 and the Shadow over the Paris Agreement," *Australian Outlook*, Nov. 6, 2017, http://www.internationalaffairs.org.au/australianoutlook/bonn-climate-negotiations-shadow-trump/; Frank Jotzo, Joanna Depledge, and Harald Winkler, "US and International Climate Policy under President Trump," *Climate Policy* 18 (2018): 813, 813–814.

[122] See Jotzo et al., *id.* at 814; Rajamani and Brunnée, *supra* note 119, at 59, 547–548.

In other words, the Paris Agreement's non-binding normative expectations did have interpretative salience and significant impact on legal argumentation around the downgrading option. In the end, the United States opted not to downgrade but to withdraw from the Paris Agreement.[123]

2. Substantive Obligation of Conduct

This second of the aforementioned shifts in the substance of the regime, the move to an open-textured obligation of conduct, may hold the potential for dilution of international legal argumentation. Since the standard of conduct is merely to "pursue" domestic mitigation action "with a view" to achieving "the objectives" of the NDCs, interpretative reasoning and legal assessment will be challenging. The standard lacks clarity and is only indirectly tied to the agreement's normative expectations. That is, a party's pursuit of mitigation action is to be geared to the objectives of its NDC. The NDC, in turn, is subject to the expectations of ambition, progression, and CBDRRC.[124] Nonetheless, it is conceivable that the Paris Agreement's normative expectations, which help define its standards of due diligence,[125] could evolve over time through the parties' argumentative practice. Hence, the fact that an obligation is an obligation of conduct alone does not prevent the emergence of patterns of legal argumentation. After all, debates about the parameters of due diligence are quintessentially legal debates.[126] However, the prospects for this evolution may be slim, given the third shift encapsulated in the Paris Agreement, to which I now turn.

C. From Legal Accountability to Performance Assessment

The Kyoto Protocol's regime of binding emission targets and related procedural obligations went hand in hand with a noncompliance procedure designed to ensure systematic compliance assessment in relation to these core obligations. Since the Kyoto Protocol ended up being supplanted by the Paris Agreement, the NCP's enforcement branch had no opportunity to develop an extensive practice regarding emission targets.[127] Still, parties appeared to take the NCP, and potential findings of noncompliance, quite seriously, notwithstanding their non-binding nature. For example, when Canada was confronted with a potential finding of noncompliance with a procedural obligation, it not only rectified the issue but also deployed procedural arguments concerning the limits of the compliance committee's mandate to have references to its past noncompliance struck from the record.[128] Furthermore,

[123] United States, "Communication Regarding Intent to Withdraw from Paris Agreement," *Media Note*, Washington, DC, Aug. 4, 2017, https://www.state.gov/communication-regarding-intent-to-withdraw-from-paris-agreement/.

[124] See Paris Agreement, *supra* note 10, arts. 3, 4.3.

[125] See, e.g., Christina Voigt and Felipe Ferreira, "'Dynamic Differentiation': The Principles of CBDR-RC, Progression and Highest Possible Ambition in the Paris Agreement," *Transnational Environmental Law* 5 (2016): 285, 302.

[126] See Brunnée, *supra* note 1, at 124–131, 201–202, 221.

[127] But note that parties actually met their Kyoto targets. See Michael Grubb, "Full Legal Compliance with the Kyoto Protocol's First Commitment Period—Some Lessons," *Climate Policy* 16 (2016): 673.

[128] See Brunnée and Toope, *Legitimacy and Legality*, *supra* note 15, at 202–203.

subsequent to Canada's withdrawal from the Protocol in 2012, the compliance committee undertook a detailed treaty-law analysis to determine what, if any, reporting and inventory commitments under the protocol Canada might still have to meet.[129]

The Paris Agreement's three-pronged approach to accountability is heavily tilted toward the parties' procedural obligations and relies predominantly on expert review rather than compliance assessment. The transparency mechanism provides for expert review of individual parties' emissions inventories and their reports on progress toward NDCs. The global stocktake process is focused on the collective, not individual, performance of parties. The agreement's compliance mechanism too is to be "expert-based," as well as "facilitative."[130] These features as such need not preclude a legal assessment, especially since some of the committee's members are international law experts.[131] However, the constraints placed on the compliance process severely limit the space for legal argumentation.

On its own initiative, the compliance committee can deal only with procedural obligations, and even here it can only engage in a "yes/no" determination regarding parties' submission of NDCs, reports or information. The committee is explicitly barred from addressing "the *content* of the contributions, communications, information and reports."[132] Only with the consent of the relevant party could the committee "engage in facilitative consideration of . . . significant and persistent inconsistencies in reporting" with the relevant guidelines.[133] This possibility might leave some scope for the emergence, through the practice of the compliance process, of an expectation that parties will consent to facilitative consideration. Such a practice, in turn, could create at least some space for legal argumentation.

Since the parties' NDCs are non-binding and self-determined by each party, it may not be surprising that the compliance assessment process does not extend to their content. But the agreement's substantive obligation "to pursue domestic mitigation measures" too is excluded from compliance review, at least from compliance review initiated by the compliance committee. That fact can be attributed to the sensitivities of some parties, especially developing country parties, with respect to any kind of international oversight of their domestic climate action.[134] It may also be connected to the fact that the relevant obligation is an obligation of conduct and that the parties did not want to provide the compliance committee with a space in which to flesh out the

[129] See UNFCCC—Compliance Committee, "Canada's withdrawal from the Kyoto Protocol and its effects on Canada's reporting obligations under the Protocol—Note by the Secretariat," CC/EB/25/2014/2 (Aug. 20, 2014), https://unfccc.int/files/kyoto_protocol/compliance/enforcement_branch/application/pdf/cc-eb-25-2014-2_canada_withdrawal_from_kp.pdf (invoking the Kyoto Protocol's withdrawal provision, and Article 70 VCLT).

[130] See *supra* Section III.C.

[131] See UNFCCC, "Committee to facilitate implementation and promote compliance referred to in Article 15, paragraph 2 of the Paris Agreement—Composition of the Committee," https://unfccc.int/process-and-meetings/bodies/constituted-bodies/committee-to-facilitate-implementation-and-promote-compliance-referred-to-in-article-15-paragraph-2#eq-1.

[132] See UNFCCC, Modalities and procedures for compliance, *supra* note 48, para. 23 (emphasis added).

[133] *Id.* at para. 22(b).

[134] See Bodansky et al., *supra* note 27, at 242.

agreement's standards of conduct, notably the standards of progression, highest possible ambition, and CBDRRC.[135]

Starkly put, the transparency and compliance components in the Paris Agreement and the COP decisions that flesh out these components treat the agreement's provisions more like technical criteria and indicators than legal standards, turning legal accountability into performance assessment. Both the technical expert review component and the truncated compliance review component point in this direction. What is of particular interest for the purposes of this volume is that this shift to performance review is brought about precisely by the fact that the compliance process, as circumscribed by the parties and absent evolution through future practice, leaves no room for legal argumentation to occur. Even formal legal obligations, like the parties' procedural obligations and their obligation to pursue domestic mitigation measures, risk becoming mere performance indicators when the space to treat them like legal norms is curtailed.[136]

VI. Concluding Observations

My exploration of the climate regime touches on many of this volume's questions about international legal argumentation outside the courtroom. Given the chapter's grounding in the interactional account of international law, it offers insight, in particular, into the background question of what constitutes a legal argument in the first place. Here, I pull together the main conclusions of the chapter.

Why does legal argumentation occur outside of courts? The experience in international environmental law indicates that the structure of the issue to be addressed is a key factor. While there may be some role for adjudication, it cannot offer solutions to complex global challenges like climate change. Problem complexity also speaks to the volume's inquiry into the nonjudicial arenas for legal argumentation. Treaty-based regimes are the most important arenas in the environmental context since they have proven best suited to tackling multifaceted, long-term issues that implicate states and non-state actors around the globe.

While this chapter has focused predominantly on inter-state argumentation, the climate regime illustrates that non-state actors too deploy legal argumentation. With respect to the purposes of legal arguments, the experience in the climate regime suggests that state actors seek to harness their enhanced persuasiveness, often for strategic reasons. The example of the debates surrounding the CBDRRC principle illustrates that states rely on norms that reinforce and legitimize their position and that other

135 See also Rajamani and Bodansky, *supra* note 41, at 1028 (noting that the Paris Agreement leaves the application of the normative expectations, "by default, to national determination"). Note also that the compliance committee is explicitly barred from changing, through its work, "the legal character of the provisions of the Paris Agreement." See UNFCCC, Modalities and procedures for compliance, *supra* note 48, para. 19(a).

136 See also Martti Koskenniemi, "The Fate of International Law: Between Technique and Politics," *Modern Law Review* 70 (2007): 1, 13 (warning that "even formally rule-like provisions (emission reduction standards) become negotiating chips in an unending process of balancing, adjusting and managing" when environmental regimes turn to experts who manage problems rather than engage with legal issues).

actors seek to dilute or shift such norms to weaken this effect. The example of the regime's consensus decision-making illustrates how states deploy procedural arguments to obstruct or slow the development of the regime in ways that they perceive to be contrary to their substantive preferences. Non-state actors, when operating within the climate regime, use legal arguments in order to influence or pressure state parties, or in order to influence the further development of the regime. Domestically, non-state actors may resort to legal argumentation for similar reasons when they engage governments. When their audience is a wider public, a simple reference to law, the Paris Agreement, for example, will often suffice to serve the purposes of these actors.

As far as the effects of legal argumentation are concerned, the interactional law framework posits, and the experience of the climate regime tends to confirm, that specific requirements of legality both constrain what can be argued in legal terms and lend distinctive persuasiveness to legal arguments, thereby helping to shape the practices of participants in a given legal regime as well as its evolution.

These observations bring me to the main question engaged by this chapter: What is a legal argument? I have argued that treaty-based regimes like the UN climate regime, which operate against the backdrop of the VCLT, are predisposed toward legal argumentation. The interactional account illuminates this point. It is not the simple fact that the climate regime is anchored in a binding agreement and governed by binding treaty law that explains why treaty-based arguments are likely to be legal in nature. Rather, in the interactional account, a legal argument is one that accords with the requirements of legality. Since the VCLT gives effect to these requirements of legality, procedural and interpretive reasoning pursuant to the VCLT can be taken to constitute instances of legal argumentation in the interactional law sense.

Another key point follows: because the interactional account defines law according to traits and practices of legality (including, in particular, legal argumentation), formal legal status is neither a necessary nor a sufficient condition for legal argumentation. Hence, as the example of the debates around COP decisions illustrates, both formally binding and non-binding norms and rules can give rise to legal argumentation, and legal argumentation can take place even as actors disagree about the formal status of the underlying norms. That is why two dimensions of the climate regime's softening—its shift toward a bottom-up/orchestration approach and its shift toward a blend of binding procedural standards and non-binding substantive standards—are unlikely to diminish the role of legal argumentation in the regime. By contrast, when the space for legal argumentation is removed or severely curtailed, even formally binding norms may fail to operate as law. Hence, the third aspect of regime's softening—the turn from legal accountability to performance assessment—points toward a much more limited role for legal argumentation going forward, notably in the climate regime's compliance process.

13
Law and Science in Environmental Governance
The Effects of Legal and Scientific Argumentation in the International Whaling Commission

Lisbeth Zimmermann

I. Introduction

Academics have been engaged in debates about the power of international law for decades. While the source of authority of international law is highly contested, most scholars agree that legal argumentation takes a form which differs from other types of argumentation. Scholars at the intersection of international law and international relations (IR) emphasize the distinct authority that is attached to legal argumentation in international politics. Even if used for strategic reasons, actors in international politics often dress their positions in legal arguments. Opinions diverge as to whether this pressure to resort to law has civilizing effects, constraining the use of open power politics, or whether it is a mere fig leaf covering up hegemonic power constellations.

In the field of environmental governance and environmental law, a similar debate exists about scientific argumentation. Science and technology studies, in particular, have pointed out how "science" is used as a resource of authority and legitimacy in international politics—and how scientific argumentation centrally shapes debates in this field.[1] The debates show surprising parallels. Moreover, the logics of legal and scientific argumentation are oftentimes intertwined in the institutional structure of environmental regimes.[2]

But which type of argumentation do states prefer in environmental politics, and with what effects? I will analyze the dispute around a moratorium on commercial whaling in the context of the International Whaling Commission (IWC)—a highly

[1] Rolf Lidskog and Göran Sundqvist, "The Role of Science in Environmental Regimes: The Case of LRTAP," *European Journal of International Relations* 8 (2002): 77; Silke Beck et al., "Towards a Reflexive Turn in the Governance of Global Environmental Expertise. The Cases of the IPCC and the IPBES," *GAIA—Ecological Perspectives for Science and Society* 23 (2014): 80; Sheila Jasanoff, "Just Evidence: The Limits of Science in the Legal Process," *Journal of Law, Medicine & Ethics: A Journal of the American Society of Law, Medicine & Ethics* 34 (2006): 328.

[2] Oren Perez, "The Hybrid Legal-Scientific Dynamic of Transnational Scientific Institutions," *European Journal of International Law* 26 (2015): 391.

Lisbeth Zimmermann, *Law and Science in Environmental Governance* In: *Talking International Law*. Edited by: Ian Johnstone and Steven Ratner, Oxford University Press. © Lisbeth Zimmermann 2021. DOI: 10.1093/oso/9780197588437.003.0013

controversial issue creating such a "toxic" atmosphere in the IWC temporarily that other international organizations on wildlife management and environmental protection were careful to avoid the issue of whaling. Anti-whaling and pro-whaling states have fought over the dominance of *preservation* versus *conservation* as a leading paradigm in the organization for decades. I analyze the types of argumentation *challengers* of the commercial whaling ban used to put the ban into question—legal, scientific, or other forms of arguments, and with what effects. While the role of so-called norm entrepreneurs and their argumentative strategies has been widely studied,[3] this is less true for the challengers. This contribution to the volume therefore explores the types of argumentation used by state representatives to contest rules in the context of multilateral organizations. How do they make use of the "power of law" in disputes about international rules?

Based on a qualitative content analysis of types of arguments used by norm challengers in IWC debates from 1986 to 2016, I show that in the highly contested context of the IWC, legal and scientific argumentation dominate. Yet other types of normative argumentation are surprisingly widespread. For the highly politicized topic of whaling, moral arguments are used intensively to fight over hearts and minds. I also find a division of labor with regard to types of argumentation: while substantive legal and normative arguments were used to fundamentally challenge the ban in an emotional way,[4] scientific and procedural legal arguments were more often used in technical debates to discuss concrete resolutions and policy proposals. Moreover, institutional contexts matter for the effects of different types of argumentation. When comparing the strategies for evading the moratorium, Japan became enmeshed in "scientific discourse," which was hard to settle in the institutional setting of the IWC, while Norway and Iceland, fearing an endless debate, mostly used a "legal" strategy, where institutional mechanisms in the IWC to deal with these arguments were missing.

I will provide an overview of the regulation of whaling and the moratorium on commercial whaling in the second section. The third section discusses the similarities of and differences between legal and scientific argumentation. The fourth section gives a general overview of which types of contestation were used in debates in the IWC and finds that legal and scientific contestation were—surprisingly—not omnipresent and were used for different objectives. When comparing country strategies to circumvent the moratorium, however, Japan used a different type of argumentation from that of Norway and Iceland. The institutional structure of the IWC shaped the reaction to these different argumentative strategies, as I show in Section V.

[3] Most importantly, Martha Finnemore and Kathryn Sikkink, "International Norm Dynamics and Political Change," *International Organization* 52 (1998): 887; Margaret E. Keck and Kathryn Sikkink, *Activists Beyond Borders: Advocacy Networks in International Politics* (Ithaca: Cornell University Press, 1998).

[4] Wouter Werner, chapter 10, and Edward Kwakwa, chapter 14, both in this volume.

II. The Moratorium on Commercial Whaling: Complete Preservation

Whaling was not a polarized topic prior to the 1970s. It had been a widespread practice in the United States and many European countries since the late eighteenth century and became more industrialized in the twentieth century. International regulation of the whaling of so-called "great whales" existed early on (International Agreement for the Regulation of Whaling, 1937; International Convention on the Regulation of Whaling (ICRW), 1946). The conventions were early examples of international treaties that included conservation requirements.[5] The ICRW presents the conservation of whale stocks as a central objective; linked to the objective of ensuring the "orderly development of the whaling industry" (Preamble, ICRW), however. The contracting states were, in practice, mostly oriented toward ensuring profits for the whaling industry. Scientific advice did not have any tempering effects on whaling quotas. Accordingly, whale stocks were dwindling in the twentieth century. Overexploitation led to many whale stocks becoming critically endangered.[6]

Because of this trend, as well as technological advances,[7] the whaling industry became less and less profitable in many Western states. We also observe the rise of environmental and animal rights movements in the 1970s and 1980s. All these factors brought about a policy change in many Western states, such as the United States, Great Britain, and Australia, leading to a halt of industrialized whaling. In addition, these states switched to outspoken support of a ban on whaling at the international level.

A change of the underlying convention was out of reach given the diverging positions of member states of the IWC at that time. The proponents of a whaling ban therefore opted for a change of the IWC schedule setting whaling quotas. Only the accession of new anti-whaling members (for the growth in number of contracting states, see Figure 13.1), as well as the proposal of a temporarily limited ban, helped secure the necessary three-quarters majority for a moratorium on commercial whaling in 1982.[8]

This moratorium banned any commercial whaling activities of IWC members. However, the IWC members did not pass a permanent ban. The IWC members could only agree to a compromise version,[9] where the

> catch limits for the killing for commercial purposes of whales from all stocks for the 1986 coastal and the 1985/86 pelagic seasons and thereafter shall be zero. This provision will be kept under review, based upon the best scientific advice, and by 1990 at the latest the Commission will undertake a comprehensive assessment of the effects

[5] Malgosia Fitzmaurice, "International Convention for the Regulation of Whaling: Introductory Note," http://legal.un.org/avl/ha/icrw/icrw.html; Kurkpatrick Dorsey, *Whales and Nations: Environmental Diplomacy on the High Seas* (Seattle: University of Washington Press, 2013).

[6] Johan N. Tønnessen and Arne O. Johnsen, *The History of Modern Whaling* (Berkeley: University of California Press, 1982); Dorsey, *supra* note 5.

[7] Petroleum had increasingly displaced whale blubber in many products.

[8] On the development of the commercial whaling moratorium, see Charlotte Epstein, *The Power of Words in International Relations: Birth of an Anti-whaling Discourse* (Cambridge, MA: MIT Press, 2008).

[9] Mostly to gain the support of Spain for a "yes" vote.

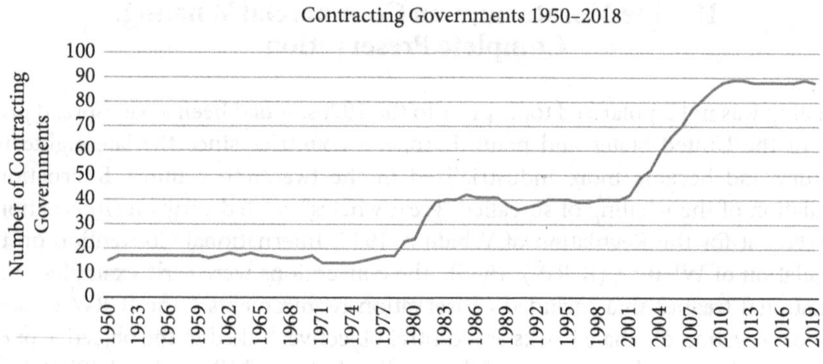

Figure 13.1 IWC membership 1950–2019

> of this decision on whale stocks and consider modification of this provision and the establishment of other catch limits. (IWC Schedule, para. 10(e))

This temporal formulation led to major disputes in the 1990s after the IWC's Scientific Committee had passed a new, risk-averse algorithm to calculate sustainable whaling quotas for non-endangered stocks. It became clear that the anti-whaling states understood the moratorium as a permanent measure, which they were not easily willing to lift.[10]

Two major exemptions to the moratorium exist: the IWC allows quotas for Indigenous whaling (called "aboriginal subsistence whaling" in the IWC context), which are considered "non-commercial" hunts—without this category being officially part of the ICRW. Limited quotas exist for the Inuit in Greenland (Denmark: minke whales, bowhead whales, fin whales, humpback whales) and Alaska (United States: bowhead whales), as well as for the Siberian Chukotka (Russia: bowhead and gray whales) and for whalers on the island of Bequia (St. Vincent and the Grenadines: humpback whales).[11] Moreover, the ICRW includes a paragraph which allows for domestically issued permits to hunt whales for scientific purposes.[12]

Several remaining whaling states lodged objections to the moratorium (a possibility under the ICRW) in the 1980s. Because of US pressure, most states withdrew these and halted commercial whaling after the moratorium came into force in 1986.

[10] Subsequent debates focused on a monitoring and sanctioning regime—but no agreement or compromise was forthcoming between pro-whaling and anti-whaling states.

[11] Canada allows for locally managed Indigenous hunts. It left the IWC after the passage of the moratorium. Moreover, the Indigenous hunt by the Makah tribe (United States) has been allowed by the IWC but is still pending. The Philippines banned whaling in 1997, although some ongoing local whaling might exist. Indigenous hunting in Indonesia also exists.

[12] "Notwithstanding anything contained in this Convention, any Contracting Government may grant to any of its nationals a special permit authorizing that national to kill, take, and treat whales for purposes of scientific research subject to such restrictions as to number and subject to such other conditions as the Contracting Government thinks fit, and the killing, taking, and treating of whales in accordance with the provisions of this Article shall be exempt from the operation of this Convention. Each Contracting Government shall report at once to the Commission all such authorizations which it has granted. Each Contracting Government may at any time revoke any such special permit which it has granted." ICRW, art. VIII (1).

Norway and Russia kept their objections in place but ceased commercial whaling activities. This trend changed in the 1990s (see Section V).

In sum, the moratorium on commercial whaling developed into a permanent measure. The underlying ICRW is a rather old international treaty, intended originally as an instrument for conservation and resource management. It now sits oddly between more paradigms in wildlife management: of preservation on the one hand, and conservation and sustainable use on the other hand. In addition, it only includes a soft self-monitoring mechanism and no internal adjudication processes in the IWC,[13] leaving ample room for interpretation, contestation, and evasion.

III. The Authority of Legal and Scientific Argumentation

In IR research on the emergence, diffusion, contestation, and erosion of international laws and norms, formal international institutionalization and legal argumentative processes play a central role. For example, scholars point out that formalized international institutions provide procedures to deal with contestation and to formulate rules on how to react to norm violations. They often also establish adjudication processes or fair institutional settings for interpreting international norms.[14]

Yet research in this field pays less attention to the specific role of legal argumentation—in particular, to the role of legal argumentation in the contestation of international rules. If states want to challenge an international rule, do they invoke legal arguments, because they assume that this will bolster the authority of their claims? Or does such legal argumentation have unintended effects, by drawing challengers into a legal discourse and thereby excluding more radical positions, channeling, and taming conflict?

A. The Power of Legal Argumentation

Both these potential effects of legal argumentation have been at the center of a debate in constructivist IR research and international law. Scholars have been particularly interested in legal discourse and the process of legal justification. For Chris Reus-Smit, law is the imagined realm "of institutionalized action in which certain

[13] External adjudication is available, such as the ICJ or potentially the International Tribunal for the Law of the Sea.

[14] Adam Bower, "Contesting the International Criminal Court: Bashir, Kenyatta, and the Status of the Nonimpunity Norm in World Politics," *Journal of Global Security Studies* 4 (2019): 88; Jutta Brunnée and Stephen J. Toope, "Norm Robustness and Contestation in International Law: Self-Defense against Nonstate Actors," *Journal of Global Security Studies* 4 (2019): 73; Richard Price, "Syria and the Chemical Weapons Taboo," *Journal of Global Security Studies* 4 (2019): 37; Averell Schmidt and Kathryn Sikkink, "Breaking the Ban? The Heterogeneous Impact of US Contestation of the Torture Norm," *Journal of Global Security Studies* 4 (2019): 105; Lisbeth Zimmermann et al., "Why International Norms Decline: Taming Contestation in Fair International Institutions" (under review); but see also Sarah Percy, "What Makes a Norm Robust: The Norm Against Female Combat," *Journal of Global Security Studies* 4 (2019): 123.

'political' types of behavior are foreclosed and other 'legal' types are licensed and empowered."[15] Actors perceive legal arguments to be more legitimate and successful.[16] Adam Bower also emphasizes this point in his study on how the United States fought the International Criminal Court:

> When actors argue via legal means they seek to validate particular behaviours or policies as conforming to, or violating, established principles, rules, and norms. . . . These can be distinguished from, and are inter-subjectively recognized as superior to, more politicised forms of rhetoric that explicitly invoke self-interest.[17]

Moreover, this has "taming" effects. Ian Johnstone stresses the shared/intersubjective presuppositions and understandings in legal interpretive communities which constrain the use of arguments and the particular form of discourse.[18] The constraining force of legal arguments might even be a good thing normatively speaking, shielding discourses from open power-play, at least in a situation where actors are engaged in a Habermasian version of deliberation or "communicative action."[19] Jutta Brunnée and Stephen Toope point to the interactional elements of legal discourse, which create "incremental contestation" rather than open contestation of a norm's validity, which "helps to account for the robustness of law, and its capacity to provide stability."[20] Similarly, Bower stresses that legal discourse is perceived by actors of international politics as "more technocratic and impartial in contrast to an unregulated political realm in which material power is expected to dominate."[21] Use of legal discourse might therefore shield international norms and institutions from more radical challenges and norm weakening.[22]

By pointing out these particular effects of legal argumentation, Bower, at the same time, claims there is a clear dichotomy between legal arguments and "politicised forms of rhetoric."[23] This is too simplistic a classification: it suggests actors in international politics use either legal arguments or politicized arguments—there is nothing in between. Steven Ratner gives a more nuanced overview.[24] He studies how

[15] Christian Reus-Smit, ed., *The Politics of International Law* (Cambridge: Cambridge University Press, 2004), 37.

[16] Ingo Venzke, chapter 2, in this volume.

[17] Adam Bower, "Arguing with Law: Strategic Legal Argumentation, US Diplomacy, and Debates over the International Criminal Court," *Review of International Studies* 41 (2015): 337, 339.

[18] Ian Johnstone, "Security Council Deliberations: The Power of the Better Argument," *European Journal of International Law* 14 (2003): 437.

[19] *Id.* 453–454.

[20] Brunnée and Toope, *supra* note 14, at 73.

[21] Bower, *supra* note 17, at 346.

[22] Bower, *supra* note 14; Jutta Brunnée and Stephen J. Toope, "Constructivism and International Law," in *Interdisciplinary Perspectives on International Law and International Relations. The State of the Art*, edited by Jeffrey L. Dunoff and Mark A. Pollack (Cambridge: Cambridge University Press, 2013), 119. Brunnée and Toope point out that, in this field of research, we learn much about the processes of legal argumentation, but much less about the nature of obligation which gives legal arguments their special authority.

[23] Bower, *supra* note 17, at 343.

[24] Steven R. Ratner, "Law Promotion Beyond Law Talk: The Red Cross, Persuasion, and the Laws of War," *European Journal of International Law* 22 (2011): 459; Steven R. Ratner, "Persuading to Comply: On the Deployment and Avoidance of Legal Argumentation," in *Interdisciplinary Perspectives on International Law and International Relations*, *supra* note 22, at 568.

norm proponents (such as the International Committee of the Red Cross (ICRC) or the Organization for Security and Co-operation in Europe) use different types of arguments and vary their strategy according to setting and context—he distinguishes humanitarian, political, economic, pragmatic, moral, and customary justifications.[25] He would still refer to these justifications as being part of an "indirect" legal discourse, as the actors aim at creating compliance with the law. They are using other types of arguments to achieve this beyond the courtroom.[26] We can imagine informal meetings of ICRC employees with non-state armed groups where conversations hardly refer to "law" at all.[27] Ratner claims that the more public and the more legally embedded a context, the more likely becomes direct legal justification:

> Those disputes currently governed by a thick legal regime are likely to elicit more dense and direct legal argumentation by persuading entities than are other disputes, where greater legal leeway will result in reliance on alternative forms of argument.[28]

In sum, international law and IR scholars assume that legal argumentation comes with a perceived special authority, which might even tame more radical positions. Legal argumentation, they contend, also dominates institutionalized international contexts. Others argue from a more critical perspective that legal argumentation is far from a shield against open power-play. They highlight the power relations and biases which shape legal discourses and legal proceedings,[29] as well as the contested nature of legal discourse, which uses a "shared" language of authority while remaining at the same time always ambiguous and contested. David Kennedy explores this point in depth: on the one hand, legal knowledge brings about a depoliticization of "rule," pressing it into a "language of law."[30] On the other hand, professional knowledge and legal expertise are constantly used in the context of struggles over policy.

B. The Power of Scientific Argumentation

A comparable debate exists on the role of scientific arguments in the context of environmental governance. Scholars attach similar functions to scientific as to legal argumentation.[31] Like legal expertise, scientific expertise is a source of authority and

[25] Slightly different, Dimitrov distinguishes pragmatic, moral, legal, procedural, and ideological argumentation. Radoslav Dimitrov, "The Politics of Persuasion: UN Climate Change Negotiations," in *Handbook of Global Environmental Politics*, edited by Peter Dauvergne (Cheltenham, UK; Northampton, MA: Edward Elgar Publishing, 2012), 72, 78.

[26] Ratner, "Persuading to Comply," *supra* note 24.

[27] Hyeran Jo, chapter 9, in this volume.

[28] Ratner, "Persuading to Comply," *supra* note 24, at 581–582. See also Steven Ratner, chapter 6, in this volume.

[29] Adriana Sinclair, "Law, Caution: Towards a Better Understanding of Law for IR Theorists," *Review of International Studies* 37 (2011): 1095.

[30] David Kennedy, *A World of Struggle: How Power, Law and Expertise Shape Global Political Economy* (Woodstock, UK: Princeton University Press, 2016).

[31] This debate in IR is linked to a wider branch of research dealing with the field of knowledge and expertise, e.g., Karin Knorr-Cetina, *Epistemic Cultures: How the Sciences Make Knowledge* (Cambridge, MA: Harvard University Press, 1999). Scholars would point out that knowledge and expertise are not objective but are only perceived as such by actors in a relational process; see Annabelle Littoz-Monnet,

legitimacy. This expertise, the argument goes, helps an "actor's voice" to be "heard, recognized, and believed."[32] Scholars have, for example, pointed to the power of epistemic communities. These are networks "of professionals with recognized expertise and competence in a particular domain and an authoritative claim to policy-relevant knowledge within that domain or issue area,"[33] whose science-based arguments have particular influence. Researchers were interested in understanding when such knowledge became influential and what type of institutional process increased its authority.[34]

Like critical research on international law, science and technology studies have criticized this approach to studying epistemic networks as being too static. Science and technology studies are interested in how knowledge is created and (re)presented as authoritative and uncontested.[35] They try to uncover the ambiguities, political choices, and contestation that are hidden within scientific knowledge and arguments when they enter policy processes. One well-studied example is the work of the Intergovernmental Panel on Climate Change (IPCC), an organization collecting and presenting expert knowledge on climate change to policymakers. While the production of documents such as reports and indicators involves struggles and contestation, this "knowledge" only becomes authoritative when it is presented as univocal to the public.[36]

The underlying assumptions are similar to those that underlie legal argumentation: scientific arguments (if presented as consensual and unambiguous[37]) create legitimacy and authority for policy claims—in particular in the field of environmental governance. Scientific discourse is said to have constraining powers similar to legal discourse. Moreover, as critical approaches point out in both fields, legal and scientific expertise are presented as being fixed and objective, while in fact they are constantly contested. Interestingly, in the field of environmental governance, we find both logics—legal and scientific—to be highly intertwined.[38] Institutions in this field use different types of scientific bodies or advisory boards, which have "the difficult task of translating complex scientific findings into legal prescriptions."[39]

"Production and Uses of Expertise by International Bureaucracies," in *The Politics of Expertise in International Organizations. How International Bureaucracies Produce and Mobilize Knowledge*, edited by Annabelle Littoz-Monnet (Abingdon: Routledge, 2017), 1, 2.

[32] Michael N. Barnett and Martha Finnemore, *Rules for the World: International Organizations in Global Politics* (Ithaca: Cornell University Press, 2004), 20.

[33] Peter M. Haas, "Introduction: Epistemic Communities and International Policy Coordination," *International Organization* 46 (1992): 1, 3.

[34] Aarti Gupta et al., "Science Networks," in *Global Environmental Governance Reconsidered. Earth System Governance*, edited by Frank Biermann and Philipp Pattberg (Cambridge, MA: MIT Press, 2012), 69; Peter Haas and Casey Stevens, "Organized Science, Usable Knowledge, and Multilateral Environmental Governance," in *Governing the Air: The Dynamics of Science, Policy, and Citizen Interaction*, edited by Rolf Lidskog and Göran Sundqvist (Cambridge, MA: MIT Press, 2011), 125.

[35] Sheila Jasanoff, "Science and Norms in Global Environmental Regimes," in *Earthly Goods. Environmental Change and Social Justice*, edited by Fen Osler Hampson and Judith Reppy (Ithaca, NY: Cornell University Press, 1996), 173.

[36] Beck et al., *supra* note 1.

[37] Gupta et al., *supra* note 34.

[38] Perez, *supra* note 2.

[39] *Id.* 395.

Why do we commonly differentiate the two, however, rather than treat both as the same type of argumentation? Law might be a more organized professional discipline, where substance, as well as the processes of teaching and practicing international law, might be more standardized (while international law theory is, of course, very diverse). "Science," as such, is much more disparate. Yet, like law, "science" is linked to different disciplines or thematic areas with specific professional backgrounds, preferred theoretical approaches and standards, and intersubjective ways of sense-making. These backgrounds often conflict in the context of environmental international organizations. One example is the IWC's Scientific Committee, which went from being a meeting of statisticians to one that was also frequented by marine biologists. The two groups were shaped by different professional cultures and approaches which regularly clashed in meetings.

Others point to different types of "truth-finding" linked to science or law: the first being uncoordinated, network-like inquiry and deliberation, the other being hierarchical.[40] Again, this does not seem to describe accurately much legal argumentation in the international context, which often takes place (at least formally) in nonhierarchical settings. Still, in an ideal version, "[e]pistemic authority . . . emerges spontaneously through the network dynamic of scientific contestation. Legal authority is [at least often] grounded . . . in formal constitutional structures."[41] Legal argumentation is the art of interpretation of legal norms,[42] while scientific argumentation relates to the process of research and knowledge production. It is linked to a dynamic and contested process of producing (limited) intersubjective validity of certain claims. While perhaps functioning in a similar way, the reference points (legal norms versus knowledge production) and the logic of contestation differ.

Yet which of these two sources of authority do norm challengers use in their arguments in the context of environmental governance? Do challengers in a "thick" regime context such as the IWC make use of mostly legal arguments? Or is environmental governance dominated by science-based arguments? And what effect does the use of one or the other have on debates?

IV. Division of Labor: Emotional and Technical

To answer these questions, I have analyzed the debates inside the IWC. This is the central international institution dealing with whaling, since the coming into force of the commercial whaling ban in 1986.[43] I qualitatively coded contestation of the whaling moratorium by IWC member states as well as contestation aimed at the widening of existing exemptions (use of scientific permits, Indigenous whaling, as well as a proposal of an exemption for small-type coastal whaling by Japan) as reproduced in

[40] *Id.* 396.

[41] *Id.* 397.

[42] Mary Ellen O'Connell, *The Art of Law in the International Community* (Cambridge University Press, 2019). See also Ingo Venzke, chapter 2, and Ian Johnstone, chapter 7, both in this volume.

[43] The Convention on International Trade in Endangered Species of Wild Fauna and Flora deals with trade of endangered species, including whales. It also follows IWC decisions on whaling issues.

verbatim records and the chair's reports of IWC meetings between 1986 and 2016.[44] This chapter therefore focuses on argumentation by state representatives in a multilateral forum challenging an existing regulation. Taking up Johnstone and Ratner's list of potential purposes set out in chapter 1 of this volume: the challengers only in a limited way want to *persuade* others of their position, as they do not expect that to happen in this forum. Rather, they want to *legitimate their actions* (whaling), *resist pressure* (to stop whaling), change the narrative that the pro-whaling states are the "bad guys" (*change the normative climate*), and *assert authority* in their domestic audiences.

I distinguish three types of argumentation, which I found in all four different lines of dispute (the whaling moratorium, use of scientific permits, Indigenous whaling, as well as a proposed exemption for small-type coastal whaling by Japan). *Legal arguments* are a first category of argumentation, using the "maximum" definition offered by Johnstone and Ratner in chapter 1. This includes (1) references to the *substantive dimension*, thus references to law, rights, or broad paradigms, such as sustainability (as, for example, laid down in the Rio Declaration on Environment and Development from 1992), human and Indigenous rights, state sovereignty, or the right to self-determination. This also includes (2) a *procedural/institutional dimension*, referring, that is, to the necessary institutional process for making a decision, that activities were transparent and complied with existing rules, that necessary information was submitted, or that there were institutional similarities between different kinds of whaling. This also includes criticism of certain institutional processes, for example, as being too bureaucratic. I distinguish these from a second category, *scientific arguments*, arguing, for example, that specific whale stocks were healthy and could be used sustainably; or that certain data had been verified. I also code an argument as "scientific" if it posited that scientific "back-up" existed for certain claims (for example, by independent research or by the IWC Scientific Committee). A third category I examined were other *normative or policy-related arguments*, referring, for example, to the socioeconomic situations of hunters or local communities, or the humane treatment of animals, but also references to coercive power and colonialism (see Annex).

Figure 13.2 presents the percentage of contracting states that used the three types in contestation statements at IWC meetings over time—separately presenting the substantive and procedural arguments.[45] At a general level, we observe that challengers of the whaling moratorium grew more and more dissatisfied in the 1990s and early 2000s. Japan also proactively tried to win new IWC members to support pro-whaling positions (as did the anti-whaling side for anti-whaling positions). Overall, an increasing share of contracting states contested the whaling moratorium. This culminated in an IWC meeting in 2006, where the pro-whaling position briefly gained a majority. The subsequent drop in contestation is due to a joint negotiation process which started in 2008. This joint search for a compromise failed at the IWC 2010

[44] The IWC met annually until 2012 and changed to biannual meetings since then. IWC meetings had verbatim records up to the meeting in 2000. Later, only audio live recordings and chair reports of the meetings exist. I have opted to code the chair reports—which, I admit, give a highly summarized version of state arguments.

[45] 1994 is not included as the existing verbatim record is not complete.

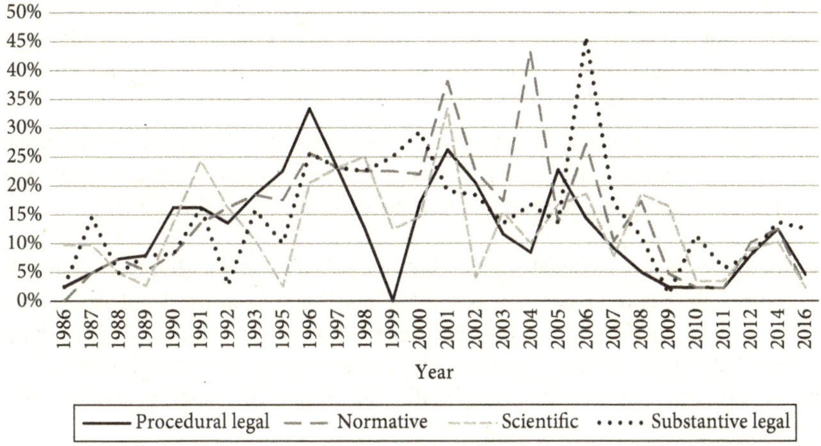

Figure 13.2 Percentage of contracting states using specific type of contestation at IWC meetings

meeting, however. Afterward, contestation picked up again but is not back to the level of the early 2000s. As a consequence, Japan finally decided to quit the IWC in 2018.[46]

With regard to the types of argumentation used, we observe a mishmash (see Figure 13.2). There is no single dominant line of contestation—members neither use only legal nor only scientific arguments, although legal arguments (procedural and substantive) are more common.

Indeed, in contrast to the expectation that we would observe more direct legal argumentation in dense legal environments, normative arguments—referring to cultural practices or suffering of local communities—are an important part of contestation and were used more frequently when the dispute over whaling heated up in the early 2000s. The specifics of the whaling issue—including both a high level of politicization and of legal vagueness—might explain the divergences from the theoretical assumptions about legal argumentation. It seems that the whaling ban is less a fight about lawful versus unlawful behavior (perhaps because the legal situation is so fuzzy, as discussed below), but more of an issue of "hearts and minds," of moral right versus moral wrong on both sides, of killing sentient beings versus making use of natural food resources.

The statements using normative justifications remain at a general level and use very emotional language, often referring to hardship, coercion, and imperialism. Examples are the following:

> As long history has shown, Iceland will not yield to any threat of political compulsion or economic coercion. (Iceland, Verbatim Records 1987, 20)

[46] See also Nicole Deitelhoff and Lisbeth Zimmermann, "Things We Lost in the Fire: How Different Types of Contestation Affect the Robustness of International Norms," *International Studies Review* 22 (2020): 51.

> We express our sympathy and understanding for the Japanese communities' people for experiencing a diverse effect, distress and hardship in culture, way of life, religion and so on caused by giving up community-based whaling heritage since [the] moratorium. (China, IWC Verbatim Record 1994, 62)
>
> Japan mentioned that some believe whaling to be immoral. It noted that the coastal whaling communities, while taking whales, also respect them and furthermore do not try to impose their own morals on others. (Japan, Chair's Report 2006, 28–29)

While we might expect legal argumentation to deal mostly with more technical interpretations of existing rules, this is not the case for substantive legal arguments in the IWC context. In the IWC, substantive legal arguments remain at a highly abstract level, similar to normative arguments, often referring to cultural rights or sustainability as main paradigms, only occasionally pointing to the existing specific exemptions. Examples being the following:

> [W]e feel ... the need of coastal people to utilise the marine resources that can be harvested sustainably is a fundamental principle in international law which is a question that this organisation cannot re-write. There's a fact that both in the Convention of the Law of the Sea and in more recent soft law documents like the agenda 21 from Rio, the principle of sustainable use is the over-riding principle. (Norway, IWC Verbatim Report, 1997, 69–70)
>
> Norway no longer accepts what she perceives as cultural imperialism imposed by the majority of the members of the IWC on the local communities of the nation and peoples who want to exercise their sovereign cultural right. (Norway, IWC Verbatim Record 1992, 21)

Legal procedural arguments and scientific arguments, in contrast, were mostly used in debates about specific proposals and resolutions on the widening of Indigenous hunting quotas, or the detailed nature of scientific whaling:

> I simply want to say that from a Danish point of view we see absolutely no problem in increased catch limits for aboriginal subsistence whaling ... if they meet recognised needs in the aboriginal populations. (Denmark, IWC Verbatim Record 1995, 150)
>
> [T]he IWC has no conservation reason to reject Japan's request since the North Pacific minke whale stock is healthy. (Japan, Chair's Report 2001, 24)
>
> A humble number of one hundred animals will be sampled and these numbers of samples in no way produce adverse effect to the stocks that was so reported and discussed and recognised by the Scientific Committee. (Japan, IWC Verbatim Record, 1997, 140)

In sum, substantive legal argumentation and normative argumentation were often used by states to formulate their general fundamental opposition to the moratorium and to resist pressure. States furthered their interpretation, legitimated their actions, and voiced fundamental opposition to the moratorium by prioritizing sustainable use over preservation. They also used rather emotional and expressive language for this, describing themselves as victims in the IWC.[47] A taming effect of using substantive legal anguage could therefore not be observed. This pattern might be due to the highly politicized context with rather vague legal rules.

Yet, at the same time, detailed debates on policy proposals and resolutions enabling or constraining specific behavior were also taking place. Here, contesting states were using procedural legal and scientific argumentation to legitimate their positions, in line with the procedural requirements in the IWC.[48] Types of argumentation therefore reflected a division of labor, where normative and substantive legal argumentation were doing the emotional[49] and legal procedural and scientific argumentation the technical work.

V. Legal or Scientific Argumentation: Comparing Country Strategies

A comparison of strategies by states which not only contest but openly evade the moratorium on commercial whaling can also give us some insight into the effects of different types of argumentation.

Of course, as I have shown above, the main pro-whaling countries—Iceland, Norway, and Japan—all use a mixture of arguments to justify their positions in the IWC. They differ, however, with regard to which strategy they used for evading the moratorium. While Japan invoked the exemption for scientific whaling for thirty years, Norway and Iceland have both stopped their scientific whaling programs and nowadays invoke their objection to the moratorium to support whaling. As the following section will show, the effects of these different strategies were very much shaped by the institutional settings available to consider and respond to the different types of argumentation.

A. Scientific Whaling as Japanese Strategy

After withdrawing its objection to the moratorium in the 1980s,[50] Japan decided to use the ICRW exemption on scientific permits to keep alive a whaling industry (which did not succeed in the long term, however, and turned into a heavily subsidized enterprise). These scientific programs have been very controversial. Since the start of these programs, critical voices have complained that the quotas given out by the Japanese government for these hunts were not scientifically justified, that findings of these programs were not necessary for management decisions, and that lethal whaling was not essential for answering the scientific questions of the programs. Moreover, they argued that whale meat from these hunts should not enter Japanese markets.[51]

[47] On this expressive, emotional aspect of law, see also Wouter Werner, chapter 10, in this volume.
[48] See also Bruno Stagno-Ugarte, chapter 8, in this volume.
[49] See also Wouter Werner, chapter 10, in this volume.
[50] On the US-Japanese negotiations, see M. Strausz, "Executives, Legislatures, and Whales: The Birth of Japan's Scientific Whaling Regime," *International Relations of the Asia-Pacific* 14 (2014): 455.
[51] E.g., Phillip J. Clapham et al., "Whaling as Science," *BioScience* 53 (2003): 210.

Japan has kept up the programs despite strong criticism and has significantly increased the number of caught whales as well as the targeted species (from some stocks which are considered rather healthy, such as minke whales in the Antarctic, to some which are considered more endangered, like humpbacks) in the early 2000s.[52]

Given that Japan used the exemption for scientific whaling, much of the debates focused on the scientific value of the Japanese whaling. The legal basis for the exemption, a very imprecise permission for states to hand out permits for scientific whaling, sparked little controversy—and the sovereign right to give out such permits was regularly invoked by Japan. The discussions instead focused on the scientific value of whaling, which, critics argued, was a necessary condition to use this exemption.

While the ICRW does not name an institutional format to discuss scientific whaling permits, the IWC, as an environmental governance institution, is centrally built on the logic of scientific advice. This led to intense debates at the annual meetings of the IWC Scientific Committee as well as at the general IWC meetings on the scientific value of the Japanese research. Huge delegations—in particular, from Australia, the United Kingdom, and the United States on one side, and Japan on the other—waged a rather repetitive war of scientific arguments. Of course, these scientific discourses link back to law: if the scientific value cannot be proven, the Japanese use of scientific permits might be illegal—although the IWC itself has no institutional mechanisms to make such a decision. Just the existence of the institutional format to process this type of argumentation, however, put Japan in a defensive position.

After a major renegotiation process on the commercial whaling ban failed in 2010 ("Future of the IWC" process), Australia brought the issue before the International Court of Justice (ICJ).[53] The Court decided that the program in question (JARPA II) was not for the "purposes of scientific research."[54] This was not a complete victory of the anti-whaling side, however. The ICJ did not rule that Japan could no longer give out scientific permits (in fact, Japan restarted two adapted programs shortly after the decision), nor did it ban whale meat from such hunts from entering the Japanese market. Still, while the legal decision did not immediately stop Japanese scientific whaling, the importance of these programs being "for the purposes of scientific research" was invoked centrally by anti-whaling states at an IWC meeting following the decision that even intensified the pressure on Japan.[55]

Both the long-term struggle over the scientific merits of the Japanese whaling programs in the IWC and the ICJ decision of the importance of "the purpose of science" put Japan in a position of constant justification of its programs in the IWC

[52] Numbers slightly declined in the 2010s. Commercial whaling quotas by the government given out after Japan's IWC withdrawal are also lower than the quotas in the early 2000s.

[53] On possible motivations for this move, see Shirley V. Scott, "Australia's Decision to Initiate Whaling in the Antarctic: Winning the Case versus Resolving the Dispute," *Australian Journal of International Affairs* 68 (2013): 1. New Zealand joined in 2012 with a Declaration of Intervention; see Whaling in the Antarctic (Australia v. Japan), Declaration of Intervention of the Government of New Zealand, Nov. 20, 2012, https://www.icj-cij.org/files/case-related/148/17256.pdf.

[54] Whaling in the Antarctic (Australia v. Japan, New Zealand Intervening), 2014 ICJ Rep., at 226. On the decision, see also Richard Caddell, "Science Friction: Antarctic Research Whaling and the International Court of Justice," *Journal of Environmental Law* 26 (2014): 331.

[55] See IWC Chair's Report 2016 (6.2 as well as 14). Anti-whalers also used the momentum to establish a Working Group reviewing Special Permit Programs outside the Scientific Committee.

context. This might have affected the final decision of Japan to withdraw from the IWC in 2018.

B. Legal Objections as Norwegian and Icelandic Strategy

Norway and Iceland chose a different strategy. The ICRW includes the possibility of lodging objections against decisions of the IWC amending the IWC schedule (ICRW, Article V(3)). Both Norway and Iceland first lodged objections against the moratorium decision. Iceland withdrew this objection in the 1980s, based on threats of sanctions by the US and consumer boycotts.[56] Norway, in contrast, held tight and left the objection in place. Both countries halted commercial whaling—and started small research whaling programs.

When it became clear to both countries that the anti-whaling states were not willing to lift the moratorium in the 1990s, and that giving out scientific permits was highly controversial inside the IWC, they both reacted. Norway, as a surprise to the anti-whaling countries, restarted commercial whaling.[57] Iceland withdrew from the treaty in 1992 but rejoined in 2002—this time with a new objection against the moratorium in place. This move has been disputed. It is the only new membership the IWC plenary voted upon.[58] IWC members still disagree about whether the re-entry of Iceland with an objection in place was legal. In the following years, Iceland first started a scientific whaling program and then restarted commercial whaling in 2008.

Norway and Iceland mostly pointed to their objection: commercial whaling was linked to their sovereign right and not illegal. Both Norway and Iceland emphasized that they supported whaling activities based on a sustainability paradigm embedded in other regimes of environmental governance (see Section V.A). They fought off criticism by their reference to law.[59]

In this case, a specific institutional format to deal with this legal strategy of evasion was missing. The vague formulation of the ICRW (allowing explicitly for objections) made it difficult to challenge the legal argumentation. Japan became enmeshed in a detailed battle about the scientific quality of its programs. In contrast, Norway and Iceland have seen less direct attacks on their whaling programs by the other IWC members—they are hardly dealt with at IWC meetings. In the 1990s, Norway's resumption of commercial whaling saw several resolutions condemning this behavior.

[56] See Anne Brydon, "The Predicament of Nature: Keiko the Whale and the Cultural Politics of Whaling in Iceland," *Anthropological Quarterly* 79 (2006): 225, 231–235; Arne Kalland, *Unveiling the Whale: Discourses on Whales and Whaling, Vol. 12, Studies in Environmental Anthropology and Ethnobiology* (New York: Berghahn, 2009), 140.

[57] Steinar Andresen, "Science and Policy in the International Whaling Commission," in *Contesting Global Environmental Knowledge, Norms, and Governance, Transforming Environmental Politics and Policy*, edited by M.J. Peterson (Abingdon, Oxon, New York: Routledge, 2019), 110, 121.

[58] See IWC Chair's Report 2002 and IWC Special Meeting Chair's Report 2002.

[59] E.g., Nick Mackie, "Norwegian Whalers' Determined Position," *The Guardian*, Oct. 14, 2002, http://news.bbc.co.uk/2/hi/science/nature/2326461.stm. Julia Jabour and Rachel Lorna Johnstone, "Why Iceland Is Set to Resume Whaling Despite International Opposition," *The Conversation*, May 14, 2018, https://theconversation.com/why-iceland-is-set-to-resume-whaling-despite-international-opposition-95642.

The condemnation died down, however.[60] Similarly, Iceland's resumption of whaling saw diplomatic condemnation[61]—but hardly any open shaming by other IWC member states. Similarly, direct action by nongovernmental organizations targeted Norway and Iceland until the end of the 1980s and 1990s. Yet, since the early 2000s, action by Sea Shepherd and Greenpeace[62] only focused on the Japanese scientific whaling program in the Antarctic.[63] This difference is not due to different levels of whaling. While Japanese research whaling was the most important whaling activity in the early 2000s, this was no longer the case in the 2010s. In this period, Icelandic and Norwegian commercial whaling dominated.[64]

Of course, there might be other reasons why Iceland and Norway saw fewer attacks. In the early 2000s, their programs were smaller and mostly focused on minke whales, which were not considered endangered in the targeted stocks. They also kept these activities to their exclusive economic zones. Some participants in the processes argue that the lesser targeting of Norway, for example, is due to political dealmaking in the background—when the United States needed support to uphold Indigenous whaling in exchange for fewer direct attacks on Norway.[65] Still, it seems that the use of the different evasion strategies led to the prevalence of different types of argumentation: scientific in the case of Japan and legal in the case of Norway and Iceland. The institutional structures of the IWC shaped how other states were able to react: the perceived "misuse" of science by Japan led to constant attacks in the institutional venue specifically dedicated to scientific advisory work in the IWC. Showing the priority of the scientific basis for their programs was certainly difficult for Japan. This situation, together with the decision by the ICJ on scientific whaling, surely influenced Japan's withdrawal from the IWC in 2018. A similar forum was not available to counter the legal argumentation by Norway and Iceland—and IWC member states also had less opportunity to successfully counter the legal interpretation.

VI. Conclusion

In sum, constructivist research in both IR and international law has lately focused on the specific power of legal argumentation, often focusing on its "taming" effects.

60 IWC resolutions are available at https://archive.iwc.int/pages/search.php?search=%21collection72&k=.

61 See Wikileaks Cable: 09STATE99783, 24.09.2009; Wikileaks Cable: 09REYKJAVIK37, 20.02.2009; Wikileaks Cable: 09REYKJAVIK36, 18.02.2009.

62 Greenpeace stopped direct action in the 1990s and stopped following Japanese whaling ships in 2008. Justin McCurry, "Greenpeace Calls Off Japanese Anti-Whaling Mission," *The Guardian*, Nov. 4, 2008, https://www.theguardian.com/environment/2008/nov/04/whaling-japan; see also Rik Scarce, *Eco-Warriors: Understanding the Radical Environmental Movement* (London: Routledge, 2016), ch. 4.

63 Anti-whaling NGOs of course keep up the shaming of Norwegian and Icelandic whaling, Sandra Altherr, "Iceland's Whaling Comeback: Preparations for the Resumption of Whaling," http://www.hsi.org/assets/pdfs/icelands_whaling_comeback_pt1.pdf; Sandra Altherr et al., "Frozen in Time: How Modern Norway Clings to Its Whaling Past," https://awionline.org/sites/default/files/uploads/documents/AWI-ML-NorwayReport-2016.pdf.

64 Figures on the different types of whaling are available at https://iwc.int/whaling.

65 Interviews with former/current members of Norwegian and US delegation to IWC at the IWC 2016 and IWC Scientific Committee meeting 2016 in Slovenia.

In the field of environmental governance, IR research has also studied the power of scientific argumentation. Both occur in international organizations dealing with environmental governance. If states challenge international rules in such institutional settings, which type of argumentation do they use and with what effects?

Based on the analysis of the disputes over whaling in the IWC, I showed that legal and scientific argumentation were frequently used to add authority to positions, yet in unexpected ways. In the highly politicized case of whaling with vague rules, normative arguments were more widespread than existing research would assume for a formalized setting like the IWC. But also substantive legal arguments were often used in an emotional way to justify the general opposition of the whaling moratorium and to express how "victimized" the pro-whaling state felt. Thus, legal argumentation served as a way of expressing fundamental opposition. The technical debates on resolutions and policy decisions, in contrast, were mostly shaped by procedural legal and scientific argumentation.

When comparing strategies by the major whaling countries—Norway, Iceland, and Japan—to evade the moratorium, we see major differences. Norway and Iceland focused on legal discourse by emphasizing their objections to the moratorium. In contrast, Japan got enmeshed in a discourse about science when using the exemption for scientific permits. Norway and Iceland saw much less condemnation than Japan. Japan has become the major "rogue state" in the whaling debate—it had to face endless challenges to the scientific merits of its programs at every IWC meeting and has been the only target of direct action by Greenpeace and Sea Shepherd since the early 2000s. A reaction to this was the Japanese withdrawal from the IWC in 2018. While there are certainly many other reasons for different treatment of Norway, Iceland, and Japan, the specific institutional structure of the IWC, as a resource management/environmental protection organization based importantly on scientific advice, could be used for an ongoing fight over "science" much better than for a fight over "law."

These findings enlarge the debate on the power of legal argumentation. Existing research on international law often contrasts legal argumentation dichotomously with "politicized" argumentation. This contribution shows that it is important to compare the usage of several types of argumentation, including scientific, policy-related, or normative. We currently know too little about the logic and authority of these diverse types of argumentation in different contexts. Yet as this chapter showed, there is a surprising amount of similarities between legal and other types of argumentation. Also, actors do not prefer one type of argumentation over the other but use them in a "division of labor" to achieve different objectives. Future research should therefore focus less on the "uniqueness" of legal argumentation and explore the joint production of authority of diverse types of argumentation, the interplay as well as similarities and differences.

Furthermore, the effects of these types of argumentation are not straightforward but depend on many conditions. We need to explore what kind of expertise comes with authority in specific policy fields (environmental, humanitarian, security). We might, for example, observe that political arguments and those that refer to national security are more accepted and widespread in debates about arms treaties than in debates about humanitarian aid. Moreover, do we observe dominant transnational expert groups for a specific governance issue—which might determine if certain types of argumentation have more authority? For example, when arguing over the control of drugs, using legal arguments might be more widespread in the context of the UN Office on Drugs and Crime, where people come from a criminal justice background, than in the World Health Organization, where people prefer a focus on health and science and reject a "criminalization" of the issue. Last but not least, what specific setting the debate is embedded in might centrally shape the types of arguments used and how arguments are dealt with and reacted to; relevant factors could be the institutional setting, the precision of underlying international rules, as well as the level of politicization of issues, as we have seen in the case of whaling. In sum, such a comparative research program, bridging several research traditions and exploring legal argumentation in different contexts, can expand and deepen existing productive research at the intersection of international law and international relations.

Annex

Coding for Different Types of Argumentation

Categories	Arguments Coded
Scientific	Support from Scientific Committee for whaling
	Management method verified scientifically
	Many stocks healthy; sustainable whaling possible
	Scientific data sufficient for whaling
	Other scientific data on whaling biased
	International scientific backing for whaling
	Lethal research on whales necessary
Legal (substantive)	Conservation/sustainable use as central paradigm
	Development as central paradigm
	Priority of state sovereignty
	Priority of self-determination
	Priority of food security
	Priority of cultural identity
	Priority of human rights
	Whaling in line with existing IWC rules
Legal (procedural)	National monitoring mechanisms in place
	All procedural aspects fulfilled
	Precedents exist
	Necessary transparency exists
	Avoid overbureaucratization
	Procedural standards too high to implement

Categories	Arguments Coded
Normative/policy	Negative effects of moratorium too high
	Moratorium the product of power asymmetries/colonialism/coercion
	Moratorium destroys culture
	Moratorium brings about human suffering
	Whaling not in humane
	Health and nutritional needs of population more important

14

International Legal Argumentation on Intellectual Property

Two Snaphots from the World Intellectual Property Organization

*Edward Kwakwa**

I. Introduction

International legal argumentation outside the courtroom appears in most, if not all, areas of international law. This chapter will focus on international legal argumentation as it plays out in the field of international intellectual property (IP) law. In particular, it addresses the process of the Uniform Domain Name Dispute Resolution Policy (UDRP) at the World Intellectual Property Organization (WIPO) and looks at the WIPO Intergovernmental Committee on Intellectual Property and Genetic Resources, Traditional Knowledge and Folklore (IGC). The IGC is a body at WIPO that is, in accordance with its mandate, undertaking text-based negotiations with the objective of reaching agreement on a text(s) of an international legal instrument(s) to ensure the effective protection of traditional knowledge (TK), traditional cultural expressions (TCEs), and genetic resources (GRs).

The choice of the UDRP and the IGC is aimed at exploring legal argumentation in the IP context in two different but somewhat related settings: the UDRP constitutes a quasi-judicial or alternative form of dispute resolution, while the IGC is an intergovernmental committee that has an explicit treaty-making or other norm-setting mandate. Both examples are processes administered by WIPO, and they also represent two of the most high-profile and most publicized WIPO processes that entail extensive legal argumentation outside the courtroom. As will be shown in this chapter, in the case of the UDRP, legal argumentation invokes strict administrative and quasi-judicial criteria that individuals and companies must follow in order to enhance the chance of winning their cases brought before the UDRP. As a result of legal arguments used by trademark owners and the tendency of UDRP Panelists to follow earlier Panelists' decisions, a body of jurisprudence has been established that facilitates greater certainty and predictability of decisions under the UDRP. In the case of the IGC, while WIPO

* The views expressed here are my personal views and are not necessarily shared by the World Intellectual Property Organization or its member states.

Edward Kwakwa, *International Legal Argumentation on Intellectual Property* In: *Talking International Law.*
Edited by: Ian Johnstone and Steven Ratner, Oxford University Press. © Edward Kwakwa 2021.
DOI: 10.1093/oso/9780197588437.003.0014

member states and other non-state observers are striving to agree on the adoption of an international legal instrument, the arguments used are not only legal but also moral, philosophical, economic, and other types of arguments. While argumentation is yet to result in concrete international legal outcomes, it has already significantly shaped national and regional legislation on the protection of TK.

The chapter is organized as follows. Section II provides a brief description of WIPO, the main multilateral organization responsible for the promotion of the protection of IP; Section III describes the subject of IP in the context of international legal argumentation in general. Based on this, Section IV analyzes the UDRP and the IGC in the context of international legal argumentation outside the courtroom. The chapter ends with some concluding observations.

For purposes of this chapter, I use the term "argument" to refer to a statement that is used to try to convince others about the correctness of one's position or opinion. The word "legal" simply describes arguments as they relate to the law. Thus, I use "legal argumentation" to refer to a statement or set of statements, frequently but not always relating to the law, that are used for various and varied reasons by different actors.[1]

II. The World Intellectual Property Organization

The Convention Establishing the World Intellectual Property Organization (the WIPO Convention) was signed in 1967 and entered into force in 1970.[2] Although the WIPO Convention was signed in 1967, the Organization's origins predate the WIPO Convention to 1883 and 1886, the years in which the Paris Convention for the Protection of Industrial Property[3] and the Berne Convention for the Protection of Literary and Artistic Works were adopted.[4]

WIPO is dedicated to promoting innovation and creativity for the economic, social, and cultural development of all countries, through a balanced and effective international IP system. It is responsible for promoting the protection of IP throughout the world and for the administration of various multilateral treaties that address the legal and administrative aspects of IP. The Secretariat of WIPO comprises about thirteen hundred staff members from some one hundred twenty-five countries. The budget of the Organization for the 2020–2021 biennium is approximately US$900 million.[5]

[1] Actors engaging in international legal argumentation include national as well as international state and non-state entities. Such actors often use legal argumentation for a variety of reasons, such as: to persuade; in pursuance of a mandate; or to try to change or affect the normative climate. See generally Ian Johnstone and Steven Ratner, chapter 1, in this volume.

[2] Convention Establishing the World Intellectual Property Organization, July 14, 1967, 828 UNTS 3 (last amended Sept. 28, 1979). For a detailed account of the history of WIPO, see generally World Intellectual Property Organization, *Introduction to Intellectual Property, Theory and Practice* (Geneva: WIPO, 1997).

[3] Paris Convention for the Protection of Industrial Property, Mar. 20, 1883, 828 UNTS 305 (last revised July 14, 1967).

[4] Berne Convention for the Protection of Literary and Artistic Works, Sept. 9, 1886, 828 UNTS 221 (last revised July 24, 1971).

[5] The equivalent in Swiss Francs is CHF 882.8 million. See Program and Budget 2020–2021, https://www.wipo.int/export/sites/www/about-wipo/en/budget/pdf/budget_2020_2021.pdf.

Unlike the rest of the UN system, WIPO is largely self-financing. The Organization generates about 95 percent of its income from fees paid by private sector users of the international registration services provided by the WIPO Secretariat.[6] Less than 5 percent of the Organization's income is received from its 193 member states, and the remaining income comes from the sale of WIPO publications, fees related to the arbitration and mediation services provided by WIPO, and interest earnings.[7]

III. IP and International Legal Argumentation

The international community has witnessed a phenomenal increase in the global innovative economy. This has been accompanied by a concomitant increase in the importance of IP rights, thus increasing the number of worldwide IP assets and registrations for protection of such assets. Quite naturally, this increase in ownership and filing of IP assets has resulted in an increase in IP-related disputes. There has thus been a corresponding increase in international legal argumentation in the IP arena, both inside and outside the courtroom.

Legal argumentation in the courtroom includes venues such as the World Trade Organization (WTO) dispute settlement panels and Appellate Body.[8] Legal argumentation in the courtroom also takes place in national and regional courts on IP.[9]

Argumentation outside the courtroom, on the other hand, includes the norm-setting processes through which new IP treaties are adopted at WIPO and other relevant institutions. In this regard, WIPO currently administers some twenty-six treaties dealing with various subjects of international IP law. In respect of the circumstances leading to the adoption of each of those twenty-six treaties, the normal process was the prior establishment of a Committee of Experts, which starts work on the textual formulation of a treaty. This is then passed on to the relevant subject matter's Standing

[6] Some of the WIPO treaties relating to patents, trademarks, and industrial designs ensure that a single international registration or filing will have effect in any of the designated or relevant member states. General information is available at http://www.wipo.int/about-wipo/en.

[7] For a comprehensive overview of WIPO, see generally Carolyn Deere Birkbeck, *The World Intellectual Property Organization (WIPO): A Reference Guide* (Cheltenham: Edward Elgar, 2016).

[8] An example of IP legal argumentation in the courtroom can be gleaned from one of the WTO's recent and most far-reaching and publicized cases, the so-called Tobacco Plain Packaging Cases. Australia enacted the Tobacco Plain Packaging Act (TPP), essentially to discourage the use of tobacco products. Australia's TPP legislation was challenged at the WTO on the grounds, *inter alia*, that the TPP measures imposed special requirements and prohibitions on use that unjustifiably encumbered the use of marks in the course of trade. A WTO Panel ruled in 2018 in favor of Australia, a decision upheld by the Appellate Body in 2020. See WT/DS435/AB/R and WT/DS441/AB/R, https://www.wto.org/english/tratop_e/dispu_e/435_441abr_e.pdf.

[9] For example, the Federal Patent Court of Switzerland is the court of first instance for all civil law disputes on patents. See generally "Efficiency and Effectiveness in the Proceedings before the Federal Patent Court of Switzerland: Contribution Prepared by Dr. Dieter Brandle, President, Federal Patent Court, St. Gallen, Switzerland," Doc. WIPO/ACE/12/6, at 14, https://www.wipo.int/edocs/mdocs/enforcement/en/wipo_ace_12/wipo_ace_12_6.pdf. Indeed, several countries have now established, or are considering establishing, specialized IP jurisdictions. See "Adjudicating Intellectual Property Disputes—An International Chamber of Commerce (ICC) Report on Specialized Intellectual Property Jurisdictions Worldwide," Contribution by the ICC, Doc. WIPO/ACE/11/7, at 28, https://www.wipo.int/edocs/mdocs/enforcement/en/wipo_ace11_7.pdf.

Committee (SC). WIPO has an SC for each of the three substantive IP areas—the Standing Committee on the Law of Patents (SCP); the Standing Committee on the Law of Trademarks, Industrial Designs and Geographical Indications (SCT); and the Standing Committee on the Law of Copyright and Related Rights (SCCR). The SCs are the WIPO member state bodies in which discussions take place for the progressive development of international IP law. When work in any particular area of an SC's competence reaches a sufficiently mature nature, that SC recommends to the WIPO General Assembly (GA) any further action that it considers appropriate, including the convening of a diplomatic conference for the purpose of concluding a treaty or adopting other instruments, such as declarations or resolutions.

Through their deliberations and participation in the various Committees of Experts, SCs, and the GA, WIPO member states and observers engage in various forms of legal argumentation outside the courtroom.[10] In respect of each of the above stages, from the initial Committee of Experts, through the SC, and ending up with the GA, participation (and therefore legal argumentation) is open not just to the 193 member states of WIPO but also to some 435 accredited observers, mostly comprised of organizations, civil society, and industry or business entities. The observers comprise some 75 intergovernmental organizations (IGOs), 262 international nongovernmental organizations (international NGOs), and 98 national nongovernmental organizations (national NGOs).[11]

A different form of legal argumentation in the IP field takes place through the processes of the registration systems. As is well known, IP is territorial in nature. The territoriality of IP implies that IP rights are generally acquired on a territory-by-territory basis. For example, as a prerequisite for acquiring a patent right for an invention in Ghana, an inventor must register his or her invention with the competent patent authorities in Ghana (in this case, the Registrar-General of Ghana). This also applies in respect of applications for patent protection on a regional basis, such as through the African Regional Intellectual Property Organization (ARIPO) or the European Patent Organization. As a necessary part of such applications, applicants engage in legal argumentation by articulating reasons why their inventions satisfy the legal criteria required for the grant of patent protection.

This type of legal argumentation is normally conducted by individuals or companies applying for IP titles. The extent to which such legal arguments will succeed will almost invariably be a function of whether those legal arguments are accepted by

[10] For example, during the thirtieth session of the SCP, the delegations of France and Spain argued for an urgent need for the SCP to discuss and take positions on the relationship between artificial intelligence and the patent system. See Revised Proposal of Document SCP/28/7 by the Delegations of France and Spain, Document prepared by the Secretariat for the 30th session of the SCP, June 24 to 27, 2019, https://www.wipo.int/edocs/mdocs/scp/en/scp_30/scp_30_9.pdf. See also Report of the Standing Committee on the Law of Patents, 30th Session, at para. 16, Doc. SCP/30/11, Dec. 6, 2019, https://www.wipo.int/edocs/mdocs/scp/en/scp_30/scp_30_11.pdf (statement by Uganda, on behalf of the African Group, noting the importance of the SCP as a multilateral forum for discussions and norm-setting in international patent law, and stating that "patents in principle promoted innovation by providing incentives to invest in research and development, to enhance socio-economic development [and] . . . a balance between the interests of rights holders and public access to knowledge and innovation must be maintained.").

[11] For a full list of the observers at WIPO, see Doc. BIG/158/32, http://www.wipo.int/export/sites/www/members/en/docs/observers.pdf.

the competent IP authorities as complying with the laid-down legal prerequisites for obtaining IP protection in the area concerned. In respect of patents, for example, it is now generally accepted internationally, and in most national legal systems, that inventions, whether they are products or processes, will be given patent protection only insofar as the inventors can show that their inventions "are new, involve an inventive step and are capable of industrial application."[12]

It should be recalled that WIPO does not have the type of enforcement mandate that exists at the WTO. This may well explain why one would be hard pressed to find any WIPO member state meetings or fora at which states seek to argue that others are breaching or are failing to comply with their obligations under IP treaties.

Nevertheless, states and observer organizations engage in legal argumentation not tied to a specific IP issue in WIPO and other IP fora. As I have written recently, the IP system now tends to be more polarized and politicized:

> Tensions underlying some of these questions have led to a schism between the general position of developed countries, on the one hand, and developing countries, on the other. To characterize the positions very broadly, debates on IP matters in all relevant fora in the last several years generally trend toward developed countries insisting that we maintain the traditional practice of protecting IP rights *per se*, and developing countries insisting that we protect IP rights only in such a manner as to ensure that other important social and economic goals are attained.[13]

To be sure, WIPO is not the only forum where broad or generalized legal argumentation takes place in respect of IP matters. An example of competing types of argumentation can be seen in the ongoing discussions at the WTO regarding the relationship between the TRIPS Agreement and the Convention on Biological Diversity (CBD).[14] Most developing countries take the position that the TRIPs Agreement should be amended to introduce a mandatory disclosure requirement in patent applications. For example, at the WTO's TRIPS Council meeting on October 19–20, 2017, India argued that the TRIPS Agreement should be amended to include a new Article 29*bis* for disclosure of origin of genetic resources and/or associated TK. A "mandatory disclosure requirement in patent applications to include disclosure of origin and evidence of prior informed consent and access and benefit sharing, would, in addition to combating bio-piracy, further strengthen the credibility of the patent system by facilitating assessment of the novelty and inventiveness criteria."[15] Several developed

[12] See Agreement on Trade-Related Aspects of Intellectual Property Rights, art. 27, https://www.wto.org/english/docs_e/legal_e/31bis_trips_01_e.htm.

[13] See Edward Kwakwa, "Intellectual Property," in *The Oxford Handbook of United Nations Treaties*, edited by Simon Chesterman, David Malone, and Santiago Villalpando (Oxford: Oxford University Press, 2019), 363, 367–374.

[14] *Id.*

[15] See Doc. IP/C/M/87/Add.1 (Feb. 7, 2018), at 12; see also Statement by Haiti on behalf of the least-developed countries (LDC) Group ("the TRIPS Agreement should be amended to include a provision making it mandatory to disclose the origin of genetic resources and traditional knowledge when filing a patent application"; "LDCs are . . . often victims of bio-piracy. Therefore, the disclosure of the origin of genetic resources and traditional knowledge would allow for these dishonest practices to be combatted effectively, and facilitate the sharing of the benefits gained from the exploitation of such resources." Doc. IP/C/M/87/Add.1 (Feb. 7, 2018), at 9.

countries, on the other hand, take the position that there is no inconsistency between the TRIPs Agreement and the CBD. Thus Japan, for example, argued at the WTO that it was "firmly convinced that the disclosure requirement would discourage industries from conducting research and development activities on biological materials overseas," and that "the disclosure requirement is not an adequate means for dealing with such misappropriation, so therefore, we have to avoid including it in the intellectual property system."[16]

It is significant that even after more than a decade of debating this issue at the WTO's TRIPS Council, and notwithstanding consistent legal argumentation for and against amending the TRIPS Agreement, there have been no outcomes in terms of new legal instruments. This result could, in large part, be attributable to the politicized nature of the WTO and other fora discussions on the matter.

Under WIPO's auspices, the most direct form of legal argumentation outside the courtroom by individuals and companies takes place in the UDRP, to which I will now turn.

IV. The Uniform Domain Name Dispute Resolution Policy

WIPO has an Arbitration and Mediation Center (the WIPO Center)[17] that acts as an international resource for time- and cost-effective alternatives to court litigation of IP disputes, generally known as alternative dispute resolution (ADR). The WIPO Center acts as an administrator of cases and a provider of legal and organizational expertise in ADR, including the Uniform Domain Name Dispute Resolution Policy (UDRP).[18] The UDRP is perhaps one of the best examples of the effective use of international legal argumentation outside the courtroom. The UDRP was adopted by the Internet Corporation for Assigned Names and Numbers (ICANN) in 1999 on the basis of recommendations made by WIPO after the First WIPO Internet Domain Name Process.[19] The UDRP only deals with the resolution of disputes involving trademarks, one of the distinct types of IP whose protection WIPO has an explicit mandate to promote.

[16] See Doc. IP/C/M/87/Add.1 (Feb. 7, 2018), at 10; see also statement by Canada, TRIPs Council meeting on 19–20 October 2017 ("Canada continues to firmly believe that the TRIPs Agreement and the CBD are complementary and that there is therefore no need to amend the TRIPs Agreement in this regard.") *Id.* at 10.

[17] For a comprehensive history of the WIPO Center, see Heike Wollgast and Andrzej Gadkowski, "Arbitration and Mediation Center: World Intellectual Property Organization (WIPO)," *Max Planck Encyclopedias of International Law* (Oxford: Oxford University Press, 2019).

[18] WIPO is one of six dispute resolution providers under the UDRP. Other dispute resolution providers are: the Arab Center for Domain Name Dispute Resolution (ACDR); the Asian Domain Name Dispute Resolution Centre; the Canadian International Internet Dispute Resolution Centre (CIIDRC); the Arbitration Center attached to the Czech Chamber of Commerce and the Agricultural Chamber of the Czech Republic (the Czech Arbitration Court); and the National Arbitration Forum.

[19] The Management of Internet Domain Names and Addresses: Intellectual Property Issues—Final Report of the First WIPO Internet Domain Name Process, WIPO Publication No. 439, http://www.wipo.int/amc/en/processes/process1/report. Although ICANN was reorganized recently, that reorganization has no bearing on the adoption or implementation of the UDRP.

The UDRP works in a simple and efficient manner: a Complaint is filed by a party asserting trademark rights (the "Complainant") with the WIPO Center, often through a simple email.[20] The WIPO Center requests the Registrar[21] of the domain name(s) in dispute to lock the domain name (pending resolution of the dispute, and in order to avoid its use or transfer by any party during the dispute proceedings).[22] The WIPO Center then reviews the Complaint for administrative compliance with the UDRP Rules and notifies the Respondent of the Complaint.[23] The Respondent is given twenty days within which to file a Response to the Complaint.[24] The WIPO Center appoints a one- or three-person Panel, and the Panel issues a decision within fourteen calendar days.[25]

A Complainant has to satisfy a three-step requirement in order to win a case. According to the UDRP Rules, a Panel will issue an order for the transfer (or cancellation)[26] of the domain name if the following three criteria are satisfied:

1. the domain name is identical or confusingly similar to a trademark or service mark in which the Complainant has rights; and
2. the domain name holder has no rights or legitimate interests in respect of the domain name; and
3. the domain name has been registered and is being used in bad faith.[27]

This three-step requirement constitutes the universe of options within which Complainants and Defendants can make their legal arguments. The extent to which a Complaint would include any references to international or IP law is a function of whether such arguments are able to shed light on or substantiate attempts to satisfy any of the three criteria listed above but is generally quite limited. In respect of criterion 1, for example (whether a domain name is "identical or confusingly similar" to a trademark or service mark in which the Complainant has rights), the Complainant is only required to prove a fact—that the Complainant has rights in a trademark or service mark that is "identical or confusingly similar" to the domain name in dispute. The UDRP Rules themselves explain the notion of "identical or confusingly similar." Thus, the Complainant's only argumentation would be to prove the factual existence

[20] See Rules for Uniform Domain Name Dispute Resolution Policy [hereinafter UDRP Rules], para. 3(a), https://www.icann.org/resources/pages/udrp-rules-2015-03-11-en.

[21] The Registrars of domain names are the technical entities, accredited by ICANN, with which companies and individuals can register domain names.

[22] UDRP Rules, para. 4.

[23] *Id.* paras. 2(a) and 4(c).

[24] *Id.* para. 5(a).

[25] *Id.* para. 15(b). UDRP Panels generally comprise external, independent trademark law experts, appointed by the WIPO Center or nominated by the parties from a list of hundreds of experts. See http://www.wipo.int/amc/en/domains/panel/panelists.html ("The persons appearing on the WIPO Center's list of Domain Name Panelists have been selected on the basis of their well-established reputation for their impartiality, sound judgment and experience as decision-makers, as well as their substantive experience in the areas of international trademark law, electronic commerce and internet-related issues. The WIPO Center's list is international, consisting of some 400 Panelists from over 50 countries, many of whom are multi-lingual.").

[26] The remedy of cancellation is rarely sought by parties, due to the risk of a canceled domain name being quickly snapped up again, including by third parties. Remedies under the UDRP are limited to transfer or cancellation. No costs or damages are awarded under the UDRP.

[27] UDRP Rules, para. 4(a).

and ownership of a trademark (which comes with its concomitant rights), followed by an elaboration of how identical or confusingly similar the Complainant's trademark is to the domain name in dispute. Similarly, in respect of criterion 3, for example (the domain name "has been registered and is being used in bad faith"), all the Complainant needs to establish, by way of legal argumentation, is the fact that the Defendant has registered and is using the disputed domain name in bad faith. Again, the UDRP Rules give specific examples of what is meant by "bad faith" registration and use.

A UDRP Panel's decision is based solely on written evidence; there are no in-person hearings. At the end of ten calendar days, absent a domestic court challenge, the ICANN-appointed Registrar implements the Panel's decision.[28]

In short, the UDRP is not a judicial or court-administered process but an administrative procedure that relies essentially on built-in technological measures to implement the Panels' decisions. This is because Panels' decisions are notified to the Registrar by the WIPO Center. The Registrar is then obliged to implement the remedy decided by the Panel. The Registrar literally implements or enforces the Panel's decision by the press of a button—by transferring or canceling the domain name, depending on the Panel's holding.

While the UDRP may have certain characteristics of court procedures and is often compared to an arbitration process, it differs from an arbitration in various respects, including in its relationship to the court system. The UDRP does not prevent either party from submitting a dispute to a competent court of justice: however, very few cases that have been decided under the UDRP have been brought before a court. And in those few instances where UDRP decisions have been appealed to a court, the courts have generally validated the actions or holdings of the earlier UDRP Panel.[29] And in general, domestic courts that adjudicate the matter anew have reached the same conclusion as did the UDRP Panel.[30]

Since its inception in 1999, the Center has administered over forty-eight thousand UDRP-based cases, covering over eighty-five thousand domain names.[31] In the twenty years of its formation and administration, the UDRP has established a comprehensive jurisprudence through an administrative process, and in the absence of judicial procedures. While the UDRP does not follow a doctrine of precedent as such, it is rare for any UDRP Panelists to write a decision without citation to prior UDRP case law. In the case of *Canada,dbaeResolution v. eResolution.com*, for example, the Panel stated as follows:

[28] *Id.* para. 4(k).

[29] See, e.g., the landmark Canadian case of Tucows.Com Co. v. Lojas Renner S.A., 2011 ONCA 548, para. 28, reproduced at https://www.wipo.int/amc/en/domains/challenged/index.html (referring to WIPO Case D2009-0637 in respect of the domain name renner.com).

[30] See Selected UDRP-related Court Cases, http://www.wipo.int/amc/en/domains/challenged.

[31] See http://www.wipo.int/amc/en/domains/statistics. Recent filing now also includes disputes concerning COVID-19–related domain names, such as: coronagileadsciences.com, dettolhandsanitizer.com, facebookcovid19.com, and sanofivaccine.com. See "WIPO Cybersquatting Case Filing Surges During COVID-19 Crisis," https://www.wipo.int/amc/en/news/2020/cybersquatting_covid19.html?utm_source=W.

> Although entitled to consider principles of law deemed applicable, [the Panel found it] unnecessary to do so in any depth. The jurisprudence which is being rapidly developed by a wide variety of Panelists world-wide under the ICANN Policy provides a fruitful source of precedent.[32]

Indeed, UDRP Panels have consistently used prior cases as persuasive precedents to help navigate a variety of substantive as well as procedural matters. Another example was the case of *J.P. Morgan v. Resource Marketing*, in respect of the domain name jpmorgan.com, in which the Complainant argued for the inadmissibility of the Respondent's late reply. In so doing, the Complainant cited *Talk City, Inc. v. Robertson*[33] as precedent for his argument. The Panel decided to accept the late reply because, in the Panel's view, the Respondent's late reply was within the parameters of a similarly late Reply accepted in the earlier case *Talk City*. The Panel was unpersuaded by four other precedents because "the distinguished Panelists in [those four] cases did not discuss this issue, [and] the Panel in the present case [*JP Morgan*] did not have the benefit of their reasoning."[34]

The jurisprudence has clearly been created through successive international legal argumentation processes at the UDRP stage where Complainants and Respondents make their respective arguments in order to win a case. While the UDRP as a matter of course does not operate on a strict doctrine of precedent, the emergence of a body of jurisprudence shows an undeniable truth—that precedent matters. It suggests a confirmation of the principle that like cases ought to be treated alike, thus demonstrating that the pull of precedent is central to the power of legal argumentation. This also shows that the pull of precedent relates to the principle of certainty. Knowing what the law is enables people to act accordingly. In this regard, it is recalled that the WIPO Center maximizes transparency of process and outcome by posting all WIPO UDRP Panel decisions on its publicly accessible website.[35] It may well be that such publication of UDRP opinions on the WIPO website has further encouraged the practice of relying on or citing previous Panel decisions.

It is also arguable that the UDRP, while not a judicial process, is nevertheless very similar to a regular judicial model or court process. In such a situation, argumentation "outside" the courtroom may, for all practical purposes, be no different from argumentation "inside" the courtroom. The clear and strict three-step criteria required by the UDRP probably accounts for this similarity.

The role of the WIPO Secretariat in the administration of the UDRP process is very clear. The WIPO Secretariat, represented by the WIPO Center, plays more of an

[32] See Canada,dbaeResolution v. eResolution.com (3636275, D2000-0110, WIPO, Apr. 10, 2000).

[33] Case regarding the domain name talk-city.com, D2000-0009.

[34] *Id.* See also Time Inc. v. Chip Cooper (D2000-1342, WIPO, Feb. 13, 2001, in respect of the domain name lifemagazine.com), in which the Panel "believes potential users of the UDRP are entitled to some degree of predictability," and if "a principle enunciated in a decision is well-reasoned and repeatedly adopted by other panels, the majority believes that absent compelling reasons which require a determination otherwise, the rule established should be respected ... [u]sers of the internet are better served through panel decisions that promote consistency and predictability." See also Pantalon Retail India Limited v. RareNames, WebReg (D2010-0587, WIPO, June 21, 2010, where the Panel notes that "a strong body of precedent ... is strongly persuasive" even if not binding).

[35] See http://www.wipo.int/amc/en/domains/search/legalindex.jsp.

administrative role than a legal role. WIPO administers the UDRP process on a not-for-profit basis. It is the parties to the dispute who engage in direct legal argumentation in order to substantiate their allegations in a case. The WIPO Center itself engages in no legal argumentation at all. This is seen as a necessity, given the potential for conflict between WIPO UDRP Panels' decisions and WIPO's role as the administrator of a trademark registration system through which the majority of UDRP Complainants may have ultimately acquired their trademarks. And by refraining from participating in any legal argumentation, the WIPO Secretariat also enhances the perceived neutrality and objectivity of the UDRP process as administered by WIPO.[36]

The UDRP has become one of the most popular means of settling disputes in the IP arena, because of its obvious advantages. First, it is widely used by default, for the simple reason that all domain name registrants must agree, in advance, to be bound by the UDRP in the event of a dispute concerning the domain name. This is a condition of all ICANN-imposed registration agreements.[37] Second, the UDRP is attractive because it is a cost-effective alternative to litigation. To be sure, it only costs US$1,500.[38] The UDRP is also popular because it is a predictable means of resolving clear cases of cybersquatting. It is internationally enforceable by means of technology, thus obviating the difficulty of enforcing decisions across borders. Finally, parties in dispute are not required by the UDRP to retain counsel, thus further reducing the general costs associated with normal litigation. The absence of counsel does not seem to affect the nature of the argumentation, as the argumentation is based strictly on the three-step criteria or requirements of the UDRP.

In short, the UDRP is highly valued and very popular because of its speed, user-friendliness, low cost, ease of international application, and enforcement by technological means. All these factors have made the UDRP a popular tool for trademark owners to protect their rights without going to a court of law. In so doing, trademark owners have generally resorted to legal arguments tailored to establish the three criteria required by the UDRP, for purposes of winning their cases at the UDRP. This has enabled the UDRP to establish a body of jurisprudence and a cadre of Panelists who invariably rely on earlier Panelists' decisions, in deference to the principle of *stare decisis*.

The UDRP seems to demonstrate the possibility of having legal argumentation, decision-making according to quasi-legal criteria, and a strong deference to precedent, all in the absence of a court.

[36] On the UDRP generally, as well as online dispute resolution as an alternative to face-to-face dispute resolution, see generally Ethan Katsh and Colin Rule, "What We Know and Need to Know about Online Dispute Resolution," *South Carolina Law Review* 67 (2016): 329. See also Tony Willoughby, "Domain Name Disputes: The UDRP 10 Years On," *Journal of Intellectual Property Law & Practice* 4 (2009): 714.

[37] The UDRP, in effect, is based on a mandatory "contract web" between ICANN, the domain name Registrars, and the domain name Registrants. While it is not arbitration per se, it is designed to allow trademark owners to resolve their clear cases of abusive domain name registration and use by allowing direct enforcement of Panel decisions through Registrars, without going to court, but while preserving court options.

[38] This is the cost for a single Panelist. The UDRP Rules provide that a Complainant pays the entire fee for that proceeding. See UDRP, para. 4(g). But in the case where the Respondent requests a three-person Panel, the cost of US$4,500 is shared equally between the two parties. UDRP Rules, paras. 5(b)(iv), 5(d).

V. The WIPO Intergovernmental Committee on Intellectual Property and Genetic Resources, Traditional Knowledge and Folklore

As far back as 2000, the member states of WIPO established the Intergovernmental Committee on Intellectual Property and Genetic Resources, Traditional Knowledge and Folklore (IGC). The mandate of the IGC is to undertake text-based negotiations with the objective of reaching agreement on the texts of international legal instruments, which will ensure the effective protection of TK, TCEs, and GRs. As stated in WIPO's Background Brief on the subject, the "[i]mpetus [for the establishment of the IGC] came from a growing sense in developing countries that folklore embodies creativity and was part of the cultural identity of indigenous and local communities; it was therefore seen as worthy of IP protection, especially since new technologies were making folklore increasingly vulnerable to expropriation and misuse."[39]

In pursuit of this mandate, the IGC has met in forty sessions to date.[40] In the course of these sessions so far, participants in the IGC have used various means of legal argumentation to try to suggest what should be the framework for an international legal regime governing the protection of TK, TCEs, and GRs. In general, legal argumentation in favor of establishing new legal instruments has been conducted mostly by developing countries and Indigenous and other local communities.[41] The trend stems from the increasing realization of the commercial value derived from TK and, in particular, its potential to contribute to economic growth for developing countries and least-developed countries (LDCs). The majority of the world's TK is owned by, or created by, communities in these developing countries and LDCs. And the introduction of new technologies, such as biotechnology, brought to the fore the considerable economic value of GRs and associated TK, which were increasingly being used in patentable inventions.[42]

At its thirty-eighth session, for example, the delegation of Morocco, speaking on behalf of the Group of African States, stated: "TK and TCEs had, for a long time, enriched and assisted communities and nations throughout the world and contributed to their autonomy. The IP regime did not provide sufficient protection to those assets. The absence of any legally binding instruments allowed continued misappropriation, and contributed to an imbalance in the global IP system. It wished to improve, enrich

[39] See WIPO Background Brief No. 2, "The WIPO Intergovernmental Committee on Intellectual Property and Genetic Resources, Traditional Knowledge and Folklore" (2016).

[40] The IGC had been scheduled to have its forty-first meeting in March 2020, and its forty-second meeting in June 2020. Both sessions had to be postponed as a result of the COVID-19 pandemic. For a summary of all forty sessions to date, see https://www.wipo.int/meetings/en/topic.jsp?group_id=110.

[41] The IGC currently has some 404 IGOs and NGOs accredited to it and participating in its deliberations. For the full list of IGC-accredited observers, see https://www.wipo.int/export/sites/www/tk/en/igc/pdf/igc_observers.pdf.

[42] See WIPO Background Brief No. 2, *supra* note 39 ("As a result, many people began to argue that the patent regime should help to prevent misappropriation and promote fair benefit sharing between holders of those assets (mostly biodiversity-rich countries) and those with the modern technologies to access and use them. IP issues regarding access to GRs and associated TK came into the agenda of the WIPO Standing Committee on Patents in the late 1990s, and were raised in the preparatory work leading up to the WIPO Diplomatic Conference for the adoption of a new Patent Law Treaty in 2000.").

and strengthen the transparency of the current IP system and make it more inclusive, to ensure protection for GRs, TCEs and TK."[43]

To be sure, some developed countries also resort to arguments to counter those positions. At the thirty-eighth session of the IGC, for example, the delegation of Japan suggested that the IGC was not ready to discuss legal issues relating to the protection of TK and TCEs because "even after many years of discussion, the IGC had not been able to find a common understanding on the fundamental issues, namely, objectives, beneficiaries, subject matter, and definition of misappropriation . . . the IGC needed to reach a common understanding on the definitions of TK and TCEs first, before starting negotiating the texts."[44] And at the thirtieth session of the IGC, the US delegation "disagreed with the suggestion that a disclosure requirement would introduce legal certainty, just because it would supposedly introduce minimum and maximum standards internationally. The strongest legal certainty was no disclosure requirement. . . . [T]he premise that an international legal standard was necessary for legal certainty was false. . . . [The delegation] remained deeply concerned that new patent disclosure requirements would actually add new uncertainties in the patent system, particularly where the sanctions for noncompliance included invalidation of a patent."[45] Thus both states effectively argued in legal terms against the need for new law.

In the IGC (as well as non-WIPO fora), Indigenous and other local communities are increasingly involved in discussions on IP and TK, where they have cited legal instruments as well as invoked policy arguments. They have generally condemned misappropriation of their knowledge and cultural heritage, the lack of recognition by the IP regime of their collective ownership rights over their IP, and the need to recognize customary practices and laws regulating access, control, and management of their TK.[46]

The representative of the Native American Rights Fund, speaking on behalf of the Indigenous Caucus at the tenth meeting of the IGC, stated:

> [WIPO] Member States had to recognize the rights in the United Nations Declaration on the Rights of Indigenous Peoples ("UNDRIP"), the International Labour Organization Convention No. 169 ("ILO 169 Convention"), and other instruments of international, domestic, and indigenous law, as well as indigenous customary law. Under those, indigenous peoples enjoyed legal peoplehood, self-determination, and the right to maintain indigenous cosmologies, spirituality and lifeways. . . . Anyone

[43] See Report of the Intergovernmental Committee on Intellectual Property and Genetic Resources, Traditional Knowledge and Folklore, 38th Session, Geneva, December 10–14, 2018, Doc. WIPO/GRTKF/IC/38/16 (Mar. 22, 2019).

[44] See *id.*, para. 24.

[45] See Doc. WIPO/GRTKF/IC/30/10 (Sept. 23, 2016), at para. 191. See also statement by the Delegation of Sweden (opining on the nature of any instrument being negotiated at the IGC): "any instrument on TK should be non-binding, flexible and sufficiently clear." Doc. WIPO/GRTKF/IC/27/10 (July 2, 2014), at para. 76.

[46] See, e.g., Joint Statement of the Indigenous Peoples Council on Biocolonialism (IPCB), Call of the Earth/Llamado de le Terra (COE), & International Indian Treaty Council (IITC) during the 10th session of the IGC, http://www.ipcb.org/issues/intellect-prop/files/igc10_tk.html. See also Doc. WIPO/GRTKF/IGC/7/Prov2, para. 135 (statement by representative of the Saami Council).

> who wanted to exploit or use TK or TCEs should be required to use due diligence to discover potential owners and engage in free, prior, and informed consent to determine whether they could legally access and use the TK and TCEs.... Much TK and many TCEs had been taken from them historically and economically without their free, prior and informed consent.[47]

As seen in this excerpt, legal argumentation in the IGC has sometimes relied on existing bodies of law. An obvious example is the reliance on human rights law, where some of the policy objectives are drawn from Article 31 of the UNDRIP:

> Indigenous peoples have the right to maintain, control, protect and develop their cultural heritage, traditional knowledge and traditional cultural expressions.... In conjunction with indigenous peoples, States shall take effective measures to recognize and protect the exercise of these rights.[48]

The work of the IGC, as well as its deliberations, are infused with appeals to or reliance on existing bodies of law or ongoing work in related fora and institutions, including national legal systems. For example, the IGC's work on the relationship between IP, TK, and GRs partly "stems from concerns regarding the role that IP protection should play in achieving global policy objectives as varied as the conservation of biodiversity (as enshrined in the Convention on Biological Diversity, 1992), food security, free and fair trade, and development."[49] The delegation of Lithuania, speaking on behalf of the Group of Central European and Baltic States, also explained, at the thirty-eighth session of the IGC, that it

> attached great importance to well-balanced IP regimes, which stimulated innovation and creativity and therefore supported economic and social developments as well as the welfare of all groups of population. It favored an evidence-based approach, as it was important to draw lessons from the most recent experiences in various Member States while elaborating their existing national legislation and measures for protecting TK and TCEs. Such crucial aspects as legal certainty and economic, social

[47] *Id.*

[48] UN Declaration on the Rights of Indigenous Peoples, art. 31, GA Res. 61/295 (Sept. 13, 2007). The 2007 Declaration constitutes the most comprehensive international instrument on the rights of Indigenous peoples. Almost all UN member states have endorsed the instrument, including the four countries that had initially voted against it.

[49] See WIPO Background Brief No. 2, *supra* note 39, at 1. Discussions at the IGC have also invoked the Convention on Biological Diversity (CBD), the Nagoya Protocol on Access to Genetic Resources and the Fair and Equitable Sharing of Benefits Arising from their Utilization (the Nagoya Protocol), the International Treaty on Plant Genetic Resources for Food and Agriculture, UNESCO's 2005 Convention for the Protection and Promotion of the Diversity of Cultural Expressions, as well as UNESCO's 2003 Convention for the Safeguarding of Intangible Cultural Heritage. Article 8(j) of the CBD requires parties, subject to their national laws, to "respect, preserve and maintain knowledge, innovations and practices of indigenous and local communities embodying traditional lifestyles relevant for the conservation and sustainable use of biological diversity." The CBD also addresses the issues of access and benefit sharing. The Nagoya Protocol deals with TK associated with GRs, and addresses issues such as prior and informed consent, equitable remuneration, and maintenance of community laws and procedures, as well as customary use and exchange.

and cultural impacts should be carefully considered before reaching an agreement on any particular outcome.[50]

The WIPO Secretariat itself tries to avoid taking specific positions or engaging in direct legal argumentation in the course of the IGC's work. In general, the WIPO Secretariat tends to limit its role to facilitating the work of the IGC. In particular, it provides secretariat and administrative support, including organizing consultations and providing briefings, preparing and translating documentation, and generally assisting the chairs of the IGC in the performance of their functions. This is all consistent with the IGC's status as an intergovernmental process that is member state–driven. Admittedly, secretariats in other intergovernmental organizations may be more activist in their pronouncements and more assertive (or intrusive) in intergovernmental legal debates and processes. That would seem to be more easily carried out, and indeed expected, in human rights and other related organizations with mandates that arguably encourage activist secretariats, but not in an IP organization with no express mandate for enforcement, and where member states would therefore expect from the Secretariat neutrality (or abstention).

The Secretariat has nonetheless taken occasional initiatives. For example, as far back as 2005, noticing that no member state "had formally proposed a comprehensive draft instrument," the WIPO Secretariat "published the working documents on TK and TCEs as concise 'draft articles.' "[51] These draft articles were, in effect, a comprehensive set of legal arguments outside the courtroom. While they may have been shelved or dismissed by some member states, they had the effect of galvanizing other member states into taking needed action at the time.[52] Such actions and legal argumentation by the Secretariat, while rare, obviously had the semblance of neutrality, and thus greater credibility, than would have been the case for legal argumentation by member states. The WIPO Secretariat similarly prepared, in 2008, a document on "gap analyses" to help contribute to clarifying the issues and options to be deliberated upon by member states. Again, such initiatives by the Secretariat propelled the process forward because the initial drafts and "options" papers prepared by the Secretariat were complemented by several member state proposals, and all consolidated into single texts which became the basis for further and ongoing negotiations at the IGC.[53]

Some assert that the IGC has become an ineffective talking shop and that, after twenty years, it has no impressive achievements, despite the consistent and frequent

[50] See Report of the Intergovernmental Committee, *supra* note 43, at para. 16; *id.* at para. 42 (Mr. Shapiro, Co-Chair of the Ad Hoc Expert Group, explaining that "a number of experts [in the IGC Ad Hoc Expert Group] observed that certain UNESCO Conventions complemented the IGC's work on the protection of TK and TCEs and encouraged continued cooperation between WIPO and UNESCO on areas of common interest.").

[51] See Wend Wendland, "Protecting Indigenous Knowledge: A Personal Perspective on International Negotiations at WIPO," *WIPO Magazine*, Dec. 2019, at 2, https://www.wipo.int/wipo_magazine/en/2019/06/article_0004.html.

[52] *Id.* (explaining that "[a]t the Member states' request, the WIPO Secretariat prepared materials on the 'international dimension' of the IGC's work and analyses of gaps between the protections provided by the IP system and the needs and aspirations of indigenous peoples and local communities and other *demandeurs*").

[53] See WIPO Background Brief No. 2, *supra* note 39.

international legal argumentation there.[54] But legal argumentation does not necessarily take place with the expectation that it will result in specific legal outcomes. Nor is it always driven by specific legal motives. As Ian Johnstone points out, at least three distinct purposes are plausible reasons why legal argumentation occurs outside of courts: "to persuade, to affect instrumental calculations of interest, and to change the normative climate."[55] In the IGC context, so far, the first two purposes seem to have been achieved.

A considerable amount of progress has been achieved to date, even if no international legal instrument or other specific international norms have been set. Discussions in the IGC have engendered recommendations for the amendment of some patent law systems to introduce disclosure requirements.[56] There has been a significant growth in the number of national and regional laws relating to the protection of TK, TCEs, and GRs.[57] The IGC process has also stimulated increased recognition of TK within the patent system; WIPO "has developed, and regularly updates, an online database of relevant contractual practices"; and "[u]nder the auspices of the IGC, WIPO has carried out numerous studies and developed other resources (such as glossaries, surveys of national experiences, a laws database and training programs), which have proved useful for member states and others."[58] The WIPO Secretariat has also established a very comprehensive web page that provides information on local, national, and regional community experiences regarding IP and TK, TCEs, and GRs.[59] This would all seem to suggest that argumentation in the IGC has already had far-reaching and concrete outcomes. The different types of argumentation have had an obvious impact in encouraging states to adopt national and regional legislation that comports with the essence of the arguments that have been made in the course of the IGC processes. Yet in terms of ultimate impact and effects, there does not seem to be a discernible difference between argumentation that is strictly legal and argumentation that is more economic, pragmatic, or policy-oriented.

[54] See, e.g., Center for International Environmental Law Brief, "The Gap Between Indigenous Peoples' Demands and WIPO's Framework on Traditional Knowledge," https://www.ciel/org/Publications/WIPO_Gap_Sept07.pdf ("after ten sessions of the IGC, indigenous and other local communities continue to reiterate their concerns and reservations regarding the work of the IGC," and "[a]nother concern is the slow pace of work and the unwillingness of some industrialized countries, eg the United States and Japan, to work towards a final outcome. A more significant concern is the substantive approach and content of the IGC framework, including inadequate consideration of indigenous and other local communities' rights and views."). *Id.* at 2.

[55] Ian Johnstone, chapter 7, in this volume.

[56] In some national legal systems, where GRs and associated TK are used in an invention, the applicant is required to furnish, as a prerequisite for grant of patents, evidence of prior and informed consent, and fair and equitable benefit-sharing.

[57] Certain countries have national legislation that protects TK. Others have national legislation that protects GRs. See generally Marisella Ouma, "Traditional Knowledge: The Challenges Facing International Lawmakers," *WIPO Magazine*, Feb. 2017, https://www.wipo.int/wipo_magazine/en/2017/01/article_0003.html. At the regional level, see the African Regional Intellectual Property Organization's Swakopmund Protocol on the Protection of Traditional Knowledge and Expressions of Folklore, https://www.aripo.org/wp-content/uploads/2019/06/Swakopmund-Protocoal-on-the-Protection-of-Traditional-Knowledge-and-Expressions-of-Folklore-2019.pdf. The Swakopmund Protocol was adopted by ARIPO member states in 2011 and entered into force in 2015.

[58] See generally WIPO Background Brief No. 2, *supra* note 39, at 3.

[59] See https://www.wipo.int/tk/en/resources/tk_experiences.html.

VI. Conclusion

We have looked at the IP field in general and, in particular, at the UDRP process and the IGC process as they play out in WIPO. It is evident that international legal argumentation plays a prominent part in both processes. While the IGC process entails mostly argumentation by states, that of the UDRP is exclusively argumentation by private parties or non-state entities.

Based on the examples shown in this chapter, one can confidently conclude that, in the IP field, international legal argumentation takes place on a daily basis, almost as a matter of course in the two specific processes demonstrated here. By virtue of the structure of the UDRP Rules, argumentation at the UDRP tends to follow a more precedent-oriented and quasi-judicial routine. By virtue of the IGC's political and member state–driven nature, on the other hand, argumentation at the IGC has tended to rely not just on legality but sometimes also on morality, on religion, on economics, and even on emotions. Indeed, as Wouter Werner ably demonstrates in his chapter in this volume, emotions are effectively communicated through legal argumentation outside the courtroom.[60]

In both the UDRP and the IGC processes, argumentation has clearly had effects in shaping the direction of national laws, of administrative issuances, and of regional instruments. This chapter has demonstrated that the UDRP has generally followed precedent. Indeed, such precedent setting is itself a form of legal argumentation. While legal argumentation in the UDRP seems to have established a clear jurisprudence as well as a practice of following precedents, that in the IGC has yet to result in specific legal outcomes, such as an international legal instrument, an authoritative declaration, a resolution of the WIPO GA, or some other form of soft law. It is, however, significant that considerable achievements have already been made in the protection of TK, TCEs, and GRs at the national and regional levels. These achievements have been largely a result of the ongoing work of the IGC and the frequent and extensive international legal and other argumentation that has taken place in that forum over the last twenty years.

[60] See Wouter Werner, chapter 10, in this volume. And for the role of emotional and moral arguments, see Lisbeth Zimmermann, chapter 13, also in this volume.

15
Arguing about Trade Law Beyond the Courtroom

Kathleen Claussen

International trade law, unlike many other areas of international law, benefits from a set of long-standing widely agreed binding and enforceable rules. Since 1947, international trade law premised on the principles set out in the General Agreement on Tariffs and Trade (GATT) has continued to grow. The World Trade Organization (WTO), founded in 1994, added dozens of additional rules to the GATT foundation and a more rigorous dispute settlement mechanism. These rules expanded the reach of trade law to new areas of public policy. With this expansion, trade law became not just *relevant* to domestic regulatory policy but also in some ways *determinative* of the contours of domestic regulatory space. The playing field grew and with that more players became necessarily versed in trade law, its attributes, and its areas of controversy. As a result, today, argumentation regarding the reach, content, and contours of trade law occurs in multiple fora.

This chapter reviews trade law argumentation in settings outside of the WTO dispute settlement mechanism. By "trade law argumentation," I refer to advocacy that invokes substantive international trade law principles, not just political statements that promote a particular trade policy. Even so limited, the expanse of the possible areas where one might find such argumentation remains broad. I focus here on two novel data sets of arguments growing out of recent events: first, state reactions to the US imposition of special tariffs on steel and aluminum and on products from China; second, comments by US legislators in congressional debates. Each set engages a very different set of speakers across a range of experiences. And each yields different lessons about the purposes and effects of trade law argumentation outside the courtroom.

I. Trade's Courtroom and Broadening Interpretive Communities

The international trade law regime is composed of a dense web of international agreements primarily under the auspices or reflecting the norms of the WTO: norms in support of liberalization in the cross-border movement of goods and services. The WTO agreements are at the figurative center of the regime. They have been supplemented by numerous bilateral and plurilateral agreements, mostly in the form of free trade agreements (FTAs). It is a highly codified system with complex instruments

Kathleen Claussen, *Arguing about Trade Law Beyond the Courtroom* In: *Talking International Law*. Edited by: Ian Johnstone and Steven Ratner, Oxford University Press. © Kathleen Claussen 2021. DOI: 10.1093/oso/9780197588437.003.0015

in many subject areas. Most of its content is enforceable through dispute settlement procedures.

The WTO dispute settlement mechanism is the closest thing trade law has to an international courtroom.[1] Members bring and resolve disputes in accordance with the WTO Dispute Settlement Understanding. But the WTO provides far more than a courtroom. The institution is a place of exchange, consultation, debate, and engagement on trade issues.[2] In the committees of the WTO, members regularly discuss state measures as consistent or problematic under the WTO rules. Having such a forum for regular state engagement on the legal provisions of the institution has a significant impact on the strength, impact, and entrenchment of those rules, especially as they have grown in complexity and reach.[3]

In addition to providing this institutional structure, the creation of the WTO expanded trade law in content. Negotiations in the 1960s and 1970s shifted attention from the reduction of traditional tariff barriers to the elimination of "non-tariff barriers" to trade such as licensing requirements, health and safety regulations, and other administrative measures that could be considered discriminatory to foreign business. As the concept of trade has expanded outward so has conversation about trade law in domestic policymaking conversations. States widely rely on trade rules when developing an expansive set of policies in a way that would have been highly unlikely a half century ago.

Accordingly, trade law's public consciousness has grown quickly and widely and with it the interpretive communities of trade law. Those communities extend trade rules and define their content, especially within the WTO. There, Ian Johnstone has noted previously, trade law's discursivity is clearly seen.[4] That is also true outside the WTO where trade law is taken up and argued by non-trade experts and non-bureaucrats. These arguments beyond trade law's conventional courtroom bring trade law home and help to overcome democratic deficits perceived in the system.[5] One now locates trade law and its argumentation in previously unexpected places: op-eds

[1] To be sure, national courts likewise play a significant role in litigating trade rules as do administrative trade remedies agencies. See generally Kathleen Claussen, "Trade Administration," *Virginia Law Review* 107 (2021): 845; Joel Trachtman, "The Domain of WTO Dispute Resolution," *Harvard International Law Journal* 40 (1999): 333.

[2] See, e.g., Marc L. Busch, Eric Reinhardt, and Gregory Shaffer, "Does Legal Capacity Matter? A Survey of WTO Members," *World Trade Review* 8 (2009): 559.

[3] See Devin McDaniels, Ana Cristina Molina, and Erik N. Wijkström, "A Closer Look at WTO's Third Pillar: How WTO Committees Influence Regional Trade Agreements," *Journal of International Economic Law* 21 (2018): 815; Inveer Manak, "Enforcing International Trade Law in the World Trade Organization's Committees: Courting Third Party Opinion" (PhD Dissertation, Georgetown University-Graduate School of Arts and Sciences 2019).

[4] Ian Johnstone, *The Power of Deliberation: International Law, Politics and Organizations* (New York: Oxford University Press, 2011) (commenting that one primary function of an interpretive community is that it defines, interprets, and extends the rules of international life thereby having an impact on the evolution of the law); 183–190 (on trade and interpretive communities).

[5] See J.H.H. Weiler, "The Rule of Lawyers and the Ethos of Diplomats: Reflections on WTO Dispute Settlement," in *Efficiency, Equity, Legitimacy: The Multilateral Trading System at the Millennium*, edited by R. Porter et al. (Cambridge & Washington, DC: Center for Business and Government Harvard University & Brookings Institution Press, 2002); Gregory C. Shaffer, "The World Trade Organization Under Challenge: Democracy and the Law and Politics of the WTO's Treatment of Trade and Environment Matters," *Harvard Environmental Law Review* 25 (2001): 1.

in national newspapers; press releases that make headlines in local or regional media; other international settings like the G20; legislative bodies; domestic courts; and electoral debates, to name a few. This creates a practical problem for any study of this nature: how to fashion tools for finding trade law argumentation as well as for understanding it across widely varying circumstances.[6]

For this chapter, I have selected two spaces outside the WTO where trade law argumentation occurs. The first is a rather traditional state setting; I look at arguments by states in official statements or in comments by state executives to the press. Some of these comments are made unilaterally by states while some respond to and are in conversation with other states. The second space is that of domestic lawmakers. I review trade law arguments made by one group: members of the US Congress, on the floor of the legislature. I call the former "external trade law argumentation" and the latter "internal trade law argumentation," choosing these terms to reflect what the evidence suggests is the speaker's primary audience in each setting. While there are undoubtedly multiple audiences in any area of international legal argumentation,[7] I consider the primary audience for external lawmaking argumentation to be other states, and the primary audience for internal lawmaking argumentation to be a mix of the domestic public and other domestic lawmakers. Across both types, practitioners and policymakers manage trade law discussions through the reinforcement of existing norms and in some cases through contesting their application with diverse aims.

I have chosen these two sets recognizing that they have some features in common, but they also demonstrate clear differences about trade law's argumentation in these distinct settings. On the one hand, both sets confirm the robust use of trade law argumentation outside the courtroom. They reveal that trade law argumentation occurs in many settings—public statements in major media, the floor of legislatures, and electoral debates, among them—by very different actors—lawmakers in executive and legislative capacities—with audiences including other states, other actors within their own governments, and both international and domestic publics. Comparing the two sets also reveals at least one distinction in the way trade law arguments are made by the different actors in each setting. Broadly speaking, each set uses different levels of generality to reach their respective overlapping but contrasting audiences. In the case of states engaged in the reasonably singular purpose of persuading other states to change their trade measures, they use rather low-intensity-styled arguments, invoking legal principles in broader political rhetoric, and they do so often in conjunction with action they are taking in the courtroom where their legal arguments are more detailed. By contrast, the deployment of trade law argumentation in domestic

[6] One such unexpected site as this volume went to press in April 2021 was US President Joe Biden's speech in a joint session to the US Congress. Biden made an apparently off-the-cuff comment that his proposed revised Buy American program would "not violate any trade agreement." See Dan DuPont, "Biden: 'Buy American' Plans Won't Violate Trade Agreements," *Inside U.S. Trade*, Apr. 28, 2021. Michael Reisman has identified this as a challenge to international law more generally. See W. Michael Reisman, "The Quest for World Order and Human Dignity in the Twenty-First Century: Constitutive Process and Individual Commitment, General Course on Public International Law," *Collected Courses of the Hague Academy of International Law* 351 (2012): 13, 135–37.

[7] Those audiences have only grown in size, nature, and complexity with globalization. Reisman, *supra* note 6, at 138 (noting that the audience also communicates, drawing on its collective experience and ascribing expectations about authority and control even to the communicators themselves).

settings by legislators is often carried out with significant nuance. Thus, whereas states tend to speak in generalities on the world stage, domestic lawmakers necessarily examine and invoke specific aspects of international trade law in service of individual policy modifications. The remainder of the chapter unpacks how this is so.

II. External Trade Law Argumentation

This section takes up external trade law arguments by government leaders in response to the major shift in trade law precipitated by the Trump administration beginning in 2018. The implementation by the United States since 2018 of additional, special tariffs on products from multiple countries on the basis of national security has changed the landscape of trade law. It has tested the strength, weight, and reach of rules thought to be well entrenched and widely shared. Many states, including the United States, continue to speak in terms of trade rules, but recently they have done so in creative, public, and often defensive ways that shed new light on trade law's normalization outside the trade courtroom.[8]

A. National Security Tariffs

On March 8, 2018, after concluding that certain steel mill products and types of aluminum were being imported to the United States at such levels so as to "threaten to impair the national security" of the United States, President Trump issued two proclamations imposing new special duties on US imports of those products. Seeing these moves as contrary to long-standing international trade law rules, US trading partners responded swiftly, speaking first outside of the trade courtroom as is customary at the WTO. On March 23, 2018, over forty members took the floor at the WTO Council for Trade on Goods to express concern about the consistency of the US measure with WTO rules.[9] There and in the days that followed, leaders of those states and others also issued public statements about the US tariffs. This was the first wave of external trade law argumentation in response to exceptional US trade action. These statements preceded any legal action these states would take by several days and in some cases by several weeks.

Three types of arguments from state leaders quickly surfaced. First, states like Russia and the European Union made arguments maintaining expressly or implicitly that the US action was a violation of WTO rules. Within the WTO Council, the representative

[8] Caution is in order here: this study looked only at statements made in English and made public through major world news sources. The fact that the statements were made in English is an important limitation and signal of the data. For those countries where English is not the principal language, the message was most clearly intended to be heard on the international stage rather than domestically.

[9] WTO Council for Trade in Goods, "WTO Members Raise Concerns over US Tariffs on Steel and Aluminum at Goods Council," Mar. 23, 2018, https://www.wto.org/english/news_e/news18_e/good_23mar18_e.htm (concerns expressed by Russia, Japan, Venezuela, Brazil, New Zealand, Turkey, Korea, Hong Kong, Singapore, Thailand, Pakistan, Norway, Australia, India, El Salvador, Switzerland, Paraguay, Guatemala, and Kazakhstan).

of the Russian Federation argued that the US tariffs exceeded US bound rates under WTO rules.[10] The European Union issued a statement saying that the US measure could not be justified using the WTO exception for national security actions found in Article XXI of the GATT.[11] Second, leaders made public arguments indicating that they would retaliate in light of the US violation of the rules. For one, French President Emmanuel Macron said: "If attacked, we will respond without weakness. Everyone needs to understand this, and I think I can say that the American strategy is a bad strategy.... We talk about everything, in principle, with a friendly country that respects the rules of the W.T.O. We talk about nothing, in principle, when it is with a gun to our head."[12] Third, leaders made largely political and institutional arguments about the Trump administration's disregard for the trade law system. The European Union's foreign policy chief asserted that the European Union would "send a strong message on where the European Union stands in relation to trade: no protectionism."[13] A Chinese Commerce Ministry representative issued a statement that China "is absolutely not afraid of a trade war" and hoped that "the United States [would] pause on the brink of a precipice."[14] These three types of arguments were often expressed together, but the first concerning rule violation was the most prevalent.

The United States, for its part, did not use the language of international trade rules in its announcement about the tariffs or in its subsequent responses until several weeks had passed. In its first public statement after the imposition of the tariffs, the US Trade Representative (USTR) made a short comment in support of the president's action.[15] In April, in response to China's request for consultations at the WTO, the United States made public a letter that it had sent to the Chinese government rejecting China's legal arguments about the tariffs as inapposite.[16] It was not until the end of June, more than three months after the implementation of the tariff action and long after most comments from other states, that the USTR argued that the action was consistent with WTO rules, claiming an exception.[17] The United States subsequently began dispute settlement proceedings against those trading partners for their retaliatory tariffs, taking the position that its steel and aluminum tariffs were consistent with WTO law, so any retaliation against the United States was necessarily not. This exchange of rules debates, cases, and retaliation continued for more than two years.

[10] *Id.*

[11] *Id.*

[12] "Strong Reactions to U.S. Trade Moves," *New York Times*, Mar. 24, 2018, https://www.nytimes.com/2018/03/24/business/trade-tariffs-quotes-reactions.html.

[13] *Id.*

[14] *Id.*

[15] Office of the U.S. Trade Representative, "USTR Robert Lighthizer's Statement on President Trump's Decisions on Imported Steel and Aluminum," Mar. 8, 2018, https://ustr.gov/about-us/policy-offices/press-office/press-releases/2018/february/ustr-robert-lighthizer%E2%80%99s-statement.

[16] Letter of Ambassador Dennis Shea, Permanent Mission of the United States to the World Trade Organization to Ambassador Zhang Xiangchen, Permanent Mission of the People's Republic of China, Apr. 4, 2018.

[17] Office of the U.S. Trade Representative, "Statement by Ambassador Robert E. Lighthizer on Retaliatory Duties," June 26, 2018, https://ustr.gov/about-us/policy-offices/press-office/press-releases/2018/june/statement-ambassador-robert-e.

B. China Tariffs

The experience and display of external legal argumentation in the case of the national security tariff was similar to that in response to another round of US tariffs implemented around the same time on products from China. The Trump administration levied these tariffs on products from China on the basis that China was engaged in an act, policy, or practice—theft of trade secrets from US companies and other restrictive intellectual property measures—that was unreasonable or unjustifiable and burdened or restricted US commerce.[18] The United States implemented tariffs on Chinese products in four waves continuing into 2021, despite the conclusion of an agreement between the two countries that came into effect in early 2020.

Again, states, and importantly not just China, responded to the US action invoking WTO mechanisms including the WTO dispute settlement system, but not exclusively those mechanisms. On March 26, 2018, at a meeting of the WTO Goods Council, several states took the floor to argue about the application of the rules: both that the United States was acting contrary to them and that any response would be consistent with them.[19] Outside the WTO, in public statements, world leaders again spoke out about the importance of trade law in respect of the US actions. Macron argued that the United States should work multilaterally and through the WTO to manage trade issues.[20] Interestingly, the WTO leadership likewise issued a public statement in favor of the institution, emphasizing that such trade actions would put the rules under stress. WTO Deputy Director-General Alan Wolff made a statement urging members to "rededicate" themselves to the organization amidst the rising tensions surrounding tariffs as well as China's rising international ambitions.[21] Each of these arguments sought to reinforce principal trade law norms and to discourage the continuance of the US action.

C. Implications

This review of external trade law argumentation from 2018 to 2020 yields some preliminary conclusions about *how* and *why* state actors engage in trade law argumentation outside the courtroom, and *which state actors* are most active.

With respect to *who* is engaging in legal argumentation, the data show a diverse group of states, from El Salvador to Russia. However, most of the comments made entirely outside the WTO system were made by major world powers. Many smaller states participated in the Council for Trade in Goods discussion, but very few made

[18] 19 U.S.C. §§ 2411–2420.

[19] WTO, "US 'Section 301' Action against China's Intellectual Property Regime Questioned at WTO Goods Council," Mar. 26, 2018, https://www.wto.org/english/news_e/news18_e/good_28mar18_e.htm.

[20] Macron stated that "commercial war," deregulation, and nationalism will not remedy the challenges spurred by globalization. "Macron Warns against 'Commercial War,' Urges Embrace of Multilateralism," *Inside U.S. Trade*, Apr. 25, 2018, https://insidetrade.com/trade/macron-warns-against-%E2%80%98commercial-war%E2%80%99-urges-embrace-multilateralism.

[21] See "WTO Deputy Calls for Reinvestment in WTO amid Growing Pressures," *Inside U.S. Trade*, June 13, 2018, https://insidetrade.com/daily-news/wto-deputy-calls-reinvestment-wto-amid-growing-pressures.

public statements outside of the WTO, which likely limited their exposure. Using the institution was likely a safer and more trusted space for those small states.[22] In other words, trade law argumentation outside the WTO has a price; thus, public statements criticizing the United States may not be available to all states equally. Bigger economies can more easily take ownership of the conversation, which in turn affects the growth and shape of the interpretive landscape. They have more staff that can provide trade law expertise; they have access to venues and global media outlets; and they are able to offer comments in English with little difficulty. The collection of arguments here also indicates that external trade law argumentation allows EU member states to speak up and speak freely on trade matters, whereas the European Union speaks with one voice at the WTO.

Given that the data set focused on comments by states about the US tariff policy, it is unsurprising that the main *purpose* behind these arguments was to persuade the United States to change its ways. But there were likely secondary purposes.[23] For one, the public statements buttressed the statements that many were making inside the courtroom. Some states played "by the book"—that is, they commenced dispute settlement proceedings[24] or they raised concerns in WTO committees—while others chose to retaliate.[25] Many did both. India, for example, threatened retaliation, publicly invoking the rules, while it also requested dispute settlement consultations at the WTO.[26] Some governments used external trade law argumentation as a means to negotiate an alternative route with the United States. For one, Brazil agreed to quotas to avoid the steel and aluminum tariffs.[27] For the most part, on these occasions, the courtroom actions were portrayed as side thoughts to the public spars over the application of the rules, though both were mounted in increasing numbers throughout the summer of 2018, especially as new potential tariffs were announced.[28]

[22] See generally Manak, *supra* note 3.

[23] Steven Ratner has outlined factors at work in persuasion that influence the success of external argumentation: (1) the nature of the normative question; (2) the nature of the parties; (3) the traits and identity of the persuading entity; and, (4) the persuasive process setting (public or private). See generally Steven R. Ratner, "Law Promotion Beyond Law Talk: The Red Cross, Persuasion, and the Laws of War," *European Journal of International Law* 22 (2011): 459.

[24] China requested WTO dispute consultations with the United States regarding certain US duties imposed on imports of steel and aluminum. WTO, "China Initiates WTO Dispute Complaint against US Tariffs on Steel, Aluminium Products," Apr. 9, 2018, https://www.wto.org/english/news_e/news18_e/ds544rfc_09apr18_e.htm.

[25] See, e.g., WTO, "The European Union Launches Safeguard Investigation on Certain Steel Products," Mar. 27, 2018, https://www.wto.org/english/news_e/news18_e/safe_eec_27mar18_e.htm.

[26] WTO, "India Initiates WTO Dispute Complaint against US Steel, Aluminium Duties," May 23, 2018, https://www.wto.org/english/news_e/news18_e/ds547rfc_23may18_e.htm; "India and EU Give WTO Lists of US Goods for Potential Tariff Retaliation," *CNBC*, May 18, 2018, https://www.cnbc.com/2018/05/18/india-and-eu-give-wto-lists-of-us-goods-for-potential-tariff-retaliation.html. See also "Japan Signals Intent to Withdraw WTO Concessions in Response to Section 232 Tariffs," *Inside U.S. Trade*, May 18, 2018, https://insidetrade.com/daily-news/japan-signals-intent-withdraw-wto-concessions-response-section-232-tariffs#:~:text=Japan%20will%20soon%20file%20its,sources%20familiar%20with%20the%20action.

[27] "U.S. Cuts Off Brazil Tariff Talks, Adopts Steel Import Quotas," *Reuters*, May 2, 2018, https://www.reuters.com/article/us-usa-trade-brazil/u-s-cuts-off-brazil-tariff-talks-adopts-steel-import-quotas-idUSKBN1I31ZD?il=0.

[28] See WTO, "Members Raise Concerns over US Section 232 Investigation on Automobiles and Automotive Parts," July 3 & 4, 2018, https://www.wto.org/english/news_e/news18_e/good_03jul18_e.htm (over forty WTO members expressing concern).

This mix of adjudicative action and external trade law argumentation helps us understand how states use the two in parallel. They both activate the trade law courtroom and take their arguments outside the courtroom.[29] But rather than use external trade law argumentation to significantly expand or elaborate the content or scope of trade law rules or fill gaps that cannot be filled through the courtroom process, governments are making arguments that track substantially in very general terms the arguments that these states ultimately articulate in the courtroom. That this is so confirms that international trade law plays out in diffuse discursive processes apart from the courtroom, even if the courtroom is seen by most trade scholars as the gold standard. It is too early to tell how the disputes against the United States or brought by the United States will come out, but because that process takes many months, the external legal argumentation allows states to articulate publicly their interpretations of the trade law rules before and while they file any submissions to a panel. Accordingly, one additional motivation may be to provide a public preview to states' courtroom commentary.

The collection studied here also reveals several effects of external trade law argumentation, many of which extend far beyond this response to the Trump administration tariffs. First, external trade law argumentation provided states with an opportunity to control the narrative. They used trade law arguments to make the issue of the US tariffs a legal rather than a political one, diffusing tensions among trading partners. The United States' own delay in invoking international trade law arguments was perceived by some commentators to suggest uncertainty about the strength of its argument or perhaps an internal divide within the US government as to which course to take, but it also demonstrated an interest on the part of the United States to pursue the issue politically rather than legally. Through their invocation of the rules, these other states' arguments reinforced the application of the rules.

Second, such reinforcement helps enhance the legitimacy of trade law, its institutions, and the trade rule of law.[30] I attribute much of states' abilities to engage in such institutional reinforcement to the fact that trade law has an enforceable set of rules that have in turn formed the foundation for a new set of tools for actors to use in their policy debates. Trade disputes both get to court and have a life outside of the courtroom. They are used together with the rules to reinforce that trade commitments, unlike many others in international law, are readily enforceable.

Third, the external trade law arguments presented here re-emphasized the application and continued relevance of the rules in a controversial area where and when dispute settlement ultimately may prove unsatisfactory. As compared to the legal narrative and institutional legitimacy effects, this separate effect evidences the instrumentalization of legal argument outside the courtroom to achieve the goals likewise sought inside the courtroom. Through these external statements that stress the importance of the rules, state actors sought to precipitate change in

[29] See also Johnstone, *supra* note 4, at 34 (discussing the use of legal arguments to enhance perceptions of obligation); and Stephen Mathias and Nicolas Perez, chapter 16, in this volume (on the United Nations' use of legal argumentation to governments for eventual use in domestic courts).

[30] Monica Hakimi and Ingo Venzke each likewise take up the legitimization effects of such argumentation in chapter 3 and chapter 2, respectively, in this volume.

US policy and to influence domestic legal choices, just as the dispute settlement process might ordinarily do. That states chose to use the public sphere may reflect the challenges facing WTO dispute settlement of late. Given the absence of any functioning WTO Appellate Body at the time of writing, WTO dispute settlement may end in a stalemate. Accordingly, in this instance at least, WTO members may rely more heavily on the public space to articulate such arguments and justify their own responses.

Relatedly and as noted, few external trade law arguments outside the courtroom take issue with the substance of the rules. While states regularly contest the future of rule reform and negotiation of new rules, those types of arguments permeate the popular space less frequently. Rather, the legal argumentation outside the WTO dispute settlement system as seen here often concerns trade law's coverage and application. These arguments nearly all reflect broad statements about inconsistency of this particular action with the rules, but that is not necessarily generalizable.

Fourth, whether intended or not, external trade law argumentation expands the legal community and brings the rules more directly into the public consciousness. The arguments presented here reveal a level of acceptance with and familiarity of trade law in popular speech. Each of the arguments captured by this study could have been made (and likely was also made) by private note or in the course of dispute settlement.[31] By broadcasting this message, however, the trade law conversation reaches everyday citizens. Thus, external trade law argumentation broadens the scope of trade-interested parties and internalizes trade law norms with domestic and foreign audiences.[32]

Finally, the external trade law response to the Trump administration actions also tells us something about the moments in which public-facing trade law argumentation may become more salient. During complex negotiations for trade agreements, one could anticipate that external trade argumentation may increase. Governments alert stakeholders as to their anticipated negotiating positions. They articulate arguments for selected language to be codified in those agreements. By contrast, in this instance, the data show that states are equally willing to advance trade law arguments in potential litigation contexts as well.

But how does external trade argumentation compare with the type of international trade law arguments that may be made to a primarily domestic audience? Would we expect the same motivations and effects in a very different forum than major media outlets and press releases? The next section turns to internal trade law argumentation where we see some different motivations given the starkly different setting and speakers, but, surprisingly, there are some similarities in effect.

[31] See, e.g., "Turkey Challenges Section 232 Tariff Expansion in WTO Safeguards Committee," *Inside U.S. Trade*, Apr. 2, 2020, https://insidetrade.com/daily-news/turkey-challenges-section-232-tariff-expansion-wto-safeguards-committee.

[32] See Janet K. Levit, "Bottom-Up International Lawmaking: Reflections on the New Haven School of International Law," *Yale Journal of International Law* 32 (2007): 393 (noting the significance of other actors in trade law conversations); Johnstone, *supra* note 4, at 34.

III. Internal Trade Law Argumentation

This section reviews what I call "internal trade law argumentation." Here, I refer to arguments made by individuals to a primarily internal, that is, domestic, audience. Internal trade law arguments can be found among media statements by private sector or civil society leaders, or on popular blogs and in op-eds by scholars, or they may be statements by legislators during legislative debate. For this chapter, I focus on the latter. I present here preliminary results derived from a new and original data set of trade law arguments made on the floor of the US Congress by members of Congress and comments of certain interest groups or individuals submitted to Congress and entered into the record in the course of debate.[33] These arguments were offered between 2008 and 2019.

The US Congress is a rather unique body for a case study in trade law argumentation.[34] First, Congress is the branch of the US government that has the lead on US trade lawmaking according to the US Constitution.[35] Congress has delegated much of that responsibility to the executive over the last century, but it nevertheless maintains ultimate authority with respect to tariffs and matters of foreign commerce facing the United States. Second, Congress has exhibited a mixed view on trade over time. Since 1934, Congress by at least a narrow majority has appeared to favor trade liberalization—the lowering of barriers to trade with US trading partners. It regularly provided the US president with the power to negotiate the reciprocal reduction of tariff rates. Despite that legislative choice, congressional records reveal that a significant minority in the Congress often doubted whether lowering barriers to trade, or more accurately, giving the president the ability to lower barriers to trade was the preferred policy for the United States.[36]

Congress's engagement with international trade law rules that themselves promote liberalization could be seen as a sign of its acceptance of trade liberalization as the default position now codified at the international level. On the other hand, the trade law argumentation occurring in Congress could just as well reject the content or the application of international trade law rules to US domestic law reflecting the maintenance of ambiguity in Congress's position toward trade liberalization and trade law. Thus, the tone and content of congressional arguments about trade law help us understand and even predict the future direction of trade law as advanced by one of its most important proponents. The regular invocation of international trade law rules in the Congressional Record suggests that there is more to congressional interest in trade law than meets the eye.

[33] I examine only statements offered on the House or Senate floors and not in committees. There are expert conversations about trade law occurring regularly in US congressional committees, to be sure. I chose to exclude those to be able to isolate the most important and most forceful comments made to an entire chamber of Congress among a range of participants—not just those members that specialize in international trade in their respective committees.

[34] Others have considered international law in Congress—see, e.g., Kevin L. Cope, "Congress's International Legal Discourse," *Michigan Law Review* 113 (2015): 1115.

[35] U.S. Const., art. I, § 8, cl. 1 and cl. 3.

[36] One can see this in the constant renewal of trade negotiating authority given to the executive branches in fits and starts since its original delegation in 1934, among other evidence. See Claussen, *supra* note 1, at Part I.

Examining the congressional arguments in the data set reveals that the nature, content, and purpose of the arguments diverge. Five general types of trade law arguments appear as identified by their primary purpose or driving message: (1) law-embracing: arguments advocating for a particular domestic policy action because it is consistent with trade rules or would correct US policy in favor of consistency with trade rules; (2) law-cautioning: arguments that adopting a particular policy will create a litigation risk at the WTO or otherwise put the United States at fault; (3) enforcement: arguments in favor of the United States enforcing international trade law rules where a trading partner has implemented a problematic measure; (4) reprisal: arguments in favor of retaliation as justified by trade law typically after the United States has shown a trading partner to have violated trade rules; and (5) institutional critique: arguments criticizing trade law rules or arguing about the limitations of the rules. The arguments do not break down evenly across the five categories, however, nor are the lines between them totally solid. I will focus here on some highlights, turning first to the biggest category—the law-embracing category, and then turn to the rest, noting their fuzzy boundaries.

A. US Policy Advocacy Arguments

The largest group of arguments from US legislators—roughly one-third—comprise the "law-embracing" category: arguments advocating a particular domestic policy action consistent with the rules or clarifying the content of the rules. Members of the US Congress regularly refer to the WTO or FTA rules as a means of influencing the trajectory of US law and domestic policy, both for and against, but they more often use international trade law to support taking action that they maintain is consistent with the rules or that would make US action more consistent with international rules. For example, in 2012, three representatives advocated for the passage of legislation that would clarify the ability of the United States to apply countervailing duties in response to state subsidies by US partners in line with WTO rules.[37] In 2011, senators argued for passage of a bill that would enable the United States to enhance the WTO rules to combat China's trade practices.[38]

Members have also called for reform of US law to be consistent with WTO obligations or with decisions reached in WTO dispute settlement. The most well known instance of such a debate had to do with the US Country of Origin Labeling (COOL) requirements. The US COOL statutes and regulations were the subject of a contentious dispute at the WTO. Canada and Mexico challenged the treatment accorded to imported Canadian cattle and hogs and imported Mexican cattle under the COOL regime.[39] After the panel and the WTO Appellate Body

[37] See, e.g., Statement of Representatives Dave Camp, Charles Boustany, and Renee Ellmers, Congressional Record, 2012.

[38] Statement of Senator Debbie Stabenow, Congressional Record, 2011 (arguing that China is cheating and taking illegal actions under the WTO and the bill under consideration would help address the cheating and rule-breaking).

[39] See United States—Certain Country of Origin Labelling (COOL) Requirements, DS384, 386, https://www.wto.org/english/tratop_e/dispu_e/cases_e/ds384_e.htm.

determined that the US measures violated WTO rules, the Obama administration attempted to work with Congress to amend the legislation. Several members of Congress spoke about the WTO ruling and even engaged with the merits of the decision in nuanced ways.[40] Some argued that repeal was necessary for consistency with international law, while others noted findings of the WTO panel that acknowledged the legitimacy of the measures even if inconsistent.[41] Still others saw extensions for future FTAs.[42] The COOL situation was not the only such instance of members taking these sorts of positions, however; members have likewise considered legislation on aircraft subsidies and other trade topics in similar terms.[43]

Across the last decade, members of Congress have regularly referred to WTO rules or WTO dispute settlement decisions as a justification for US legislative outcomes.[44] They have also occasionally defended proposed US measures as WTO-compliant in the face of challenge by foreign trading partners. For example, in a Senate debate in 2016, Senator John Boozman, senator from Arkansas, argued that a proposed catfish inspection rule did not violate WTO rules, contrary to the positions of fish import lobbyists and Vietnam, because it would apply equally to imported and domestic fish.[45]

Are these invocations of international trade law representative of a form of legal opportunism in which members look for support for their political gains and employ references to the rules when the rules seem to favor them, but they do not do so when unfavorable?[46] Or do these comments by members reflect their true position as legal enthusiasts, particularly when it comes to trade? The data set is too limited to answer these questions with certainty. At the very least, however, one can conclude that members of Congress are engaging with international trade law as another tool in their arsenal for policy advocacy.

[40] See, e.g., Statement of Representative Mike Conaway, Congressional Record, 2015 (arguing that a WTO panel ruled that US labeling requirements for beef and pork are unavoidably discriminatory under COOL, so repeal of COOL is the only way to bring the United States into compliance with its WTO obligations and avoid retaliation).

[41] See, e.g., Statement of Representative Collin Peterson, Congressional Record, 2015 (arguing that repealing COOL to avoid WTO sanctions for discriminatory behavior is not the most reasonable solution, because the WTO has said that COOL is a legitimate goal).

[42] See, e.g., Statement of Representative Brian Schatz, Congressional Record, 2015 (arguing that the WTO panel's conclusions would have reverberating effects on FTAs and investor-state dispute settlement outcomes).

[43] See, e.g., Statement of Representative Russ Carnahan, Congressional Record, 2010 (arguing that the United States should make it difficult for contractors to work with Airbus since the WTO decided that Airbus received illegal subsidies).

[44] See, e.g., Statement of Senator Jeff Sessions, Congressional Record, 2011 (arguing that the Currency Exchange Rate Oversight Reform Act should be passed because it would productively incorporate WTO rules into US administrative processes); Statement of Senator Patty Murray, Congressional Record, 2010 (arguing that the Defense Level Playing Field Act ought to take into account the WTO Airbus subsidy ruling).

[45] Statement of Senator John Boozman, Congressional Record, 2016.

[46] The challenge of answering these questions increases when legislators change views on trade law issues. Compare Statement of Senator Rob Portman, Congressional Record, 2011 (arguing that the United States should work through the WTO to address China), with Statement of Senator Rob Portman, Congressional Record, 2019 (arguing that the WTO was insufficient to address the threat of China's rise).

B. Arguments Using Trade Law as Sword or Shield

Another third of congressional trade law arguments from the last decade are offensive and defensive arguments, falling in the "enforcement" and "law-cautioning" categories: arguments in favor of the United States enforcing international trade law rules where a trading partner has implemented a problematic measure, and arguments that adopting a particular policy will create a litigation risk at the WTO or otherwise put the United States at fault. First, members sometimes advocate US bill passage or executive action that will help the United States enforce rules against a trading partner.[47] This is a common argument in congressional debates about aircraft subsidies, for instance, or in those having to do with China's trade practices.[48] Second and in nearly equal number, members have used the WTO rules to argue that certain US policies ought to be avoided. For example, over the period studied here, different members warned that the failure to bring US cotton industries into compliance with WTO rules could lead to US WTO violations.[49] Likewise, in a House debate in 2010, various representatives took the position that the proposed Currency Reform for Fair Trade Act would violate trade rules and that the measure would be subject to challenge at the WTO.[50]

Very few—roughly 10 percent—of the trade law arguments in the data set fall in the institutional critique category; that is, few criticize trade law rules or argue about the limitations of the rules.[51] This may be the result of the US separation of trade law powers between the branches. The US executive branch is responsible for negotiations and rule interpretation on behalf of the United States; it regularly makes such criticisms in Geneva. Where legislators have concerns about rule language, they are more likely to voice those to the USTR who speaks on their behalf. An equally small group of internal trade law arguments advocate retaliation as justified by trade law.[52]

The remaining 10 percent of internal trade law arguments is a mixed bag, defying classification in any one area. They do not have an obvious trigger such as a particular incident or announced policy. As is true for other arguments discussed above, these arguments vary widely, especially with respect to target. Some trade law arguments in the mixed bag as well as across the various categories are issue-specific, such as

[47] See, e.g., Statements of Representatives David Dreier, Billy Long, and Tom Reed, Congressional Record, 2012 (arguing that the United States needs to repeal the Jackson-Vanik provision so the country can be on equal playing field for exports with other states once Russia joins WTO).

[48] See, e.g., Statement of Senator Maria Cantwell, Congressional Record, 2017 (arguing that the United States should enforce WTO rules against the European Union after WTO rulings on airplane subsidies); Statement of Senator Sherrod Brown, Congressional Record, 2011 (arguing that China cheats in the WTO, leading to loss of jobs).

[49] See, e.g., Statement of Senator Richard Lugar, Congressional Record, 2008; Statement of Senator Jeff Flake, Congressional Record, 2010 (arguing that the US cotton program needs to be reformed to be consistent with WTO subsidy rues).

[50] Statements of Representative Chris Van Hollen and others, Congressional Record, 2010.

[51] See, e.g., Statements of Senators Orrin Hatch, Jefferson Sessions, and James Lankford, and of Representative Linda Sánchez, Congressional Record, 2011–2019 (arguing that FTA or WTO rules do not work for the United States in various respects).

[52] See, e.g., Statement of Representative DeLauro, Congressional Record, 2009 (arguing that the WTO recently found Airbus is receiving illegal subsidies and US Department of Defense should take this into consideration when considering bids for next-generation air refueling tanker contract).

dealing with policies of China or Russia, but some are also systemic or address broad engagement with trade law institutions.

C. Trade Law Arguments to Congress

The Congressional Record also features statements by individuals appearing before Congress who have made international trade law arguments. These individuals and interest groups typically make arguments advocating for a policy course in light of the rules or expressing concern about the possible inconsistency of proposed legislation with the WTO rules. For example, in 2011, an industry association argued to Congress that "China's blocking and filtering measures, and the fog of uncertainty surrounding what China's censors will and will not permit, violate numerous of China's international obligations, including provisions of the GATS Article 111:4 (and other provisions) and China's WTO Protocol of Accession."[53]

Others have used trade law arguments to raise concern about US policy choices, given what they considered to be the insufficient proposed international trade law rules. Labor and industry groups made arguments in 2011, for instance, about the US-Korea FTA. The United Steelworkers argued that Congress should reject the agreement because it would allow Korea, according to the Steelworkers, to avoid countervailing and anti-dumping duties by shipping through third countries and lacks safeguards to protect against these practices. The American Manufacturing Trade Action Coalition likewise advocated against the FTA because Korea had sixteen trade remedies orders against it and, according to the Coalition, had been hostile to imports by creating non-tariff barriers to trade. Even US state governments have had occasion to make trade law arguments to members of Congress about trade issues affecting their economies.[54]

D. Implications

Taken together, the use of international trade law argumentation in the US Congress signals a shift in the content of legislative interest in international trade law. This evidence counters a perception among some policymakers that US institutions, and particularly the Congress, lost their regulatory policy space to overly constraining international rules.[55] But this is not the dominant message of legislators today who

[53] Statement of Gilbert Kaplan on behalf of the US Committee to Support Trade Laws, Congressional Record, 2011. Other examples abound. For instance, in a statement delivered to and entered into the record of the US House of Representatives, the US Chamber of Commerce argued that if the House were to pass legislation constraining what could pass through Keystone XL Pipeline it would be subject to the same criticisms as China was in a recent case China lost at the WTO about export restraints on raw materials. See Statement of Bruce Josten on behalf of the US Chamber of Commerce, Congressional Record, 2012.

[54] Statement on behalf of the legislature of the state of Utah, Congressional Record, 2009 (arguing that US trading partners may attempt to bring further claims against federal and state gambling laws under trade and investment agreements that lack the "public morals" exception found in the WTO General Agreement on Trade in Services).

[55] "Episode 111: Trade Policy Under Trump," *Trade Talks Podcast*, Nov. 25, 2019.

appear to have accepted, even if reluctantly, the international trade law system. Many members of Congress appear to acknowledge as given, and binding, not just the basic trade law rules in the GATT but also the norms that are now firm in the other WTO agreements. Members of Congress do not regularly argue on the legislative floor that trade law is overly constraining. In most instances, they use trade law instrumentally. Few of the arguments surveyed here criticize the content or constraints of the rules; rather, legislators regularly work within them and deploy them to their advantage for the advancement of domestic policy decisions. Accordingly, regardless of the topic or substance of the argument, there is a sense of cooperation with international trade rules that dominates congressional trade law argumentation.

Given that the earlier typology of arguments examined each statement on the basis of motivation, what of the effects? Looking at the arguments on a case-by-case basis, members occasionally achieved their stated aims with respect to particular legislation. It is difficult to make any causal claims as to the influence of the international trade law argument in those scenarios or to track precisely which bills in which categories succeeded or failed, but the general takeaway is one of relevance of international trade law and the evolution of US policymaking to be both cognizant of and perhaps more consistent with international trade norms.

Apart from these legislative outcomes, internal trade law argumentation has still other effects. Importantly, the proliferation of these arguments strengthens the role of the US Congress in the regulation of foreign commerce. US lawmakers rely on the rules to advance both domestic and international policies. This approach turns traditional trade law process somewhat on its head: when it comes to international trade law in the United States for the past thirty years, often the executive acts while the legislature reacts, but these data show that legislators are themselves speakers and progenitors of trade law argumentation, and not just in directing the executive.[56]

Internal trade law arguments also enhance the embeddedness of trade law norms in domestic lawmaking processes. The expressions from constituents and civil society likewise have socialized the international trade law rules to the public and to members of Congress. To be responsive, members must educate themselves and their staff about trade law issues. In fact, both the House and the Senate employ specialized committee staff to deal with trade law issues apart from individual members' staff that may be trained in this field.[57]

As a result, there is a robust public platform for international trade law in the US media. The same groups—members of Congress, other politicians, scholars, industry groups, and others from civil society—regularly make international trade law arguments in popular US news sources such as in the opinion pages of the *New York Times* and *Wall Street Journal*.[58] There, the audience is clearly more mixed, but the outcome

[56] Cf. Rebecca Ingber, "Congressional Administration of Foreign Affairs," *Virginia Law Review* 106 (2020): 395 (discussing the controls Congress maintains over the executive branch in the executive's foreign affairs powers).

[57] This fact is not unique to trade, but is nevertheless representative of trade's importance.

[58] See, e.g., "China's High Trade Barriers," U.S. Business and Industry Council, Letter to the Editor, *New York Times*, Dec. 21, 2011, https://www.nytimes.com/2011/12/21/opinion/chinas-high-trade-barriers.html (arguing that China has been allowed to keep unusually high economic barriers to trade because American companies lobbied for a good deal for China and that new WTO protections for Chinese exports encourage American companies to offshore jobs); "Trump Lies. China Thrives," Letter to the

is largely the same: the normalization of international trade law in public space. Just as shown above with the widening interpretive community through external trade law argumentation, trade law is increasingly ingrained in public speech beyond trade law experts to policymakers and media influencers. In effect, trade law is widely shared and owned by diverse constituencies. This phenomenon is partly spurred by the twenty-first-century ready availability of global communications, but the decentralization of international trade law argumentation is especially notable.

These examples tell a reasonably rosy story of international trade law's proliferation. This glimpse into internal trade law argumentation where most of the comments employ the rules to domestic ends suggests a threshold level of support for trade law institutions. It suggests that trade law matters to the US public. It strengthens trade law institutions, such that when they come under attack a broad base of support for them has been socialized through the legal community.[59] The data explored here reflect a particularly meaningful level of acceptance as they extend across parts of the government and to the public. The arguments seen here are also emblematic of the many decentralized international lawmaking processes that are especially prevalent in trade given trade's expansion throughout the regulatory state. There is increased comfort and familiarity with international trade law in Congress that signify a degree of acceptance in the legislative body, all the more significant given its mixed history on the matter.

Nevertheless, there are potential downsides to this type of argumentation by non-specialist audiences like members of Congress. For example, the increased use of trade law argumentation could have a negative impact on the perceived meaning of underlying legal norms. Legislators speak with foreign delegations and trading partners with some frequency. In fact, in some instances, foreign delegations have served as greater sources of information on trade negotiations to legislative staff than the executive branch. But legislators' invocations of trade norms either with foreign delegations or in congressional debate could confuse the public as to precisely what international trade law is or what its institutions do. Many of the statements reviewed

Editor, *New York Times*, June 7, 2017, https://www.nytimes.com/2017/06/07/opinion/trump-china-trade.html (arguing that even though China agreed to let in US credit card companies like Visa and Mastercard, it was because it was required to do so under WTO rules, it dragged its feet in letting them in, and now they will struggle to compete against Chinese card companies like UnionPay); "A Costly Anachronism," *New York Times*, Feb. 28, 2012, https://www.nytimes.com/2012/02/28/opinion/a-costly-anachronism.html (editorial arguing that if Congress does not repeal the Jackson-Vanik amendment soon, the United States will be in violation of WTO rules and American exporters will pay higher tariffs than competitors for access to Russian markets); "Why I Support a Border-Adjustment Tax," *New York Times*, Mar. 30, 2017, https://www.nytimes.com/2017/03/30/opinion/why-i-support-a-border-adjustment-tax.html (arguing that the United States should adopt a border-adjustment tax even though the WTO may disapprove of it as an import barrier or export subsidy and that nevertheless the WTO would probably approve of it because WTO panels have approved of similar consumption taxes that foreign competitors collect).

[59] On certain occasions, Congress has been quite express about its support and interest in the functioning of the WTO. For a recent example, see H. Res. 746, 116th Congress (2019), in which a bipartisan group of House members "express[] the sense of the House of Representatives that the United States should reaffirm its commitment as a member of the [WTO] and work with other WTO members to achieve reforms at the WTO."

for this study demonstrated a degree of ambiguity or arguably a misunderstanding of trade law norms.

This depiction of external trade law argumentation also shows the dynamism and iterativeness of trade law. Unlike domestic legal constraints, compliance with international trade law under the WTO system is reasonably flexible and negotiable. In the trade dispute settlement system, states may choose among remedies. For example, where a panel identifies a measure to violate WTO rules, the member in question may choose to bring that measure into compliance or it may choose to enter into an arrangement where the challenging member is compensated in trade terms at a level reciprocal to the cost of the violative measure. Incorporating trade law norms into domestic conversations may shape community expectations in favor of compliance. Where political challenges make reform of domestic trade policies difficult, using the language of trade law with greater frequency may establish that law as a basis for change to help overcome those challenges. Thus, making arguments on the floor of the US Congress may be jurisgenerative, supplementing legal transformation at the international level with ideas and interpretations deployed in domestic settings. As legislators and other actors argue about trade law's application and translate trade law norms into their everyday speech, they serve both explanatory and argumentative functions; not only may they achieve domestic policy aims, but they also help explain and interpret international trade law in ways that may inform legal development internationally.[60] The data reflect regular engagement with trade law, lending support for the idea that trade law is always moving and shaping activity not just at the international level but also at the domestic level.

Finally, we may draw additional conclusions as to what types of arguments are *not* found in the data set. For example, we have not (yet) seen arguments about the Trump administration's tariff policies that were the focus of Section II. While that conversation is ongoing in committees and among certain members, there is no legislation on the floor of the Congress for consideration at this time or in the time frame of reference. In any event, debates about that issue have centered on the separation of trade law powers between Congress and the executive, and not on whether the Trump administration was acting consistently with WTO or other trade law rules. This distinction highlights another noteworthy point about the data set. Rarely do legislators invoke trade law on the floor of Congress to exert pressure on the executive for a particular course of action. This is likely the case because (1) members of the two branches frequently meet in private, and (2) the more natural setting to make those sorts of statements (which are indeed very common) is at a congressional hearing. Further, Congress can effect change in the executive's course through legislation such as Trade Promotion Authority legislation when it comes up for renewal. This may also be the case because the Congress is somewhat powerless to employ trade law in this manner. Congress does not appear to use trade law argumentation to take ownership of the legal issue area as a matter of course. The far more common purpose of internal trade law argumentation is persuasion as to domestic, legislative policy choices and actions.

[60] Thinking about trade law argumentation in this way provides a useful complement to transnational legal process theories that consider the trickle-down effect of international law.

IV. Conclusion

At both the international and domestic levels, this widespread use of trade law has a self-perpetuating effect: it protects international trade law institutions, including their dispute settlement features, when those institutions come under political or geoeconomic stress. Both sets of arguments reflect a normalization of trade law, but they also illustrate that the process is imperfect and our information is incomplete. Trade law rules have become entrenched in popular vocabulary to some degree even if no single theory explains what is happening in this space nor do we fully understand the panoply of lawmaking and law-shaping effects. At a time when the future of our multilateral trade law system has come into question, external and internal trade law argumentation outside the courtroom is especially important. The courtroom may fade, but the rules will be reinforced in myriad ways in other settings as seen here.

To be sure, my intent is to provide the groundwork for a continuing analysis of trade law argumentation and to do so through two short illustrations, but there is much more work to be done. This is a preliminary, narrowly focused study with room for much more. The popularization and acculturation of international trade law norms demand greater scholarly attention. The occasion of the 2020 coronavirus pandemic and economic measures taken in response proves fertile ground for evaluating how states choose to engage in external trade law argumentation—or not—when it is not just the United States but nearly all states affected in some way. Moreover, future studies could take a closer look at audiences to aggregate the responses among different constituencies and examine how successful certain types of arguments are in achieving desired policy ends or compliance with the law. The data here suggest that triggering domestic policies that accord with international trade law may be a long-term goal that requires much greater embeddedness than that seen at present. Further, although this study looks at just one moment in time, a longitudinal analysis may reflect what I suspect would be an increase in the use of international trade law arguments especially since 1994. Finally, as this volume addresses numerous fields within international law, this chapter has hypothesized that differences in argumentation across those field are in part attributable to trade law's codified, binding, and enforceable nature, but more work could be done on other possible contributing factors. These projects, necessarily inchoate and indefinite, will surely yield additional fruit for this important conversation.

16
The Privileges and Immunities of the United Nations

*Stephen Mathias and Nicolas Perez**

I. Introduction

Shedding some light on the legal argumentation developed outside the courtroom by the United Nations in relation to its privileges and immunities and those of its personnel is a complex task. For purposes of this chapter, the term "legal argumentation" shall be understood as the sum of legal arguments developed by the Organization, including the Secretariat, the Agencies, Funds, and Programs as well as the missions deployed in the field, and communicated, through a variety of forms, to a wide array of stakeholders and interlocutors, both internal (UN departments, agencies, funds, or programs) and external (member states, private entities, other international organizations). While the Office of Legal Affairs (OLA) constitutes the primary source of legal advice for the Secretariat, multiple actors, both at UN Headquarters and in the field, are involved in the collection of facts required to form a specific legal argumentation. The need to also take into account operational and political considerations creates a unique and intricate environment for the United Nations' legal officers.

The United Nations' legal argumentation most often aims, in relation to privileges and immunities, at ensuring that a specific dispute involving the United Nations as a whole and/or one of its personnel will be solved in accordance with the specific status enjoyed by the United Nations and its personnel under international law. Thus, the dispute will not be brought before the court of a member state or, in cases where legal proceedings have already been engaged, those proceedings are terminated pursuant to the applicable framework. Rather, the purpose of the argumentation is generally to persuade specific national representatives and authorities—Permanent Missions, Foreign Ministries, Ministries of Justice, national courts—to adopt the legal position set forth by the United Nations.[1] This legal position is generally presented in solely legal terms: the UN

* The views expressed in this chapter are the authors' personal views and do not necessarily reflect the views of the United Nations.

[1] See the developments regarding the motives for legal argumentation proposed by Ian Johnstone, chapter 7, and by Scott P. Sheeran, chapter 4, both in this volume.

Stephen Mathias and Nicolas Perez, *The Privileges and Immunities of the United Nations* In: *Talking International Law.* Edited by: Ian Johnstone and Steven Ratner, Oxford University Press. © Stephen Mathias and Nicolas Perez 2021. DOI: 10.1093/oso/9780197588437.003.0016

position should be adopted because it is legally correct. Other considerations are secondary, if presented at all. OLA is normally seeking to present, outside the courtroom, the exact same legal argumentation that lawyers and counsels would use, in a courtroom, to convince a judicial authority. It is generally dealing directly, however, only with political entities, such as Permanent Missions, Foreign Ministries, and Ministries of Justice. In the most complex situations, the legal argumentation developed on behalf of the Organization will complement, or sometimes be reinforced by, political argumentation developed by other UN bodies or departments, to which OLA will not necessarily be privy. The scope of our analysis will, however, be limited to the legal argumentation developed by OLA and will therefore not refer to any political arguments that the Organization may have put forward in the different cases analyzed below.

The recognition of privileges and immunities can be sensitive for both member states and international organizations since it sometimes gives rise, within the general population and the media, to a feeling that the normal course of justice has not been followed in a given situation. While diplomatic privileges and immunities are distinct from those applicable to international organizations and their personnel, the political and reputational risks associated with the assertion of privileges and immunities are similar for states and international organizations. While this chapter does not include a discussion of the internal decision processes of the United Nations, assertions of immunities are always carefully weighed, taking into consideration not only their potential impact on the United Nations' reputation but also, and primarily, their consequences on its ability to fulfill its mandate. Relevant departments, as well as field offices and missions, are always consulted prior to any assertion of privileges or immunities and reminded that the Secretary-General is under a legal obligation to waive the immunity of UN personnel in any case where, in his or her opinion, the immunity would impede the course of justice and it can be waived without prejudice to the United Nations' interests.[2] Those considerations are not unique to the United Nations, or to international organizations in general, since states face the same challenges in relation to their own diplomats and representatives. However, once the decision to assert the privileges and immunities has been taken, the specificity of the legal argumentation which is developed in respect of the United Nations resurfaces.

In order to better understand the legal argumentation relating to UN privileges and immunities developed by the Organization, as well as its specificities, it will be appropriate to distinguish two types of rationale for this legal argumentation:

- Argumentation to ensure the proper implementation of the existing legal framework or principles (Section II);

[2] Convention on the Privileges and Immunities of the United Nations, Feb. 13, 1946, 1 UNTS 15, art. V, sec. 20, and art. VI, sec. 23.

- Argumentation to support the development of privileges and immunities not expressly provided in the existing legal framework that are necessary for the activities of the Organization (Section III).

II. Legal Argumentation by the United Nations Related to the Implementation of the Existing Legal Framework

Privileges and immunities are critical to ensure that the United Nations' mandate is being implemented properly, in full independence and without any undue interference. This was recognized early in the history of the United Nations by member states, which included in the Charter itself a specific provision stating that the "Organization shall enjoy in the territory of each of its Members such privileges and immunities as are necessary for the fulfilment of its purposes" and led to the adoption, by the General Assembly in 1946, of the Convention on the Privileges and Immunities of the United Nations.[3] The 1946 Convention is not, however, the only legal instrument defining and detailing the United Nations' privileges and immunities. Each UN Headquarters office and field mission, as well as each project activity of the United Nations and its funds or programs, is also usually governed by a specific host country agreement or a generic convention (such as the UN Development Programme (UNDP)'s Standard Basic Assistance Agreement). The drafting, negotiation, and review of this type of instrument continue to constitute a major part of the activities of OLA.

The United Nations sometimes finds itself in the unusual situation of having to defend its privileges and immunities, and those of its personnel, against the very states which, through their accession to the Charter, the 1946 Convention, and/or specific mission agreements, have recognized that such privileges and immunities are "necessary for the fulfilment of its purposes" (Article 105). Even in circumstances where the legal dispute has been initiated by an entity other that a member state, such as an individual, a private company, or a nongovernmental organization, the purpose of the legal argumentation put forward by the United Nations will always be to convince the member state that this dispute be resolved pursuant to the specific legal principles applicable to the Organization. These legal principles can usually be divided into two main topics: the privileges and immunities of the individuals associated with the United Nations (representatives of member states, UN officials, and experts on mission for the United Nations), and those of the Organization itself.

A. Reaffirming the Applicability of Privileges and Immunities to Nationals in Their Home Country

OLA has observed a recent trend toward a more restrictive approach of member states to the granting of privileges and immunities to their nationals present on their territory but working for the United Nations. In many negotiations aiming at the

[3] *Id.*

conclusion of host country agreements for the establishment of a new UN office in a member state, or for the organization of a conference or a training on the territory of a member state, the United Nations has had to face demands from host states aiming at explicitly excluding their nationals from the benefits of the privileges and immunities accorded to them under the 1946 Convention.

The arguments used by member states are usually drawn from their domestic legal order. For example, the principle of equality of citizens before the law, enshrined or not in the state constitution, is often put forward as the basis on which to refuse to agree to provide privileges and immunities to national staff members, in order to prevent what is characterized as discrimination among nationals. Some member states note that any legal instrument that would provide such privileges and immunities to some of their citizens would necessarily have to be presented to their Parliament, which would cause delays that are often incompatible with the schedule of the planned activity or the opening of the UN facility.

In such cases, and when the member state concerned is a party to the 1946 Convention, OLA will endeavor to negotiate indirectly, through the relevant department, fund, or program, suggesting a number of core principles. First, the United Nations will typically remind the member state (through its Permanent Mission or its Ministry of Foreign Affairs) of its obligations under international law by pointing out that the provisions of the 1946 Convention related to officials (Article V) and experts on mission (Article VI) do not contain any exceptions based on the nationality of those individuals or on the territories on which they are present. For the United Nations, the only recognized exception relates to members of the staff "recruited locally and [. . .] assigned to hourly rates."[4] The applicability of the privileges and immunities detailed in those articles of the 1946 Convention to a member of the UN personnel on the territory of his or her own state of nationality has therefore already been recognized and accepted by every party to the 1946 Convention. The United Nations will then indicate that both the text of the 1946 Convention and customary international law would prevent a state to refer to its domestic legal order to justify its nonobservance of an international legal obligation. Indeed, pursuant to Section 34 of the 1946 Convention, "when an instrument of accession is deposited on behalf of any Member, the Member will be in a position under its own law to give effect to the terms of this Convention." Furthermore, Article 27 of the Vienna Convention on the Law of Treaties, which codified customary international law on that point, a state cannot "invoke the provisions of its internal law as justification for its failure to perform a treaty."

In most cases, this two-part legal argumentation, conveyed informally with the assistance of relevant UN entities or formally through a Note Verbale, will be sufficient to result in the recognition of the applicability of the privileges and immunities granted under the 1946 Convention to nationals of the host country authorities. In some instances, the OLA legal argumentation is used by one Ministry—for instance, the Ministry of Foreign Affairs—to demonstrate to another Ministry—for instance, the Ministry of Finance—that the legal principles

[4] GA Res. 76 (I) (Dec. 7, 1946).

are clear and that the applicability of the privileges and immunities cannot lawfully be called into question.

However, the legal argumentation put forward by the Organization in those cases is not necessarily successful, and in 1989, a difference of interpretation between the United Nations and a member state on this subject escalated and ultimately resulted in a request by the Economic and Social Council for an advisory opinion of the International Court of Justice. On May 24, 1989, the Economic and Social Council (ECOSOC) requested an advisory opinion from the International Court of Justice (ICJ) on "the legal question of the applicability of Article VI, Section 22, of the Convention on the Privileges and Immunities of the United Nations" in the case of Dumitru Mazilu as Special Rapporteur of the Sub-Commission on Prevention of Discrimination and Protection of Minorities. The Court's advisory opinion[5] confirmed the interpretation of OLA and of many member states and concluded that the privileges and immunities accorded by the 1946 Convention to experts on mission "may be invoked as against the State of nationality or of residence unless a reservation to Section 22 of the General Convention has been validly made by that State."[6] Beyond this result, it is important to observe that, through the request by the ECOSOC for an advisory opinion of the ICJ, legal argumentation which was initially prepared as internal UN documentation was brought to the attention of a judicial body and member states.

Following a request for an ICJ advisory opinion, the Secretariat has indeed the task to provide the Court, pursuant to Article 65 of its statute, with "all documents likely to throw light upon the question." In this case, the dossier transmitted to the Court was over one hundred sixty pages long and contained materials related to the request (such as the relevant facts of the case, reports, resolutions, and correspondence); general documentation regarding the status of experts on mission and the 1946 Convention; and copies of two OLA memoranda from 1988 addressed to the Under-Secretary-General for Human Rights. These internal memoranda, conveying the legal views of OLA to the relevant senior UN official and dated well before the request for an advisory opinion, were thus communicated officially to the Court, which then transmitted them to member states intervening in its proceedings.

Not only did this case reinforce, in the eyes of member states and other UN departments, the weight of OLA's arguments and opinion in relation to the interpretation of the 1946 Convention, but it also illustrated that, for the United Nations, the line between internal legal argumentation and a legal argumentation which will be used in court can sometimes be difficult to draw. The consequences of this advisory opinion of the ICJ must, however, not be overstated as many member states have, since then, continued to argue against the applicability of the privileges and immunities to their own nationals in their home country.

[5] Applicability of Article VI, Section 22, of the Convention on the Privileges and Immunities of the United Nations, Advisory Opinion, 1989 ICJ Rep., at 177.

[6] *Id.* 196, para. 52.

B. Ensuring Respect for the Functional Immunity of UN Personnel

Although the United Nations' member states have all recognized that a form of immunity from prosecution of UN officials is necessary for the implementation of its mandate, their choice has been, as exemplified by the adoption of the 1946 Convention by the General Assembly, to provide in most cases and excepting only the most senior personnel, a type of immunity distinct from the established concept of diplomatic immunity. This choice is justified by the broad nature of diplomatic immunity and the perceived need to distinguish between the status of diplomats and that of international civil servants in the light of the nature and functions of an international organization as compared to a state. The immunity from legal process accorded to most UN personnel is therefore limited, under the 1946 Convention, to "words spoken or written, and all acts performed by them in their official capacity" (Sections 17 and 22). This functional immunity offers the necessary compromise between the protection of the independence of the UN personnel and the need to hold them accountable under specific circumstances.

Despite the wide consensus for this level of protection, its implementation in some cases has proven to be a challenging task for which the legal argumentation prepared by the Secretariat has had to be carefully tailored. In one notable example, an arms expert appointed by the Secretary-General to one of the panels of experts of the Security Council was arrested at an airport in his home state while officially traveling for the United Nations. The Secretariat immediately mobilized legal and operational resources both at Headquarters and in the field to provide support to this expert. Once confirmation of the arrest was obtained by UN representatives in the country concerned, legal argumentation was prepared by OLA along the following lines: inquiring about the reasons for the arrest; explaining the legal status under the 1946 Convention of members of the Security Council's panels of experts; and insisting on the immediate release of the expert. OLA drafted and issued Notes Verbales addressed, through the Permanent Mission of the state, to the Ministry of Foreign Affairs. They indicated that, as a member of a panel of experts, the subject had the legal status of an expert on mission for the United Nations, as defined in Article VI of the 1946 Convention, and that he was therefore covered by the privileges and immunities in its Section 22, including "immunity from personal arrest or detention and from seizure of [his] personal baggage," as well as "in respect of words spoken or written and acts done by [him] in the course of the performance of [his] mission, immunity from legal process of every kind."

The process by which OLA communicates with member states, through Permanent Missions to Ministries of Foreign Affairs, and from those Ministries to Ministries of Justice and perhaps from those Ministries to courts, suggests that such Notes must be convincing not only to diplomats and practitioners of international law but also potentially to judicial authorities specialized in criminal law but often unfamiliar with the intricacies of privileges and immunities, given that the Notes may be presented in court in essentially unchanged form. In such a case, the Secretariat's efforts are not limited to Notes Verbales. To ensure that its legal argumentation aiming at the immediate release of the expert was as effective and far-reaching as possible, the

United Nations deployed a wide array of means to convey its message: in addition to its formal Notes Verbales, the Secretariat made use of numerous meetings with diplomats and/or legal advisers of the Permanent Mission concerned, briefings to the relevant UN bodies and interested member states, and repeated press statements by the UN Spokesperson, as well as regular contacts with the lawyers and the family of the expert.

In each of those meetings, the purpose of the arguments put forward by the United Nations varied based on the identity and nature of the counterparts. When the Secretary-General or the Legal Counsel were meeting with the national authorities or representatives of the member state concerned, the objective was to remind them of their obligations under international law and to convince them that functional immunity was applicable. When discussing the case with the media or with the lawyers and family of the expert, the objective was to keep them abreast of the United Nations' efforts to secure the release of the expert. While the legal argumentation was still at the heart of the discussions, the purpose of those meetings was not to convince but to simply provide the rationale justifying the demand formulated by the Organization. These various meetings were frequently conducted in the absence of an OLA representative, and the strategy and style of argumentation was determined by other Secretariat officials. The legal argument established the context in which other strategies of argumentation may have been employed.[7]

Shortly after the initial Notes Verbales were sent, OLA received the first official communication from the relevant state in the form of a Note Verbale explaining that the expert had entered the country using his national passport and denying that any privileges or immunities applied to him in his home country. Pursuant to the longstanding interpretation of the 1946 Convention previously mentioned, OLA replied, via another Note Verbale, that the applicability of the immunities of experts on mission in their home states had been recognized explicitly by the ICJ in the *Mazilu* case and that the nationality of an expert could therefore not be relied upon by a member state to deny functional immunity. OLA continued to issue Notes Verbales to this effect as the detention of the expert continued, reminding the state of its obligations under the 1946 Convention and consequently of the need to release the expert without further delay. OLA did not receive any official reply to its Notes Verbales during this period and only learned through its contacts with lawyers hired by the expert that criminal proceedings were continuing and that specific criminal charges had been brought against him.

Following a series of meetings between the UN Legal Counsel and the Permanent Representative of the state concerned, and at the point when the details of the criminal charges were informally communicated to OLA, it became clear that the crux of the matter was whether the actions constituting the alleged criminal conduct had been performed by the expert in the course of his official duty for the United Nations. As a result, more than a month after the arrest and despite the absence of an official reply to its legal argumentation, OLA received, from the authorities of the state, a dossier containing copies of judicial documents and materials related to the case. This dossier

[7] For other examples where the nature of the audience is particularly important to the purpose of legal argumentation, see Hyeran Jo, chapter 9, and Lisbeth Zimmermann, chapter 13, both in this volume.

was submitted in support of the state's position that the acts allegedly committed by the expert were not related to his official functions and that his functional immunity could therefore not prevent its prosecution.

At this stage, the United Nations' task had to evolve from one of purely legal analysis (reminding of existing legal obligations) to a mixed one (including assessing facts so as to determine if a legal framework was applicable). Following a careful review of the documents, the United Nations determined that the acts allegedly committed by the expert could not be detached from the conduct of his official UN duties. OLA then formally notified the member state concerned, through another Note Verbale, that the functional immunity from legal process accorded to the expert was expressly maintained and requested his immediate release and the discontinuation of the judicial proceedings. Following this assessment, the release of the expert was ordered by a court in the state concerned, and he was authorized to leave the country. However, the charges have not, to this date, been dropped, and the United Nations still engages with relevant national authorities to achieve that final objective. The United Nations is therefore not in a position, at this stage, to know whether its legal argumentation was successful or if the expert was released for purely procedural reasons.

This example illustrates one of the difficulties faced by the United Nations, which is that it is often not informed of the specific rationale behind a certain decision made or a specific new position taken by a member state or one of its judicial bodies. Assessing the effectiveness and persuasive power of a specific legal argumentation developed by OLA can therefore be difficult. However, in this case, as in many others, it could be argued that, although the legal argumentation may have not in fact convinced the relevant judicial authorities on the merits, the existence of the legal argumentation of the United Nations has possibly played a critical role in facilitating the decision of the government or the court to abide by international law.

One of the key elements of this case was the ability of the United Nations, or, more specifically, of the Secretary-General acting through the Legal Counsel, to be the sole authority in determining whether acts committed by a UN expert were performed in the course of official duty. The 1946 Convention is explicit on this point: "The Secretary-General shall have the right and the duty to waive the immunity of any expert in any case where, in his opinion, the immunity would impede the course of justice and it can be waived without prejudice to the interests of the UN."[8]

This authority granted by the member states can be explained by the Secretary-General's status as the Chief Administrative Officer, and thus best placed to know the exact outlines of the official duty of an official of the Organization or one of its experts on mission and whether a specific activities was conducted in the course of this official duty. The fact that the immunity can only be waived when, in the opinion of the Secretary-General, it is possible to do so in accordance with the criteria provided by Article V, Section 20, and Article VI, Section 23, may have been intended by the drafters of the 1946 Convention to ensure that member states would not be put in a position to authoritatively decide where the official duty of an international civil

[8] Art. V, sec. 20, and art. VI, sec. 23.

servant begins or ends, thus avoiding disputes as to the extent of the activities of the Organization and its personnel.

Nevertheless, the defense of this prerogative was one of the elements brought by the Secretary-General to the ICJ's attention in the dossier constituted after the request for an advisory opinion by the Economic and Social Council in the case later known as Difference Relating to Immunity from Legal Process of a Special Rapporteur of the Commission on Human Rights (also known as the "Cumaraswamy Case"). The Secretary-General took the opportunity of the dossier communicated to the Court to remind it and the state parties to the 1946 Convention of its interpretation of Articles V and VI. In this case again, the formal communication to the ICJ was for the United Nations a convenient and effective way of also informing member states of its legal argumentation. However, the Court elected to follow another interpretation of the 1946 Convention, supported by some member states through their written statements to the Court. It indicated in its advisory opinion that, although it is up to the Secretary-General "to assess whether its agents acted within the scope of their functions and, where he so concludes, to protect these agents, including experts on mission, by asserting their immunity,"[9] such "finding, and its documentary expression, creates a presumption which can only be set aside for the most compelling reasons and is thus to be given the greatest weight by national courts."[10]

C. Protecting the Immunity of the Organization Itself

The provisions of the 1946 Convention related to UN personnel are preceded by provisions detailing the privileges and immunities applicable to the Organization itself. Ensuring the implementation by the state parties of those provisions also in some cases constitutes a challenge for the Secretariat and OLA.

A recent situation relates to the 2010 catastrophic outbreak of cholera in Haiti. It occurred in the context of the presence of the UN Stabilization Mission in Haiti (MINUSTAH) established by Security Council Resolution 1542 (2004)[11] to support the government in ensuring a secure and stable environment; assist in the restoration and maintenance of the rule of law, public safety, and public order in Haiti; support Haiti's constitutional and political processes; support efforts by the government to promote human rights; and monitor and report on the human rights situation in the country. This outbreak happened within ten months of the devastating earthquake that struck the island and left close to two hundred thousand people dead and one million displaced; it proved to be the worst episode of cholera in recent history, with over nine thousand casualties according to the World Health Organization. Acts by MINUSTAH and by UN peacekeepers from Nepal were alleged to have caused or contributed to the outbreak.

[9] Difference Relating to Immunity from Legal Process of a Special Rapporteur of the Commission on Human Rights, Advisory Opinion, 1999 ICJ Rep., at 87, para. 60.

[10] *Id.* para. 61.

[11] SC Res. 1542 (Apr. 30, 2004).

The United Nations' position with respect to claims brought against it on the basis of these allegations was set forth in a letter sent, on November 25, 2014, by Mr. Pedro Medrano, Assistant Secretary-General and Senior Coordinator for Cholera Response,[12] to the special rapporteur on adequate housing as a component of the right to an adequate standard of living, and on the right to nondiscrimination in this context; the Independent Expert on the situation of human rights in Haiti; the special rapporteur on the right of everyone to the enjoyment of the highest attainable standard of physical and mental health; and the special rapporteur on the human right to safe drinking water and sanitation.[13]

A number of claims were brought against the United Nations in respect of the outbreak. For purposes of pursuing their claims, the claimants requested the establishment of a standing claims commission under the MINUSTAH Status-of-Forces-Agreement (SOFA) concluded between the United Nations and the government of Haiti.[14] Paragraph 55 of the MINUSTAH SOFA provided that any dispute or claim of a private law character, not resulting from the operational necessity of MINUSTAH, to which the mission or any member thereof was a party and over which the courts of Haiti did not have jurisdiction because of any provision of the SOFA, had to be settled by a standing claims commission to be established for that purpose.

Paragraph 55 of the MINUSTAH SOFA was an implementation of Section 29(a) of the 1946 Convention, which provides that the United Nations shall make provisions for appropriate modes of settlement of disputes of a private law character to which the United Nations is a party. Section 29(a) is by its terms limited to the consideration of private law claims. In the practice of the Organization, disputes of a private law character have been understood to be disputes of the type that arise between two private parties. Claims under Section 29(a) are distinct from public law claims, which are understood as claims that would arise between an individual and a public authority, such as a state. On the international level, these claims may be addressed in various ways, such as through political, diplomatic, or other means, including a body established for that specific purpose.

Claims "based on political or policy-related grievances,"[15] such as those "related to actions or decisions taken by the Security Council or the General Assembly,"[16] are excluded from the scope of any obligation to provide an appropriate mode of settlement. That is, in contrast to claims arising from circumstances in which the United Nations is acting like a private person, claims attacking the political or policymaking functions of the Organization are not private law in character. In this context, an assertion that the United Nations has not adopted or implemented certain policies or practices does not generate a dispute of a private law character.

[12] Available on the website of the Office of the High Commissioner for Human Rights, https://spcommreports.ohchr.org/TMResultsBase/DownLoadFile?gId=32377.

[13] For an alternative view, see Scott P. Sheeran, chapter 4, in this volume.

[14] July 9, 2004, 2271 UNTS 235.

[15] UN Doc. A/C.5/49/65, Report of the Secretary-General on procedures in place for implementation of article VIII, section 29, of the Convention on the Privileges and Immunities of the UN, adopted by the General Assembly on Feb. 13, 1946, para. 23.

[16] *Id.*

When assessing a claim under Section 29(a), the Organization does not rely solely on the allegations of the claim itself but also assesses the character of the claim in the context of all its circumstances. The mere allegation of tortious conduct does not make a claim one of a private law character. The nature of the duty allegedly owed by the Organization, the nature of the conduct or activity at issue, and other relevant circumstances are all pertinent to determining whether the claim involves a dispute of a private law character.

With respect to the cholera outbreak in Haiti, the claimants alleged that the United Nations breached its duty to adequately screen troops from Nepal for cholera, a country where cholera was endemic, by ignoring the risk of asymptomatic carriage and only requiring testing where individuals presented active symptoms and, further, that they failed to administer prophylaxis prior to their departure. They contended that the actions alleged above violated Haitian law, including the Haitian Constitution, the Haitian Penal Code, and the Haitian Civil Code. Additionally, claimants contended that the United Nations acted in violation of petitioners' rights under international human rights law.

The United Nations carefully considered the claims and the circumstances in which they arose. The claims raised broad issues of policy that arose out of the functions of the United Nations as an international organization. As such, they could not form the basis of a claim of a private law character. Accordingly, the Legal Counsel of the United Nations informed the claimants that the claim was not receivable pursuant to Section 29 of the General Convention, as these claims would necessarily involve a review of political and policy matters.

Following this decision, the claimants instituted several cases against the United Nations in the courts of the United States.[17] Under Section 2 of the 1946 Convention, the United Nations is immune from every form of legal process unless it has previously and expressly waived its immunity. This immunity is required in order for it to be able to conduct its mandated operations, which are not for its benefit but for the common interests of its member states. Without immunity, international organizations would be reluctant to establish offices, implement projects, and conduct operations in their member states. With respect to these cases, the United Nations maintained its immunity, and the United States filed statements of interest informing the courts of its immunity. This immunity was respected by US courts, and the cases have been dismissed.[18]

On December 1, 2016, Secretary-General Ban Ki-Moon officially and formally apologized to the people of Haiti, expressing deep regret for the loss of life and suffering caused by the country's cholera epidemic, and acknowledging that the United Nations "did not do enough with regard to the cholera outbreak and its spread in Haiti" and that it had a "moral responsibility to those who have been most directly

[17] Jean-Robert et al. v. United Nations et al.; Georges et al. v. United Nations et al.; Marie Laventure et al. v. United Nations et al., 279 F. Supp. 3d 394 (E.D.N.Y. 2017).

[18] Decision of the District Court of the Southern District of New York, dated Jan. 20, 2015, in relation to Jean-Robert v. United Nations; Georges v. United Nations, 834 F. 3d 88 (2d Cir. 2016); Marie Laventure v. United Nations, 104 S. Ct. 108 (2019).

affected." The United Nations continues to engage actively in ongoing efforts to eradicate cholera in Haiti and support communities affected by cholera.

III. UN Legal Argumentation in Relation to the Development of New Privileges and Immunities

The tremendous evolution in both the methods and activities of the United Nations on the territories of its member states and the pressure of operational necessity associated with the multiplication of multifaceted missions in the field have created a gap in some cases between the tools detailed in the mid-1940s in the Convention on the Privileges and Immunities of the United Nations and the requirements of modern UN operations.

Given the legal complexities and political sensitivities that would be triggered by any call by the United Nations to revisit the provisions of the 1946 Convention, the United Nations has seen the need, in close cooperation with its member states, to forge new legal tools and principles to strengthen the privileges and immunities regime to reflect those "necessary for the fulfilment of [the] purposes" of the Organization (Article 105). This includes innovations in respect of (1) ad hoc instruments relevant to member states not parties to the 1946 Convention; (2) new categories of UN personnel not envisioned seventy years ago; and (3) matters not directly addressed by the 1946 Convention.

A. Assertions of Privileges and Immunities in States Not Party to the 1946 Convention

If the large number of states parties to the 1946 Convention (162 to date[19]) is a tribute to the undeniable success of this instrument, many UN member states are still not parties. As a result, the United Nations could potentially conduct activities on the territory of member states not bound to recognize the privileges and immunities in the Convention; in such cases, it would rely solely on Articles 104 and 105 of the Charter with respect to its activities in those states. However, since the protection afforded by privileges and immunities are, in the United Nations' opinion, legally and operationally necessary to the implementation of the United Nations' mandate, the Organization has regarded it as appropriate to conclude an ad hoc instrument explicitly stating and detailing the legal framework of any UN presence and activity to be conducted on the territory of a state not party to the 1946 Convention.

It is important to highlight a critical difference between the privileges and immunities of the United Nations and those applicable to states, including their diplomatic and consular missions or personnel. The United Nations' privileges and immunities, just like those of other international organizations, are generally treaty-based (at the

[19] Available at https://treaties.un.org/Pages/ViewDetails.aspx?src=IND&mtdsg_no=III-1&chapter=3&lang=en.

very least, they rely on the organization's constitutive agreement). They therefore differ significantly from jurisdictional immunities of states, which are a part of customary international law as recently codified in the 2004 UN Convention on Jurisdictional Immunities of States and their Property, adopted by the General Assembly[20] (though not yet in force). In addition, when a state acts as a private person in a commercial context (*jure gestionis*), and not in its role as a sovereign power (*jure imperii*), immunity does not generally apply. But the UN Charter and the 1946 Convention do not distinguish between *jure gestionis* and *jure imperii*. This full immunity explains why the United Nations is under the obligation, pursuant to Article VIII, Section 29 of the 1946 Convention, to make provisions for appropriate modes of settlement of, *inter alia*, "disputes arising out of contracts or other disputes of a private law nature to which the United Nations is a party."

However, the actual content of an instrument defining the legal status of the United Nations and its personnel and its activities on the territory of a member state can sometimes generate lengthy and complex debates involving OLA. To convince a member state of the nature and extent of the privileges and immunities to be included in the bilateral agreement (often labeled as a "host country agreement" or a "status of mission agreement") to be signed with the United Nations, the legal argumentation relies again on Article 105, under which the United Nations' members recognize that "the Organization shall enjoy in the territory of each of its Members such privileges and immunities as are necessary for the fulfilment of its purposes" (paragraph 1) and that "[r]epresentatives of the Members of the United Nations and officials of the Organization shall similarly enjoy such privileges and immunities as are necessary for the independent exercise of their functions in connection with the Organization" (paragraph 2). The necessary character of those privileges and immunities is illustrated by the decisions of the Security Council to include, in recent resolutions creating a new peacekeeping or special political mission, a specific paragraph requesting the Secretary-General and the host state to conclude, usually within thirty days, a status of mission, or status of forces, agreement. Recognizing the need for privileges and immunities to be provided even to the first civilian and military personnel to be deployed in the host country, the Council also often decides, acting under Chapter VII of the Charter, to provisionally apply, pending the conclusion of a specific ad hoc agreement, the model status-of-forces agreement dated October 9, 1990.[21]

Some privileges and immunities are often easily accepted by a member state not party to the 1946 Convention. Indeed, the United Nations usually does not meet any resistance or reluctance in relation to the immunity from legal process of officials and of the Organization itself or regarding the inviolability of UN premises and archives. While they sometimes constitute a sensitive matter, the privilege to have banking accounts and hold funds without any "financial controls, regulations or moratoria of any kind"[22] or the immunity of international staff from local "taxation on the salaries and

[20] GA Res. 59/38 (Dec. 2, 2004).

[21] See, e.g., SC Res. 2100 (Apr. 25, 2013), para. 33, in relation to the United Nations Multidimensional Integrated Stabilization Mission in Mali (MINUSMA) or SC Res. 2149 (Apr. 10, 2014), para. 41, in relation to the United Nations Multidimensional Integrated Stabilization Mission in the Central African Republic (MINUSCA).

[22] Art. II, sec. 5, of the 1946 Convention.

emoluments paid to them by the United Nations"[23] are also acknowledged without complex negotiations.

However, OLA is often required to insist on the need to accord local staff the same immunities granted to international staff (including in relation to taxation on salaries and emoluments paid by the United Nations). On this issue, the arguments developed earlier in relation to the absence of difference between local and international officials under the 1946 Convention, including the ICJ's advisory opinion in the *Mazilu* case, are useful but not always convincing to a state that is not party to this Convention. In such cases, OLA would point out that, in place of national taxation, the General Assembly, in 1948, adopted a Staff Assessment Plan designed "to impose a direct assessment on UN staff members which is comparable to national income taxes."[24] The total funds collected from this assessment are distributed among member states in proportion to their contributions to the assessed budget of the United Nations. Any taxation by a member state on its nationals working for the United Nations in their home country would thus constitute double taxation on those officials and increase the financial burden of the United Nations and its member states. In addition, such measures are viewed by the United Nations as inconsistent with their obligations under the Charter. In this regard, the Report of the Committee on the San Francisco Conference responsible for the drafting of Article 105 pointed out that "if there is one principle certain it is that no Member State may hinder in any way the working of the Organization or take any measure the effect of which might be to increase its burden financial or otherwise."[25]

Another rationale for agreeing in any ad hoc bilateral agreement on a provision granting immunity from taxation to national staff lies in the need for the United Nations to see all its officials, irrespective of their nationality, treated equally, and in the fact that the United Nations will not accept a situation in which some would be taxed and some would not. Ultimately, the United Nations would also argue that no member state should derive any national financial advantage from the presence on its territory of staff of international organizations who receive salaries and emoluments from the funds of these organizations.

While the initial rounds of negotiations on those matters are most often conducted by the relevant substantive department or office directly with the Permanent Mission of the member state concerned, technical legal debates regarding Article 105 of the Charter, the *Mazilu* case or the *travaux préparatoires* of the Charter will usually require the direct intervention of OLA, which may take over the negotiations. In such cases, OLA will always engage, through the Permanent Mission, with host country teams, normally led by the Ministry of Foreign Affairs, which would also include ministries of justice and finance. A formal engagement will therefore take place through an exchange of Notes Verbales annexing the revised host country agreement but may also include direct negotiations at UN Headquarters or through teleconference.

[23] *Id.* art. V, sec. 17.

[24] GA Res. 239 (III) (Nov. 18, 1948).

[25] Documents of the UN Conference on International Organization, "Report of Commission IV on Judicial Organization," Vol. 13, at 705.

B. Categories of Persons to Whom Privileges and Immunities Necessary for Fulfillment of the United Nations' Purposes May Be Extended

As noted earlier, the 1946 Convention refers to representatives of member states (Article IV), officials (Article V), and experts on mission for the United Nations (Article VI). In 1946, the drafters of this Convention as well as the states that negotiated it could not imagine that, a few decades later, new categories of individuals would be associated with the conduct of the UN operations and activities to whom privileges and immunities should be extended. Two examples are contractors hired to provide goods and services to UN missions deployed in the field and lawyers defending individuals prosecuted by the International Criminal Tribunal for Rwanda (ICTR).

1. Contractors for UN Operations

As a result of the expansion and growth of peacekeeping operations, the United Nations was forced, from the middle of the 1990s, to rely increasingly on commercial firms to provide services and perform tasks traditionally performed by military personnel made available by member states. The contractors' functions in the context of UN peacekeeping operations are commercial, ranging from the procurement of goods and the supply of services to construction and catering services. However, difficulties faced by the companies and their employees to reliably and safely fulfill their contractual obligations have forced the Organization to consider options to facilitate their work.

Under the 1946 Convention, the only category of covered personnel that may have potentially been broad enough to encompass the type of activities conducted by contractors was the "Experts on Mission for the UN" referred to in Article VI. However, Article VI does not include any definition. Therefore, when considering whether contractors could be considered as experts on mission, OLA looked at the relevant practice of the United Nations and jurisprudence of the ICJ. In its advisory opinion on the *Mazilu* case[26] discussed above, the Court considered that experts on mission "have been entrusted with mediation, with preparing reports, preparing studies, investigations or finding and establishing facts."[27] This description of the scope of functions of experts on mission conformed in a general sense to the United Nations and state practice, and it therefore raised the question of whether recourse to Section 22 of the Convention (within Article VI) would provide adequate protection in respect of contractors.

As a result, it seemed prudent for the United Nations to enter into negotiations with member states, including parties to the 1946 Convention, to introduce, in the bilateral instruments defining the legal status of a peacekeeping or a special political mission, provisions to detail the privileges and immunities of contractors. Those negotiations would be based on the same principles in relation to member states not party to the 1946 Convention, notably the operational requirements of the missions

[26] *Supra* note 5.
[27] *Id.* 194, para. 48.

and the necessity of such facilities for the fulfillment of the United Nations' purposes. Efforts by the United Nations on this matter have been successful, and most of the status of forces or status of mission agreements of the operations currently used contain provisions granting contractors with certain facilities such as exemption from taxation or favorable treatment for visa purposes.

However, even in circumstances where host states of UN missions or activities have accepted provisions related to contractors, the actual daily implementation often proves difficult. The critical nature of the goods and services provided to UN operations by contractors (ranging from transport and security to medical assistance and telecommunications) causes the United Nations to closely monitor this implementation so as to prevent, or at least mitigate, any risk of service disruption.

For example, although host governments still retain primary responsible for the security and safety of UN personnel and premises on their territory, the limited capacity and resource constraints of some governments as well as the volatile security situation in some countries have forced the United Nations to hire the services of private companies to provide armed and unarmed security services inside UN compounds. In some instances, local authorities have been inclined to demand, despite a status of forces or mission agreement, payment for the issuance to contractors of visas, work permits, and licenses. Their attempts to contest the applicability of any exemption from taxes that may have been negotiated and included in the agreement with the host state often require the intervention of UN legal officers in the field and sometimes escalate to OLA. In such cases, the United Nations' argumentation is often limited to reminders of the host state's international legal obligations and to direct engagement, including at the highest level in the country concerned or in New York, with local authorities. The goal is to demonstrate that any failure to abide by the agreement could negatively impact the lives of UN personnel and jeopardize the United Nations' ability to implement its mandate.

2. Counsel at the ICTR

In May 2010, the Registrar of the ICTR informed OLA that the counsel for one of the individuals prosecuted by the Tribunal had been arrested in Rwanda. While the circumstances and reasons for the arrest were not immediately clear, the Registrar indicated that the counsel's visit to Rwanda was not in connection with his mandate as counsel with the ICTR. However, it quickly appeared from the charges and from arguments used by the prosecutor and a local court on the issue of bail that there was in fact some link between the arrest of the counsel and his activity before the ICTR. The local prosecutor had indeed made several references to cases before the ICTR, and the local court pointed out many of the arguments developed by that counsel at the ICTR in the defense of his client.

Because part of the case leveled against the counsel had derived from the words he spoke and statements he made in his case before the ICTR, the United Nations had to determine whether he had immunity in relation to acts done or words spoken or written in the course of his official duty. The two most relevant legal instruments were the Statute of the ICTR (the Statute) and the Memorandum of Understanding between the United Nations and Rwanda to regulate matters of mutual concern relating to the Office in Rwanda of the International Tribunal for Rwanda of June 3, 1999 (the MOU).[28]

The Statute did not mention any privileges or immunities accorded to defense counsels, but its Article 29(4) provided that "persons, including the accused, required at the seat or meeting place of the International Tribunal for Rwanda shall be accorded such treatment as is necessary for the proper functioning of the International Tribunal for Rwanda." While the Statute did not define the treatment accorded under Article 29(4), OLA concluded that, at a minimum, such treatment would include, pursuant to Principle 20 of the United Nations' Basic Principles on the Role of Lawyers,[29] immunity from legal process for words spoken or written and acts done in their capacity as defense counsel. As part of Security Council Resolution 955 (1994),[30] adopted under Chapter VII, the Statute was binding on all states, including Rwanda, which therefore had an obligation to accord to the defense counsel treatment necessary for the proper functioning of the ICTR. Furthermore, OLA determined that defense counsels would fall, under the MOU, in the category of "other persons assigned to the Office" and would thus be entitled to privileges and immunities accorded to experts on mission for the United Nations under Article VI of the 1946 Convention. As indicated earlier, those privileges and immunities include, pursuant to Section 22, immunity from personal arrest and from legal process of every kind in respect to words spoken or written and acts done by them in the course of the performance of their mission. This analysis was communicated by OLA to the president of the ICTR. It is, however, not clear to the authors how or whether it was ever brought to the attention of the relevant national authorities.

The counsel was released by the authorities of Rwanda after a couple of weeks in detention. The Appeals Chamber of the ICTR issued a ruling on October 6, 2010, in which it stated that the criminal proceedings against the counsel were in violation of "his functional immunity from legal process for words spoken or written in the course of his functions before the Tribunal."[31] The Appeals Chamber also considered that such proceedings "interfered with the proper functioning of the Tribunal, which required that Defence Counsel be free to advance arguments in their client's case without fear of prosecution."[32]

These two examples illustrate the complexity of the legal argumentation that the United Nations has to develop, using a wide array of instruments ranging from a resolution of the Security Council under Chapter VII to non-binding principles, to convince member states of the need to ensure the legal protection of individuals whose activities are seen as critical or at least appropriate to the implementation of the United Nations' mandate.

The role of OLA in such cases is to develop legal arguments in support of positions that the United Nations has determined to be appropriate and to set forth those arguments in specifically legal terms. It may be that other parts of the United Nations are

[28] 2066 UNTS 6.
[29] UN Doc. A/CONF.144/28/Rev.1.
[30] SC Res. 955 (Nov. 8, 1994).
[31] Case No. ICTR-98-41-A, Decision dated Oct. 6, 2010, para. 29.
[32] *Id.*

simultaneously making other types of arguments to the same or other interlocutors, but, as noted above, OLA does not directly participate in the non-legal diplomacy that may be undertaken.

C. Resisting the Recent Trend Requiring the United Nations to Engage in National Social Security Schemes

While the previous examples related to new categories of beneficiaries, in another situation the absence of specific terms in the 1946 Convention has led some member states to question the United Nations' practice in relation to its own privileges and immunities.

For the last decade or so, the United Nations has witnessed the multiplication of domestic legislation or regulations regarding the mandatory participation of employers and employees in national social security schemes, pension mechanisms, or health insurance programs. While the United Nations favors increasing social coverage of workers and employees around the world, it has taken a firm stance against member states which, despite the absence of any exemption related to social security in the 1946 Convention, insisted on the mandatory participation of the United Nations and its officials to those mechanisms. Indeed, it has been the consistent practice and policy of the United Nations for more than five decades that mandatory contributions for such programs under national legislation are considered a form of direct taxation.

Under Section 7(a) of the 1946 Convention, "the United Nations, its assets, income and other property shall be exempt from all direct taxes." A similar immunity has been accorded, under Section 18(b), to UN officials, including those recruited locally and not assigned to hourly rates, who "shall be exempt from taxation on the salaries and emoluments paid to them by the United Nations." Therefore, the United Nations is of the view that the United Nations and its officials will not pay any contributions or perform any other actions in relation to social security schemes under national legislation.

While the participation in national social security schemes remains possible for staff members on a purely voluntary basis, the United Nations and its officials' exemption from mandatory contributions is further evidenced by the Organization's own comprehensive social security scheme. The establishment of such scheme is required under Regulation 6.2 of the UN Staff Regulations,[33] established by the General Assembly according to Article 101 of the Charter. Pursuant to the Staff Regulations, the Secretary-General has promulgated Rule 6.1 (participation in the UN Joint Staff Pension Fund), Rule 6.2 (sick leave), Rule 6.3 (maternity and paternity leave), Rule 6.4 (compensation for death, injury, or illness attributable to service), Rule 6.5 (compensation for loss or damage to personal effects attributable to service), and Rule 6.6 (medical insurance). With the exception of Rule 6.6—where staff members "may be required to participate ... under conditions established by the Secretary-General"—the UN social security system is compulsory. With regard to service contractors, the

[33] Secretary-General's Bulletin, Staff Regulations and Rules of the UN, UN Doc. ST/SGB/2018/1.

United Nations' general policy is that, when calculating remuneration for such types of contracts, factors such as social security and/or pension are included. It is up to the service contract holder to then make contributions to social security or pension schemes. Accordingly, this policy excludes any direct payments by the United Nations to member states with respect to its contractors.

Explaining the intricacies of the internal rules and regulations of the United Nations as well as the practice in relation to the provisions of the 1946 Convention to member states, whose only objective is often to simply have the most comprehensive schemes of social guarantees, often proves to be a challenging task. In some countries, unfortunately, the dispute with local authorities on this matter has not yet been solved despite years of direct engagement by OLA and local UN representatives.

* * *

The topics on which the United Nations has developed, over the last seventy-five years, legal argumentation in relation to its privileges and immunities are probably as diverse as its member states. However, the examples detailed above reveal that two constants remain in that argumentation developed by the United Nations outside of the courtroom regardless of the objective: on one end, reliance on the *treaty-based nature of the privileges and immunities* granted to the Organization and its personnel, and on the other, the ultimate grounding of privileges and immunities in the principle of *necessity*, which always depends, at one level or another, on the consent of member states.[34]

As indicated earlier, the specific treaty-based regime setting forth UN privileges and immunities makes clear the distinction between UN privileges and immunities and diplomatic and consular privileges and immunities. In relation to the proper and complete implementation of the 1946 Convention, the task faced by OLA is sometimes less to convince than to recall. The United Nations will therefore draw extensively, and almost exclusively, on the provisions of the 1946 Convention and, in such cases, the heart of the argumentation will always be a clear and unequivocal reminder of letter, nature, and extent of the obligations accepted by member states which have become parties to the 1946 Convention.

On the other end, in relation to the expansion of the privileges and immunities sought by the Organization, the absence of explicit provisions in the 1946 Convention forces OLA to construct a specific argumentation aiming, this time, at convincing member states. However, although the objective of the argumentation is now different, the treaty-nature of privileges and immunities granted by states to international organizations still requires references to a written instrument. This is the reason why the Charter, and more specifically its Article 105, which was at the heart of the process that led to the 1946 Convention, remains the foundation stone of any argumentation aiming at convincing member states that a specific privilege or immunity not explicitly mentioned in the Convention should nevertheless be granted to the United Nations or its personnel. While the power and in some sense constitutional aura associated with the UN Charter certainly assists OLA to convince member states,

[34] See the developments proposed by Ian Johnstone in relation to consent, chapter 7, in this volume.

those characteristics of the Charter also require the Organization to exercise tact and finesse in developing and presenting legal argumentation based on Article 105.

The second constant or common denominator that stands behind all these illustrations is precisely the one embodied directly within Article 105: the notion of necessity. Ultimately, this is the reason why legal arguments used outside the courtroom by the United Nations are often similar, regardless of whether their purpose is to remind a member state to properly implement the existing legal framework or principles or to convince that member state to accept the development of privileges and immunities not expressly provided in the existing legal framework. It is only because they are necessary for the fulfillment of the United Nations' purposes and the implementation of its mandate that the privileges and immunities in the 1946 Convention exist. It is only because member states value the United Nations' operations and activities that they are willing to grant it these extraordinary privileges and immunities and are sometimes willing, often after involvement by OLA, to accept any arguments of the United Nations in that regard.

The good relations established and maintained by the UN Legal Counsel and OLA in general with the permanent representatives to the United Nations and their legal advisers are critical to ensuring that the argumentation developed by OLA be properly received and understood at the level of the Permanent Missions and relayed to the capital. Therefore, Permanent Missions, and more broadly Ministries of Foreign Affairs, are key interlocutors in the effort to ensure that the legal argumentation developed by the Organization will be brought to the attention of the relevant national authorities. It is ultimately those authorities whom the Organization wishes to persuade to uphold the legal framework granted to the United Nations. The legal argumentation presented by the United Nations in support of its privileges and immunities has at its core the maintenance of the legal regime, which makes it possible for the Organization to carry out its functions.

PART V

17

Toward a Theory of Legal Argumentation

Ian Johnstone and Steven Ratner

The studies presented in this volume offer a broad sample of the global issues, legal regimes, actors, and venues that constitute the process of international legal argumentation outside of courts. Our authors have presented both outsiders' perspectives on the use of legal argumentation as well as insiders' direct experiences in the deployment of legal arguments in diverse settings. They show that states and non-state actors have used a range of argumentative strategies to further their interests and assert their identities. Though actors evince various motives for using these arguments, and the argumentation can result in sometimes unintended effects, the participants involved see a value in adding law to their conversations—or diplomatic shouting matches—about matters of bilateral, regional, or global concern. The richness and variety of legal argumentation, including its co-mingling with other sorts of arguments, stands in sharp contrast to the sometimes formulaic sorts of arguments made in front of courts and tribunals.

The essays also demonstrate the limitations of existing theories about international law when it comes to legal argumentation. As discussed in Chapter 1, those theories generally address how international law evolves, how states express legal commitments, and the reasons states comply with or violate them. But they offer precious little guidance about the microprocess of direct communication witnessed in this volume. In particular, other than perhaps some antiquated version of realism (which would regard legal argumentation as pure theater), none of the theories explain what actors understand they are doing when they make a "legal argument," the reasons they use legal argumentation, and the effects of legal argumentation, including the relevance of the institutional settings, audiences, and thickness of legal regimes for legal argumentation. While legal scholars have at times addressed these issues regarding courtroom argumentation, the variety of nonjudicial argumentation demands a deeper level of inquiry. Moreover, various strands of international relations theories have expounded on the purposes and effects of argumentation generally, but mostly without delving into the specificities of *legal* argumentation.

This conclusion aims to push forward on constructing a theory of nonjudicial legal argumentation. Like all theories in the social sciences, a theory on this subject must at a minimum show a good fit with the behavior of the actors described in the preceding chapters and, at the same time, be generalizable to the countless scenarios not discussed in this volume. Such generalizability promotes prediction, so that observers of future arguments will not only understand them better while they are happening, but even predict the responses they elicit and the ultimate effects of the argumentative

Ian Johnstone and Steven Ratner, *Toward a Theory of Legal Argumentation* In: *Talking International Law*. Edited by: Ian Johnstone and Steven Ratner, Oxford University Press. © Ian Johnstone and Steven Ratner 2021.
DOI: 10.1093/oso/9780197588437.003.0017

exchange. And because law is also a normative field, a theory can also (though it need not) be oriented around certain normative commitments, such as compliance with international law, solution to global problems, or promotion of human rights. In that light, we seek to pull together key strands from the chapters that should, or at least could, be part of a theory of legal argumentation. Indeed, these areas of commonality and generalizability might be the basis for multiple, even competing, theories of legal argumentation, depending on one's theoretical orientation on other aspects of international law. Because our focus is on laying the groundwork for future theory, we do not seek in this conclusion to provide a full descriptive synthesis or summary of all the chapters.

I. Diversity in What Counts as a Legal Argument

In the judicial setting, lawyers and judges are generally of a similar mindset when it comes to a legal versus a non-legal argument. Legal arguments (1) consist of claims that the law prohibits, permits, or precludes certain conduct; and (2) invoke as "law" only the tribunal's understanding of what is in and what is out—with Article 38 of the Statute of the International Court of Justice as a key reference point (though not the endpoint) for international courts, and constitutional rules of recognition for domestic courts. The chapters in this volume do not, however, adopt a single definition of a legal argument. This catholicism is not simply a matter of the author's choice. Rather, each author's understanding of a legal argument reflects the ways that actors perceive of a legal argument in that particular context (though the authors also make their own choices as to what counts as a legal argument, including claims or positions that the actors might not have consciously identified as legal). In the microprocess of communication in nonjudicial settings, participants think of something as a legal argument, and react to it, in various ways.

Thus, the actors discussed in some chapters rely on the more conventional, judicially originated conception noted above. Their claims invoke traditional prescriptive processes or sources, such as treaty or custom, to ground a claim of prohibited, permitted, or required conduct. Actors see a strong legal claim as one grounded in the most authoritative or legitimate of sources, the multilateral treaty. Thus the United Nations' lawyers argue for privileges and immunities by citing chapter and verse of the 1946 Convention on Privileges and Immunities or the UN Charter (Mathias and Perez); most disagreements about non-proliferation are grounded in the language of the Nuclear Non-Proliferation Treaty (NPT) (Johnstone); disputes over the ban on whaling are made in terms of the 1946 Convention on the Regulation of Whaling (Zimmermann); and arguments about the permissibility of retaliatory tariffs rely on the World Trade Organization (WTO) agreements (Claussen). And of course, arguments about the use of force center on the meaning of Article 2(4) and Chapter VII of the UN Charter (Hakimi and Sheeran).

Yet the volume also presents other understandings of a legal argument. With respect to *sources*, in multiple settings the actors make legal arguments based on the resolutions of international organizations, including those not legally binding. At the regional level, legal argumentation in the African Union (AU), whether over unconstitutional changes of government or its relationship with the International Criminal Court (ICC), invokes prior AU resolutions (Negm and Werner). At the global level, debates in and around the Security Council about women, peace, and security emphasize non-binding Chapter VI resolutions or preambles to resolutions (Heathcote). Equally important, rules primarily focused on procedural matters—even unwritten ones—have great legal weight, such as those within the Security Council (Stagno-Ugarte), those governing how parties to the Paris Agreement are supposed to set and improve their national commitments (Brunnée), and those governing challenges to domain names in the World Intellectual Property Organization (WIPO) (Kwakwa). Indeed, the range of acceptable sources for a legal argument can change over time, as is clear in the evolution of argumentation under the climate regime to include non-binding and procedural rules.

As for the *underlying communication* grounded in those sources, legal argumentation for some actors means discourse about the terms of a document representing a formal, normative commitment (whether or not legally binding), even if those seeking to shape its content are arguing mostly about good policy. What makes these arguments legal is that they aim to shape the content of a document that the parties regard as more than merely a political statement. This instantiation is seen most clearly in the arguments in the AU over its resolutions on unconstitutional takeovers (Negm) and the ICC (Werner). It is also seen in the debates leading to outcome statements in intergovernmental meetings, such as the NPT review conferences (Johnstone), the International Whaling Commission (IWC) (Zimmermann), and the UN Group of Governmental Experts on cyber norms (Ratner).

But a legal argument is not limited to a communication about the current state of the law—what we think of as legal interpretation. It includes claims about the desired *future direction* of the law. Narrow understandings of legal argumentation also miss the reality that arguments about whether one party is complying with the law, and the meaning of that law, are often part of debates about the future direction of the law—thus blurring the line between interpretation and prescription. This dynamic is seen in the strategies of states responding to cyber misconduct (Ratner), low commitments to climate change mitigation (Brunnée), or the lack of protection of intellectual property rights for Indigenous peoples (Kwakwa). Parties may not even be aware when they are interpreting the law that they are simultaneously offering arguments about the future direction of the law, as arguments about the meaning of the obligation on the nuclear weapons states to negotiate disarmament ended up laying the foundation for the treaty banning nuclear weapons (Johnstone).

The case studies suggest that understandings of what constitutes a legal argument, or a good one, may be traceable to the subject area. With regard to international peace and security, the chapters by Hakimi, Sheeran, Heathcote, and Ratner all show an attachment to the UN Charter, core treaties, and key Security Council resolutions. Any legal argument will include those; and any argument not including them is likely to be a bad legal argument or not legal at all. For human rights, the chapters by Jo and Stagno-Ugarte suggest a hierarchy of instruments to invoke, with the top shared by the two covenants (and perhaps the Torture Convention), the Geneva Conventions, and the ICC Statute. And for UN privileges and immunities, Mathias and Perez show the centrality of the 1946 Convention. But for a regional organization like the AU, Negm and Werner show that its constitutive act will be at the same level as the instruments noted above. For the other areas of cooperation, such as climate, whaling, cybersecurity, trade, and intellectual property, the mix seems to be more fluid, with a combination of procedural instruments and soft law playing a role. We will have more to say about these distinctions in Section V below.

These lived experiences of what constitutes a legal argument represent a challenge to traditional sources doctrine as well as some lawyers' or political scientists' intuitions about the nature of a legal argument. At the same time, we acknowledge the danger in considering or labeling every argument that loosely touches on law as a legal argument, for at that point it becomes difficult to ascertain the distinctiveness of a legal argument in terms of its motivations and effects. The independent variable has slipped away from our analysis. So, for example, we do need to draw some line that would exclude the casual mention of a legal instrument, or the mere usage of a legal instrument for a policy debate (lest every debate over the funding of a UN agency be considered legal simply because it ends up in a General Assembly resolution). We do not propose where exactly to draw that line but agree some parameters must be set.

II. Theorizing Motivations

Our introduction suggested several possible motivations for actors to engage in legal argumentation based largely on theoretical work on why actors choose to express commitments in legal form.

A. A Tentative Compilation of Motives

Our case studies lend support to that list, but they also reveal additional motivations as well as some possible patterns that would form the basis for future theory. Below is a list of motives. It is important to stress that these are not mutually exclusive. Indeed, it is reasonable to assume that most actors have multiple motives for making a legal argument—just as they have multiple motives for behavior. Moreover, the motives may vary depending on the audience. For example, geopolitical adversaries may doubt they will be able to persuade their rival of the merits of a legal argument but may do it anyway in order to undermine the adversary's clout in an intergovernmental body while seeking to persuade a domestic audience of the correctness of their own position.

- True persuasion: to convince the interlocutor or other audiences of the merits of the legal claim in order to change their behavior or their policy positions;

- Strategic argumentation: to change the behavior or policy position of the interlocutor or other audiences without necessarily changing their minds about the legal merits;[1]
- Resistance to pressure: to deflect criticism or defend one's own conduct or policy position by recourse to a legal argument;
- Legitimation or delegitimation: to establish the credibility or acceptability of the entity making the argument to key constituencies, international or domestic;
- Assertion of authority: to demonstrate to various audiences that the entity making the argument has a right to participate in the international legal process;
- Shaping future directions in the law: to create or dispel expectations among various audiences regarding future prescription, whether through hard law or otherwise;
- Alteration of the normative climate: to change targets' perceptions about the underlying legal landscape and thus reframe their views about the relevant law;
- Promotion of a mandate: to invoke law for instrumental purposes associated with an existing agenda on the international stage;
- Assertion of ownership of an issue: to claim a distinct authority to speak on behalf of a particular issue due to the speaker's connection to it;
- Obfuscation of the real issue at stake: to distract attention from the fundamental policy or moral disagreements by introducing competing legal arguments;
- Suppression or silencing of voices: to assert a dominant role on a legal issue through argumentation that marginalizes the roles of other actors.

B. Actual vs. Imputed Motives

The compilation of motives offered here is not a product of scientific observation. Motivations are only sometimes evident; often they must be inferred. Thus, on the one hand, some of the practitioner (or former practitioner) authors confirm certain motivations in their chapters—the UN lawyers Mathias and Perez make clear that they are trying to persuade UN member states to comply with their legal obligations to grant privileges and immunities; Stagno-Ugarte and other UN delegates were invoking the crimes in the ICC Statute to change the normative climate and push the Security Council to stronger action; Negm's account shows that the AU's member states argued in terms of AU law to persuade coup organizers to give up power; and Claussen's view is that members of the US Congress invoke trade law to persuade other legislators, or constituents, that a particular US policy or law on trade needs to change, or to justify existing policy.

On the other hand, other authors, observers rather than direct participants in the arguments, tend to attribute motivations based on behavior. Thus, Ratner infers from the

[1] As a practical matter, actors engaging in legal argumentation may be indifferent between these first two motives, seeking first and foremost to change the behavior or policy position of the target(s) of the argument. See, e.g., Ian Johnstone, "Security Council Deliberations: The Power of the Better Argument," *European Journal of International Law* 14 (2003): 437, 453–455; Steven R. Ratner, "Law Promotion Beyond Law Talk: The Red Cross, Persuasion, and the Laws of War," *European Journal of International Law* 22 (2011): 459, 499–501.

thin legal landscape on cybersecurity that states are motivated by a felt need to shape the future of the law rather than comply with existing law; Jo examines the quest of non-state armed groups for legitimacy in front of other international actors and sees that acceptance as motivating their endorsement of certain international humanitarian norms; Werner argues that the AU was seeking to express its African identity on issues of international justice; and Zimmermann suggests, based on the political dynamics within the IWC, that some whaling states invoke the language of the Whaling Convention because they believe it provides the best argument to justify their behavior.

The divergence between knowledge of actual motives and imputation of likely motives opens up an area for future research. More qualitative research involving interviews with actors about their reasons for choosing a legal argument, already undertaken by a few scholars, seems essential. Venzke's research agenda addressing the ways actors react to legal versus non-legal arguments may offer a window into why actors would be motivated to use legal arguments in the first place.

C. Venues and Audiences

One central factor for determining an actor's motive or motives for using a legal argument is the nature of the *venue* in which it makes an argument and, relatedly, the perceived *audience(s)* for it. Though more work remains to link venue and audience to motives, the case studies reveal some hypotheses. First, it is possible that actors in smaller settings are more single-minded in their motivation for using a legal argument, as in the UN legal counsel's focus in private bilateral talks on persuading parties to the 1946 privileges and immunities convention to comply with their duties, non-state armed groups' quest for legitimation with humanitarian organizations or peace negotiators, or the work of technical committees under the Paris Climate Accord to persuade parties to improve their reporting. The legal argumentation in front of WIPO's center for resolving disputes over domain names is also singular in its purpose—to persuade the panel to protect their claimant's domain name.

On the other hand, in formal settings of international organizations, whether at the NPT Review Conferences, at WIPO negotiations on traditional knowledge, at the IWC, or in the Security Council, the audiences are much larger, including states, as well as nongovernmental organizations and domestic audiences—what might be termed international public opinion. In front of those large audiences, actors would seem to have multiple purposes for using an international legal argument—including to persuade others to comply with law, to serve strategic purposes (e.g., to gain allies), to legitimate their own conduct, and/or to try to change the normative landscape. Thus, actors seem to have these motivations (and others) in UN debates over nonproliferation, the use of force, women and armed conflict, and responses to human rights atrocities. Even in the regional context, the argumentative strategy of the AU regarding the ICC seems motivated by both a need to reflect African solidarity and values—thereby asserting ownership over the issue—as well as to persuade the ICC Prosecutor not to bring cases against African leaders.

Second, the chapters suggest that the "legalization" of the venue matters (and by that term, we are distinguishing it from the legalization of the overall governance arrangements for an issue of international concern, the key concern for international relations theorists). Where substantive and procedural rules define or circumscribe the debates and discourse, or lawyers play an important role in that discourse, all actors will see advantages to using legal arguments. (Or perhaps they are simply persuaded by lawyers in their midst that it is in their interest to make legal arguments.) One can contrast the WIPO's center on domain names—an administrative body with characteristics of a tribunal—or the UN's Office of Legal Affairs' interactions with legal officials in member states over privileges and immunities—a conversation among lawyers—with the IWC or the committees under the Paris Accord, dominated by technical experts and not lawyers. Somewhere in the middle might be the Security Council, which is dominated by diplomats and politicians, yet where lawyers (particularly from P5 missions) draft or pore over resolutions and the entire process is overlaid and influenced by precedents and rules. Women's advocacy groups navigating the Council have needed to engage with its legalized aspects, yet they are also concerned that various precedents and linkages across resolutions will either dilute or corrupt the agenda regarding women, peace, and security (Heathcote).

Third, within an international organization, the Secretariat's role may affect the role of legal argumentation and the motivations of actors for using it. In the AU, the Legal Counsel is critical to preparing AU responses to unconstitutional coups; but in other organizations, the lawyers play more background roles, as in the WIPO Secretariat's role regarding the domain name center. Further complicating the issue in the UN context is that the Secretariat is a multiheaded creature. As Stagno-Ugarte's account of its responses to atrocities indicates, some of its officials (e.g., from the Office of the High Commissioner for Human Rights) may be willing to invoke atrocity crimes as others (in New York) shy away from it; and the views of UN lawyers are not generally public.

Fourth, the extent to which domestic audiences are closely following the issue seems to affect parties' reasons to use a legal argument. In the trade context, Claussen argues that some members of the US Congress see WTO law as strengthening their case in front of other legislators and constituents to justify or change US policy. In the security context, non-state armed groups who see themselves as representing a certain population see law as offering domestic (and not merely international) legitimacy. If domestic audiences are not as engaged, as might be the case with arguments over cyber norms, intellectual property, or non-proliferation, actors will have fewer reasons to use legal arguments—although those reasons will still be strong enough to lead them to use a legal argument.

D. Timing and Sequence

In addition to audiences and venues, *timing* seems to affect an actor's motives for using a legal argument. In the cybersecurity context, actors in the *ex ante* (pre-incident) phase of legal argumentation are making claims at a somewhat more abstract level and primarily motivated by shaping future law; in the *ex post* phase, where they are responding to a particular incident, different motivations kick in, such as preserving one's options. Regarding climate change, the reasons for legal argumentation shifted: before the Paris Agreement, states invoked the law to change the normative environment and legal landscape; since then, they have been focused on getting states to meet their commitments and ratchet them up. In the non-proliferation context, the reasons also shifted from trying to pressure nuclear weapon states to live up to their disarmament obligation to trying to persuade non-nuclear weapon states to join the Treaty on the Prohibition of Nuclear Weapons. Regarding human rights atrocities, states at the Security Council invoke international crimes to stop ongoing atrocities, to prevent future atrocities, and to promote individual accountability through referral to the ICC. And non-state armed actors have been particularly motivated to use international legal argumentation during peace negotiations as a way of legitimizing themselves in front of international audiences. Future research could also address timing more systematically to see how it affects parties' motivations to engage in legal argument.

E. Avoidance of Legal Argument

The chapters also offer a snapshot into the reasons that actors deliberately avoid international legal argumentation or move back and forth between legal and non-legal arguments (as defined by the speaker). The case studies suggest a number of motivations for avoidance:

(1) A sense that other arguments are more likely to resonate with, or persuade, an audience based on the argument's claim to authority, the target's own background, or other factors. This point, emphasized by Venzke, is at the core of states' choices to use scientific rather than legal arguments to justify the whaling ban (Zimmermann), or non-state armed groups' choices to use traditional values rather than international humanitarian law to justify their behavior to local populations (Jo).

(2) A desire to avoid tying one's hands in the future, as made clear by avoidance of legal argumentation in response to some cyberattacks (Ratner). The push for non-binding substantive norms in the climate regime (Brunnée), as well as the slow progress toward a binding instrument on the protection of traditional knowledge (Kwakwa), may also stem from this motivation.

(3) Political concerns, including the desire to avoid offending certain actors, which seems to describe the choice of some UN Secretariat officials to avoid invoking ICC crimes to describe Syrian governmental atrocities (Stagno-Ugarte). The desire to avoid offense, of course, may be a part of a broader political strategy, for example, to broker deals between warring parties. In the AU, nuanced argumentation about how to respond to the unconstitutional change of government in Sudan was designed to facilitate a transition to democracy there (Negm).

(4) Lack of concern for the law, whether writ large or out of a choice to avoid getting bogged down in specific legal rules. This avoidance can be a form of hegemonic assertion, as suggested by Hakimi and Claussen regarding the United States; but it motivates other states or non-state armed groups seeking to bolster their reputation by showing their lack of concern for—or overt rejection of—rules to which they never consented (Jo). Concerns about hegemony in the UN Security

Council inform the skepticism of some women's groups about the direction the women, peace, and security agenda has taken there (Heathcote).

(5) Bona fide uncertainty about the meaning of international law, as seen again in the cyber context. In these situations, actors are still working through their views on the state of existing law or its desired direction, including thinking about the ways that certain audiences might react to their views. This factor goes beyond factor (2)'s narrow focus on preserving options.

The chapters also show actors ready to switch from engagement to avoidance, often depending on the venue, audience, and timing, as made clear regarding whaling and non-state armed groups. Indeed, where an actor wants to make an argument simultaneously in front of multiple audiences (for instance, within a large international organization), the speaker may be torn, as it were, to use a legal argument that will resonate with some audiences but motivated to avoid one for one of the reasons noted above (in particular the first three). These choices face the AU in its policy toward the ICC, many actors in front of the Security Council, and US trade officials seeking to justify retaliatory measures to WTO officials and other governments, on the one hand, or domestic constituencies, on the other.

III. From Motives to Effects: The Outputs of International Legal Argumentation

All the chapters in this volume devote significant attention to the effects of international legal argumentation. As stated in our introduction, scholars within international relations and international law have offered theories about the effects of legalization on (mostly state) behavior under the general umbrella of "Why do states comply with or violate international law?" But our goal has been not to discern or theorize the effects of *legalization*, but rather about the effects of *legal argumentation*. The second is not simply a proxy for the first. Actors in highly legalized regimes may refrain from legal arguments, as seen regarding climate change and whaling; and actors in thinly legalized regimes may make legal arguments, as seen regarding cybersecurity and intellectual property protection for traditional knowledge.

A. A Tentative Compilation of Effects

Our introduction identified some possible effects of legal argumentation. Here we identify those effects borne out by the cases. That list begins with a reframing of the intended effects or motivations mentioned in Section II.A above—because sometimes the argument achieves its intended purpose, or it achieves another purpose on that list:

- True persuasion, where the interlocutor is convinced of the merits of the legal claim and changes its behavior or policy;
- Strategic effects, where the behavior or policy of the interlocutor or other audiences changes, even if its views on the legal merits does not;

- Resistance to pressure, where the argument deflects criticism of a conduct or policy;
- Legitimation or delegitimation, where the entity asserts its credibility, reputation, or acceptability to key constituencies, international or domestic;
- Assertion of authority, where the actor demonstrates it has a right to participate in the international legal process;
- Shaping the future directions in the law, where the actor alters expectations regarding future prescription;
- Alteration of the normative climate, where the argument changes and reframes targets' perceptions about the underlying legal landscape;
- Promotion of a mandate, where the argument advances an existing agenda on the international stage;
- Assertion of ownership of an issue, where the entity gains a distinct authority to speak on behalf of a particular issue;
- Obfuscation of the real issue at stake, whereby competing legal arguments distract the audience's attention from the fundamental policy or moral disagreements;
- Suppression or silencing of voices, where the argument dominates other legal arguments or claims by less powerful voices.

Our volume includes a number of examples of arguments that seem to have achieved their intended purpose. The US legal argumentation for strategic purposes against Iran kept together the P5+1 coalition throughout the negotiation of the Iran nuclear accords. Companies using legal arguments in front of the WIPO's domain name center have persuaded it and received the protection sought. States arguing in the Security Council that certain atrocities amount to ICC crimes have twice prevailed in convincing the Council's members to refer those cases to the ICC (even as they failed regarding Syria). And non-state armed groups may have improved their reputation with some international actors by agreeing to abide by some norms of international humanitarian law.

But states may use legal argumentation for one purpose and achieve something unintended, whether in addition to their original goal or instead of it. Johnstone shows how non-nuclear weapons states arguing to the nuclear weapon states that the NPT required negotiations in good faith instead seem to have changed the legal landscape and laid the groundwork for the prohibition treaty; and Heathcote observes that states' expression of concern about women in war through invocation of the Security Council's women, peace, and security resolutions end up opening the door to challenges to those resolutions as not reflecting women's concerns.

Indeed, our cases point to some effects that actors simply do not normally intend at all, so we add these effects to the list above:

- Promotion of the rule of law generally or of specific legal regimes, whereby the argument promotes a respect for the role of international law in international relations;
- Constituting or expanding a legal community, whereby the process of argumentation creates new connections and mutual commitments among actors.

Thus, for example, Hakimi suggests that states trying to persuade other states that their use of force was consistent with the UN Charter end up promoting the rule of law more generally by treating different audiences seriously; Claussen argues that invocation of international trade law by members of the US Congress have resulted in its "normalization ... in public space." Werner's study shows how legal argumentation creates new emotional and political connections within the AU; and Sheeran suggests that arguments can hide more fundamental issues and agendas about power within the Security Council.

B. Epistemology, Again

Each of these effects of argumentation supports Hurd's key observations about the role of international law generally, namely, as (1) constraining behavior; (2) enabling behavior; and (3) framing the way actors think about global issues.[2] Yet, as with motives, the epistemological question looms large. As Venzke's chapter emphasizes, that challenge is as great, perhaps greater, for gauging an argument's effects as for determining an actor's motives. Was it the argument that changed minds of listeners (or altered the normative environment, or something else)? Or the speaker? Or the venue? Or the audience? Or simply power politics? Or all of them? As with a theory about motives, scholars may have to impute effects (and thus causation, for an effect requires a cause) based on observable facts. Some explanations will be more convincing than others; and some may ultimately be verifiable, more or less, through quantitative and qualitative research, such as that proposed by Venzke. But other effects, for instance, that legal argumentation promotes the rule of law, seem rather intangible, based on a reconstruction of the facts rather than the facts themselves.

C. Causal Factors

The causation challenge requires identifying whether and how the communication entailed in international legal argumentation changes something about the issue being argued about or perhaps something else. We do not underestimate the difficulty of tracing and explaining the effects of a verbal communication in a setting—unlike (for the most part) a courtroom—where so many other factors can influence outcomes. But our case studies offer some important starting points.

First, the *connections and shared commitments* among the actors on the different ends of the communication seem to matter. The AU's resolutions invoking its Constitutive Act have bite with its members because of their shared commitments to the Union and its values; the sense among members of the US Congress that the United States should not violate the WTO Agreements makes legal arguments important to

[2] Ian Hurd, "The International Rule of Law: Law and the Limits of Politics," *Ethics and International Affairs* 28 (2014): 39, 42–48.

them; the desire of non-nuclear weapons states for a nuclear-free world mean that arguments for filling a gap in the NPT would change the normative landscape over time; the sense by all states that the United Nations needs privileges and immunities makes legal arguments by the United Nations ultimately quite persuasive. On the other hand, the merely superficial commitment by key members of the Security Council to combat impunity for serious international crimes, or act on the Responsibility to Protect, makes legal claims grounded in the ICC's list of crimes fall short in the case of Syria; and the fundamental disagreements over whaling between Norway and Japan, on the one hand, and the other IWC states, on the other hand, meant that arguments about the meaning of "scientific" under the Whaling Convention would not go far in changing behavior—and scientific arguments would prove more important to various audiences.

Second, the nature of the *venues and audiences* might play a role. Large venues, with global audiences, seem especially conducive to the possibility that a legal argument will affect the normative landscape, or the rule of law generally. But they may be less likely to succeed in persuading a state to comply with international law (or otherwise change its behavior), because the target of the communication may be on the defensive in front of so many other states. So while legal arguments in the Security Council's debates on atrocity prevention, women and armed conflict, or self-defense might lead over time to changed attitudes about those legal regimes, they may not persuade an actor violating the law to change its conduct—an irony, given the Security Council's mandated role in the Charter to respond to breaches of the peace. Conversely, they may persuade an actor to change its conduct without necessarily changing attitudes about the legal regime. In smaller venues, such as the private conversations between the United Nations' lawyers and their governmental interlocutors over privileges and immunities, or the WIPO's domain name dispute resolution process, legal argumentation would seem to have a better chance at persuading parties; the Iran nuclear deal talks, held in secret among a small group of states, may have similarly been an example of smaller venues as more promising for persuasion.

As is clear from our lists, sometimes the arguer is seeking expression of support from an ally, which would be more meaningful in a large public setting than quietly behind the scenes. Other times it may be a vote for or against a resolution, for example, in the Security Council or African Union. The argumentation there could be either in public or behind the scenes, if all the speaker cares about is the outcome—not the reasons for it. If the argument is deployed to urge the creation of a new legal instrument (a cyber treaty, the Paris Agreement, the Treaty on the Prohibition of Nuclear Weapons), presumably it would have wider impact if made to a large audience. If it is to lay the foundations for peace talks with a non-state armed group, a quieter approach may bear more fruit.

Another causal factor for effectiveness may concern the *reputation and expertise* of those engaging in legal argumentation. Thus, Japan's reputation as a state committed to whaling made its legal arguments about the meaning of the IWC rather unconvincing to most states, and did not seem to have helped its reputation with others; Russia's assistance to Syria seems to have made its arguments about Syria implausible to most members of the Security Council; the Trump administration's alienation of many audiences suggested that its arguments over both the Syria strike and global trade did not change many minds; and some non-state armed groups may be more convincing than others in shoring up their reputation through recourse to international legal argumentation based on their own practices in wartime. Reputation is central to several theories of compliance, as noted in the introduction to this volume. Indeed, as the list of motivations and effects makes clear, not only is an interlocutor's reputation a causal factor for the success of its argument, reputation may motivate, and improve from, a legal argument. Or, in some cases, overt rejection of legal argumentation can serve instrumental and identity-related purposes, just as embracing it can.

Finally, some of the case studies suggest that, as lawyers would hope, the *quality of a legal argument* matters for its effectiveness. A challenge for any theory of legal argumentation outside of courts is to distinguish good legal arguments from bad. After all, if the matter is not subject to authoritative judicial resolution, who decides what counts as a good argument? Some of our authors stipulate that the answer is embedded in the professional discipline of international law. Brunnée points to certain "traits of legality" that actors respect in the application and interpretation of relevant norms; failure to respect those traits undermines the force of the argument. Johnstone refers to the "interpretive community" of international lawyers that structure and constrain argumentation about non-proliferation, in effect rendering judgment on what constitutes a good (or at least better) legal argument in that sphere. Stagno-Ugarte regrets the failure of some Council members to call out mass atrocities for what they are, instead using vague language that points to elements of a specific crime without naming the crime itself. Implicitly, he is suggesting that dissimulation about what is at stake is a bad legal argument.

On the other hand, strong legal arguments do not always fare better than merely plausible ones. In the cyber context, states seem to have accepted as legal rules for cyber conduct both well-accepted principles of state responsibility, for example, that a government is responsible for the acts of its organs, and more controversial positions, for example, that a state has a due diligence responsibility to prevent private actors from engaging in cyberattacks. Sheeran observes that the analytically detailed legal reasoning typical of adjudicative settings is unsuited to the culture of the Security Council and may be less effective than a less positivist legal argument that leverages extralegal factors—arising from international relations, diplomacy, policy considerations, and international values. Hakimi refrains from distinguishing between good and bad arguments, suggesting that as long as the argument is legal in kind and engaged with seriously, it can advance the international rule of law. Taken as a whole, the chapters in this book show that identifying what constitutes a good legal argument is no easy task, which should not be surprising given how much legal argumentation occurs outside the disciplining force of the courtroom. While it seems intuitive that the quality of a legal argument matters—arguments that conform with accepted parameters of legal interpretation and discourse are more likely to resonate than those that are wildly far-fetched—more research needs to be done on the precise effects of good versus plausible versus obviously specious argumentation.

IV. The Contours of the Legal Landscape

Although we have sought to distinguish between the modes, motives, and effects of legalization, on the one hand, and legal argumentation, on the other, we agree that the thickness or thinness of the legal landscape regarding an issue plays a role in legal argumentation. As discussed earlier, the nature of the legal landscape constitutes what the relevant actors regard as a legal argument, or a good one, in the first place. Certainly, the chapters demonstrate that in situations with a thick set of binding legal instruments, actors will invoke them, and perhaps stay away from soft law altogether. Thus, the United Nations' lawyers will invoke the 1946 Convention on privileges and immunities but, it seems, not much soft law; states arguing over non-proliferation will rely primarily on the NPT; arguments over the legality of the use of force or the role of the Security Council in response to force will invoke the Charter and Council resolutions first and foremost; and since 2015, the Paris Agreement is a sort of alpha and omega when it comes to climate change. The possibility that actors may have fundamental disagreements over the meaning of these hard instruments does not cause parties to avoid invoking them, but, as Hakimi posits regarding the *jus ad bellum*, all the more reason to argue in terms of them. Yet as Zimmermann and Jo point out, even where the landscape is thick with hard law, actors may rely on non-legal arguments, which may well prove more effective in achieving some goals with some audiences.

On the other hand, if the landscape is thick, but that thickness includes instruments other than traditional hard law, parties will invoke them as well—a challenge to the orthodox understanding of "sources" of international law.[3] Thus, for many issues, the hard/soft law distinction does not seem important to the form of an argument, the motives for making one, nor even the effects thereof. The use of soft law in the case of intellectual property, climate change, and AU resolutions on unconstitutional changes of government does not seem fundamentally different in these aspects compared to hard law. In the context of women, peace, and security, debates are organized around non-binding Security Council resolutions or non-binding preambles in binding resolutions as well as influential UN reports, with formal bindingness seemingly not that important. And the cyber security case suggests that even when the landscape is very thin overall, with only a consensus on some basic principles, parties will still make legal arguments with a goal of shaping the future direction of the law.

V. Does Consistency Matter in Legal Argumentation?

International lawyers have long recognized that one of reasons states follow international law, and are restrained from violating or misinterpreting it, is through what Georges Scelle called the "dédoublement fonctionnel"—the reality that the same actors (often governmental officials) both make legal arguments and respond to

[3] For further reflections, see Steven R. Ratner, "War/Crimes and the Limits of the Doctrine of Sources," in *The Oxford Handbook of the Sources of International Law*, edited by Samantha Besson and Jean d'Aspremont (Oxford: Oxford University Press, 2017), 912. See also José Alvarez, *The Impact of International Organizations on International Law* (Leiden: Brill Nijhoff, 2017), 47–48.

them. As a result, actors look beyond their immediate interests in considering or responding to conduct, including through accompanying legal arguments, to think about what would happen if, respectively, another state undertook that conduct toward them (or toward an ally), or they (or an ally) wished to undertake that conduct in the future. This mechanism thus sees legal argumentation as enforcing the law through what Jon Elster calls the "civilizing force of hypocrisy."[4] Or, as François de la Rochefoucauld wrote, "hypocrisy is the homage vice pays to virtue."[5] It would suggest that a desire for consistency will affect the content of a legal argument; and that consistency will also influence an argument's effects, for example, insofar as a baldly hypocritical claim would have less influence on audiences than one reconcilable with earlier positions.

Indeed, legal argumentation by its very nature is designed to promote consistency. This follows from the basic principle of justice that like cases ought to be treated alike, and from standard techniques of legal argumentation, such as the invocation of precedent and appeals to analogy. While consistency may be the hobgoblin of little minds, it is hard to deny that—for better or worse—it is embedded in the structure of legal argumentation. From that perspective, invoking a legal argument is an advocacy tool that makes it more difficult, though of course not impossible, for states to behave hypocritically. By engaging in legal argumentation, one signals that the law has value, even if one's professed commitment to it is not genuine.

Despite the importance of this factor for thinking about compliance, the case studies leave the role of consistency somewhat elusive. On the one hand, for example, the United States was clearly circumspect in making legal claims in response to cyberattacks for fear of tying its hands in the future, or having to make a later argument that would be inconsistent with its earlier position. And, as pointed out by Mathias and Perez, part of the persuasiveness of the United Nations' claims regarding privileges and immunities is that it makes the same principled claims regardless of the potential violator (although the United Nations has no incentive to take any other position); and Kwakwa notes that precedent counts for a great deal in the rulings within the WIPO's domain name dispute settlement process. On the other hand, the potential of appearing hypocritical does not seem to have affected US arguments regarding recent tariffs, or the use of force, though it may well be the case that those less-than-principled arguments have harmed US foreign policy interests. Hypocritical arguments may nonetheless have some benefits for an actor, for instance, with domestic audiences that do not realize that the actor's argument is inconsistent with previous positions. And an argument by a state that is inconsistent with an earlier view may be evidence that the legal landscape is changing—that the actor is not being inconsistent, but rather changing its mind.

[4] Jon Elster, "Deliberation and Constitution Making," in *Deliberative Democracy* (Cambridge: Cambridge University Press, 1998).

[5] François de la Rochefoucauld, *Maximes* (Paris: chez Claude Barbin, 5th ed. 1678), 218.

VI. A Place for Legal Argumentation within Normative Theories?

The foregoing chapters contain the building blocks for future theoretical work on how, why, and to what end international actors use legal arguments in nonjudicial settings. But as much theory within international law, international relations, and international ethics advances or assumes certain normative commitments, it is worth considering whether the insights of these chapters can inform normative theory. While recognizing the range and diversity (methodically and disciplinarily) of such theories, we might nonetheless consider the relevance of international legal argumentation from the perspective of four broad normative orientations or commitments.

For theories oriented toward promoting *compliance with international law*—a significant strand among international legal scholarship—the essays in this volume confirm that actors are sometimes motivated to use legal arguments for this purpose, and that certain contextual factors associated with a legal argument can contribute to its ability to induce compliance. At a minimum, then, theorists and practitioners seeking to promote compliance with existing rules need to consider the role of a good legal argument in that process and not assume that compliance is dictated solely by structural factors about the parties or contextual factors about the particular dispute. At the same time, some chapters, such as those on the use of force and international trade, show that some legal arguments are not motivated by a wish to get another actor to comply with international law, but rather by other interests of the relevant actor, even though the actor's message may sound like it is aimed at compliance. Thus theories and practitioners should not assume that states are concerned about compliance just because they say they are.

More generally, the insights from the cases can complement, rather than displace other theories suggesting why actors comply with international law. Regarding motives, dissecting the motivations for legal arguments may reveal new understandings about why states do or do not care about their own or others' compliance with international law. Regarding effects, although the cases suggest that arguments can matter for compliance, much remains to be studied and theorized about how much they matter compared to structural and contextual factors.

For actors or observers concerned about *solving global cooperation* problems (where legal compliance is not the main driver of a solution), the chapters confirm the perhaps obvious observation that states will use legal arguments to advance those goals in certain normative environments and settings but will deploy non-legal arguments as well. More important, as we see with cybersecurity, climate change, and non-proliferation, legal argumentation among multiple actors can be evidence of, or a precursor to, new norm-making and lawmaking to solve global cooperation problems. Whether it is a *prerequisite* for such new norms and law is a harder question. Legal arguments might even contribute to a broader culture of respect for the rule of law that makes the ground more fertile for arriving at solutions to global problems.

For actors concerned about *power dynamics among states and hegemony*, the chapters may confirm some of their assumptions and arguments about powerful states. A number of the studies show powerful states using strained legal arguments aimed more at gaining allies than at demonstrating any commitment to their own or others' compliance with international law. The deafness of two members of the Permanent Five to respond to strong legal arguments about war crimes in Syria suggests the limits of a good legal argument. But legal arguments can be used to resist hegemony (or at least an actor's perception of it), as seen in the AU's strategy toward the ICC, which it saw as reflecting a Western hegemonic model of international criminal justice. On the other hand, the cases reveal some shortcomings of a model of state behavior that identifies certain conduct as distinctively hegemonic, for the same tactics of legal argumentation used by powerful states to justify their behavior are used by other states, such as Japan regarding whaling, or non-state armed groups seeking international recognition.

Lastly, for theories oriented around the fate of *disempowered groups and communities* within states—including human rights–oriented theories—the studies show both promises and dangers from the use of legal arguments in various settings. On the one hand, the arguments by some states that Syrian atrocities constituted ICC crimes galvanized international attention (though with few concrete results in the Security Council); and non-state armed groups seemed to have attained an opportunity to partake in international legal argumentation. On the other hand, the study on the women, peace, and security agenda suggests that arguments in favor of disempowered groups may be co-opted for other purposes by states; and that states deploying a legal argument that facially seems concerned with disempowered groups may actually be motivated by other interests.

VII. Conclusion

The studies in this volume are, we hope, just the beginning of further inquiry into the role of international legal argumentation in global affairs. By peering into nonjudicial venues, they force us to re-examine and unpack just what constitutes a legal argument in the places where they are most likely to be made. We have begun to ask what actors perceive as the added value of a legal argumentation to their discourse with other actors, and what the added value actually turns out to be. In addressing these questions, the cases demonstrate the need for multiple analytical and disciplinary lenses and, in addition, the contribution of practitioners' perspectives on what is happening in various venues where legal arguments are made.

Looking ahead, we hope others will take up some of the unfinished business of this project. And we hope that future approaches to legal argumentation will work outside existing boxes—subsets or derivations of theories of compliance—to zero in on a specific process of communication central to international relations and law. That future work will, we think, reveal just how consequential international legal argumentation can be for those making the arguments and, even more crucially, for the audiences that hear them.

Index